# Scala Cookbook

*Alvin Alexander*

Beijing · Cambridge · Farnham · Köln · Sebastopol · Tokyo

**Scala Cookbook**

by Alvin Alexander

Copyright © 2013 Alvin Alexander. All rights reserved.

Printed in the United States of America.

Published by O'Reilly Media, Inc., 1005 Gravenstein Highway North, Sebastopol, CA 95472.

O'Reilly books may be purchased for educational, business, or sales promotional use. Online editions are also available for most titles (*http://my.safaribooksonline.com*). For more information, contact our corporate/institutional sales department: 800-998-9938 or *corporate@oreilly.com*.

| | |
|---|---|
| **Editor:** Courtney Nash | **Indexer:** Ellen Troutman |
| **Production Editor:** Rachel Steely | **Cover Designer:** Karen Montgomery |
| **Copyeditor:** Kim Cofer | **Interior Designer:** David Futato |
| **Proofreader:** Linley Dolby | **Illustrator:** Rebecca Demarest |

August 2013:     First Edition

**Revision History for the First Edition:**

2013-07-30:    First release

See *http://oreilly.com/catalog/errata.csp?isbn=9781449339616* for release details.

ISBN: 978-1-449-33961-6

[LSI]

*For my mom, who loves cookbooks.*

# Table of Contents

# Preface

This is a cookbook of problem-solving recipes about Scala, the most interesting programming language I've ever used. The book contains solutions to more than 250 common problems, shown with possibly more than 700 examples. (I haven't counted, but I suspect that's true.)

There are a few unique things about this book:

- As a cookbook, it's intended to save you time by providing solutions to the most common problems you'll encounter.

- Almost all of the examples are shown in the Scala interpreter. As a result, whether you're sitting by a computer, on a plane, or reading in your favorite recliner, you get the benefit of seeing their exact output. (Which often leads to, "Ah, so that's how that works.")

- The book covers not only the Scala language, but also has large chapters on Scala tools and libraries, including SBT, actors, the collections library (more than 100 pages), and JSON processing.

Just prior to its release, the book was updated to cover Scala 2.10.x and SBT 0.12.3.

## The Scala Language

My (oversimplified) Scala elevator pitch is that it's a child of Ruby and Java: it's light, concise, and readable like Ruby, but it compiles to class files that you package as JAR files that run on the JVM; it uses traits and mixins, and feels dynamic, but it's statically typed. It uses the Actor model to simplify concurrent programming so you can keep those multicore processors humming. The name Scala comes from the word *scalable*, and true to that name, it's used to power the busiest websites in the world, including Twitter, Netflix, Tumblr, LinkedIn, Foursquare, and many more.

In my opinion, Scala is not a good language for teaching a Programming 101 class. Instead, it's a power language created for the professional programmer. Don't let that scare you, though. If you were my own brother and about to start a new project and could choose any programming language available, without hesitation I'd say, "Use Scala."

Here are a few more nuggets about Scala:

- It's a modern programming language created by Martin Odersky (the father of `javac`), influenced by Java, Ruby, Smalltalk, ML, Haskell, Erlang, and others.
- It's a *pure* object-oriented programming (OOP) language. Every variable is an object, and every "operator" is a method.
- It's also a functional programming (FP) language, so you can pass functions around as variables. You can write your code using OOP, FP, or both.
- Scala code runs on the JVM and lets you use the wealth of Java libraries that have been developed over the years.
- You can be productive on Day 1, but the language is deep, so as you go along you'll keep learning and finding newer, better ways to write code. Scala will change the way you think about programming—and that's a good thing.

Of all of Scala's benefits, what I like best is that it lets you write concise, readable code. The time a programmer spends *reading* code compared to the time spent *writing* code is said to be at least a 10:1 ratio, so writing code that's concise and readable is a big deal. Because Scala has these attributes, programmers say that it's *expressive*.

## Solutions

I've always bought O'Reilly cookbooks for the solutions, and that's what this book is about: solving problems.

When using a cookbook, I usually think, "I have this problem, I need to iterate over the elements in an `Array`, what's the best way to do that?" I like to look at the table of contents, find a recipe, implement the solution, and move on. I tried to write each recipe with this use case in mind.

However, with a modern language like Scala, it may end up that I phrased my question wrong. Because of my prior programming experience I may have thought, "I need to iterate over the elements in an `Array`," but in reality my deeper *intent* was to loop over those elements for a reason, such as to transform them into a new collection. So it's nice when a recipe says, "Hey, I know you're here to read about how to loop over the elements in an `Array`, here's how you do that":

```
for (i <- Array(1,2,3)) println(i)
```

"But, if what you're really trying to do is transform those elements into a new collection, what you want is a for/yield expression or `map` method":

```
// for/yield
scala> for (i <- Array(1,2,3)) yield i * 2
res0: Array[Int] = Array(2, 4, 6)

// map
scala> Array(1,2,3).map(_ * 2)
res1: Array[Int] = Array(2, 4, 6)
```

(More on that _ character shortly.)

To create the list of problems and solutions, I followed the "Eat your own dog food" (*http://bit.ly/18gySAa*) philosophy. The recipes come from my own experience of creating Scala scripts, web applications, web services, Swing applications, and actor-based systems. As I developed the applications I needed, I encountered problems like these:

- Scala files tend to be very small; what's the proper way to organize an application?
- It looks like SBT is the best build tool for Scala, but it's different than Ant or Maven; how do I compile and package applications, and work with dependencies?
- Constructors are really different than Java; how do I create them? What code is generated when I declare constructor parameters and class fields?
- Actors are cool; how do I write a complete actor-based application?
- What, I shouldn't use `null` values anymore? Why not? How do I code without them?
- I can pass a function around like any other variable? How do I do that, and what's the benefit?
- Why are there so many collections classes, and why does each collection class have so many methods?
- I have all of this legacy Java code; can I still use it in Scala? If so, how?
- I'm starting to grok this. Now I need to know, what are the top five or ten "best practices" of writing Scala code?

Truthfully, I fell fast in love with everything about Scala except for one thing: the collections library seemed large and intimidating. I really enjoyed using Scala so I kept using the language, but whenever I needed a collection, I used a trusty old Java collection.

Then one day I got up the courage to dive into the collections library. I thought I'd hate it, but after struggling with it for a while, I suddenly "got" it. The light bulb went on over my head, and I suddenly understood not only the collections, but several other concepts I had been struggling with as well. I realized the collections library writers aren't crazy; they're brilliant.

Once I understood the collections library, I quit writing so many for loops, and started using collection methods like filter, foreach, and map. They made coding easier, and made my code more concise. These days I can't imagine a better way to write code like this:

```
// filter the items in a list
scala> val nums = List(1,2,3,4,5).filter(_ < 4)
nums: List[Int] = List(1, 2, 3)
```

The _ wildcard character is discussed in several recipes, but as you can infer from that example, it's a placeholder for each element in the collection. The filter method loops through each element in the list, calling your _ < 4 function on each iteration. That Scala one-liner is the equivalent of this Java code:

```
Integer[] intArray = {1,2,3,4,5};
List<Integer> nums = Arrays.asList(intArray);
List<Integer> filteredNums = new LinkedList<Integer>();
for (int n: nums) {
   if (n < 4) filteredNums.add(n);
}
```

The next example takes this a step further. It filters the elements as in the previous example, and then multiplies each element by the number 2 using the map method:

```
// filter the items, then double them
scala> val nums = List(1,2,3,4,5).filter(_ < 4).map(_ * 2)
nums: List[Int] = List(2, 4, 6)
```

If you think about how much code would be required to write this expression in another language, I think you'll agree that Scala is expressive.

(If you're new to Scala, examples like this are broken down into smaller chunks in the recipes.)

## Audience

This book is intended for programmers who want to be able to quickly find solutions to problems they'll encounter when using Scala and its libraries and tools. I hope it will also be a good tool for developers who want to learn Scala. I'm a big believer in "learning by example," and this book is chock full of examples.

I generally assume that you have some experience with another programming language like C, C++, Java, Ruby, C#, PHP, Python, or similar. My own experience is with those languages, so I'm sure my writing is influenced by that background.

Another way to describe the audience for this book involves looking at different levels of software developers. In the article at scala-lang.org (*http://bit.ly/13KwDa4*), Martin Odersky defines the following levels of computer programmers:

- Level A1: Beginning application programmer
- Level A2: Intermediate application programmer
- Level A3: Expert application programmer
- Level L1: Junior library designer
- Level L2: Senior library designer
- Level L3: Expert library designer

This book is primarily aimed at the application developers in the A1, A2, A3, and L1 categories. While helping those developers is my primary goal, I hope that L2 and L3 developers can also benefit from the many examples in this book—especially if they have no prior experience with functional programming, or they want to quickly get up to speed with Scala and its tools and libraries.

## Contents of This Book

The first three chapters in this book cover some of the nuts and bolts of the Scala language.

Chapter 1, *Strings*, provides recipes for working with strings. Scala gets its basic String functionality from Java, but with the power of *implicit conversions*, Scala adds new functionality to strings through classes like StringLike and StringOps, which let Scala treat a String as a sequence of Char. The last recipe in the chapter shows how to add your own behavior to a String (or any other class) by creating an implicit conversion.

Chapter 2, *Numbers*, provides recipes for working with Scala's numeric types. There are no ++ and -- operators for working with numbers, and this chapter explains why, and demonstrates the other methods you can use. It also shows how to handle large numbers, currency, and how to compare floating-point numbers.

Chapter 3, *Control Structures*, demonstrates Scala's built-in control structures, starting with if/then statements and for loops, and then provides solutions for working with for/yield loops (for comprehensions) and for expressions with embedded if statements (guards). Because match expressions are so important to Scala, several recipes show how to use them to solve a variety of problems.

The next five chapters continue to cover the Scala syntax, with an emphasis on organizing your projects with classes, methods, objects, traits, and packaging. Recipes on classes, methods, objects, and traits place an emphasis on object-oriented programming techniques.

Chapter 4, *Classes and Properties*, provides examples related to Scala classes and fields. Because Scala constructors are very different than Java constructors, several recipes show the ins and outs of writing both primary and auxiliary constructors. The chapter also shows how to override the accessor and mutator methods that Scala automatically generates for your val and var variables. Several recipes show what *case classes* are and how to use them, and how to write equals methods.

Chapter 5, *Methods*, shows how to define methods to accept parameters, return values, use parameter names when calling methods, set default values for method parameters, create varargs fields, and write methods to support a fluent style of programming.

Chapter 6, *Objects*, covers "all things object." Like Java, Scala uses the word *object* to refer to an instance of a class, but Scala also has an object keyword. This chapter covers topics like class casting, how to launch an application with an object, how to create the equivalent of Java's static members, and how to write a class with a companion object so you can create new instances of a class without using the new keyword.

Chapter 7, *Packaging and Imports*, provides examples of Scala's package and import statements, which provide more capabilities than the same Java keywords. This includes how to use the curly brace style for packaging, how to hide and rename members when you import them, and more.

Chapter 8, *Traits*, provides examples of the Scala trait. It begins by showing how to use a trait like a Java interface, and then gets into more advanced topics, such as how to use traits as "mixins," and limit which members a trait can be mixed into using a variety of methods.

Although much of the book demonstrates functional programming (FP) techniques, Chapter 9, *Functional Programming*, combines many FP recipes into one location. Solutions show how to define anonymous functions (function literals) and use them in a variety of situations. Recipes demonstrate how to define a method that accepts a function argument, how to return a function from a function, and how to use closures and partially applied functions.

The Scala collections library is rich and deep, so Chapter 10, *Collections*, and Chapter 11, *List, Array, Map, Set (and More)*, provide more than 100 pages of collection-related solutions.

Recipes in Chapter 10, *Collections*, help you choose collection classes for specific needs, and then help you choose and use methods within a collection to solve specific problems, such as transforming one collection into a new collection, filtering a collection, and creating subgroups of a collection. More than 60 pages of recipes demonstrate solutions for writing for loops, for/yield expressions, using methods like filter, foreach, groupBy, map, and many more.

Chapter 11, *List, Array, Map, Set (and More)*, continues where Chapter 10, *Collections*, leaves off, providing solutions for those specific collection types, as well as recipes for the Queue, Stack, and Range classes.

Chapter 12, *Files and Processes*, begins by providing solutions about reading and writing files with Scala, including CSV. After that, because the Scala library makes it much (much!) easier to work with external processes than Java, a collection of recipes demonstrates how to execute external commands and work with their I/O.

Chapter 13, *Actors and Concurrency*, provides solutions for the wonderful world of building concurrent applications (and engaging those multicore CPUs) with the Scala Actors library. Recipes in this chapter show solutions to common problems using the industrial-strength Akka Actors library that was integrated into the 2.10.x Scala release. Examples show how to build actor-based applications from the ground up, how to send messages to actors, how to receive and work with messages in actors, and how to kill actors and shut down the system. It also shows easy ways to run concurrent tasks with a Future, a terrific way to run simple computations in parallel.

Chapter 14, *Command-Line Tasks*, combines a collection of recipes centered around using Scala at the command line. It begins by showing tips on how to use the Scala REPL, and then shows how to use command-line tools like `scalac`, `scala`, `scaladoc`, and `fsc`. It also provides recipes showing how to use Scala as a scripting language, including how to precompile your Scala scripts to make them run faster.

Chapter 15, *Web Services*, shows how to use Scala on both the client and server sides of web services. On the server side, it shows how to use Scalatra and the Play Framework to develop RESTful web services, including how to use Scalatra with MongoDB. For both client and server code, it shows how to serialize and deserialize JSON and how to work with HTTP headers.

Chapter 16, *Databases and Persistence*, provides examples of how to interact with databases from Scala, including working with traditional SQL databases using JDBC and Spring JDBC, along with extensive coverage of how to work with MongoDB, a popular "NoSQL" database.

Chapter 17, *Interacting with Java*, shows how to solve the few problems you'll encounter when working with Java code. While Scala code often *just works* when interacting with Java, there are a few gotchas. This chapter shows how to resolve problems related to the differences in the collections libraries, as well as problems you can run into when calling Scala code from Java.

Chapter 18, *The Simple Build Tool (SBT)*, is a comprehensive guide to the de-facto build tool for Scala applications. It starts by showing several ways to create an SBT project directory structure, and then shows how to include managed and unmanaged dependencies, build your projects, generate Scaladoc for your projects, deploy your projects, and more. Though I strongly recommend learning SBT, a recipe also shows how to use Ant to compile Scala projects.

Chapter 19, *Types*, provides recipes for working with Scala's powerful type system. Starting right from the introduction, concepts such as type variance, bounds, and constraints are demonstrated by example. Recipes demonstrate how to declare generics in class and method definitions, implement "duck typing," and how to control which types your traits can be mixed into.

Chapter 20, *Idioms*, is unique for a cookbook, but because this is a book of solutions, I think it's important to have a section dedicated to showing the best practices, i.e., how to write code "the Scala way." Recipes show how to create methods with no side effects, how to work with immutable objects and collection types, how to think in terms of *expressions* (rather than statements), how to use pattern matching, and how to eliminate null values in your code.

## Online Bonus Chapters

Because Scala is an incredibly rich and deep language, an additional three chapters consisting of more than 130 pages of *Scala Cookbook* content are available for readers who wish to explore Scala further. These bonus chapters are:

- *XML and XPath*
- *Testing and Debugging*
- *The Play Framework*

These chapters are available in PDF format, and can be downloaded at *http://exam ples.oreilly.com/9781449339616-files/*.

## Installing the Software

Installing Scala is simple and should just take a few minutes.

On Unix systems (including Mac OS X), download the software from the Scala download page (*http://bit.ly/10WFP7t*) to a directory on your computer like *$HOME/scala*, and then add these lines to your *$HOME/.bash_profile* file (or its equivalent, depending on which login shell you're using):

```
export SCALA_HOME=/Users/Al/scala
PATH=$PATH:/Users/Al/scala/bin
```

Once you've done this, when you open a new terminal window, you should have access to the scala and scalac commands at your command line.

You can follow a similar process if you're using Microsoft Windows, or you can use an MSI installer. See the Scala download page (*http://www.scala-lang.org/downloads*) for more information.

# How the Code Listings Work

Most of the code listings in the book are shown in the Scala "Read-Eval-Print-Loop," or *REPL*. If you've used `irb` with Ruby, the concept is the same: you type an expression, and the REPL evaluates the expression and prints the resulting output.

In the REPL examples, the code that's shown in a bold font is what you type, and all the text that isn't bold is output from the REPL.

You start the REPL from your operating system command line by executing the `scala` command:

```
$ scala
Welcome to Scala version 2.10.1
Type in expressions to have them evaluated.
Type :help for more information.

scala> _
```

Once the REPL has started, just type your expressions as input, and the REPL will evaluate them and show their output:

```
scala> val hello = "Hello, world"
hello: String = Hello, world

scala> Array(1,2,3).foreach(println)
1
2
3
```

The REPL is demonstrated more in the Chapter 1 introduction and Recipe 14.1, "Getting Started with the Scala REPL". Recipe 14.4 takes this a step further and shows how to customize the REPL environment.

# Conventions Used in This Book

The following typographical conventions are used in this book:

*Italic*
> Indicates new terms, URLs, email addresses, filenames, and file extensions.

`Constant width`
> Used for program listings, as well as within paragraphs to refer to program elements such as variable or function names, databases, data types, environment variables, statements, and keywords.

**`Constant width bold`**
> Shows commands or other text that should be typed literally by the user.

*Constant width italic*

Shows text that should be replaced with user-supplied values or by values determined by context.

This icon signifies a tip, suggestion, or general note.

This icon indicates a warning or caution.

# Using Code Examples

This book is here to help you get your job done. In general, if this book includes code examples, you may use the code in your programs and documentation. You do not need to contact us for permission unless you're reproducing a significant portion of the code. For example, writing a program that uses several chunks of code from this book does not require permission. Selling or distributing a CD-ROM of examples from O'Reilly books does require permission. Answering a question by citing this book and quoting example code does not require permission. Incorporating a significant amount of example code from this book into your product's documentation does require permission.

Supplemental material (code examples, exercises, etc.) is available for download at *https://github.com/alvinj*.

We appreciate, but do not require, attribution. An attribution usually includes the title, author, publisher, and ISBN. For example: "*Scala Cookbook* by Alvin Alexander (O'Reilly). Copyright 2013 Alvin Alexander, 978-1-449-33961-6."

If you feel your use of code examples falls outside fair use or the permission given above, feel free to contact us at *permissions@oreilly.com*.

# Safari® Books Online

Safari Books Online (*www.safaribooksonline.com*) is an on-demand digital library that delivers expert content in both book and video form from the world's leading authors in technology and business.

Technology professionals, software developers, web designers, and business and creative professionals use Safari Books Online as their primary resource for research, problem solving, learning, and certification training.

Safari Books Online offers a range of product mixes and pricing programs for organizations, government agencies, and individuals. Subscribers have access to thousands of books, training videos, and prepublication manuscripts in one fully searchable database from publishers like O'Reilly Media, Prentice Hall Professional, Addison-Wesley Professional, Microsoft Press, Sams, Que, Peachpit Press, Focal Press, Cisco Press, John Wiley & Sons, Syngress, Morgan Kaufmann, IBM Redbooks, Packt, Adobe Press, FT Press, Apress, Manning, New Riders, McGraw-Hill, Jones & Bartlett, Course Technology, and dozens more. For more information about Safari Books Online, please visit us online.

## How to Contact Us

Please address comments and questions concerning this book to the publisher:

O'Reilly Media, Inc.
1005 Gravenstein Highway North
Sebastopol, CA 95472
800-998-9938 (in the United States or Canada)
707-829-0515 (international or local)
707-829-0104 (fax)

We have a web page for this book, where we list errata, examples, and any additional information. You can access this page at *http://oreil.ly/Scala_CB*.

To comment or ask technical questions about this book, send an email to *bookquestions@oreilly.com*.

For more information about our books, courses, conferences, and news, see our website at *http://www.oreilly.com*.

Find us on Facebook: *http://facebook.com/oreilly*

Follow us on Twitter: *http://twitter.com/oreillymedia*

Watch us on YouTube: *http://www.youtube.com/oreillymedia*

## Acknowledgments

Writing a book this large takes a lot of work, and I'd like to thank my editor, Courtney Nash, for keeping me sane during the speed bumps and generally being encouraging throughout the process.

Kim Cofer was the copy editor for this book, and I'd like to thank her for helping whip the book into shape, correcting my grammar issues regardless of how many times I repeated them, and for having good discussions about how to handle several issues in this book.

This book grew from about 540 pages during the first review to roughly 700 pages in its final release, and much of that was due to reviewers. All of the reviewers were helpful in different ways, but I'd especially like to thank Eric Torreborre (*http://etorreborre.blog spot.com/*) and Ryan LeCompte (*https://twitter.com/ryanlecompte*) for making it all the way through different versions of the book. Additional thanks go out to Rudi Farkas, Rahul Phulore, Jason Swartz, Hugo Sereno Ferreira, and Dean Wampler.

I'd also like to thank my friends and family members who encouraged me throughout the process. A special thanks goes to my sister Melissa, who helped bring my initial plain, wiki-style text into Microsoft Word, and styled everything correctly.

Finally, I'd like to thank Martin Odersky and his team for creating such an interesting programming language. I also owe his Programming Methods Laboratory at EFPL a special thank you for letting me use the Scala collections performance tables shown in Recipe 10.4.

# CHAPTER 1

# Strings

## Introduction

At first glance, a Scala `String` appears to be just a Java `String`. For instance, when you work in the Scala *Read-Evaluate-Print-Loop* (REPL) environment (see Figure 1-1) and print the name of a `String` literal, the REPL feedback tells you the type is `java.lang.String`:

```
scala> "Hello, world".getClass.getName
res0: String = java.lang.String
```

*Figure 1-1. The Scala REPL is an interactive environment where you can test Scala statements*

Indeed, a Scala `String` *is* a Java `String`, so you can use all the normal Java string methods. You can create a string variable, albeit in the Scala way:

```
val s = "Hello, world"
```

You can get the length of a string:

```
s.length  // 12
```

You can concatenate strings:

```
val s = "Hello" + " world"
```

These are all familiar operations. But because Scala offers the magic of *implicit conversions*, `String` instances also have access to all the methods of the `StringOps` class, so you can do many other things with them, such as treating a `String` instance as a sequence of characters. As a result, you can iterate over every character in the string using the `foreach` method:

```
scala> "hello".foreach(println)
h
e
l
l
o
```

You can treat a `String` as a sequence of characters in a `for` loop:

```
scala> for (c <- "hello") println(c)
h
e
l
l
o
```

You can also treat it as a sequence of bytes:

```
scala> s.getBytes.foreach(println)
104
101
108
108
111
```

Because there are many methods available on sequential collections, you can also use other functional methods like `filter`:

```
scala> val result = "hello world".filter(_ != 'l')
result: String = heo word
```

It's an oversimplification to say that this functionality comes from the StringOps class, but it's a useful illusion. The reality is that *some* of this functionality comes from StringOps, some comes from StringLike, some from WrappedString, and so on. If you dig into the Scala source code, you'll see that the rabbit hole goes deep, but it begins with the implicit conversion from String to StringOps in the Predef object.

When first learning Scala, take a look at the source code for the Predef object. It provides nice examples of many Scala programming features.

Figure 1-2, taken from the StringOps class Scaladoc page, shows the supertypes and type hierarchy for the StringOps class.

*Figure 1-2. Supertypes and type hierarchy information for the StringOps class*

## Add Methods to Closed Classes

Even though the String class is declared as final in Java, you've seen that Scala somehow adds new functionality to it. This happens through the power of *implicit conversions*. Recipe 1.9, "Accessing a Character in a String", demonstrates how to add your own methods to the String class using this technique.

As one more example of how this pattern helps a Scala String have both string and collection features, the following code uses the drop and take methods that are available on Scala sequences, along with the capitalize method from the StringOps class:

```
scala> "scala".drop(2).take(2).capitalize
res0: String = Al
```

In this chapter you'll see examples like this, and many more.

---

### How Did the Preceding Example Work?

The `drop` and `take` methods are demonstrated in Chapter 10, but in short, `drop` is a collection method that drops (discards) the number of elements that are specified from the beginning of the collection and keeps the remaining elements. When it's called on your string as `drop(2)`, it drops the first two characters from the string (`sc`), and returns the remaining elements:

```
scala> "scala".drop(2)
res0: String = ala
```

Next, the `take(2)` method retains the first two elements from the collection it's given, and discards the rest:

```
scala> "scala".drop(2).take(2)
res1: String = al
```

Finally, you treat the output from the `take(2)` method call like a `String` once again and call the `capitalize` method to get what you want:

```
scala> "scala".drop(2).take(2).capitalize
res2: String = Al
```

The `capitalize` method is in the `StringOps` class, but as a practical matter, you generally don't have to worry about that. When you're writing code in an IDE like Eclipse or IntelliJ and invoke the code assist keystroke, the `capitalize` method will appear in the list along with all the other methods that are available on a `String`.

If you're not familiar with chaining methods together like this, it's known as a *fluent* style of programming. See Recipe 5.9, "Supporting a Fluent Style of Programming", for more information.

---

# 1.1. Testing String Equality

## Problem

You want to compare two strings to see if they're equal, i.e., whether they contain the same sequence of characters.

## Solution

In Scala, you compare two `String` instances with the `==` operator. Given these strings:

```
scala> val s1 = "Hello"
s1: String = Hello
```

```
scala> val s2 = "Hello"
s2: String = Hello

scala> val s3 = "H" + "ello"
s3: String = Hello
```

You can test their equality like this:

```
scala> s1 == s2
res0: Boolean = true

scala> s1 == s3
res1: Boolean = true
```

A pleasant benefit of the == method is that it doesn't throw a NullPointerException on a basic test if a String is null:

```
scala> val s4: String = null
s4: String = null

scala> s3 == s4
res2: Boolean = false

scala> s4 == s3
res3: Boolean = false
```

If you want to compare two strings in a case-insensitive manner, you can convert both strings to uppercase or lowercase and compare them with the == method:

```
scala> val s1 = "Hello"
s1: String = Hello

scala> val s2 = "hello"
s2: String = hello

scala> s1.toUpperCase == s2.toUpperCase
res0: Boolean = true
```

However, be aware that calling a method on a null string can throw a NullPointerException:

```
scala> val s1: String = null
s1: String = null

scala> val s2: String = null
s2: String = null

scala> s1.toUpperCase == s2.toUpperCase
java.lang.NullPointerException  // more output here ...
```

To compare two strings while ignoring their case, you can also fall back and use the equalsIgnoreCase of the Java String class:

```
scala> val a = "Marisa"
a: String = Marisa

scala> val b = "marisa"
b: String = marisa

scala> a.equalsIgnoreCase(b)
res0: Boolean = true
```

## Discussion

In Scala, you test object equality with the == method. This is different than Java, where you use the equals method to compare two objects.

In Scala, the == method defined in the AnyRef class first checks for null values, and then calls the equals method on the first object (i.e., this) to see if the two objects are equal. As a result, you don't have to check for null values when comparing strings.

 In idiomatic Scala, you *never* use null values. The discussion in this recipe is intended to help you understand how == works if you encounter a null value, presumably from working with a Java library, or some other library where null values were used.

If you're coming from a language like Java, any time you feel like using a null, use an Option instead. (I find it helpful to imagine that Scala doesn't even have a null keyword.) See Recipe 20.6, "Using the Option/Some/None Pattern", for more information and examples.

For more information on defining equals methods, see Recipe 4.15, "Defining an equals Method (Object Equality)".

# 1.2. Creating Multiline Strings

## Problem

You want to create multiline strings within your Scala source code, like you can with the "heredoc" syntax of other languages.

## Solution

In Scala, you create multiline strings by surrounding your text with three double quotes:

```
val foo = """This is
    a multiline
    String"""
```

# Discussion

Although this works, the second and third lines in this example will end up with white-space at the beginning of their lines. If you print the string, it looks like this:

```
This is
    a multiline
    String
```

You can solve this problem in several different ways. First, you can left-justify every line after the first line of your string:

```
val foo = """This is
a multiline
String"""
```

A cleaner approach is to add the `stripMargin` method to the end of your multiline string and begin all lines after the first line with the pipe symbol (|):

```
val speech = """Four score and
              |seven years ago""".stripMargin
```

If you don't like using the | symbol, you can use any character you like with the `stripMargin` method:

```
val speech = """Four score and
              #seven years ago""".stripMargin('#')
```

All of these approaches yield the same result, a multiline string with each line of the string left justified:

```
Four score and
seven years ago
```

This results in a true multiline string, with a hidden \n character after the word "and" in the first line. To convert this multiline string into one continuous line you can add a `replaceAll` method after the `stripMargin` call, replacing all newline characters with blank spaces:

```
val speech = """Four score and
              |seven years ago
              |our fathers""".stripMargin.replaceAll("\n", " ")
```

This yields:

```
Four score and seven years ago our fathers
```

Another nice feature of Scala's multiline string syntax is that you can include single- and double-quotes without having to escape them:

```
val s = """This is known as a
         |"multiline" string
         |or 'heredoc' syntax.""". stripMargin.replaceAll("\n", " ")
```

This results in this string:

```
This is known as a "multiline" string or 'heredoc' syntax.
```

# 1.3. Splitting Strings

## Problem

You want to split a string into parts based on a field separator, such as a string you get from a comma-separated value (CSV) or pipe-delimited file.

## Solution

Use one of the `split` methods that are available on `String` objects:

```
scala> "hello world".split(" ")
res0: Array[java.lang.String] = Array(hello, world)
```

The `split` method returns an array of `String` elements, which you can then treat as a normal Scala `Array`:

```
scala> "hello world".split(" ").foreach(println)
hello
world
```

## Discussion

The string that the `split` method takes can be a regular expression, so you can split a string on simple characters like a comma in a CSV file:

```
scala> val s = "eggs, milk, butter, Coco Puffs"
s: java.lang.String = eggs, milk, butter, Coco Puffs

// 1st attempt
scala> s.split(",")
res0: Array[java.lang.String] = Array(eggs, " milk", " butter", " Coco Puffs")
```

Using this approach, it's best to trim each string. Use the `map` method to call `trim` on each string before returning the array:

```
// 2nd attempt, cleaned up
scala> s.split(",").map(_.trim)
res1: Array[java.lang.String] = Array(eggs, milk, butter, Coco Puffs)
```

You can also split a string based on a regular expression. This example shows how to split a string on whitespace characters:

```
scala> "hello world, this is Al".split("\\s+")
res0: Array[java.lang.String] = Array(hello, world,, this, is, Al)
```

### About that split method...

The `split` method is overloaded, with some versions of the method coming from the Java `String` class and some coming from the Scala `StringLike` class. For instance, if you call `split` with a `Char` argument instead of a `String` argument, you're using the `split` method from `StringLike`:

```
// split with a String argument
scala> "hello world".split(" ")
res0: Array[java.lang.String] = Array(hello, world)

// split with a Char argument
scala> "hello world".split(' ')
res1: Array[String] = Array(hello, world)
```

The subtle difference in that output—`Array[java.lang.String]` versus `Array[String]`—is a hint that something is different, but as a practical matter, this isn't important. Also, with the Scala IDE project integrated into Eclipse, you can see where each method comes from when the Eclipse "code assist" dialog is displayed. (IntelliJ IDEA and NetBeans may show similar information.)

# 1.4. Substituting Variables into Strings

## Problem

You want to perform variable substitution into a string, like you can do with other languages, such as Perl, PHP, and Ruby.

## Solution

Beginning with Scala 2.10 you can use *string interpolation* in a manner similar to other languages like Perl, PHP, and Ruby.

To use basic string interpolation in Scala, precede your string with the letter s and include your variables inside the string, with each variable name preceded by a $ character. This is shown in the `println` statement in the following example:

```
scala> val name = "Fred"
name: String = Fred

scala> val age = 33
age: Int = 33

scala> val weight = 200.00
weight: Double = 200.0

scala> println(s"$name is $age years old, and weighs $weight pounds.")
Fred is 33 years old, and weighs 200.0 pounds.
```

According to the official Scala string interpolation documentation (*http://bit.ly/1ahuxxB*), when you precede your string with the letter s, you're creating a *processed* string literal. This example uses the "s string interpolator," which lets you embed variables inside a string, where they're replaced by their values. As stated in the documentation, "Prepending s to any string literal allows the usage of variables directly in the string."

## Using expressions in string literals

In addition to putting variables inside strings, you can include expressions inside a string by placing the expression inside curly braces. According to the official string interpolation documentation (*http://bit.ly/1ahuxxB*), "Any arbitrary expression can be embedded in ${}."

In the following example, the value 1 is added to the variable age inside the string:

```
scala> println(s"Age next year: ${age + 1}")
Age next year: 34
```

This example shows that you can use an equality expression inside the curly braces:

```
scala> println(s"You are 33 years old: ${age == 33}")
You are 33 years old: true
```

You'll also need to use curly braces when printing object fields. The following example shows the correct approach:

```
scala> case class Student(name: String, score: Int)
defined class Student

scala> val hannah = Student("Hannah", 95)
hannah: Student = Student(Hannah,95)

scala> println(s"${hannah.name} has a score of ${hannah.score}")
Hannah has a score of 95
```

Attempting to print the values of the object fields without wrapping them in curly braces results in the wrong information being printed out:

```
// error: this is intentionally wrong
scala> println(s"$hannah.name has a score of $hannah.score")
Student(Hannah,95).name has a score of Student(Hannah,95).score
```

Because $hannah.name wasn't wrapped in curly braces, the wrong information was printed; in this case, the toString output of the hannah variable.

## s is a method

The s that's placed before each string literal is actually a method. Though this seems slightly less convenient than just putting variables inside of strings, there are at least two benefits to this approach:

- Scala provides other off-the-shelf interpolation functions to give you more power.
- You can define your own string interpolation functions.

To see why this is a good thing, let's look at another string interpolation function.

### The f string interpolator (printf style formatting)

In the example in the Solution, the `weight` was printed as `200.0`. This is okay, but what can you do if you want to add more decimal places to the weight, or remove them entirely?

This simple desire leads to the "f string interpolator," which lets you use `printf` style formatting specifiers inside strings. The following examples show how to print the `weight`, first with two decimal places:

```
scala> println(f"$name is $age years old, and weighs $weight%.2f pounds.")
Fred is 33 years old, and weighs 200.00 pounds.
```

and then with no decimal places:

```
scala> println(f"$name is $age years old, and weighs $weight%.0f pounds.")
Fred is 33 years old, and weighs 200 pounds.
```

As demonstrated, to use this approach, just follow these steps:

1. Precede your string with the letter `f`.
2. Use `printf` style formatting specifiers immediately after your variables.

The most common `printf` format specifiers are shown in Table 1-1 in the Discussion.

Though these examples used the `println` method, it's important to note that you can use string interpolation in other ways. For instance, you can assign the result of a variable substitution to a new variable, similar to calling `sprintf` in other languages:

```
scala> val out = f"$name, you weigh $weight%.0f pounds."
out: String = Fred, you weigh 200 pounds.
```

### The raw interpolator

In addition to the `s` and `f` string interpolators, Scala 2.10 includes another interpolator named `raw`. The `raw` interpolator "performs no escaping of literals within the string." The following example shows how `raw` compares to the `s` interpolator:

```
scala> s"foo\nbar"
res0: String =
foo
```

```
bar

scala> raw"foo\nbar"
res1: String = foo\nbar
```

The raw interpolator is useful when you want to avoid having a sequence of characters like \n turn into a newline character.

### Create your own interpolator

In addition to the s, f, and raw interpolators that are built into Scala 2.10, you can define your own interpolators. See the official Scala String Interpolation documentation (*http://bit.ly/1ahuxxB*) for an example of how to create your own interpolator.

 String interpolation does not work with pattern-matching statements in Scala 2.10. This feature is planned for inclusion in Scala 2.11.

## Discussion

Prior to version 2.10, Scala didn't include the string interpolation functionality just described. If you need to use a release prior to Scala 2.10 for some reason, the solution is to call the format method on a string, as shown in the following examples:

```
scala> val name = "Fred"
name: java.lang.String = Fred

scala> val age = 33
age: Int = 33

scala> val s = "%s is %d years old".format(name, age)
s: String = Fred is 33 years old

scala> println("%s is %d years old".format(name, age))
Fred is 33 years old
```

Just as with the string interpolation capability shown in the Solution, you can use this approach anywhere you want to format a string, such as a toString method:

```
override def toString: String =
  "%s %s, age %d".format(firstName, lastName, age)
```

With either of these approaches, you can format your variables using all the usual printf specifiers. The most common format specifiers are shown in Table 1-1.

*Table 1-1. Common printf style format specifiers*

| Format specifier | Description |
| --- | --- |
| %c | Character |
| %d | Decimal number (integer, base 10) |
| %e | Exponential floating-point number |
| %f | Floating-point number |
| %i | Integer (base 10) |
| %o | Octal number (base 8) |
| %s | A string of characters |
| %u | Unsigned decimal (integer) number |
| %x | Hexadecimal number (base 16) |
| %% | Print a "percent" character |
| \% | Print a "percent" character |

## See Also

- This `printf` cheat sheet shows more format specifiers and examples (*http://bit.ly/ 16EPKxn*)
- This Oracle `Formatter` page (*http://bit.ly/1azIsTh*) shows examples and details
- The official Scala String Interpolation documentation (*http://bit.ly/1ahuxxB*)

# 1.5. Processing a String One Character at a Time

## Problem

You want to iterate through each character in a string, performing an operation on each character as you traverse the string.

## Solution

Depending on your needs and preferences, you can use the `map` or `foreach` methods, a `for` loop, or other approaches. Here's a simple example of how to create an uppercase string from an input string, using `map`:

```
scala> val upper = "hello, world".map(c => c.toUpper)
upper: String = HELLO, WORLD
```

As you'll see in many examples throughout this book, you can shorten that code using the magic of Scala's underscore character:

```
scala> val upper = "hello, world".map(_.toUpper)
upper: String = HELLO, WORLD
```

With any collection—such as a sequence of characters in a string—you can also chain collection methods together to achieve a desired result. In the following example, the filter method is called on the original String to create a new String with all occurrences of the lowercase letter "L" removed. That String is then used as input to the map method to convert the remaining characters to uppercase:

```
scala> val upper = "hello, world".filter(_ != 'l').map(_.toUpper)
upper: String = HEO, WORD
```

When you first start with Scala, you may not be comfortable with the map method, in which case you can use Scala's for loop to achieve the same result. This example shows another way to print each character:

```
scala> for (c <- "hello") println(c)
h
e
l
l
o
```

To write a for loop to work like a map method, add a yield statement to the end of the loop. This for/yield loop is equivalent to the first two map examples:

```
scala> val upper = for (c <- "hello, world") yield c.toUpper
upper: String = HELLO, WORLD
```

Adding yield to a for loop essentially places the result from each loop iteration into a temporary holding area. When the loop completes, all of the elements in the holding area are returned as a single collection.

This for/yield loop achieves the same result as the third map example:

```
val result = for {
  c <- "hello, world"
  if c != 'l'
} yield c.toUpper
```

Whereas the map or for/yield approaches are used to transform one collection into another, the foreach method is typically used to operate on each element without returning a result. This is useful for situations like printing:

```
scala> "hello".foreach(println)
h
e
l
l
o
```

## Discussion

Because Scala treats a string as a sequence of characters—and because of Scala's background as both an object-oriented *and* functional programming language—you can iterate over the characters in a string with the approaches shown. Compare those examples with a common Java approach:

```
String s = "Hello";
StringBuilder sb = new StringBuilder();
for (int i = 0; i < s.length(); i++) {
  char c = s.charAt(i);
  // do something with the character ...
  // sb.append ...
}
String result = sb.toString();
```

You'll see that the Scala approach is more concise, but still very readable. This combination of conciseness and readability lets you focus on solving the problem at hand. Once you get comfortable with Scala, it feels like the imperative code in the Java example obscures your business logic.

Wikipedia describes *imperative programming* like this:

> Imperative programming is a programming paradigm that describes computation in terms of statements that change a program state ... imperative programs define sequences of commands for the computer to perform.

This is shown in the Java example, which defines a series of explicit statements that tell a computer how to achieve a desired result.

### Understanding how map works

Depending on your coding preferences, you can pass large blocks of code to a map method. These two examples demonstrate the syntax for passing an algorithm to a map method:

```
// first example
"HELLO".map(c => (c.toByte+32).toChar)

// second example
"HELLO".map{ c =>
  (c.toByte+32).toChar
}
```

Notice that the algorithm operates on one Char at a time. This is because the map method in this example is called on a String, and map treats a String as a sequential collection of Char elements. The map method has an implicit loop, and in that loop, it passes one Char at a time to the algorithm it's given.

Although this algorithm it still short, imagine for a moment that it is longer. In this case, to keep your code clear, you might want to write it as a method (or function) that you can pass into the map method.

To write a method that you can pass into map to operate on the characters in a String, define it to take a single Char as input, then perform the logic on that Char inside the method. When the logic is complete, return whatever it is that your algorithm returns. Though the following algorithm is still short, it demonstrates how to create a custom method and pass that method into map:

```
// write your own method that operates on a character
scala> def toLower(c: Char): Char = (c.toByte+32).toChar
toLower: (c: Char)Char

// use that method with map
scala> "HELLO".map(toLower)
res0: String = hello
```

As an added benefit, the same method also works with the for/yield approach:

```
scala> val s = "HELLO"
s: java.lang.String = HELLO

scala> for (c <- s) yield toLower(c)
res1: String = hello
```

 I've used the word "method" in this discussion, but you can also use functions here instead of methods. What's the difference between a method and a function?

Here's a quick look at a *function* equivalent to this toLower method:

```
val toLower = (c: Char) => (c.toByte+32).toChar
```

This function can be passed into map in the same way the previous toLower method was used:

```
scala> "HELLO".map(toLower)
res0: String = hello
```

For more information on functions and the differences between methods and functions, see Chapter 9, *Functional Programming*.

### A complete example

The following example demonstrates how to call the getBytes method on a String, and then pass a block of code into a foreach method to help calculate an Adler-32 checksum value on a String:

```
package tests

/**
```

```
   * Calculate the Adler-32 checksum using Scala.
   * @see http://en.wikipedia.org/wiki/Adler-32
   */
object Adler32Checksum {

  val MOD_ADLER = 65521

  def main(args: Array[String]) {
    val sum = adler32sum("Wikipedia")
    printf("checksum (int) = %d\n", sum)
    printf("checksum (hex) = %s\n", sum.toHexString)
  }

  def adler32sum(s: String): Int = {
    var a = 1
    var b = 0
    s.getBytes.foreach{char =>
      a = (char + a) % MOD_ADLER
      b = (b + a) % MOD_ADLER
    }
    // note: Int is 32 bits, which this requires
    b * 65536 + a      // or (b << 16) + a
  }

}
```

The getBytes method returns a sequential collection of bytes from a String as follows:

```
scala> "hello".getBytes
res0: Array[Byte] = Array(104, 101, 108, 108, 111)
```

Adding the foreach method call after getBytes lets you operate on each Byte value:

```
scala> "hello".getBytes.foreach(println)
104
101
108
108
111
```

You use foreach in this example instead of map, because the goal is to loop over each Byte in the String, and do something with each Byte, but you don't want to return anything from the loop.

## See Also

- Under the covers, the Scala compiler translates a for loop into a foreach method call. This gets more complicated if the loop has one or more if statements (guards) or a yield expression. This is discussed in detail in Recipe 3.1, "Looping with for and foreach" and I also provide examples on my website at alvinalexander.com (*http://bit.ly/1bvk82T*). The full details are presented in Section 6.19 (*http://bit.ly/158qP62*) of the current Scala Language Specification.

- The Adler-32 checksum algorithm (*http://en.wikipedia.org/wiki/Adler-32*)

# 1.6. Finding Patterns in Strings

## Problem

You need to determine whether a String contains a regular expression pattern.

## Solution

Create a Regex object by invoking the .r method on a String, and then use that pattern with findFirstIn when you're looking for one match, and findAllIn when looking for all matches.

To demonstrate this, first create a Regex for the pattern you want to search for, in this case, a sequence of one or more numeric characters:

```
scala> val numPattern = "[0-9]+".r
numPattern: scala.util.matching.Regex = [0-9]+
```

Next, create a sample String you can search:

```
scala> val address = "123 Main Street Suite 101"
address: java.lang.String = 123 Main Street Suite 101
```

The findFirstIn method finds the first match:

```
scala> val match1 = numPattern.findFirstIn(address)
match1: Option[String] = Some(123)
```

(Notice that this method returns an Option[String]. I'll dig into that in the Discussion.)

When looking for multiple matches, use the findAllIn method:

```
scala> val matches = numPattern.findAllIn(address)
matches: scala.util.matching.Regex.MatchIterator = non-empty iterator
```

As you can see, findAllIn returns an iterator, which lets you loop over the results:

```
scala> matches.foreach(println)
123
101
```

If findAllIn doesn't find any results, an empty iterator is returned, so you can still write your code just like that—you don't need to check to see if the result is null. If you'd rather have the results as an Array, add the toArray method after the findAllIn call:

```
scala> val matches = numPattern.findAllIn(address).toArray
matches: Array[String] = Array(123, 101)
```

If there are no matches, this approach yields an empty `Array`. Other methods like `toList`, `toSeq`, and `toVector` are also available.

# Discussion

Using the `.r` method on a `String` is the easiest way to create a `Regex` object. Another approach is to import the `Regex` class, create a `Regex` instance, and then use the instance in the same way:

```
scala> import scala.util.matching.Regex
import scala.util.matching.Regex

scala> val numPattern = new Regex("[0-9]+")
numPattern: scala.util.matching.Regex = [0-9]+

scala> val address = "123 Main Street Suite 101"
address: java.lang.String = 123 Main Street Suite 101

scala> val match1 = numPattern.findFirstIn(address)
match1: Option[String] = Some(123)
```

Although this is a bit more work, it's also more obvious. I've found that it can be easy to overlook the `.r` at the end of a `String` (and then spend a few minutes wondering how the code I saw could possibly work).

### Handling the Option returned by findFirstIn

As mentioned in the Solution, the `findFirstIn` method finds the first match in the `String` and returns an `Option[String]`:

```
scala> val match1 = numPattern.findFirstIn(address)
match1: Option[String] = Some(123)
```

The Option/Some/None pattern is discussed in detail in Recipe 20.6, but the simple way to think about an `Option` is that it's a container that holds either zero or one values. In the case of `findFirstIn`, if it succeeds, it returns the string "123" as a `Some(123)`, as shown in this example. However, if it fails to find the pattern in the string it's searching, it will return a `None`, as shown here:

```
scala> val address = "No address given"
address: String = No address given

scala> val match1 = numPattern.findFirstIn(address)
match1: Option[String] = None
```

To summarize, a method defined to return an `Option[String]` will either return a `Some(String)`, or a `None`.

The normal way to work with an `Option` is to use one of these approaches:

- Call `getOrElse` on the value.

- Use the `Option` in a match expression.
- Use the `Option` in a `foreach` loop.

Recipe 20.6 describes those approaches in detail, but they're demonstrated here for your convenience.

With the `getOrElse` approach, you attempt to "get" the result, while also specifying a default value that should be used if the method failed:

```
scala> val result = numPattern.findFirstIn(address).getOrElse("no match")
result: String = 123
```

Because an `Option` is a collection of zero or one elements, an experienced Scala developer will also use a `foreach` loop in this situation:

```
numPattern.findFirstIn(address).foreach { e =>
  // perform the next step in your algorithm,
  // operating on the value 'e'
}
```

A match expression also provides a very readable solution to the problem:

```
match1 match {
  case Some(s) => println(s"Found: $s")
  case None =>
}
```

See Recipe 20.6 for more information.

To summarize this approach, the following REPL example shows the complete process of creating a `Regex`, searching a `String` with `findFirstIn`, and then using a `foreach` loop on the resulting match:

```
scala> val numPattern = "[0-9]+".r
numPattern: scala.util.matching.Regex = [0-9]+

scala> val address = "123 Main Street Suite 101"
address: String = 123 Main Street Suite 101

scala> val match1 = numPattern.findFirstIn(address)
match1: Option[String] = Some(123)

scala> match1.foreach { e =>
     |     println(s"Found a match: $e")
     | }
Found a match: 123
```

## See Also

- The `StringOps` class (*http://bit.ly/1bvlHxv*)
- The `Regex` class (*http://bit.ly/18eabYK*)

- Recipe 20.6, "Using the Option/Some/None Pattern" provides more information on `Option`

# 1.7. Replacing Patterns in Strings

## Problem

You want to search for regular-expression patterns in a string, and replace them.

## Solution

Because a `String` is immutable, you can't perform find-and-replace operations directly on it, but you can create a new `String` that contains the replaced contents. There are several ways to do this.

You can call `replaceAll` on a `String`, remembering to assign the result to a new variable:

```
scala> val address = "123 Main Street".replaceAll("[0-9]", "x")
address: java.lang.String = xxx Main Street
```

You can create a regular expression and then call `replaceAllIn` on that expression, again remembering to assign the result to a new string:

```
scala> val regex = "[0-9]".r
regex: scala.util.matching.Regex = [0-9]

scala> val newAddress = regex.replaceAllIn("123 Main Street", "x")
newAddress: String = xxx Main Street
```

To replace only the first occurrence of a pattern, use the `replaceFirst` method:

```
scala> val result = "123".replaceFirst("[0-9]", "x")
result: java.lang.String = x23
```

You can also use `replaceFirstIn` with a `Regex`:

```
scala> val regex = "H".r
regex: scala.util.matching.Regex = H

scala> val result = regex.replaceFirstIn("Hello world", "J")
result: String = Jello world
```

## See Also

Recipe 1.6, "Finding Patterns in Strings" for examples of how to find patterns in strings

# 1.8. Extracting Parts of a String That Match Patterns

## Problem

You want to extract one or more parts of a string that match the regular-expression patterns you specify.

## Solution

Define the regular-expression patterns you want to extract, placing parentheses around them so you can extract them as "regular-expression groups." First, define the desired pattern:

```
val pattern = "([0-9]+) ([A-Za-z]+)".r
```

Next, extract the regex groups from the target string:

```
val pattern(count, fruit) = "100 Bananas"
```

This code extracts the numeric field and the alphabetic field from the given string as two separate variables, count and fruit, as shown in the Scala REPL:

```
scala> val pattern = "([0-9]+) ([A-Za-z]+)".r
pattern: scala.util.matching.Regex = ([0-9]+) ([A-Za-z]+)

scala> val pattern(count, fruit) = "100 Bananas"
count: String = 100
fruit: String = Bananas
```

## Discussion

The syntax shown here may feel a little unusual because it seems like you're defining pattern as a val field twice, but this syntax is more convenient and readable in a real-world example.

Imagine you're writing the code for a search engine like Google, and you want to let people search for movies using a wide variety of phrases. To be really convenient, you'll let them type any of these phrases to get a listing of movies near Boulder, Colorado:

```
"movies near 80301"
"movies 80301"
"80301 movies"
"movie: 80301"
"movies: 80301"
"movies near boulder, co"
"movies near boulder, colorado"
```

One way you can allow all these phrases to be used is to define a series of regular-expression patterns to match against them. Just define your expressions, and then attempt to match whatever the user types against all the possible expressions you're willing to allow.

For example purposes, you'll just allow these two simplified patterns:

```
// match "movies 80301"
val MoviesZipRE = "movies (\\d{5})".r

// match "movies near boulder, co"
val MoviesNearCityStateRE = "movies near ([a-z]+), ([a-z]{2})".r
```

Once you've defined the patterns you want to allow, you can match them against whatever text the user enters, using a match expression. In this example, you'll call a fictional method named getSearchResults when a match occurs:

```
textUserTyped match {
  case MoviesZipRE(zip) => getSearchResults(zip)
  case MoviesNearCityStateRE(city, state) => getSearchResults(city, state)
  case _ => println("did not match a regex")
}
```

As you can see, this syntax makes your match expressions very readable. For both patterns you're matching, you call an overloaded version of the getSearchResults method, passing it the zip field in the first case, and the city and state fields in the second case.

The two regular expressions shown in this example will match strings like this:

```
"movies 80301"
"movies 99676"
"movies near boulder, co"
"movies near talkeetna, ak"
```

It's important to note that with this technique, the regular expressions must match the *entire* user input. With the regex patterns shown, the following strings will fail because they have a blank space at the end of the line:

```
"movies 80301 "
"movies near boulder, co "
```

You can solve this particular problem by trimming the input string or using a more complicated regular expression, which you'll want to do anyway in the "real world."

As you can imagine, you can use this same pattern-matching technique in many different circumstances, including matching date and time formats, street addresses, people's names, and many other situations.

## See Also

- Recipe 3.7, "Using a Match Expression Like a switch Statement" for more match expression examples
- Recipe 14.12, "Prompting for Input from a Scala Shell Script" shows another example of this technique

# 1.9. Accessing a Character in a String

## Problem

You want to get a character at a specific position in a string.

## Solution

You *could* use the Java charAt method:

```
scala> "hello".charAt(0)
res0: Char = h
```

However, the preferred approach is to use Scala's Array notation:

```
scala> "hello"(0)
res1: Char = h

scala> "hello"(1)
res2: Char = e
```

## Discussion

When looping over the characters in a string, you'll normally use the map or foreach methods, but if for some reason those approaches won't work for your situation, you can treat a String as an Array, and access each character with the array notation shown.

The Scala array notation is different than Java because in Scala it's really a method call, with some nice syntactic sugar added. You write your code like this, which is convenient and easy to read:

```
scala> "hello"(1)
res0: Char = e
```

But behind the scenes, Scala converts your code into this:

```
scala> "hello".apply(1)
res1: Char = e
```

This little bit of syntactic sugar is explained in detail in Recipe 6.8, "Creating Object Instances Without Using the new Keyword".

# 1.10. Add Your Own Methods to the String Class

## Problem

Rather than create a separate library of String utility methods, like a StringUtilities class, you want to add your own behavior(s) to the String class, so you can write code like this:

```
"HAL".increment
```

Instead of this:

```
StringUtilities.increment("HAL")
```

## Solution

In Scala 2.10, you define an implicit class, and then define methods within that class to implement the behavior you want.

You can see this in the REPL. First, define your implicit class and method(s):

```
scala> implicit class StringImprovements(s: String) {
     | def increment = s.map(c => (c + 1).toChar)
     | }
defined class StringImprovements
```

Then invoke your method on any String:

```
scala> val result = "HAL".increment
result: String = IBM
```

In real-world code, this is just slightly more complicated. According to SIP-13, Implicit Classes (*http://bit.ly/10WqdRi*), "An implicit class must be defined in a scope where method definitions are allowed (not at the top level)." This means that your implicit class must be defined inside a class, object, or package object.

### Put the implicit class in an object

One way to satisfy this condition is to put the implicit class inside an object. For instance, you can place the StringImprovements implicit class in an object such as a StringUtils object, as shown here:

```
package com.alvinalexander.utils

object StringUtils {
  implicit class StringImprovements(val s: String) {
    def increment = s.map(c => (c + 1).toChar)
```

```
    }
  }
```

You can then use the `increment` method somewhere else in your code, after adding the proper `import` statement:

```
package foo.bar

import com.alvinalexander.utils.StringUtils._

object Main extends App {
  println("HAL".increment)
}
```

## Put the implicit class in a package object

Another way to satisfy the requirement is to put the implicit class in a *package object*. With this approach, place the following code in a file named *package.scala*, in the appropriate directory. If you're using SBT, you should place the file in the *src/main/scala/com/alvinalexander* directory of your project, containing the following code:

```
package com.alvinalexander

package object utils {

  implicit class StringImprovements(val s: String) {
    def increment = s.map(c => (c + 1).toChar)
  }

}
```

When you need to use the `increment` method in some other code, use a slightly different `import` statement from the previous example:

```
package foo.bar

import com.alvinalexander.utils._

object MainDriver extends App {
  println("HAL".increment)
}
```

 See Recipe 6.7, "Putting Common Code in Package Objects" for more information about package objects.

### Using versions of Scala prior to version 2.10

If for some reason you need to use a version of Scala prior to version 2.10, you'll need to take a slightly different approach. In this case, define a method named increment in a normal Scala class:

```
class StringImprovements(val s: String) {
  def increment = s.map(c => (c + 1).toChar)
}
```

Next, define another method to handle the implicit conversion:

```
implicit def stringToString(s: String) = new StringImprovements(s)
```

The String parameter in the stringToString method essentially links the String class to the StringImprovements class.

Now you can use increment as in the earlier examples:

```
"HAL".increment
```

Here's what this looks like in the REPL:

```
scala> class StringImprovements(val s: String) {
     |    def increment = s.map(c => (c + 1).toChar)
     | }
defined class StringImprovements

scala> implicit def stringToString(s: String) = new StringImprovements(s)
stringToString: (s: String)StringImprovements

scala> "HAL".increment
res0: String = IBM
```

## Discussion

As you just saw, in Scala, you can add new functionality to closed classes by writing implicit conversions and bringing them into scope when you need them. A major benefit of this approach is that you don't have to extend existing classes to add the new functionality. For instance, there's no need to create a new class named MyString that extends String, and then use MyString throughout your code instead of String; instead, you define the behavior you want, and then add that behavior to *all* String objects in the current scope when you add the import statement.

Note that you can define as many methods as you need in your implicit class. The following code shows both increment and decrement methods, along with a method named hideAll that returns a String with all characters replaced by the * character:

```
implicit class StringImprovements(val s: String) {
  def increment = s.map(c => (c + 1).toChar)
  def decrement = s.map(c => (c - 1).toChar)
```

```
    def hideAll = s.replaceAll(".", "*")
}
```

Notice that except for the `implicit` keyword before the class name, the `StringImprovements` class and its methods are written as usual.

By simply bringing the code into scope with an `import` statement, you can use these methods, as shown here in the REPL:

```
scala> "HAL".increment
res0: String = IBM
```

Here's a simplified description of how this works:

1. The compiler sees a string literal "HAL."
2. The compiler sees that you're attempting to invoke a method named `increment` on the `String`.
3. Because the compiler can't find that method on the `String` class, it begins looking around for implicit conversion methods that are in scope and accepts a `String` argument.
4. This leads the compiler to the `StringImprovements` class, where it finds the `increment` method.

That's an oversimplification of what happens, but it gives you the general idea of how implicit conversions work.

 For more details on what's happening here, see SIP-13, Implicit Classes (*http://bit.ly/10WqdRi*).

### Annotate your method return type

It's recommended that the return type of implicit method definitions should be annotated. If you run into a situation where the compiler can't find your implicit methods, or you just want to be explicit when declaring your methods, add the return type to your method definitions.

In the `increment`, `decrement`, and `hideAll` methods shown here, the return type of `String` is made explicit:

```
implicit class StringImprovements(val s: String) {
  // being explicit that each method returns a String
  def increment: String = s.map(c => (c + 1).toChar)
  def decrement: String = s.map(c => (c - 1).toChar)
  def hideAll: String = s.replaceAll(".", "*")
}
```

### Returning other types

Although all of the methods shown so far have returned a String, you can return any type from your methods that you need. The following class demonstrates several different types of string conversion methods:

```
implicit class StringImprovements(val s: String) {
  def increment = s.map(c => (c + 1).toChar)
  def decrement = s.map(c => (c - 1).toChar)
  def hideAll: String = s.replaceAll(".", "*")
  def plusOne = s.toInt + 1
  def asBoolean = s match {
    case "0" | "zero" | "" | " " => false
    case _ => true
  }
}
```

With these new methods you can now perform Int and Boolean conversions, in addition to the String conversions shown earlier:

```
scala> "4".plusOne
res0: Int = 5

scala> "0".asBoolean
res1: Boolean = false

scala> "1".asBoolean
res2: Boolean = true
```

Note that all of these methods have been simplified to keep them short and readable. In the real world, you'll want to add some error-checking.

# CHAPTER 2

# Numbers

## Introduction

In Scala, all the numeric types are objects, including Byte, Char, Double, Float, Int, Long, and Short. These seven numeric types extend the AnyVal trait, as do the Unit and Boolean classes, which are considered to be "nonnumeric value types."

As shown in Table 2-1, the seven built-in numeric types have the same data ranges as their Java primitive equivalents.

*Table 2-1. Data ranges of Scala's built-in numeric types*

| Data type | Range |
| --- | --- |
| Char | 16-bit unsigned Unicode character |
| Byte | 8-bit signed value |
| Short | 16-bit signed value |
| Int | 32-bit signed value |
| Long | 64-bit signed value |
| Float | 32-bit IEEE 754 single precision float |
| Double | 64-bit IEEE 754 single precision float |

In addition to those types, Boolean can have the values true or false.

If you ever need to know the exact values of the data ranges, you can find them in the Scala REPL:

```
scala> Short.MinValue
res0: Short = -32768

scala> Short.MaxValue
res1: Short = 32767
```

```
scala> Int.MinValue
res2: Int = -2147483648

scala> Float.MinValue
res3: Float = -3.4028235E38
```

In addition to these basic numeric types, it's helpful to understand the BigInt and BigDecimal classes, as well as the methods in the scala.math package. These are all covered in this chapter.

## Complex Numbers and Dates

If you need more powerful math classes than those that are included with the standard Scala distribution, check out the Spire project (*https://github.com/non/spire*), which includes classes like Rational, Complex, Real, and more; and ScalaLab (*http://code.google.com/p/scalalab/*), which offers Matlab-like scientific computing in Scala.

For processing dates, the Java Joda Time (*http://joda-time.sourceforge.net/*) project is popular and well documented. A project named nscala-time (*https://github.com/nscala-time/nscala-time*) implements a Scala wrapper around Joda Time, and lets you write date expressions in a more Scala-like way, including these examples:

```
DateTime.now    // returns org.joda.time.DateTime
DateTime.now + 2.months
DateTime.nextMonth < DateTime.now + 2.months
(2.hours + 45.minutes + 10.seconds).millis
```

# 2.1. Parsing a Number from a String

## Problem

You want to convert a String to one of Scala's numeric types.

## Solution

Use the to* methods that are available on a String (courtesy of the StringLike trait):

```
scala> "100".toInt
res0: Int = 100

scala> "100".toDouble
res1: Double = 100.0

scala> "100".toFloat
res2: Float = 100.0

scala> "1".toLong
res3: Long = 1
```

```
scala> "1".toShort
res4: Short = 1

scala> "1".toByte
res5: Byte = 1
```

Be careful, because these methods can throw the usual Java `NumberFormatException`:

```
scala> "foo".toInt
java.lang.NumberFormatException: For input string: "foo"
    at java.lang.NumberFormatException.forInputString(NumberFormatException.java)
    at java.lang.Integer.parseInt(Integer.java:449)
    ... more output here ...
```

`BigInt` and `BigDecimal` instances can also be created directly from strings (and can also throw a `NumberFormatException`):

```
scala> val b = BigInt("1")
b: scala.math.BigInt = 1

scala> val b = BigDecimal("3.14159")
b: scala.math.BigDecimal = 3.14159
```

### Handling a base and radix

If you need to perform calculations using bases other than 10, you'll find the `toInt` method in the Scala `Int` class doesn't have a method that lets you pass in a base and radix. To solve this problem, use the `parseInt` method in the `java.lang.Integer` class, as shown in these examples:

```
scala> Integer.parseInt("1", 2)
res0: Int = 1

scala> Integer.parseInt("10", 2)
res1: Int = 2

scala> Integer.parseInt("100", 2)
res2: Int = 4

scala> Integer.parseInt("1", 8)
res3: Int = 1

scala> Integer.parseInt("10", 8)
res4: Int = 8
```

If you're a fan of implicit conversions, you can create an implicit class and method to help solve the problem. As described in Recipe 1.10, "Add Your Own Methods to the String Class" create the implicit conversion as follows:

```
implicit class StringToInt(s: String) {
  def toInt(radix: Int) = Integer.parseInt(s, radix)
}
```

Defining this implicit class (and bringing it into scope) adds a `toInt` method that takes a radix argument to the `String` class, which you can now call instead of calling `Integer.parseInt`:

```
scala> implicit class StringToInt(s: String) {
     | def toInt(radix: Int) = Integer.parseInt(s, radix)
     | }
defined class StringToInt

scala> "1".toInt(2)
res0: Int = 1

scala> "10".toInt(2)
res1: Int = 2

scala> "100".toInt(2)
res2: Int = 4

scala> "100".toInt(8)
res3: Int = 64

scala> "100".toInt(16)
res4: Int = 256
```

See Recipe 1.10 for more details on how to implement this solution outside of the REPL.

## Discussion

If you've used Java to convert a `String` to a numeric data type, then the `NumberFormatException` is familiar. However, Scala doesn't have checked exceptions, so you'll probably want to handle this situation differently.

First, you don't have to declare that Scala methods can throw an exception, so it's perfectly legal to declare a Scala method like this:

```
// not required to declare "throws NumberFormatException"
def toInt(s: String) = s.toInt
```

If you're going to allow an exception to be thrown like this, callers of your method might appreciate knowing that this can happen. Consider adding a Scaladoc comment to your method in this case.

If you prefer to declare that your method can throw an exception, mark it with the `@throws` annotation, as shown here:

```
@throws(classOf[NumberFormatException])
def toInt(s: String) = s.toInt
```

This approach is required if the method will be called from Java code, as described in Recipe 17.2, "Add Exception Annotations to Scala Methods to Work with Java".

However, in Scala, situations like this are often handled with the Option/Some/None pattern, as described in Recipe 20.6, "Using the Option/Some/None Pattern". With this approach, define the toInt method like this:

```
def toInt(s: String):Option[Int] = {
  try {
    Some(s.toInt)
  } catch {
    case e: NumberFormatException => None
  }
}
```

Now you can call the toInt method in several different ways, depending on your needs. One way is with getOrElse:

```
println(toInt("1").getOrElse(0))    // 1
println(toInt("a").getOrElse(0))    // 0

// assign the result to x
val x = toInt(aString).getOrElse(0)
```

Another approach is to use a match expression. You can write a match expression to print the toInt result like this:

```
toInt(aString) match {
  case Some(n) => println(n)
  case None => println("Boom! That wasn't a number.")
}
```

You can also write a match expression as follows to assign the result to a variable:

```
val result = toInt(aString) match {
  case Some(x) => x
  case None => 0  // however you want to handle this
}
```

If these examples haven't yet sold you on the Option/Some/None approach, you'll see in Chapter 10 and Chapter 11 that this pattern is incredibly helpful and convenient when working with collections.

## Alternatives to Option

If you like the Option/Some/None concept, but need access to the exception information, there are several additional possibilities:

- Try, Success, and Failure (introduced in Scala 2.10)
- Either, Left, and Right

These alternate approaches are discussed in Recipe 20.6, "Using the Option/Some/None Pattern". (The new Try/Success/Failure approach is especially appealing.)

## See Also

- Recipe 20.6, "Using the Option/Some/None Pattern"
- The `StringLike` trait (*http://bit.ly/18bCByX*)

# 2.2. Converting Between Numeric Types (Casting)

## Problem

You want to convert from one numeric type to another, such as from an `Int` to a `Double`.

## Solution

Instead of using the "cast" approach in Java, use the `to*` methods that are available on all numeric types. These methods can be demonstrated in the REPL (note that you need to hit Tab at the end of the first example):

```
scala> val b = a.to[Tab]
toByte      toChar      toDouble   toFloat    toInt       toLong
toShort     toString

scala> 19.45.toInt
res0: Int = 19

scala> 19.toFloat
res1: Float = 19.0

scala> 19.toDouble
res2: Double = 19.0

scala> 19.toLong
res3: Long = 19

scala> val b = a.toFloat
b: Float = 1945.0
```

## Discussion

In Java, you convert from one numeric type to another by casting the types, like this:

```
int a = (int) 100.00;
```

But in Scala, you use the `to*` methods, as shown in this recipe.

If you want to avoid potential conversion errors when casting from one numeric type to another, you can use the related `isValid` methods to test whether the type can be converted before attempting the conversion. For instance, a `Double` object (via `RichDouble`) has methods like `isValidInt` and `isValidShort`:

```
scala> val a = 1000L
a: Long = 1000

scala> a.isValidByte
res0: Boolean = false

scala> a.isValidShort
res1: Boolean = true
```

## See Also

The `RichDouble` class (*http://bit.ly/14O87Sn*)

# 2.3. Overriding the Default Numeric Type

## Problem

Scala automatically assigns types to numeric values when you assign them, and you need to override the default type it assigns as you create a numeric field.

## Solution

If you assign 1 to a variable, Scala assigns it the type `Int`:

```
scala> val a = 1
a: Int = 1
```

The following examples show one way to override simple numeric types:

```
scala> val a = 1d
a: Double = 1.0

scala> val a = 1f
a: Float = 1.0

scala> val a = 1000L
a: Long = 1000
```

Another approach is to annotate the variable with a type, like this:

```
scala> val a = 0: Byte
a: Byte = 0

scala> val a = 0: Int
a: Int = 0

scala> val a = 0: Short
a: Short = 0
```

```
scala> val a = 0: Double
a: Double = 0.0

scala> val a = 0: Float
a: Float = 0.0
```

Spacing after the colon isn't important, so you can use this format, if preferred:

```
val a = 0:Byte
```

According to the Scala Style Guide (*http://bit.ly/13ljL33*), those examples show the preferred style for annotating types, but personally I prefer the following syntax when assigning types to variables, specifying the type after the variable name:

```
scala> val a:Byte = 0
a: Byte = 0

scala> val a:Int = 0
a: Int = 0
```

You can create hex values by preceding the number with a leading 0x or 0X, and you can store them as an Int or Long:

```
scala> val a = 0x20
a: Int = 32

// if you want to store the value as a Long
scala> val a = 0x20L
a: Long = 32
```

 In some rare instances, you may need to take advantage of *type ascription*. Stack Overflow (*http://bit.ly/1ahyUbN*) shows a case where it's advantageous to upcast a String to an Object. The technique is shown here:

```
scala> val s = "Dave"
s: String = Dave

scala> val p = s: Object
p: Object = Dave
```

As you can see, the technique is similar to this recipe. This upcasting is known as *type ascription*. The official Scala documentation describes type ascription as follows:

> Ascription is basically just an up-cast performed at compile time for the sake of the type checker. Its use is not common, but it does happen on occasion. The most often seen case of ascription is invoking a varargs method with a single Seq parameter.

## Discussion

It's helpful to know about this approach when creating object instances. The general syntax looks like this:

```
// general case
var [name]:[Type] = [initial value]

// example
var a:Short = 0
```

This form can be helpful when you need to initialize numeric `var` fields in a class:

```
class Foo {
  var a: Short = 0      // specify a default value
  var b: Short = _      // defaults to 0
}
```

As shown, you can use the underscore character as a placeholder when assigning an initial value. This works when creating class variables, but doesn't work in other places, such as inside a method. For numeric types this isn't an issue—you can just assign the type the value zero—but with most other types, you can use this approach inside a method:

```
var name = null.asInstanceOf[String]
```

Better yet, use the `Option`/`Some`/`None` pattern. It helps eliminate `null` values from your code, which is a very good thing. You'll see this pattern used in the best Scala libraries and frameworks, such as the Play Framework. An excellent example of this approach is shown in Recipe 12.4, "How to Process Every Character in a Text File".

See Recipe 20.5, "Eliminate null Values from Your Code" and Recipe 20.6, "Using the Option/Some/None Pattern" for more discussion of this important topic.

## See Also

- The Scala Style Guide (*http://docs.scala-lang.org/style*)
- The Stack Overflow URL (*http://bit.ly/1ahyUbN*) mentioned in the note in the Solution

# 2.4. Replacements for ++ and −−

## Problem

You want to increment or decrement numbers using operators like ++ and −− that are available in other languages, but Scala doesn't have these operators.

## Solution

Because val fields are immutable, they can't be incremented or decremented, but var Int fields can be mutated with the += and -= methods:

```
scala> var a = 1
a: Int = 1

scala> a += 1

scala> println(a)
2

scala> a -= 1

scala> println(a)
1
```

As an added benefit, you use similar methods for multiplication and division:

```
scala> var i = 1
i: Int = 1

scala> i *= 2

scala> println(i)
2

scala> i *= 2

scala> println(i)
4

scala> i /= 2

scala> println(i)
2
```

Note that these symbols aren't operators; they're implemented as methods that are available on Int fields declared as a var. Attempting to use them on val fields results in a compile-time error:

```
scala> val x = 1
x: Int = 1

scala> x += 1
<console>:9: error: value += is not a member of Int
              x += 1
                ^
```

As mentioned, the symbols +=, -=, *=, and /= aren't operators, they're *methods*. This approach of building functionality with libraries instead of operators is a consistent pattern in Scala. Actors, for instance, are not built into the language, but are instead implemented as a library. See the Dr. Dobbs link in the See Also for Martin Odersky's discussion of this philosophy.

## Discussion

Another benefit of this approach is that you can call methods of the same name on other types besides Int. For instance, the Double and Float classes have methods of the same name:

```
scala> var x = 1d
x: Double = 1.0

scala> x += 1

scala> println(x)
2.0

scala> var x = 1f
x: Float = 1.0

scala> x += 1

scala> println(x)
2.0
```

## See Also

Martin Odersky discusses how Actors are added into Scala as a library on drdobbs.com. (*http://ubm.io/12JCypq*)

# 2.5. Comparing Floating-Point Numbers

## Problem

You need to compare two floating-point numbers, but as in some other programming languages, two floating-point numbers that *should* be equivalent may not be.

## Solution

As in Java and many other languages, you solve this problem by creating a method that lets you specify the precision for your comparison. The following "approximately equals" method demonstrates the approach:

```
def ~=(x: Double, y: Double, precision: Double) = {
  if ((x - y).abs < precision) true else false
}
```

You can use this method like this:

```
scala> val a = 0.3
a: Double = 0.3

scala> val b = 0.1 + 0.2
b: Double = 0.30000000000000004

scala> ~=(a, b, 0.0001)
res0: Boolean = true

scala> ~=(b, a, 0.0001)
res1: Boolean = true
```

## Discussion

When you begin working with floating-point numbers, you quickly learn that 0.1 plus 0.1 is 0.2:

```
scala> 0.1 + 0.1
res38: Double = 0.2
```

But 0.1 plus 0.2 isn't exactly 0.3:

```
scala> 0.1 + 0.2
res37: Double = 0.30000000000000004
```

This subtle inaccuracy makes comparing two floating-point numbers a real problem:

```
scala> val a = 0.3
a: Double = 0.3

scala> val b = 0.1 + 0.2
b: Double = 0.30000000000000004

scala> a == b
res0: Boolean = false
```

As a result, you end up writing your own functions to compare floating-point numbers with a precision (or tolerance).

As you saw in Recipe 1.11, you can define an implicit conversion to add a method like this to the Double class. This makes the following code very readable:

```
if (a ~= b) ...
```

Or, you can add the same method to a utilities object, if you prefer:

```
object MathUtils {
  def ~=(x: Double, y: Double, precision: Double) = {
    if ((x - y).abs < precision) true else false
```

```
    }
  }
```

which you can then invoke like a static method:

```
println(MathUtils.~=(a, b, 0.000001))
```

With an implicit conversion, the name ~= is very readable, but in a utilities object like this, it doesn't look quite right, so it might be better named `approximatelyEqual`, `equalWithinTolerance`, or some other name.

### See Also

- Floating-point accuracy problems (*Floating-point accuracy problems*)
- Arbitrary-precision arithmetic (*http://bit.ly/18SxYNc*)
- What every computer scientist should know about floating-point arithmetic (*http://bit.ly/18SxXZy*)

# 2.6. Handling Very Large Numbers

## Problem

You're writing an application and need to use very large integer or decimal numbers.

## Solution

Use the Scala `BigInt` and `BigDecimal` classes. You can create a `BigInt`:

```
scala> var b = BigInt(1234567890)
b: scala.math.BigInt = 1234567890
```

or a `BigDecimal`:

```
scala> var b = BigDecimal(123456.789)
b: scala.math.BigDecimal = 123456.789
```

Unlike their Java equivalents, these classes support all the operators you're used to using with numeric types:

```
scala> b + b
res0: scala.math.BigInt = 2469135780

scala> b * b
res1: scala.math.BigInt = 1524157875019052100

scala> b += 1
```

```
scala> println(b)
1234567891
```

You can convert them to other numeric types:

```
scala> b.toInt
res2: Int = 1234567891

scala> b.toLong
res3: Long = 1234567891

scala> b.toFloat
res4: Float = 1.23456794E9

scala> b.toDouble
res5: Double = 1.234567891E9
```

To help avoid errors, you can also test them first to see if they can be converted to other numeric types:

```
scala> b.isValidByte
res6: Boolean = false

scala> b.isValidChar
res7: Boolean = false

scala> b.isValidShort
res8: Boolean = false

scala> if (b.isValidInt) b.toInt
res9: AnyVal = 1234567890
```

## Discussion

Although the Scala `BigInt` and `BigDecimal` classes are backed by the Java `BigInteger` and `BigDecimal` classes, they are simpler to use than their Java counterparts. As you can see in the examples, they work just like other numeric types, and they're also mutable (as you saw in the += example). These are nice improvements over the Java classes.

Before using `BigInt` or `BigDecimal`, you can check the maximum values that the other Scala numeric types can handle in Table 1-1, or by checking their `MaxValue` in the REPL:

```
scala> Byte.MaxValue
res0: Byte = 127

scala> Short.MaxValue
res1: Short = 32767

scala> Int.MaxValue
res2: Int = 2147483647

scala> Long.MaxValue
```

```
res3: Long = 9223372036854775807

scala> Double.MaxValue
res4: Double = 1.7976931348623157E308
```

Depending on your needs, you may also be able to use the PositiveInfinity and NegativeInfinity of the standard numeric types:

```
scala> Double.PositiveInfinity
res0: Double = Infinity

scala> Double.NegativeInfinity
res1: Double = -Infinity

scala> 1.7976931348623157E308 > Double.PositiveInfinity
res45: Boolean = false
```

## See Also

- The Java BigInteger class (*http://bit.ly/1ORHkE0*)
- The Scala BigInt class (*http://bit.ly/13FUtUH*)
- The Scala BigDecimal class (*http://bit.ly/1b7tLWP*)

# 2.7. Generating Random Numbers

## Problem

You need to create random numbers, such as when testing an application, performing a simulation, and many other situations.

## Solution

Create random numbers with the Scala scala.util.Random class. You can create random integers:

```
scala> val r = scala.util.Random
r: scala.util.Random = scala.util.Random@13eb41e5

scala> r.nextInt
res0: Int = -1323477914
```

You can limit the random numbers to a maximum value:

```
scala> r.nextInt(100)
res1: Int = 58
```

In this use, the Int returned is between 0 (inclusive) and the value you specify (exclusive), so specifying 100 returns an Int from 0 to 99.

You can also create random `Float` values:

```
// returns a value between 0.0 and 1.0
scala> r.nextFloat
res2: Float = 0.50317204
```

You can create random `Double` values:

```
// returns a value between 0.0 and 1.0
scala> r.nextDouble
res3: Double = 0.6946000981900997
```

You can set the seed value using an `Int` or `Long` when creating the `Random` object:

```
scala> val r = new scala.util.Random(100)
r: scala.util.Random = scala.util.Random@bbf4061
```

You can also set the seed value after a `Random` object has been created:

```
r.setSeed(1000L)
```

## Discussion

The `Random` class handles all the usual use cases, including creating numbers, setting the maximum value of a random number range, and setting a seed value. You can also generate random characters:

```
// random characters
scala> r.nextPrintableChar
res0: Char = H

scala> r.nextPrintableChar
res1: Char = r
```

Scala makes it easy to create a random-length range of numbers, which is especially useful for testing:

```
// create a random length range
scala> var range = 0 to r.nextInt(10)
range: scala.collection.immutable.Range.Inclusive = Range(0, 1, 2, 3)

scala> range = 0 to r.nextInt(10)
range: scala.collection.immutable.Range.Inclusive = Range(0, 1)
```

You can add a `for/yield` loop to modify the numbers:

```
scala> for (i <- 0 to r.nextInt(10)) yield i * 2
res0: scala.collection.immutable.IndexedSeq[Int] = Vector(0, 2, 4)
```

You can easily create random-length ranges of other types. Here's a random-length collection of up to 10 `Float` values:

```
scala> for (i <- 0 to r.nextInt(10)) yield (i * r.nextFloat)
res1: scala.collection.immutable.IndexedSeq[Float] =
  Vector(0.0, 0.71370363, 1.0783684)
```

Here's a random-length collection of "printable characters":

```
scala> for (i <- 0 to r.nextInt(10)) yield r.nextPrintableChar
res2: scala.collection.immutable.IndexedSeq[Char] = Vector(x, K, ^, z, w)
```

Be careful with the `nextPrintableChar` method. A better approach may be to control the characters you use, as shown in my "How to create a list of alpha or alphanumeric characters" article, shown in the See Also.

Conversely, you can create a sequence of known length, filled with random numbers:

```
scala> for (i <- 1 to 5) yield r.nextInt(100)
res3: scala.collection.immutable.IndexedSeq[Int] = Vector(88, 94, 58, 96, 82)
```

## See Also

- The Scala Random class (*http://bit.ly/12wYbIE*)
- Recipe 11.29, "Using a Range", provides examples of how to create and use ranges
- My article (*http://bit.ly/12t4iT2*) on how to create a list of alpha or alphanumeric characters
- An additional recipe for generating random strings (*http://bit.ly/11Jw6nw*)

# 2.8. Creating a Range, List, or Array of Numbers

## Problem

You need to create a range, list, or array of numbers, such as in a `for` loop, or for testing purposes.

## Solution

Use the to method of the `Int` class to create a `Range` with the desired elements:

```
scala> val r = 1 to 10
r: scala.collection.immutable.Range.Inclusive = Range(1, 2, 3, 4, 5,
    6, 7, 8, 9, 10)
```

You can set the step with the by method:

```
scala> val r = 1 to 10 by 2
r: scala.collection.immutable.Range = Range(1, 3, 5, 7, 9)

scala> val r = 1 to 10 by 3
r: scala.collection.immutable.Range = Range(1, 4, 7, 10)
```

Ranges are commonly used in `for` loops:

```
scala> for (i <- 1 to 5) println(i)
1
2
3
4
5
```

When creating a Range, you can also use until instead of to:

```
scala> for (i <- 1 until 5) println(i)
1
2
3
4
```

## Discussion

Scala makes it easy to create a range of numbers. The first three examples shown in the Solution create a Range. You can easily convert a Range to other sequences, such as an Array or List, like this:

```
scala> val x = 1 to 10 toArray
x: Array[Int] = Array(1, 2, 3, 4, 5, 6, 7, 8, 9, 10)

scala> val x = 1 to 10 toList
x: List[Int] = List(1, 2, 3, 4, 5, 6, 7, 8, 9, 10)
```

Although this *infix notation* syntax is clear in many situations (such as for loops), it's generally preferable to use this syntax:

```
scala> val x = (1 to 10).toList
x: List[Int] = List(1, 2, 3, 4, 5, 6, 7, 8, 9, 10)

scala> val x = (1 to 10).toArray
x: Array[Int] = Array(1, 2, 3, 4, 5, 6, 7, 8, 9, 10)
```

The magic that makes this process work is the to and until methods, which you'll find in the RichInt class. When you type the following portion of the code, you're actually invoking the to method of the RichInt class:

```
1 to
```

You can demonstrate that to is a method on an Int by using this syntax in the REPL:

```
1.to(10)
```

 Although the infix notation (1 to 10) shown in most of these examples can make your code more readable, Rahul Phulore has a post on Stack Overflow where he advises against using it for anything other than internal DSLs. The link to that post is shown in the See Also.

---

Combine this with Recipe 2.7, "Generating Random Numbers" and you can create a random-length range, which can be useful for testing:

```
scala> var range = 0 to scala.util.Random.nextInt(10)
range: scala.collection.immutable.Range.Inclusive = Range(0, 1, 2, 3)
```

By using a range with the for/yield construct, you don't have to limit your ranges to sequential numbers:

```
scala> for (i <- 1 to 5) yield i * 2
res0: scala.collection.immutable.IndexedSeq[Int] = Vector(2, 4, 6, 8, 10)
```

You also don't have to limit your ranges to just integers:

```
scala> for (i <- 1 to 5) yield i.toDouble
res1: scala.collection.immutable.IndexedSeq[Double] =
    Vector(1.0, 2.0, 3.0, 4.0, 5.0)
```

## See Also

- The Scala RichInt class (*http://bit.ly/179yv9F*)
- Rahul Phulore's post (*http://bit.ly/12meut4*), where he advises not using the infix notation

# 2.9. Formatting Numbers and Currency

## Problem

You want to format numbers or currency to control decimal places and commas, typically for printed output.

## Solution

For basic number formatting, use the f string interpolator shown in Recipe 1.4, "Substituting Variables into Strings":

```
scala> val pi = scala.math.Pi
pi: Double = 3.141592653589793

scala> println(f"$pi%1.5f")
3.14159
```

A few more examples demonstrate the technique:

```
scala> f"$pi%1.5f"
res0: String = 3.14159

scala> f"$pi%1.2f"
res1: String = 3.14
```

```
scala> f"$pi%06.2f"
res2: String = 003.14
```

If you're using a version of Scala prior to 2.10, or prefer the explicit use of the format method, you can write the code like this instead:

```
scala> "%06.2f".format(pi)
res3: String = 003.14
```

A simple way to add commas is to use the getIntegerInstance method of the java.text.NumberFormat class:

```
scala> val formatter = java.text.NumberFormat.getIntegerInstance
formatter: java.text.NumberFormat = java.text.DecimalFormat@674dc

scala> formatter.format(10000)
res0: String = 10,000

scala> formatter.format(1000000)
res1: String = 1,000,000
```

You can also set a locale with the getIntegerInstance method:

```
scala> val locale = new java.util.Locale("de", "DE")
locale: java.util.Locale = de_DE

scala> val formatter = java.text.NumberFormat.getIntegerInstance(locale)
formatter: java.text.NumberFormat = java.text.DecimalFormat@674dc

scala> formatter.format(1000000)
res2: String = 1.000.000
```

You can handle floating-point values with a formatter returned by getInstance:

```
scala> val formatter = java.text.NumberFormat.getInstance
formatter: java.text.NumberFormat = java.text.DecimalFormat@674dc

scala> formatter.format(10000.33)
res0: String = 10,000.33
```

For currency output, use the getCurrencyInstance formatter:

```
scala> val formatter = java.text.NumberFormat.getCurrencyInstance
formatter: java.text.NumberFormat = java.text.DecimalFormat@67500

scala> println(formatter.format(123.456789))
$123.46

scala> println(formatter.format(1234.56789))
$1,234.57

scala> println(formatter.format(12345.6789))
$12,345.68
```

```
scala> println(formatter.format(123456.789))
$123,456.79
```

This approach handles international currency:

```
scala> import java.util.{Currency, Locale}
import java.util.{Currency, Locale}

scala> val de = Currency.getInstance(new Locale("de", "DE"))
de: java.util.Currency = EUR

scala> formatter.setCurrency(de)

scala> println(formatter.format(123456.789))
EUR123,456.79
```

## Discussion

This recipe falls back to the Java approach for printing currency and other formatted numeric fields, though of course the currency solution depends on how you handle currency in your applications. In my work as a consultant, I've seen most companies handle currency using the Java `BigDecimal` class, and others create their own custom currency classes, which are typically wrappers around `BigDecimal`.

## See Also

- My `printf` cheat sheet (*http://bit.ly/12wZQhk*).
- The Joda Money library (*http://bit.ly/13V30BZ*) is a Java library for handling currency, and is currently at version 0.8.
- JSR 354: Money and Currency API, is also being developed in the Java Community Process. See jcp.org (*http://bit.ly/12t62Ma*) for more information.

# CHAPTER 3
# Control Structures

## Introduction

The control structures in Scala start off similar to their Java counterparts, and then diverge in some wonderful ways. For instance, Scala's if/then/else structure is similar to Java, but can also be used to return a value. As a result, though Java has a special syntax for a ternary operator, in Scala you just use a normal if statement to achieve the ternary effect:

```
val x = if (a) y else z
```

The try/catch/finally structure is similar to Java, though Scala uses pattern matching in the catch clause. This differs from Java, but because it's consistent with other uses of pattern matching in Scala, it's easy to remember.

When you get to the for loop, things really start to get interesting. Its basic use is similar to Java, but with the addition of *guards* and other conveniences, the Scala for loop rapidly departs from its Java counterpart. For instance, in Scala you *could* write two for loops as follows to read every line in a file and then operate on each character in each line:

```
for (line <- source.getLines) {
  for {
    char <- line
    if char.isLetter
  } // char algorithm here ...
}
```

But with Scala's for loop mojo, you can write this code even more concisely:

```
for {
  line <- source.getLines
  char <- line
  if char.isLetter
} // char algorithm here ...
```

The rabbit hole goes even deeper, because a Scala *for comprehension* lets you easily apply an algorithm to one collection to generate a new collection:

```scala
scala> val nieces = List("emily", "hannah", "mercedes", "porsche")
nieces: List[String] = List(emily, hannah, mercedes, porsche)

scala> for (n <- nieces) yield n.capitalize
res0: List[String] = List(Emily, Hannah, Mercedes, Porsche)
```

Similarly, in its most basic use, a Scala *match expression* can look like a Java `switch` statement, but because you can match any object, extract information from matched objects, add guards to `case` statements, return values, and more, match expressions are a major feature of the Scala language.

# 3.1. Looping with for and foreach

## Problem

You want to iterate over the elements in a collection, either to operate on each element in the collection, or to create a new collection from the existing collection.

## Solution

There are many ways to loop over Scala collections, including `for` loops, `while` loops, and collection methods like `foreach`, `map`, `flatMap`, and more. This solution focuses primarily on the `for` loop and `foreach` method.

Given a simple array:

```scala
val a = Array("apple", "banana", "orange")
```

I prefer to iterate over the array with the following `for` loop syntax, because it's clean and easy to remember:

```scala
scala> for (e <- a) println(e)
apple
banana
orange
```

When your algorithm requires multiple lines, use the same `for` loop syntax, and perform your work in a block:

```scala
scala> for (e <- a) {
     |   // imagine this requires multiple lines
     |   val s = e.toUpperCase
     |   println(s)
     | }
APPLE
BANANA
ORANGE
```

### Returning values from a for loop

Those examples perform an operation using the elements in an array, but they don't return a value you can use, such as a new array. In cases where you want to build a new collection from the input collection, use the `for`/`yield` combination:

```
scala> val newArray = for (e <- a) yield e.toUpperCase
newArray: Array[java.lang.String] = Array(APPLE, BANANA, ORANGE)
```

The `for`/`yield` construct returns a value, so in this case, the array `newArray` contains uppercase versions of the three strings in the initial array. Notice that an input `Array` yields an `Array` (and not something else, like a `Vector`).

When your algorithm requires multiple lines of code, perform the work in a block after the `yield` keyword:

```
scala> val newArray = for (e <- a) yield {
     |     // imagine this requires multiple lines
     |     val s = e.toUpperCase
     |     s
     | }
newArray: Array[java.lang.String] = Array(APPLE, BANANA, ORANGE)
```

### for loop counters

If you need access to a counter inside a `for` loop, use one of the following approaches. First, you can access array elements with a counter like this:

```
for (i <- 0 until a.length) {
  println(s"$i is ${a(i)}")
}
```

That loops yields this output:

```
0 is apple
1 is banana
2 is orange
```

Scala collections also offer a `zipWithIndex` method that you can use to create a loop counter:

```
scala> for ((e, count) <- a.zipWithIndex) {
     |     println(s"$count is $e")
     | }
0 is apple
1 is banana
2 is orange
```

See Recipe 10.11, "Using zipWithIndex or zip to Create Loop Counters", for more examples of how to use `zipWithIndex`.

### Generators and guards

On a related note, the following example shows how to use a `Range` to execute a loop three times:

```
scala> for (i <- 1 to 3) println(i)
1
2
3
```

The 1 to 3 portion of the loop creates a `Range`, as shown in the REPL:

```
scala> 1 to 3
res0: scala.collection.immutable.Range.Inclusive = Range(1, 2, 3)
```

Using a `Range` like this is known as using a *generator*. The next recipe demonstrates how to use this technique to create multiple loop counters.

Recipe 3.3 demonstrates how to use guards (`if` statements in `for` loops), but here's a quick preview:

```
scala> for (i <- 1 to 10 if i < 4) println(i)
1
2
3
```

### Looping over a Map

When iterating over keys and values in a `Map`, I find this to be the most concise and readable `for` loop:

```
val names = Map("fname" -> "Robert",
                "lname" -> "Goren")
for ((k,v) <- names) println(s"key: $k, value: $v")
```

See Recipe 11.17, "Traversing a Map" for more examples of how to iterate over the elements in a `Map`.

## Discussion

An important lesson from the `for` loop examples is that when you use the `for/yield` combination with a collection, you're building and returning a new collection, but when you use a `for` loop *without* `yield`, you're just operating on each element in the collection —you're not creating a new collection. The `for/yield` combination is referred to as a *for comprehension*, and in its basic use, it works just like the `map` method. It's discussed in more detail in Recipe 3.4, "Creating a for Comprehension (for/yield Combination)".

In some ways Scala reminds me of the Perl slogan, "There's more than one way to do it," and iterating over a collection provides some great examples of this. With the wealth of methods that are available on collections, it's important to note that a `for` loop may not even be the best approach to a particular problem; the methods `foreach`, `map`, `flatMap`, `collect`, `reduce`, etc., can often be used to solve your problem without requiring an explicit `for` loop.

For example, when you're working with a collection, you can also iterate over each element by calling the `foreach` method on the collection:

```
scala> a.foreach(println)
apple
banana
orange
```

When you have an algorithm you want to run on each element in the collection, just use the anonymous function syntax:

```
scala> a.foreach(e => println(e.toUpperCase))
APPLE
BANANA
ORANGE
```

As before, if your algorithm requires multiple lines, perform your work in a block:

```
scala> a.foreach { e =>
     |    val s = e.toUpperCase
     |    println(s)
     | }
APPLE
BANANA
ORANGE
```

### How for loops are translated

As you work with Scala, it's helpful to understand how `for` loops are translated by the compiler. The Scala Language Specification (*http://www.scala-lang.org/node/198*) provides details on precisely how a `for` loop is translated under various conditions. I encourage you to read the Specification for details on the rules, but a simplification of those rules can be stated as follows:

1. A simple `for` loop that iterates over a collection is translated to a `foreach` method call on the collection.

2. A `for` loop with a *guard* (see Recipe 3.3) is translated to a sequence of a `withFilter` method call on the collection followed by a `foreach` call.

3. A `for` loop with a `yield` expression is translated to a `map` method call on the collection.

4. A `for` loop with a `yield` expression and a guard is translated to a `withFilter` method call on the collection, followed by a `map` method call.

Again, the Specification is more detailed than this, but those statements will help get you started in the right direction.

These statements can be demonstrated with a series of examples. Each of the following examples starts with a for loop, and the code in each example will be compiled with the following scalac command:

```
$ scalac -Xprint:parse Main.scala
```

This command provides some initial output about how the Scala compiler translates the for loops into other code.

As a first example, start with the following code in a file named *Main.scala*:

```
class Main {
    for (i <- 1 to 10) println(i)
}
```

This code is intentionally small and trivial so you can see how the for loop is translated by the compiler.

When you compile this code with the scalac -Xprint:parse command, the full output looks like this:

```
$ scalac -Xprint:parse Main.scala

[[syntax trees at end of parser]] // Main.scala
package <empty> {
  class Main extends scala.AnyRef {
    def <init>() = {
      super.<init>();
      ()
    };
    1.to(10).foreach(((i) => println(i)))
  }
}
```

For this example, the important part of the output is the area that shows the for loop was translated by the compiler into the following code:

```
1.to(10).foreach(((i) => println(i)))
```

As you can see, the Scala compiler translates a simple for loop over a collection into a foreach method call on the collection.

 If you compile the file with the -Xprint:all option instead of -Xprint:parse, you'll see that the code is further translated into the following code:

```
scala.this.Predef.intWrapper(1).to(10).foreach[Unit]
    (((i: Int) => scala.this.Predef.println(i)))
```

The code continues to get more and more detailed as the compiler phases continue, but for this demonstration, only the first step in the translation process is necessary.

Note that although I use a `Range` in these examples, the compiler behaves similarly for other collections. For example, if I replace the `Range` in the previous example with a `List`, like this:

```
// original List code
val nums = List(1,2,3)
for (i <- nums) println(i)
```

the `for` loop is still converted by the compiler into a `foreach` method call:

```
// translation performed by the compiler
nums.foreach(((i) => println(i)))
```

Given this introduction, the following series of examples demonstrates how various `for` loops are translated by the Scala 2.10 compiler. Here's the first example again, showing both the *input* code I wrote and the *output* code from the compiler:

```
// #1 - input (my code)
for (i <- 1 to 10) println(i)

// #1 - compiler output
1.to(10).foreach(((i) => println(i)))
```

Next, I'll use the same `for` loop but add a guard condition (an `if` statement) to it:

```
// #2 - input code
for {
  i <- 1 to 10
  if i % 2 == 0
} println(i)

// #2 - translated output
1.to(10).withFilter(((i) => i.$percent(2).$eq$eq(0))).foreach(((i) =>
    println(i)))
```

As shown, a simple, single guard is translated into a `withFilter` method call on the collection, followed by a `foreach` call.

The same `for` loop with two guards is translated into two `withFilter` calls:

```
// #3 - input code
for {
  i <- 1 to 10
  if i != 1
  if i % 2 == 0
} println(i)

// #3 - translated output
1.to(10).withFilter(((i) => i.$bang$eq(1)))
        .withFilter(((i)
    => i.$percent(2).$eq$eq(0))).foreach(((i) => println(i)))
```

Next, I'll add a `yield` statement to the initial `for` loop:

```
// #4 - input code
for { i <- 1 to 10 } yield i

// #4 - output
1.to(10).map(((i) => i))
```

As shown, when a `yield` statement is used, the compiler translates the `for/yield` code into a `map` method call on the collection.

Here's the same `for/yield` combination with a guard added in:

```
// #5 - input code (for loop, guard, and yield)
for {
  i <- 1 to 10
  if i % 2 == 0
} yield i

// #5 - translated code
1.to(10).withFilter(((i) => i.$percent(2).$eq$eq(0))).map(((i) => i))
```

As in the previous examples, the guard is translated into a `withFilter` method call, and the `for/yield` code is translated into a `map` method call.

These examples demonstrate how the translations are made by the Scala compiler, and I encourage you to create your own examples to see how they're translated by the compiler into other code. The `-Xprint:parse` option shows a small amount of compiler output, while the `-Xprint:all` option produces hundreds of lines of output for some of these examples, showing all the steps in the compilation process.

For more details, see the Scala Language Specification for exact rules on the `for` loop translation process. The details are currently in Section 6.19, "For Comprehensions and For Loops," of the Specification.

## See Also

The Scala Language Specification (*http://www.scala-lang.org/node/198*) in PDF format

# 3.2. Using for Loops with Multiple Counters

## Problem

You want to create a loop with multiple counters, such as when iterating over a multi-dimensional array.

## Solution

You can create a `for` loop with two counters like this:

```
scala> for (i <- 1 to 2; j <- 1 to 2) println(s"i = $i, j = $j")
i = 1, j = 1
i = 1, j = 2
i = 2, j = 1
i = 2, j = 2
```

When doing this, the preferred style for multiline for loops is to use curly brackets:

```
for {
  i <- 1 to 2
  j <- 1 to 2
} println(s"i = $i, j = $j")
```

Similarly, you can use three counters like this:

```
for {
  i <- 1 to 3
  j <- 1 to 5
  k <- 1 to 10
} println(s"i = $i, j = $j, k = $k")
```

This is useful when looping over a multidimensional array. Assuming you create a small two-dimensional array like this:

```
val array = Array.ofDim[Int](2,2)
array(0)(0) = 0
array(0)(1) = 1
array(1)(0) = 2
array(1)(1) = 3
```

you can print each element of the array like this:

```
scala> for {
     |    i <- 0 to 1
     |    j <- 0 to 1
     | } println(s"($i)($j) = ${array(i)(j)}")
(0)(0) = 0
(0)(1) = 1
(1)(0) = 2
(1)(1) = 3
```

## Discussion

Ranges created with the <- symbol in for loops are referred to as *generators*, and you can easily use multiple generators in one loop.

As shown in the examples, the recommended style for writing longer for loops is to use curly braces:

```
for {
  i <- 1 to 2
  j <- 2 to 3
} println(s"i = $i, j = $j")
```

This style is more scalable than other styles; in this case, "scalable" means that it continues to be readable as you add more generators and guards to the expression.

## See Also

The Scala Style Guide page on formatting control (*http://bit.ly/15oazgY*) structures

# 3.3. Using a for Loop with Embedded if Statements (Guards)

## Problem

You want to add one or more conditional clauses to a `for` loop, typically to filter out some elements in a collection while working on the others.

## Solution

Add an `if` statement after your generator, like this:

```
// print all even numbers
scala> for (i <- 1 to 10 if i % 2 == 0) println(i)
2
4
6
8
10
```

or using the preferred curly brackets style, like this:

```
for {
  i <- 1 to 10
  if i % 2 == 0
} println(i)
```

These `if` statements are referred to as filters, filter expressions, or *guards*, and you can use as many guards as are needed for the problem at hand. This loop shows a hard way to print the number 4:

```
for {
  i <- 1 to 10
  if i > 3
  if i < 6
  if i % 2 == 0
} println(i)
```

## Discussion

Using guards with `for` loops can make for concise and readable code, but you can also use the traditional approach:

```
for (file <- files) {
  if (hasSoundFileExtension(file) && !soundFileIsLong(file)) {
    soundFiles += file
  }
}
```

However, once you become comfortable with Scala's `for` loop syntax, I think you'll find it makes the code more readable, because it separates the looping and filtering concerns from the business logic:

```
for {
  file <- files
  if passesFilter1(file)
  if passesFilter2(file)
} doSomething(file)
```

As a final note, because guards are generally intended to filter collections, you may want to use one of the many filtering methods that are available to collections (`filter`, `take`, `drop`, etc.) instead of a `for` loop, depending on your needs.

# 3.4. Creating a for Comprehension (for/yield Combination)

## Problem

You want to create a new collection from an existing collection by applying an algorithm (and potentially one or more guards) to each element in the original collection.

## Solution

Use a `yield` statement with a `for` loop and your algorithm to create a new collection from an existing collection.

For instance, given an array of lowercase strings:

```
scala> val names = Array("chris", "ed", "maurice")
names: Array[String] = Array(chris, ed, maurice)
```

you can create a new array of capitalized strings by combining `yield` with a `for` loop and a simple algorithm:

```
scala> val capNames = for (e <- names) yield e.capitalize
capNames: Array[String] = Array(Chris, Ed, Maurice)
```

Using a `for` loop with a `yield` statement is known as a *for comprehension*.

If your algorithm requires multiple lines of code, perform the work in a block after the yield keyword:

```scala
scala> val lengths = for (e <- names) yield {
     |     // imagine that this required multiple lines of code
     |     e.length
     | }
lengths: Array[Int] = Array(5, 2, 7)
```

Except for rare occasions, the collection type returned by a for comprehension is the same type that you begin with. For instance, if the collection you're looping over is an ArrayBuffer:

```scala
var fruits = scala.collection.mutable.ArrayBuffer[String]()
fruits += "apple"
fruits += "banana"
fruits += "orange"
```

the collection your loop returns will also be an ArrayBuffer:

```scala
scala> val out = for (e <- fruits) yield e.toUpperCase
out: scala.collection.mutable.ArrayBuffer[java.lang.String] =
    ArrayBuffer(APPLE, BANANA, ORANGE)
```

If your input collection is a List, the for/yield loop will return a List:

```scala
scala> val fruits = "apple" :: "banana" :: "orange" :: Nil
fruits: List[java.lang.String] = List(apple, banana, orange)

scala> val out = for (e <- fruits) yield e.toUpperCase
out: List[java.lang.String] = List(APPLE, BANANA, ORANGE)
```

## Discussion

If you're new to using yield with a for loop, it can help to think of the loop like this:

- When it begins running, the for/yield loop immediately creates a new, empty collection that is of the same type as the input collection. For example, if the input type is a Vector, the output type will also be a Vector. You can think of this new collection as being like a bucket.

- On each iteration of the for loop, a new output element is created from the current element of the input collection. When the output element is created, it's placed in the bucket.

- When the loop finishes running, the entire contents of the bucket are returned.

That's a simplification of the process, but I find it helpful when explaining the process.

Writing a basic for/yield expression without a guard is just like calling the map method on a collection. For instance, the following for comprehension converts all the strings in the fruits collection to uppercase:

```
scala> val out = for (e <- fruits) yield e.toUpperCase
out: List[String] = List(APPLE, BANANA, ORANGE)
```

Calling the map method on the collection does the same thing:

```
scala> val out = fruits.map(_.toUpperCase)
out: List[String] = List(APPLE, BANANA, ORANGE)
```

When I first started learning Scala, I wrote all of my code using for/yield expressions until the map light bulb went on one day.

## See Also

- Comparisons between for comprehensions and map are shown in more detail in Recipe 10.13, "Transforming One Collection to Another with for/yield" and Recipe 10.14, "Transforming One Collection to Another with map".

- The official Scala website (*http://bit.ly/1ahFWNJ*) offers an introduction to sequence comprehensions

# 3.5. Implementing break and continue

## Problem

You have a situation where you need to use a break or continue construct, but Scala doesn't have break or continue keywords.

## Solution

It's true that Scala doesn't have break and continue keywords, but it does offer similar functionality through scala.util.control.Breaks.

The following code demonstrates the Scala "break" and "continue" approach:

```
package com.alvinalexander.breakandcontinue

import util.control.Breaks._

object BreakAndContinueDemo extends App {

  println("\n=== BREAK EXAMPLE ===")
  breakable {
    for (i <- 1 to 10) {
      println(i)
      if (i > 4) break  // break out of the for loop
    }
  }

  println("\n=== CONTINUE EXAMPLE ===")
```

```
    val searchMe = "peter piper picked a peck of pickled peppers"
    var numPs = 0
    for (i <- 0 until searchMe.length) {
      breakable {
        if (searchMe.charAt(i) != 'p') {
          break  // break out of the 'breakable', continue the outside loop
        } else {
          numPs += 1
        }
      }
    }
    println("Found " + numPs + " p's in the string.")
}
```

Here's the output from the code:

```
=== BREAK EXAMPLE ===
1
2
3
4
5

=== CONTINUE EXAMPLE ===
Found 9 p's in the string.
```

(The "pickled peppers" example comes from a continue example in the Java documentation. More on this at the end of the recipe.)

The following discussions describe how this code works.

### The break example

The break example is pretty easy to reason about. Again, here's the code:

```
breakable {
  for (i <- 1 to 10) {
    println(i)
    if (i > 4) break  // break out of the for loop
  }
}
```

In this case, when i becomes greater than 4, the break "keyword" is reached. At this point an exception is thrown, and the for loop is exited. The breakable "keyword" essentially catches the exception, and the flow of control continues with any other code that might be after the breakable block.

Note that break and breakable aren't actually keywords; they're methods in scala.util.control.Breaks. In Scala 2.10, the break method is declared as follows to throw an instance of a BreakControl exception when it's called:

```
private val breakException = new BreakControl

def break(): Nothing = { throw breakException }
```

The `breakable` method is defined to catch a `BreakControl` exception, like this:

```
def breakable(op: => Unit) {
    try {
      op
    } catch {
      case ex: BreakControl =>
        if (ex ne breakException) throw ex
    }
  }
```

 See Recipe 3.18 for examples of how to implement your own control structures in a manner similar to the Breaks library.

### The continue example

Given the explanation for the `break` example, you can now reason about how the "continue" example works. Here's the code again:

```
val searchMe = "peter piper picked a peck of pickled peppers"
var numPs = 0

for (i <- 0 until searchMe.length) {
  breakable {
    if (searchMe.charAt(i) != 'p') {
      break  // break out of the 'breakable', continue the outside loop
    } else {
      numPs += 1
    }
  }
}

println("Found " + numPs + " p's in the string.")
```

Following the earlier explanation, as the code walks through the characters in the `String` variable named `searchMe`, if the current character is not the letter p, the code breaks out of the `if`/`then` statement, and the loop continues executing.

As before, what really happens is that the `break` method is reached, an exception is thrown, and that exception is caught by `breakable`. The exception serves to break out of the `if`/`then` statement, and catching it allows the `for` loop to continue executing with the next element.

### General syntax

The general syntax for implementing break and continue functionality is shown in the following examples, which are partially written in pseudocode, and compared to their Java equivalents.

To implement a *break*, this Scala:

```
breakable {
  for (x <- xs) {
    if (cond)
      break
  }
}
```

corresponds to this Java:

```
for (X x : xs) {
  if (cond) break;
}
```

To implement *continue* functionality, this Scala:

```
for (x <- xs) {
  breakable {
    if (cond)
      break
  }
}
```

corresponds to this Java:

```
for (X x : xs) {
  if (cond) continue;
}
```

### About that continue example...

The continue example shown is a variation of the Java `continue` example shown on the Oracle website (*http://bit.ly/11JCuuZ*). If you know Scala, you know that there are better ways to solve this particular problem. For instance, a direct approach is to use the `count` method with a simple anonymous function:

```
val count = searchMe.count(_ == 'p')
```

When this code is run, `count` is again 9.

### Nested loops and labeled breaks

In some situations, you may need nested break statements. Or, you may prefer labeled break statements. In either case, you can create labeled breaks as shown in the following example:

```
package com.alvinalexander.labeledbreaks

object LabeledBreakDemo extends App {

  import scala.util.control._

  val Inner = new Breaks
  val Outer = new Breaks
```

```
Outer.breakable {
  for (i <- 1 to 5) {
    Inner.breakable {
      for (j <- 'a' to 'e') {
        if (i == 1 && j == 'c') Inner.break else println(s"i: $i, j: $j")
        if (i == 2 && j == 'b') Outer.break
      }
    }
  }
}
```

In this example, if the first `if` condition is met, an exception is thrown and caught by `Inner.breakable`, and the outer `for` loop continues. But if the second `if` condition is triggered, control of flow is sent to `Outer.breakable`, and both loops are exited. Running this object results in the following output:

```
i: 1, j: a
i: 1, j: b
i: 2, j: a
```

Use the same approach if you prefer labeled breaks. This example shows how you can use the same technique with just one `break` method call:

```
import scala.util.control._

val Exit = new Breaks
Exit.breakable {
  for (j <- 'a' to 'e') {
    if (j == 'c') Exit.break else println(s"j: $j")
  }
}
```

## Discussion

If you don't like using `break` and `continue`, there are several other ways to attack these problems.

For instance, if you want to add monkeys to a barrel, but only until the barrel is full, you can use a simple boolean test to break out of a `for` loop:

```
var barrelIsFull = false
for (monkey <- monkeyCollection if !barrelIsFull) {
  addMonkeyToBarrel(monkey)
  barrelIsFull = checkIfBarrelIsFull
}
```

Another approach is to place your algorithm inside a function, and then return from the function when the desired condition is reached. In the following example, the `sumToMax` function returns early if `sum` becomes greater than `limit`:

```
// calculate a sum of numbers, but limit it to a 'max' value
def sumToMax(arr: Array[Int], limit: Int): Int = {
  var sum = 0
  for (i <- arr) {
    sum += i
    if (sum > limit) return limit
  }
  sum
}
val a = Array.range(0,10)
println(sumToMax(a, 10))
```

A common approach in functional programming is to use recursive algorithms. This is demonstrated in a recursive approach to a *factorial* function, where the condition n == 1 results in a break from the recursion:

```
def factorial(n: Int): Int = {
  if (n == 1) 1
  else n * factorial(n - 1)
}
```

Note that this example does not use *tail recursion* and is therefore not an optimal approach, especially if the starting value n is very large. A more optimal solution takes advantage of tail recursion:

```
import scala.annotation.tailrec

def factorial(n: Int): Int = {
  @tailrec def factorialAcc(acc: Int, n: Int): Int = {
    if (n <= 1) acc
    else factorialAcc(n * acc, n - 1)
  }
  factorialAcc(1, n)
}
```

Note that you can use the @tailrec annotation in situations like this to confirm that your algorithm is tail recursive. If you use this annotation and your algorithm isn't tail recursive, the compiler will complain. For instance, if you attempt to use this annotation on the first version of the factorial method, you'll get the following compile-time error:

```
Could not optimize @tailrec annotated method factorial: it contains a recursive
call not in tail position
```

## See Also

The Java continue example mentioned can be found on the Oracle website (*http://bit.ly/11JCuuZ*).

There are many Scala recursive factorial examples on the Internet; here are two of the best discussions:

- A nice discussion about tail recursion and trampolines (*http://bit.ly/136lkGa*)
- Tail-call optimization in Scala (*http://bit.ly/12mjhKQ*)

# 3.6. Using the if Construct Like a Ternary Operator

## Problem

You'd like to use a Scala `if` expression like a ternary operator to solve a problem in a concise, expressive way.

## Solution

This is a bit of a trick problem, because unlike Java, in Scala there is no special ternary operator; just use an `if`/`else` expression:

```
val absValue = if (a < 0) -a else a
```

Because an `if` expression returns a value, you can embed it into a print statement:

```
println(if (i == 0) "a" else "b")
```

You can use it in another expression, such as this portion of a `hashCode` method:

```
hash = hash * prime + (if (name == null) 0 else name.hashCode)
```

## Discussion

The Java documentation page shown in the See Also states that the Java conditional operator `?:` "is known as the *ternary operator* because it uses three operands." Unlike some other languages, Scala doesn't have a special operator for this use case.

In addition to the examples shown, the combination of (a) `if` statements returning a result, and (b) Scala's syntax for defining methods makes for concise code:

```
def abs(x: Int) = if (x >= 0) x else -x
def max(a: Int, b: Int) = if (a > b) a else b
val c = if (a > b) a else b
```

## See Also

"Equality, Relational, and Conditional Operators" on the Java Tutorials page (*http://bit.ly/1ahGfYY*)

# 3.7. Using a Match Expression Like a switch Statement

## Problem

You have a situation where you want to create something like a simple Java integer-based switch statement, such as matching the days in a week, months in a year, and other situations where an integer maps to a result.

## Solution

To use a Scala match expression like a Java switch statement, use this approach:

```
// i is an integer
i match {
  case 1  => println("January")
  case 2  => println("February")
  case 3  => println("March")
  case 4  => println("April")
  case 5  => println("May")
  case 6  => println("June")
  case 7  => println("July")
  case 8  => println("August")
  case 9  => println("September")
  case 10 => println("October")
  case 11 => println("November")
  case 12 => println("December")
  // catch the default with a variable so you can print it
  case whoa  => println("Unexpected case: " + whoa.toString)
}
```

That example shows how to take an action based on a match. A more functional approach returns a value from a match expression:

```
val month = i match {
  case 1  => "January"
  case 2  => "February"
  case 3  => "March"
  case 4  => "April"
  case 5  => "May"
  case 6  => "June"
  case 7  => "July"
  case 8  => "August"
  case 9  => "September"
  case 10 => "October"
  case 11 => "November"
  case 12 => "December"
  case _  => "Invalid month"  // the default, catch-all
}
```

### The @switch annotation

When writing simple match expressions like this, it's recommend to use the @switch annotation. This annotation provides a warning at compile time if the switch can't be compiled to a tableswitch or lookupswitch.

Compiling your match expression to a tableswitch or lookupswitch is better for performance, because it results in a branch table rather than a decision tree. When a value is given to the expression, it can jump directly to the result rather than working through the decision tree.

Here's the official description from the @switch annotation documentation (*http://bit.ly/12x5MHd*):

> "An annotation to be applied to a match expression. If present, the compiler will verify that the match has been compiled to a tableswitch or lookupswitch, and issue an error if it instead compiles into a series of conditional expressions."

The effect of the @switch annotation is demonstrated with a simple example. First, place the following code in a file named *SwitchDemo.scala*:

```
// Version 1 - compiles to a tableswitch
import scala.annotation.switch

class SwitchDemo {

  val i = 1
  val x = (i: @switch) match {
    case 1  => "One"
    case 2  => "Two"
    case _  => "Other"
  }

}
```

Then compile the code as usual:

```
$ scalac SwitchDemo.scala
```

Compiling this class produces no warnings and creates the *SwitchDemo.class* output file. Next, disassemble that file with this javap command:

```
$ javap -c SwitchDemo
```

The output from this command shows a tableswitch, like this:

```
16:   tableswitch{ //1 to 2
            1: 50;
            2: 45;
            default: 40 }
```

This shows that Scala was able to optimize your match expression to a tableswitch. (This is a good thing.)

Next, make a minor change to the code, replacing the integer literal 2 with a value:

```
import scala.annotation.switch

// Version 2 - leads to a compiler warning
class SwitchDemo {

  val i = 1
  val Two = 2                    // added
  val x = (i: @switch) match {
    case 1   => "One"
    case Two => "Two"            // replaced the '2'
    case _   => "Other"
  }

}
```

Again, compile the code with `scalac`, but right away you'll see a warning message:

```
$ scalac SwitchDemo.scala
SwitchDemo.scala:7: warning: could not emit switch for @switch annotated match
  val x = (i: @switch) match {
          ^
one warning found
```

This warning message is saying that neither a `tableswitch` nor `lookupswitch` could be generated for the match expression. You can confirm this by running the `javap` command on the *SwitchDemo.class* file that was generated. When you look at that output, you'll see that the `tableswitch` shown in the previous example is now gone.

In his book, *Scala In Depth* (Manning), Joshua Suereth states that the following conditions must be true for Scala to apply the `tableswitch` optimization:

1. The matched value must be a known integer.

2. The matched expression must be "simple." It can't contain any type checks, `if` statements, or extractors.

3. The expression must also have its value available at compile time.

4. There should be more than two `case` statements.

For more information on how JVM switches work, see the Oracle document, Compiling Switches (*http://bit.ly/11JFVSH*).

## Discussion

As demonstrated in other recipes, you aren't limited to matching only integers; the match expression is incredibly flexible:

```
def getClassAsString(x: Any): String = x match {
  case s: String => s + " is a String"
```

```
    case i: Int => "Int"
    case f: Float => "Float"
    case l: List[_] => "List"
    case p: Person => "Person"
    case _ => "Unknown"
}
```

## Handling the default case

The examples in the Solution showed the two ways you can handle the default, "catch all" case. First, if you're not concerned about the value of the default match, you can catch it with the _ wildcard:

```
case _ => println("Got a default match")
```

Conversely, if you are interested in what fell down to the default match, assign a variable name to it. You can then use that variable on the right side of the expression:

```
case default => println(default)
```

Using the name default often makes the most sense and leads to readable code, but you can use any legal name for the variable:

```
case oops => println(oops)
```

You can generate a MatchError if you don't handle the default case. Given this match expression:

```
i match {
  case 0 => println("0 received")
  case 1 => println("1 is good, too")
}
```

if i is a value other than 0 or 1, the expression throws a MatchError:

```
scala.MatchError: 42 (of class java.lang.Integer)
  at .<init>(<console>:9)
  at .<clinit>(<console>)
    much more error output here ...
```

So unless you're intentionally writing a *partial function*, you'll want to handle the default case. (See Recipe 9.8, "Creating Partial Functions", for more information on partial functions.)

## Do you really need a switch statement?

Of course you don't really need a switch statement if you have a data structure that maps month numbers to month names. In that case, just use a Map:

```
val monthNumberToName = Map(
    1  -> "January",
    2  -> "February",
    3  -> "March",
    4  -> "April",
    5  -> "May",
```

```
    6  -> "June",
    7  -> "July",
    8  -> "August",
    9  -> "September",
   10 -> "October",
   11 -> "November",
   12 -> "December"
)

val monthName = monthNumberToName(4)
println(monthName)  // prints "April"
```

## See Also

- The @switch annotation documentation (*http://bit.ly/12x5MHd*).
- The Oracle document, Compiling Switches (*http://bit.ly/11JFVSH*), discusses the tableswitch and lookupswitch.
- A tableswitch and lookupswitch (*http://bit.ly/16yPJem*) differences discussion.

# 3.8. Matching Multiple Conditions with One Case Statement

## Problem

You have a situation where several match conditions require that the same business logic be executed, and rather than repeating your business logic for each case, you'd like to use one copy of the business logic for the matching conditions.

## Solution

Place the match conditions that invoke the same business logic on one line, separated by the | (pipe) character:

```
val i = 5
i match {
  case 1 | 3 | 5 | 7 | 9 => println("odd")
  case 2 | 4 | 6 | 8 | 10 => println("even")
}
```

This same syntax works with strings and other types. Here's an example based on a String match:

```
val cmd = "stop"
cmd match {
  case "start" | "go" => println("starting")
  case "stop" | "quit" | "exit" => println("stopping")
```

```
  case _ => println("doing nothing")
}
```

This example shows how to match multiple case objects:

```
trait Command
case object Start extends Command
case object Go extends Command
case object Stop extends Command
case object Whoa extends Command

def executeCommand(cmd: Command) = cmd match {
  case Start | Go => start()
  case Stop | Whoa => stop()
}
```

As demonstrated, the ability to define multiple possible matches for each case statement can simplify your code.

## See Also

See Recipe 3.13, "Adding if Expressions (Guards) to Case Statements", for a related approach.

# 3.9. Assigning the Result of a Match Expression to a Variable

## Problem

You want to return a value from a match expression and assign it to a variable, or use a match expression as the body of a method.

## Solution

To assign a variable to the result of a match expression, insert the variable assignment before the expression, as with the variable evenOrOdd in this example:

```
val evenOrOdd = someNumber match {
  case 1 | 3 | 5 | 7 | 9 => println("odd")
  case 2 | 4 | 6 | 8 | 10 => println("even")
}
```

This approach is commonly used to create short methods or functions. For example, the following method implements the Perl definitions of true and false:

```
def isTrue(a: Any) = a match {
  case 0 | "" => false
  case _ => true
}
```

You'll hear that Scala is an "expression-oriented programming (EOP) language," which Wikipedia defines as, "a programming language where every (or nearly every) construction is an expression and thus yields a value." The ability to return values from if statements and match expressions helps Scala meet this definition.

## See Also

- Recipe 20.3, "Think "Expression-Oriented Programming""
- The Expression-Oriented Programming page on Wikipedia (*http://bit.ly/1b7B6FE*)

# 3.10. Accessing the Value of the Default Case in a Match Expression

## Problem

You want to access the value of the default, "catch all" case when using a match expression, but you can't access the value when you match it with the _ wildcard syntax.

## Solution

Instead of using the _ wildcard character, assign a variable name to the default case:

```
i match {
  case 0 => println("1")
  case 1 => println("2")
  case default => println("You gave me: " + default)
}
```

By giving the default match a variable name, you can access the variable on the right side of the statement.

## Discussion

The key to this recipe is in using a variable name for the default match instead of the usual _ wildcard character.

The name you assign can be any legal variable name, so instead of naming it default, you can name it something else, such as whoa:

```
i match {
  case 0 => println("1")
  case 1 => println("2")
  case whoa => println("You gave me: " + whoa)
}
```

It's important to provide a default match. Failure to do so can cause a `MatchError`:

```
scala> 3 match {
     |    case 1 => println("one")
     |    case 2 => println("two")
     |    // no default match
     | }
scala.MatchError: 3 (of class java.lang.Integer)
many more lines of output ...
```

# 3.11. Using Pattern Matching in Match Expressions

## Problem

You need to match one or more patterns in a match expression, and the pattern may be a constant pattern, variable pattern, constructor pattern, sequence pattern, tuple pattern, or type pattern.

## Solution

Define a `case` statement for each pattern you want to match. The following method shows examples of many different types of patterns you can use in match expressions:

```
def echoWhatYouGaveMe(x: Any): String = x match {

    // constant patterns
    case 0 => "zero"
    case true => "true"
    case "hello" => "you said 'hello'"
    case Nil => "an empty List"

    // sequence patterns
    case List(0, _, _) => "a three-element list with 0 as the first element"
    case List(1, _*) => "a list beginning with 1, having any number of elements"
    case Vector(1, _*) => "a vector starting with 1, having any number of elements"

    // tuples
    case (a, b) => s"got $a and $b"
    case (a, b, c) => s"got $a, $b, and $c"

    // constructor patterns
    case Person(first, "Alexander") => s"found an Alexander, first name = $first"
    case Dog("Suka") => "found a dog named Suka"

    // typed patterns
    case s: String => s"you gave me this string: $s"
    case i: Int => s"thanks for the int: $i"
    case f: Float => s"thanks for the float: $f"
    case a: Array[Int] => s"an array of int: ${a.mkString(",")}"
    case as: Array[String] => s"an array of strings: ${as.mkString(",")}"
```

```
    case d: Dog => s"dog: ${d.name}"
    case list: List[_] => s"thanks for the List: $list"
    case m: Map[_, _] => m.toString

    // the default wildcard pattern
    case _ => "Unknown"
}
```

The large match expression in this method shows the different categories of patterns described in the book, *Programming in Scala* (Artima), by Odersky, et al, including constant patterns, sequence patterns, tuple patterns, constructor patterns, and typed patterns.

You can test this match expression in a variety of ways. For the purposes of this example, I created the following object to test the echoWhatYouGaveMe method:

```
object LargeMatchTest extends App {

    case class Person(firstName: String, lastName: String)
    case class Dog(name: String)

    // trigger the constant patterns
    println(echoWhatYouGaveMe(0))
    println(echoWhatYouGaveMe(true))
    println(echoWhatYouGaveMe("hello"))
    println(echoWhatYouGaveMe(Nil))

    // trigger the sequence patterns
    println(echoWhatYouGaveMe(List(0,1,2)))
    println(echoWhatYouGaveMe(List(1,2)))
    println(echoWhatYouGaveMe(List(1,2,3)))
    println(echoWhatYouGaveMe(Vector(1,2,3)))

    // trigger the tuple patterns
    println(echoWhatYouGaveMe((1,2)))           // two element tuple
    println(echoWhatYouGaveMe((1,2,3)))         // three element tuple

    // trigger the constructor patterns
    println(echoWhatYouGaveMe(Person("Melissa", "Alexander")))
    println(echoWhatYouGaveMe(Dog("Suka")))

    // trigger the typed patterns
    println(echoWhatYouGaveMe("Hello, world"))
    println(echoWhatYouGaveMe(42))
    println(echoWhatYouGaveMe(42F))
    println(echoWhatYouGaveMe(Array(1,2,3)))
    println(echoWhatYouGaveMe(Array("coffee", "apple pie")))
    println(echoWhatYouGaveMe(Dog("Fido")))
    println(echoWhatYouGaveMe(List("apple", "banana")))
    println(echoWhatYouGaveMe(Map(1->"Al", 2->"Alexander")))
```

```
    // trigger the wildcard pattern
    println(echoWhatYouGaveMe("33d"))

}
```

Running this object results in the following output:

```
zero
true
you said 'hello'
an empty List

a three-element list with 0 as the first element
a list beginning with 1 and having any number of elements
a list beginning with 1 and having any number of elements
a vector beginning with 1 and having any number of elements
a list beginning with 1 and having any number of elements

got 1 and 2
got 1, 2, and 3

found an Alexander, first name = Melissa
found a dog named Suka

you gave me this string: Hello, world
thanks for the int: 42
thanks for the float: 42.0
an array of int: 1,2,3
an array of strings: coffee,apple pie
dog: Fido
thanks for the List: List(apple, banana)
Map(1 -> Al, 2 -> Alexander)

you gave me this string: 33d
```

Note that in the match expression, the List and Map statements that were written like this:

```
case list: List[_] => s"thanks for the List: $list"
case m: Map[_, _] => m.toString
```

could have been written as this instead:

```
case m: Map[a, b] => m.toString
case list: List[x] => s"thanks for the List: $list"
```

I prefer the underscore syntax because it makes it clear that I'm not concerned about what's stored in the List or Map. Actually, there are times that I might be interested in what's stored in the List or Map, but because of type erasure in the JVM, that becomes a difficult problem.

When I first wrote this example, I wrote the `List` expression as follows:

```
case l: List[Int] => "List"
```

If you're familiar with *type erasure* on the Java platform, you may know that this won't work. The Scala compiler kindly lets you know about this problem with this warning message:

```
Test1.scala:7: warning: non-variable type argument Int in type pattern
List[Int] is unchecked since it is eliminated by erasure
    case l: List[Int] => "List[Int]"
         ^
```

If you're not familiar with type erasure, I've included a link in the See Also section of this recipe that describes how it works on the JVM.

## Discussion

Typically when using this technique, your method will expect an instance that inherits from a base class or trait, and then your `case` statements will reference subtypes of that base type. This was inferred in the echoWhatYouGaveMe method, where every Scala type is a subtype of Any. The following code shows a more obvious example of this technique.

In my Blue Parrot application (*http://alvinalexander.com/blueparrot*), which either plays a sound file or "speaks" the text it's given at random intervals, I have a method that looks like this:

```
import java.io.File

sealed trait RandomThing

case class RandomFile(f: File) extends RandomThing
case class RandomString(s: String) extends RandomThing

class RandomNoiseMaker {

  def makeRandomNoise(t: RandomThing) = t match {
    case RandomFile(f) => playSoundFile(f)
    case RandomString(s) => speak(s)
  }

}
```

The makeRandomNoise method is declared to take a RandomThing type, and then the match expression handles its two subtypes, RandomFile and RandomString.

### Patterns

The large match expression in the Solution shows a variety of patterns that are defined in the book *Programming in Scala*. These patterns are briefly described in the following paragraphs.

*Constant patterns*

A constant pattern can only match itself. Any literal may be used as a constant. If you specify a 0 as the literal, only an `Int` value of 0 will be matched. Examples:

```
case 0 => "zero"
case true => "true"
```

*Variable patterns*

This was not shown in the large match example in the Solution—it's discussed in detail in Recipe 3.10, "Accessing the Value of the Default Case in a Match Expression"—but a *variable pattern* matches any object just like the _ wildcard character. Scala binds the variable to whatever the object is, which lets you use the variable on the right side of the `case` statement. For example, at the end of a match expression you can use the _ wildcard character like this to catch "anything else":

```
case _ => s"Hmm, you gave me something ..."
```

But with a variable pattern you can write this instead:

```
case foo => s"Hmm, you gave me a $foo"
```

See Recipe 3.10 for more information.

*Constructor patterns*

The *constructor pattern* lets you match a constructor in a `case` statement. As shown in the examples, you can specify constants or variable patterns as needed in the constructor pattern:

```
case Person(first, "Alexander") => s"found an Alexander, first name = $first"
case Dog("Suka") => "found a dog named Suka"
```

*Sequence patterns*

You can match against sequences like `List`, `Array`, `Vector`, etc. Use the _ character to stand for one element in the sequence, and use _* to stand for "zero or more elements," as shown in the examples:

```
case List(0, _, _) => "a three-element list with 0 as the first element"
case List(1, _*) => "a list beginning with 1, having any number of elements"
case Vector(1, _*) => "a vector beginning with 1 and having any number …"
```

*Tuple patterns*

As shown in the examples, you can match *tuple patterns* and access the value of each element in the tuple. You can also use the _ wildcard if you're not interested in the value of an element:

```
case (a, b, c) => s"3-elem tuple, with values $a, $b, and $c"
case (a, b, c, _) => s"4-elem tuple: got $a, $b, and $c"
```

*Type patterns*

In the following example, `str: String` is a *typed pattern*, and `str` is a *pattern variable*:

```
case str: String => 's"you gave me this string: $str"
```

As shown in the examples, you can access the pattern variable on the right side of the expression after declaring it.

## Adding variables to patterns

At times you may want to add a variable to a pattern. You can do this with the following general syntax:

```
variableName @ pattern
```

As the book, *Programming in Scala*, states, "This gives you a variable-binding pattern. The meaning of such a pattern is to perform the pattern match as normal, and if the pattern succeeds, set the variable to the matched object just as with a simple variable pattern."

The usefulness of this is best shown by demonstrating the problem it solves. Suppose you had the List pattern that was shown earlier:

```
case List(1, _*) => "a list beginning with 1, having any number of elements"
```

As demonstrated, this lets you match a List whose first element is 1, but so far, the List hasn't been accessed on the right side of the expression. When accessing a List, you know that you can do this:

```
case list: List[_] => s"thanks for the List: $list"
```

so it seems like you should try this with a sequence pattern:

```
case list: List(1, _*) => s"thanks for the List: $list"
```

Unfortunately, this fails with the following compiler error:

```
Test2.scala:22: error: '=>' expected but '(' found.
    case list: List(1, _*) => s"thanks for the List: $list"
                   ^
one error found
```

The solution to this problem is to add a variable-binding pattern to the sequence pattern:

```
case list @ List(1, _*) => s"$list"
```

This code compiles, and works as expected, giving you access to the List on the right side of the statement.

The following code demonstrates this example and the usefulness of this approach:

```
case class Person(firstName: String, lastName: String)

object Test2 extends App {

  def matchType(x: Any): String = x match {

    //case x: List(1, _*) => s"$x"          // doesn't compile
```

```
    case x @ List(1, _*) => s"$x"          // works; prints the list

    //case Some(_) => "got a Some"         // works, but can't access the Some
    //case Some(x) => s"$x"                // works, returns "foo"
    case x @ Some(_) => s"$x"             // works, returns "Some(foo)"

    case p @ Person(first, "Doe") => s"$p"  // works, returns "Person(John,Doe)"

  }

  println(matchType(List(1,2,3)))              // prints "List(1, 2, 3)"
  println(matchType(Some("foo")))              // prints "Some(foo)"
  println(matchType(Person("John", "Doe")))    // prints "Person(John,Doe)"

}
```

In the two List examples inside the match expression, the commented-out line of code won't compile, but the second example shows how to assign the variable x to the List object it matches. When this line of code is matched with the `println(matchType(List(1,2,3)))` call, it results in the output List(1, 2, 3).

The first Some example shows that you can match a Some with the approach shown, but you can't access its information on the righthand side of the expression. The second example shows how you can access the value inside the Some, and the third example takes this a step further, giving you access to the Some object itself. When it's matched by the second println call, it prints Some(foo), demonstrating that you now have access to the Some object.

Finally, this approach is used to match a Person whose last name is Doe. This syntax lets you assign the result of the pattern match to the variable p, and then access that variable on the right side of the expression.

### Using Some and None in match expressions

To round out these examples, you'll often use Some and None with match expressions. For instance, assume you have a **toInt** method defined like this:

```
def toInt(s: String): Option[Int] = {
  try {
    Some(Integer.parseInt(s.trim))
  } catch {
    case e: Exception => None
  }
}
```

In some situations, you may want to use this method with a match expression, like this:

```
toInt("42") match {
  case Some(i) => println(i)
  case None => println("That wasn't an Int.")
}
```

Inside the match expression you just specify the Some and None cases as shown to handle the success and failure conditions. See Recipe 20.6 for more examples of using Option, Some, and None.

## See Also

- A discussion of getting around type erasure when using match expressions on Stack Overflow (*http://bit.ly/15odxST*)
- My Blue Parrot application (*http://alvinalexander.com/blueparrot*)
- The "Type Erasure" documentation (*http://bit.ly/139WrFj*)

# 3.12. Using Case Classes in Match Expressions

## Problem

You want to match different case classes (or case objects) in a match expression, such as when receiving messages in an actor.

## Solution

Use the different patterns shown in the previous recipe to match case classes and objects, depending on your needs.

The following example demonstrates how to use patterns to match case classes and case objects in different ways, depending primarily on what information you need on the right side of each case statement. In this example, the Dog and Cat case classes and the Woodpecker case object are different subtypes of the Animal trait:

```
trait Animal
case class Dog(name: String) extends Animal
case class Cat(name: String) extends Animal
case object Woodpecker extends Animal

object CaseClassTest extends App {

  def determineType(x: Animal): String = x match {
    case Dog(moniker) => "Got a Dog, name = " + moniker
    case _:Cat => "Got a Cat (ignoring the name)"
    case Woodpecker => "That was a Woodpecker"
    case _ => "That was something else"
  }
```

```
println(determineType(new Dog("Rocky")))
println(determineType(new Cat("Rusty the Cat")))
println(determineType(Woodpecker))

}
```

When the code is compiled and run, the output is:

```
Got a Dog, name = Rocky
Got a Cat (ignoring the name)
That was a Woodpecker
```

In this example, if the Dog class is matched, its name is extracted and used in the print statement on the right side of the expression. To show that the variable name used when extracting the name can be any legal variable name, I use the name moniker.

When matching a Cat, I want to ignore the name, so I use the syntax shown to match any Cat instance. Because Woodpecker is defined as a case object and has no name, it is also matched as shown.

# 3.13. Adding if Expressions (Guards) to Case Statements

## Problem

You want to add qualifying logic to a case statement in a match expression, such as allowing a range of numbers, or matching a pattern, but only if that pattern matches some additional criteria.

## Solution

Add an if *guard* to your case statement. Use it to match a range of numbers:

```
i match {
  case a if 0 to 9 contains a => println("0-9 range: " + a)
  case b if 10 to 19 contains b => println("10-19 range: " + b)
  case c if 20 to 29 contains c => println("20-29 range: " + c)
  case _ => println("Hmmm...")
}
```

Use it to match different values of an object:

```
num match {
  case x if x == 1 => println("one, a lonely number")
  case x if (x == 2 || x == 3) => println(x)
  case _ => println("some other value")
}
```

You can reference class fields in your if guards. Imagine here that x is an instance of a Stock class that has symbol and price fields:

```
stock match {
  case x if (x.symbol == "XYZ" && x.price < 20) => buy(x)
  case x if (x.symbol == "XYZ" && x.price > 50) => sell(x)
  case _ => // do nothing
}
```

You can also extract fields from case classes and use those in your guards:

```
def speak(p: Person) = p match {
  case Person(name) if name == "Fred" => println("Yubba dubba doo")
  case Person(name) if name == "Bam Bam" => println("Bam bam!")
  case _ => println("Watch the Flintstones!")
}
```

## Discussion

You can use this syntax whenever you want to add simple matches to your case statements on the left side of the expression.

Note that all of these examples could be written by putting the if tests on the right side of the expressions, like this:

```
case Person(name) =>
  if (name == "Fred") println("Yubba dubba doo")
  else if (name == "Bam Bam") println("Bam bam!")
```

However, for many situations, your code will be simpler and easier to read by joining the if guard directly with the case statement.

# 3.14. Using a Match Expression Instead of isInstanceOf

## Problem

You want to write a block of code to match one type, or multiple different types.

## Solution

You *can* use the isInstanceOf method to test the type of an object:

```
if (x.isInstanceOf[Foo]) { do something ...
```

However, some programmers discourage this approach, and in other cases, it may not be convenient. In these instances, you can handle the different expected types in a match expression.

For example, you may be given an object of unknown type, and want to determine if the object is an instance of a Person:

```
def isPerson(x: Any): Boolean = x match {
  case p: Person => true
```

```
    case _ => false
  }
```

Or you may be given an object that extends a known supertype, and then want to take different actions based on the exact subtype. In the following example, the `printInfo` method is given a `SentientBeing`, and then handles the subtypes differently:

```
trait SentientBeing
trait Animal extends SentientBeing
case class Dog(name: String) extends Animal
case class Person(name: String, age: Int) extends SentientBeing

// later in the code ...
def printInfo(x: SentientBeing) = x match {
  case Person(name, age) => // handle the Person
  case Dog(name) => // handle the Dog
}
```

## Discussion

As shown, a match expression lets you match multiple types, so using it to replace the `isInstanceOf` method is just a natural use of the `case` syntax and the general pattern-matching approach used in Scala applications.

In simple examples, the `isInstanceOf` method can be a simpler approach to determining whether an object matches a type:

```
if (o.isInstanceOf[Person]) { // handle this ...
```

However, with more complex needs, a match expression is more readable than an `if`/`else` statement.

# 3.15. Working with a List in a Match Expression

## Problem

You know that a `List` data structure is a little different than other collection data structures. It's built from *cons* cells and ends in a `Nil` element. You want to use this to your advantage when working with a match expression, such as when writing a recursive function.

## Solution

You can create a `List` like this:

```
val x = List(1, 2, 3)
```

or like this, using cons cells and a `Nil` element:

```
val y = 1 :: 2 :: 3 :: Nil
```

---

When writing a recursive algorithm, you can take advantage of the fact that the last element in a List is a Nil object. For instance, in the following listToString method, if the current element is not Nil, the method is called recursively with the remainder of the List, but if the current element is Nil, the recursive calls are stopped and an empty String is returned, at which point the recursive calls unwind:

```
def listToString(list: List[String]): String = list match {
  case s :: rest => s + " " + listToString(rest)
  case Nil => ""
}
```

Running this example in the REPL yields the following result:

```
scala> val fruits = "Apples" :: "Bananas" :: "Oranges" :: Nil
fruits: List[java.lang.String] = List(Apples, Bananas, Oranges)

scala> listToString(fruits)
res0: String = "Apples Bananas Oranges "
```

The same approach of (a) handling the Nil condition and (b) handling the remainder of the List can be used when dealing with a List of other types:

```
def sum(list: List[Int]): Int = list match {
  case Nil => 1
  case n :: rest => n + sum(rest)
}

def multiply(list: List[Int]): Int = list match {
  case Nil => 1
  case n :: rest => n * multiply(rest)
}
```

These methods are demonstrated in the REPL:

```
scala> val nums = List(1,2,3,4,5)
nums: List[Int] = List(1, 2, 3, 4, 5)

scala> sum(nums)
res0: Int = 16

scala> multiply(nums)
res1: Int = 120
```

## Discussion

When using this recipe, be sure to handle the Nil case, or you'll get the following error in the REPL:

```
warning: match is not exhaustive!
```

In the real world (outside the REPL), you'll get a MatchError:

```
Exception in thread "main" scala.MatchError: List()
(of class scala.collection.immutable.Nil$)
```

## See Also

Recipe 3.11, "Using Pattern Matching in Match Expressions", for more examples of using a match expression with multiple types

# 3.16. Matching One or More Exceptions with try/catch

## Problem

You want to catch one or more exceptions in a try/catch block.

## Solution

The Scala try/catch/finally syntax is similar to Java, but it uses the match expression approach in the catch block:

```
val s = "Foo"
try {
  val i = s.toInt
} catch {
  case e: Exception => e.printStackTrace
}
```

When you need to catch and handle multiple exceptions, just add the exception types as different case statements:

```
try {
  openAndReadAFile(filename)
} catch {
  case e: FileNotFoundException => println("Couldn't find that file.")
  case e: IOException => println("Had an IOException trying to read that file")
}
```

## Discussion

As shown, the Scala match expression syntax is used to match different possible exceptions. If you're not concerned about which specific exceptions might be thrown, and want to catch them all and do something with them (such as log them), use this syntax:

```
try {
  openAndReadAFile("foo")
} catch {
  case t: Throwable => t.printStackTrace()
}
```

You can also catch them all and ignore them like this:

```
try {
  val i = s.toInt
} catch {
  case _: Throwable => println("exception ignored")
}
```

As with Java, you can throw an exception from a catch clause, but because Scala doesn't have checked exceptions, you don't need to specify that a method throws the exception. This is demonstrated in the following example, where the method isn't annotated in any way:

```
// nothing required here
def toInt(s: String): Option[Int] =
  try {
    Some(s.toInt)
  } catch {
    case e: Exception => throw e
  }
```

If you prefer to declare the exceptions that your method throws, or you need to interact with Java, add the @throws annotation to your method definition:

```
@throws(classOf[NumberFormatException])
def toInt(s: String): Option[Int] =
  try {
    Some(s.toInt)
  } catch {
    case e: NumberFormatException => throw e
  }
```

## See Also

- Recipe 5.8, "Declaring That a Method Can Throw an Exception" for more examples of declaring that a method can throw an exception

- Recipe 2.1, "Parsing a Number from a String" for more examples of a toInt method

# 3.17. Declaring a Variable Before Using It in a try/catch/finally Block

## Problem

You want to use an object in a try block, and need to access it in the finally portion of the block, such as when you need to call a close method on an object.

## Solution

In general, declare your field as an Option before the try/catch block, then create a Some inside the try clause. This is shown in the following example, where the fields in and out are declared before the try/catch block, and assigned inside the try clause:

```
import java.io._

object CopyBytes extends App {

  var in = None: Option[FileInputStream]
  var out = None: Option[FileOutputStream]

  try {
    in = Some(new FileInputStream("/tmp/Test.class"))
    out = Some(new FileOutputStream("/tmp/Test.class.copy"))
    var c = 0
    while ({c = in.get.read; c != -1}) {
      out.get.write(c)
    }
  } catch {
    case e: IOException => e.printStackTrace
  } finally {
    println("entered finally ...")
    if (in.isDefined) in.get.close
    if (out.isDefined) out.get.close
  }

}
```

In this code, in and out are assigned to None before the try clause, and then reassigned to Some values inside the try clause if everything succeeds. Therefore, it's safe to call in.get and out.get in the while loop, because if an exception had occurred, flow control would have switched to the catch clause, and then the finally clause before leaving the method.

Normally I tell people that I wish the get and isDefined methods on Option would be deprecated, but this is one of the few times where I think their use is acceptable, and they lead to more readable code.

Another approach you can employ inside the try clause is to use the foreach approach with a Some:

```
try {
  in = Some(new FileInputStream("/tmp/Test.class"))
  out = Some(new FileOutputStream("/tmp/Test.class.copy"))
  in.foreach { inputStream =>
    out.foreach { outputStream =>
      var c = 0
      while ({c = inputStream.read; c != -1}) {
        outputStream.write(c)
```

```
      }
    }
  }
} // ...
```

This is still readable with two variables, and eliminates the `get` method calls, but wouldn't be practical with more variables.

## Discussion

One key to this recipe is knowing the syntax for declaring `Option` fields that aren't initially populated:

```
var in = None: Option[FileInputStream]
var out = None: Option[FileOutputStream]
```

I had a hard time remembering this until I came up with a little mnemonic, "Var x has No Option yeT," where I capitalize the "T" there to stand for "type." In my brain it looks like this:

```
var x has No Option[yeT]
```

From there it's a simple matter to get to this:

```
var x = None: Option[Type]
```

When I first started working with Scala, the only way I could think to write this code was using `null` values. The following code demonstrates the approach I used in an application that checks my email accounts. The `store` and `inbox` fields in this code are declared as `null` fields that have the `Store` and `Folder` types (from the *javax.mail* package):

```
// (1) declare the null variables
var store: Store = null
var inbox: Folder = null

try {
  // (2) use the variables/fields in the try block
  store = session.getStore("imaps")
  inbox = getFolder(store, "INBOX")
  // rest of the code here ...
  catch {
    case e: NoSuchProviderException => e.printStackTrace
    case me: MessagingException => me.printStackTrace
} finally {
  // (3) call close() on the objects in the finally clause
  if (inbox != null) inbox.close
  if (store != null) store.close
}
```

However, working in Scala gives you a chance to forget that null values even exist, so this is *not* a recommended approach. See Recipe 20.5, "Eliminate null Values from Your Code", for examples of how to rid your code of null values.

## See Also

The code shown in this recipe is a Scala version of this Oracle "Byte Streams" example (*http://bit.ly/1ahHPtP*).

# 3.18. Creating Your Own Control Structures

## Problem

You want to define your own control structures to improve the Scala language, simplify your own code, or create a DSL for others to use.

## Solution

The creators of the Scala language made a conscious decision not to implement some keywords in Scala, and instead implemented functionality through Scala libraries. This was demonstrated in Recipe 3.5, "Implementing break and continue", which showed that although the Scala language doesn't have break and continue keywords, you can achieve the same functionality through library methods.

As a simple example of creating what appears to be a control structure, imagine for a moment that for some reason you don't like the while loop and want to create your own whilst loop, which you can use like this:

```
package foo

import com.alvinalexander.controls.Whilst._

object WhilstDemo extends App {

  var i = 0
  whilst (i < 5) {
    println(i)
    i += 1
  }

}
```

To create your own whilst control structure, define a function named whilst that takes two parameter lists. The first parameter list handles the test condition—in this case, i < 5—and the second parameter list is the block of code the user wants to run.

You could implement this as a method that's just a wrapper around the `while` operator:

```
// 1st attempt
def whilst(testCondition: => Boolean)(codeBlock: => Unit) {
  while (testCondition) {
    codeBlock
  }
}
```

But a more interesting approach is to implement the `whilst` method without calling `while`. This is shown in a complete object here:

```
package com.alvinalexander.controls

import scala.annotation.tailrec

object Whilst {

  // 2nd attempt
  @tailrec
  def whilst(testCondition: => Boolean)(codeBlock: => Unit) {
    if (testCondition) {
      codeBlock
      whilst(testCondition)(codeBlock)
    }
  }

}
```

In this code, the `testCondition` is evaluated once, and if the condition is true, the `codeBlock` is executed, and then `whilst` is called recursively. This approach lets you keep checking the condition without needing a `while` or `for` loop.

## Discussion

In the second `whilst` example, I used a recursive call to keep the loop running, but in a simpler example, you don't need recursion. For example, assume you want a control structure that takes two test conditions, and if both evaluate to true, you'll run a block of code that's supplied. An expression using that control structure might look like this:

```
doubleif(age > 18)(numAccidents == 0) { println("Discount!") }
```

In this case, define a function that takes three parameter lists:

```
// two 'if' condition tests
def doubleif(test1: => Boolean)(test2: => Boolean)(codeBlock: => Unit) {
  if (test1 && test2) {
    codeBlock
  }
}
```

Because doubleif only needs to perform one test and doesn't need to loop indefinitely, there's no need for a recursive call in its method body. It simply checks the two test conditions, and if they evaluate to true, the codeBlock is executed.

## See Also

- One of my favorite uses of this technique is shown in the book, *Beginning Scala* (Apress), by David Pollak. I describe how it works on my website (*http://bit.ly/ 12JL0Fp*).

- The Scala Breaks class is demonstrated in Recipe 3.5. Its source code is simple, and provides another example of how to implement a control structure (*http://bit.ly/ 16yPb8n*).

# CHAPTER 4

# Classes and Properties

## Introduction

Although Scala and Java share many similarities, the declaration of classes, class constructors, and the control of field visibility are some of the biggest differences between the two languages. Whereas Java tends to be more verbose (yet obvious), Scala is more concise, and the code you write ends up generating other code.

Recipes in this chapter will help you get through the initial learning curve related to Scala classes and fields by demonstrating how class constructors work, and the code the Scala compiler generates on your behalf when you declare constructor parameters and class fields using the `val`, `var`, and `private` keywords.

Because the Scala compiler generates accessors and mutators based on your field declarations, you may wonder how to override those methods, and this chapter provides recipes showing how to override that generated code.

Additionally, because Scala automatically sets the field type based on the value you assign, you may wonder, "What happens when a field has no initial value?" For instance, you may want to create an uninitialized field as an instance of an `Address` class. As you think about this you start typing the following code, and then wonder how to complete it:

```
var address = ?      // how to create an uninitialized Address?
```

This chapter shows the solution to that problem, demonstrates how declaring a class as a *case class* results in more than 20 additional methods being generated, shows how to write `equals` methods that work with class inheritance, and much more.

In Java, it seems correct to refer to *accessor* and *mutator* methods as "getter" and "setter" methods, primarily because of the JavaBeans standard. In this chapter, I use the terms interchangeably, but to be clear, Scala does not follow the JavaBeans naming convention for accessor and mutator methods.

# 4.1. Creating a Primary Constructor

## Problem

You want to create a primary constructor for a class, and you quickly find that the approach is different than Java.

## Solution

The primary constructor of a Scala class is a combination of:

- The constructor parameters
- Methods that are called in the body of the class
- Statements and expressions that are executed in the body of the class

Fields declared in the body of a Scala class are handled in a manner similar to Java; they are assigned when the class is first instantiated.

The following class demonstrates constructor parameters, class fields, and statements in the body of a class:

```
class Person(var firstName: String, var lastName: String) {

  println("the constructor begins")

  // some class fields
  private val HOME = System.getProperty("user.home")
  var age = 0

  // some methods
  override def toString = s"$firstName $lastName is $age years old"
  def printHome { println(s"HOME = $HOME") }
  def printFullName { println(this) }  // uses toString

  printHome
  printFullName
  println("still in the constructor")

}
```

Because the methods in the body of the class are part of the constructor, when an instance of a `Person` class is created, you'll see the output from the `println` statements at the beginning and end of the class declaration, along with the call to the `printHome` and `printFullName` methods near the bottom of the class:

```
scala> val p = new Person("Adam", "Meyer")
the constructor begins
HOME = /Users/Al
Adam Meyer is 0 years old
still in the constructor
```

## Discussion

If you're coming to Scala from Java, you'll find that the process of declaring a primary constructor in Scala is quite different. In Java it's fairly obvious when you're in the main constructor and when you're not, but Scala blurs this distinction. However, once you understand the approach, it also makes your class declarations more concise than Java class declarations.

In the example shown, the two constructor arguments `firstName` and `lastName` are defined as `var` fields, which means that they're variable, or mutable; they can be changed after they're initially set. Because the fields are mutable, Scala generates both accessor and mutator methods for them. As a result, given an instance p of type `Person`, you can change the values like this:

```
p.firstName = "Scott"
p.lastName = "Jones"
```

and you can access them like this:

```
println(p.firstName)
println(p.lastName)
```

Because the `age` field is declared as a `var`, it's also visible, and can be mutated and accessed:

```
p.age = 30
println(p.age)
```

The field `HOME` is declared as a `private val`, which is like making it `private` and `final` in a Java class. As a result, it can't be accessed directly by other objects, and its value can't be changed.

When you call a method in the body of the class—such as the call near the bottom of the class to the `printFullName` method—that method call is also part of the constructor. You can verify this by compiling the code to a *Person.class* file with `scalac`, and then decompiling it back into Java source code with a tool like the JAD decompiler (*http://www.varaneckas.com/jad/*). After doing so, this is what the `Person` class constructor looks like:

```
public Person(String firstName, String lastName)
{
  super();
  this.firstName = firstName;
  this.lastName = lastName;
  Predef$.MODULE$.println("the constructor begins");
  age = 0;
  printHome();
  printFullName();
  Predef$.MODULE$.println("still in the constructor");
}
```

This clearly shows the printHome and printFullName methods call in the Person constructor, as well as the initial age being set.

When the code is decompiled, the constructor parameters and class fields appear like this:

```
private String firstName;
private String lastName;
private final String HOME = System.getProperty("user.home");
private int age;
```

 Anything defined within the body of the class other than method declarations is a part of the primary class constructor. Because auxiliary constructors must always call a previously defined constructor in the same class, auxiliary constructors will also execute the same code.

### A comparison with Java

The following code shows the equivalent Java version of the Person class:

```
// java
public class Person {

  private String firstName;
  private String lastName;
  private final String HOME = System.getProperty("user.home");
  private int age;

  public Person(String firstName, String lastName) {
    super();
    this.firstName = firstName;
    this.lastName = lastName;
    System.out.println("the constructor begins");
    age = 0;
    printHome();
    printFullName();
    System.out.println("still in the constructor");
  }
```

```
public String firstName() { return firstName; }
public String lastName() { return lastName; }
public int age() { return age; }

public void firstName_$eq(String firstName) {
  this.firstName = firstName;
}

public void lastName_$eq(String lastName) {
  this.lastName = lastName;
}

public void age_$eq(int age) {
  this.age = age;
}

public String toString() {
  return firstName + " " + lastName + " is " + age + " years old";
}

public void printHome() {
  System.out.println(HOME);
}

public void printFullName() {
  System.out.println(this);
}

}
```

As you can see, this is quite a bit lengthier than the equivalent Scala code. With constructors, I find that Java code is more verbose, but obvious; you don't have to reason much about what the compiler is doing for you.

### Those _$eq methods

The names of the mutator methods that are generated may look a little unusual:

```
public void firstName_$eq(String firstName) { ...
public void age_$eq(int age) { ...
```

These names are part of the Scala syntactic sugar for mutating var fields, and not anything you normally have to think about. For instance, the following Person class has a var field named name:

```
class Person {
  var name = ""
  override def toString = s"name = $name"
}
```

Because name is a var field, Scala generates accessor and mutator methods for it. What you don't normally see is that when the code is compiled, the mutator method is named name_$eq. You don't see that because with Scala's syntactic sugar, you mutate the field like this:

```
p.name = "Ron Artest"
```

However, behind the scenes, Scala converts that line of code into this code:

```
p.name_$eq("Ron Artest")
```

To demonstrate this, you can run the following object that calls the mutator method in both ways (not something that's normally done):

```
object Test extends App {

    val p = new Person

    // the 'normal' mutator approach
    p.name = "Ron Artest"
    println(p)

    // the 'hidden' mutator method
    p.name_$eq("Metta World Peace")
    println(p)

}
```

When this code is run, it prints this output:

```
name = Ron Artest
name = Metta World Peace
```

Again, there's no reason to call the name_$eq method in the real world, but when you get into overriding mutator methods, it's helpful to understand how this translation process works.

### Summary

As shown with the equivalent Scala and Java classes, the Java code is verbose, but it's also straightforward. The Scala code is more concise, but you have to look at the constructor parameters to understand whether getters and setters are being generated for you, and you have to know that any method that's called in the body of the class is really being called from the primary constructor. This was a little confusing when I first started working with Scala, but it quickly became second nature.

# 4.2. Controlling the Visibility of Constructor Fields

## Problem

You want to control the visibility of fields that are used as constructor parameters in a Scala class.

# Solution

As shown in the following examples, the visibility of constructor fields in a Scala class is controlled by whether the fields are declared as val, var, without either val or var, and whether private is also added to the fields.

Here's the short version of the solution:

- If a field is declared as a var, Scala generates both getter and setter methods for that field.
- If the field is a val, Scala generates only a getter method for it.
- If a field doesn't have a var or val modifier, Scala gets conservative, and doesn't generate a getter or setter method for the field.
- Additionally, var and val fields can be modified with the private keyword, which prevents getters and setters from being generated.

See the examples that follow for more details.

### var fields

If a constructor parameter is declared as a var, the value of the field *can* be changed, so Scala generates both getter and setter methods for that field. In the following examples, the constructor parameter name is declared as a var, so the field can be accessed and mutated:

```
scala> class Person(var name: String)
defined class Person

scala> val p = new Person("Alvin Alexander")
p: Person = Person@369e58be

// getter
scala> p.name
res0: String = Alvin Alexander

// setter
scala> p.name = "Fred Flintstone"
p.name: String = Fred Flintstone

scala> p.name
res1: String = Fred Flintstone
```

As shown, Scala does not follow the JavaBean naming convention when generating accessor and mutator methods.

## val fields

If a constructor field is defined as a `val`, the value of the field *can't* be changed once it's been set; it's immutable (like `final` in Java). Therefore it makes sense that it should have an accessor method, and should *not* have a mutator method:

```
scala> class Person(val name: String)
defined class Person

scala> val p = new Person("Alvin Alexander")
p: Person = Person@3f9f332b

scala> p.name
res0: String = Alvin Alexander

scala> p.name = "Fred Flintstone"
<console>:11: error: reassignment to val
       p.name = "Fred Flintstone"
              ^
```

The last example fails because a mutator method is not generated for a `val` field.

## Fields without val or var

When neither `val` nor `var` are specified on constructor parameters, the visibility of the field becomes very restricted, and Scala doesn't generate accessor or mutator methods:

```
scala> class Person(name: String)
defined class Person

scala> val p = new Person("Alvin Alexander")
p: Person = Person@144b6a6c

scala> p.name
<console>:12: error: value name is not a member of Person
              p.name
                 ^
```

## Adding private to val or var

In addition to these three basic configurations, you can add the `private` keyword to a `val` or `var` field. This keyword prevents getter and setter methods from being generated, so the field can only be accessed from within members of the class:

```
scala> class Person(private var name: String) { def getName {println(name)} }
defined class Person

scala> val p = new Person("Alvin Alexander")
p: Person = Person@3cb7cee4

scala> p.name
<console>:10: error: variable name in class Person cannot be accessed in Person
              p.name
                 ^
```

```
scala> p.getName
Alvin Alexander
```

Attempting to access `p.name` fails because a getter method is not generated for the `name` field, so callers can't access it directly, but `p.getName` works because it can access the name field.

## Discussion

If this is a little confusing, it helps to think about the choices the compiler has when generating code for you. When a field is defined as a `val`, by definition its value can't be changed, so it makes sense to generate a getter, but no setter. By definition, the value of a `var` field *can* be changed, so generating both a getter and setter make sense for it.

The `private` setting on a constructor parameter gives you additional flexibility. When it's added to a `val` or `var` field, the getter and setter methods are generated as before, but they're marked `private`. (I rarely use this feature, but it's there if you need it.)

The accessors and mutators that are generated for you based on these settings are summarized in Table 4-1.

*Table 4-1. The effect of constructor parameter settings*

| Visibility | Accessor? | Mutator? |
|---|---|---|
| var | Yes | Yes |
| val | Yes | No |
| Default visibility (no var or val) | No | No |
| Adding the private keyword to var or val | No | No |

You can also manually add your own accessor and mutator methods. See Recipe 4.6, "Overriding Default Accessors and Mutators", for more information.

### Case classes

Parameters in the constructor of a *case class* differ from these rules in one way. Case class constructor parameters are `val` by default. So if you define a case class field without adding `val` or `var`, like this:

```
case class Person(name: String)
```

you can still access the field, just as if it were defined as a `val`:

```
scala> val p = Person("Dale Cooper")
p: Person = Person(Dale Cooper)

scala> p.name
res0: String = Dale Cooper
```

Although this is slightly different than a "regular" class, it's a nice convenience and has to do with the way case classes are intended to be used in functional programming, i.e., as immutable records. See Recipe 4.14, "Generating Boilerplate Code with Case Classes", for more information about how case classes work.

# 4.3. Defining Auxiliary Constructors

## Problem

You want to define one or more auxiliary constructors for a class to give consumers of the class different ways to create object instances.

## Solution

Define the auxiliary constructors as methods in the class with the name this. You can define multiple auxiliary constructors, but they must have different signatures (parameter lists). Also, each constructor must call one of the previously defined constructors.

The following example demonstrates a primary constructor and three auxiliary constructors:

```
// primary constructor
class Pizza (var crustSize: Int, var crustType: String) {

  // one-arg auxiliary constructor
  def this(crustSize: Int) {
    this(crustSize, Pizza.DEFAULT_CRUST_TYPE)
  }

  // one-arg auxiliary constructor
  def this(crustType: String) {
    this(Pizza.DEFAULT_CRUST_SIZE, crustType)
  }

  // zero-arg auxiliary constructor
  def this() {
    this(Pizza.DEFAULT_CRUST_SIZE, Pizza.DEFAULT_CRUST_TYPE)
  }

  override def toString = s"A $crustSize inch pizza with a $crustType crust"

}

object Pizza {
  val DEFAULT_CRUST_SIZE = 12
  val DEFAULT_CRUST_TYPE = "THIN"
}
```

Given these constructors, the same pizza can be created in the following ways:

```
val p1 = new Pizza(Pizza.DEFAULT_CRUST_SIZE, Pizza.DEFAULT_CRUST_TYPE)
val p2 = new Pizza(Pizza.DEFAULT_CRUST_SIZE)
val p3 = new Pizza(Pizza.DEFAULT_CRUST_TYPE)
val p4 = new Pizza
```

## Discussion

There are several important points to this recipe:

- Auxiliary constructors are defined by creating methods named this.
- Each auxiliary constructor must begin with a call to a previously defined constructor.
- Each constructor must have a different signature.
- One constructor calls another constructor with the name this.

In the example shown, all of the auxiliary constructors call the primary constructor, but this isn't necessary; an auxiliary constructor just needs to call one of the previously defined constructors. For instance, the auxiliary constructor that takes the crustType parameter could have been written like this:

```
def this(crustType: String) {
  this(Pizza.DEFAULT_CRUST_SIZE)
  this.crustType = Pizza.DEFAULT_CRUST_TYPE
}
```

Another important part of this example is that the crustSize and crustType parameters are declared in the primary constructor. This isn't necessary, but doing this lets Scala generate the accessor and mutator methods for those parameters for you. You could start to write a similar class as follows, but this approach requires more code:

```
class Pizza () {

  var crustSize = 0
  var crustType = ""

  def this(crustSize: Int) {
    this()
    this.crustSize = crustSize
  }

  def this(crustType: String) {
    this()
    this.crustType = crustType
  }
```

```
// more constructors here ...

override def toString = s"A $crustSize inch pizza with a $crustType crust"

}
```

To summarize, if you want the accessors and mutators to be generated for you, put them in the primary constructor.

 Although the approach shown in the Solution is perfectly valid, before creating multiple class constructors like this, take a few moments to read Recipe 4.5, "Providing Default Values for Constructor Parameters". Using that recipe can often eliminate the need for multiple constructors.

### Generating auxiliary constructors for case classes

A *case class* is a special type of class that generates a *lot* of boilerplate code for you. Because of the way they work, adding what appears to be an auxiliary constructor to a case class is different than adding an auxiliary constructor to a "regular" class. This is because they're not really constructors: they're `apply` methods in the companion object of the class.

To demonstrate this, assume that you start with this case class in a file named *Person.scala*:

```
// initial case class
case class Person (var name: String, var age: Int)
```

This lets you create a new `Person` instance without using the new keyword, like this:

```
val p = Person("John Smith", 30)
```

This appears to be a different form of a constructor, but in fact, it's a little syntactic sugar —a factory method, to be precise. When you write this line of code:

```
val p = Person("John Smith", 30)
```

behind the scenes, the Scala compiler converts it into this:

```
val p = Person.apply("John Smith", 30)
```

This is a call to an `apply` method in the companion object of the `Person` class. You don't see this, you just see the line that you wrote, but this is how the compiler translates your code. As a result, if you want to add new "constructors" to your case class, you write new `apply` methods. (To be clear, the word "constructor" is used loosely here.)

For instance, if you decide that you want to add auxiliary constructors to let you create new `Person` instances (a) without specifying any parameters, and (b) by only specifying their name, the solution is to add `apply` methods to the companion object of the `Person` case class in the *Person.scala* file:

```
// the case class
case class Person (var name: String, var age: Int)

// the companion object
object Person {

  def apply() = new Person("<no name>", 0)
  def apply(name: String) = new Person(name, 0)

}
```

The following test code demonstrates that this works as desired:

```
object CaseClassTest extends App {

  val a = Person()              // corresponds to apply()
  val b = Person("Pam")         // corresponds to apply(name: String)
  val c = Person("William Shatner", 82)

  println(a)
  println(b)
  println(c)

  // verify the setter methods work
  a.name = "Leonard Nimoy"
  a.age = 82
  println(a)
}
```

This code results in the following output:

```
Person(<no name>,0)
Person(Pam,0)
Person(William Shatner,82)
Person(Leonard Nimoy,82)
```

## See Also

- Recipe 6.8, "Creating Object Instances Without Using the new Keyword", demonstrates how to implement the `apply` method in a companion object so you can create instances of a class without having to use the new keyword (or declare your class as a case class).

- Recipe 4.5, "Providing Default Values for Constructor Parameters", demonstrates an approach that can often eliminate the need for auxiliary constructors.

- Recipe 4.14, "Generating Boilerplate Code with Case Classes", details the nuts and bolts of how case classes work.

# 4.4. Defining a Private Primary Constructor

## Problem

You want to make the primary constructor of a class private, such as to enforce the Singleton pattern.

## Solution

To make the primary constructor private, insert the `private` keyword in between the class name and any parameters the constructor accepts:

```
// a private no-args primary constructor
class Order private { ...

// a private one-arg primary constructor
class Person private (name: String) { ...
```

As shown in the REPL, this keeps you from being able to create an instance of the class:

```
scala> class Person private (name: String)
defined class Person

scala> val p = new Person("Mercedes")
<console>:9: error: constructor Person in class Person cannot be accessed
in object $iw
       val p = new Person("Mercedes")
                   ^
```

## Discussion

A simple way to enforce the Singleton pattern in Scala is to make the primary constructor `private`, then put a `getInstance` method in the *companion object* of the class:

```
class Brain private {
  override def toString = "This is the brain."
}

object Brain {
  val brain = new Brain
  def getInstance = brain
}

object SingletonTest extends App {

  // this won't compile
  // val brain = new Brain
```

```
// this works
val brain = Brain.getInstance
println(brain)
}
```

You don't have to name the accessor method `getInstance`; it's only used here because of the Java convention.

> A *companion object* is simply an `object` that's defined in the same file as a `class`, where the object and class have the same name. If you declare a class named `Foo` in a file named *Foo.scala*, and then declare an object named `Foo` in that same file, the `Foo` object is the companion object for the `Foo` class.
>
> A companion object has several purposes, and one purpose is that any method declared in a companion object will appear to be a static method on the object. See Recipe 6.6 for more information on creating the equivalent of Java's static methods, and Recipe 6.8 for examples of how (and why) to define `apply` methods in a companion object.

### Utility classes

Depending on your needs, creating a private class constructor may not be necessary at all. For instance, in Java you'd create a file utilities class by defining static methods in a Java class, but in Scala you do the same thing by putting all the methods in a Scala *object*:

```
object FileUtils {

  def readFile(filename: String) = {
    // code here ...
  }

  def writeToFile(filename: String, contents: String) {
    // code here ...
  }
}
```

This lets consumers of your code call these methods like this:

```
val contents = FileUtils.readFile("input.txt")
FileUtils.writeToFile("output.txt", content)
```

Because only an object is defined, code like this won't compile:

```
val utils = new FileUtils  // won't compile
```

So in this case, there's no need for a private class constructor; just don't define a class.

# 4.5. Providing Default Values for Constructor Parameters

## Problem

You want to provide a default value for a constructor parameter, which gives other classes the option of specifying that parameter when calling the constructor, or not.

## Solution

Give the parameter a default value in the constructor declaration. Here's a simple declaration of a Socket class with one constructor parameter named timeout that has a default value of 10000:

```
class Socket (val timeout: Int = 10000)
```

Because the parameter is defined with a default value, you can call the constructor without specifying a timeout value, in which case you get the default value:

```
scala> val s = new Socket
s: Socket = Socket@7862af46

scala> s.timeout
res0: Int = 10000
```

You can also specify the desired timeout value when creating a new Socket:

```
scala> val s = new Socket(5000)
s: Socket = Socket@6df5205c

scala> s.timeout
res1: Int = 5000
```

If you prefer the approach of using named parameters when calling a constructor (or method), you can also use this approach to construct a new Socket:

```
scala> val s = new Socket(timeout=5000)
s: Socket = Socket@52aaf3d2

scala> s.timeout
res0: Int = 5000
```

## Discussion

This recipe demonstrates a powerful feature that can eliminate the need for auxiliary constructors. As shown in the Solution, the following single constructor is the equivalent of two constructors:

```
class Socket (val timeout: Int = 10000)
```

If this feature didn't exist, two constructors would be required to get the same functionality; a primary one-arg constructor and an auxiliary zero-args constructor:

```
class Socket(val timeout: Int) {

    def this() = this(10000)
    override def toString = s"timeout: $timeout"

}
```

## Multiple parameters

Taking this approach a step further, you can provide default values for multiple constructor parameters:

```
class Socket(val timeout: Int = 1000, val linger: Int = 2000) {
    override def toString = s"timeout: $timeout, linger: $linger"
}
```

Though you've defined only one constructor, your class now appears to have three constructors:

```
scala> println(new Socket)
timeout: 1000, linger: 2000

scala> println(new Socket(3000))
timeout: 3000, linger: 2000

scala> println(new Socket(3000, 4000))
timeout: 3000, linger: 4000
```

## Using named parameters

As shown in the Solution, you can also provide the names of constructor parameters when creating objects, in a manner similar to Objective-C and other languages. This means you can also create new Socket instances like this:

```
println(new Socket(timeout=3000, linger=4000))
println(new Socket(linger=4000, timeout=3000))
println(new Socket(timeout=3000))
println(new Socket(linger=4000))
```

See Recipe 5.4, "Using Parameter Names When Calling a Method", for more examples of how to use parameter names in method calls.

# See Also

Recipe 4.3, "Defining Auxiliary Constructors", for more information on creating auxiliary class constructors

# 4.6. Overriding Default Accessors and Mutators

## Problem

You want to override the getter or setter methods that Scala generates for you.

## Solution

This is a bit of a trick problem, because you can't override the getter and setter methods Scala generates for you, at least not if you want to stick with the Scala naming conventions. For instance, if you have a class named `Person` with a constructor parameter named `name`, and attempt to create getter and setter methods according to the Scala conventions, your code won't compile:

```
// error: this won't work
class Person(private var name: String) {
  // this line essentially creates a circular reference
  def name = name
  def name_=(aName: String) { name = aName }
}
```

Attempting to compile this code generates three errors:

```
Person.scala:3: error: overloaded method name needs result type
  def name = name
          ^
Person.scala:4: error: ambiguous reference to overloaded definition,
both method name_= in class Person of type (aName: String)Unit
and  method name_= in class Person of type (x$1: String)Unit
match argument types (String)
  def name_=(aName: String) { name = aName }
          ^
Person.scala:4: error: method name_= is defined twice
  def name_=(aName: String) { name = aName }
      ^
three errors found
```

I'll examine these problems more in the Discussion, but the short answer is that both the constructor parameter and the getter method are named `name`, and Scala won't allow that.

To solve this problem, change the name of the field you use in the class constructor so it won't collide with the name of the getter method you want to use. A common approach is to add a leading underscore to the parameter name, so if you want to manually create a getter method called `name`, use the parameter name `_name` in the constructor, then declare your getter and setter methods according to the Scala conventions:

```
class Person(private var _name: String) {
  def name = _name                              // accessor
```

```
    def name_=(aName: String) { _name = aName }  // mutator
}
```

Notice the constructor parameter is declared `private` and `var`. The `private` keyword keeps Scala from exposing that field to other classes, and the `var` lets the value of the field be changed.

Creating a getter method named `name` and a setter method named `name_=` conforms to the Scala convention and lets a consumer of your class write code like this:

```
val p = new Person("Jonathan")
p.name = "Jony"      // setter
println(p.name)      // getter
```

If you don't want to follow this Scala naming convention for getters and setters, you can use any other approach you want. For instance, you can name your methods `getName` and `setName`, following the JavaBean style. (However, if JavaBeans are what you really want, you may be better off using the `@BeanProperty` annotation, as described in Recipe 17.6, "When Java Code Requires JavaBeans".)

## Discussion

When you define a constructor parameter to be a `var` field, Scala makes the field private to the class and automatically generates getter and setter methods that other classes can use to access the field. For instance, given a simple class like this:

```
class Stock (var symbol: String)
```

after the class is compiled with `scalac`, you'll see this signature when you disassemble it with `javap`:

```
$ javap Stock
```

```
public class Stock extends java.lang.Object{
    public java.lang.String symbol();
    public void symbol_$eq(java.lang.String);
    public Stock(java.lang.String);
}
```

You can see that the Scala compiler generated two methods: a getter named `symbol` and a setter named `symbol_$eq`. This second method is the same as a method you'd name `symbol_=`, but Scala needs to translate the = symbol to `$eq` to work with the JVM.

That second method name is a little unusual, but it follows a Scala convention, and when it's mixed with some syntactic sugar, it lets you set the `symbol` field on a `Stock` instance like this:

```
stock.symbol = "GOOG"
```

The way this works is that behind the scenes, Scala converts that line of code into this line of code:

```
stock.symbol_$eq("GOOG")
```

You generally never have to think about this, unless you want to override the mutator method.

## Summary

As shown in the Solution, the recipe for overriding default getter and setter methods is:

1. Create a `private var` constructor parameter with a name you want to reference from within your class. In the example in the Solution, the field is named _name.

2. Define getter and setter names that you want other classes to use. In the Solution the getter name is name, and the setter name is name_= (which, combined with Scala's syntactic sugar, lets users write p.name = "Jony").

3. Modify the body of the getter and setter methods as desired.

It's important to remember the `private` setting on your field. If you forget to control the access with `private` (or `private[this]`), you'll end up with getter/setter methods for the field you meant to hide. For example, in the following code, I intentionally left the `private` modifier off of the _symbol constructor parameter:

```
// intentionally left the 'private' modifier off _symbol
class Stock (var _symbol: String) {

  // getter
  def symbol = _symbol

  // setter
  def symbol_= (s: String) {
    this.symbol = s
    println(s"symbol was updated, new value is $symbol")
  }

}
```

Compiling and disassembling this code shows the following class signature, including two methods I "accidentally" made visible:

```
public class Stock extends java.lang.Object{
    public java.lang.String _symbol();            // error
    public void _symbol_$eq(java.lang.String);    // error
    public java.lang.String symbol();
    public void symbol_$eq(java.lang.String);
    public Stock(java.lang.String);
}
```

Correctly adding `private` to the _symbol field results in the correct signature in the disassembled code:

```
public class Stock extends java.lang.Object{
    public java.lang.String symbol();             // println(stock.symbol)
```

```
    public void symbol_$eq(java.lang.String);   // stock.symbol = "AAPL"
    public Stock(java.lang.String);
}
```

Note that while these examples used fields in a class constructor, the same principles hold true for fields defined inside a class.

# 4.7. Preventing Getter and Setter Methods from Being Generated

## Problem

When you define a class field as a var, Scala automatically generates getter and setter methods for the field, and defining a field as a val automatically generates a getter method, but you don't want either a getter or setter.

## Solution

Define the field with the private or private[this] access modifiers, as shown with the currentPrice field in this example:

```
class Stock {

    // getter and setter methods are generated
    var delayedPrice: Double = _

    // keep this field hidden from other classes
    private var currentPrice: Double = _
}
```

When you compile this class with scalac, and then disassemble it with javap, you'll see this interface:

```
// Compiled from "Stock.scala"
public class Stock extends java.lang.Object implements scala.ScalaObject{
    public double delayedPrice();
    public void delayedPrice_$eq(double);
    public Stock();
}
```

This shows that getter and setter methods are defined for the delayedPrice field, and there are no getter or setter methods for the currentPrice field, as desired.

## Discussion

Defining a field as private limits the field so it's only available to instances of the same class, in this case instances of the Stock class. To be clear, any instance of a Stock class can access a private field of any other Stock instance.

As an example, the following code yields `true` when the `Driver` object is run, because the `isHigher` method in the `Stock` class can access the `price` field both (a) in its object, and (b) in the other `Stock` object it's being compared to:

```
class Stock {
    // a private field can be seen by any Stock instance
    private var price: Double = _
    def setPrice(p: Double) { price = p }
    def isHigher(that: Stock): Boolean = this.price > that.price
}

object Driver extends App {

    val s1 = new Stock
    s1.setPrice(20)

    val s2 = new Stock
    s2.setPrice(100)

    println(s2.isHigher(s1))

}
```

### Object-private fields

Defining a field as `private[this]` takes this privacy a step further, and makes the field *object-private*, which means that it can only be accessed from the object that contains it. Unlike `private`, the field can't also be accessed by other instances of the same type, making it more private than the plain `private` setting.

This is demonstrated in the following example, where changing `private` to `private[this]` in the `Stock` class no longer lets the `isHigher` method compile:

```
class Stock {
    // a private[this] var is object-private, and can only be seen
    // by the current instance
    private[this] var price: Double = _

    def setPrice(p: Double) { price = p }

    // error: this method won't compile because price is now object-private
    def isHigher(that: Stock): Boolean = this.price > that.price
}
```

Attempting to compile this class generates the following error:

```
Stock.scala:5: error: value price is not a member of Stock
    def isHigher(that: Stock): Boolean = this.price > that.price
                                                            ^
one error found
```

# 4.8. Assigning a Field to a Block or Function

## Problem

You want to initialize a field in a class using a block of code, or by calling a function.

## Solution

Set the field equal to the desired block of code or function. Optionally, define the field as `lazy` if the algorithm requires a long time to run.

In the following example, the field `text` is set equal to a block of code, which either returns (a) the text contained in a file, or (b) an error message, depending on whether the file exists and can be read:

```
class Foo {

  // set 'text' equal to the result of the block of code
  val text = {
    var lines = ""
    try {
      lines = io.Source.fromFile("/etc/passwd").getLines.mkString
    } catch {
      case e: Exception => lines = "Error happened"
    }
    lines
  }

  println(text)
}

object Test extends App {
  val f = new Foo
}
```

Because the assignment of the code block to the `text` field and the `println` statement are both in the body of the `Foo` class, they are in the class's constructor, and will be executed when a new instance of the class is created. Therefore, compiling and running this example will either print the contents of the file, or the "Error happened" message from the `catch` block.

In a similar way, you can assign a class field to the results of a method or function:

```
class Foo {
  import scala.xml.XML

  // assign the xml field to the result of the load method
  val xml = XML.load("http://example.com/foo.xml")
```

```
    // more code here ...
  }
```

## Discussion

When it makes sense, define a field like this to be `lazy`, meaning it won't be evaluated until it is accessed. To demonstrate this, ignore the potential for errors and shorten the class to this:

```
class Foo {
  val text =
    io.Source.fromFile("/etc/passwd").getLines.foreach(println)
}

object Test extends App {
  val f = new Foo
}
```

When this code is compiled and run on a Unix system, the contents of the */etc/passwd* file are printed. That's interesting, but notice what happens when you change the block to define the `text` field as `lazy`:

```
class Foo {
  lazy val text =
    io.Source.fromFile("/etc/passwd").getLines.foreach(println)
}

object Test extends App {
  val f = new Foo
}
```

When this code is compiled and run, there is no output, because the `text` field isn't initialized until it's accessed. That's how a `lazy` field works.

Defining a field as `lazy` is a useful approach when the field might not be accessed in the normal processing of your algorithms, or if running the algorithm will take a long time, and you want to defer that to a later time.

# 4.9. Setting Uninitialized var Field Types

## Problem

You want to set the type for an uninitialized `var` field in a class, so you begin to write code like this:

```
var x =
```

and then wonder how to finish writing the expression.

## Solution

In general, define the field as an `Option`. For certain types, such as `String` and numeric fields, you can specify default initial values.

For instance, imagine that you're starting a social network, and to encourage people to sign up, you only ask for a username and password during the registration process. Therefore, you define `username` and `password` as fields in your class constructor:

```
case class Person(var username: String, var password: String) ...
```

However, later on, you'll also want to get other information from users, including their age, first name, last name, and address. Declaring those first three `var` fields is simple:

```
var age = 0
var firstName = ""
var lastName = ""
```

But what do you do when you get to the address?

The solution is to define the `address` field as an `Option`, as shown here:

```
case class Person(var username: String, var password: String) {

    var age = 0
    var firstName = ""
    var lastName = ""
    var address = None: Option[Address]

}

case class Address(city: String, state: String, zip: String)
```

Later, when a user provides an address, you can assign it using a `Some[Address]`, like this:

```
val p = Person("alvinalexander", "secret")
p.address = Some(Address("Talkeetna", "AK", "99676"))
```

When you need to access the `address` field, there are a variety of approaches you can use, and these are discussed in detail in Recipe 20.6. As one example, if you want to print the fields of an `Address`, calling `foreach` on the `address` field works well:

```
p.address.foreach { a =>
    println(a.city)
    println(a.state)
    println(a.zip)
}
```

If the field hasn't been assigned, `address` is a `None`, and calling `foreach` on it does no harm, the loop is just skipped over. If the `address` field is assigned, it will be a `Some[Address]`, so the `foreach` loop will be entered and the data printed.

## Discussion

In a related situation, setting the type on numeric `var` fields can occasionally be interesting. For instance, it's easy to create an `Int` or `Double` field:

```
var i = 0    // Int
var d = 0.0  // Double
```

In those cases, the compiler automatically defaults to the desired types, but what if you want a different numeric type? This approach lets you give each field the proper type, and a default value:

```
var b: Byte  = 0
var c: Char  = 0
var f: Float = 0
var l: Long  = 0
var s: Short = 0
```

## See Also

- The `Option` class (*http://bit.ly/16yQhkp*)

- Don't set fields like this to `null`; Scala provides a terrific opportunity for you to get away from ever using `null` values again. See Recipe 20.5, "Eliminate null Values from Your Code", for ways to eliminate common uses of `null` values.

- In many Scala frameworks, such as the Play Framework, fields like this are commonly declared as `Option` values. See Recipe 20.6, "Using the Option/Some/None Pattern", for a detailed discussion of this approach.

# 4.10. Handling Constructor Parameters When Extending a Class

## Problem

You want to extend a base class, and need to work with the constructor parameters declared in the base class, as well as new parameters in the subclass.

## Solution

Declare your base class as usual with `val` or `var` constructor parameters. When defining a subclass constructor, leave the `val` or `var` declaration off of the fields that are common to both classes. Then define new constructor parameters in the subclass as `val` or `var` fields, as usual.

For example, first define a `Person` base class:

```
class Person (var name: String, var address: Address) {
  override def toString = if (address == null) name else s"$name @ $address"
}
```

Next define `Employee` as a subclass of `Person`, so that it takes the constructor parameters `name`, `address`, and `age`. The `name` and `address` parameters are common to the parent `Person` class, so leave the `var` declaration off of those fields, but `age` is new, so declare it as a `var`:

```
class Employee (name: String, address: Address, var age: Int)
extends Person (name, address) {
  // rest of the class
}
```

With this `Employee` class and an `Address` case class:

```
case class Address (city: String, state: String)
```

you can create a new `Employee` as follows:

```
val teresa = new Employee("Teresa", Address("Louisville", "KY"), 25)
```

By placing all that code in the REPL, you can see that all of the fields work as expected:

```
scala> teresa.name
res0: String = Teresa

scala> teresa.address
res1: Address = Address(Louisville,KY)

scala> teresa.age
res2: Int = 25
```

## Discussion

To understand how constructor parameters in a subclass work, it helps to understand how the Scala compiler translates your code. Because the following `Person` class defines its constructor parameters as `var` fields:

```
class Person (var name: String, var address: Address) {
  override def toString = if (address == null) name else s"$name @ $address"
}
```

the Scala compiler generates both accessor and mutator methods for the class. You can demonstrate this by compiling and then disassembling the `Person` class.

First, put this code in a file named *Person.scala*:

```
case class Address (city: String, state: String)

class Person (var name: String, var address: Address) {
  override def toString = if (address == null) name else s"$name @ $address"
}
```

Then compile the code with `scalac`, and disassemble the *Person.class* file with `javap`:

```
$ javap Person
Compiled from "Person.scala"
public class Person extends java.lang.Object implements scala.ScalaObject{
  public java.lang.String name();
  public void name_$eq(java.lang.String);
  public Address address();
  public void address_$eq(Address);
  public java.lang.String toString();
  public Person(java.lang.String, Address);
}
```

As shown, the `Person` class contains the `name`, `name_$eq`, `address`, and `address_$eq` methods, which are the accessor and mutator methods for the `name` and `address` fields. (See Recipe 6.8 for an explanation of how those mutator methods work.)

This raises the question, if you define an `Employee` class that extends `Person`, how should you handle the `name` and `address` fields in the `Employee` constructor? Assuming `Employee` adds no new parameters, there are at least two main choices:

```
// Option 1: define name and address as 'var'
class Employee (var name: String, var address: Address)
extends Person (name, address) { ... }

// Option 2: define name and address without var or val
class Employee (name: String, address: Address)
extends Person (name, address) { ... }
```

Because Scala has already generated the getter and setter methods for the `name` and `address` fields in the `Person` class, the solution is to declare the `Employee` constructor without `var` declarations:

```
// this is correct
class Employee (name: String, address: Address)
extends Person (name, address) { ... }
```

Because you don't declare the parameters in `Employee` as `var`, Scala won't attempt to generate methods for those fields. You can demonstrate this by adding the `Employee` class definition to the code in *Person.scala*:

```
case class Address (city: String, state: String)
class Person (var name: String, var address: Address) {
  override def toString = if (address == null) name else s"$name @ $address"
}
class Employee (name: String, address: Address)
extends Person (name, address) {
  // code here ...
}
```

Compiling the code with `scalac` and then disassembling the *Employee.class* file with `javap`, you see the following, expected result:

```
$ javap Employee
Compiled from "Person.scala"
public class Employee extends Person implements scala.ScalaObject{
    public Employee(java.lang.String, Address);
}
```

The Employee class extends Person, and Scala did not generate any methods for the name and address fields. Therefore, the Employee class inherits that behavior from Person.

While this example shows how Scala works with var fields, you can follow the same line of reasoning with val fields as well.

# 4.11. Calling a Superclass Constructor

## Problem

You want to control the superclass constructor that's called when you create constructors in a subclass.

## Solution

This is a bit of a trick question, because you *can* control the superclass constructor that's called by the primary constructor in a subclass, but you *can't* control the superclass constructor that's called by an auxiliary constructor in the subclass.

When you define a subclass in Scala, you control the superclass constructor that's called by its primary constructor when you define the extends portion of the subclass declaration. For instance, in the following code, the Dog class is defined to call the primary constructor of the Animal class, which is a one-arg constructor that takes name as its parameter:

```
class Animal (var name: String) {
  // ...
}
class Dog (name: String) extends Animal (name) {
  // ...
}
```

However, if the Animal class has multiple constructors, the primary constructor of the Dog class can call any of those constructors.

For example, the primary constructor of the Dog class in the following code calls the one-arg auxiliary constructor of the Animal class by specifying that constructor in its extends clause:

```
// (1) primary constructor
class Animal (var name: String, var age: Int) {
```

```
    // (2) auxiliary constructor
    def this (name: String) {
      this(name, 0)
    }

    override def toString = s"$name is $age years old"
}

// calls the Animal one-arg constructor
class Dog (name: String) extends Animal (name) {
  println("Dog constructor called")
}
```

Alternatively, it could call the two-arg primary constructor of the Animal class:

```
// call the two-arg constructor
class Dog (name: String) extends Animal (name, 0) {
  println("Dog constructor called")
}
```

## Auxiliary constructors

Regarding auxiliary constructors, because the first line of an auxiliary constructor must be a call to another constructor of the current class, there is no way for auxiliary constructors to call a superclass constructor.

As you can see in the following code, the primary constructor of the Employee class can call any constructor in the Person class, but the auxiliary constructors of the Employee class must call a previously defined constructor of its own class with the this method as its first line:

```
case class Address (city: String, state: String)
case class Role (role: String)

class Person (var name: String, var address: Address) {

  // no way for Employee auxiliary constructors to call this constructor
  def this (name: String) {
    this(name, null)
    address = null
  }

  override def toString = if (address == null) name else s"$name @ $address"

}

class Employee (name: String, role: Role, address: Address)
extends Person (name, address) {

  def this (name: String) {
    this(name, null, null)
  }
```

```
    def this (name: String, role: Role) {
      this(name, role, null)
    }

    def this (name: String, address: Address) {
      this(name, null, address)
    }

}
```

Therefore, there's no direct way to control which superclass constructor is called from an auxiliary constructor in a subclass. In fact, because each auxiliary constructor must call a previously defined constructor in the same class, all auxiliary constructors will eventually call the same superclass constructor that's called from the subclass's primary constructor.

# 4.12. When to Use an Abstract Class

## Problem

Scala has traits, and a trait is more flexible than an abstract class, so you wonder, "When should I use an abstract class?"

## Solution

There are two main reasons to use an abstract class in Scala:

- You want to create a base class that requires constructor arguments.
- The code will be called from Java code.

Regarding the first reason, traits don't allow constructor parameters:

```
// this won't compile
trait Animal(name: String)
```

So, use an abstract class whenever a base behavior must have constructor parameters:

```
abstract class Animal(name: String)
```

Regarding the second reason, if you're writing code that needs to be accessed from Java, you'll find that Scala traits with implemented methods can't be called from Java code. If you run into this situation, see Recipe 17.7, "Wrapping Traits with Implementations", for solutions to that problem.

## Discussion

Use an abstract class instead of a trait when the base functionality must take constructor parameters. However, be aware that a class can extend only one abstract class.

Abstract classes work just like Java in that you can define some methods that have complete implementations, and other methods that have no implementation and are therefore abstract. To declare that a method is abstract, just leave the body of the method undefined:

```
def speak    // no body makes the method abstract
```

There is no need for an **abstract** keyword; simply leaving the body of the method undefined makes it abstract. This is consistent with how abstract methods in traits are defined.

In the following example, the methods save, update, and delete are defined in the abstract class BaseController, but the connect, getStatus, and set-ServerName methods have no method body, and are therefore abstract:

```
abstract class BaseController(db: Database) {

    def save { db.save }
    def update { db.update }
    def delete { db.delete }

    // abstract
    def connect

    // an abstract method that returns a String
    def getStatus: String

    // an abstract method that takes a parameter
    def setServerName(serverName: String)
}
```

When a class extends the BaseController class, it must implement the connect, getStatus, and setServerName methods, or be declared abstract. Attempting to extend BaseController without implementing those methods yields a "class needs to be abstract" error, as shown in the REPL:

```
scala> class WidgetController(db: Database) extends BaseController(db)
<console>:9: error: class WidgetController needs to be abstract, since:
method setServerName in class BaseController of type (serverName: String)Unit
is not defined
method getStatus in class BaseController of type => String is not defined
method connect in class BaseController of type => Unit is not defined
       class WidgetController(db: Database) extends BaseController(db)
             ^
```

Because a class can extend only one abstract class, when you're trying to decide whether to use a trait or abstract class, always use a trait, unless you have this specific need to have constructor arguments in your base implementation.

# 4.13. Defining Properties in an Abstract Base Class (or Trait)

## Problem

You want to define abstract or concrete properties in an abstract base class (or trait) that can be referenced in all child classes.

## Solution

You can declare both `val` and `var` fields in an abstract class (or trait), and those fields can be abstract or have concrete implementations. All of these variations are shown in this recipe.

### Abstract val and var fields

The following example demonstrates an `Animal` trait with abstract `val` and `var` fields, along with a simple concrete method named `sayHello`, and an override of the `toString` method:

```
abstract class Pet (name: String) {
  val greeting: String
  var age: Int
  def sayHello { println(greeting) }
  override def toString = s"I say $greeting, and I'm $age"
}
```

The following `Dog` and `Cat` classes extend the `Animal` class and provide values for the greeting and age fields. Notice that the fields are again specified as `val` or `var`:

```
class Dog (name: String) extends Pet (name) {
  val greeting = "Woof"
  var age = 2
}

class Cat (name: String) extends Pet (name) {
  val greeting = "Meow"
  var age = 5
}
```

The functionality can be demonstrated with a simple driver object:

```
object AbstractFieldsDemo extends App {
  val dog = new Dog("Fido")
  val cat = new Cat("Morris")

  dog.sayHello
  cat.sayHello

  println(dog)
  println(cat)
```

```
    // verify that the age can be changed
    cat.age = 10
    println(cat)
}
```

The resulting output looks like this:

```
Woof
Meow
I say Woof, and I'm 2
I say Meow, and I'm 5
I say Meow, and I'm 10
```

Concrete field implementations are presented in the Discussion, because it helps to understand how the Scala compiler translates your code in the preceding examples.

## Discussion

As shown, you can declare abstract fields in an abstract class as either val or var, depending on your needs. The way abstract fields work in abstract classes (or traits) is interesting:

- An abstract var field results in getter and setter methods being generated for the field.

- An abstract val field results in a getter method being generated for the field.

- When you define an abstract field in an abstract class or trait, the Scala compiler does *not* create a field in the resulting code; it only generates the methods that correspond to the val or var field.

In the example shown in the Solution, if you look at the code that's created by scalac using the -Xprint:all option, or by decompiling the resulting *Pet.class* file, you won't find greeting or age fields. For instance, if you decompile the class, the output shows only methods in the class, no fields:

```
import scala.*;
import scala.runtime.BoxesRunTime;

public abstract class Pet
{
  public abstract String greeting();
  public abstract int age();
  public abstract void age_$eq(int i);

  public void sayHello() {
    Predef$.MODULE$.println(greeting());
  }

  public String toString(){
```

```
      // code omitted
    }

    public Pet(String name){}
}
```

Because of this, when you provide concrete values for these fields in your concrete classes, you must again define your fields to be val or var. Because the fields don't actually exist in the abstract base class (or trait), the override keyword is not necessary.

As another result of this, you may see developers define a def that takes no parameters in the abstract base class rather than defining a val. They can then define a val in the concrete class, if desired. This technique is demonstrated in the following code:

```
abstract class Pet (name: String) {
  def greeting: String
}

class Dog (name: String) extends Pet (name) {
  val greeting = "Woof"
}

object Test extends App {
  val dog = new Dog("Fido")
  println(dog.greeting)
}
```

Given this background, it's time to examine the use of concrete val and var fields in abstract classes.

## Concrete val fields in abstract classes

When defining a concrete val field in an abstract class, you can provide an initial value, and then override that value in concrete subclasses:

```
abstract class Animal {
  val greeting = "Hello"              // provide an initial value
  def sayHello { println(greeting) }
  def run
}

class Dog extends Animal {
  override val greeting = "Woof"      // override the value
  def run { println("Dog is running") }
}
```

In this example, the greeting variable is created in both classes. To demonstrate this, running the following code:

```
abstract class Animal {
  val greeting = { println("Animal"); "Hello" }
}
```

```
class Dog extends Animal {
  override val greeting = { println("Dog"); "Woof" }
}

object Test extends App {
  new Dog
}
```

results in this output, showing that both values are created:

```
Animal
Dog
```

To prove this, you can also decompile both the Animal and Dog classes, where you'll find the greeting declared like this:

```
private final String greeting = "Hello";
```

To prevent a concrete val field in an abstract base class from being overridden in a subclass, declare the field as a final val:

```
abstract class Animal {
  final val greeting = "Hello"    // made the field 'final'
}

class Dog extends Animal {
  val greeting = "Woof"          // this line won't compile
}
```

## Concrete var fields in abstract classes

You can also give var fields an initial value in your trait or abstract class, and then refer to them in your concrete subclasses, like this:

```
abstract class Animal {
  var greeting = "Hello"
  var age = 0
  override def toString = s"I say $greeting, and I'm $age years old."
}

class Dog extends Animal {
  greeting = "Woof"
  age = 2
}
```

In this case, these fields are declared and assigned in the abstract base class, as shown in the decompiled code for the Animal class:

```
private String greeting;
private int age;
```

```
public Animal(){
  greeting = "Hello";
  age = 0;
}

// more code ...
```

Because the fields are declared and initialized in the abstract Animal base class, there's no need to redeclare the fields as val or var in the concrete Dog subclass.

You can verify this by looking at the code the Scala compiler generates for the Dog class. When you compile the code with scalac -Xprint:all, and look at the last lines of output, you'll see how the compiler has converted the Dog class:

```
class Dog extends Animal {
  def <init>(): Dog = {
    Dog.super.<init>();
    Dog.this.greeting_=("Woof");
    Dog.this.age_=(2);
    ()
  }
}
```

Because the fields are concrete fields in the abstract base class, they just need to be reassigned in the concrete Dog class.

### Don't use null

As discussed in many recipes in this book, including Recipe 20.5, "Eliminate null Values from Your Code", you shouldn't use null values in these situations. If you're tempted to use a null, instead initialize the fields using the Option/Some/None pattern. The following example demonstrates how to initialize val and var fields with this approach:

```
trait Animal {
  val greeting: Option[String]
  var age: Option[Int] = None
  override def toString = s"I say $greeting, and I'm $age years old."
}

class Dog extends Animal {
  val greeting = Some("Woof")
  age = Some(2)
}

object Test extends App {
  val d = new Dog
  println(d)
}
```

Running this Test object yields the following output:

```
I say Some(Woof), and I'm Some(2) years old.
```

See Recipe 5.2, "Calling a Method on a Superclass", for more examples of how to call methods on superclasses.

# 4.14. Generating Boilerplate Code with Case Classes

## Problem

You're working with match expressions, actors, or other situations where you want to use the *case class* syntax to generate boilerplate code, including accessor and mutator methods, along with `apply`, `unapply`, `toString`, `equals`, and `hashCode` methods, and more.

## Solution

Define your class as a *case class*, defining any parameters it needs in its constructor:

```
// name and relation are 'val' by default
case class Person(name: String, relation: String)
```

Defining a class as a case class results in a lot of boilerplate code being generated, with the following benefits:

- An `apply` method is generated, so you don't need to use the new keyword to create a new instance of the class.
- Accessor methods are generated for the constructor parameters because case class constructor parameters are `val` by default. Mutator methods are also generated for parameters declared as `var`.
- A good, default `toString` method is generated.
- An `unapply` method is generated, making it easy to use case classes in match expressions.
- `equals` and `hashCode` methods are generated.
- A `copy` method is generated.

When you define a class as a case class, you don't have to use the new keyword to create a new instance:

```
scala> case class Person(name: String, relation: String)
defined class Person

// "new" not needed before Person
scala> val emily = Person("Emily", "niece")
emily: Person = Person(Emily,niece)
```

Case class constructor parameters are `val` by default, so accessor methods are generated for the parameters, but mutator methods are not generated:

```
scala> emily.name
res0: String = Emily

scala> emily.name = "Fred"
<console>:10: error: reassignment to val
       emily.name = "Fred"
                  ^
```

By defining a case class constructor parameter as a `var`, both accessor and mutator methods are generated:

```
scala> case class Company (var name: String)
defined class Company

scala> val c = Company("Mat-Su Valley Programming")
c: Company = Company(Mat-Su Valley Programming)

scala> c.name
res0: String = Mat-Su Valley Programming

scala> c.name = "Valley Programming"
c.name: String = Valley Programming
```

Case classes also have a good default `toString` method implementation:

```
scala> emily
res0: Person = Person(Emily,niece)
```

Because an `unapply` method is automatically created for a case class, it works well when you need to extract information in match expressions, as shown here:

```
scala> emily match { case Person(n, r) => println(n, r) }
(Emily,niece)
```

Case classes also have generated `equals` and `hashCode` methods, so instances can be compared:

```
scala> val hannah = Person("Hannah", "niece")
hannah: Person = Person(Hannah,niece)

scala> emily == hannah
res1: Boolean = false
```

A case class even creates a `copy` method that is helpful when you need to clone an object, and change some of the fields during the process:

```
scala> case class Employee(name: String, loc: String, role: String)
defined class Employee

scala> val fred = Employee("Fred", "Anchorage", "Salesman")
fred: Employee = Employee(Fred,Anchorage,Salesman)
```

```
scala> val joe = fred.copy(name="Joe", role="Mechanic")
joe: Employee = Employee(Joe,Anchorage,Mechanic)
```

# Discussion

Case classes are primarily intended to create "immutable records" that you can easily use in pattern-matching expressions. Indeed, pure FP developers look at case classes as being similar to immutable records found in ML, Haskell, and other languages.

Perhaps as a result of this, case class constructor parameters are val by default. As a reviewer of this book with an FP background wrote, "Case classes allow var fields, but then you are subverting their very purpose."

## Generated code

As shown in the Solution, when you create a case class, Scala generates a wealth of code for your class. To see the code that's generated for you, first compile a simple case class, then disassemble it with javap. For example, put this code in a file named *Person.scala*:

```
case class Person(var name: String, var age: Int)
```

Then compile the file:

```
$ scalac Person.scala
```

This creates two class files, *Person.class* and *Person$.class*. Disassemble *Person.class* with this command:

```
$ javap Person
```

This results in the following output, which is the public signature of the class:

```
Compiled from "Person.scala"
public class Person extends java.lang.Object ↵
implements scala.ScalaObject,scala.Product,scala.Serializable{
  public static final scala.Function1 tupled();
  public static final scala.Function1 curry();
  public static final scala.Function1 curried();
  public scala.collection.Iterator productIterator();
  public scala.collection.Iterator productElements();
  public java.lang.String name();
  public void name_$eq(java.lang.String);
  public int age();
  public void age_$eq(int);
  public Person copy(java.lang.String, int);
  public int copy$default$2();
  public java.lang.String copy$default$1();
  public int hashCode();
  public java.lang.String toString();
  public boolean equals(java.lang.Object);
  public java.lang.String productPrefix();
```

```
    public int productArity();
    public java.lang.Object productElement(int);
    public boolean canEqual(java.lang.Object);
    public Person(java.lang.String, int);
}
```

Then disassemble *Person$.class*:

```
$ javap Person$

Compiled from "Person.scala"
public final class Person$ extends scala.runtime.AbstractFunction2 ↵
implements scala.ScalaObject,scala.Serializable{
    public static final Person$ MODULE$;
    public static {};
    public final java.lang.String toString();
    public scala.Option unapply(Person);
    public Person apply(java.lang.String, int);
    public java.lang.Object readResolve();
    public java.lang.Object apply(java.lang.Object, java.lang.Object);
}
```

As you can see, Scala generates a *lot* of source code when you declare a class as a case class.

As a point of comparison, if you remove the keyword case from that code (making it a "regular" class), compile it, and then disassemble it, Scala only generates the following code:

```
public class Person extends java.lang.Object{
    public java.lang.String name();
    public void name_$eq(java.lang.String);
    public int age();
    public void age_$eq(int);
    public Person(java.lang.String, int);
}
```

That's a big difference. The case class results in 22 more methods than the "regular" class. If you need the functionality, this is a good thing. However, if you don't need all this additional functionality, consider using a "regular" class declaration instead. For instance, if you just want to be able to create new instances of a class without the new keyword, like this:

```
val p = Person("Alex")
```

create an apply method in the companion object of a "regular" class, as described in Recipe 6.8, "Creating Object Instances Without Using the new Keyword". Remember, there isn't anything in a case class you can't code for yourself.

## See Also

- Recipe 4.3, "Defining Auxiliary Constructors", shows how to write additional apply methods so a case class can appear to have multiple constructors.

- A discussion of extractors on the official Scala website (*http://bit.ly/1dzQ301*).

# 4.15. Defining an equals Method (Object Equality)

## Problem

You want to define an equals method for your class so you can compare object instances to each other.

## Solution

Like Java, you define an equals method (and hashCode method) in your class to compare two instances, but unlike Java, you then use the == method to compare the equality of two instances.

There are many ways to write equals methods. The following example shows one possible way to define an equals method and its corresponding hashCode method:

```
class Person (name: String, age: Int) {

  def canEqual(a: Any) = a.isInstanceOf[Person]

  override def equals(that: Any): Boolean =
    that match {
      case that: Person => that.canEqual(this) && this.hashCode == that.hashCode
      case _ => false
  }

  override def hashCode:Int = {
    val prime = 31
    var result = 1
    result = prime * result + age;
    result = prime * result + (if (name == null) 0 else name.hashCode)
    return result
  }

}
```

This example shows a modified version of a hashCode method that Eclipse generated for a similar Java class. It also uses a canEqual method, which will be explained shortly.

With the equals method defined, you can compare instances of a Person with ==, as demonstrated in the following tests:

```
import org.scalatest.FunSuite

class PersonTests extends FunSuite {

  // these first two instances should be equal
  val nimoy = new Person("Leonard Nimoy", 82)
  val nimoy2 = new Person("Leonard Nimoy", 82)
  val shatner = new Person("William Shatner", 82)
  val ed = new Person("Ed Chigliak", 20)

  // all tests pass
  test("nimoy    == nimoy")   { assert(nimoy == nimoy) }
  test("nimoy    == nimoy2")  { assert(nimoy == nimoy2) }
  test("nimoy2   == nimoy")   { assert(nimoy2 == nimoy) }
  test("nimoy    != shatner") { assert(nimoy != shatner) }
  test("shatner != nimoy")    { assert(shatner != nimoy) }
  test("nimoy    != null")    { assert(nimoy != null) }
  test("nimoy    != String")  { assert(nimoy != "Leonard Nimoy") }
  test("nimoy    != ed")      { assert(nimoy != ed) }

}
```

As noted in the code comments, all of these tests pass.

 These tests were created with the ScalaTest FunSuite, which is similar to writing unit tests with JUnit.

## Discussion

The first thing to know about Scala and the equals method is that, unlike Java, you compare the equality of two objects with ==. In Java, the == operator compares "reference equality," but in Scala, == is a method you use on each class to compare the equality of two instances, calling your equals method under the covers.

As mentioned, there are many ways to implement equals methods, and the code in the Solution shows just one possible approach. The book *Programming in Scala* contains one chapter of more than 25 pages on "object equality," so this is a big topic.

An important benefit of the approach shown in the Solution is that you can continue to use it when you use inheritance in classes. For instance, in the following code, the Employee class extends the Person class that's shown in the Solution:

```
class Employee(name: String, age: Int, var role: String)
extends Person(name, age)
{

  override def canEqual(a: Any) = a.isInstanceOf[Employee]
```

```
override def equals(that: Any): Boolean =
  that match {
    case that: Employee =>
      that.canEqual(this) && this.hashCode == that.hashCode
    case _ => false
  }

override def hashCode:Int = {
  val ourHash = if (role == null) 0 else role.hashCode
  super.hashCode + ourHash
}

}
```

This code uses the same approach to the canEqual, equals, and hashCode methods, and I like that consistency. Just as important as the consistency is the accuracy of the approach, especially when you get into the business of comparing instances of a child class to instances of any of its parent classes. In the case of the Person and Employee code shown, these classes pass all of the following tests:

```
class EmployeeTests extends FunSuite with BeforeAndAfter {

  // these first two instance should be equal
  val eNimoy1 = new Employee("Leonard Nimoy", 82, "Actor")
  val eNimoy2 = new Employee("Leonard Nimoy", 82, "Actor")
  val pNimoy = new Person("Leonard Nimoy", 82)
  val eShatner = new Employee("William Shatner", 82, "Actor")

  test("eNimoy1 == eNimoy1") { assert(eNimoy1 == eNimoy1) }
  test("eNimoy1 == eNimoy2") { assert(eNimoy1 == eNimoy2) }
  test("eNimoy2 == eNimoy1") { assert(eNimoy2 == eNimoy1) }
  test("eNimoy  != pNimoy")  { assert(eNimoy1 != pNimoy) }
  test("pNimoy  != eNimoy")  { assert(pNimoy != eNimoy1) }

}
```

All the tests pass, including the comparison of the eNimoy and pNimoy objects, which are instances of the Employee and Person classes, respectively.

### Theory

The Scaladoc for the equals method of the Any class states, "any implementation of this method should be an *equivalence relation*." The documentation states that an equivalence relation should have these three properties:

- It is *reflexive*: for any instance x of type Any, x.equals(x) should return true.

- It is *symmetric*: for any instances x and y of type Any, x.equals(y) should return true if and only if y.equals(x) returns true.

- It is *transitive*: for any instances x, y, and z of type AnyRef, if x.equals(y) returns true and y.equals(z) returns true, then x.equals(z) should return true.

Therefore, if you override the equals method, you should verify that your implementation remains an equivalence relation.

## See Also

- The Artima website has an excellent related article titled How to Write an Equality Method in Java (*http://bit.ly/13a2sBR*).
- Eric Torreborre shares an excellent canEqual example on GitHub (*http://bit.ly/1bvBjkK*).
- "Equivalence relation" defined on Wikipedia (*http://bit.ly/18SIt2U*).
- The Scala Any class (*http://bit.ly/18bM1KZ*).

# 4.16. Creating Inner Classes

## Problem

You want to create a class as an inner class to help keep the class out of your public API, or to otherwise encapsulate your code.

## Solution

Declare one class inside another class. In the following example, a case class named Thing is declared inside of a class named PandorasBox:

```
class PandorasBox {

  case class Thing (name: String)

  var things = new collection.mutable.ArrayBuffer[Thing]()
  things += Thing("Evil Thing #1")
  things += Thing("Evil Thing #2")

  def addThing(name: String) { things += new Thing(name) }

}
```

This lets users of PandorasBox access the collection of things inside the box, while code outside of PandorasBox generally doesn't have to worry about the concept of a Thing:

```
object ClassInAClassExample extends App {

  val p = new PandorasBox
  p.things.foreach(println)

}
```

As shown, you can access the things in PandorasBox with the things method. You can also add new things to PandorasBox by calling the addThing method:

```
p.addThing("Evil Thing #3")
p.addThing("Evil Thing #4")
```

## Discussion

The concept of a "class within a class" is different in Scala than in Java. As described on the official Scala website (*http://www.scala-lang.org/node/115*), "Opposed to Java-like languages where such inner classes are members of the enclosing class, in Scala, such inner classes are bound to the outer object." The following code demonstrates this:

```
object ClassInObject extends App {

  // inner classes are bound to the object
  val oc1 = new OuterClass
  val oc2 = new OuterClass
  val ic1 = new oc1.InnerClass
  val ic2 = new oc2.InnerClass
  ic1.x = 10
  ic2.x = 20
  println(s"ic1.x = ${ic1.x}")
  println(s"ic2.x = ${ic2.x}")
}

class OuterClass {
  class InnerClass {
    var x = 1
  }
}
```

Because inner classes are bound to their object instances, when that code is run, it prints the following output:

```
ic1.x = 10
ic2.x = 20
```

There are many other things you can do with inner classes, such as include a class inside an object or an object inside a class:

```
object InnerClassDemo2 extends App {

  // class inside object
  println(new OuterObject.InnerClass().x)
```

```scala
    // object inside class
    println(new OuterClass().InnerObject.y)

}

object OuterObject {
  class InnerClass {
    var x = 1
  }
}

class OuterClass {
  object InnerObject {
    val y = 2
  }
}
```

## See Also

The Scala website has a page on Inner Classes (*http://bit.ly/13G0DnG*).

# CHAPTER 5
# Methods

## Introduction

Conceptually, Scala methods are similar to Java methods in that they are behaviors you add to a class. However, they differ significantly in their implementation details. The following example shows some of the differences between Java and Scala when defining a simple method that takes an integer argument and returns a string:

```
// java
public String doSomething(int x) {
  // code here
}

// scala
def doSomething(x: Int): String = {
  // code here
}
```

This is just a start, though. Scala methods can be written even more concisely. This method takes an Int, adds 1 to it, and returns the resulting Int value:

```
def plusOne(i: Int) = i + 1
```

Notice that the return type didn't have to be specified, and parentheses around the short method body aren't required.

In addition to the differences shown in these simple examples, there are other differences between Java and Scala methods, including:

- Specifying method access control (visibility)
- The ability to set default values for method parameters

- The ability to specify the names of method parameters when calling a method
- How you declare the exceptions a method can throw
- Using varargs fields in methods

This chapter demonstrates all of these method-related features.

# 5.1. Controlling Method Scope

## Problem

Scala methods are public by default, and you want to control their scope in ways similar to Java.

## Solution

Scala lets you control method visibility in a more granular and powerful way than Java. In order from "most restrictive" to "most open," Scala provides these scope options:

- Object-private scope
- Private
- Package
- Package-specific
- Public

These scopes are demonstrated in the examples that follow.

### Object-private scope

The most restrictive access is to mark a method as *object-private*. When you do this, the method is available only to the current instance of the current object. Other instances of the same class cannot access the method.

You mark a method as object-private by placing the access modifier `private[this]` before the method declaration:

```
private[this] def isFoo = true
```

In the following example, the method `doFoo` takes an instance of a `Foo` object, but because the `isFoo` method is declared as an object-private method, the code won't compile:

```
class Foo {

  private[this] def isFoo = true

  def doFoo(other: Foo) {
    if (other.isFoo) {  // this line won't compile
```

```
      // ...
    }
  }

}
```

The code won't compile because the current Foo instance can't access the isFoo method of the other instance, because isFoo is declared as private[this]. As you can see, the object-private scope is extremely restrictive.

### Private scope

A slightly less restrictive access is to mark a method private, which makes the method available to (a) the current class and (b) other instances of the current class. This is the same as marking a method private in Java. By changing the access modifier from private[this] to private, the code will now compile:

```
class Foo {

  private def isFoo = true

  def doFoo(other: Foo) {
    if (other.isFoo) {  // this now compiles
      // ...
    }

  }
}
```

By making a method private, it is not available to subclasses. The following code won't compile because the heartBeat method is private to the Animal class:

```
class Animal {
  private def heartBeat {}
}

class Dog extends Animal {
  heartBeat  // won't compile
}
```

### Protected scope

Marking a method protected makes the method available to subclasses, so the following code will compile:

```
class Animal {
  protected def breathe {}
}

class Dog extends Animal {
  breathe
}
```

The meaning of protected is slightly different in Scala than in Java. In Java, protected methods can be accessed by other classes in the same package, but this isn't true in Scala. The following code won't compile because the Jungle class can't access the breathe method of the Animal class, even though they're in the same package:

```scala
package world {

  class Animal {
    protected def breathe {}
  }

  class Jungle {
    val a = new Animal
    a.breathe    // error: this line won't compile
  }

}
```

### Package scope

To make a method available to all members of the current package—what would be called "package scope" in Java—mark the method as being private to the current package with the private[packageName] syntax.

In the following example, the method doX can be accessed by other classes in the same package (the model package), but the method doY is available only to the Foo class:

```scala
package com.acme.coolapp.model {

  class Foo {
    private[model] def doX {}
    private def doY {}
  }

  class Bar {
    val f = new Foo
    f.doX  // compiles
    f.doY  // won't compile
  }

}
```

### More package-level control

Beyond making a method available to classes in the current package, Scala gives you more control and lets you make a method available at different levels in a class hierarchy. The following example demonstrates how you can make the methods doX, doY, and doZ available to different package levels:

```scala
package com.acme.coolapp.model {
  class Foo {
    private[model] def doX {}
```

```
      private[coolapp] def doY {}
      private[acme] def doZ {}
   }
}

import com.acme.coolapp.model._

package com.acme.coolapp.view {
  class Bar {
    val f = new Foo
    f.doX  // won't compile
    f.doY
    f.doZ
  }
}

package com.acme.common {
  class Bar {
    val f = new Foo
    f.doX  // won't compile
    f.doY  // won't compile
    f.doZ
  }
}
```

In this example, the methods can be seen as follows:

- The method doX can be seen by other classes in the model package (com.acme.coolapp.model).
- The method doY can be seen by all classes under the coolapp package level.
- The method doZ can be seen by all classes under the acme level.

As you can see, this approach allows a fine-grained level of access control.

### Public scope

If no access modifier is added to the method declaration, the method is public. In the following example, any class in any package can access the doX method:

```
package com.acme.coolapp.model {
  class Foo {
    def doX {}
  }
}

package org.xyz.bar {
  class Bar {
    val f = new com.acme.coolapp.model.Foo
    f.doX
  }
}
```

## Discussion

The Scala approach to access modifiers is different than Java. Though it offers more power than Java, it's also a little more complicated.

Table 5-1 describes the levels of access control that were demonstrated in the examples in the Solution.

*Table 5-1. Descriptions of Scala's access control modifiers*

| Access modifier | Description |
| --- | --- |
| private[this] | The method is available only to the current instance of the class it's declared in. |
| private | The method is available to the current instance and other instances of the class it's declared in. |
| protected | The method is available only to instances of the current class and subclasses of the current class. |
| private[model] | The method is available to all classes beneath the com.acme.coolapp.model package. |
| private[coolapp] | The method is available to all classes beneath the com.acme.coolapp package. |
| private[acme] | The method is available to all classes beneath the com.acme package. |
| (no modifier) | The method is public. |

# 5.2. Calling a Method on a Superclass

## Problem

To keep your code DRY ("Don't Repeat Yourself"), you want to invoke a method that's already defined in a parent class or trait.

## Solution

In the basic use case, the syntax to invoke a method in an immediate parent class is the same as Java: Use super to refer to the parent class, and then provide the method name. The following Android method (written in Scala) demonstrates how to call a method named onCreate that's defined in the Activity parent class:

```
class WelcomeActivity extends Activity {
  override def onCreate(bundle: Bundle) {
    super.onCreate(bundle)
    // more code here ...
  }
}
```

As with Java, you can call multiple superclass methods if necessary:

```
class FourLeggedAnimal {
  def walk { println("I'm walking") }
  def run { println("I'm running") }
}
```

```
class Dog extends FourLeggedAnimal {
  def walkThenRun {
    super.walk
    super.run
  }
}
```

Running this code in the Scala REPL yields:

```
scala> val suka = new Dog
suka: Dog = Dog@239bf795

scala> suka.walkThenRun
I'm walking
I'm running
```

## Controlling which trait you call a method from

If your class inherits from multiple traits, and those traits implement the same method, you can select not only a method name, but also a trait name when invoking a method using super. For instance, given this class hierarchy:

```
trait Human {
  def hello = "the Human trait"
}

trait Mother extends Human {
  override def hello = "Mother"
}

trait Father extends Human {
  override def hello = "Father"
}
```

The following code shows different ways to invoke the hello method from the traits the Child class inherits from. This example shows that by mixing in the Human, Mother, and Father traits, you can call super.hello, or be more specific by calling super[Mother].hello, super[Father].hello, or super[Human].hello:

```
class Child extends Human with Mother with Father {
  def printSuper  = super.hello
  def printMother = super[Mother].hello
  def printFather = super[Father].hello
  def printHuman  = super[Human].hello
}
```

If you construct a test object to run this code:

```
object Test extends App {
  val c = new Child
  println(s"c.printSuper  = ${c.printSuper}")
  println(s"c.printMother = ${c.printMother}")
```

```
    println(s"c.printFather = ${c.printFather}")
    println(s"c.printHuman  = ${c.printHuman}")
}
```

you can see the output:

```
c.printSuper  = Father
c.printMother = Mother
c.printFather = Father
c.printHuman  = the Human trait
```

As shown, when a class inherits from multiple traits, and those traits have a common method name, you can choose which trait to run the method from with the `super[traitName].methodName` syntax.

Note that when using this technique, you can't continue to reach up through the parent class hierarchy unless you directly extend the target class or trait using the `extends` or `with` keywords. For instance, the following code won't compile because `Dog` doesn't directly extend the `Animal` trait:

```
trait Animal {
  def walk { println("Animal is walking") }
}

class FourLeggedAnimal extends Animal {
  override def walk { println("I'm walking on all fours") }
}

class Dog extends FourLeggedAnimal {
  def walkThenRun {
    super.walk                      // works
    super[FourLeggedAnimal].walk    // works
    super[Animal].walk              // error: won't compile
  }
}
```

If you attempt to compile the code, you'll get the error, "Animal does not name a parent class of class Dog." You can get around that error by adding `with Animal` to your class declaration (but whether or not that's really a good idea is another story):

```
class Dog extends FourLeggedAnimal with Animal {
```

# 5.3. Setting Default Values for Method Parameters

## Problem

You want to set default values for method parameters so the method can optionally be called without those parameters having to be assigned.

## Solution

Specify the default value for parameters in the method signature. In the following code, the timeout field is assigned a default value of 5000, and the protocol field is given a default value of "http":

```
class Connection {
  def makeConnection(timeout: Int = 5000, protocol:  = "http") {
    println("timeout = %d, protocol = %s".format(timeout, protocol))
    // more code here
  }
}
```

This method can now be called in the following ways:

```
c.makeConnection()
c.makeConnection(2000)
c.makeConnection(3000, "https")
```

The results are demonstrated in the REPL:

```
scala> val c = new Connection
c: Connection = Connection@385db088

scala> c.makeConnection()
timeout = 5000, protocol = http

scala> c.makeConnection(2000)
timeout = 2000, protocol = http

scala> c.makeConnection(3000, "https")
timeout = 3000, protocol = https
```

Note that empty parentheses are used in the first example. Attempting to call this method without parentheses results in an error:

```
scala> c.makeConnection
<console>:10: error: missing arguments for method makeConnection in Connection;
follow this method with `_' to treat it as a partially applied function
            c.makeConnection
             ^
```

The reason for this error is discussed in Recipe 9.6, "Using Partially Applied Functions".

If you like to call methods with the names of the method parameters, the method makeConnection can also be called in these ways:

```
c.makeConnection(timeout=10000)
c.makeConnection(protocol="https")
c.makeConnection(timeout=10000, protocol="https")
```

## Discussion

Just as with constructor parameters, you can provide default values for method arguments. Because you have provided defaults, the consumer of your method can either supply an argument to override the default or skip the argument, letting it use its default value.

Arguments are assigned from left to right, so the following call assigns no arguments and uses the default values for both `timeout` and `protocol`:

```
c.makeConnection()
```

This call sets `timeout` to 2000 and leaves `protocol` to its default:

```
c.makeConnection(2000)
```

This call sets both the `timeout` and `protocol`:

```
c.makeConnection(3000, "https")
```

Note that you can't set the `protocol` only with this approach, but as shown in the Solution, you can use a named parameter:

```
c.makeConnection(protocol="https")
```

If your method provides a mix of some fields that offer default values and others that don't, list the fields that have default values last. To demonstrate the problem, the following example assigns a default value to the first argument and does not assign a default to the second argument:

```
class Connection {
  // intentional error
  def makeConnection(timeout: Int = 5000, protocol: String) {
    println("timeout = %d, protocol = %s".format(timeout, protocol))
    // more code here
  }
}
```

This code compiles, but you won't be able to take advantage of the default, as shown in the REPL errors:

```
scala> c.makeConnection(1000)
<console>:10: error: not enough arguments for method makeConnection:
(timeout: Int, protocol: String)Unit.
Unspecified value parameter protocol.
              c.makeConnection(1000)
                      ^

scala> c.makeConnection("https")
<console>:10: error: not enough arguments for method makeConnection:
(timeout: Int, protocol: String)Unit.
Unspecified value parameter protocol.
```

```
        c.makeConnection("https")
                   ^
```

By changing the method so the first field doesn't have a default and the last field does, the default method call can now be used:

```
class Connection {
  // corrected implementation
  def makeConnection(timeout: Int, protocol: String = "http") {
    println("timeout = %d, protocol = %s".format(timeout, protocol))
    // more code here
  }
}
```

```
scala> c.makeConnection(1000)
timeout = 1000, protocol = http
```

```
scala> c.makeConnection(1000, "https")
timeout = 1000, protocol = https
```

# 5.4. Using Parameter Names When Calling a Method

## Problem

You prefer a coding style where you specify the method parameter names when calling a method.

## Solution

The general syntax for calling a method with named parameters is this:

```
methodName(param1=value1, param2=value2, ...)
```

This is demonstrated in the following example.

Given this definition of a Pizza class:

```
class Pizza {
  var crustSize = 12
  var crustType = "Thin"
  def update(crustSize: Int, crustType: String) {
    this.crustSize = crustSize
    this.crustType = crustType
  }
  override def toString = {
    "A %d inch %s crust pizza.".format(crustSize, crustType)
  }
}
```

you can create a Pizza:

```
val p = new Pizza
```

You can then update the `Pizza`, specifying the field names and corresponding values when you call the `update` method:

```
p.update(crustSize = 16, crustType = "Thick")
```

This approach has the added benefit that you can place the fields in any order:

```
p.update(crustType = "Pan", crustSize = 14)
```

## Discussion

You can confirm that this example works by running it in the Scala REPL:

```
scala> val p = new Pizza
p: Pizza = A 12 inch Thin crust pizza.

scala> p.updatePizza(crustSize = 16, crustType = "Thick")

scala> println(p)
A 16 inch Thick crust pizza.

scala> p.updatePizza(crustType = "Pan", crustSize = 14)

scala> println(p)
A 14 inch Pan crust pizza.
```

The ability to use named parameters when calling a method is available in other languages, including Objective-C. Although this approach is more verbose, it can also be more readable.

This technique is especially useful when several parameters have the same type, such as having several `Boolean` or `String` parameters in a method. For instance, compare this method call:

```
engage(true, true, true, false)
```

to this one:

```
engage(speedIsSet = true,
       directionIsSet = true,
       picardSaidMakeItSo = true,
       turnedOffParkingBrake = false)
```

When a method specifies default values for its parameters, as demonstrated in Recipe 5.3, you can use this approach to specify only the parameters you want to override.

For instance, the `scala.xml.Utility` object has a method named `serialize` that takes seven parameters. However, default values are defined for each parameter in the method declaration, so if you need to change only one parameter, such as whether you want comments stripped from the output, you need to specify only that one parameter, in addition to your XML node:

```
Utility.serialize(myNode, stripComments = true)
```

The combination of these two recipes makes for a powerful approach.

# 5.5. Defining a Method That Returns Multiple Items (Tuples)

## Problem

You want to return multiple values from a method, but don't want to wrap those values in a makeshift class.

## Solution

Although you can return objects from methods just as in other OOP languages, Scala also lets you return multiple values from a method using *tuples*. First, define a method that returns a tuple:

```
def getStockInfo = {
  // other code here ...
  ("NFLX", 100.00, 101.00) // this is a Tuple3
}
```

Then call that method, assigning variable names to the expected return values:

```
val (symbol, currentPrice, bidPrice) = getStockInfo
```

Running this example in the REPL demonstrates how this works:

```
scala> val (symbol, currentPrice, bidPrice) = getStockInfo
symbol: java.lang.String = NFLX
currentPrice: Double = 100.0
bidPrice: Double = 101.0
```

## Discussion

In Java, when it would be convenient to be able to return multiple values from a method, the typical workaround is to return those values in a one-off "wrapper" class. For instance, you might create a temporary wrapper class like this:

```
// java
public class StockInfo {
  String symbol;
  double currentPrice;
  double bidPrice;

  public StockInfo(String symbol, double currentPrice, double bidPrice) {
    this.symbol = symbol;
    this.currentPrice = currentPrice;
    this.bidPrice = bidPrice;
```

```
        }
    }
```

Then you could return an instance of this class from a method, like this:

```
    return new StockInfo("NFLX", 100.00, 101.00);
```

In Scala you don't need to create a wrapper like this; you can just return the data as a tuple.

### Working with tuples

In the example shown in the Solution, the getStockInfo method returned a tuple with three elements, so it is a Tuple3. Tuples can contain up to 22 variables and are implemented as Tuple1 through Tuple22 classes. As a practical matter, you don't have to think about those specific classes; just create a new tuple by enclosing elements inside parentheses, as shown.

To demonstrate a Tuple2, if you wanted to return only two elements from a method, just put two elements in the parentheses:

```
    def getStockInfo = ("NFLX", 100.00)

    val (symbol, currentPrice) = getStockInfo
```

If you don't want to assign variable names when calling the method, you can set a variable equal to the tuple the method returns, and then access the tuple values using the following tuple underscore syntax:

```
scala> val result = getStockInfo
x: (java.lang.String, Double, Double) = (NFLX,100.0)

scala> result._1
res0: java.lang.String = NFLX

scala> result._2
res1: Double = 100.0
```

As shown, tuple values can be accessed by position as result._1, result._2, and so on. Though this approach can be useful in some situations, your code will generally be clearer if you assign variable names to the values:

```
    val (symbol, currentPrice) = getStockInfo
```

## See Also

- The Tuple3 class (*http://bit.ly/1dzLfl0*)
- Recipe 10.27, "Tuples, for When You Just Need a Bag of Things" for more tuple examples

# 5.6. Forcing Callers to Leave Parentheses off Accessor Methods

## Problem

You want to enforce a coding style where getter/accessor methods can't have parentheses when they are invoked.

## Solution

Define your getter/accessor method without parentheses after the method name:

```scala
class Pizza {
  // no parentheses after crustSize
  def crustSize = 12
}
```

This forces consumers of your class to call `crustSize` without parentheses:

```scala
scala> val p = new Pizza
p: Pizza = Pizza@3a3e8692

// this fails because of the parentheses
scala> p.crustSize()
<console>:10: error: Int does not take parameters
              p.crustSize()
                       ^

// this works
scala> p.crustSize
res0: Int = 12
```

 Coming from a Java background, I originally named this method getCrustSize, but the Scala convention is to drop "get" from methods like this, hence the method name crustSize.

## Discussion

The recommended strategy for calling getter methods that have no side effects is to leave the parentheses off when calling the method. As stated in the Scala Style Guide (*http://docs.scala-lang.org/style/*):

> Methods which act as accessors of any sort ... should be declared *without* parentheses, except if they have side effects.

According to the style guide, because a simple accessor method like crustSize does not have side effects, it should not be called with parentheses, and this recipe demonstrates how to enforce this convention.

Although this recipe shows how to force callers to leave parentheses off methods when calling simple getters, there is no way to force them to use parentheses for side-effecting methods. This is only a convention, albeit a convention that I like and use these days. Although it's usually obvious that a method named `printStuff` is probably going to print some output, a little warning light goes off in my head when I see it called as `printStuff()` instead.

---

### Side Effects

It's said that a purely functional program has no side effects. So what is a side effect?

According to Wikipedia, a function is said to have a side effect "if, in addition to returning a value, it also modifies some state or has an observable interaction with calling functions or the outside world."

Side effects include things like:

- Writing or printing output.
- Reading input.
- Mutating the state of a variable that was given as input, changing data in a data structure, or modifying the value of a field in an object.
- Throwing an exception, or stopping the application when an error occurs.
- Calling other functions that have side effects.

In theory, pure functions are much easier to test. Imagine writing an addition function, such as +. Given the two numbers 1 and 2, the result will always be 3. A pure function like this is a simple matter of (a) immutable data coming in, and (b) a result coming out; nothing else happens. Because a function like this has no side effects, it's simple to test.

See Recipe 20.1, "Create Methods with No Side Effects (Pure Functions)", for more details on writing pure functions. Also, see the Wikipedia discussion on side effects in functional programming (FP) applications for more details and examples (*http://bit.ly/1dzLoeB*).

---

## See Also

The Scala Style Guide on naming conventions and parentheses (*http://bit.ly/16E1Ir4*)

# 5.7. Creating Methods That Take Variable-Argument Fields

## Problem

To make a method more flexible, you want to define a method parameter that can take a variable number of arguments, i.e., a varargs field.

## Solution

Define a *varargs* field in your method declaration by adding a * character after the field type:

```
def printAll(strings: String*) {
  strings.foreach(println)
}
```

Given that method declaration, the printAll method can be called with zero or more parameters:

```
// these all work
printAll()
printAll("foo")
printAll("foo", "bar")
printAll("foo", "bar", "baz")
```

### Use _* to adapt a sequence

As shown in the following example, you can use Scala's _* operator to adapt a sequence (Array, List, Seq, Vector, etc.) so it can be used as an argument for a varargs field:

```
// a sequence of strings
val fruits = List("apple", "banana", "cherry")

// pass the sequence to the varargs field
printAll(fruits: _*)
```

If you come from a Unix background, it may be helpful to think of _* as a "splat" operator. This operator tells the compiler to pass each element of the sequence to printAll as a separate argument, instead of passing fruits as a single argument.

## Discussion

When declaring that a method has a field that can contain a variable number of arguments, the varargs field must be the last field in the method signature. Attempting to define a field in a method signature *after* a varargs field is an error:

```
scala> def printAll(strings: String*, i: Int) {
     |     strings.foreach(println)
     | }
```

```
<console>:7: error: *-parameter must come last
       def printAll(strings: String*, i: Int) {
                    ^
```

As an implication of that rule, a method can have only one varargs field.

As demonstrated in the Solution, if a field is a varargs field, you don't have to supply any arguments for it. For instance, in a method that has only one varargs field, you can call it with no arguments:

```
scala> def printAll(numbers: Int*) {
     |    numbers.foreach(println)
     | }
printAll: (numbers: Int*)Unit

scala> printAll()
```

This case reveals some of the inner workings of how Scala handles varargs fields. By defining a varargs method that can take multiple integers, and then calling that method (a) with arguments, and (b) without arguments, you can see how Scala handles the two situations:

```
def printAll(numbers: Int*) {
  println(numbers.getClass)
}

scala> printAll(1, 2, 3)
class scala.collection.mutable.WrappedArray$ofInt

scala> printAll()
class scala.collection.immutable.Nil$
```

While the first situation reveals how Scala handles the normal "one or more arguments" situation, treating the "no args" situation as a Nil$ in the second situation keeps your code from throwing a NullPointerException.

Although the resulting types are different, as a practical matter, this isn't too important. You'll typically use a loop inside a method to handle a varargs field, and either of the following examples work fine whether the method is called with zero or multiple parameters:

```
// version 1
def printAll(numbers: Int*) {
  numbers.foreach(println)
}

// version 2
def printAll(numbers: Int*) {
  for (i <- numbers) println
}
```

# 5.8. Declaring That a Method Can Throw an Exception

## Problem

You want to declare that a method can throw an exception, either to alert callers to this fact or because your method will be called from Java code.

## Solution

Use the `@throws` annotation to declare the exception(s) that can be thrown. To declare that one exception can be thrown, place the annotation just before the method signature:

```
@throws(classOf[Exception])
override def play {
  // exception throwing code here ...
}
```

To indicate that a method can throw multiple exceptions, list them all before the method signature:

```
@throws(classOf[IOException])
@throws(classOf[LineUnavailableException])
@throws(classOf[UnsupportedAudioFileException])
def playSoundFileWithJavaAudio {
  // exception throwing code here ...
}
```

## Discussion

The two examples shown are from an open source project I created that lets developers play WAV, AIFF, MP3, and other types of sound files. I declared that these two methods can throw exceptions for two reasons. First, whether the consumers are using Scala or Java, if they're writing robust code, they'll want to know that something failed.

Second, if they're using Java, the `@throws` annotation is the Scala way of providing the throws method signature to Java consumers. It's equivalent to declaring that a method throws an exception with this Java syntax:

```
public void play() throws FooException {
  // code here ...
}
```

It's important to note that Scala's philosophy regarding checked exceptions is different than Java's. Scala doesn't require that methods declare that exceptions can be thrown, and it also doesn't require calling methods to catch them. This is easily demonstrated in the REPL:

```
// 1) it's not necessary to state that a method throws an exception
scala> def boom {
     |   throw new Exception
     | }
boom: Unit

// 2) it's not necessary to wrap 'boom' in a try/catch block, but ...
scala> boom
java.lang.Exception
    at .boom(<console>:8)
    // much more exception output here ...
```

Although Scala doesn't require that exceptions are checked, if you fail to test for them, they'll blow up your code just like they do in Java. In the following example, the second `println` statement is never reached because the `boom` method throws its exception:

```
object BoomTest extends App {

  def boom { throw new Exception }

  println("Before boom")

  boom

  // this line is never reached
  println("After boom")

}
```

---

## Java Exception Types

As a quick review, Java has (a) checked exceptions, (b) descendants of `Error`, and (c) descendants of `RuntimeException`. Like checked exceptions, `Error` and `RuntimeException` have many subclasses, such as `RuntimeException`'s famous offspring, `NullPointerException`.

According to the Java documentation for the `Exception` class (*http://bit.ly/12ADsbu*), "The class `Exception` and any subclasses that are not also subclasses of `RuntimeException` are checked exceptions. Checked exceptions need to be declared in a method or constructor's throws clause if they can be thrown by the execution of the method or constructor and propagate outside the method or constructor boundary."

The following links provide more information on Java exceptions and exception handling:

- The Three Kinds of (Java) Exceptions (*http://bit.ly/12DBv9y*)
- Unchecked Exceptions—The Controversy (*http://bit.ly/18jrDLf*)
- Wikipedia discussion of checked exceptions (*http://bit.ly/17fSC64*)

---

- Java tutorial on exception handling (*http://bit.ly/12Q9ltg*)
- Java `Exception` class (*http://bit.ly/12ADsbu*)

## See Also

Recipe 17.2, "Add Exception Annotations to Scala Methods to Work with Java", for other examples of adding exception annotations to methods

# 5.9. Supporting a Fluent Style of Programming

## Problem

You want to create an API so developers can write code in a fluent (*http://bit.ly/15xKqN2*) programming style, also known as method chaining (*http://bit.ly/1dzLUJC*).

## Solution

A fluent style of programming lets users of your API write code by chaining method calls together, as in this example:

```
person.setFirstName("Leonard")
      .setLastName("Nimoy")
      .setAge(82)
      .setCity("Los Angeles")
      .setState("California")
```

To support this style of programming:

- If your class can be extended, specify `this.type` as the return type of fluent style methods.

- If you're sure that your class won't be extended, you can optionally return `this` from your fluent style methods.

The following code demonstrates how to specify `this.type` as the return type of the set* methods:

```scala
class Person {

  protected var fname = ""
  protected var lname = ""

  def setFirstName(firstName: String): this.type = {
    fname = firstName
    this
  }
```

```
    def setLastName(lastName: String): this.type = {
      lname = lastName
      this
    }

}

class Employee extends Person {

  protected var role = ""

  def setRole(role: String): this.type = {
    this.role = role
    this
  }
  override def toString = {
    "%s, %s, %s".format(fname, lname, role)
  }

}
```

The following test object demonstrates how these methods can be chained together:

```
object Main extends App {

  val employee = new Employee

  // use the fluent methods
  employee.setFirstName("Al")
          .setLastName("Alexander")
          .setRole("Developer")
  println(employee)

}
```

## Discussion

If you're sure your class won't be extended, specifying this.type as the return type of your set* methods isn't necessary; you can just return the this reference at the end of each fluent style method. This is shown in the addTopping, setCrustSize, and setCrustType methods of the following Pizza class, which is declared to be final:

```
final class Pizza {

  import scala.collection.mutable.ArrayBuffer

  private val toppings = ArrayBuffer[String]()
  private var crustSize = 0
  private var crustType = ""

  def addTopping(topping: String) = {
    toppings += topping
```

```
    this
  }

  def setCrustSize(crustSize: Int) = {
    this.crustSize = crustSize
    this
  }

  def setCrustType(crustType: String) = {
    this.crustType = crustType
    this
  }

  def print() {
    println(s"crust size: $crustSize")
    println(s"crust type: $crustType")
    println(s"toppings:   $toppings")
  }

}
```

This class is demonstrated with the following driver program:

```
object FluentPizzaTest extends App {

  val p = new Pizza
  p.setCrustSize(14)
   .setCrustType("thin")
   .addTopping("cheese")
   .addTopping("green olives")
   .print()

}
```

This results in the following output:

```
crust size: 14
crust type: thin
toppings:   ArrayBuffer(cheese, green olives)
```

Returning this in your methods works fine if you're sure your class won't be extended, but if your class can be extended—as in the first example where the Employee class extended the Person class—explicitly setting this.type as the return type of your set* methods ensures that the fluent style will continue to work in your subclasses. In this example, this makes sure that methods like setFirstName on an Employee object return an Employee reference and not a Person reference.

## See Also

- Definition of a fluent interface (*http://bit.ly/15xKqN2*)
- Method chaining (*http://bit.ly/1dzLUJC*)
- Martin Fowler's discussion of a fluent interface (*http://bit.ly/144R7t4*)

CHAPTER 6

# Objects

## Introduction

The word "object" has a dual meaning in Scala. As with Java, you use it to refer to an instance of a class, but in Scala, `object` is also a keyword.

The first three recipes in this chapter look at an object as an instance of a class, show how to cast objects from one type to another, demonstrate the Scala equivalent of Java's `.class` approach, and show how to determine the class of an object.

The remaining recipes demonstrate how the `object` keyword is used for other purposes. You'll see how to use it to launch Scala applications and to create Singletons. There's also a special type of object known as a *package object*. Using a package object is entirely optional, but it provides a nice little out-of-the-way place where you can put code that's common to all classes and objects in a particular package level in your application. For instance, Scala's root-level package object contains many lines of code like this:

```
type Throwable = java.lang.Throwable
type Exception = java.lang.Exception
type Error = java.lang.Error

type Seq[+A] = scala.collection.Seq[A]
val Seq = scala.collection.Seq
```

Declaring those type definitions in Scala's root package object helps to make the rest of the code a little bit cleaner, and also keeps these definitions from cluttering up other files.

You'll also see how to create a *companion object* to solve several problems. For instance, one use of a companion object is to create the equivalent of Java's static members. You can also use a companion object so consumers of its corresponding class won't need to use the new keyword to create an instance of the class. For example, notice how the new keyword isn't required before each `Person` instance in this code:

```
val siblings = List(Person("Kim"), Person("Julia"), Person("Kenny"))
```

These solutions, and a few more, are presented in this chapter.

# 6.1. Object Casting

## Problem

You need to cast an instance of a class from one type to another, such as when creating objects dynamically.

## Solution

Use the `asInstanceOf` method to cast an instance to the desired type. In the following example, the object returned by the `lookup` method is cast to an instance of a class named `Recognizer`:

```
val recognizer = cm.lookup("recognizer").asInstanceOf[Recognizer]
```

This Scala code is equivalent to the following Java code:

```
Recognizer recognizer = (Recognizer)cm.lookup("recognizer");
```

The `asInstanceOf` method is defined in the Scala `Any` class and is therefore available on all objects.

## Discussion

In dynamic programming, it's often necessary to cast from one type to another. This approach is needed when using the Spring Framework and instantiating beans from an application context file:

```
// open/read the application context file
val ctx = new ClassPathXmlApplicationContext("applicationContext.xml")

// instantiate our dog and cat objects from the application context
val dog = ctx.getBean("dog").asInstanceOf[Animal]
val cat = ctx.getBean("cat").asInstanceOf[Animal]
```

It's used when reading a YAML configuration file:

```
val yaml = new Yaml(new Constructor(classOf[EmailAccount]))
val emailAccount = yaml.load(text).asInstanceOf[EmailAccount]
```

The example shown in the Solution comes from code I wrote to work with an open source Java speech recognition library named Sphinx-4. With this library, many properties are defined in an XML file, and then you create recognizer and microphone objects dynamically. In a manner similar to Spring, this requires reading an XML configuration file, then casting instances to the specific types you want:

```
val cm = new ConfigurationManager("config.xml")

// instance of Recognizer
val recognizer = cm.lookup("recognizer").asInstanceOf[Recognizer]

// instance of Microphone
val microphone = cm.lookup("microphone").asInstanceOf[Microphone]
```

The asInstanceOf method isn't limited to only these situations. You can use it to cast numeric types:

```
scala> val a = 10
a: Int = 10

scala> val b = a.asInstanceOf[Long]
b: Long = 10

scala> val c = a.asInstanceOf[Byte]
c: Byte = 10
```

It can be used in more complicated code, such as when you need to interact with Java and send it an array of Object instances:

```
val objects = Array("a", 1)
val arrayOfObject = objects.asInstanceOf[Array[Object]]
AJavaClass.sendObjects(arrayOfObject)
```

It's demonstrated in Chapter 15 like this:

```
import java.net.{URL, HttpURLConnection}
val connection = (new URL(url)).openConnection.asInstanceOf[HttpURLConnection]
```

Be aware that as with Java, this type of coding can lead to a ClassCastException, as demonstrated in this REPL example:

```
scala> val i = 1
i: Int = 1

scala> i.asInstanceOf[String]
ClassCastException: java.lang.Integer cannot be cast to java.lang.String
```

As usual, use a try/catch expression to handle this situation.

## See Also

- Recipe 2.2, "Converting Between Numeric Types (Casting)", for more numeric type casting recipes
- The Any class (*http://bit.ly/14TRvZk*)
- The Sphinx-4 project (*http://bit.ly/15HDPBX*)

# 6.2. The Scala Equivalent of Java's .class

## Problem

When an API requires that you pass in a Class, you'd call `.class` on an object in Java, but that doesn't work in Scala.

## Solution

Use the Scala `classOf` method instead of Java's `.class`. The following example shows how to pass a class of type `TargetDataLine` to a method named `DataLine.Info`:

```
val info = new DataLine.Info(classOf[TargetDataLine], null)
```

By contrast, the same method call would be made like this in Java:

```
// java
info = new DataLine.Info(TargetDataLine.class, null);
```

The `classOf` method is defined in the Scala `Predef` object and is therefore available in all classes without requiring an import.

## Discussion

This approach also lets you begin with simple reflection techniques. The following REPL example demonstrates how to access the methods of the `String` class:

```
scala> val stringClass = classOf[String]
stringClass: Class[String] = class java.lang.String

scala> stringClass.getMethods
res0: Array[java.lang.reflect.Method] = Array(public boolean
java.lang.String.equals(java.lang.Object), public java.lang.String
(output goes on for a while ...)
```

## See Also

- Oracle's "Retrieving Class Objects" document (*http://bit.ly/1dzQk36*)
- The Scala `Predef` object (*http://bit.ly/11QI0fF*)

# 6.3. Determining the Class of an Object

## Problem

Because you don't have to explicitly declare types with Scala, you may occasionally want to print the class/type of an object to understand how Scala works, or to debug code.

## Solution

When you want to learn about the types Scala is automatically assigning on your behalf, call the `getClass` method on the object.

For instance, when I was first trying to understand how varargs fields work, I called `getClass` on a method argument, and found that the class my method was receiving varied depending on the situation. Here's the method declaration:

```
def printAll(numbers: Int*) {
  println("class: " + numbers.getClass)
}
```

Calling the `printAll` method with and without arguments demonstrates the two classes Scala assigns to the numbers field under the different conditions:

```
scala> printAll(1, 2, 3)
class scala.collection.mutable.WrappedArray$ofInt

scala> printAll()
class scala.collection.immutable.Nil$
```

This technique can be very useful when working with something like Scala's XML library, so you can understand which classes you're working with in different situations. For instance, the following example shows that the `<p>` tag contains one child element, which is of class `scala.xml.Text`:

```
scala> val hello = <p>Hello, world</p>
hello: scala.xml.Elem = <p>Hello, world</p>

scala> hello.child.foreach(e => println(e.getClass))
class scala.xml.Text
```

However, by adding a `<br/>` tag inside the `<p>` tags, there are now three child elements of two different types:

```
scala> val hello = <p>Hello, <br/>world</p>
hello: scala.xml.Elem = <p>Hello, <br/>world</p>

scala> hello.child.foreach(e => println(e.getClass))
class scala.xml.Text
class scala.xml.Elem
class scala.xml.Text
```

When you can't see information like this in your IDE, using this `getClass` approach is very helpful.

## Discussion

When I can't see object types in an IDE, I write little tests like this in the REPL. The usual pattern is to call getClass on the object of interest, passing in different parameters to see how things work:

```
scala> def printClass(c: Any) { println(c.getClass) }
printClass: (c: Any)Unit

scala> printClass(1)
class java.lang.Integer

scala> printClass("yo")
class java.lang.String
```

In the first example shown in the Solution, the types Scala assigns to the number parameter don't matter too much; it was more a matter of curiosity about how things work. The actual method looks like the following code, and for my purposes, the only important thing is that each class Scala uses supports a foreach method:

```
def printAll(numbers: Int*) {
  numbers.foreach(println)
}
```

As desired, this method can be called with and without parameters:

```
scala> printAll(1,2,3)
1
2
3

scala> printAll()
(no output)
```

# 6.4. Launching an Application with an Object

## Problem

You want to start an application with a main method, or provide the entry point for a script.

## Solution

There are two ways to create a launching point for your application: define an object that extends the App trait, or define an object with a properly defined main method.

For the first solution, define an object that extends the App trait. Using this approach, the following code creates a simple but complete Scala application:

```
object Hello extends App {
  println("Hello, world")
}
```

The code in the body of the `object` is automatically run, just as if it were inside a `main` method.

Just save that code to a file named *Hello.scala*, compile it with `scalac`, and then run it with `scala`, like this:

```
$ scalac Hello.scala

$ scala Hello
Hello, world
```

When using this approach, any command-line arguments to your application are implicitly available through an `args` object, which is inherited from the App trait. The `args` object is an instance of `Array[String]`, just as if you had declared a `main` method yourself. The following code demonstrates how to use the `args` object:

```
object Hello extends App {
  if (args.length == 1)
    println(s"Hello, ${args(0)}")
  else
    println("I didn't get your name.")
}
```

After it's been compiled, this program yields the following results:

```
$ scala Hello
I didn't get your name.

$ scala Hello Joe
Hello, Joe
```

The second approach to launching an application is to manually implement a `main` method with the correct signature in an `object`, in a manner similar to Java:

```
object Hello2 {
  def main(args: Array[String]) {
    println("Hello, world")
  }
}
```

This is also a simple but complete application.

## Discussion

Note that in both cases, Scala applications are launched from an *object*, not a class.

I tend to use the App trait for both scripts and larger applications, but you can use either approach. I recommend reviewing the source code for the App trait to better understand what it performs. The source code is available from the URL in the See Also section.

The Scaladoc for the `App` trait currently includes two caveats:

1. It should be noted that this trait is implemented using the `DelayedInit` functionality, which means that fields of the object will not have been initialized before the `main` method has been executed.

2. It should also be noted that the `main` method will not normally need to be overridden: the purpose is to turn the whole class body into the "main method." You should only choose to override it if you know what you are doing.

See the Scaladoc for the `App` and `DelayedInit` traits for more information.

## See Also

- The `App` trait (*http://bit.ly/1bgzCsJ*).
- The `DelayedInit` trait (*http://bit.ly/1anQNpz*).
- The shell script examples in Chapter 14 demonstrate more examples of the `App` trait.

# 6.5. Creating Singletons with object

## Problem

You want to create a Singleton object to ensure that only one instance of a class exists.

## Solution

Create Singleton objects in Scala with the `object` keyword. For instance, you might create a Singleton object to represent something like a keyboard, mouse, or perhaps a cash register in a pizza restaurant:

```
object CashRegister {
  def open { println("opened") }
  def close { println("closed") }
}
```

With `CashRegister` defined as an object, there can be only one instance of it, and its methods are called just like static methods on a Java class:

```
object Main extends App {
  CashRegister.open
  CashRegister.close
}
```

This pattern is also common when creating utility methods, such as this `DateUtils` object:

```
import java.util.Calendar
import java.text.SimpleDateFormat

object DateUtils {

  // as "Thursday, November 29"
  def getCurrentDate: String = getCurrentDateTime("EEEE, MMMM d")

  // as "6:20 p.m."
  def getCurrentTime: String = getCurrentDateTime("K:m aa")

  // a common function used by other date/time functions
  private def getCurrentDateTime(dateTimeFormat: String): String = {
    val dateFormat = new SimpleDateFormat(dateTimeFormat)
    val cal = Calendar.getInstance()
    dateFormat.format(cal.getTime())
  }

}
```

Because these methods are defined in an object instead of a class, they can be called in the same way as a static method in Java:

```
scala> DateUtils.getCurrentTime
res0: String = 10:13 AM

scala> DateUtils.getCurrentDate
res1: String = Friday, July 6
```

Singleton objects also make great reusable messages when using actors. If you have a number of actors that can all receive start and stop messages, you can create Singletons like this:

```
case object StartMessage
case object StopMessage
```

You can then use those objects as messages that can be sent to actors:

```
inputValve ! StopMessage
outputValve ! StopMessage
```

See Chapter 13, *Actors and Concurrency*, for more examples of this approach.

## Discussion

In addition to creating objects in this manner, you can give the appearance that a class has both static and nonstatic methods using an approach known as a "companion object." See the following recipe for examples of that approach.

# 6.6. Creating Static Members with Companion Objects

## Problem

You want to create a class that has instance methods and static methods, but unlike Java, Scala does not have a `static` keyword.

## Solution

Define nonstatic (instance) members in your *class*, and define members that you want to appear as "static" members in an *object* that has the same name as the class, and is in the same file as the class. This object is known as a *companion object*.

Using this approach lets you create what appear to be static members on a class (both fields and methods), as shown in this example:

```
// Pizza class
class Pizza (var crustType: String) {
  override def toString = "Crust type is " + crustType
}

// companion object
object Pizza {
  val CRUST_TYPE_THIN = "thin"
  val CRUST_TYPE_THICK = "thick"
  def getFoo = "Foo"
}
```

With the `Pizza` class and `Pizza` object defined in the same file (presumably named *Pizza.scala*), members of the `Pizza` object can be accessed just as static members of a Java class:

```
println(Pizza.CRUST_TYPE_THIN)
println(Pizza.getFoo)
```

You can also create a new `Pizza` instance and use it as usual:

```
var p = new Pizza(Pizza.CRUST_TYPE_THICK)
println(p)
```

If you're coming to Scala from a language other than Java, "static" methods in Java are methods that can be called directly on a class, without requiring an instance of the class. For instance, here's an example of a method named increment in a Scala object named StringUtils:

```
object StringUtils {
    def increment(s: String) = s.map(c => (c + 1).toChar)
}
```

Because it's defined inside an object (not a class), the increment method can be called directly on the StringUtils object, without requiring an instance of StringUtils to be created:

```
scala> StringUtils.increment("HAL")
res0: String = IBM
```

In fact, when an object is defined like this without a corresponding class, you *can't* create an instance of it. This line of code won't compile:

```
val utils = new StringUtils
```

## Discussion

Although this approach is different than Java, the recipe is straightforward:

- Define your class and object in the same file, giving them the same name.
- Define members that should appear to be "static" in the object.
- Define nonstatic (instance) members in the class.

### Accessing private members

It's also important to know that a class and its companion object can access each other's private members. In the following code, the "static" method double in the object can access the private variable secret of the class Foo:

```
class Foo {
  private val secret = 2
}

object Foo {
  // access the private class field 'secret'
  def double(foo: Foo) = foo.secret * 2
}

object Driver extends App {
  val f = new Foo
  println(Foo.double(f))  // prints 4
}
```

Similarly, in the following code, the instance member `printObj` can access the private field `obj` of the object `Foo`:

```
class Foo {
  // access the private object field 'obj'
  def printObj { println(s"I can see ${Foo.obj}") }
}

object Foo {
  private val obj = "Foo's object"
}

object Driver extends App {
  val f = new Foo
  f.printObj
}
```

# 6.7. Putting Common Code in Package Objects

## Problem

You want to make functions, fields, and other code available at a package level, without requiring a class or object.

## Solution

Put the code you want to make available to all classes within a package in a *package object*.

By convention, put your code in a file named *package.scala* in the directory where you want your code to be available. For instance, if you want your code to be available to all classes in the `com.alvinalexander.myapp.model` package, create a file named *package.scala* in the *com/alvinalexander/myapp/model* directory of your project.

In the *package.scala* source code, remove the word `model` from the end of the package statement, and use that name to declare the name of the package object. Including a blank line, the first three lines of your file will look like this:

```
package com.alvinalexander.myapp

package object model {
```

Now write the rest of your code as you normally would. The following example shows how to create a field, method, enumeration, and type definition in your package object:

```
package com.alvinalexander.myapp

package object model {

  // field
  val MAGIC_NUM = 42
```

```scala
  // method
  def echo(a: Any) { println(a) }

  // enumeration
  object Margin extends Enumeration {
    type Margin = Value
    val TOP, BOTTOM, LEFT, RIGHT = Value
  }

  // type definition
  type MutableMap[K, V] = scala.collection.mutable.Map[K, V]
  val MutableMap = scala.collection.mutable.Map
}
```

You can now access this code directly from within other classes, traits, and objects in the package com.alvinalexander.myapp.model as shown here:

```scala
package com.alvinalexander.myapp.model

object MainDriver extends App {

  // access our method, constant, and enumeration
  echo("Hello, world")
  echo(MAGIC_NUM)
  echo(Margin.LEFT)

  // use our MutableMap type (scala.collection.mutable.Map)
  val mm = MutableMap("name" -> "Al")
  mm += ("password" -> "123")
  for ((k,v) <- mm) printf("key: %s, value: %s\n", k, v)
}
```

## Discussion

The most confusing part about package objects is where to put them, along with what their package and object names should be.

Where to put them isn't too hard; by convention, create a file named *package.scala* in the directory where you want your code to be available. In the example shown, I want the package code to be available in the com.alvinalexander.myapp.model package, so I put the file *package.scala* in the *com/alvinalexander/myapp/model* source code directory:

```
+-- com
    +-- alvinalexander
        +-- myapp
            +-- model
                +-- package.scala
```

In regards to the first few lines of the *package.scala* source code, simply start with the usual name of the package:

```
package com.alvinalexander.myapp.model
```

Then take the name of the last package level (`model`) off that statement, leaving you with this:

```
package com.alvinalexander.myapp
```

Then use that name (`model`) as the name of your package object:

```
package object model {
```

As shown earlier, the first several lines of your *package.scala* file will look like this:

```
package com.alvinalexander.myapp

package object model {
```

The Scala package object documentation (*http://bit.ly/14OaFQi*) states, "Any kind of definition that you can put inside a class, you can also put at the top level of a package." In my experience, package objects are a great place to put methods and functions that are common to the package, as well as constants, enumerations, and implicit conversions.

As described in the second page of the Scala package object documentation (*http://bit.ly/1anQR8M*), "The standard Scala package also has its package object. Because `scala._` is automatically imported into every Scala file, the definitions of this object are available without prefix." If you create something like a `StringBuilder` or `Range`, you're using this code.

## See Also

Scala's root package object is full of type aliases, like these:

```
type Throwable = java.lang.Throwable
type Exception = java.lang.Exception
type Error     = java.lang.Error

type RuntimeException     = java.lang.RuntimeException
type NullPointerException = java.lang.NullPointerException
type ClassCastException   = java.lang.ClassCastException
```

Like the `Predef` object, its source code is worth looking at if you want to know more about how Scala works. You can find its source by following the "source" link on its Scaladoc page (*http://bit.ly/13lmCc9*).

- An introduction to package objects (*http://bit.ly/14OaFQi*)
- The Scala package object (*http://bit.ly/1anQR8M*)

# 6.8. Creating Object Instances Without Using the new Keyword

## Problem

You've seen that Scala code looks cleaner when you don't always have to use the new keyword to create a new instance of a class, like this:

```
val a = Array(Person("John"), Person("Paul"))
```

So you want to know how to write your code to make your classes work like this.

## Solution

There are two ways to do this:

- Create a companion object for your class, and define an apply method in the companion object with the desired constructor signature.
- Define your class as a *case class*.

You'll look at both approaches next.

### Creating a companion object with an apply method

To demonstrate the first approach, define a Person class and Person object in the same file. Define an apply method in the object that takes the desired parameters. This method is essentially the constructor of your class:

```
class Person {
  var name: String = _
}

object Person {
  def apply(name: String): Person = {
    var p = new Person
    p.name = name
    p
  }
}
```

Given this definition, you can create new Person instances without using the new keyword, as shown in these examples:

```
val dawn = Person("Dawn")
val a = Array(Person("Dan"), Person("Elijah"))
```

The apply method in a companion object is treated specially by the Scala compiler and lets you create new instances of your class without requiring the new keyword. (More on this in the Discussion.)

### Declare your class as a case class

The second solution to the problem is to declare your class as a *case class*, defining it with the desired constructor:

```
case class Person (var name: String)
```

This approach also lets you create new class instances without requiring the new keyword:

```
val p = Person("Fred Flinstone")
```

With case classes, this works because the case class generates an `apply` method in a companion object for you. However, it's important to know that a case class creates *much more code* for you than just the `apply` method. This is discussed in depth in the Discussion.

## Discussion

An `apply` method defined in the companion object of a class is treated specially by the Scala compiler. There is essentially a little syntactic sugar baked into Scala that converts this code:

```
val p = Person("Fred Flinstone")
```

into this code:

```
val p = Person.apply("Fred Flinstone")
```

The `apply` method is basically a factory method, and Scala's little bit of syntactic sugar lets you use the syntax shown, creating new class instances without using the new keyword.

### Providing multiple constructors with additional apply methods

To create multiple constructors when manually defining your own `apply` method, just define multiple `apply` methods in the companion object that provide the constructor signatures you want:

```
class Person {
  var name = ""
  var age = 0
}

object Person {

  // a one-arg constructor
  def apply(name: String): Person = {
    var p = new Person
    p.name = name
    p
  }
```

```
    // a two-arg constructor
    def apply(name: String, age: Int): Person = {
      var p = new Person
      p.name = name
      p.age = age
      p
    }
}
```

You can now create a new `Person` instance in these ways:

```
val fred = Person("Fred")
val john = Person("John", 42)
```

I'm using the term "constructor" loosely here, but each `apply` method does define a different way to construct an instance.

### Providing multiple constructors for case classes

To provide multiple constructors for a case class, it's important to know what the `case class` declaration actually does.

If you look at the code the Scala compiler generates for the case class example, you'll see that see it creates two output files, *Person$.class* and *Person.class*. If you disassemble *Person$.class* with the `javap` command, you'll see that it contains an `apply` method, along with many others:

```
$ javap Person$
Compiled from "Person.scala"
public final class Person$ extends scala.runtime.AbstractFunction1
implements scala.ScalaObject,scala.Serializable{
    public static final Person$ MODULE$;
    public static {};
    public final java.lang.String toString();
    public scala.Option unapply(Person);
    public Person apply(java.lang.String); // the apply method (returns a Person)
    public java.lang.Object readResolve();
    public java.lang.Object apply(java.lang.Object);
}
```

You can also disassemble *Person.class* to see what it contains. For a simple class like this, it contains an additional 20 methods; this hidden bloat is one reason some developers don't like case classes.

 See Recipe 4.14, "Generating Boilerplate Code with Case Classes", for a thorough discussion of what code is generated for case classes, and why.

Note that the `apply` method in the disassembled code accepts one `String` argument:

```
public Person apply(java.lang.String);
```

That `String` corresponds to the `name` field in your case class constructor:

```
case class Person (var name: String)
```

So, it's important to know that when a case class is created, it writes the accessor and (optional) mutator methods *only* for the default constructor. As a result, (a) it's best to define all class parameters in the default constructor, and (b) write `apply` methods for the auxiliary constructors you want.

This is demonstrated in the following code, which I place in a file named *Person.scala*:

```
// want accessor and mutator methods for the name and age fields
case class Person (var name: String, var age: Int)

// define two auxiliary constructors
object Person {

  def apply() = new Person("<no name>", 0)
  def apply(name: String) = new Person(name, 0)

}
```

Because `name` and `age` are declared as `var` fields, accessor and mutator methods will both be generated. Also, two `apply` methods are declared in the object: a no-args constructor, and a one-arg constructor.

As a result, you can create instances of your class in three different ways, as demonstrated in the following code:

```
object Test extends App {

  val a = Person()
  val b = Person("Al")
  val c = Person("William Shatner", 82)

  println(a)
  println(b)
  println(c)

  // test the mutator methods
  a.name = "Leonard Nimoy"
  a.age = 82
  println(a)
}
```

Running this test object results in the following output:

```
Person(<no name>,0)
Person(Al,0)
Person(William Shatner,82)
Person(Leonard Nimoy,82)
```

For more information on case classes, see Recipe 4.14, "Generating Boilerplate Code with Case Classes".

# 6.9. Implement the Factory Method in Scala with apply

## Problem

To let subclasses declare which type of object should be created, and to keep the object creation point in one location, you want to implement the factory method in Scala.

## Solution

One approach to this problem is to take advantage of how a Scala companion object's apply method works. Rather than creating a "get" method for your factory, you can place the factory's decision-making algorithm in the apply method.

For instance, suppose you want to create an Animal factory that returns instances of Cat and Dog classes, based on what you ask for. By writing an apply method in the companion object of an Animal class, users of your factory can create new Cat and Dog instances like this:

```
val cat = Animal("cat")  // creates a Cat
val dog = Animal("dog")  // creates a Dog
```

To implement this behavior, create a parent Animal trait:

```
trait Animal {
  def speak
}
```

In the same file, create (a) a companion object, (b) the classes that extend the base trait, and (c) a suitable apply method:

```
object Animal {

  private class Dog extends Animal {
    override def speak { println("woof") }
  }

  private class Cat extends Animal {
    override def speak { println("meow") }
  }

  // the factory method
  def apply(s: String): Animal = {
    if (s == "dog") new Dog
    else new Cat
  }
}
```

This lets you run the desired code:

```
val cat = Animal("cat")  // returns a Cat
val dog = Animal("dog")  // returns a Dog
```

You can test this by pasting the `Animal` trait and object into the REPL, and then issuing these statements:

```
scala> val cat = Animal("cat")
cat: Animal = Animal$Cat@486f8860

scala> cat.speak
meow

scala> val dog = Animal("dog")
dog: Animal = Animal$Dog@412798c1

scala> dog.speak
woof
```

As you can see, this approach works as desired.

## Discussion

You have a variety of ways to implement this solution, so experiment with different approaches, in particular how you want to make the `Cat` and `Dog` classes accessible. The idea of the factory method is to make sure that concrete instances can only be created through the factory; therefore, the class constructors should be hidden from all other classes. The code here shows one possible solution to this problem.

If you don't like using the `apply` method as the factory interface, you can create the usual "get" method in the companion object, as shown in the `getAnimal` method here:

```
// an alternative factory method (use one or the other)
def getAnimal(s: String): Animal = {
  if (s == "dog") return new Dog
  else return new Cat
}
```

Using this method instead of the `apply` method, you now create new `Animal` instances like this:

```
val cat = Animal.getAnimal("cat")  // returns a Cat
val dog = Animal.getAnimal("dog")  // returns a Dog
```

Either approach is fine; consider this recipe as a springboard for your own solution.

## See Also

Recipe 6.8 for more examples of implementing the `apply` method

# CHAPTER 7

# Packaging and Imports

## Introduction

Scala's packaging approach is similar to Java, but it's more flexible. In addition to using the package statement at the top of a class file, you can use a curly brace packaging style, similar to C++ and C# namespaces.

The Scala approach to importing members is also similar to Java, and more flexible. With Scala you can:

- Place import statements anywhere
- Import classes, packages, or objects
- Hide and rename members when you import them

All of these approaches are demonstrated in this chapter.

It's helpful to know that in Scala, two packages are implicitly imported for you:

- `java.lang._`
- `scala._`

In Scala, the _ character is similar to the * character in Java, so these statements refer to every member in those packages.

In addition to those packages, all members from the `scala.Predef` object are imported into your applications implicitly.

A great suggestion from the book *Beginning Scala* by David Pollak (Apress), is to dig into the source code of the `Predef` object (*http://bit.ly/11QI0fF*). The code isn't too long, and it demonstrates many of the features of the Scala language. Many implicit conversions are brought into scope by the `Predef` object, as well as methods like `println`, `readLine`, `assert`, and `require`.

# 7.1. Packaging with the Curly Braces Style Notation

## Problem

You want to use a nested style package notation, similar to the namespace notation in C++ and C#.

## Solution

Wrap one or more classes in a set of curly braces with a package name, as shown in this example:

```
package com.acme.store {
  class Foo { override def toString = "I am com.acme.store.Foo" }
}
```

The canonical name of the class is `com.acme.store.Foo`. It's just as though you declared the code like this:

```
package com.acme.store

class Foo { override def toString = "I am com.acme.store.Foo" }
```

With this approach, you can place multiple packages in one file. You can also nest packages using this "curly braces" style.

The following example creates three `Foo` classes, all of which are in different packages, to demonstrate how to include one package inside another:

```
// a package containing a class named Foo
package orderentry {
  class Foo { override def toString = "I am orderentry.Foo" }
}

// one package nested inside the other
package customers {
  class Foo { override def toString = "I am customers.Foo" }

  package database {
    // this Foo is different than customers.Foo or orderentry.Foo
    class Foo { override def toString = "I am customers.database.Foo" }
  }
}

// a simple object to test the packages and classes
object PackageTests extends App {
  println(new orderentry.Foo)
```

```
    println(new customers.Foo)
    println(new customers.database.Foo)
  }
```

If you place this code in a file, and then compile and run it, you'll get the following output:

```
I am orderentry.Foo
I am customers.Foo
I am customers.database.Foo
```

This demonstrates that each Foo class is indeed in a different package.

As shown in the first example, package names don't have to be limited to just one level. You can define multiple levels of depth at one time:

```
package com.alvinalexander.foo {
  class Foo { override def toString = "I am com.alvinalexander.foo.Foo" }
}
```

## Discussion

You can create Scala packages with the usual Java practice of declaring a package name at the top of the file:

```
package foo.bar.baz

class Foo {
  override def toString = "I'm foo.bar.baz.Foo"
}
```

In most cases, I use this packaging approach, but because Scala code can be much more concise than Java, the alternative curly brace packaging syntax can be very convenient when you want to declare multiple classes and packages in one file.

# 7.2. Importing One or More Members

## Problem

You want to import one or more members into the scope of your current program.

## Solution

This is the syntax for importing one class:

```
import java.io.File
```

You can import multiple classes the Java way:

```
import java.io.File
import java.io.IOException
import java.io.FileNotFoundException
```

Or you can import several classes the Scala way:

```
import java.io.{File, IOException, FileNotFoundException}
```

Use the following syntax to import everything from the `java.io` package:

```
import java.io._
```

The _ character in this example is similar to the * wildcard character in Java. If the _ character feels unusual, it helps to know that it's used consistently throughout the Scala language as a wildcard character, and that consistency is very nice.

## Discussion

The concept of importing code into the current scope is similar between Java and Scala, but Scala is more flexible. Scala lets you:

- Place import statements anywhere, including the top of a class, within a class or object, within a method, or within a block of code
- Import classes, packages, or objects
- Hide and rename members when you import them

Syntactically, the two big differences are the curly brace syntax, known as the *import selector clause*, and the use of the _ wildcard character instead of Java's * wildcard. The advantages of the import selector clause are demonstrated further in Recipes 7.3 and 7.4.

### Placing import statements anywhere

In Scala you can place an import statement anywhere. For instance, because Scala makes it easy to include multiple classes in the same file, you may want to separate your import statements so the common imports are declared at the top of the file, and the imports specific to each class are within each class specification:

```
package foo

import java.io.File
import java.io.PrintWriter

class Foo {
  import javax.swing.JFrame   // only visible in this class
  // ...
}

class Bar {
  import scala.util.Random    // only visible in this class
```

```
    // ...
}
```

You can also place import statements inside methods, functions, or blocks:

```scala
class Bar {
  def doBar = {
    import scala.util.Random
    println("")
  }
}
```

See Recipe 7.6, "Using Import Statements Anywhere", for more examples and details about the use of import statements.

# 7.3. Renaming Members on Import

## Problem

You want to rename members when you import them to help avoid namespace collisions or confusion.

## Solution

Give the class you're importing a new name when you import it with this syntax:

```scala
import java.util.{ArrayList => JavaList}
```

Then, within your code, refer to the class by the alias you've given it:

```scala
val list = new JavaList[String]
```

You can also rename multiple classes at one time during the import process:

```scala
import java.util.{Date => JDate, HashMap => JHashMap}
```

Because you've created these aliases during the import process, the original (real) name of the class can't be used in your code. For instance, in the last example, the following code will fail because the compiler can't find the `java.util.HashMap` class:

```scala
// error: this won't compile because HashMap was renamed
// during the import process
val map = new HashMap[String, String]
```

## Discussion

As shown, you can create a new name for a class when you import it, and can then refer to it by the new name, or alias. The book *Programming in Scala*, by Odersky, et al (Artima). The book refers to this as a *renaming clause*.

This can be very helpful when trying to avoid namespace collisions and confusion. Class names like `Listener`, `Message`, `Handler`, `Client`, `Server`, and many more are all very common, and it can be helpful to give them an alias when you import them.

From a strategy perspective, you can either rename all classes that might be conflicting or confusing:

```
import java.util.{HashMap => JavaHashMap}
import scala.collection.mutable.{Map => ScalaMutableMap}
```

or you can just rename one class to clarify the situation:

```
import java.util.{HashMap => JavaHashMap}
import scala.collection.mutable.Map
```

As an interesting combination of several recipes, not only can you rename classes on import, but you can even rename class members. As an example of this, in shell scripts I tend to rename the `println` method to a shorter name, as shown here in the REPL:

```
scala> import System.out.{println => p}
import System.out.{println=>p}

scala> p("hello")
hello
```

# 7.4. Hiding a Class During the Import Process

## Problem

You want to hide one or more classes while importing other members from the same package.

## Solution

To hide a class during the import process, use the renaming syntax shown in Recipe 7.3, "Renaming Members on Import", but point the class name to the _ wildcard character. The following example hides the `Random` class, while importing everything else from the `java.util` package:

```
import java.util.{Random => _, _}
```

This can be confirmed in the REPL:

```
scala> import java.util.{Random => _, _}
import java.util.{Random=>_, _}

// can't access Random
scala> val r = new Random
<console>:10: error: not found: type Random
       val r = new Random
                   ^
```

```
// can access other members
scala> new ArrayList
res0: java.util.ArrayList[Nothing] = []
```

In that example, the following portion of the code is what "hides" the Random class:

```
import java.util.{Random => _}
```

The second _ character inside the curly braces is the same as stating that you want to import everything else in the package, like this:

```
import java.util._
```

Note that the _ import wildcard must be in the last position. It yields an error if you attempt to use it in other positions:

```
scala> import java.util.{_, Random => _}
<console>:1: error: Wildcard import must be in last position
       import java.util.{_, Random => _}
                         ^
```

This is because you may want to hide multiple members during the import process, and to do, so you need to list them first.

To hide multiple members, list them before using the final wildcard import:

```
scala> import java.util.{List => _, Map => _, Set => _, _}
import java.util.{List=>_, Map=>_, Set=>_, _}

scala> new ArrayList
res0: java.util.ArrayList[Nothing] = []
```

This ability to hide members on import is useful when you need many members from one package, and therefore want to use the _ wildcard syntax, but you also want to hide one or more members during the import process, typically due to naming conflicts.

# 7.5. Using Static Imports

## Problem

You want to import members in a way similar to the Java static import approach, so you can refer to the member names directly, without having to prefix them with their class name.

## Solution

Use this syntax to import all members of the Java Math class:

```
import java.lang.Math._
```

You can now access these members without having to precede them with the class name:

```
scala> import java.lang.Math._
import java.lang.Math._

scala> val a = sin(0)
a: Double = 0.0

scala> val a = cos(PI)
a: Double = -1.0
```

The Java Color class also demonstrates the usefulness of this technique:

```
scala> import java.awt.Color._
import java.awt.Color._

scala> println(RED)
java.awt.Color[r=255,g=0,b=0]

scala> val currentColor = BLUE
currentColor: java.awt.Color = java.awt.Color[r=0,g=0,b=255]
```

Enumerations are another great candidate for this technique. Given a Java enum like this:

```
package com.alvinalexander.dates;

public enum Day {
    SUNDAY, MONDAY, TUESDAY, WEDNESDAY, THURSDAY, FRIDAY, SATURDAY
}
```

you can import and use this enumeration in a Scala program like this:

```
import com.alvinalexander.dates.Day._

// somewhere after the import statement
if (date == SUNDAY || date == SATURDAY) println("It's the weekend.")
```

## Discussion

Although some developers don't like static imports, I find that this approach makes enums more readable. Just specifying the name of a class or enum before the constant makes the code less readable:

```
if (date == Day.SUNDAY || date == Day.SATURDAY) {
    println("It's the weekend.")
}
```

With the static import approach there's no need for the leading "Day." in the code, and it's easier to read.

# 7.6. Using Import Statements Anywhere

## Problem

You want to use an import statement anywhere, generally to limit the scope of the import, to make the code more clear, or to organize your code.

## Solution

You can place an import statement almost anywhere inside a program. As with Java, you can import members at the top of a class definition, and then use the imported resource later in your code:

```
package foo

import scala.util.Random

class ImportTests {
  def printRandom {
    val r = new Random
  }
}
```

You can import members inside a class:

```
package foo

class ImportTests {
  import scala.util.Random
  def printRandom {
    val r = new Random
  }
}
```

This limits the scope of the import to the code in the class that comes after the import statement.

You can limit the scope of an import to a method:

```
def getRandomWaitTimeInMinutes: Int = {
  import com.alvinalexander.pandorasbox._
  val p = new Pandora
  p.release
}
```

You can even place an import statement inside a block, limiting the scope of the import to only the code that follows the statement, inside that block. In the following example, the field r1 is declared correctly, because it's within the block and after the import statement, but the declaration for field r2 won't compile, because the Random class is not in scope at that point:

```
def printRandom {
  {
    import scala.util.Random
    val r1 = new Random    // this is fine
  }
  val r2 = new Random      // error: not found: type Random
}
```

## Discussion

Import statements are read in the order of the file, so where you place them in a file also limits their scope. The following code won't compile because I attempt to reference the Random class before the import statement is declared:

```
// this doesn't work because the import is after the attempted reference
class ImportTests {
  def printRandom {
    val r = new Random    // fails
  }
}
import scala.util.Random
```

When you want to include multiple classes and packages in one file, you can combine import statements and the curly brace packaging approach to limit the scope of the import statements, as shown in these examples:

```
package orderentry {
  import foo._
  // more code here ...
}

package customers {
  import bar._
  // more code here ...

  package database {
    import baz._
    // more code here ...
  }
}
```

In this example, members can be accessed as follows:

- Code in the orderentry package can access members of foo, but can't access members of bar or baz.

- Code in customers and customers.database can't access members of foo.

- Code in customers can access members of bar.

- Code in customers.database can access members in bar and baz.

The same concept applies when defining multiple classes in one file:

```
package foo

// available to all classes defined below
import java.io.File
import java.io.PrintWriter

class Foo {
  // only available inside this class
  import javax.swing.JFrame
  // ...
}

class Bar {
  // only available inside this class
  import scala.util.Random
  // ...
}
```

Although placing import statements at the top of a file or just before they're used can be a matter of style, I find this flexibility to be useful when placing multiple classes or packages in one file. In these cases, it's nice to keep the imports in a small scope to limit namespace issues, and also to make the code easier to refactor as it grows.

# CHAPTER 8

# Traits

## Introduction

In its most basic use, a Scala trait is just like a Java interface. When you're faced with situations where you would have used an interface in Java, just think "trait" in Scala.

Just as Java classes can implement multiple interfaces, Scala classes can extend multiple traits. As you'll see in the recipes in this chapter, this is done with the extends and with keywords, so when a class (or object) extends multiple traits, you'll see code like this:

```
class Woodpecker extends Bird with TreeScaling with Pecking
```

However, using traits as interfaces only scratches the surface of what they can do. Traits have much more power than Java interfaces because, just like abstract methods in Java, they can also have implemented methods. However, unlike Java's abstract classes, you can mix more than one trait into a class, and a trait can also control what classes it can be mixed into.

This chapter provides examples of the many uses of Scala traits.

## 8.1. Using a Trait as an Interface

### Problem

You're used to creating interfaces in other languages like Java and want to create something like that in Scala.

### Solution

You can use a trait just like a Java interface. As with interfaces, just declare the methods in your trait that you want extending classes to implement:

```
trait BaseSoundPlayer {
  def play
  def close
  def pause
  def stop
  def resume
}
```

If the methods don't take any argument, you only need to declare the names of the methods after the def keyword, as shown. If a method should require parameters, list them as usual:

```
trait Dog {
  def speak(whatToSay: String)
  def wagTail(enabled: Boolean)
}
```

When a class extends a trait, it uses the extends and with keywords. When extending one trait, use extends:

```
class Mp3SoundPlayer extends BaseSoundPlayer { ...
```

When extending a class and one or more traits, use extends for the class, and with for subsequent traits:

```
class Foo extends BaseClass with Trait1 with Trait2 { ...
```

When a class extends multiple traits, use extends for the first trait, and with for subsequent traits:

```
class Foo extends Trait1 with Trait2 with Trait3 with Trait4 { ...
```

Unless the class implementing a trait is abstract, it must implement all of the abstract trait methods:

```
class Mp3SoundPlayer extends BaseSoundPlayer {
  def play   { // code here ... }
  def close  { // code here ... }
  def pause  { // code here ... }
  def stop   { // code here ... }
  def resume { // code here ... }
}
```

If a class extends a trait but does not implement the abstract methods defined in that trait, it must be declared abstract:

```
// must be declared abstract because it does not implement
// all of the BaseSoundPlayer methods
abstract class SimpleSoundPlayer extends BaseSoundPlayer {
  def play { ... }
  def close { ... }
}
```

In other uses, one trait can extend another trait:

```
trait Mp3BaseSoundFilePlayer extends BaseSoundFilePlayer {
  def getBasicPlayer: BasicPlayer
  def getBasicController: BasicController
  def setGain(volume: Double)
}
```

## Discussion

As demonstrated, at their most basic level, traits can be used just like Java interfaces. In your trait, just declare the methods that need to be implemented by classes that want to extend your trait.

Classes extend your trait using either the extends or with keywords, according to these simple rules:

- If a class extends one trait, use the extends keyword.
- If a class extends multiple traits, use extends for the first trait and with to extend (mix in) the other traits.
- If a class extends a class (or abstract class) and a trait, always use extends before the class name, and use with before the trait name(s).

You can also use fields in your traits. See the next recipe for examples.

As shown in the WaggingTail trait in the following example, not only can a trait be used like a Java interface, but it can also provide method implementations, like an abstract class in Java:

```
abstract class Animal {
  def speak
}

trait WaggingTail {
  def startTail { println("tail started") }
  def stopTail { println("tail stopped") }
}

trait FourLeggedAnimal {
  def walk
  def run
}

class Dog extends Animal with WaggingTail with FourLeggedAnimal {
  // implementation code here ...
  def speak { println("Dog says 'woof'") }
  def walk { println("Dog is walking") }
  def run { println("Dog is running") }
}
```

This ability is discussed in detail in Recipe 8.3, "Using a Trait Like an Abstract Class".

When a class has multiple traits, such as the `WaggingTail` and `FourLeggedAnimal` traits in this example, those traits are said to be *mixed in* to the class. The term "mixed in" is also used when extending a single object instance with a trait, like this:

```
val f = new Foo with Trait1
```

This feature is discussed more in Recipe 8.8, "Adding a Trait to an Object Instance".

# 8.2. Using Abstract and Concrete Fields in Traits

## Problem

You want to put abstract or concrete fields in your traits so they are declared in one place and available to all types that implement the trait.

## Solution

Define a field with an initial value to make it *concrete*; otherwise, don't assign it an initial value to make it *abstract*. This trait shows several examples of abstract and concrete fields with var and val types:

```
trait PizzaTrait {
  var numToppings: Int       // abstract
  var size = 14              // concrete
  val maxNumToppings = 10    // concrete
}
```

In the class that extends the trait, you'll need to define the values for the abstract fields, or make the class abstract. The following `Pizza` class demonstrates how to set the values for the `numToppings` and `size` fields in a concrete class:

```
class Pizza extends PizzaTrait {
  var numToppings = 0        // 'override' not needed
  size = 16                  // 'var' and 'override' not needed
}
```

## Discussion

As shown in the example, fields of a trait can be declared as either var or val. You don't need to use the override keyword to override a var field in a subclass (or trait), but you do need to use it to override a val field:

```
trait PizzaTrait {
  val maxNumToppings: Int
}

class Pizza extends PizzaTrait {
  override val maxNumToppings = 10  // 'override' is required
}
```

Overriding var and val fields is discussed more in Recipe 4.13, "Defining Properties in an Abstract Base Class (or Trait)".

# 8.3. Using a Trait Like an Abstract Class

## Problem

You want to use a trait as something like an abstract class in Java.

## Solution

Define methods in your trait just like regular Scala methods. In the class that extends the trait, you can override those methods or use them as they are defined in the trait.

In the following example, an implementation is provided for the speak method in the Pet trait, so implementing classes don't have to override it. The Dog class chooses not to override it, whereas the Cat class does:

```
trait Pet {
  def speak { println("Yo") }    // concrete implementation
  def comeToMaster              // abstract method
}

class Dog extends Pet {
  // don't need to implement 'speak' if you don't need to
  def comeToMaster { ("I'm coming!") }
}

class Cat extends Pet {
  // override the speak method
  override def speak { ("meow") }
  def comeToMaster { ("That's not gonna happen.") }
}
```

If a class extends a trait without implementing its abstract methods, it must be defined as abstract. Because FlyingPet does not implement comeToMaster, it must be declared as abstract:

```
abstract class FlyingPet extends Pet {
  def fly { ("I'm flying!") }
}
```

## Discussion

Although Scala has abstract classes, it's much more common to use traits than abstract classes to implement base behavior. A class can extend only one abstract class, but it can implement multiple traits, so using traits is more flexible.

## See Also

- Like Java, you use `super.foo` to call a method named `foo` in an immediate super-class. When a class mixes in multiple traits—and those traits implement a method declared by a common ancestor—you can be more specific, and specify which trait you'd like to invoke a method on. See Recipe 5.2, "Calling a Method on a Super-class", for more information.

- See Recipe 4.12, "When to Use an Abstract Class", for information on when to use an abstract class instead of a trait. (Spoiler: Use an abstract class (a) when you want to define a base behavior, and that behavior requires a constructor with parameters, and (b) in some situations when you need to interact with Java.)

# 8.4. Using Traits as Simple Mixins

## Problem

You want to design a solution where multiple traits can be mixed into a class to provide a robust design.

## Solution

To implement a simple *mixin*, define the methods you want in your trait, then add the trait to your class using `extends` or `with`. For instance, the following code defines a `Tail` trait:

```
trait Tail {
  def wagTail { println("tail is wagging") }
  def stopTail { println("tail is stopped") }
}
```

You can use this trait with an abstract `Pet` class to create a `Dog`:

```
abstract class Pet (var name: String) {
  def speak // abstract
  def ownerIsHome { println("excited") }
  def jumpForJoy { println("jumping for joy") }
}

class Dog (name: String) extends Pet (name) with Tail {
  def speak { println("woof") }
  override def ownerIsHome {
    wagTail
    speak
  }
}
```

The Dog class extends the abstract class Pet and mixes in the Tail trait, and can use the methods defined by both Pet and Tail:

```
object Test extends App {
  val zeus = new Dog("Zeus")
  zeus.ownerIsHome
  zeus.jumpForJoy
}
```

In summary, the Dog class gets behavior from both the abstract Pet class and the Tail trait; this is something you can't do in Java.

 To see a great demonstration of the power of mixins, read Artima's short "Stackable Trait Pattern" article (*http://bit.ly/17fZTma*). By defining traits and classes as *base*, *core*, and *stackable* components, they demonstrate how sixteen different classes can be derived from three traits by "stacking" the traits together.

## See Also

When you develop traits, you may want to limit the classes they can be mixed into. The classes a trait can be mixed into can be limited using the following techniques:

- Recipe 8.5 shows how to limit which classes can use a trait by declaring inheritance.
- Recipe 8.6 shows how to mark traits so they can only be used by subclasses of a certain type.
- Recipe 8.7 demonstrates the technique to use to make sure a trait can only be mixed into classes that have a specific method.
- Also, see Artima's "Stackable Trait Pattern" article (*http://bit.ly/17fZTma*).

# 8.5. Limiting Which Classes Can Use a Trait by Inheritance

## Problem

You want to limit a trait so it can only be added to classes that extend a superclass or another trait.

## Solution

Use the following syntax to declare a trait named TraitName, where TraitName can only be mixed into classes that extend a type named SuperThing, where SuperThing may be a trait, class, or abstract class:

```
trait [TraitName] extends [SuperThing]
```

For instance, in the following example, `Starship` and `StarfleetWarpCore` both extend the common superclass `StarfleetComponent`, so the `StarfleetWarpCore` trait *can* be mixed into the `Starship` class:

```
class StarfleetComponent
trait StarfleetWarpCore extends StarfleetComponent
class Starship extends StarfleetComponent with StarfleetWarpCore
```

However, in the following example, the `Warbird` class *can't* extend the `StarfleetWarpCore` trait, because `Warbird` and `StarfleetWarpCore` don't share the same superclass:

```
class StarfleetComponent
trait StarfleetWarpCore extends StarfleetComponent
class RomulanStuff

// won't compile
class Warbird extends RomulanStuff with StarfleetWarpCore
```

Attempting to compile this second example yields this error:

```
error: illegal inheritance; superclass RomulanStuff
 is not a subclass of the superclass StarfleetComponent
 of the mixin trait StarfleetWarpCore
class Warbird extends RomulanStuff with StarfleetWarpCore
                                        ^
```

## Discussion

A trait inheriting from a class is not a common occurrence, and in general, Recipes 8.6 and Recipe 8.7 are more commonly used to limit the classes a trait can be mixed into.

However, when this situation occurs, you can see how inheritance can be used. As long as a class and a trait share the same superclass (`Starship` and `StarfleetWarpCore` extend `StarfleetComponent`) the code will compile, but if the superclasses are different (`Warbird` and `StarfleetWarpCore` have different superclasses), the code will not compile.

As a second example, in modeling a large pizza store chain that has a corporate office and many small retail stores, the legal department creates a rule that people who deliver pizzas to customers must be a subclass of `StoreEmployee` and cannot be a subclass of `CorporateEmployee`. To enforce this, begin by defining your base classes:

```
abstract class Employee
class CorporateEmployee extends Employee
class StoreEmployee extends Employee
```

Someone who delivers food can only be a `StoreEmployee`, so you enforce this requirement in the `DeliversFood` trait using inheritance like this:

```
trait DeliversFood extends StoreEmployee
```

Now you can define a `DeliveryPerson` class like this:

```
// this is allowed
class DeliveryPerson extends StoreEmployee with DeliversFood
```

Because the `DeliversFood` trait can only be mixed into classes that extend `StoreEmployee`, the following line of code won't compile:

```
// won't compile
class Receptionist extends CorporateEmployee with DeliversFood
```

## Discussion

It seems rare that a trait and a class the trait will be mixed into should both have the same superclass, so I suspect the need for this recipe is also rare. When you want to limit the classes a trait can be mixed into, don't create an artificial inheritance tree to use this recipe; use one of the following recipes instead.

## See Also

- Recipe 8.6 to see how to mark traits so they can only be used by subclasses of a certain type
- Recipe 8.7 to make sure a trait can only be mixed into a class that has a specific method

# 8.6. Marking Traits So They Can Only Be Used by Subclasses of a Certain Type

## Problem

You want to mark your trait so it can only be used by types that extend a given base type.

## Solution

To make sure a trait named `MyTrait` can only be mixed into a class that is a subclass of a type named `BaseType`, begin your trait with a `this: BaseType =>` declaration, as shown here:

```
trait MyTrait {
  this: BaseType =>
```

For instance, to make sure a `StarfleetWarpCore` can only be used in a `Starship`, mark the `StarfleetWarpCore` trait like this:

```
trait StarfleetWarpCore {
  this: Starship =>
  // more code here ...
}
```

Given that declaration, this code will work:

```
class Starship
class Enterprise extends Starship with StarfleetWarpCore
```

But other attempts like this will fail:

```
class RomulanShip
// this won't compile
class Warbird extends RomulanShip with StarfleetWarpCore
```

This second example fails with an error message similar to this:

```
error: illegal inheritance;
self-type Warbird does not conform to StarfleetWarpCore's selftype
StarfleetWarpCore with Starship
class Warbird extends RomulanShip with StarfleetWarpCore
                                      ^
```

## Discussion

As shown in the error message, this approach is referred to as a *self type*. The Scala Glossary (*http://bit.ly/15xVIAX*) includes this statement as part of its description of a self type:

> "Any concrete class that mixes in the trait must ensure that its type conforms to the trait's self type."

A trait can also require that any type that wishes to extend it must extend multiple other types. The following WarpCore definition requires that any type that wishes to mix it in must extend WarpCoreEjector and FireExtinguisher, in addition to extending Starship:

```
trait WarpCore {
  this: Starship with WarpCoreEjector with FireExtinguisher =>
}
```

Because the following Enterprise definition matches that signature, this code compiles:

```
class Starship
trait WarpCoreEjector
trait FireExtinguisher

// this works
class Enterprise extends Starship
  with WarpCore
  with WarpCoreEjector
  with FireExtinguisher
```

However, if the `Enterprise` doesn't extend `Starship`, `WarpCoreEjector`, and `FireExtinguisher`, the code won't compile. Once again, the compiler shows that the self-type signature is not correct:

```
// won't compile
class Enterprise extends Starship with WarpCore with WarpCoreEjector

error: illegal inheritance;
self-type Enterprise does not conform to WarpCore's selftype WarpCore
with Starship with WarpCoreEjector with FireExtinguisher

class Enterprise extends Starship with WarpCore with WarpCoreEjector
                                                 ^
```

## See Also

- Recipe 8.5 shows how to limit which classes can use a trait by declaring inheritance
- Recipe 8.7 demonstrates the technique to use to make sure a trait can only be mixed into classes that have a specific method
- The Scala Glossary (*http://bit.ly/15xVIAX*)

# 8.7. Ensuring a Trait Can Only Be Added to a Type That Has a Specific Method

## Problem

You only want to allow a trait to be mixed into a type (class, abstract class, or trait) that has a method with a given signature.

## Solution

Use a variation of the self-type syntax that lets you declare that any class that attempts to mix in the trait must implement the method you specify.

In the following example, the `WarpCore` trait requires that any classes that attempt to mix it in must have an `ejectWarpCore` method:

```
trait WarpCore {
  this: { def ejectWarpCore(password: String): Boolean } =>
}
```

It further states that the `ejectWarpCore` method must accept a `String` argument and return a `Boolean` value.

The following definition of the `Enterprise` class meets these requirements, and will therefore compile:

```
class Starship {
  // code here ...
}

class Enterprise extends Starship with WarpCore {
  def ejectWarpCore(password: String): Boolean = {
    if (password == "password") {
      println("ejecting core")
      true
    } else {
      false
    }
  }
}
```

A trait can also require that a class have multiple methods. To require more than one method, just add the additional method signatures inside the block:

```
trait WarpCore {
  this: {
    def ejectWarpCore(password: String): Boolean
    def startWarpCore: Unit
  } =>
}

class Starship

class Enterprise extends Starship with WarpCore {
  def ejectWarpCore(password: String): Boolean = {
    if (password == "password") { println("core ejected"); true } else false
  }
  def startWarpCore { println("core started") }
}
```

## Discussion

This approach is known as a *structural type*, because you're limiting what classes the trait can be mixed into by stating that the class must have a certain structure, i.e., the methods you've defined. In the examples shown, limits were placed on what classes the `WarpCore` trait can be mixed into.

## See Also

- Recipe 8.5 shows how to limit which classes can use a trait by declaring inheritance.
- Recipe 8.6 shows how to mark traits so they can only be used by subclasses of a certain type.

# 8.8. Adding a Trait to an Object Instance

## Problem

Rather than add a trait to an entire class, you just want to add a trait to an object instance when the object is created.

## Solution

Add the trait to the object when you construct it. This is demonstrated in a simple example:

```
class DavidBanner

trait Angry {
  println("You won't like me ...")
}

object Test extends App {
  val hulk = new DavidBanner with Angry
}
```

When you compile and run this code, it will print, "You won't like me ...", because the hulk object is created when the DavidBanner class is instantiated with the Angry trait, which has the print statement shown in its constructor.

## Discussion

As a more practical matter, you might mix in something like a debugger or logging trait when constructing an object to help debug that object:

```
trait Debugger {
  def log(message: String) {
    // do something with message
  }
}

// no debugger
val child = new Child

// debugger added as the object is created
val problemChild = new ProblemChild with Debugger
```

This makes the log method available to the problemChild instance.

# 8.9. Extending a Java Interface Like a Trait

## Problem

You want to implement a Java interface in a Scala application.

## Solution

In your Scala application, use the `extends` and `with` keywords to implement your Java interfaces, just as though they were Scala traits.

Given these three Java interfaces:

```java
// java
public interface Animal {
  public void speak();
}

public interface Wagging {
  public void wag();
}

public interface Running {
  public void run();
}
```

you can create a `Dog` class in Scala with the usual `extends` and `with` keywords, just as though you were using traits:

```scala
// scala
class Dog extends Animal with Wagging with Running {
  def speak { println("Woof") }
  def wag { println("Tail is wagging!") }
  def run { println("I'm running!") }
}
```

The difference is that Java interfaces don't implement behavior, so if you're defining a class that extends a Java interface, you'll need to implement the methods, or declare the class abstract.

# Functional Programming

## Introduction

Scala is both an object-oriented programming (OOP) and a functional programming (FP) language. This chapter demonstrates functional programming techniques, including the ability to define functions and pass them around as instances. Just like you create a `String` instance in Java and pass it around, you can define a function as a variable and pass it around. I'll demonstrate many examples and advantages of this capability in this chapter.

As a language that supports functional programming, Scala encourages an expression-oriented programming (EOP) model (*http://bit.ly/1b7B6FE*). Simply put, in EOP, every statement (expression) yields a value. This paradigm can be as obvious as an `if/else` statement returning a value:

```
val greater = if (a > b) a else b
```

It can also be as surprising as a `try/catch` statement returning a value:

```
val result = try {
  aString.toInt
} catch {
  case _ => 0
}
```

Although EOP is casually demonstrated in many examples in this book, it's helpful to be consciously aware of this way of thinking in the recipes that follow.

# 9.1. Using Function Literals (Anonymous Functions)

## Problem

You want to use an anonymous function—also known as a *function literal*—so you can pass it into a method that takes a function, or to assign it to a variable.

## Solution

Given this List:

```
val x = List.range(1, 10)
```

you can pass an anonymous function to the List's filter method to create a new List that contains only even numbers:

```
val evens = x.filter((i: Int) => i % 2 == 0)
```

The REPL demonstrates that this expression indeed yields a new List of even numbers:

```
scala> val evens = x.filter((i: Int) => i % 2 == 0)
evens: List[Int] = List(2, 4, 6, 8)
```

In this solution, the following code is a function literal (also known as an *anonymous function*):

```
(i: Int) => i % 2 == 0
```

Although that code works, it shows the most explicit form for defining a function literal. Thanks to several Scala shortcuts, the expression can be simplified to this:

```
val evens = x.filter(_ % 2 == 0)
```

In the REPL, you see that this returns the same result:

```
scala> val evens = x.filter(_ % 2 == 0)
evens: List[Int] = List(2, 4, 6, 8)
```

## Discussion

In this example, the original function literal consists of the following code:

```
(i: Int) => i % 2 == 0
```

When examining this code, it helps to think of the => symbol as a *transformer*, because the expression transforms the parameter list on the left side of the symbol (an Int named i) into a new result using the algorithm on the right side of the symbol (in this case, an expression that results in a Boolean).

As mentioned, this example shows the long form for defining an anonymous function, which can be simplified in several different ways. The first example shows the most explicit form:

```
val evens = x.filter((i: Int) => i % 2 == 0)
```

Because the Scala compiler can infer from the expression that i is an Int, the Int declaration can be dropped off:

```
val evens = x.filter(i => i % 2 == 0)
```

Because Scala lets you use the _ wildcard instead of a variable name when the parameter appears only once in your function, this code can be simplified even more:

```
val evens = x.filter(_ % 2 == 0)
```

In other examples, you can simplify your anonymous functions further. For instance, beginning with the most explicit form, you can print each element in the list using this anonymous function with the foreach method:

```
x.foreach((i:Int) => println(i))
```

As before, the Int declaration isn't required:

```
x.foreach((i) => println(i))
```

Because there is only one argument, the parentheses around the i parameter aren't needed:

```
x.foreach(i => println(i))
```

Because i is used only once in the body of the function, the expression can be further simplified with the _ wildcard:

```
x.foreach(println(_))
```

Finally, if a function literal consists of one statement that takes a single argument, you need not explicitly name and specify the argument, so the statement can finally be reduced to this:

```
x.foreach(println)
```

# 9.2. Using Functions as Variables

## Problem

You want to pass a function around like a variable, just like you pass String, Int, and other variables around in an object-oriented programming language.

## Solution

Use the syntax shown in Recipe 9.1 to define a function literal, and then assign that literal to a variable.

The following code defines a function literal that takes an Int parameter and returns a value that is twice the amount of the Int that is passed in:

```
(i: Int) => { i * 2 }
```

As mentioned in Recipe 9.1, you can think of the => symbol as a *transformer*. In this case, the function transforms the Int value i to an Int value that is twice the value of i.

You can now assign that function literal to a variable:

```
val double = (i: Int) => { i * 2 }
```

The variable double is an instance, just like an instance of a String, Int, or other type, but in this case, it's an instance of a function, known as a *function value*. You can now invoke double just like you'd call a method:

```
double(2)   // 4
double(3)   // 6
```

Beyond just invoking double like this, you can also pass it to any method (or function) that takes a function parameter with its signature. For instance, because the map method of a sequence is a generic method that takes an input parameter of type A and returns a type B, you can pass the double method into the map method of an Int sequence:

```
scala> val list = List.range(1, 5)
list: List[Int] = List(1, 2, 3, 4)

scala> list.map(double)
res0: List[Int] = List(2, 4, 6, 8)
```

Welcome to the world of functional programming.

## Discussion

You can declare a function literal in at least two different ways. I generally prefer the following approach, which implicitly infers that the following function's return type is Boolean:

```
val f = (i: Int) => { i % 2 == 0 }
```

In this case, the Scala compiler is smart enough to look at the body of the function and determine that it returns a Boolean value. As a human, it's also easy to look at the code on the right side of the expression and see that it returns a Boolean, so I usually leave the explicit Boolean return type off the function declaration.

However, if you prefer to explicitly declare the return type of a function literal, or want to do so because your function is more complex, the following examples show different forms you can use to explicitly declare that your function returns a Boolean:

```
val f: (Int) => Boolean = i => { i % 2 == 0 }
val f: Int => Boolean = i => { i % 2 == 0 }
val f: Int => Boolean = i => i % 2 == 0
val f: Int => Boolean = _ % 2 == 0
```

A second example helps demonstrate the difference of these approaches. These functions all take two Int parameters and return a single Int value, which is the sum of the two input values:

```
// implicit approach
val add = (x: Int, y: Int) => { x + y }
val add = (x: Int, y: Int) => x + y

// explicit approach
val add: (Int, Int) => Int = (x,y) => { x + y }
val add: (Int, Int) => Int = (x,y) => x + y
```

As shown, the curly braces around the body of the function in these simple examples are optional, but they are required when the function body grows to more than one expression:

```
val addThenDouble: (Int, Int) => Int = (x,y) => {
  val a = x + y
  2 * a
}
```

### Using a method like an anonymous function

Scala is very flexible, and just like you can define an anonymous function and assign it to a variable, you can also define a method and then pass it around like an instance variable. Again using a modulus example, you can define a method in any of these ways:

```
def modMethod(i: Int) = i % 2 == 0
def modMethod(i: Int) = { i % 2 == 0 }
def modMethod(i: Int): Boolean = i % 2 == 0
def modMethod(i: Int): Boolean = { i % 2 == 0 }
```

Any of these methods can be passed into collection methods that expect a function that has one Int parameter and returns a Boolean, such as the filter method of a List[Int]:

```
val list = List.range(1, 10)
list.filter(modMethod)
```

Here's what that looks like in the REPL:

```
scala> def modMethod(i: Int) = i % 2 == 0
modMethod: (i: Int)Boolean

scala> val list = List.range(1, 10)
list: List[Int] = List(1, 2, 3, 4, 5, 6, 7, 8, 9)

scala> list.filter(modMethod)
res0: List[Int] = List(2, 4, 6, 8)
```

As noted, this is similar to the process of defining a function literal and assigning it to a variable. The following function works just like the previous method:

```
val modFunction = (i: Int) => i % 2 == 0
list.filter(modFunction)
```

At a coding level, the obvious difference is that modMethod is a *method* defined in a class, whereas modFunction is a *function* that's assigned to a variable. Under the covers, modFunction is an instance of the Function1 (*http://bit.ly/13KD90C*) trait (*http://bit.ly/13KD90C*), which defines a function that takes one argument. (The scala package defines other similar traits, including Function0, Function2, and so on, up to Function22.)

### Assigning an existing function/method to a function variable

Continuing our exploration, you can assign an existing method or function to a function variable. For instance, you can create a new function named c from the scala.math.cos method using either of these approaches:

```
scala> val c = scala.math.cos _
c: Double => Double = <function1>

scala> val c = scala.math.cos(_)
c: Double => Double = <function1>
```

This is called a *partially applied function*. It's partially applied because the cos method requires one argument, which you have not yet supplied (more on this in Recipe 9.6).

Now that you have c, you can use it just like you would have used cos:

```
scala> c(0)
res0: Double = 1.0
```

If you're not familiar with this syntax, this is a place where the REPL can be invaluable. If you attempt to assign the cos function/method to a variable, the REPL tells you what's wrong:

```
scala> val c = scala.math.cos
<console>:11: error: missing arguments for method cos in class MathCommon;
follow this method with `_' to treat it as a partially applied function
       val c = scala.math.cos
                         ^
```

The following example shows how to use this same technique on the scala.math.pow method, which takes two parameters:

```
scala> val p = scala.math.pow(_, _)
pow: (Double, Double) => Double = <function2>

scala> p(scala.math.E, 2)
res0: Double = 7.3890560989306495
```

If this seems like an interesting language feature, but you're wondering where it would be useful, see Recipe 9.6, "Using Partially Applied Functions", for more information.

Summary notes:

- Think of the => symbol as a transformer. It transforms the input data on its left side to some new output data, using the algorithm on its right side.
- Use def to define a method, val, to create a function.
- When assigning a function to a variable, a *function literal* is the code on the right side of the expression.
- A *function value* is an object, and extends the FunctionN traits in the main scala package, such as Function0 for a function that takes no parameters.

## See Also

The Function1 trait (*http://bit.ly/13KD90C*)

# 9.3. Defining a Method That Accepts a Simple Function Parameter

## Problem

You want to create a method that takes a simple function as a method parameter.

## Solution

This solution follows a three-step process:

1. Define your method, including the signature for the function you want to take as a method parameter.
2. Define one or more functions that match this signature.
3. Sometime later, pass the function(s) as a parameter to your method.

To demonstrate this, define a method named executeFunction, which takes a function as a parameter. The method will take one parameter named callback, which is a function. That function must have no input parameters and must return nothing:

```
def executeFunction(callback:() => Unit) {
  callback()
}
```

Two quick notes:

- The `callback:()` syntax defines a function that has no parameters. If the function had parameters, the types would be listed inside the parentheses.
- The `=> Unit` portion of the code indicates that this method returns nothing.

I'll discuss this syntax more shortly.

Next, define a function that matches this signature. The following function named `sayHello` takes no input parameters and returns nothing:

```
val sayHello = () => { println("Hello") }
```

In the last step of the recipe, pass the `sayHello` function to the `executeFunction` method:

```
executeFunction(sayHello)
```

The REPL demonstrates how this works:

```
scala> def executeFunction(callback:() => Unit) { callback() }
executeFunction: (callback: () => Unit)Unit

scala> val sayHello = () => { println("Hello") }
sayHello: () => Unit = <function0>

scala> executeFunction(sayHello)
Hello
```

## Discussion

There isn't anything special about the `callback` name used in this example. When I first learned how to pass functions to methods, I preferred the name `callback` because it made the meaning clear, but it's just the name of a method parameter. These days, just as I often name an `Int` parameter `i`, I name a function parameter `f`:

```
def executeFunction(f:() => Unit) {
  f()
}
```

The part that is special is that the function that's passed in must match the function signature you define. In this case, you've declared that the function that's passed in must take no arguments and must return nothing:

```
f:() => Unit
```

The general syntax for defining a function as a method parameter is:

```
parameterName: (parameterType(s)) => returnType
```

In the example, the `parameterName` is `f`, the `parameterType` is empty because you don't want the function to take any parameters, and the return type is `Unit` because you don't want the function to return anything:

```
executeFunction(f:() => Unit)
```

To define a function that takes a `String` and returns an `Int`, use one of these two signatures:

```
executeFunction(f:String => Int)
executeFunction(f:(String) => Int)
```

See the next recipe for more function signature examples.

---

## Scala's Unit

The Scala `Unit` shown in these examples is similar to Java's `Void` class. It's used in situations like this to indicate that the function returns nothing ... or perhaps nothing of interest.

As a quick look into its effect, first define a method named `plusOne`, which does what its name implies:

```
scala> def plusOne(i: Int) = i + 1
plusOne: (i: Int)Int

scala> plusOne(1)
res0: Int = 2
```

When it's called, `plusOne` adds 1 to its input parameter, and returns that result as an `Int`.

Now, modify `plusOne` to declare that it returns `Unit`:

```
scala> def plusOne(i: Int): Unit = i + 1
plusOne: (i: Int)Unit

scala> plusOne(1)
(returns nothing)
```

Because you explicitly stated that `plusOne` returns `Unit`, there's no result in the REPL when `plusOne(1)` is called.

This isn't a common use of `Unit`, but it helps to demonstrate its effect.

---

## See Also

Scala's *call-by-name* functionality provides a very simple way to pass a block of code into a function or method. See Recipe 19.8, "Building Functionality with Types", for several call-by-name examples.

# 9.4. More Complex Functions

## Problem

You want to define a method that takes a function as a parameter, and that function may have one or more input parameters, and may also return a value.

## Solution

Following the approach described in the previous recipe, define a method that takes a function as a parameter. Specify the function signature you expect to receive, and then execute that function inside the body of the method.

The following example defines a method named exec that takes a function as an input parameter. That function must take one Int as an input parameter and return nothing:

```
def exec(callback: Int => Unit) {
  // invoke the function we were given, giving it an Int parameter
  callback(1)
}
```

Next, define a function that matches the expected signature. The following plusOne function matches that signature, because it takes an Int argument and returns nothing:

```
val plusOne = (i: Int) => { println(i+1) }
```

Now you can pass plusOne into the exec function:

```
exec(plusOne)
```

Because the function is called inside the method, this prints the number 2.

Any function that matches this signature can be passed into the exec method. To demonstrate this, define a new function named plusTen that also takes an Int and returns nothing:

```
val plusTen = (i: Int) => { println(i+10) }
```

Now you can pass it into your exec function, and see that it also works:

```
exec(plusTen)    // prints 11
```

Although these examples are simple, you can see the power of the technique: you can easily swap in interchangeable algorithms. As long as your function signature matches what your method expects, your algorithms can do anything you want. This is comparable to swapping out algorithms in the OOP *Strategy* design pattern.

## Discussion

The general syntax for describing a function as a method parameter is this:

```
parameterName: (parameterType(s)) => returnType
```

Therefore, to define a function that takes a `String` and returns an `Int`, use one of these two signatures:

```
executeFunction(f:(String) => Int)
```

```
// parentheses are optional when the function has only one parameter
executeFunction(f:String => Int)
```

To define a function that takes two `Int`s and returns a `Boolean`, use this signature:

```
executeFunction(f:(Int, Int) => Boolean)
```

The following `exec` method expects a function that takes `String`, `Int`, and `Double` parameters and returns a `Seq[String]`:

```
exec(f:(String, Int, Double) => Seq[String])
```

As shown in the Solution, if a function doesn't return anything, declare its return type as `Unit`:

```
exec(f:(Int) => Unit)
exec(f:Int => Unit)
```

### Passing in a function with other parameters

A function parameter is just like any other method parameter, so a method can accept other parameters in addition to a function.

The following code demonstrates this in a simple example. First, define a simple function:

```
val sayHello = () => println("Hello")
```

Next, define a method that takes this function as a parameter and also takes a second `Int` parameter:

```
def executeXTimes(callback:() => Unit, numTimes: Int) {
  for (i <- 1 to numTimes) callback()
}
```

Next, pass the function value and an `Int` into the method:

```
scala> executeXTimes(sayHello, 3)
Hello
Hello
Hello
```

Though that was a simple example, this technique can be used to pass variables into the method that can then be used by the function, inside the method body. To see how this works, create a method named `executeAndPrint` that takes a function and two `Int` parameters:

```
def executeAndPrint(f:(Int, Int) => Int, x: Int, y: Int) {
  val result = f(x, y)
  println(result)
}
```

This method is more interesting than the previous method, because it takes the Int parameters it's given and passes those parameters to the function it's given in this line of code:

```
val result = f(x, y)
```

To show how this works, create two functions that match the signature of the function that executeAndPrint expects, a sum function and a multiply function:

```
val sum = (x: Int, y: Int) => x + y
val multiply = (x: Int, y: Int) =>  x * y
```

Now you can call executeAndPrint like this, passing in the different functions, along with two Int parameters:

```
executeAndPrint(sum, 2, 9)        // prints 11
executeAndPrint(multiply, 3, 9)   // prints 27
```

This is cool, because the executeAndPrint method doesn't know what algorithm is actually run. All it knows is that it passes the parameters x and y to the function it is given and then prints the result from that function. This is similar to defining an interface in Java and then providing concrete implementations of the interface in multiple classes.

Here's one more example of this three-step process:

```
// 1 - define the method
def exec(callback: (Any, Any) => Unit, x: Any, y: Any) {
  callback(x, y)
}

// 2 - define a function to pass in
val printTwoThings =(a: Any, b: Any) => {
  println(a)
  println(b)
}

// 3 - pass the function and some parameters to the method
case class Person(name: String)
exec(printTwoThings, "Hello", Person("Dave"))
```

Note that in all of the previous examples where you created functions with the val keyword, you could have created methods, and the examples would still work. For instance, you can define printTwoThings as a method, and exec still works:

```
// 2a - define a method to pass in
def printTwoThings (a: Any, b: Any) {
  println(a)
```

```
    println(b)
  }

  // 3a - pass the printTwoThings method to the exec method
  case class Person(name: String)
  exec(printTwoThings, "Hello", Person("Dave"))
```

Behind the scenes, there are differences between these two approaches—for instance, a function implements one of the Function0 to Function22 traits—but Scala is forgiving, and lets you pass in either a method or function, as long as the signature is correct.

# 9.5. Using Closures

## Problem

You want to pass a function around like a variable, and while doing so, you want that function to be able to refer to one or more fields that were in the same scope as the function when it was declared.

## Solution

To demonstrate a closure in Scala, use the following simple (but complete) example:

```
package otherscope {

  class Foo {
    // a method that takes a function and a string, and passes the string into
    // the function, and then executes the function
    def exec(f:(String) => Unit, name: String) {
      f(name)
    }
  }

}

object ClosureExample extends App {

  var hello = "Hello"
  def sayHello(name: String) { println(s"$hello, $name") }

  // execute sayHello from the exec method foo
  val foo = new otherscope.Foo
  foo.exec(sayHello, "Al")

  // change the local variable 'hello', then execute sayHello from
  // the exec method of foo, and see what happens
  hello = "Hola"
  foo.exec(sayHello, "Lorenzo")

}
```

To test this code, save it as a file named *ClosureExample.scala*, then compile and run it. When it's run, the output will be:

```
Hello, Al
Hola, Lorenzo
```

If you're coming to Scala from Java or another OOP language, you might be asking, "How could this possibly work?" Not only did the sayHello method reference the variable hello from within the exec method of the Foo class on the first run (where hello was no longer in scope), but on the second run, it also picked up the change to the hello variable (from Hello to Hola). The simple answer is that Scala supports closure functionality, and this is how closures work.

As Dean Wampler and Alex Payne describe in their book *Programming Scala* (O'Reilly), there are two *free variables* in the sayHello method: name and hello. The name variable is a formal parameter to the function; this is something you're used to.

However, hello is not a formal parameter; it's a reference to a variable in the enclosing scope (similar to the way a method in a Java class can refer to a field in the same class). Therefore, the Scala compiler creates a closure that encompasses (or "closes over") hello.

 You could continue to pass the sayHello method around so it gets farther and farther away from the scope of the hello variable, but in an effort to keep this example simple, it's only passed to one method in a class in a different package. You can verify that hello is not in scope in the Foo class by attempting to print its value in that class or in its exec method, such as with println(hello). You'll find that the code won't compile because hello is not in scope there.

## Discussion

In my research, I've found many descriptions of closures, each with slightly different terminology. Wikipedia defines a closure like this:

> "In computer science, a closure (also lexical closure or function closure) is a function together with a referencing environment for the non-local variables of that function. A closure allows a function to access variables outside its immediate lexical scope."

In his excellent article, Closures in Ruby (*http://bit.ly/12DOhF7*), Paul Cantrell states, "a closure is a block of code which meets three criteria." He defines the criteria as follows:

1. The block of code can be passed around as a value, and

2. It can be executed on demand by anyone who has that value, at which time

3. It can refer to variables from the context in which it was created (i.e., it is closed with respect to variable access, in the mathematical sense of the word "closed").

Personally, I like to think of a closure as being like quantum entanglement, which Einstein referred to as "a spooky action at a distance." Just as quantum entanglement begins with two elements that are together and then separated—but somehow remain aware of each other—a closure begins with a function and a variable defined in the same scope, which are then separated from each other. When the function is executed at some other point in space (scope) and time, it is magically still aware of the variable it referenced in their earlier time together, and even picks up any changes to that variable.

As shown in the Solution, to create a closure in Scala, just define a function that refers to a variable that's in the same scope as its declaration. That function can be used later, even when the variable is no longer in the function's current scope, such as when the function is passed to another class, method, or function.

Any time you run into a situation where you're passing around a function, and wish that function could refer to a variable like this, a closure can be a solution. The variable can be a collection, an `Int` you use as a counter or limit, or anything else that helps to solve a problem. The value you refer to can be a `val`, or as shown in the example, a `var`.

### A second example

If you're new to closures, another example may help demonstrate them. First, start with a simple function named `isOfVotingAge`. This function tests to see if the `age` given to the function is greater than or equal to 18:

```
val isOfVotingAge = (age: Int) => age >= 18
isOfVotingAge(16)  // false
isOfVotingAge(20)  // true
```

Next, to make your function more flexible, instead of hardcoding the value 18 into the function, you can take advantage of this closure technique, and let the function refer to the variable `votingAge` that's in scope when you define the function:

```
var votingAge = 18
val isOfVotingAge = (age: Int) => age >= votingAge
```

When called, `isOfVotingAge` works as before:

```
isOfVotingAge(16)  // false
isOfVotingAge(20)  // true
```

You can now pass `isOfVotingAge` around to other methods and functions:

```
def printResult(f: Int => Boolean, x: Int) {
  println(f(x))
}
printResult(isOfVotingAge, 20)  // true
```

Because you defined votingAge as a var, you can reassign it. How does this affect printResult? Let's see:

```
// change votingAge in one scope
votingAge = 21

// the change to votingAge affects the result
printResult(isOfVotingAge, 20)  // now false
```

Cool. The field and function are still entangled.

### Using closures with other data types

In the two examples shown so far, you've worked with simple String and Int fields, but closures can work with any data type, including collections. For instance, in the following example, the function named addToBasket is defined in the same scope as an ArrayBuffer named fruits:

```
import scala.collection.mutable.ArrayBuffer
val fruits = ArrayBuffer("apple")

// the function addToBasket has a reference to fruits
val addToBasket = (s: String) => {
  fruits += s
  println(fruits.mkString(", "))
}
```

As with the previous example, the addToBasket function can now be passed around as desired, and will always have a reference to the fruits field. To demonstrate this, define a method that accepts a function with addToBasket's signature:

```
def buyStuff(f: String => Unit, s: String) {
  f(s)
}
```

Then pass addToBasket and a String parameter to the method:

```
scala> buyStuff(addToBasket, "cherries")
cherries

scala> buyStuff(addToBasket, "grapes")
cherries, grapes
```

As desired, the elements are added to your ArrayBuffer.

Note that the buyStuff method would typically be in another class, but this example demonstrates the basic idea.

## A comparison to Java

If you're coming to Scala from Java, or an OOP background in general, it may help to see a comparison between this closure technique and what you can currently do in Java. (In Java, there are some closure-like things you can do with inner classes, and closures are intended for addition to Java 8 in Project Lambda (*http://bit.ly/13lvtdW*). But this example attempts to show a simple OOP example.)

The following example shows how a sayHello method and the helloPhrase string are encapsulated in the class Greeter. In the main method, the first two examples with Al and Lorenzo show how the sayHello method can be called directly.

At the end of the main method, the greeter instance is passed to an instance of the Bar class, and greeter's sayHello method is executed from there:

```
public class SimulatedClosure {

    public static void main (String[] args) {
        Greeter greeter = new Greeter();
        greeter.setHelloPhrase("Hello");
        greeter.sayHello("Al");         // "Hello, Al"

        greeter.setHelloPhrase("Hola");
        greeter.sayHello("Lorenzo");    // "Hola, Lorenzo"

        greeter.setHelloPhrase("Yo");
        Bar bar = new Bar(greeter);     // pass the greeter instance to a new Bar
        bar.sayHello("Adrian");         // invoke greeter.sayHello via Bar
    }

}

class Greeter {

    private String helloPhrase;

    public void setHelloPhrase(String helloPhrase) {
        this.helloPhrase = helloPhrase;
    }

    public void sayHello(String name) {
        System.out.println(helloPhrase + ", " + name);
    }

}

class Bar {

    private Greeter greeter;

    public Bar (Greeter greeter) {
        this.greeter = greeter;
```

```
    }

    public void sayHello(String name) {
      greeter.sayHello(name);
    }

  }
```

Running this code prints the following output:

```
Hello, Al
Hola, Lorenzo
Yo, Adrian
```

The end result is similar to the Scala closure approach, but the big differences in this example are that you're passing around a Greeter instance (instead of a function), and sayHello and the helloPhrase are encapsulated in the Greeter class. In the Scala closure solution, you passed around a function that was coupled with a field from another scope.

## See Also

- The voting age example in this recipe was inspired by Mario Gleichmann's example in Functional Scala: Closures (*http://bit.ly/15y1SRx*).

- Paul Cantrell's article, Closures in Ruby (*http://bit.ly/12DOhF7*).

- Recipe 3.18, "Creating Your Own Control Structures", demonstrates the use of multiple parameter lists.

- Java 8's Project Lambda (*http://bit.ly/13lvtdW*).

# 9.6. Using Partially Applied Functions

## Problem

You want to eliminate repetitively passing variables into a function by (a) passing common variables into the function to (b) create a new function that is preloaded with those values, and then (c) use the new function, passing it only the unique variables it needs.

## Solution

The classic example of a partially applied function begins with a simple sum function:

```
val sum = (a: Int, b: Int, c: Int) => a + b + c
```

There's nothing special about this sum function, it's just a normal function. But things get interesting when you supply two of the parameters when calling the function, but don't provide the third parameter:

```
val f = sum(1, 2, _: Int)
```

Because you haven't provided a value for the third parameter, the resulting variable f is a *partially applied function*. You can see this in the REPL:

```
scala> val sum = (a: Int, b: Int, c: Int) => a + b + c
sum: (Int, Int, Int) => Int = <function3>

scala> val f = sum(1, 2, _: Int)
f: Int => Int = <function1>
```

The result in the REPL shows that f is a function that implements the function1 trait, meaning that it takes one argument. Looking at the rest of the signature, you see that it takes an Int argument, and returns an Int value.

When you give f an Int, such as the number 3, you magically get the sum of the three numbers that have been passed into the two functions:

```
scala> f(3)
res0: Int = 6
```

The first two numbers (1 and 2) were passed into the original sum function; that process created the new function named f, which is a partially applied function; then, some time later in the code, the third number (3) was passed into f.

## Discussion

In functional programming languages, when you call a function that has parameters, you are said to be applying the function to the parameters. When all the parameters are passed to the function—something you always do in Java—you have fully applied the function to all of the parameters. But when you give only a subset of the parameters to the function, the result of the expression is a partially applied function.

As demonstrated in the example, this partially applied function is a variable that you can pass around. This variable is called a *function value*, and when you later provide all the parameters needed to complete the function value, the original function is executed and a result is yielded.

This technique has many advantages, including the ability to make life easier for the consumers of a library you create. For instance, when working with HTML, you may want a function that adds a prefix and a suffix to an HTML snippet:

```
def wrap(prefix: String, html: String, suffix: String) = {
  prefix + html + suffix
}
```

If at a certain point in your code, you know that you always want to add the same prefix and suffix to different HTML strings, you can apply those two parameters to the function, without applying the html parameter:

```
val wrapWithDiv = wrap("<div>", _: String, "</div>")
```

Now you can call the new wrapWithDiv function, just passing it the HTML you want to wrap:

```
scala> wrapWithDiv("<p>Hello, world</p>")
res0: String = <div><p>Hello, world</p></div>

scala> wrapWithDiv("<img src=\"/images/foo.png\" />")
res1: String = <div><img src="/images/foo.png" /></div>
```

The wrapWithDiv function is preloaded with the <div> tags you applied, so it can be called with just one argument: the HTML you want to wrap.

As a nice benefit, you can still call the original wrap function if you want:

```
wrap("<pre>", "val x = 1", "</pre>")
```

You can use partially applied functions to make programming easier by binding some arguments—typically some form of local arguments—and leaving the others to be filled in.

# 9.7. Creating a Function That Returns a Function

## Problem

You want to return a function (algorithm) from a function or method.

## Solution

Define a function that returns an algorithm (an anonymous function), assign that to a new function, and then call that new function.

The following code declares an anonymous function that takes a String argument and returns a String:

```
(s: String) => { prefix + " " + s }
```

You can return that anonymous function from the body of another function as follows:

```
def saySomething(prefix: String) = (s: String) => {
  prefix + " " + s
}
```

Because saySomething returns a function, you can assign that resulting function to a variable. The saySomething function requires a String argument, so give it one as you create the resulting function sayHello:

```
val sayHello = saySomething("Hello")
```

The sayHello function is now equivalent to your anonymous function, with the prefix set to hello. Looking back at the anonymous function, you see that it takes a String parameter and returns a String, so you pass it a String:

```
sayHello("Al")
```

Here's what these steps look like in the REPL:

```
scala> def saySomething(prefix: String) = (s: String) => {
     |    prefix + " " + s
     | }
saySomething: (prefix: String)String => java.lang.String

scala> val sayHello = saySomething("Hello")
sayHello: String => java.lang.String = <function1>

scala> sayHello("Al")
res0: java.lang.String = Hello Al
```

## Discussion

If you're new to functional programming, it can help to break this down a little. You can break the expression down into its two components. On the left side of the = symbol you have a normal method declaration:

```
def saySomething(prefix: String)
```

On the right side of the = is a function literal (also known as an anonymous function):

```
(s: String) => { prefix + " " + s }
```

### Another example

As you can imagine, you can use this approach any time you want to encapsulate an algorithm inside a function. A bit like a Factory or Strategy pattern, the function your method returns can be based on the input parameter it receives. For example, create a greeting method that returns an appropriate greeting based on the language specified:

```
def greeting(language: String) = (name: String) => {
  language match {
    case "english" => "Hello, " + name
    case "spanish" => "Buenos dias, " + name
  }
}
```

If it's not clear that greeting is returning a function, you can make the code a little more explicit:

```
def greeting(language: String) = (name: String) => {
  val english = () => "Hello, " + name
  val spanish = () => "Buenos dias, " + name
  language match {
```

```
      case "english" => println("returning 'english' function")
                        english()
      case "spanish" => println("returning 'spanish' function")
                        spanish()
  }
}
```

Here's what this second method looks like when it's invoked in the REPL:

```
scala> val hello = greeting("english")
hello: String => java.lang.String = <function1>

scala> val buenosDias = greeting("spanish")
buenosDias: String => java.lang.String = <function1>

scala> hello("Al")
returning 'english' function
res0: java.lang.String = Hello, Al

scala> buenosDias("Lorenzo")
returning 'spanish' function
res1: java.lang.String = Buenos dias, Lorenzo
```

You can use this recipe any time you want to encapsulate one or more functions behind a method, and is similar in that effect to the Factory and Strategy patterns.

## See Also

My Java Factory Pattern example (*http://bit.ly/15HJ30l*)

# 9.8. Creating Partial Functions

## Problem

You want to define a function that will only work for a subset of possible input values, or you want to define a series of functions that only work for a subset of input values, and combine those functions to completely solve a problem.

## Solution

A *partial function* is a function that does not provide an answer for every possible input value it can be given. It provides an answer only for a subset of possible data, and defines the data it can handle. In Scala, a partial function can also be queried to determine if it can handle a particular value.

As a simple example, imagine a normal function that divides one number by another:

```
val divide = (x: Int) => 42 / x
```

As defined, this function blows up when the input parameter is zero:

```
scala> divide(0)
java.lang.ArithmeticException: / by zero
```

Although you can handle this particular situation by catching and throwing an exception, Scala lets you define the `divide` function as a `PartialFunction`. When doing so, you also explicitly state that the function is defined when the input parameter is not zero:

```
val divide = new PartialFunction[Int, Int] {
  def apply(x: Int) = 42 / x
  def isDefinedAt(x: Int) = x != 0
}
```

With this approach, you can do several nice things. One thing you can do is test the function before you attempt to use it:

```
scala> divide.isDefinedAt(1)
res0: Boolean = true

scala> if (divide.isDefinedAt(1)) divide(1)
res1: AnyVal = 42

scala> divide.isDefinedAt(0)
res2: Boolean = false
```

This isn't all you can do with partial functions. You'll see shortly that other code can take advantage of partial functions to provide elegant and concise solutions.

Whereas that `divide` function is explicit about what data it handles, partial functions are often written using `case` statements:

```
val divide2: PartialFunction[Int, Int] = {
  case d: Int if d != 0 => 42 / d
}
```

Although this code doesn't explicitly implement the `isDefinedAt` method, it works exactly the same as the previous `divide` function definition:

```
scala> divide2.isDefinedAt(0)
res0: Boolean = false

scala> divide2.isDefinedAt(1)
res1: Boolean = true
```

### The PartialFunction explained

The `PartialFunction` Scaladoc describes a partial function in this way:

> A partial function of type PartialFunction[A, B] is a unary function where the domain does not necessarily include all values of type A. The function isDefinedAt allows [you] to test dynamically if a value is in the domain of the function.

This helps to explain why the last example with the match expression (case statement) works: the isDefinedAt method dynamically tests to see if the given value is in the domain of the function (i.e., it is handled, or accounted for).

The signature of the PartialFunction trait looks like this:

```
trait PartialFunction[-A, +B] extends (A) => B
```

As discussed in other recipes, the => symbol can be thought of as a transformer, and in this case, the (A) => B can be interpreted as a function that transforms a type A into a resulting type B.

The example method transformed an input Int into an output Int, but if it returned a String instead, it would be declared like this:

```
PartialFunction[Int, String]
```

For example, the following method uses this signature:

```
// converts 1 to "one", etc., up to 5
val convertLowNumToString = new PartialFunction[Int, String] {
  val nums = Array("one", "two", "three", "four", "five")
  def apply(i: Int) = nums(i-1)
  def isDefinedAt(i: Int) = i > 0 && i < 6
}
```

### orElse and andThen

A terrific feature of partial functions is that you can chain them together. For instance, one method may only work with even numbers, and another method may only work with odd numbers. Together they can solve all integer problems.

In the following example, two functions are defined that can each handle a small number of Int inputs, and convert them to String results:

```
// converts 1 to "one", etc., up to 5
val convert1to5 = new PartialFunction[Int, String] {
  val nums = Array("one", "two", "three", "four", "five")
  def apply(i: Int) = nums(i-1)
  def isDefinedAt(i: Int) = i > 0 && i < 6
}

// converts 6 to "six", etc., up to 10
val convert6to10 = new PartialFunction[Int, String] {
  val nums = Array("six", "seven", "eight", "nine", "ten")
  def apply(i: Int) = nums(i-6)
  def isDefinedAt(i: Int) = i > 5 && i < 11
}
```

Taken separately, they can each handle only five numbers. But combined with orElse, they can handle ten:

```
scala> val handle1to10 = convert1to5 orElse convert6to10
handle1to10: PartialFunction[Int,String] = <function1>
```

```
scala> handle1to10(3)
res0: String = three

scala> handle1to10(8)
res1: String = eight
```

The orElse method comes from the Scala PartialFunction trait, which also includes the andThen method to further help chain partial functions together.

## Discussion

It's important to know about partial functions, not just to have another tool in your toolbox, but because they are used in the APIs of some libraries, including the Scala collections library.

One example of where you'll run into partial functions is with the collect method on collections' classes. The collect method takes a partial function as input, and as its Scaladoc describes, collect "Builds a new collection by applying a partial function to all elements of this list on which the function is defined."

For instance, the divide function shown earlier is a partial function that is not defined at the Int value zero. Here's that function again:

```
val divide: PartialFunction[Int, Int] = {
  case d: Int if d != 0 => 42 / d
}
```

If you attempt to use this function with the map method, it will explode with a MatchError:

```
scala> List(0,1,2) map { divide }
scala.MatchError: 0 (of class java.lang.Integer)
stack trace continues ...
```

However, if you use the same function with the collect method, it works fine:

```
scala> List(0,1,2) collect { divide }
res0: List[Int] = List(42, 21)
```

This is because the collect method is written to test the isDefinedAt method for each element it's given. As a result, it doesn't run the divide algorithm when the input value is 0 (but does run it for every other element).

You can see the collect method work in other situations, such as passing it a List that contains a mix of data types, with a function that works only with Int values:

```
scala> List(42, "cat") collect { case i: Int => i + 1 }
res0: List[Int] = List(43)
```

Because it checks the isDefinedAt method under the covers, collect can handle the fact that your anonymous function can't work with a String as input.

The PartialFunction Scaladoc demonstrates this same technique in a slightly different way. In the first example, it shows how to create a list of even numbers by defining a PartialFunction named isEven, and using that function with the collect method:

```
scala> val sample = 1 to 5
sample: scala.collection.immutable.Range.Inclusive = Range(1, 2, 3, 4, 5)

scala> val isEven: PartialFunction[Int, String] = {
     |  case x if x % 2 == 0 => x + " is even"
     | }
isEven: PartialFunction[Int,String] = <function1>

scala> val evenNumbers = sample collect isEven
evenNumbers: scala.collection.immutable.IndexedSeq[String] =
  Vector(2 is even, 4 is even)
```

Similarly, an isOdd function can be defined, and the two functions can be joined by orElse to work with the map method:

```
scala> val isOdd: PartialFunction[Int, String] = {
     |  case x if x % 2 == 1 => x + " is odd"
     | }
isOdd: PartialFunction[Int,String] = <function1>

scala> val numbers = sample map (isEven orElse isOdd)
numbers: scala.collection.immutable.IndexedSeq[String] =
    Vector(1 is odd, 2 is even, 3 is odd, 4 is even, 5 is odd)
```

 Portions of this recipe were inspired by Erik Bruchez's blog post, titled, "Scala partial functions (without a PhD)."

## See Also

- Erik Bruchez's blog post (*http://bit.ly/15xZNVE*)
- PartialFunction trait (*http://bit.ly/18YmK9Z*)
- Wikipedia definition of a partial function (*http://bit.ly/1dzVkF5*)

# 9.9. A Real-World Example

## Problem

Understanding functional programming concepts is one thing; putting them into practice in a real project is another. You'd like to see a real example of them in action.

# Solution

To demonstrate some of the techniques introduced in this chapter, the following example shows one way to implement Newton's Method, a mathematical method that can be used to solve the roots of equations.

As you can see from the code, the method named newtonsMethod takes functions as its first two parameters. It also takes two other Double parameters, and returns a Double. The two functions that are passed in should be the original equation (fx) and the derivative of that equation (fxPrime).

The method newtonsMethodHelper also takes two functions as parameters, so you can see how the functions are passed from newtonsMethod to newtonsMethodHelper.

Here is the complete source code for this example:

```
object NewtonsMethod {

  def main(args: Array[String]) {
    driver
  }

  /**
   * A "driver" function to test Newton's method.
   * Start with (a) the desired f(x) and f'(x) equations,
   * (b) an initial guess and (c) tolerance values.
   */
  def driver {
    // the f(x) and f'(x) functions
    val fx = (x: Double) => 3*x + math.sin(x) - math.pow(math.E, x)
    val fxPrime = (x: Double) => 3 + math.cos(x) - math.pow(Math.E, x)

    val initialGuess = 0.0
    val tolerance = 0.00005

    // pass f(x) and f'(x) to the Newton's Method function, along with
    // the initial guess and tolerance
    val answer = newtonsMethod(fx, fxPrime, initialGuess, tolerance)

    println(answer)
  }

  /**
   * Newton's Method for solving equations.
   * @todo check that |f(xNext)| is greater than a second tolerance value
   * @todo check that f'(x) != 0
   */
  def newtonsMethod(fx: Double => Double,
                    fxPrime: Double => Double,
                    x: Double,
                    tolerance: Double): Double = {
    var x1 = x
```

```
    var xNext = newtonsMethodHelper(fx, fxPrime, x1)
    while (math.abs(xNext - x1) > tolerance) {
      x1 = xNext
      println(xNext) // debugging (intermediate values)
      xNext = newtonsMethodHelper(fx, fxPrime, x1)
    }

    xNext
  }

  /**
   * This is the "x2 = x1 - f(x1)/f'(x1)" calculation
   */
  def newtonsMethodHelper(fx: Double => Double,
                          fxPrime: Double => Double,
                          x: Double): Double = {
    x - fx(x) / fxPrime(x)
  }

}
```

## Discussion

As you can see, a majority of this code involves defining functions, passing those functions to methods, and then invoking the functions from within a method.

The method name newtonsMethod will work for any two functions fx and fxPrime, where fxPrime is the derivative of fx (within the limits of the "to do" items that are not implemented).

To experiment with this example, try changing the functions fx and fxPrime, or implement the @todo items in newtonsMethod.

 The algorithm shown comes from an old textbook titled *Applied Numerical Analysis*, by Gerald and Wheatley, where the approach was demonstrated in pseudocode.

## See Also

- More details on this example (*http://bit.ly/13dPSpJ*)
- Newton's Method (*http://bit.ly/18jyRiv*)

# CHAPTER 10

# Collections

## Introduction

Scala's collection classes are rich, deep, and differ significantly from the Java collections, all of which makes learning them a bit of a speed bump for developers coming to Scala from Java.

When a Java developer first comes to Scala, she might think, "Okay, I'll use lists and arrays, right?" Well, not really. The Scala List class is very different from the Java List classes—including the part where it's immutable—and although the Scala Array is an improvement on the Java array in most ways, it's not even recommended as the "go to" sequential collection class.

Because there are many collections classes to choose from, and each of those classes offers many methods, a goal of this chapter (and the next) is to help guide you through this plethora of options to find the solutions you need. Recipes will help you decide which collections to use in different situations, and also choose a method to solve a problem. To help with this, the methods that are common to all collections are shown in this chapter, and methods specific to collections like List, Array, Map, and Set are shown in Chapter 11.

### A Few Important Concepts

There are a few important concepts to know when working with the methods of the Scala collection classes:

- What a predicate is
- What an anonymous function is
- Implied loops

A *predicate* is simply a method, function, or anonymous function that takes one or more parameters and returns a Boolean value. For instance, the following method returns true or false, so it's a predicate:

```
def isEven (i: Int) = if (i % 2 == 0) true else false
```

That's a simple concept, but you'll hear the term so often when working with collection methods that it's important to mention it.

The concept of an *anonymous function* is also important. They're described in depth in Recipe 9.1, but here's an example of the long form for an anonymous function:

```
(i: Int) => i % 2 == 0
```

Here's the short form of the same function:

```
_ % 2 == 0
```

That doesn't look like much by itself, but when it's combined with the filter method on a collection, it makes for a lot of power in just a little bit of code:

```
scala> val list = List.range(1, 10)
list: List[Int] = List(1, 2, 3, 4, 5, 6, 7, 8, 9)

scala> val events = list.filter(_ % 2 == 0)
events: List[Int] = List(2, 4, 6, 8)
```

This is a nice lead-in into the third topic: *implied loops*. As you can see from that example, the filter method contains a loop that applies your function to every element in the collection and returns a new collection. You could live without the filter method and write equivalent code like this:

```
for {
  e <- list
  if e % 2 == 0
} yield e
```

But I think you'll agree that the filter approach is both more concise and easier to read.

Collection methods like filter, foreach, map, reduceLeft, and many more have loops built into their algorithms. As a result, you'll write far fewer loops when writing Scala code than with another language like Java.

# 10.1. Understanding the Collections Hierarchy

## Problem

The Scala collections hierarchy is very rich (deep and wide), and understanding how it's organized can be helpful when choosing a collection to solve a problem.

## Solution

Figure 10-1, which shows the traits from which the Vector class inherits, demonstrates some of the complexity of the Scala collections hierarchy.

*Figure 10-1. The traits inherited by the Vector class*

Because Scala classes can inherit from traits, and well-designed traits are granular, a class hierarchy can look like this. However, don't let Figure 10-1 throw you for a loop: you don't need to know all those traits to use a Vector. In fact, using a Vector is straightforward:

```
val v = Vector(1, 2, 3)
v.sum                  // 6
v.filter(_ > 1)        // Vector(2, 3)
v.map(_ * 2)           // Vector(2, 4, 6)
```

At a high level, Scala's collection classes begin with the Traversable and Iterable traits, and extend into the three main categories of sequences (Seq), sets (Set), and maps (Map). Sequences further branch off into *indexed* and *linear* sequences, as shown in Figure 10-2.

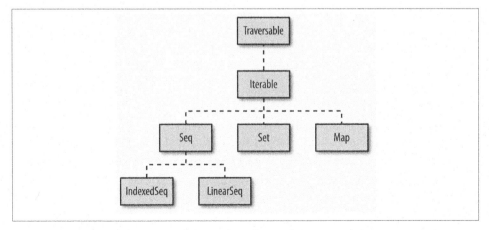

*Figure 10-2. A high-level view of the Scala collections*

The Traversable trait lets you traverse an entire collection, and its Scaladoc states that it "implements the behavior common to all collections in terms of a foreach method," which lets you traverse the collection repeatedly.

The Iterable trait defines an *iterator*, which lets you loop through a collection's elements one at a time, but when using an iterator, the collection can be traversed only once, because each element is consumed during the iteration process.

### Sequences

Digging a little deeper into the *sequence* hierarchy, Scala contains a large number of sequences, many of which are shown in Figure 10-3.

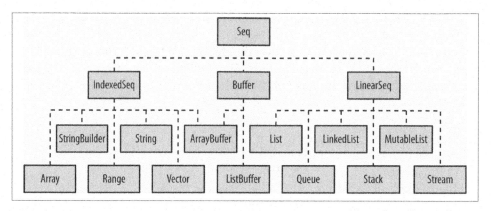

*Figure 10-3. A portion of the Scala sequence hierarchy*

These traits and classes are described in Tables 10-1 through 10-4.

As shown in Figure 10-3, sequences branch off into two main categories: *indexed sequences* and *linear sequences* (linked lists). An IndexedSeq indicates that random access of elements is efficient, such as accessing an Array element as arr(5000). By default, specifying that you want an IndexedSeq with Scala 2.10.x creates a Vector:

```
scala> val x = IndexedSeq(1,2,3)
x: IndexedSeq[Int] = Vector(1, 2, 3)
```

A LinearSeq implies that the collection can be efficiently split into head and tail components, and it's common to work with them using the head, tail, and isEmpty methods. Note that creating a LinearSeq creates a List, which is a singly linked list:

```
scala> val seq = scala.collection.immutable.LinearSeq(1,2,3)
seq: scala.collection.immutable.LinearSeq[Int] = List(1, 2, 3)
```

## Maps

Like a Java `Map`, Ruby `Hash`, or Python dictionary, a Scala `Map` is a collection of key/value pairs, where all the keys must be unique. The most common map classes are shown in Figure 10-4.

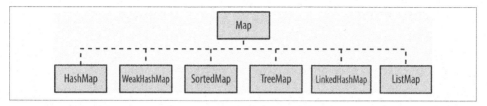

*Figure 10-4. Common map classes*

Map traits and classes are discussed in Table 10-5. When you just need a simple, *immutable* map, you can create one without requiring an import:

```
scala> val m = Map(1 -> "a", 2 -> "b")
m: scala.collection.immutable.Map[Int,java.lang.String] = Map(1 -> a, 2 -> b)
```

The *mutable* map is not in scope by default, so you must import it (or specify its full path) to use it:

```
scala> val m = collection.mutable.Map(1 -> "a", 2 -> "b")
m: scala.collection.mutable.Map[Int,String] = Map(2 -> b, 1 -> a)
```

## Sets

Like a Java `Set`, a Scala `Set` is a collection of unique elements. The common set classes are shown in Figure 10-5.

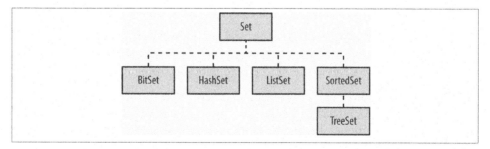

*Figure 10-5. Common set classes*

Set traits and classes are discussed in Table 10-6, but as a quick preview, if you just need an immutable set, you can create it like this, without needing an import statement:

```
scala> val set = Set(1, 2, 3)
set: scala.collection.immutable.Set[Int] = Set(1, 2, 3)
```

Just like a map, if you want to use a mutable set, you must import it, or specify its complete path:

```
scala> val s = collection.mutable.Set(1, 2, 3)
s: scala.collection.mutable.Set[Int] = Set(1, 2, 3)
```

### More collection classes

There are many additional collection traits and classes, including `Stream`, `Queue`, `Stack`, and `Range`. You can also create *views* on collections (like a database view); use iterators; and work with the `Option`, `Some`, and `None` types as collections. All of these classes (and objects) are demonstrated in this and the next chapter.

### Strict and lazy collections

Collections can also be thought of in terms of being *strict* or *lazy*. See the next recipe for a discussion of these terms.

# 10.2. Choosing a Collection Class

## Problem

You want to choose a Scala collection class to solve a particular problem.

## Solution

There are three main categories of collection classes to choose from:

- Sequence
- Map
- Set

A *sequence* is a linear collection of elements and may be indexed or linear (a linked list). A *map* contains a collection of key/value pairs, like a Java `Map`, Ruby `Hash`, or Python dictionary. A *set* is a collection that contains no duplicate elements.

In addition to these three main categories, there are other useful collection types, including `Stack`, `Queue`, and `Range`. There are a few other classes that act like collections, including tuples, enumerations, and the `Option/Some/None` and `Try/Success/Failure` classes.

### Choosing a sequence

When choosing a *sequence* (a sequential collection of elements), you have two main decisions:

- Should the sequence be indexed (like an array), allowing rapid access to any elements, or should it be implemented as a linked list?
- Do you want a mutable or immutable collection?

As of Scala 2.10, the recommended, general-purpose, "go to" sequential collections for the combinations of mutable/immutable and indexed/linear are shown in Table 10-1.

*Table 10-1. Scala's general-purpose sequential collections*

|  | Immutable | Mutable |
| --- | --- | --- |
| Indexed | Vector | ArrayBuffer |
| Linear (Linked lists) | List | ListBuffer |

As an example of reading that table, if you want an immutable, indexed collection, in general you should use a Vector; if you want a mutable, indexed collection, use an ArrayBuffer (and so on).

While those are the general-purpose recommendations, there are many more sequence alternatives. The most common *immutable* sequence choices are shown in Table 10-2.

*Table 10-2. Main immutable sequence choices*

|  | IndexedSeq | LinearSeq | Description |
| --- | --- | --- | --- |
| List |  | ✓ | A singly linked list. Suited for recursive algorithms that work by splitting the head from the remainder of the list. |
| Queue |  | ✓ | A first-in, first-out data structure. |
| Range | ✓ |  | A range of integer values. |
| Stack |  | ✓ | A last-in, first-out data structure. |
| Stream |  | ✓ | Similar to List, but it's lazy and persistent. Good for a large or infinite sequence, similar to a Haskell List. |
| String | ✓ |  | Can be treated as an immutable, indexed sequence of characters. |
| Vector | ✓ |  | The "go to" immutable, indexed sequence. The Scaladoc describes it as, "Implemented as a set of nested arrays that's efficient at splitting and joining." |

The most common *mutable* sequence choices are shown in Table 10-3. Queue and Stack are also in this table because there are mutable and immutable versions of these classes.

*Table 10-3. Main mutable sequence choices*

|  | IndexedSeq | LinearSeq | Description |
| --- | --- | --- | --- |
| Array | ✓ |  | Backed by a Java array, its elements are mutable, but it can't change in size. |
| ArrayBuffer | ✓ |  | The "go to" class for a mutable, sequential collection. The amortized cost for appending elements is constant. |

| | IndexedSeq | LinearSeq | Description |
|---|---|---|---|
| ArrayStack | ✓ | | A last-in, first-out data structure. Prefer over `Stack` when performance is important. |
| DoubleLinkedList | | ✓ | Like a singly linked list, but with a `prev` method as well. The documentation (*http://bit.ly/1albKiD*) states, "The additional links make element removal very fast." |
| LinkedList | | ✓ | A mutable, singly linked list. |
| ListBuffer | | ✓ | Like an `ArrayBuffer`, but backed by a list. The documentation (*http://bit.ly/1albKiD*) states, "If you plan to convert the buffer to a list, use `ListBuffer` instead of `ArrayBuffer`." Offers constant-time prepend and append; most other operations are linear. |
| MutableList | | ✓ | A mutable, singly linked list with constant-time append. |
| Queue | | ✓ | A first-in, first-out data structure. |
| Stack | | ✓ | A last-in, first-out data structure. (The documentation suggests that an `ArrayStack` is slightly more efficient.) |
| StringBuilder | ✓ | | Used to build strings, as in a loop. Like the Java `StringBuilder`. |

In addition to the information shown in these tables, performance can be a consideration. See Recipe 10.4, "Understanding the Performance of Collections", if performance is important to your selection process.

When creating an API for a library, you may want to refer to your sequences in terms of their superclasses. Table 10-4 shows the traits that are often used when referring generically to a collection in an API.

*Table 10-4. Traits commonly used in library APIs*

| Trait | Description |
|---|---|
| IndexedSeq | Implies that random access of elements is efficient. |
| LinearSeq | Implies that linear access to elements is efficient. |
| Seq | Used when it isn't important to indicate that the sequence is indexed or linear in nature. |

Of course if the collection you're returning can be *very* generic, you can also refer to the collections as `Iterable` or `Traversable`. This is the rough equivalent of declaring that a Java method returns `Collection`.

You can also learn more about declaring the type a method returns by looking at the "code assist" tool in your IDE. For instance, when I create a new `Vector` in Eclipse and then look at the methods available on a `Vector` instance, I see that the methods return types such as `GenSeqLike`, `IndexedSeqLike`, `IterableLike`, `TraversableLike`, and `TraversableOnce`. You don't have to be this specific with the types your methods return—certainly not initially—but it's usually a good practice to identify the *intent* of what you're really returning, so you can declare these more specific types once you get used to them.

## Choosing a map

Choosing a map class is easier than choosing a sequence. There are the base mutable and immutable map classes, a `SortedMap` trait to keep elements in sorted order by key, a `LinkedHashMap` to store elements in insertion order, and a few other maps for special purposes. These options are shown in Table 10-5. (Quotes in the descriptions come from the Scaladoc for each class.)

*Table 10-5. Common map choices, including whether immutable or mutable versions are available*

| | Immutable | Mutable | Description |
|---|---|---|---|
| HashMap | ✓ | ✓ | The immutable version "implements maps using a hash trie"; the mutable version "implements maps using a hashtable." |
| LinkedHashMap | | ✓ | "Implements mutable maps using a hashtable." Returns elements by the order in which they were inserted. |
| ListMap | ✓ | ✓ | A map implemented using a list data structure. Returns elements in the opposite order by which they were inserted, as though each element is inserted at the head of the map. |
| Map | ✓ | ✓ | The base map, with both mutable and immutable implementations. |
| SortedMap | ✓ | | A base trait that stores its keys in sorted order. (Creating a variable as a `SortedMap` currently returns a `TreeMap`.) |
| TreeMap | ✓ | | An immutable, sorted map, implemented as a red-black tree. |
| WeakHashMap | | ✓ | A hash map with weak references, it's a wrapper around `java.util.WeakHashMap`. |

You can also create a thread-safe mutable map by mixing the `SynchronizedMap` trait into the map implementation you want. See the map discussion in the Scala Collections Overview (*http://bit.ly/13lzu1T*) for more information.

## Choosing a set

Choosing a set is similar to choosing a map. There are base mutable and immutable set classes, a `SortedSet` to return elements in sorted order by key, a `LinkedHashSet` to store elements in insertion order, and a few other sets for special purposes. The common classes are shown in Table 10-6. (Quotes in the descriptions come from the Scaladoc for each class.)

*Table 10-6. Common set choices, including whether immutable or mutable versions are available*

| | Immutable | Mutable | |
|---|---|---|---|
| BitSet | ✓ | ✓ | A set of "non-negative integers represented as variable-size arrays of bits packed into 64-bit words." Used to save memory when you have a set of integers. |
| HashSet | ✓ | ✓ | The immutable version "implements sets using a hash trie"; the mutable version "implements sets using a hashtable." |

| | Immutable | Mutable | |
|---|:---:|:---:|---|
| LinkedHashSet | | ✓ | A mutable set implemented using a hashtable. Returns elements in the order in which they were inserted. |
| ListSet | ✓ | | A set implemented using a list structure. |
| TreeSet | ✓ | ✓ | The immutable version "implements immutable sets using a tree." The mutable version is a mutable SortedSet with "an immutable AVL Tree as underlying data structure." |
| Set | ✓ | ✓ | Generic base traits, with both mutable and immutable implementations. |
| SortedSet | ✓ | ✓ | A base trait. (Creating a variable as a SortedSet returns a TreeSet.) |

You can also create a thread-safe mutable set by mixing the SynchronizedSet trait into the set implementation you want. See the Scala Collections Overview discussion of maps and sets (*http://bit.ly/13lzu1T*) for more information.

## Types that act like collections

Scala offers many other collection types, and some types that act like collections. Table 10-7 provides descriptions of several types that act somewhat like collections, even though they aren't.

*Table 10-7. Other collections classes (and types that act like collections)*

| | Description |
|---|---|
| Enumeration | A finite collection of constant values (i.e., the days in a week or months in a year). |
| Iterator | An iterator isn't a collection; instead, it gives you a way to access the elements in a collection. It does, however, define many of the methods you'll see in a normal collection class, including foreach, map, flatMap, etc. You can also convert an iterator to a collection when needed. |
| Option | Acts as a collection that contains zero or one elements. The Some class and None object extend Option. Some is a container for one element, and None holds zero elements. |
| Tuple | Supports a heterogeneous collection of elements. There is no one "Tuple" class; tuples are implemented as case classes ranging from Tuple1 to Tuple22, which support 1 to 22 elements. |

## Strict and lazy collections

To understand strict and lazy collections, it helps to first understand the concept of a transformer method. A *transformer method* is a method that constructs a new collection from an existing collection. This includes methods like map, filter, reverse, etc.—any method that transforms the input collection to a new output collection.

Given that definition, collections can also be thought of in terms of being strict or lazy. In a *strict* collection, memory for the elements is allocated immediately, and all of its elements are immediately evaluated when a transformer method is invoked. In a *lazy* collection, memory for the elements is not allocated immediately, and transformer methods do not construct new elements until they are demanded.

All of the collection classes except `Stream` are strict, but the other collection classes can be converted to a lazy collection by creating a *view* on the collection. See Recipe 10.24, "Creating a Lazy View on a Collection", for more information on this approach.

## See Also

- In addition to my own experience using the collections, most of the information used to create these tables comes from the Scaladoc of each type, and the Scala Collections Overview documentation (*http://bit.ly/1bCEnM3*).
- Recipe 10.1, "Understanding the Collections Hierarchy".
- Recipe 10.4, "Understanding the Performance of Collections".

# 10.3. Choosing a Collection Method to Solve a Problem

## Problem

There is a large number of methods available to Scala collections, and you need to choose a method to solve a problem.

## Solution

The Scala collection classes provide a wealth of methods that can be used to manipulate data. Most methods take either a function or a predicate as an argument. (A *predicate* is just a function that returns a Boolean.)

The methods that are available are listed in two ways in this recipe. In the next few paragraphs, the methods are grouped into categories to help you easily find what you need. In the tables that follow, a brief description and method signature is provided.

### Methods organized by category

*Filtering methods*

Methods that can be used to filter a collection include `collect`, `diff`, `distinct`, `drop`, `dropWhile`, `filter`, `filterNot`, `find`, `foldLeft`, `foldRight`, `head`, `headOption`, `init`, `intersect`, `last`, `lastOption`, `reduceLeft`, `reduceRight`, `remove`, `slice`, `tail`, `take`, `takeWhile`, and `union`.

*Transformer methods*

Transformer methods take at least one input collection to create a new output collection, typically using an algorithm you provide. They include `+`, `++`, `-`, `--`, `diff`, `distinct`, `collect`, `flatMap`, `map`, `reverse`, `sortWith`, `takeWhile`, `zip`, and `zipWithIndex`.

*Grouping methods*

These methods let you take an existing collection and create multiple groups from that one collection. These methods include `groupBy`, `partition`, `sliding`, `span`, `splitAt`, and `unzip`.

*Informational and mathematical methods*

These methods provide information about a collection, and include `canEqual`, `contains`, `containsSlice`, `count`, `endsWith`, `exists`, `find`, `forAll`, `has-DefiniteSize`, `indexOf`, `indexOfSlice`, `indexWhere`, `isDefinedAt`, `isEmpty`, `lastIndexOf`, `lastIndexOfSlice`, `lastIndexWhere`, `max`, `min`, `nonEmpty`, `product`, `segmentLength`, `size`, `startsWith`, `sum`. The methods `foldLeft`, `foldRight`, `reduceLeft`, and `reduceRight` can also be used with a function you supply to obtain information about a collection.

*Others*

A few other methods are hard to categorize, including `par`, `view`, `flatten`, `foreach`, and `mkString`. `par` creates a parallel collection from an existing collection; `view` creates a lazy view on a collection (see Recipe 10.24); `flatten` converts a list of lists down to one list; `foreach` is like a for loop, letting you iterate over the elements in a collection; `mkString` lets you build a `String` from a collection.

There are even more methods than those listed here. For instance, there's a collection of `to*` methods that let you convert the current collection (a `List`, for example) to other collection types (`Array`, `Buffer`, `Vector`, etc.). Check the Scaladoc for your collection class to find more built-in methods.

## Common collection methods

The following tables list the most common collection methods.

Table 10-8 lists methods that are common to all collections via `Traversable`. The following symbols are used in the first column of the table:

- c refers to a collection
- f refers to a function
- p refers to a predicate
- n refers to a number
- op refers to a simple operation (usually a simple function)

Additional methods for mutable and immutable collections are listed in Tables 10-9 and 10-10, respectively.

*Table 10-8. Common methods on Traversable collections*

| Method | Description |
| --- | --- |
| c collect f | Builds a new collection by applying a partial function to all elements of the collection on which the function is defined. |
| c count p | Counts the number of elements in the collection for which the predicate is satisfied. |
| c1 diff c2 | Returns the difference of the elements in c1 and c2. |
| c drop n | Returns all elements in the collection except the first n elements. |
| c dropWhile p | Returns a collection that contains the "longest prefix of elements that satisfy the predicate." |
| c exists p | Returns true if the predicate is true for any element in the collection. |
| c filter p | Returns all elements from the collection for which the predicate is true. |
| c filterNot p | Returns all elements from the collection for which the predicate is false. |
| c find p | Returns the first element that matches the predicate as Some[A]. Returns None if no match is found. |
| c flatten | Converts a collection of collections (such as a list of lists) to a single collection (single list). |
| c flatMap f | Returns a new collection by applying a function to all elements of the collection c (like map), and then flattening the elements of the resulting collections. |
| c foldLeft(z)(op) | Applies the operation to successive elements, going from left to right, starting at element z. |
| c foldRight(z)(op) | Applies the operation to successive elements, going from right to left, starting at element z. |
| c forAll p | Returns true if the predicate is true for all elements, false otherwise. |
| c foreach f | Applies the function f to all elements of the collection. |
| c groupBy f | Partitions the collection into a Map of collections according to the function. |
| c hasDefiniteSize | Tests whether the collection has a finite size. (Returns false for a Stream or Iterator, for example.) |
| c head | Returns the first element of the collection. Throws a NoSuchElementException if the collection is empty. |
| c headOption | Returns the first element of the collection as Some[A] if the element exists, or None if the collection is empty. |
| c init | Selects all elements from the collection except the last one. Throws an UnsupportedOperationException if the collection is empty. |
| c1 intersect c2 | On collections that support it, it returns the intersection of the two collections (the elements common to both collections). |
| c isEmpty | Returns true if the collection is empty, false otherwise. |
| c last | Returns the last element from the collection. Throws a NoSuchElementException if the collection is empty. |
| c lastOption | Returns the last element of the collection as Some[A] if the element exists, or None if the collection is empty. |
| c map f | Creates a new collection by applying the function to all the elements of the collection. |
| c max | Returns the largest element from the collection. |
| c min | Returns the smallest element from the collection. |

| Method | Description |
|---|---|
| c nonEmpty | Returns `true` if the collection is not empty. |
| c par | Returns a parallel implementation of the collection, e.g., `Array` returns `ParArray`. |
| c partition p | Returns two collections according to the predicate algorithm. |
| c product | Returns the multiple of all elements in the collection. |
| c reduceLeft op | The same as `foldLeft`, but begins at the first element of the collection. |
| c reduceRight op | The same as `foldRight`, but begins at the last element of the collection. |
| c reverse | Returns a collection with the elements in reverse order. (Not available on `Traversable`, but common to most collections, from `GenSeqLike`.) |
| c size | Returns the size of the collection. |
| c slice(from, to) | Returns the interval of elements beginning at element `from` and ending at element `to`. |
| c sortWith f | Returns a version of the collection sorted by the comparison function f. |
| c span p | Returns a collection of two collections; the first created by `c.takeWhile(p)`, and the second created by `c.dropWhile(p)`. |
| c splitAt n | Returns a collection of two collections by splitting the collection c at element n. |
| c sum | Returns the sum of all elements in the collection. |
| c tail | Returns all elements from the collection except the first element. |
| c take n | Returns the first n elements of the collection. |
| c takeWhile p | Returns elements from the collection while the predicate is `true`. Stops when the predicate becomes `false`. |
| c1 union c2 | Returns the union (all elements) of two collections. |
| c unzip | The opposite of `zip`, breaks a collection into two collections by dividing each element into two pieces, as in breaking up a collection of `Tuple2` elements. |
| c view | Returns a nonstrict (lazy) view of the collection. |
| c1 zip c2 | Creates a collection of pairs by matching the element 0 of c1 with element 0 of c2, element 1 of c1 with element 1 of c2, etc. |
| c zipWithIndex | Zips the collection with its indices. |

## Mutable collection methods

Table 10-9 shows the common methods for mutable collections. (Although these are all methods, they're often referred to as operators, because that's what they look like.)

*Table 10-9. Common operators (methods) on mutable collections*

| Operator (method) | Description |
|---|---|
| c += x | Adds the element x to the collection c. |
| c += (x,y,z) | Adds the elements x, y, and z to the collection c. |
| c1 ++= c2 | Adds the elements in the collection c2 to the collection c1. |
| c -= x | Removes the element x from the collection c. |
| c -= (x,y,z) | Removes the elements x , y, and z from the collection c. |

| Operator (method) | Description |
| --- | --- |
| c1 --= c2 | Removes the elements in the collection c2 from the collection c1. |
| c(n) = x | Assigns the value x to the element c(n). |
| c clear | Removes all elements from the collection. |
| c remove n<br>c.remove(n, len) | Removes the element at position n, or the elements beginning at position n and continuing for length len. |

There are additional methods, but these are the most common. See the Scaladoc for the mutable collection you're working with for more methods.

### Immutable collection operators

Table 10-10 shows the common methods for working with immutable collections. Note that immutable collections can't be modified, so the result of each expression in the first column must be assigned to a new variable. (Also, see Recipe 10.6 for details on using a mutable variable with an immutable collection.)

*Table 10-10. Common operators (methods) on immutable collections*

| Operator (method) | Description |
| --- | --- |
| c1 ++ c2 | Creates a new collection by appending the elements in the collection c2 to the collection c1. |
| c :+ e | Returns a new collection with the element e appended to the collection c. |
| e +: c | Returns a new collection with the element e prepended to the collection c. |
| e :: list | Returns a List with the element e prepended to the List named list. (:: works only on List.) |
| c drop n<br>c dropWhile p<br>c filter p<br>c filterNot p<br>c head<br>c tail<br>c take n<br>c takeWhile p | The two methods - and -- have been deprecated, so use the filtering methods listed in Table 10-8 to return a new collection with the desired elements removed. Examples of some of these filtering methods are shown here. |

Again, this table lists only the most common methods available on immutable collections. There are other methods available, such as the -- method on a Set. See the Scaladoc for your current collection for even more methods.

### Maps

Maps have additional methods, as shown in Table 10-11. In this table, the following symbols are used in the first column:

- m refers to a map
- mm refers to a mutable map
- k refers to a key

- p refers to a predicate (a function that returns `true` or `false`)
- v refers to a map value
- c refers to a collection

*Table 10-11. Common methods for immutable and mutable maps*

| Map method | Description |
| --- | --- |
| **Methods for immutable maps** | |
| m - k | Returns a map with the key k (and its corresponding value) removed. |
| m - (k1, k2, k3) | Returns a map with the keys k1, k2, and k3 removed. |
| m -- c<br>m -- List(k1, k2) | Returns a map with the keys in the collection removed. (Although List is shown, this can be any sequential collection.) |
| **Methods for mutable maps** | |
| mm += (k -> v)<br>mm += (k1 -> v1, k2 -> v2) | Add the key/value pair(s) to the mutable map mm. |
| mm ++= c<br>mm ++= List(3 -> "c") | Add the elements in the collection c to the mutable map mm. |
| mm -= k<br>mm -= (k1, k2, k3) | Remove map entries from the mutable map mm based on the given key(s). |
| mm --= c | Remove the map entries from the mutable map mm based on the keys in the collection c. |
| **Methods for both mutable and immutable maps** | |
| m(k) | Returns the value associated with the key k. |
| m contains k | Returns true if the map m contains the key k. |
| m filter p | Returns a map whose keys and values match the condition of the predicate p. |
| m filterKeys p | Returns a map whose keys match the condition of the predicate p. |
| m get k | Returns the value for the key k as Some[A] if the key is found, None otherwise. |
| m getOrElse(k, d) | Returns the value for the key k if the key is found, otherwise returns the default value d. |
| m isDefinedAt k | Returns true if the map contains the key k. |
| m keys | Returns the keys from the map as an Iterable. |
| m keyIterator | Returns the keys from the map as an Iterator. |
| m keySet | Returns the keys from the map as a Set. |
| m mapValues f | Returns a new map by applying the function f to every value in the initial map. |
| m values | Returns the values from the map as an Iterable. |
| m valuesIterator | Returns the values from the map as an Iterator. |

For additional methods, see the Scaladoc for the mutable (*http://bit.ly/12AQ2HY*) and immutable (*http://bit.ly/15y3BGn*) map classes.

## Discussion

As you can see, Scala collection classes contain a wealth of methods (and methods that appear to be operators). Understanding these methods will help you become more productive, because as you understand them, you'll write less code and fewer loops, and instead write short functions and predicates to work with these methods.

# 10.4. Understanding the Performance of Collections

## Problem

When choosing a collection for an application where performance is extremely important, you want to choose the right collection for the algorithm.

## Solution

In many cases, you can reason about the performance of a collection by understanding its basic structure. For instance, a List is a singly linked list. It's not indexed, so if you need to access the one-millionth element of a List as list(1000000), that will be slower than accessing the one-millionth element of an Array, because the Array is indexed, whereas accessing the element in the List requires traversing the length of the List.

In other cases, it may help to look at the tables. For instance, Table 10-13 shows that the append operation on a Vector is eC, "effectively constant time." As a result, I know I can create a large Vector in the REPL very quickly like this:

```
var v = Vector[Int]()
for (i <- 1 to 50000) v = v :+ i
```

However, as the table shows, the append operation on a List requires linear time, so attempting to create a List of the same size takes a much (much!) longer time.

With permission from EFPL (*http://lamp.epfl.ch/*), the tables in this recipe have been reproduced from scala-lang.org (*http://bit.ly/13KECnF*).

Before looking at the performance tables, Table 10-12 shows the performance characteristic keys that are used in the other tables that follow.

*Table 10-12. Performance characteristic keys for the subsequent tables*

| Key | Description |
|-----|-------------|
| C | The operation takes (fast) constant time. |
| eC | The operation takes effectively constant time, but this might depend on some assumptions, such as maximum length of a vector, or distribution of hash keys. |
| aC | The operation takes amortized constant time. Some invocations of the operation might take longer, but if many operations are performed, on average only constant time per operation is taken. |
| Log | The operation takes time proportional to the logarithm of the collection size. |

| Key | Description |
|---|---|
| L | The operation is linear, so the time is proportional to the collection size. |
| - | The operation is not supported. |

Table 10-13 shows the performance characteristics for operations on immutable and mutable sequential collections.

*Table 10-13. Performance characteristics for sequential collections*

| | head | tail | apply | update | prepend | append | insert |
|---|---|---|---|---|---|---|---|
| **Immutable** | | | | | | | |
| List | C | C | L | L | C | L | - |
| Stream | C | C | L | L | C | L | - |
| Vector | eC | eC | eC | eC | eC | eC | - |
| Stack | C | C | L | L | C | C | L |
| Queue | aC | aC | L | L | L | C | - |
| Range | C | C | C | - | - | - | - |
| String | C | L | C | L | L | L | - |
| | | | | | | | |
| **Mutable** | | | | | | | |
| ArrayBuffer | C | L | C | C | L | aC | L |
| ListBuffer | C | L | L | L | C | C | L |
| StringBuilder | C | L | C | C | L | aC | L |
| MutableList | C | L | L | L | C | C | L |
| Queue | C | L | L | L | C | C | L |
| ArraySeq | C | L | C | C | - | - | - |
| Stack | C | L | L | L | C | L | L |
| ArrayStack | C | L | C | C | aC | L | L |
| Array | C | L | C | C | - | - | - |

Table 10-14 describes the column headings used in Table 10-13.

*Table 10-14. Descriptions of the column headings for Table 10-13*

| Operation | Description |
|---|---|
| head | Selecting the first element of the sequence. |
| tail | Producing a new sequence that consists of all elements of the sequence except the first one. |
| apply | Indexing. |
| update | Functional update for immutable sequences, side-effecting update (with update) for mutable sequences. |

| Operation | Description |
|---|---|
| prepend | Adding an element to the front of the sequence. For immutable sequences, this produces a new sequence. For mutable sequences, it modifies the existing sequence. |
| append | Adding an element at the end of the sequence. For immutable sequences, this produces a new sequence. For mutable sequences, it modifies the existing sequence. |
| insert | Inserting an element at an arbitrary position in the sequence. This is supported directly only for mutable sequences. |

### Map and set performance characteristics

Table 10-15 shows the performance characteristics for maps and sets.

*Table 10-15. The performance characteristics for maps and sets*

|  | lookup | add | remove | min |
|---|---|---|---|---|
| **Immutable** | | | | |
| HashSet/HashMap | eC | eC | eC | L |
| TreeSet/TreeMap | Log | Log | Log | Log |
| BitSet | C | L | L | eC |
| ListMap | L | L | L | L |
| | | | | |
| **Mutable** | | | | |
| HashSet/HashMap | eC | eC | eC | L |
| WeakHashMap | eC | eC | eC | L |
| BitSet | C | aC | C | eC |
| TreeSet | Log | Log | Log | Log |

Table 10-16 provides descriptions for the column headings used in Table 10-15.

*Table 10-16. Descriptions of the column headings used in Table 10-15*

| Operation | Description |
|---|---|
| lookup | Testing whether an element is contained in a set, or selecting a value associated with a map key. |
| add | Adding a new element to a set or key/value pair to a map. |
| remove | Removing an element from a set or a key from a map. |
| min | The smallest element of the set, or the smallest key of a map. |

## See Also

- The tables in this recipe have been reproduced from the following URL, with permission from the Programming Methods Laboratory of EFPL (*http://bit.ly/13KECnF*).
- The Programming Methods Laboratory of EFPL (*http://lamp.epfl.ch/*).

# 10.5. Declaring a Type When Creating a Collection

## Problem

You want to create a collection of mixed types, and Scala isn't automatically assigning the type you want.

## Solution

In the following example, if you don't specify a type, Scala automatically assigns a type of Double to the list:

```
scala> val x = List(1, 2.0, 33D, 400L)
x: List[Double] = List(1.0, 2.0, 33.0, 400.0)
```

If you'd rather have the collection be of type AnyVal or Number, specify the type in brackets before your collection declaration:

```
scala> val x = List[Number](1, 2.0, 33D, 400L)
x: List[java.lang.Number] = List(1, 2.0, 33.0, 400)

scala> val x = List[AnyVal](1, 2.0, 33D, 400L)
x: List[AnyVal] = List(1, 2.0, 33.0, 400)
```

## Discussion

By manually specifying a type, in this case Number, you control the collection type. This is useful any time a list contains mixed types or multiple levels of inheritance. For instance, given this type hierarchy:

```
trait Animal
trait FurryAnimal extends Animal
case class Dog(name: String) extends Animal
case class Cat(name: String) extends Animal
```

create a sequence with a Dog and a Cat:

```
scala> val x = Array(Dog("Fido"), Cat("Felix"))
x: Array[Product with Serializable with Animal] = Array(Dog(Fido), Cat(Felix))
```

As shown, Scala assigns a type of Product with Serializable with Animal. If you just want an Array[Animal], manually specify the desired type:

```
scala> val x = Array[Animal](Dog("Fido"), Cat("Felix"))
x: Array[Animal] = Array(Dog(Fido), Cat(Felix))
```

This may not seem like a big deal, but imagine declaring a class with a method that returns this array:

```
class AnimalKingdom {
  def animals = Array(Dog("Fido"), Cat("Felix"))
}
```

When you generate the Scaladoc for this class, the `animals` method will show the "Product with Serializable" in its Scaladoc:

```
def animals: Array[Product with Serializable with Animal]
```

If you'd rather have it appear like this in your Scaladoc:

```
def animals: Array[Animal]
```

manually assign the type, as shown in the Solution:

```
def animals = Array[Animal](Dog("Fido"), Cat("Felix"))
```

# 10.6. Understanding Mutable Variables with Immutable Collections

## Problem

You may have seen that mixing a mutable variable (`var`) with an immutable collection causes surprising behavior. For instance, when you create an immutable `Vector` as a `var`, it appears you can somehow add new elements to it:

```
scala> var sisters = Vector("Melinda")
sisters: collection.immutable.Vector[String] = Vector(Melinda)

scala> sisters = sisters :+ "Melissa"
sisters: collection.immutable.Vector[String] = Vector(Melinda, Melissa)

scala> sisters = sisters :+ "Marisa"
sisters: collection.immutable.Vector[String] = Vector(Melinda, Melissa, Marisa)

scala> sisters.foreach(println)
Melinda
Melissa
Marisa
```

How can this be?

## Solution

Though it looks like you're mutating an immutable collection, what's really happening is that the `sisters` variable points to a new collection each time you use the `:+` method. The `sisters` variable is mutable—like a non-`final` field in Java—so it's actually being reassigned to a new collection during each step. The end result is similar to these lines of code:

```
var sisters = Vector("Melinda")
sisters = Vector("Melinda", "Melissa")
sisters = Vector("Melinda", "Melissa", "Marisa")
```

In the second and third lines of code, the `sisters` reference has been changed to point to a new collection.

You can demonstrate that the vector itself is immutable. Attempting to mutate one of its elements—which doesn't involve reassigning the variable—results in an error:

```
scala> sisters(0) = "Molly"
<console>:12: error: value update is not a member of
scala.collection.immutable.Vector[String]
              sisters(0) = "Molly"
              ^
```

### Summary

When you first start working with Scala, the behavior of a mutable variable with an immutable collection can be surprising. To be clear about *variables*:

- A mutable variable (`var`) can be reassigned to point at new data.
- An immutable variable (`val`) is like a `final` variable in Java; it can never be reassigned.

To be clear about *collections*:

- The elements in a mutable collection (like `ArrayBuffer`) can be changed.
- The elements in an immutable collection (like `Vector`) cannot be changed.

## See Also

Recipe 20.2, "Prefer Immutable Objects", discusses the use of mutable variables with immutable collections, and its opposite, using immutable variables with mutable collections as a "best practice."

# 10.7. Make Vector Your "Go To" Immutable Sequence

## Problem

You want a fast, general-purpose, immutable, sequential collection type for your Scala applications.

## Solution

The `Vector` class was introduced in Scala 2.8 and is now considered to be the "go to," general-purpose immutable data structure. (`Vector` is an indexed, immutable sequential collection. Use a `List` if you prefer working with a linear, immutable sequential collection. See Recipe 10.2, "Choosing a Collection Class", for more details.)

Create and use a `Vector` just like other immutable, indexed sequences. You can create them and access elements efficiently by index:

```
scala> val v = Vector("a", "b", "c")
v: scala.collection.immutable.Vector[java.lang.String] = Vector(a, b, c)

scala> v(0)
res0: java.lang.String = a
```

You can't modify a vector, so you "add" elements to an existing vector as you assign the result to a new variable:

```
scala> val a = Vector(1, 2, 3)
a: scala.collection.immutable.Vector[Int] = Vector(1, 2, 3)

scala> val b = a ++ Vector(4, 5)
b: scala.collection.immutable.Vector[Int] = Vector(1, 2, 3, 4, 5)
```

Use the `updated` method to replace one element in a `Vector` while assigning the result to a new variable:

```
scala> val c = b.updated(0, "x")
c: scala.collection.immutable.Vector[java.lang.String] = Vector(x, b, c)
```

You can also use all the usual filtering methods to get just the elements you want out of a vector:

```
scala> val a = Vector(1, 2, 3, 4, 5)
a: scala.collection.immutable.Vector[Int] = Vector(1, 2, 3, 4, 5)

scala> val b = a.take(2)
b: scala.collection.immutable.Vector[Int] = Vector(1, 2)

scala> val c = a.filter(_ > 2)
c: scala.collection.immutable.Vector[Int] = Vector(3, 4, 5)
```

In those examples, I created each variable as a `val` and assigned the output to a new variable just to be clear, but you can also declare your variable as a `var` and reassign the result back to the same variable:

```
scala> var a = Vector(1, 2, 3)
a: scala.collection.immutable.Vector[Int] = Vector(1, 2, 3)

scala> a = a ++ Vector(4, 5)
a: scala.collection.immutable.Vector[Int] = Vector(1, 2, 3, 4, 5)
```

## Discussion

The "concrete, immutable collections classes" page (*http://bit.ly/12QljTA*) from the scala-lang.org (*http://www.scala-lang.org/*) website states the following:

`Vector` is a collection type (introduced in Scala 2.8) that addresses the inefficiency for random access on lists. Vectors allow accessing any element of the list in 'effectively' constant time ... Because vectors strike a good balance between fast random selections and fast random functional updates, they are currently the default implementation of immutable indexed sequences...

In his book, *Scala In Depth* (Manning Publications), Joshua Suereth offers the rule, "When in Doubt, Use Vector." He writes, "Vector is the most flexible, efficient collection in the Scala collections library."

As noted in Recipe 10.1, if you create an instance of an `IndexedSeq`, Scala returns a `Vector`:

```
scala> val x = IndexedSeq(1,2,3)
x: IndexedSeq[Int] = Vector(1, 2, 3)
```

As a result, I've seen some developers create an `IndexedSeq` in their code, rather than a `Vector`, to be more generic and to allow for potential future changes.

### See Also

- The `Vector` class (*http://bit.ly/1bgKyXi*)
- The "concrete, immutable collections classes" discussion of the `Vector` class (*http://bit.ly/12QljTA*)

# 10.8. Make ArrayBuffer Your "Go To" Mutable Sequence

## Problem

You want to use a general-purpose, mutable sequence in your Scala applications.

## Solution

Just as the `Vector` is the recommended "go to" class for immutable, sequential collections, the `ArrayBuffer` class is recommended as the general-purpose class for *mutable* sequential collections. (`ArrayBuffer` is an indexed sequential collection. Use `ListBuffer` if you prefer a linear sequential collection that is mutable. See Recipe 10.2, "Choosing a Collection Class", for more information.)

To use an `ArrayBuffer`, first import it:

```
import scala.collection.mutable.ArrayBuffer
```

You can then create an empty `ArrayBuffer`:

```
var fruits = ArrayBuffer[String]()
var ints = ArrayBuffer[Int]()
```

Or you can create an `ArrayBuffer` with initial elements:

```
var nums = ArrayBuffer(1, 2, 3)
```

Like other mutable collection classes, you add elements using the += and ++= methods:

```
scala> var nums = ArrayBuffer(1, 2, 3)
nums: scala.collection.mutable.ArrayBuffer[Int] = ArrayBuffer(1, 2, 3)

// add one element
scala> nums += 4
res0: scala.collection.mutable.ArrayBuffer[Int] = ArrayBuffer(1, 2, 3, 4)

// add two or more elements (method has a varargs parameter)
scala> nums += (5, 6)
res1: scala.collection.mutable.ArrayBuffer[Int] = ArrayBuffer(1, 2, 3, 4, 5, 6)

// add elements from another collection
scala> nums ++= List(7, 8)
res2: scala.collection.mutable.ArrayBuffer[Int] =
    ArrayBuffer(1, 2, 3, 4, 5, 6, 7, 8)
```

You remove elements with the -= and --= methods:

```
// remove one element
scala> nums -= 9
res3: scala.collection.mutable.ArrayBuffer[Int] =
    ArrayBuffer(1, 2, 3, 4, 5, 6, 7, 8)

// remove two or more elements
scala> nums -= (7, 8)
res4: scala.collection.mutable.ArrayBuffer[Int] = ArrayBuffer(1, 2, 3, 4, 5, 6)

// remove elements specified by another sequence
scala> nums --= Array(5, 6)
res5: scala.collection.mutable.ArrayBuffer[Int] = ArrayBuffer(1, 2, 3, 4)
```

## Discussion

Those are the methods I generally use to add and remove elements from an `ArrayBuffer`. However, there are many more:

```
val a = ArrayBuffer(1, 2, 3)    // ArrayBuffer(1, 2, 3)
a.append(4)                     // ArrayBuffer(1, 2, 3, 4)
a.append(5, 6)                  // ArrayBuffer(1, 2, 3, 4, 5, 6)
a.appendAll(Seq(7,8))           // ArrayBuffer(1, 2, 3, 4, 5, 6, 7, 8)
a.clear                         // ArrayBuffer()

val a = ArrayBuffer(9, 10)      // ArrayBuffer(9, 10)
a.insert(0, 8)                  // ArrayBuffer(8, 9, 10)
a.insert(0, 6, 7)               // ArrayBuffer(6, 7, 8, 9, 10)
a.insertAll(0, Vector(4, 5))    // ArrayBuffer(4, 5, 6, 7, 8, 9, 10)
a.prepend(3)                    // ArrayBuffer(3, 4, 5, 6, 7, 8, 9, 10)
```

```
a.prepend(1, 2)                // ArrayBuffer(1, 2, 3, 4, 5, 6, 7, 8, 9, 10)
a.prependAll(Array(0))         // ArrayBuffer(0, 1, 2, 3, 4, 5, 6, 7, 8, 9, 10)

val a = ArrayBuffer.range('a', 'h') // ArrayBuffer(a, b, c, d, e, f, g)
a.remove(0)                    // ArrayBuffer(b, c, d, e, f, g)
a.remove(2, 3)                 // ArrayBuffer(b, c, g)

val a = ArrayBuffer.range('a', 'h') // ArrayBuffer(a, b, c, d, e, f, g)
a.trimStart(2)                 // ArrayBuffer(c, d, e, f, g)
a.trimEnd(2)                   // ArrayBuffer(c, d, e)
```

See the Scaladoc (*http://bit.ly/18YoNuP*) for more methods that you can use to modify an `ArrayBuffer`.

The `ArrayBuffer` Scaladoc provides these details about `ArrayBuffer` performance: "Append, update, and random access take constant time (amortized time). Prepends and removes are linear in the buffer size." The `ArrayBuffer` documentation also states, "array buffers are useful for efficiently building up a large collection whenever the new items are always added to the end."

If you need a mutable sequential collection that works more like a `List` (i.e., a linear sequence rather than an indexed sequence), use `ListBuffer` instead of `ArrayBuffer`. The Scala documentation on the `ListBuffer` states, "A `ListBuffer` is like an array buffer except that it uses a linked list internally instead of an array. If you plan to convert the buffer to a list once it is built up, use a list buffer instead of an array buffer."

## See Also

- `ArrayBuffer` discussion (*http://bit.ly/1dzXIM7*)
- `ArrayBuffer` Scaladoc (*http://bit.ly/18YoNuP*)
- `ListBuffer` discussion (*http://bit.ly/18YoTT4*)

# 10.9. Looping over a Collection with foreach

## Problem

You want to iterate over the elements in a collection with the `foreach` method.

## Solution

The `foreach` method takes a function as an argument. The function you define should take an element as an input parameter, and should not return anything. The input parameter type should match the type stored in the collection. As `foreach` executes, it passes one element at a time from the collection to your function until it reaches the last element in the collection.

The foreach method applies your function to each element of the collection, but it doesn't return a value. Because it doesn't return anything, it's said that it's used for its "side effect."

As an example, a common use of foreach is to output information:

```
scala> val x = Vector(1, 2, 3)
x: scala.collection.immutable.Vector[Int] = Vector(1, 2, 3)

scala> x.foreach((i: Int) => println(i))
1
2
3
```

That's the longhand way of writing that code. For most expressions, Scala can infer the type, so specifying i: Int isn't necessary:

```
args.foreach(i => println(i))
```

You can further shorten this expression by using the ubiquitous underscore wildcard character instead of using a temporary variable:

```
args.foreach(println(_))
```

In a situation like this, where a function literal consists of one statement that takes a single argument, it can be condensed to this form:

```
args.foreach(println)
```

For a simple case like this, the syntax in the last example is typically used.

## Discussion

As long as your function (or method) takes one parameter of the same type as the elements in the collection and returns nothing (Unit), it can be called from a foreach method. In the following example, the printIt method takes a Char, does something with it, and returns nothing:

```
def printIt(c: Char) { println(c) }
```

Because a String is a sequence of type Char, printIt can be called in a foreach method on a String as follows:

```
"HAL".foreach(c => printIt(c))
"HAL".foreach(printIt)
```

If your algorithm is used only once, you don't have to declare it as a method or function; just pass it to foreach as a function literal:

```
"HAL".foreach((c: Char) => println(c))
```

To declare a multiline function, use this format:

```
val longWords = new StringBuilder

"Hello world it's Al".split(" ").foreach{ e =>
  if (e.length > 4) longWords.append(s" $e")
  else println("Not added: " + e)
}
```

To understand this example, it may be helpful to know the `split` method used in that function creates an `Array[String]`, as shown here:

```
scala> "Hello world it's Al".split(" ")
res0: Array[java.lang.String] = Array(Hello, world, it's, Al)
```

In addition to using the `foreach` method on sequential collections, it's also available on the Map class. The `Map` implementation of `foreach` passes two parameters to your function. You can handle those parameters as a tuple:

```
val m = Map("fname" -> "Tyler", "lname" -> "LeDude")
m foreach (x => println(s"${x._1} -> ${x._2}"))
```

However, I generally prefer the following approach:

```
movieRatings.foreach {
  case(movie, rating) => println(s"key: $movie, value: $rating")
}
```

See Recipe 11.17, "Traversing a Map", for other ways to iterate over a map.

Scala's for loop provides another powerful way to iterate over the elements in a collection. See Recipe 10.10, "Looping over a Collection with a for Loop", for more information.

# 10.10. Looping over a Collection with a for Loop

## Problem

You want to loop over the elements in a collection using a for loop, possibly creating a new collection from the existing collection using the for/yield combination.

## Solution

You can loop over any `Traversable` type (basically any sequence) using a for loop:

```
scala> val fruits = Traversable("apple", "banana", "orange")
fruits: Traversable[String] = List(apple, banana, orange)

scala> for (f <- fruits) println(f)
apple
banana
```

```
orange

scala> for (f <- fruits) println(f.toUpperCase)
APPLE
BANANA
ORANGE
```

If your algorithm is long, perform the work in a block following a for loop:

```
scala> val fruits = Array("apple", "banana", "orange")
fruits: Array[String] = Array(apple, banana, orange)

scala> for (f <- fruits) {
     |     // imagine this required multiple lines
     |     val s = f.toUpperCase
     |     println(s)
     | }
APPLE
BANANA
ORANGE
```

This example shows one approach to using a counter inside a for loop:

```
scala> for (i <- 0 until fruits.size) println(s"element $i is ${fruits(i)}")
element 0 is apple
element 1 is banana
element 2 is orange
```

You can also use the zipWithIndex method when you need a loop counter:

```
scala> for ((elem, count) <- fruits.zipWithIndex) {
     |     println(s"element $count is $elem")
     | }
element 0 is apple
element 1 is banana
element 2 is orange
```

> When using zipWithIndex, consider calling view before zipWithIndex:
>
> ```
> // added a call to 'view'
> for ((elem, count) <- fruits.view.zipWithIndex) {
>   println(s"element $count is $elem")
> }
> ```
>
> See the next recipe for details.

Using zip with a Stream is another way to generate a counter:

```
scala> for ((elem,count) <- fruits.zip(Stream from 1)) {
     |     println(s"element $count is $elem")
     | }
element 1 is apple
```

```
element 2 is banana
element 3 is orange
```

See the next recipe for details on using `zipWithIndex` and `zip` to create loop counters.

If you just need to do something N times, using a `Range` works well:

```
scala> for (i <- 1 to 3) println(i)
1
2
3
```

In that example, the expression `1 to 3` creates a `Range`, which you can demonstrate in the REPL:

```
scala> 1 to 3
res0: scala.collection.immutable.Range.Inclusive = Range(1, 2, 3)
```

Again you can use a block inside curly braces when your algorithm gets long:

```
scala> for (i <- 1 to 3) {
     |    // do whatever you want in this block
     |    println(i)
     | }
1
2
3
```

### The for/yield construct

The previous examples show how to operate on each element in a sequence, but they don't return a value. As with the `foreach` examples in the previous recipe, they're used for their side effect.

To build a new collection from an input collection, use the `for/yield` construct. The following example shows how to build a new array of uppercase strings from an input array of lowercase strings:

```
scala> val fruits = Array("apple", "banana", "orange")
fruits: Array[java.lang.String] = Array(apple, banana, orange)

scala> val newArray = for (e <- fruits) yield e.toUpperCase
newArray: Array[java.lang.String] = Array(APPLE, BANANA, ORANGE)
```

The `for/yield` construct returns (yields) a new collection from the input collection by applying your algorithm to the elements of the input collection, so the array `newArray` contains uppercase versions of the three strings in the initial array. Using `for/yield` like this is known as a *for comprehension*.

If your for/yield processing requires multiple lines of code, perform the work in a block after the `yield` keyword:

```
scala> val newArray = for (fruit <- fruits) yield {
     |    // imagine this required multiple lines
     |    val upper = fruit.toUpperCase
     |    upper
     | }
newArray: Array[java.lang.String] = Array(APPLE, BANANA, ORANGE)
```

If your algorithm is long, or you want to reuse it, first define it in a method (or function):

```
def upperReverse(s: String) = {
  // imagine this is a long algorithm
  s.toUpperCase.reverse
}
```

then use the method with the for/yield loop:

```
scala> val newArray = for (fruit <- fruits) yield upperReverse(fruit)
newArray: Array[String] = Array(ELPPA, ANANAB, EGNARO)
```

### Maps

You can also iterate over a Map nicely using a for loop:

```
scala> val names = Map("fname" -> "Ed", "lname" -> "Chigliak")
names: scala.collection.immutable.Map[String,String] =
  Map(fname -> Ed, lname -> Chigliak)

scala> for ((k,v) <- names) println(s"key: $k, value: $v")
key: fname, value: Ed
key: lname, value: Chigliak
```

See Recipe 11.17, "Traversing a Map", for more examples of iterating over a map.

## Discussion

When using a for loop, the <- symbol can be read as "in," so the following statement can be read as "for i in 1 to 3, do ...":

```
for (i <- 1 to 3) { // more code here ...
```

As demonstrated in Recipe 3.3, "Using a for Loop with Embedded if Statements (Guards)", you can also combine a for loop with if statements, which are known as *guards*:

```
for {
  file <- files
  if file.isFile
  if file.getName.endsWith(".txt")
} doSomething(file)
```

See that recipe for more examples of using guards with for loops.

## See Also

- Recipe 3.3, "Using a for Loop with Embedded if Statements (Guards)"
- Recipe 10.9, "Looping over a Collection with foreach"
- Recipe 10.13, "Transforming One Collection to Another with for/yield"

# 10.11. Using zipWithIndex or zip to Create Loop Counters

## Problem

You want to loop over a sequential collection, and you'd like to have access to a counter in the loop, without having to manually create a counter.

## Solution

Use the `zipWithIndex` or `zip` methods to create a counter automatically. Assuming you have a sequential collection of days:

```
val days = Array("Sunday", "Monday", "Tuesday", "Wednesday",
                 "Thursday", "Friday", "Saturday")
```

you can print the elements in the collection with a counter using the `zipWithIndex` and `foreach` methods:

```
days.zipWithIndex.foreach {
  case(day, count) => println(s"$count is $day")
}
```

As you'll see in the Discussion, this works because `zipWithIndex` returns a series of `Tuple2` elements in an `Array`, like this:

```
Array((Sunday,0), (Monday,1), ...
```

and the `case` statement in the `foreach` loop matches a `Tuple2`.

You can also use `zipWithIndex` with a for loop:

```
for ((day, count) <- days.zipWithIndex) {
  println(s"$count is $day")
}
```

Both loops result in the following output:

```
0 is Sunday
1 is Monday
2 is Tuesday
3 is Wednesday
4 is Thursday
```

```
5 is Friday
6 is Saturday
```

When using `zipWithIndex`, the counter always starts at 0. You can also use the `zip` method with a `Stream` to create a counter. This gives you a way to control the starting value:

```
scala> for ((day,count) <- days.zip(Stream from 1)) {
     |     println(s"day $count is $day")
     | }
```

## Discussion

When `zipWithIndex` is used on a sequence, it returns a sequence of `Tuple2` elements, as shown in this example:

```
scala> val list = List("a", "b", "c")
list: List[String] = List(a, b, c)

scala> val zwi = list.zipWithIndex
zwi: List[(String, Int)] = List((a,0), (b,1), (c,2))
```

Because `zipWithIndex` creates a new sequence from the existing sequence, you may want to call `view` before invoking `zipWithIndex`, like this:

```
scala> val zwi2 = list.view.zipWithIndex
zwi2: scala.collection.SeqView[(String, Int),Seq[_]] = SeqViewZ(...)
```

As shown, this creates a lazy view on the original list, so the tuple elements won't be created until they're needed. Because of this behavior, calling `view` before calling `zipWithIndex` is recommended at the first two links in the See Also section. However, my own experience concurs with the performance shown in the third link in the See Also section, where *not* using a view performs better. If performance is a concern, try your loop both ways, and also try manually incrementing a counter.

As mentioned, the `zip` and `zipWithIndex` methods both return a sequence of `Tuple2` elements. Therefore, your `foreach` method can also look like this:

```
days.zipWithIndex.foreach { d =>
  println(s"${d._2} is ${d._1}")
}
```

However, I think the approaches shown in the Solution are more readable.

As shown in the previous recipe, you can also use a range with a `for` loop to create a counter:

```
val fruits = Array("apple", "banana", "orange")
for (i <- 0 until fruits.size) println(s"element $i is ${fruits(i)}")
```

See Recipe 10.24, "Creating a Lazy View on a Collection", for more information on using views.

## See Also

- A blog post on using `zipWithIndex` in several use cases (*http://bit.ly/12DReFU*)
- A discussion of using `zipWithIndex` in a `for` loop (*http://bit.ly/1459nCO*)
- A discussion of performance related to using a view with `zipWithIndex` (*http://bit.ly/17g4PHH*)
- `SeqView` trait (*http://bit.ly/12AQN3P*)

# 10.12. Using Iterators

## Problem

You want (or need) to work with an iterator in a Scala application.

## Solution

Although using an iterator with `hasNext()` and `next()` is a common way to loop over a collection in Java, they aren't commonly used in Scala, because Scala collections have methods like `map` and `foreach` that let you implement algorithms more concisely. To be clear, in Scala, I've never directly written code like this:

```
// don't do this
val it = collection.iterator
while (it.hasNext) ...
```

That being said, sometimes you'll run into an iterator, with one of the best examples being the `io.Source.fromFile` method. This method returns an iterator, which makes sense, because when you're working with very large files, it's not practical to read the entire file into memory.

An important part of using an iterator is knowing that it's exhausted after you use it. As you access each element, you mutate the iterator, and the previous element is discarded. For instance, if you use `foreach` to iterate over an iterator's elements, the call works the first time:

```
scala> val it = Iterator(1,2,3)
it: Iterator[Int] = non-empty iterator

scala> it.foreach(println)
1
2
3
```

But when you attempt the same call a second time, you won't get any output, because the iterator has been exhausted:

```
scala> it.foreach(println)
(no output here)
```

An iterator isn't a collection; instead, it gives you a way to access the elements in a collection, one by one. But an iterator does define many of the methods you'll see in a normal collection class, including foreach, map, flatMap, collect, etc. You can also convert an iterator to a collection when needed:

```
val it = Iterator(1,2,3)
it.toArray
```

The REPL output shows the collections you can create from an iterator:

```
scala> it.to[Tab]
toArray        toBuffer        toIndexedSeq    toIterable     toIterator
toList         toMap           toSeq           toSet          toStream
toString       toTraversable
```

## See Also

- An introduction to Scala iterators (*http://bit.ly/15HLMqB*)
- The Iterator trait (*http://bit.ly/1dzYcSo*)

# 10.13. Transforming One Collection to Another with for/yield

## Problem

You want to create a new collection from an existing collection by transforming the elements with an algorithm.

## Solution

Use the for/yield construct and your algorithm to create the new collection. For instance, starting with a basic collection:

```
scala> val a = Array(1, 2, 3, 4, 5)
a: Array[Int] = Array(1, 2, 3, 4, 5)
```

You can create a copy of that collection by just "yielding" each element (with no algorithm):

```
scala> for (e <- a) yield e
res0: Array[Int] = Array(1, 2, 3, 4, 5)
```

You can create a new collection where each element is twice the value of the original:

```
scala> for (e <- a) yield e * 2
res1: Array[Int] = Array(2, 4, 6, 8, 10)
```

You can determine the modulus of each element:

```
scala> for (e <- a) yield e % 2
res2: Array[Int] = Array(1, 0, 1, 0, 1)
```

This example converts a list of strings to uppercase:

```
scala> val fruits = Vector("apple", "banana", "lime", "orange")
fruits: Vector[String] = Vector(apple, banana, lime, orange)

scala> val ucFruits = for (e <- fruits) yield e.toUpperCase
ucFruits: Vector[String] = Vector(APPLE, BANANA, LIME, ORANGE)
```

Your algorithm can return whatever collection is needed. This approach converts the original collection into a sequence of Tuple2 elements:

```
scala> for (i <- 0 until fruits.length) yield (i, fruits(i))
res0: scala.collection.immutable.IndexedSeq[(Int, String)] =
  Vector((0,apple), (1,banana), (2,lime), (3,orange))
```

This algorithm yields a sequence of Tuple2 elements that contains each original string along with its length:

```
scala> for (f <- fruits) yield (f, f.length)
res1: Vector[(String, Int)] = Vector((apple,5), (banana,6), (lime,4), (orange,6))
```

If your algorithm takes multiple lines, include it in a block after the yield:

```
scala> val x = for (e <- fruits) yield {
     |    // imagine this required multiple lines
     |    val s = e.toUpperCase
     |    s
     | }
x: Vector[String] = List(APPLE, BANANA, LIME, ORANGE)
```

Given a Person class and a list of friend's names like this:

```
case class Person (name: String)
val friends = Vector("Mark", "Regina", "Matt")
```

a for/yield loop can yield a collection of Person instances:

```
scala> for (f <- friends) yield Person(f)
res0: Vector[Person] = Vector(Person(Mark), Person(Regina), Person(Matt))
```

You can include if statements (guards) in a for comprehension to filter elements:

```
scala> val x = for (e <- fruits if e.length < 6) yield e.toUpperCase
x: List[java.lang.String] = List(APPLE, LIME)
```

# Discussion

This combination of a for loop and yield statement is known as a *for comprehension* or *sequence comprehension*. It yields a new collection from an existing collection.

If you're new to using the for/yield construct, it can help to think that is has a bucket or temporary holding area on the side. As each element from the original collection is operated on with yield and your algorithm, it's added to that bucket. Then, when the for loop is finished iterating over the entire collection, all of the elements in the bucket are returned (yielded) by the expression.

In general, the collection type that's returned by a for comprehension will be the same type that you begin with. If you begin with an ArrayBuffer, you'll end up with an ArrayBuffer:

```
scala> val fruits = scala.collection.mutable.ArrayBuffer("apple", "banana")
fruits: scala.collection.mutable.ArrayBuffer[java.lang.String] =
    ArrayBuffer(apple, banana)

scala> val x = for (e <- fruits) yield e.toUpperCase
x: scala.collection.mutable.ArrayBuffer[java.lang.String] =
    ArrayBuffer(APPLE, BANANA)
```

A List returns a List:

```
scala> val fruits = "apple" :: "banana" :: "orange" :: Nil
fruits: List[java.lang.String] = List(apple, banana, orange)

scala> val x = for (e <- fruits) yield e.toUpperCase
x: List[java.lang.String] = List(APPLE, BANANA, ORANGE)
```

However, as shown in the Solution, this isn't always the case.

## Using guards

When you add guards to a for comprehension and want to write it as a multiline expression, the recommended coding style is to use curly braces rather than parentheses:

```
for {
  file <- files
  if hasSoundFileExtension(file)
  if !soundFileIsLong(file)
} yield file
```

This makes the code more readable, especially when the list of guards becomes long. See Recipe 3.3, "Using a for Loop with Embedded if Statements (Guards)", more information on using guards.

When using guards, the resulting collection can end up being a different size than the input collection:

```
scala> val cars = Vector("Mercedes", "Porsche", "Tesla")
cars: Vector[String] = Vector(Mercedes, Porsche, Tesla)
```

```
scala> for {
     |    c <- cars
     |    if c.startsWith("M")
     |  } yield c
res0: Vector[String] = Vector(Mercedes)
```

In fact, if none of the car names had matched the startsWith test, that code would return an empty Vector.

When I first started working with Scala I always used a for/yield expression to do this kind of work, but one day I realized that I could achieve the same result more concisely using the map method. The next recipe demonstrates how to use map to create a new collection from an existing collection.

### See Also

- Recipe 3.1, "Looping with for and foreach", provides detailed examples of how for loops are translated by the Scala compiler into foreach and map method calls.
- Recipe 3.3, "Using a for Loop with Embedded if Statements (Guards)", provides more examples of using guards.

# 10.14. Transforming One Collection to Another with map

## Problem

Like the previous recipe, you want to transform one collection into another by applying an algorithm to every element in the original collection.

## Solution

Rather than using the for/yield combination shown in the previous recipe, call the map method on your collection, passing it a function, an anonymous function, or method to transform each element. This is shown in the following examples, where each String in a List is converted to begin with a capital letter:

```
scala> val helpers = Vector("adam", "kim", "melissa")
helpers: scala.collection.immutable.Vector[java.lang.String] =
    Vector(adam, kim, melissa)

// the long form
scala> val caps = helpers.map(e => e.capitalize)
caps: scala.collection.immutable.Vector[String] = Vector(Adam, Kim, Melissa)

// the short form
```

```
scala> val caps = helpers.map(_.capitalize)
caps: scala.collection.immutable.Vector[String] = Vector(Adam, Kim, Melissa)
```

The next example shows that an array of `String` can be converted to an array of `Int`:

```
scala> val names = Array("Fred", "Joe", "Jonathan")
names: Array[java.lang.String] = Array(Fred, Joe, Jonathan)

scala> val lengths = names.map(_.length)
lengths: Array[Int] = Array(4, 3, 8)
```

The `map` method comes in handy if you want to convert a collection to a list of XML elements:

```
scala> val nieces = List("Aleka", "Christina", "Molly")
nieces: List[String] = List(Aleka, Christina, Molly)

scala> val elems = nieces.map(niece => <li>{niece}</li>)
elems: List[scala.xml.Elem] =
      List(<li>Aleka</li>, <li>Christina</li>, <li>Molly</li>)
```

Using a similar technique, you can convert the collection directly to an XML literal:

```
scala> val ul = <ul>{nieces.map(i => <li>{i}</li>)}</ul>
ul: scala.xml.Elem = <ul><li>Aleka</li><li>Christina</li><li>Molly</li></ul>
```

A function that's passed into `map` can be as complicated as necessary. An example in the Discussion shows how to use a multiline anonymous function with `map`. When your algorithm gets longer, rather than using an anonymous function, define the function (or method) first, and then pass it into `map`:

```
// imagine this is a long method
scala> def plusOne(c: Char): Char = (c.toByte+1).toChar
plusOne: (c: Char)Char

scala> "HAL".map(plusOne)
res0: String = IBM
```

When writing a method to work with `map`, define the method to take a single parameter that's the same type as the collection. In this case, `plusOne` is defined to take a `char`, because a `String` is a collection of `Char` elements. The return type of the method can be whatever you need for your algorithm. For instance, the previous `names.map(_.length)` example showed that a function applied to a `String` can return an `Int`.

Unlike the `for/yield` approach shown in the previous recipe, the `map` method also works well when writing a chain of method calls. For instance, you can split a `String` into an array of strings, then trim the blank spaces from those strings:

```
scala> val s = " eggs, milk, butter, Coco Puffs "
s: String = " eggs, milk,  butter, Coco Puffs "
```

```
scala> val items = s.split(",").map(_.trim)
items: Array[String] = Array(eggs, milk, butter, Coco Puffs)
```

This works because split creates an Array[String], and map applies the trim method
to each element in that array before returning the final array.

## Discussion

For simple cases, using map is the same as using a basic for/yield loop:

```
scala> val people = List("adam", "kim", "melissa")
people: List[java.lang.String] = List(adam, kim, melissa)

// map
scala> val caps1 = people.map(_.capitalize)
caps1: List[String] = List(Adam, Kim, Melissa)

// for/yield
scala> val caps2 = for (f <- people) yield f.capitalize
caps2: List[String] = List(Adam, Kim, Melissa)
```

But once you add a guard, a for/yield loop is no longer directly equivalent to just a
map method call. If you attempt to use an if statement in the algorithm you pass to a
map method, you'll get a very different result:

```
scala> val fruits = List("apple", "banana", "lime", "orange", "raspberry")
fruits: List[java.lang.String] = List(apple, banana, lime, orange, raspberry)

scala> val newFruits = fruits.map( f =>
     |     if (f.length < 6) f.toUpperCase
     | )
newFruits: List[Any] = List(APPLE, (), LIME, (), ())
```

You *could* filter the result *after* calling map to clean up the result:

```
scala> newFruits.filter(_ != ())
res0: List[Any] = List(APPLE, LIME)
```

But in this situation, it helps to think of an if statement as being a filter, so the correct
solution is to first filter the collection, and then call map:

```
scala> val fruits = List("apple", "banana", "lime", "orange", "raspberry")
fruits: List[String] = List(apple, banana, lime, orange, raspberry)

scala> fruits.filter(_.length < 6).map(_.toUpperCase)
res1: List[String] = List(APPLE, LIME)
```

## See Also

Recipe 3.1, "Looping with for and foreach", provides detailed examples of how
for loops are translated by the Scala compiler into foreach and map method calls.

# 10.15. Flattening a List of Lists with flatten

## Problem

You have a list of lists (a sequence of sequences) and want to create one list (sequence) from them.

## Solution

Use the `flatten` method to convert a list of lists into a single list. To demonstrate this, first create a list of lists:

```
scala> val lol = List(List(1,2), List(3,4))
lol: List[List[Int]] = List(List(1, 2), List(3, 4))
```

Calling the `flatten` method on this list of lists creates one new list:

```
scala> val result = lol.flatten
result: List[Int] = List(1, 2, 3, 4)
```

As shown, `flatten` does what its name implies, flattening the lists held inside the outer list into one resulting list.

Though I use the term "list" here, the `flatten` method isn't limited to a `List`; it works with other sequences (`Array`, `ArrayBuffer`, `Vector`, etc.) as well:

```
scala> val a = Array(Array(1,2), Array(3,4))
a: Array[Array[Int]] = Array(Array(1, 2), Array(3, 4))

scala> a.flatten
res0: Array[Int] = Array(1, 2, 3, 4)
```

In the real world, you might use `flatten` to convert a list of couples attending a wedding into a single list of all people attending the wedding. Calling `flatten` on a `List[List[String]]` does the job:

```
scala> val couples = List(List("kim", "al"), List("julia", "terry"))
couples: List[List[String]] = List(List(kim, al), List(julia, terry))

scala> val people = couples.flatten
people: List[String] = List(kim, al, julia, terry)
```

If you really want to have fun, capitalize each element in the resulting list and then sort the list:

```
scala> val people = couples.flatten.map(_.capitalize).sorted
people: List[String] = List(Al, Julia, Kim, Terry)
```

This helps to demonstrate the power of the Scala collections methods. (Imagine trying to write that code with only a `for` loop.)

---

In a social-networking application, you might do the same thing with a list of friends, and their friends:

```
val myFriends = List("Adam", "David", "Frank")
val adamsFriends = List("Nick K", "Bill M")
val davidsFriends = List("Becca G", "Kenny D", "Bill M")
val friendsOfFriends = List(adamsFriends, davidsFriends)
```

Because `friendsOfFriends` is a list of lists, you can use `flatten` to accomplish many tasks with it, such as creating a unique list of the friends of your friends:

```
scala> val uniqueFriendsOfFriends = friendsOfFriends.flatten.distinct
uniqueFriendsOfFriends: List[String] = List(Nick K, Bill M, Becca G, Kenny D)
```

The `flatten` method is useful in at least two other situations. First, because a `String` is a sequence of `Char`, you can flatten a list of strings into a list of characters:

```
scala> val list = List("Hello", "world")
list: List[java.lang.String] = List(Hello, world)

scala> list.flatten
res0: List[Char] = List(H, e, l, l, o, w, o, r, l, d)
```

Second, because an `Option` can be thought of as a container that holds zero or one elements, `flatten` has a very useful effect on a sequence of `Some` and `None` elements. It pulls the values out of the `Some` elements to create the new list, and drops the `None` elements:

```
scala> val x = Vector(Some(1), None, Some(3), None)
x: Vector[Option[Int]] = Vector(Some(1), None, Some(3), None)

scala> x.flatten
res1: Vector[Int] = Vector(1, 3)
```

# 10.16. Combining map and flatten with flatMap

## Problem

When you first come to Scala, the `flatMap` method can seem very foreign, so you'd like to understand how to use it and see where it can be applied.

## Solution

Use `flatMap` in situations where you run `map` followed by `flatten`. The specific situation is this:

- You're using `map` (or a `for`/`yield` expression) to create a new collection from an existing collection.

- The resulting collection is a list of lists.
- You call `flatten` immediately after `map` (or a `for`/`yield` expression).

When you're in this situation, you can use `flatMap` instead.

The next example shows how to use `flatMap` with an `Option`. In this example, you're told that you should calculate the sum of the numbers in a list, with one catch: the numbers are all strings, and some of them won't convert properly to integers. Here's the list:

```
val bag = List("1", "2", "three", "4", "one hundred seventy five")
```

To solve the problem, you begin by creating a "string to integer" conversion method that returns either `Some[Int]` or `None`, based on the `String` it's given:

```
def toInt(in: String): Option[Int] = {
  try {
    Some(Integer.parseInt(in.trim))
  } catch {
    case e: Exception => None
  }
}
```

With this method in hand, the resulting solution is surprisingly simple:

```
scala> bag.flatMap(toInt).sum
res0: Int = 7
```

## Discussion

To see how this works, break the problem down into smaller steps. First, here's what happens when you use `map` on the initial collection of strings:

```
scala> bag.map(toInt)
res0: List[Option[Int]] = List(Some(1), Some(2), None, Some(4), None)
```

The `map` method applies the `toInt` function to each element in the collection, and returns a list of `Some[Int]` and `None` values. But the `sum` method needs a `List[Int]`; how do you get there from here?

As shown in the previous recipe, `flatten` works very well with a list of `Some` and `None` elements. It extracts the values from the `Some` elements while discarding the `None` elements:

```
scala> bag.map(toInt).flatten
res1: List[Int] = List(1, 2, 4)
```

This makes finding the sum easy:

```
scala> bag.map(toInt).flatten.sum
res2: Int = 7
```

Now, whenever I see map followed by `flatten`, I think "flat map," so I get back to the earlier solution:

```scala
scala> bag.flatMap(toInt).sum
res3: Int = 7
```

(Actually, I think, "map flat," but the method is named `flatMap`.)

As you can imagine, once you get the original list down to a `List[Int]`, you can call any of the powerful collections methods to get what you want:

```scala
scala> bag.flatMap(toInt).filter(_ > 1)
res4: List[Int] = List(2, 4)

scala> bag.flatMap(toInt).takeWhile(_ < 4)
res5: List[Int] = List(1, 2)

scala> bag.flatMap(toInt).partition(_ > 3)
res6: (List[Int], List[Int]) = (List(4),List(1, 2))
```

As a second example of using `flatMap`, imagine you have a method that finds all the subwords from a word you give it. Skipping the implementation for a moment, if you call the method with the string then, it should work as follows:

```scala
scala> subWords("then")
res0: List[String] = List(then, hen, the)
```

(subWords should also return the string he, but it's in beta.)

With that method (mostly) working, it can be called on a list of words with map:

```scala
scala> val words = List("band", "start", "then")
words: List[java.lang.String] = List(band, start, then)

scala> words.map(subWords)
res0: List[List[String]] =
  List(List(band, and, ban), List(start, tart, star), List(then, hen, the))
```

Very cool, you have a list of subwords for all the given words. One problem, though: map gave you a list of lists. What to do? Call `flatten`:

```scala
scala> words.map(subWords).flatten
res1: List[String] = List(band, and, ban, start, tart, star, then, hen, the)
```

Success! You have a list of all the subwords from the original list of words. But notice what you did: You called map, then `flatten`. Enter "map flat," er, `flatMap`:

```scala
scala> words.flatMap(subWords)
res2: List[String] = List(band, and, ban, start, tart, star, then, hen, the)
```

General rule: Whenever you think map followed by `flatten`, use `flatMap`. Eventually your brain will skip over the intermediate steps.

As for the implementation of subWords ... well, it's a work in progress:

```
def subWords(word: String) = List(word, word.tail, word.take(word.length-1))
```

## See Also

Recipe 20.6, "Using the Option/Some/None Pattern", shows another `flatMap` example.

# 10.17. Using filter to Filter a Collection

## Problem

You want to filter the items in a collection to create a new collection that contains only the elements that match your filtering criteria.

## Solution

As listed in Recipe 10.3, "Choosing a Collection Method to Solve a Problem", a variety of methods can be used to filter the elements of an input collection to produce a new output collection. This recipe demonstrates the `filter` method.

To use `filter` on your collection, give it a predicate to filter the collection elements as desired. Your predicate should accept a parameter of the same type that the collection holds, evaluate that element, and return `true` to keep the element in the new collection, or `false` to filter it out. Remember to assign the results of the filtering operation to a new variable.

For instance, the following example shows how to create a list of even numbers from an input list using a modulus algorithm:

```
scala> val x = List.range(1, 10)
x: List[Int] = List(1, 2, 3, 4, 5, 6, 7, 8, 9)

// create a list of all the even numbers in the list
scala> val evens = x.filter(_ % 2 == 0)
evens: List[Int] = List(2, 4, 6, 8)
```

As shown, `filter` returns all elements from a sequence that return `true` when your function/predicate is called. There's also a `filterNot` method that returns all elements from a list for which your function returns `false`.

## Discussion

The main methods you can use to filter a collection are listed in Recipe 10.3, and are repeated here for your convenience: `collect`, `diff`, `distinct`, `drop`, `dropWhile`, `filter`, `filterNot`, `find`, `foldLeft`, `foldRight`, `head`, `headOption`, `init`, `intersect`, `last`, `lastOption`, `reduceLeft`, `reduceRight`, `remove`, `slice`, `tail`, `take`, `takeWhile`, and `union`.

Unique characteristics of `filter` compared to these other methods include:

- `filter` walks through all of the elements in the collection; some of the other methods stop before reaching the end of the collection.
- `filter` lets you supply a predicate (a function that returns `true` or `false`) to filter the elements.

How you filter the elements in your collection is entirely up to your algorithm. The following examples show a few ways to filter a list of strings:

```scala
scala> val fruits = Set("orange", "peach", "apple", "banana")
fruits: scala.collection.immutable.Set[java.lang.String] =
  Set(orange, peach, apple, banana)

scala> val x = fruits.filter(_.startsWith("a"))
x: scala.collection.immutable.Set[String] = Set(apple)

scala> val y = fruits.filter(_.length > 5)
y: scala.collection.immutable.Set[String] = Set(orange, banana)
```

Your filtering function can be as complicated as needed. When your algorithm gets long, you can pass a multiline block of code into `filter`:

```scala
scala> val list = "apple" :: "banana" :: 1 :: 2 :: Nil
list: List[Any] = List(apple, banana, 1, 2)

scala> val strings = list.filter {
     |    case s: String => true
     |    case _ => false
     | }
strings: List[Any] = List(apple, banana)
```

You can also put your algorithm in a separate method (or function) and then pass it into `filter`:

```scala
def onlyStrings(a: Any) = a match {
  case s: String => true
  case _ => false
}

val strings = list.filter(onlyStrings)
```

The following example demonstrates that you can filter a list as many times as needed:

```scala
def getFileContentsWithoutBlanksComments(canonicalFilename: String):
List[String] = {
  io.Source.fromFile(canonicalFilename)
           .getLines
           .toList
```

```
              .filter(_.trim != "")
              .filter(_.charAt(0) != '#')
   }
```

The two keys to using `filter` are:

- Your algorithm should return `true` for the elements you want to keep and `false` for the other elements
- Remember to assign the results of the `filter` method to a new variable; `filter` doesn't modify the collection it's invoked on

## See Also

The `collect` method can also be used as a filtering method. Because it uses partial functions, it's described in detail in Recipe 9.8, "Creating Partial Functions".

# 10.18. Extracting a Sequence of Elements from a Collection

## Problem

You want to extract a sequence of contiguous elements from a collection, either by specifying a starting position and length, or a function.

## Solution

There are quite a few collection methods you can use to extract a contiguous list of elements from a sequence, including `drop`, `dropWhile`, `head`, `headOption`, `init`, `last`, `lastOption`, `slice`, `tail`, `take`, `takeWhile`.

Given the following `Array`:

```
scala> val x = (1 to 10).toArray
x: Array[Int] = Array(1, 2, 3, 4, 5, 6, 7, 8, 9, 10)
```

The `drop` method drops the number of elements you specify from the beginning of the sequence:

```
scala> val y = x.drop(3)
y: Array[Int] = Array(4, 5, 6, 7, 8, 9, 10)
```

The `dropWhile` method drops elements as long as the predicate you supply returns `true`:

```
scala> val y = x.dropWhile(_ < 6)
y: List[Int] = List(6, 7, 8, 9, 10)
```

The dropRight method works like drop, but starts at the end of the collection and works forward, dropping elements from the end of the sequence:

```
scala> val y = x.dropRight(4)
y: Array[Int] = Array(1, 2, 3, 4, 5, 6)
```

take extracts the first N elements from the sequence:

```
scala> val y = x.take(3)
y: Array[Int] = Array(1, 2, 3)
```

takeWhile returns elements as long as the predicate you supply returns true:

```
scala> val y = x.takeWhile(_ < 5)
y: Array[Int] = Array(1, 2, 3, 4)
```

takeRight works the same way take works, but starts at the end of the sequence and moves forward, taking the specified number of elements from the end of the sequence:

```
scala> val y = x.takeRight(3)
y: Array[Int] = Array(8, 9, 10)
```

slice(from, until) returns a sequence beginning at the index from until the index until, not including until, and assuming a zero-based index:

```
scala> val peeps = List("John", "Mary", "Jane", "Fred")
peeps: List[String] = List(John, Mary, Jane, Fred)

scala> peeps.slice(1,3)
res0: List[String] = List(Mary, Jane)
```

All of these methods provide another way of filtering a collection, with their distinguishing feature being that they return a contiguous sequence of elements.

### Even more methods

There are even more methods you can use. Given this list:

```
scala> val nums = (1 to 5).toArray
nums: Array[Int] = Array(1, 2, 3, 4, 5)
```

the comments after the following expressions show the values that are returned by each expression:

```
nums.head            // 1
nums.headOption      // Some(1)
nums.init            // Array(1, 2, 3, 4)
nums.last            // 5
nums.lastOption      // Some(5)
nums.tail            // Array(2, 3, 4, 5)
```

Hopefully the use of most of those methods is obvious. Two that might need a little explanation are init and tail. The init method returns all elements from the sequence except for the last element. The `tail` method returns all of the elements except the first one.

See the Scaladoc for any sequence (`List`, `Array`, etc.) for more methods.

# 10.19. Splitting Sequences into Subsets (groupBy, partition, etc.)

## Problem

You want to partition a sequence into two or more different sequences (subsets) based on an algorithm or location you define.

## Solution

Use the `groupBy`, `partition`, `span`, or `splitAt` methods to partition a sequence into subsequences. The `sliding` and `unzip` methods can also be used to split sequences into subsequences, though `sliding` can generate many subsequences, and `unzip` primarily works on a sequence of `Tuple2` elements.

The `groupBy`, `partition`, and `span` methods let you split a sequence into subsets according to a function, whereas `splitAt` lets you split a collection into two sequences by providing an index number, as shown in these examples:

```scala
scala> val x = List(15, 10, 5, 8, 20, 12)
x: List[Int] = List(15, 10, 5, 8, 20, 12)

scala> val y = x.groupBy(_ > 10)
y: Map[Boolean,List[Int]] =
    Map(false -> List(10, 5, 8), true -> List(15, 20, 12))

scala> val y = x.partition(_ > 10)
y: (List[Int], List[Int]) = (List(15, 20, 12), List(10, 5, 8))

scala> val y = x.span(_ < 20)
y: (List[Int], List[Int]) = (List(15, 10, 5, 8), List(20, 12))

scala> val y = x.splitAt(2)
y: (List[Int], List[Int]) = (List(15, 10), List(5, 8, 20, 12))
```

The `groupBy` method partitions the collection into a `Map` of subcollections based on your function. The `true` map contains the elements for which your predicate returned `true`, and the `false` map contains the elements that returned `false`.

The `partition`, `span`, and `splitAt` methods create a `Tuple2` of sequences that are of the same type as the original collection. The `partition` method creates two lists, one containing values for which your predicate returned `true`, and the other containing the elements that returned `false`. The span method returns a `Tuple2` based on your predicate p, consisting of "the longest prefix of this list whose elements all satisfy p, and the rest of this list." The `splitAt` method splits the original list according to the element index value you supplied.

When a `Tuple2` of sequences is returned, its two sequences can be accessed like this:

```
scala> val (a,b) = x.partition(_ > 10)
a: List[Int] = List(15, 20, 12)
b: List[Int] = List(10, 5, 8)
```

The sequences in the `Map` that `groupBy` creates can be accessed like this:

```
scala> val groups = x.groupBy(_ > 10)
groups: scala.collection.immutable.Map[Boolean,List[Int]] =
  Map(false -> List(10, 5, 8), true -> List(15, 20, 12))

scala> val trues = groups(true)
trues: List[Int] = List(15, 20, 12)

scala> val falses = groups(false)
falses: List[Int] = List(10, 5, 8)
```

The `sliding(size, step)` method is an interesting creature that can be used to break a sequence into many groups. It can be called with just a `size`, or both a `size` and `step`:

```
scala> val nums = (1 to 5).toArray
nums: Array[Int] = Array(1, 2, 3, 4, 5)

// size = 2
scala> nums.sliding(2).toList
res0: List[Array[Int]] = List(Array(1, 2), Array(2, 3), Array(3, 4), Array(4, 5))

// size = 2, step = 2
scala> nums.sliding(2,2).toList
res1: List[Array[Int]] = List(Array(1, 2), Array(3, 4), Array(5))

// size = 2, step = 3
scala> nums.sliding(2,3).toList
res2: List[Array[Int]] = List(Array(1, 2), Array(4, 5))
```

As shown, `sliding` works by passing a "sliding window" over the original sequence, returning sequences of a length given by `size`. The `step` parameter lets you skip over elements, as shown in the last two examples. In my experience, the first two examples are the most useful, first with a default step size of 1, and then when `step` matches `size`.

The `unzip` method is also interesting. It can be used to take a sequence of `Tuple2` values and create two resulting lists: one that contains the first element of each tuple, and another that contains the second element from each tuple:

```
scala> val listOfTuple2s = List((1,2), ('a', 'b'))
listOfTuple2s: List[(AnyVal, AnyVal)] = List((1,2), (a,b))

scala> val x = listOfTuple2s.unzip
x: (List[AnyVal], List[AnyVal]) = (List(1, a),List(2, b))
```

For instance, given a list of couples, you can unzip the list to create a list of women and a list of men:

```
scala> val couples = List(("Kim", "Al"), ("Julia", "Terry"))
couples: List[(String, String)] = List((Kim,Al), (Julia,Terry))

scala> val (women, men) = couples.unzip
women: List[String] = List(Kim, Julia)
men: List[String] = List(Al, Terry)
```

As you might guess from its name, the unzip method is the opposite of zip:

```
scala> val women = List("Kim", "Julia")
women: List[String] = List(Kim, Julia)

scala> val men = List("Al", "Terry")
men: List[String] = List(Al, Terry)

scala> val couples = women zip men
couples: List[(String, String)] = List((Kim,Al), (Julia,Terry))
```

See the Scaladoc for any sequence (List, Array, etc.) for more methods.

# 10.20. Walking Through a Collection with the reduce and fold Methods

## Problem

You want to walk through all of the elements in a sequence, comparing two neighboring elements as you walk through the collection.

## Solution

Use the reduceLeft, foldLeft, reduceRight, and foldRight methods to walk through the elements in a sequence, applying your function to neighboring elements to yield a new result, which is then compared to the next element in the sequence to yield a new result. (Related methods, such as scanLeft and scanRight, are also shown in the Discussion.)

For example, use reduceLeft to walk through a sequence from left to right (from the first element to the last). reduceLeft starts by comparing the first two elements in the collection with your algorithm, and returns a result. That result is compared with the third element, and that comparison yields a new result. That result is compared to the fourth element to yield a new result, and so on.

If you've never used these methods before, you'll see that they give you a surprising amount of power. The best way to show this is with some examples. First, create a sample collection to experiment with:

```
scala> val a = Array(12, 6, 15, 2, 20, 9)
a: Array[Int] = Array(12, 6, 15, 2, 20, 9)
```

Given that sequence, use reduceLeft to determine different properties about the collection. The following example shows how to get the sum of all the elements in the sequence:

```
scala> a.reduceLeft(_ + _)
res0: Int = 64
```

Don't let the underscores throw you for a loop; they just stand for the two parameters that are passed into your function. You can write that code like this, if you prefer:

```
a.reduceLeft((x,y) => x + y)
```

The following examples show how to use reduceLeft to get the product of all elements in the sequence, the smallest value in the sequence, and the largest value:

```
scala> a.reduceLeft(_ * _)
res1: Int = 388800

scala> a.reduceLeft(_ min _)
res2: Int = 2

scala> a.reduceLeft(_ max _)
res3: Int = 20
```

### Show each step in the process

You can demonstrate how reduceLeft works by creating a larger function. The following function does a "max" comparison like the last example, but has some extra debugging code so you can see how reduceLeft works as it marches through the sequence. Here's the function:

```
// returns the max of the two elements
val findMax = (x: Int, y: Int) => {
  val winner = x max y
  println(s"compared $x to $y, $winner was larger")
  winner
}
```

Now call reduceLeft again on the array, this time giving it the findMax function:

```
scala> a.reduceLeft(findMax)
compared 12 to 6, 12 was larger
compared 12 to 15, 15 was larger
compared 15 to 2, 15 was larger
```

```
compared 15 to 20, 20 was larger
compared 20 to 9, 20 was larger
res0: Int = 20
```

The output shows how reduceLeft marches through the elements in the sequence, and how it called the function at each step. Here's how the process works:

- reduceLeft starts by calling findMax to test the first two elements in the array, 12 and 6. findMax returned 12, because 12 is larger than 6.

- reduceLeft takes that result (12), and calls findMax(12, 15). 12 is the result of the first comparison, and 15 is the next element in the collection. 15 is larger, so it becomes the new result.

- reduceLeft keeps taking the result from the function and comparing it to the next element in the collection, until it marches through all the elements in the collection, ending up with the result, 20.

The code that reduceLeft uses under the hood looks like this:

```
// you provide the sequence 'seq' and the function 'f'
var result = seq(0)
for (i <- 1 until seq.length) {
  val next = seq(i)
  result = f(result, next)
}
```

Feeding different algorithms into this loop lets you extract different types of information from your sequence. Wrapping the algorithm in a method also makes for very concise code.

One subtle but important note about reduceLeft: the function (or method) you supply must return the same data type that's stored in the collection. This is necessary so reduceLeft can compare the result of your function to the next element in the collection.

### Working with other sequences and types

As you can imagine, the type contained in the sequence can be anything you need. For instance, determining the longest or shortest string in a sequence of strings is a matter of walking through the elements in the sequence with a function to compare the lengths of two strings:

```
scala> val peeps = Vector("al", "hannah", "emily", "christina", "aleka")
peeps: scala.collection.immutable.Vector[java.lang.String] =
  Vector(al, hannah, emily, christina, aleka)

// longest
scala> peeps.reduceLeft((x,y) => if (x.length > y.length) x else y)
res0: String = christina
```

```
// shortest
scala> peeps.reduceLeft((x,y) => if (x.length < y.length) x else y)
res1: String = al
```

If this had been a collection of `Person` instances, you could run a similar algorithm on each person's name to get the longest and shortest names.

### foldLeft, reduceRight, and foldRight

The `foldLeft` method works just like `reduceLeft`, but it lets you set a seed value to be used for the first element. The following examples demonstrate a "sum" algorithm, first with `reduceLeft` and then with `foldLeft`, to demonstrate the difference:

```
scala> val a = Array(1, 2, 3)
a: Array[Int] = Array(1, 2, 3)

scala> a.reduceLeft(_ + _)
res0: Int = 6

scala> a.foldLeft(20)(_ + _)
res1: Int = 26

scala> a.foldLeft(100)(_ + _)
res2: Int = 106
```

In the last two examples, `foldLeft` uses `20` and then `100` for its first element, which affects the resulting sum as shown.

If you haven't seen syntax like that before, `foldLeft` takes two parameter lists. The first parameter list takes one field, the seed value. The second parameter list is the block of code you want to run (your algorithm). Recipe 3.18, "Creating Your Own Control Structures", demonstrates the use of multiple parameter lists.

The `reduceRight` and `foldRight` methods work the same as `reduceLeft` and `foldLeft`, respectively, but they begin at the end of the collection and work from right to left, i.e., from the end of the collection back to the beginning.

### The difference between reduceLeft and reduceRight

In many algorithms, it may not matter if you call `reduceLeft` or `reduceRight`. In that case, you can call `reduce` instead. The reduce Scaladoc states, "The order in which operations are performed on elements is unspecified and may be nondeterministic."

But some algorithms will yield a big difference. For example, given this `divide` function:

```
val divide = (x: Double, y: Double) => {
  val result = x / y
  println(s"divided $x by $y to yield $result")
  result
}
```

and this array:

---

```
val a = Array(1.0, 2.0, 3.0)
```

reduceLeft and reduceRight yield a significantly different result:

```
scala> a.reduceLeft(divide)
divided 1.0 by 2.0 to yield 0.5
divided 0.5 by 3.0 to yield 0.16666666666666666
res0: Double = 0.16666666666666666

scala> a.reduceRight(divide)
divided 2.0 by 3.0 to yield 0.6666666666666666
divided 1.0 by 0.6666666666666666 to yield 1.5
res1: Double = 1.5
```

### scanLeft and scanRight

Two methods named scanLeft and scanRight walk through a sequence in a manner similar to reduceLeft and reduceRight, but they return a sequence instead of a single value.

For instance, scanLeft "Produces a collection containing cumulative results of applying the operator going left to right." To understand how it works, create another function with a little debug code in it:

```
val product = (x: Int, y: Int) => {
  val result = x * y
  println(s"multiplied $x by $y to yield $result")
  result
}
```

Here's what scanLeft looks like when it's used with that function and a seed value:

```
scala> val a = Array(1, 2, 3)
a: Array[Int] = Array(1, 2, 3)

scala> a.scanLeft(10)(product)
multiplied 10 by 1 to yield 10
multiplied 10 by 2 to yield 20
multiplied 20 by 3 to yield 60
res0: Array[Int] = Array(10, 10, 20, 60)
```

As you can see, scanLeft returns a new sequence, rather than a single value. The scanRight method works the same way, but marches through the collection from right to left.

There are a few more related methods, including reduce (which was mentioned earlier), reduceLeftOption, and reduceRightOption.

If you're curious about the statement in the reduce method Scaladoc that, "The order in which operations are performed on elements is unspecified and may be nondeterministic," run this code in the REPL:

```
val findMax = (x: Int, y: Int) => {
  Thread.sleep(10)
  val winner = x max y
  println(s"compared $x to $y, $winner was larger")
  winner
}

val a = Array.range(0,50)
a.par.reduce(findMax)
```

You'll see that the elements in the sequence are indeed compared in a nondeterministic order.

# 10.21. Extracting Unique Elements from a Sequence

## Problem

You have a collection that contains duplicate elements, and you want to remove the duplicates.

## Solution

Call the `distinct` method on the collection:

```
scala> val x = Vector(1, 1, 2, 3, 3, 4)
x: scala.collection.immutable.Vector[Int] = Vector(1, 1, 2, 3, 3, 4)

scala> val y = x.distinct
y: scala.collection.immutable.Vector[Int] = Vector(1, 2, 3, 4)
```

The `distinct` method returns a new collection with the duplicate values removed. Remember to assign the result to a new variable. This is required for both immutable and mutable collections.

If you happen to need a `Set`, converting the collection to a `Set` is another way to remove the duplicate elements:

```
scala> val s = x.toSet
s: scala.collection.immutable.Set[Int] = Set(1, 2, 3, 4)
```

By definition a `Set` can only contain unique elements, so converting an `Array`, `List`, `Vector`, or other sequence to a `Set` removes the duplicates. In fact, this is how `distinct` works. The source code for the `distinct` method in `GenSeqLike` shows that it uses an instance of `mutable.HashSet`.

### Using distinct with your own classes

To use `distinct` with your own class, you'll need to implement the `equals` and `hashCode` methods. For example, the following class *will* work with `distinct` because it implements those methods:

---

```
class Person(firstName: String, lastName: String) {

  override def toString = s"$firstName $lastName"

  def canEqual(a: Any) = a.isInstanceOf[Person]

  override def equals(that: Any): Boolean =
    that match {
      case that: Person => that.canEqual(this) && this.hashCode == that.hashCode
      case _ => false
    }

  override def hashCode: Int = {
    val prime = 31
    var result = 1
    result = prime * result + lastName.hashCode;
    result = prime * result + (if (firstName == null) 0 else firstName.hashCode)
    return result
  }

}

object Person {
  def apply(firstName: String, lastName: String) =
    new Person(firstName, lastName)
}
```

You can demonstrate that this class works with distinct by placing the following code in the REPL:

```
val dale1 = new Person("Dale", "Cooper")
val dale2 = new Person("Dale", "Cooper")
val ed = new Person("Ed", "Hurley")
val list = List(dale1, dale2, ed)
val uniques = list.distinct
```

The last two lines look like this in the REPL:

```
scala> val list = List(dale1, dale2, ed)
list: List[Person] = List(Dale Cooper, Dale Cooper, Ed Hurley)

scala> val uniquePeople = list.distinct
uniquePeople: List[Person] = List(Dale Cooper, Ed Hurley)
```

If you remove either the equals method or hashCode method, you'll see that distinct won't work as desired.

## See Also

You can find the source code for the SeqLike trait (and its distinct method) by following the *Source* link on its Scaladoc page (*http://bit.ly/15fUomj*).

# 10.22. Merging Sequential Collections

## Problem

You want to join two sequences into one sequence, either keeping all of the original elements, finding the elements that are common to both collections, or finding the difference between the two sequences.

## Solution

There are a variety of solutions to this problem, depending on your needs:

- Use the ++= method to merge a sequence into a mutable sequence.
- Use the ++ method to merge two mutable or immutable sequences.
- Use collection methods like union, diff, and intersect.

Use the ++= method to merge a sequence (any TraversableOnce) into a mutable collection like an ArrayBuffer:

```
scala> val a = collection.mutable.ArrayBuffer(1,2,3)
a: scala.collection.mutable.ArrayBuffer[Int] = ArrayBuffer(1, 2, 3)

scala> a ++= Seq(4,5,6)
res0: a.type = ArrayBuffer(1, 2, 3, 4, 5, 6)
```

Use the ++ method to merge two mutable or immutable collections while assigning the result to a new variable:

```
scala> val a = Array(1,2,3)
a: Array[Int] = Array(1, 2, 3)

scala> val b = Array(4,5,6)
b: Array[Int] = Array(4, 5, 6)

scala> val c = a ++ b
c: Array[Int] = Array(1, 2, 3, 4, 5, 6)
```

You can also use methods like union and intersect to combine sequences to create a resulting sequence:

```
scala> val a = Array(1,2,3,4,5)
a: Array[Int] = Array(1, 2, 3, 4, 5)

scala> val b = Array(4,5,6,7,8)
b: Array[Int] = Array(4, 5, 6, 7, 8)

// elements that are in both collections
scala> val c = a.intersect(b)
c: Array[Int] = Array(4, 5)
```

```
// all elements from both collections
scala> val c = a.union(b)
c: Array[Int] = Array(1, 2, 3, 4, 5, 4, 5, 6, 7, 8)

// distinct elements from both collections
scala> val c = a.union(b).distinct
c: Array[Int] = Array(1, 2, 3, 4, 5, 6, 7, 8)
```

The diff method results depend on which sequence it's called on:

```
scala> val c = a diff b
c: Array[Int] = Array(1, 2, 3)

scala> val c = b diff a
c: Array[Int] = Array(6, 7, 8)
```

The Scaladoc for the diff method states that it returns, "a new list which contains all elements of this list except some of occurrences of elements that also appear in that. If an element value x appears n times in that, then the first n occurrences of x will not form part of the result, but any following occurrences will."

The objects that correspond to most collections also have a concat method:

```
scala> Array.concat(a, b)
res0: Array[Int] = Array(1, 2, 3, 4, 4, 5, 6, 7)
```

If you happen to be working with a List, the ::: method prepends the elements of one list to another list:

```
scala> val a = List(1,2,3,4)
a: List[Int] = List(1, 2, 3, 4)

scala> val b = List(4,5,6,7)
b: List[Int] = List(4, 5, 6, 7)

scala> val c = a ::: b
c: List[Int] = List(1, 2, 3, 4, 4, 5, 6, 7)
```

## Discussion

You can also use the diff method to get the *relative complement* of two sets.

 The relative complement of a set A with respect to a set B is the set of elements in B that are not in A.

On a recent project, I needed to find the elements in one list that weren't in another list. I did this by converting the lists to sets, and then using the diff method to compare the two sets. For instance, given these two arrays:

```
val a = Array(1,2,3,11,4,12,4,5)
val b = Array(6,7,4,5)
```

you can find the relative complement of each array by first converting them to sets, and then comparing them with the `diff` method:

```
// the elements in a that are not in b
scala> val c = a.toSet diff b.toSet
c: scala.collection.immutable.Set[Int] = Set(1, 2, 12, 3, 11)

// the elements in b that are not in a
scala> val d = b.toSet diff a.toSet
d: scala.collection.immutable.Set[Int] = Set(6, 7)
```

If desired, you can then sum those results to get the list of elements that are either in the first set or the second set, but not both sets:

```
scala> val complement = c ++ d
complement: scala.collection.immutable.Set[Int] = Set(1, 6, 2, 12, 7, 3, 11)
```

This works because `diff` returns a set that contains the elements in the current set (`this`) that are not in the other set (`that`).

You can also use the `--` method to get the same result:

```
scala> val c = a.toSet -- b.toSet
c: scala.collection.immutable.Set[Int] = Set(1, 2, 12, 3, 11)

scala> val d = b.toSet -- a.toSet
d: scala.collection.immutable.Set[Int] = Set(6, 7)
```

Subtracting the intersection of the two sets also yields the same result:

```
scala> val i = a.intersect(b)
i: Array[Int] = Array(4, 5)

scala> val c = a.toSet -- i.toSet
c: scala.collection.immutable.Set[Int] = Set(1, 2, 12, 3, 11)

scala> val d = b.toSet -- i.toSet
d: scala.collection.immutable.Set[Int] = Set(6, 7)
```

# 10.23. Merging Two Sequential Collections into Pairs with zip

## Problem

You want to merge data from two sequential collections into a collection of key/value pairs.

---

# Solution

Use the `zip` method to join two sequences into one:

```
scala> val women = List("Wilma", "Betty")
women: List[String] = List(Wilma, Betty)

scala> val men = List("Fred", "Barney")
men: List[String] = List(Fred, Barney)

scala> val couples = women zip men
couples: List[(String, String)] = List((Wilma,Fred), (Betty,Barney))
```

This creates an `Array` of `Tuple2` elements, which is a merger of the two original sequences.

This code shows one way to loop over the resulting collection:

```
scala> for ((wife, husband) <- couples) {
     |     println(s"$wife is married to $husband")
     | }
Wilma is married to Fred
Betty is married to Barney
```

Once you have a sequence of tuples like `couples`, you can convert it to a `Map`, which may be more convenient:

```
scala> val couplesMap = couples.toMap
couplesMap: scala.collection.immutable.Map[String,String] =
  Map(Wilma -> Fred, Betty -> Barney)
```

# Discussion

If one collection contains more items than the other collection, the items at the end of the longer collection will be dropped. In the previous example, if the `prices` collection contained only one element, the resulting collection will contain only one `Tuple2`:

```
// three elements
scala> val products = Array("breadsticks", "pizza", "soft drink")
products: Array[String] = Array(breadsticks, pizza, soft drink)

// one element
scala> val prices = Array(4)
prices: Array[Int] = Array(4)

// one resulting element
scala> val productsWithPrice = products.zip(prices)
productsWithPrice: Array[(String, Int)] = Array((breadsticks,4))
```

Note that the `unzip` method is the reverse of `zip`:

```
scala> val (a,b) = productsWithPrice.unzip
```

```
a: collection.mutable.IndexedSeq[String] =
   ArrayBuffer(breadsticks, pizza, soft drink)

b: collection.mutable.IndexedSeq[Double] =
   ArrayBuffer(4.0, 10.0, 1.5)
```

## See Also

Recipes 10.10, 10.11, and 10.19 demonstrate other uses of the zip method (and zipWithIndex).

# 10.24. Creating a Lazy View on a Collection

## Problem

You're working with a large collection and want to create a "lazy" version of it so it will only compute and return results as they are actually needed.

## Solution

Except for the Stream class, whenever you create an instance of a Scala collection class, you're creating a *strict* version of the collection. This means that if you create a collection that contains one million elements, memory is allocated for all of those elements immediately. This is the way things normally work in a language like Java.

In Scala you can optionally create a *view* on a collection. A view makes the result nonstrict, or *lazy*. This changes the resulting collection, so when it's used with a transformer method, the elements will only be calculated as they are accessed, and not "eagerly," as they normally would be. (A *transformer method* is a method that transforms an input collection into a new output collection, as described in the Discussion.)

You can see the effect of creating a view on a collection by creating one Range without a view, and a second one with a view:

```
scala> 1 to 100
res0: scala.collection.immutable.Range.Inclusive =
    Range(1, 2, 3, 4, ... 98, 99, 100)

scala> (1 to 100).view
res0: java.lang.Object with
    scala.collection.SeqView[Int,scala.collection.immutable.IndexedSeq[Int]] =
    SeqView(...)
```

Creating the Range without a view shows what you expect, a Range with 100 elements. However, the Range with the view shows different output in the REPL, showing something called a SeqView.

The signature of the SeqView shows:

- Int is the type of the view's elements.

- The `scala.collection.immutable.IndexedSeq[Int]` portion of the output indicates the type you'll get if you `force` the collection back to a "normal," strict collection.

You can see this when you `force` the view back to a normal collection:

```
scala> val view = (1 to 100).view
view: java.lang.Object with
  scala.collection.SeqView[Int,scala.collection.immutable.IndexedSeq[Int]] =
  SeqView(...)

scala> val x = view.force
x: scala.collection.immutable.IndexedSeq[Int] =
   Vector(1, 2, 3, ... 98, 99, 100)
```

There are several ways to see the effect of adding a view to a collection. First, you'll see that using a method like `foreach` doesn't seem to change when using a view:

```
(1 to 100).foreach(println)
(1 to 100).view.foreach(println)
```

Both of those expressions will print 100 elements to the console. Because `foreach` isn't a transformer method, the result is unaffected.

However, calling a `map` method with and without a view has dramatically different results:

```
scala> (1 to 100).map { _ * 2 }
res1: scala.collection.immutable.IndexedSeq[Int] =
  Vector(2, 4, 6, ... 196, 198, 200)

scala> (1 to 100).view.map { _ * 2 }
res0: scala.collection.SeqView[Int,Seq[_]] = SeqViewM(...)
```

These results are different because `map` is a transformer method. A fun way to further demonstrate this difference is with the following code:

```
val x = (1 to 1000).view.map { e =>
  Thread.sleep(10)
  e * 2
}
```

If you run that code as shown, it will return immediately, returning a `SeqView` as before. But if you remove the `view` method call, the code block will take about 10 seconds to run.

## Discussion

The Scala documentation states that a view "constructs only a proxy for the result collection, and its elements get constructed only as one demands them ... A view is a special kind of collection that represents some base collection, but implements all transformers lazily."

A *transformer* is a method that constructs a new collection from an existing collection. This includes methods like map, filter, reverse, and many more. When you use these methods, you're transforming the input collection to a new output collection.

This helps to explain why the foreach method prints the same result for a strict collection and its view: it's not a transformer method. But the map method, and other transformer methods like reverse, treat the view in a lazy manner:

```
scala> l.reverse
res0: List[Int] = List(3, 2, 1)

scala> l.view.reverse
res1: scala.collection.SeqView[Int,List[Int]] = SeqViewR(...)
```

At the end of the Solution you saw this block of code:

```
val x = (1 to 1000).view.map { e =>
  Thread.sleep(10)
  e * 2
}
```

As mentioned, that code returns a SeqView immediately. But when you go to print the elements in x, like this:

```
x.foreach(print)
```

there will be a 10 ms pause before each element is printed. The elements are being "demanded" in this line of code, so the penalty of the Thread.sleep method call is paid as each element is yielded.

### Use cases

There are two primary use cases for using a view:

- Performance
- To treat a collection like a database view

Regarding performance, assume that you get into a situation where you may (or may not) have to operate on a collection of a billion elements. You certainly want to avoid running an algorithm on a billion elements if you don't have to, so using a view makes sense here.

The second use case lets you use a Scala view on a collection just like a database view. The following examples show how a collection view works like a database view:

```
// create a normal array
scala> val arr = (1 to 10).toArray
arr: Array[Int] = Array(1, 2, 3, 4, 5, 6, 7, 8, 9, 10)
```

```
// create a view on the array
scala> val view = arr.view.slice(2, 5)
view: scala.collection.mutable.IndexedSeqView[Int,Array[Int]] = SeqViewS(...)

// modify the array
scala> arr(2) = 42

// the view is affected:
scala> view.foreach(println)
42
4
5

// change the elements in the view
scala> view(0) = 10
scala> view(1) = 20
scala> view(2) = 30

// the array is affected:
scala> arr
res0: Array[Int] = Array(1, 2, 10, 20, 30, 6, 7, 8, 9, 10)
```

Changing the elements in the array updates the view, and changing the elements referenced by the view changes the elements in the array. When you need to modify a subset of elements in a collection, creating a view on the original collection and modifying the elements in the view can be a powerful way to achieve this goal.

As a final note, don't confuse using a view with saving memory when creating a collection. Both of the following approaches will generate a "java.lang.OutOfMemoryError: Java heap space" error in the REPL:

```
val a = Array.range(0,123456789)
val a = Array.range(0,123456789).view
```

The benefit of using a view in regards to performance comes with how the view works with transformer methods.

### See Also

An introduction to Scala views (*http://bit.ly/1bgLHy8*)

# 10.25. Populating a Collection with a Range

## Problem

You want to populate a List, Array, Vector, or other sequence with a Range.

## Solution

Call the range method on sequences that support it, or create a Range and convert it to the desired sequence.

In the first approach, the range method is available on the companion object of supported types like Array, List, Vector, ArrayBuffer, and others:

```
scala> Array.range(1, 5)
res0: Array[Int] = Array(1, 2, 3, 4)

scala> List.range(0, 10)
res1: List[Int] = List(0, 1, 2, 3, 4, 5, 6, 7, 8, 9)

scala> Vector.range(0, 10, 2)
res2: collection.immutable.Vector[Int] = Vector(0, 2, 4, 6, 8)
```

For some of the collections, such as List and Array, you can also create a Range and convert it to the desired sequence:

```
scala> val a = (0 until 10).toArray
a: Array[Int] = Array(0, 1, 2, 3, 4, 5, 6, 7, 8, 9)

scala> val list = 1 to 10 by 2 toList
list: List[Int] = List(1, 3, 5, 7, 9)

scala> val list = (1 to 10).by(2).toList
list: List[Int] = List(1, 3, 5, 7, 9)
```

The REPL shows the collections that can be created directly from a Range:

```
toArray      toBuffer         toIndexedSeq    toIterable    toIterator
toList       toMap            toSeq           toSet         toStream
toString     toTraversable
```

Using this approach is useful for some collections, like Set, which don't offer a range method:

```
// intentional error
scala> val set = Set.range(0, 5)
<console>:7: error: value range is not a member of object
scala.collection.immutable.Set
       val set = Set.range(0,5)
                     ^

scala> val set = (0 until 10 by 2).toSet
set: scala.collection.immutable.Set[Int] = Set(0, 6, 2, 8, 4)
```

You can also use a Range to create a sequence of characters:

```
scala> val letters = ('a' to 'f').toList
letters: List[Char] = List(a, b, c, d, e, f)
```

```
scala> val letters = ('a' to 'f').by(2).toList
letters: List[Char] = List(a, c, e)
```

As shown in many recipes, ranges are also very useful in `for` loops:

```
scala> for (i <- 1 until 10 by 2) println(i)
1
3
5
7
9
```

## Discussion

By using the `map` method with a `Range`, you can create a sequence with elements other than type `Int` or `Char`:

```
scala> val map = (1 to 5).map(_ * 2.0)
map: collection.immutable.IndexedSeq[Double] = Vector(2.0, 4.0, 6.0, 8.0, 10.0)
```

Using a similar approach, you can also return a sequence of `Tuple2` elements:

```
scala> val map = (1 to 5).map(e => (e,e))
map: scala.collection.immutable.IndexedSeq[(Int, Int)] =
  Vector((1,1), (2,2), (3,3), (4,4), (5,5))
```

That sequence easily converts to a `Map`:

```
scala> val map = (1 to 5).map(e => (e,e)).toMap
map: scala.collection.immutable.Map[Int,Int] =
  Map(5 -> 5, 1 -> 1, 2 -> 2, 3 -> 3, 4 -> 4)
```

# 10.26. Creating and Using Enumerations

## Problem

You want to use an enumeration (a set of named values that act as constants) in your application.

## Solution

Extend the `scala.Enumeration` class to create your enumeration:

```
package com.acme.app {
  object Margin extends Enumeration {
    type Margin = Value
    val TOP, BOTTOM, LEFT, RIGHT = Value
  }
}
```

Then import the enumeration to use it in your application:

```
object Main extends App {

    import com.acme.app.Margin._

    // use an enumeration value in a test
    var currentMargin = TOP

    // later in the code ...
    if (currentMargin == TOP) println("working on Top")

    // print all the enumeration values
    import com.acme.app.Margin
    Margin.values foreach println

}
```

Enumerations are useful tool for creating groups of constants, such as days of the week, weeks of the year, and many other situations where you have a group of related, constant values.

You can also use the following approach, but it generates about four times as much code as an Enumeration, most of which you won't need if your sole purpose is to use it like an enumeration:

```
// a much "heavier" approach
package com.acme.app {
    trait Margin
    case object TOP extends Margin
    case object RIGHT extends Margin
    case object BOTTOM extends Margin
    case object LEFT extends Margin
}
```

## See Also

Scala Enumeration class (*http://bit.ly/14U04n2*)

# 10.27. Tuples, for When You Just Need a Bag of Things

## Problem

You want to create a small collection of heterogeneous elements.

## Solution

A tuple gives you a way to store a group of heterogeneous items in a container, which is useful in many situations.

Create a tuple by enclosing the desired elements between parentheses. This is a two-element tuple:

```
scala> val d = ("Debi", 95)
d: (String, Int) = (Debi,95)
```

Notice that it contains two different types. The following example shows a three-element tuple:

```
scala> case class Person(name: String)
defined class Person

scala> val t = (3, "Three", new Person("Al"))
t: (Int, java.lang.String, Person) = (3,Three,Person(Al))
```

You can access tuple elements using an underscore construct:

```
scala> t._1
res1: Int = 3

scala> t._2
res2: java.lang.String = Three

scala> t._3
res3: Person = Person(Al)
```

I usually prefer to assign them to variables using pattern matching:

```
scala> val(x, y, z) = (3, "Three", new Person("Al"))
x: Int = 3
y: String = Three
z: Person = Person(Al)
```

A nice feature of this approach is that if you don't want all of the elements from the tuple, just use the _ wildcard character in place of the elements you don't want:

```
scala> val (x, y, _) = t
x: Int = 3
y: java.lang.String = Three

scala> val (x, _, _) = t
x: Int = 3

scala> val (x, _, z) = t
x: Int = 3
z: Person = Person(Al)
```

A two-element tuple is an instance of the Tuple2 class, and a tuple with three elements is an instance of the Tuple3 class. (More on this in the Discussion.) As shown earlier, you can create a Tuple2 like this:

```
scala> val a = ("AL", "Alabama")
a: (java.lang.String, java.lang.String) = (AL,Alabama)
```

You can also create it using these approaches:

```
scala> val b = "AL" -> "Alabama"
b: (java.lang.String, java.lang.String) = (AL,Alabama)

scala> val c = ("AL" -> "Alabama")
c: (java.lang.String, java.lang.String) = (AL,Alabama)
```

When you check the class created by these examples, you'll find they're all of type Tuple2:

```
scala> c.getClass
res0: java.lang.Class[_ <: (java.lang.String, java.lang.String)] =
    class scala.Tuple2
```

This syntax is very convenient for other uses, including the creation of maps:

```
val map = Map("AL" -> "Alabama")
```

## Discussion

The tuple is an interesting construct. There is no single "Tuple" class; instead, the API defines tuple case classes from Tuple2 through Tuple22, meaning that you can have from 2 to 22 elements in a tuple.

A common use case for a tuple is returning multiple items from a method. See Recipe 5.5, "Defining a Method That Returns Multiple Items (Tuples)", for an example of this.

Though a tuple isn't a collection, you can treat a tuple as a collection when needed by creating an iterator:

```
scala> val x = ("AL" -> "Alabama")
x: (java.lang.String, java.lang.String) = (AL,Alabama)

scala> val it = x.productIterator
it: Iterator[Any] = non-empty iterator

scala> for (e <- it) println(e)
AL
Alabama
```

Be aware that like any other iterator, after it's used once, it will be exhausted. Attempting to print the elements a second time yields no output:

```
scala> for (e <- it) println(e)
// no output here
```

Create a new iterator if you need to loop over the elements a second time.

You can also convert a tuple to a collection:

```
scala> val t = ("AL", "Alabama")
t: (String, String) = (AL,Alabama)
```

```
scala> t.productIterator.toArray
res0: Array[Any] = Array(AL, Alabama)
```

## See Also

- The Tuple2 class (*http://bit.ly/15HM6FX*)
- Recipe 5.5, "Defining a Method That Returns Multiple Items (Tuples)"

# 10.28. Sorting a Collection

## Problem

You want to sort a sequential collection. Or, you want to implement the Ordered trait in a custom class so you can use the sorted method, or operators like <, <=, >, and >= to compare instances of your class.

## Solution

See Recipe 11.10, "Sorting Arrays", for information on how to sort an Array. Otherwise, use the sorted or sortWith methods to sort a collection.

The sorted method can sort collections with type Double, Float, Int, and any other type that has an implicit scala.math.Ordering:

```
scala> val a = List(10, 5, 8, 1, 7).sorted
a: List[Int] = List(1, 5, 7, 8, 10)

scala> val b = List("banana", "pear", "apple", "orange").sorted
b: List[String] = List(apple, banana, orange, pear)
```

The "rich" versions of the numeric classes (like RichInt) and the StringOps class all extend the Ordered trait, so they can be used with the sorted method. (More on the Ordered trait in the Discussion.)

The sortWith method lets you provide your own sorting function. The following examples demonstrate how to sort a collection of Int or String in both directions:

```
scala> List(10, 5, 8, 1, 7).sortWith(_ < _)
res1: List[Int] = List(1, 5, 7, 8, 10)

scala> List(10, 5, 8, 1, 7).sortWith(_ > _)
res2: List[Int] = List(10, 8, 7, 5, 1)

scala> List("banana", "pear", "apple", "orange").sortWith(_ < _)
res3: List[java.lang.String] = List(apple, banana, orange, pear)
```

```
scala> List("banana", "pear", "apple", "orange").sortWith(_ > _)
res4: List[java.lang.String] = List(pear, orange, banana, apple)
```

Your sorting function can be as complicated as it needs to be. For example, you can access methods on the elements during the sort, such as the following example, which sorts a list of strings by the string length:

```
scala> List("banana", "pear", "apple", "orange").sortWith(_.length < _.length)
res5: List[java.lang.String] = List(pear, apple, banana, orange)

scala> List("banana", "pear", "apple", "orange").sortWith(_.length > _.length)
res6: List[java.lang.String] = List(banana, orange, apple, pear)
```

In the same way the `length` method is called on a `String`, you can call a method on any class you want to sort. If your sorting method gets longer, first declare it as a method:

```
def sortByLength(s1: String, s2: String) = {
  println("comparing %s and %s".format(s1, s2))
  s1.length > s2.length
}
```

Then use it by passing it into the `sortWith` method:

```
scala> List("banana", "pear", "apple").sortWith(sortByLength)
comparing banana and pear
comparing pear and apple
comparing apple and pear
comparing banana and apple
res0: List[String] = List(banana, apple, pear)
```

## Discussion

If the type a sequence is holding doesn't have an implicit `Ordering`, you won't be able to sort it with `sorted`. For instance, given this basic class:

```
class Person (var name: String) {
  override def toString = name
}
```

create a `List[Person]`:

```
val ty = new Person("Tyler")
val al = new Person("Al")
val paul = new Person("Paul")
val dudes = List(ty, al, paul)
```

If you try to sort this list in the REPL, you'll see an error stating that the `Person` class doesn't have an implicit `Ordering`:

```
scala> dudes.sorted
<console>:13: error: No implicit Ordering defined for Person.
              dudes.sorted
                    ^
```

You can't use sorted with the Person class as it's written, but you can write a simple anonymous function to sort the Person elements by the name field using sortWith:

```scala
scala> val sortedDudes = dudes.sortWith(_.name < _.name)
sortedDudes: Array[Person] = Array(Al, Paul, Tyler)

scala> val sortedDudes = dudes.sortWith(_.name > _.name)
sortedDudes: Array[Person] = Array(Tyler, Paul, Al)
```

### Mix in the Ordered trait

If you'd rather use the Person class with the sorted method, just mix the Ordered trait into the Person class, and implement a compare method. This technique is shown in the following code:

```scala
class Person (var name: String) extends Ordered [Person]
{
  override def toString = name

  // return 0 if the same, negative if this < that, positive if this > that
  def compare (that: Person) = {
    if (this.name == that.name)
      0
    else if (this.name > that.name)
      1
    else
      -1
  }

}
```

This new Person class can be used with sorted.

The compare method is what provides the sorting capability. As shown in the comment, compare should work like this:

- Return 0 if the two objects are the same (equal, typically using the equals method of your class)
- Return a negative value if this is less than that
- Return a positive value if this is greater than that

How you determine whether one instance is greater than another instance is entirely up to your compare algorithm.

Note that because this compare algorithm only compares two String values, it could have been written like this:

```scala
def compare (that: Person) = this.name.compare(that.name)
```

However, I wrote it as shown in the first example to be clear about the approach.

An added benefit of mixing the Ordered trait into your class is that it also lets you compare object instances directly in your code:

```
if (al > ty) println("Al") else println("Tyler")
```

This works because the Ordered trait implements the <=, <, >, and >= methods, and calls your compare method to make those comparisons.

## See Also

For more information, the Ordered and Ordering Scaladoc is excellent, with good examples of this approach, and other approaches.

- The Ordering trait (*http://bit.ly/1bCFQSk*)
- The Ordered trait (*http://bit.ly/12ARfPx*)

# 10.29. Converting a Collection to a String with mkString

## Problem

You want to convert elements of a collection to a String, possibly adding a field separator, prefix, and suffix.

## Solution

Use the mkString method to print a collection as a String. Given a simple collection:

```
val a = Array("apple", "banana", "cherry")
```

you can print the collection elements using mkString:

```
scala> a.mkString
res1: String = applebananacherry
```

That doesn't look too good, so add a separator:

```
scala> a.mkString(" ")
res2: String = apple banana cherry
```

That's better. Use a comma and a space to create a CSV string:

```
scala> a.mkString(", ")
res3: String = apple, banana, cherry
```

The mkString method is overloaded, so you can also add a prefix and suffix:

```
scala> a.mkString("[", ", ", "]")
res4: String = [apple, banana, cherry]
```

If you happen to have a list of lists that you want to convert to a String, such as the following array of arrays, first `flatten` the collection, and then call `mkString`:

```
scala> val a = Array(Array("a", "b"), Array("c", "d"))
a: Array[Array[java.lang.String]] = Array(Array(a, b), Array(c, d))

scala> a.flatten.mkString(", ")
res5: String = a, b, c, d
```

## Discussion

You can also use the `toString` method on a collection, but it returns the name of the collection with the elements in the collection listed inside parentheses:

```
scala> val v = Vector("apple", "banana", "cherry")
v: scala.collection.immutable.Vector[String] = Vector(apple, banana, cherry)

scala> v.toString
res0: String = Vector(apple, banana, cherry)
```

# CHAPTER 11

# List, Array, Map, Set (and More)

## Introduction

Whereas Chapter 10 covers collections in general, this chapter provides recipes that are specific to the following collection types:

- `List`
- `Array` (and `ArrayBuffer`)
- `Map`
- `Set`

It also provides a few recipes for special-purpose collections like `Queue`, `Stack`, `Range`, and `Stream`. The following paragraphs provide a brief introduction to the `List`, `Array`, `Map`, and `Set` classes.

## List

If you're coming to Scala from Java, you'll quickly see that despite their names, the Scala `List` class is nothing like the Java `List` classes, such as the popular Java `ArrayList`. The Scala `List` class is immutable, so its size as well as the elements it refers to can't change. It's implemented as a linked list, and is generally thought of in terms of its `head`, `tail`, and `isEmpty` methods. Therefore, most operations on a `List` involve recursive algorithms, where the algorithm splits the list into its head and tail components.

## Array (and ArrayBuffer)

A Scala `Array` is an interesting collection type. The Scaladoc for the `Array` class states, "Arrays are mutable, indexed collections of values." The class is mutable in that its elements can be changed, but once the size of an `Array` is set, it can never grow or shrink.

Although the `Array` is often demonstrated in Scala examples, and often shows up in the Scala API and third-party APIs, the recommendation with Scala 2.10.x is to use the `Vector` class as your "go to" *immutable*, indexed sequence class, and `ArrayBuffer` as your *mutable*, indexed sequence of choice. In keeping with this suggestion, in my real-world code, I use `Vector` and `ArrayBuffer` for those use cases, and then convert them to an `Array` when needed.

## Maps

A Scala `Map` is a collection of key/value pairs, like a Java `Map`, Ruby `Hash`, or Python dictionary. One big difference between a Scala `Map` and the Java map classes is that the default `Map` in Scala is immutable, so if you're not used to working with immutable collections, this can be a big surprise when you attempt to add, delete, or change elements in the map. The techniques of using both immutable and mutable map traits are demonstrated in this chapter.

## Sets

A Scala `Set` is also like a Java `Set`. It's a collection that contains only unique elements, where "uniqueness" is determined by the == method of the type the set contains. If you attempt to add duplicate elements to a set, the set silently ignores the request. Scala has both mutable and immutable versions of its base `Set` implementation and offers additional set classes for other needs, such as having a sorted set.

# 11.1. Different Ways to Create and Populate a List

## Problem

You want to create and populate a `List`.

## Solution

There are many ways to create and initially populate a `List`:

```
// 1
scala> val list = 1 :: 2 :: 3 :: Nil
list: List[Int] = List(1, 2, 3)

// 2
scala> val list = List(1, 2, 3)
x: List[Int] = List(1, 2, 3)

// 3a
scala> val x = List(1, 2.0, 33D, 4000L)
x: List[Double] = List(1.0, 2.0, 33.0, 4000.0)
```

```
// 3b
scala> val x = List[Number](1, 2.0, 33D, 4000L)
x: List[java.lang.Number] = List(1, 2.0, 33.0, 4000)

// 4
scala> val x = List.range(1, 10)
x: List[Int] = List(1, 2, 3, 4, 5, 6, 7, 8, 9)

scala> val x = List.range(0, 10, 2)
x: List[Int] = List(0, 2, 4, 6, 8)

// 5
scala> val x = List.fill(3)("foo")
x: List[String] = List(foo, foo, foo)

// 6
scala> val x = List.tabulate(5)(n => n * n)
x: List[Int] = List(0, 1, 4, 9, 16)

// 7
scala> val x = collection.mutable.ListBuffer(1, 2, 3).toList
x: List[Int] = List(1, 2, 3)

// 8
scala> "foo".toList
res0: List[Char] = List(f, o, o)
```

The first two approaches shown are the most common and straightforward ways to create a List. Examples 3a and 3b show how you can manually control the List type when your collection has mixed types. When the type isn't manually set in Example 3a, it ends up as a List[Double], and in 3b it's manually set to be a List[Number].

Examples 4 through 6 show different ways to create and populate a List with data. Examples 7 and 8 show that many collection types also have a toList method that converts their data to a List.

Going back to the first example, it shows the :: method for creating a List, which will be new to Java developers. As shown, the :: method (called *cons*) takes two arguments: a *head* element, which is a single element, and a *tail*, which is another List. When a List is constructed like this, it must end with a Nil element.

It's important to know that the Scala List class is not like Java List classes, such as the Java ArrayList. For example, Recipe 17.1, "Going to and from Java Collections" shows that a java.util.List converts to a Scala Buffer or Seq, not a Scala List.

The following quote from the Scala `List` Scaladoc discusses the important properties of the `List` class:

> This class is optimal for last-in-first-out (LIFO), stack-like access patterns. If you need another access pattern, for example, random access or FIFO, consider using a collection more suited to this than `List`. `List` has `O(1)` prepend and head/tail access. Most other operations are `O(n)` on the number of elements in the list.

See Recipe 10.4, "Understanding the Performance of Collections" for more information on the `List` performance characteristics.

### See Also

- The `List` class (*http://bit.ly/15iqGNE*).
- Recipe 3.15, "Working with a List in a Match Expression", shows how to handle a `List` in a match expression, especially the `Nil` element.
- Recipe 10.4, "Understanding the Performance of Collections", discusses `List` class performance.
- Recipe 17.1, "Going to and from Java Collections", demonstrates how to convert back and forth between Scala and Java collections.

# 11.2. Creating a Mutable List

## Problem

You want to use a mutable list (a `LinearSeq`, as opposed to an `IndexedSeq`), but a `List` isn't mutable.

## Solution

Use a `ListBuffer`, and convert the `ListBuffer` to a `List` when needed.

The following examples demonstrate how to create a `ListBuffer`, and then add and remove elements, and then convert it to a `List` when finished:

```
import scala.collection.mutable.ListBuffer

var fruits = new ListBuffer[String]()

// add one element at a time to the ListBuffer
fruits += "Apple"
fruits += "Banana"
fruits += "Orange"
```

```
// add multiple elements
fruits += ("Strawberry", "Kiwi", "Pineapple")

// remove one element
fruits -= "Apple"

// remove multiple elements
fruits -= ("Banana", "Orange")

// remove multiple elements specified by another sequence
fruits --= Seq("Kiwi", "Pineapple")

// convert the ListBuffer to a List when you need to
val fruitsList = fruits.toList
```

## Discussion

Because a List is immutable, if you need to create a list that is constantly changing, the preferred approach is to use a ListBuffer while the list is being modified, then convert it to a List when a List is needed.

The ListBuffer Scaladoc states that a ListBuffer is "a Buffer implementation backed by a list. It provides constant time prepend and append. Most other operations are linear." So, don't use ListBuffer if you want to access elements arbitrarily, such as accessing items by index (like list(10000)); use ArrayBuffer instead. See Recipe 10.4, "Understanding the Performance of Collections" for more information.

Although you can't modify the elements in a List, you can create a new List from an existing one, typically prepending items to the original list with the :: method:

```
scala> val x = List(2)
x: List[Int] = List(2)

scala> val y = 1 :: x
y: List[Int] = List(1, 2)

scala> val z = 0 :: y
z: List[Int] = List(0, 1, 2)
```

This is discussed more in Recipe 11.3, "Adding Elements to a List".

# 11.3. Adding Elements to a List

## Problem

You want to add elements to a List that you're working with.

## Solution

"How do I add elements to a List?" is a bit of a trick question, because a List is immutable, so you can't actually add elements to it. If you want a List that is constantly changing, use a ListBuffer (as described in Recipe 11.2), and then convert it to a List when necessary.

To work with a List, the general approach is to prepend items to the list with the :: method while assigning the results to a new List:

```scala
scala> val x = List(2)
x: List[Int] = List(2)

scala> val y = 1 :: x
y: List[Int] = List(1, 2)

scala> val z = 0 :: y
z: List[Int] = List(0, 1, 2)
```

Rather than continually reassigning the result of this operation to a new variable, you can declare your variable as a var, and reassign the result to it:

```scala
scala> var x = List(2)
x: List[Int] = List(2)

scala> x = 1 :: x
x: List[Int] = List(1, 2)

scala> x = 0 :: x
x: List[Int] = List(0, 1, 2)
```

As these examples illustrate, the :: method is right-associative; lists are constructed from right to left, which you can see in this example:

```scala
scala> val list1 = 3 :: Nil
list1: List[Int] = List(3)

scala> val list2 = 2 :: list1
list2: List[Int] = List(2, 3)

scala> val list3 = 1 :: list2
list3: List[Int] = List(1, 2, 3)
```

Any Scala method that ends with a : character is evaluated from right to left. This means that the method is invoked on the right operand. You can see how this works by analyzing the following code, where both methods print the number 42:

```
object RightAssociativeExample extends App {
  val f1 = new Printer
  f1 >> 42
  42 >>: f1
}

class Printer {
  def >>(i: Int) { println(s"$i") }
  def >>:(i: Int) { println(s"$i") }
}
```

The two methods can also be invoked like this:

```
f1.>>(42)
f1.>>:(42)
```

but by defining the second method to end in a colon, it can be used as a right-associative operator.

Though using :: is very common, there are additional methods that let you prepend or append single elements to a List:

```
scala> val x = List(1)
x: List[Int] = List(1)

scala> val y = 0 +: x
y: List[Int] = List(0, 1)

scala> val y = x :+ 2
y: List[Int] = List(1, 2)
```

You can also merge lists to create a new list. See Recipe 11.5 for examples.

## Discussion

If you're not comfortable using a List, but want to use a mutable, linear list, see Recipe 11.2, "Creating a Mutable List" for examples of how to use the ListBuffer class. The ListBuffer is a mutable, *linear* sequence (as opposed to an *indexed* sequence, like an Array or ArrayBuffer), and is similar to working with a StringBuffer or StringBuilder in Java. Just as you'd convert those classes to a String when needed, you convert a ListBuffer to a List when needed. Programmers from other backgrounds may be more comfortable with the :: approach. A nice benefit of Scala is that it offers both options.

## See Also

- Recipe 11.2, "Creating a Mutable List"
- Recipe 10.4, "Understanding the Performance of Collections"

# 11.4. Deleting Elements from a List (or ListBuffer)

## Problem

You want to delete elements from a `List` or `ListBuffer`.

## Solution

A `List` is immutable, so you can't delete elements from it, but you can filter out the elements you don't want while you assign the result to a new variable:

```
scala> val originalList = List(5, 1, 4, 3, 2)
originalList: List[Int] = List(5, 1, 4, 3, 2)

scala> val newList = originalList.filter(_ > 2)
newList: List[Int] = List(5, 4, 3)
```

Rather than continually assigning the result of operations like this to a new variable, you can declare your variable as a `var` and reassign the result of the operation back to itself:

```
scala> var x = List(5, 1, 4, 3, 2)
x: List[Int] = List(5, 1, 4, 3, 2)

scala> x = x.filter(_ > 2)
x: List[Int] = List(5, 4, 3)
```

See Chapter 10 for other ways to get subsets of a collection using methods like `filter`, `partition`, `splitAt`, `take`, and more.

### ListBuffer

If you're going to be modifying a list frequently, it may be better to use a `ListBuffer` instead of a `List`. A `ListBuffer` is mutable, so you can remove items from it using all the methods for mutable sequences shown in Chapter 10. For example, assuming you've created a `ListBuffer` like this:

```
import scala.collection.mutable.ListBuffer
val x = ListBuffer(1, 2, 3, 4, 5, 6, 7, 8, 9)
```

You can delete one element at a time, by value:

```
scala> x -= 5
res0: x.type = ListBuffer(1, 2, 3, 4, 6, 7, 8, 9)
```

You can delete two or more elements at once:

```
scala> x -= (2, 3)
res1: x.type = ListBuffer(1, 4, 6, 7, 8, 9)
```

(That method looks like it takes a tuple, but it's actually defined to take two parameters and a third varargs field.)

You can delete elements by position:

```
scala> x.remove(0)
res2: Int = 1

scala> x
res3: scala.collection.mutable.ListBuffer[Int] = ListBuffer(4, 6, 7, 8, 9)
```

You can use remove to delete from a given starting position and provide the number of elements to delete:

```
scala> x.remove(1, 3)

scala> x
res4: scala.collection.mutable.ListBuffer[Int] = ListBuffer(4, 9)
```

You can also use - -= to delete multiple elements that are specified in another collection:

```
scala> val x = ListBuffer(1, 2, 3, 4, 5, 6, 7, 8, 9)
x: scala.collection.mutable.ListBuffer[Int] = ListBuffer↵
(1, 2, 3, 4, 5, 6, 7, 8, 9)

scala> x --= Seq(1,2,3)
res0: x.type = ListBuffer(4, 5, 6, 7, 8, 9)
```

## Discussion

When you first start using Scala, the wealth of methods whose names are only symbols (+:, /:, :::, etc.) can seem daunting, but the -= and - -= methods are used consistently across mutable collections, so it quickly becomes second nature to use them.

## See Also

- Recipes 10.17 through 10.19 show many ways to filter collections (filtering is a way of deleting).
- Recipe 10.3, "Choosing a Collection Method to Solve a Problem".

# 11.5. Merging (Concatenating) Lists

## Problem

You want to merge/concatenate the contents of two lists.

## Solution

Merge two lists using the ++, concat, or ::: methods. Given these two lists:

```
scala> val a = List(1,2,3)
a: List[Int] = List(1, 2, 3)

scala> val b = List(4,5,6)
b: List[Int] = List(4, 5, 6)
```

you can use the ++ method as shown in the following example. It's used consistently across immutable collections, so it's easy to remember:

```
scala> val c = a ++ b
c: List[Int] = List(1, 2, 3, 4, 5, 6)
```

If you work with the List class frequently, you may prefer using ::: as a way to create a new list from two existing lists:

```
scala> val c = a ::: b
c: List[Int] = List(1, 2, 3, 4, 5, 6)
```

The concat method on the List object also works:

```
scala> val c = List.concat(a, b)
c: List[Int] = List(1, 2, 3, 4, 5, 6)
```

## Discussion

Perhaps because I come from a Java background, I don't work with the List class too often, so I can't remember some of its custom methods without looking at its Scaladoc. As a result, I prefer the ++ method, because it's consistently used across immutable collections.

However, keep in mind what the List class is good at. As its Scaladoc states, "This class is optimal for last-in-first-out (LIFO), stack-like access patterns. If you need another access pattern, for example, random access or FIFO, consider using a collection more suited to this than List." See Recipe 10.4, "Understanding the Performance of Collections" for a discussion of List class performance.

## See Also

The List class (*http://bit.ly/15iqGNE*)

---

# 11.6. Using Stream, a Lazy Version of a List

## Problem

You want to use a collection that works like a List but invokes its transformer methods (map, filter, etc.) lazily.

## Solution

A Stream is like a List, except that its elements are computed lazily, in a manner similar to how a *view* creates a lazy version of a collection. Because Stream elements are computed lazily, a Stream can be long ... infinitely long. Like a view, only the elements that are accessed are computed. Other than this behavior, a Stream behaves similar to a List.

Just like a List can be constructed with ::, a Stream can be constructed with the #:: method, using Stream.empty at the end of the expression instead of Nil:

```
scala> val stream = 1 #:: 2 #:: 3 #:: Stream.empty
stream: scala.collection.immutable.Stream[Int] = Stream(1, ?)
```

The REPL output shows that the stream begins with the number 1 but uses a ? to denote the end of the stream. This is because the end of the stream hasn't been evaluated yet.

For example, given a Stream:

```
scala> val stream = (1 to 100000000).toStream
stream: scala.collection.immutable.Stream[Int] = Stream(1, ?)
```

you can attempt to access the head and tail of the stream. The head is returned immediately:

```
scala> stream.head
res0: Int = 1
```

but the tail isn't evaluated yet:

```
scala> stream.tail
res1: scala.collection.immutable.Stream[Int] = Stream(2, ?)
```

The ? symbol is the way a lazy collection shows that the end of the collection hasn't been evaluated yet.

As discussed in Recipe 10.24, "Creating a Lazy View on a Collection", *transformer methods* are computed lazily, so when transformers are called, you see the familiar ? character that indicates the end of the stream hasn't been evaluated yet:

```
scala> stream.take(3)
res0: scala.collection.immutable.Stream[Int] = Stream(1, ?)

scala> stream.filter(_ < 200)
```

```
res1: scala.collection.immutable.Stream[Int] = Stream(1, ?)

scala> stream.filter(_ > 200)
res2: scala.collection.immutable.Stream[Int] = Stream(201, ?)

scala> stream.map { _ * 2 }
res3: scala.collection.immutable.Stream[Int] = Stream(2, ?)
```

However, be careful with methods that aren't transformers. Calls to the following *strict* methods are evaluated immediately and can easily cause `java.lang.OutOfMemoryError` errors:

```
stream.max
stream.size
stream.sum
```

 *Transformer methods* are collection methods that convert a given input collection to a new output collection, based on an algorithm you provide to transform the data. This includes methods like `map`, `filter`, and `reverse`. When using these methods, you're transforming the input collection to a new output collection. Methods like `max`, `size`, and `sum` don't fit that definition, so they attempt to operate on the `Stream`, and if the `Stream` requires more memory than you can allocate, you'll get the `java.lang.OutOfMemoryError`.

As a point of comparison, if I had attempted to use a `List` in these examples, I would have encountered a `java.lang.OutOfMemory` error as soon as I attempted to create the `List`:

```
val list = (1 to 100000000).toStream
```

Using a `Stream` gives you a chance to specify a huge list, and begin working with its elements:

```
stream(0)  // returns 1
stream(1)  // returns 2
// ...
stream(10)  // returns 11
```

## See Also

- A discussion of Scala's concrete, immutable collections classes, including `Stream` (*http://bit.ly/13gh1YV*)
- Recipe 10.24, "Creating a Lazy View on a Collection"

# 11.7. Different Ways to Create and Update an Array

## Problem

You want to create and optionally populate an Array.

## Solution

There are many different ways to define and populate an Array. You can create an array with initial values, in which case Scala can determine the array type implicitly:

```
scala> val a = Array(1,2,3)
a: Array[Int] = Array(1, 2, 3)

scala> val fruits = Array("Apple", "Banana", "Orange")
fruits: Array[String] = Array(Apple, Banana, Orange)
```

If you don't like the type Scala determines, you can assign it manually:

```
// scala makes this Array[Double]
scala> val x = Array(1, 2.0, 33D, 400L)
x: Array[Double] = Array(1.0, 2.0, 33.0, 400.0)

// manually override the type
scala> val x = Array[Number](1, 2.0, 33D, 400L)
x: Array[java.lang.Number] = Array(1, 2.0, 33.0, 400)
```

You can define an array with an initial size and type, and then populate it later:

```
// create an array with an initial size
val fruits = new Array[String](3)

// somewhere later in the code ...
fruits(0) = "Apple"
fruits(1) = "Banana"
fruits(2) = "Orange"
```

You can create a var reference to an array in a class, and then assign it later:

```
// this uses a null. don't do this in the real world
var fruits: Array[String] = _

// later ...
fruits = Array("apple", "banana")
```

The following examples show a handful of other ways to create and populate an Array:

```
scala> val x = Array.range(1, 10)
x: Array[Int] = Array(1, 2, 3, 4, 5, 6, 7, 8, 9)

scala> val x = Array.range(0, 10, 2)
x: Array[Int] = Array(0, 2, 4, 6, 8)
```

```
scala> val x = Array.fill(3)("foo")
x: Array[String] = Array(foo, foo, foo)

scala> val x = Array.tabulate(5)(n => n * n)
x: Array[Int] = Array(0, 1, 4, 9, 16)

scala> val x = List(1, 2, 3).toArray
x: Array[Int] = Array(1, 2, 3)

scala> "Hello".toArray
res0: Array[Char] = Array(H, e, l, l, o)
```

## Discussion

The Array is an interesting creature: It's *mutable* in that its elements can be changed, but it's *immutable* in that its size cannot be changed. The first link in the See Also section provides this information about the Array:

> Scala arrays correspond one-to-one to Java arrays. That is, a Scala array Array[Int] is represented as a Java int[ ], an Array[Double] is represented as a Java double[ ] and a Array[String] is represented as a Java String[ ].

The Array is an *indexed* sequential collection, so accessing and changing values by their index position is straightforward and fast. Once you've created an Array, access its elements by enclosing the desired element number in parentheses:

```
scala> val a = Array(1, 2, 3)
a: Array[Int] = Array(1, 2, 3)

scala> a(0)
res0: Int = 1
```

Just as you access an array element by index, you update elements in a similar way:

```
scala> a(0) = 10

scala> a(1) = 20

scala> a(2) = 30

scala> a
res1: Array[Int] = Array(10, 20, 30)
```

## See Also

- A thorough discussion of Array, including background on its implementation (*http://bit.ly/18iQwn4*).

- Recipe 10.4, "Understanding the Performance of Collections" discusses `Array` class performance.

# 11.8. Creating an Array Whose Size Can Change (ArrayBuffer)

## Problem

You want to create an array whose size can change, i.e., a completely mutable array.

## Solution

An `Array` is mutable in that its elements can change, but its size can't change. To create a mutable, indexed sequence whose size can change, use the `ArrayBuffer` class.

To use an `ArrayBuffer`, import it into scope and then create an instance. You can declare an `ArrayBuffer` without initial elements, and then add them later:

```
import scala.collection.mutable.ArrayBuffer
var characters = ArrayBuffer[String]()
characters += "Ben"
characters += "Jerry"
characters += "Dale"
```

You can add elements when you create the `ArrayBuffer`, and continue to add elements later:

```
// initialize with elements
val characters = collection.mutable.ArrayBuffer("Ben", "Jerry")

// add one element
characters += "Dale"

// add two or more elements (method has a varargs parameter)
characters += ("Gordon", "Harry")

// add multiple elements with any TraversableOnce type
characters ++= Seq("Andy", "Big Ed")

// append one or more elements (uses a varargs parameter)
characters.append("Laura", "Lucy")
```

Those are the most common ways to add elements to an `ArrayBuffer` (and other mutable sequences). The next recipe demonstrates methods to delete `ArrayBuffer` elements.

# 11.9. Deleting Array and ArrayBuffer Elements

## Problem

You want to delete elements from an `Array` or `ArrayBuffer`.

## Solution

An `ArrayBuffer` is a mutable sequence, so you can delete elements with the usual `-=`, `--=`, `remove`, and `clear` methods.

You can remove one or more elements with `-=`:

```
import scala.collection.mutable.ArrayBuffer
val x = ArrayBuffer('a', 'b', 'c', 'd', 'e')

// remove one element
x -= 'a'

// remove multiple elements (methods defines a varargs param)
x -= ('b', 'c')
```

Use `--=` to remove multiple elements that are declared in another collection (any collection that extends `TraversableOnce`):

```
val x = ArrayBuffer('a', 'b', 'c', 'd', 'e')
x --= Seq('a', 'b')
x --= Array('c')
x --= Set('d')
```

Use the `remove` method to delete one element by its position in the `ArrayBuffer`, or a series of elements beginning at a starting position:

```
scala> val x = ArrayBuffer('a', 'b', 'c', 'd', 'e', 'f')
x: scala.collection.mutable.ArrayBuffer[Char] = ArrayBuffer(a, b, c, d, e, f)

scala> x.remove(0)
res0: Char = a

scala> x
res1: scala.collection.mutable.ArrayBuffer[Char] = ArrayBuffer(b, c, d, e, f)

scala> x.remove(1, 3)

scala> x
res2: scala.collection.mutable.ArrayBuffer[Char] = ArrayBuffer(b, f)
```

In these examples, the collection that contains the elements to be removed can be any collection that extends `TraversableOnce`, so `removeThese` can be a `Seq`, `Array`, `Vector`, and many other types that extend `TraversableOnce`.

---

The clear method removes all the elements from an ArrayBuffer:

```
scala> var a = ArrayBuffer(1,2,3,4,5)
a: scala.collection.mutable.ArrayBuffer[Int] = ArrayBuffer(1, 2, 3, 4, 5)

scala> a.clear

scala> a
res0: scala.collection.mutable.ArrayBuffer[Int] = ArrayBuffer()
```

You can also use the usual Scala filtering methods (drop, filter, take, etc.) to filter elements out of a collection; just remember to assign the result to a new variable.

## Array

The size of an Array can't be changed, so you can't directly delete elements. You can reassign the elements in an Array, which has the effect of replacing them:

```
scala> val a = Array("apple", "banana", "cherry")
a: Array[String] = Array(apple, banana, cherry)

scala> a(0) = ""

scala> a(1) = null

scala> a
res0: Array[String] = Array("", null, cherry)
```

You can also filter elements out of one array while you assign the result to a new array:

```
scala> val a = Array("apple", "banana", "cherry")
a: Array[String] = Array(apple, banana, cherry)

scala> val b = a.filter(! _.contains("apple"))
b: Array[String] = Array(banana, cherry)
```

Use other filtering methods (drop, slice, take, etc.) in the same way.

If you define the array variable as a var, you can assign the result back to itself, which gives the appearance of deleting elements using filtering:

```
scala> var a = Array("apple", "banana", "cherry")
a: Array[String] = Array(apple, banana, cherry)

scala> a = a.take(2)
a: Array[String] = [LString;@e41a882

scala> a
res0: Array[String] = Array(apple, banana)
```

# 11.10. Sorting Arrays

## Problem

You want to sort the elements in an `Array` (or `ArrayBuffer`).

## Solution

If you're working with an `Array` that holds elements that have an implicit `Ordering`, you can sort the `Array` in place using the `scala.util.Sorting.quickSort` method. For example, because the `String` class has an implicit `Ordering`, it can be used with quickSort:

```
scala> val fruits = Array("cherry", "apple", "banana")
fruits: Array[String] = Array(cherry, apple, banana)

scala> scala.util.Sorting.quickSort(fruits)

scala> fruits
res0: Array[String] = Array(apple, banana, cherry)
```

Notice that quickSort sorts the `Array` in place; there's no need to assign the result to a new variable.

This example works because the `String` class (via `StringOps`) has an implicit `Ordering`. `Sorting.quickSort` can also sort arrays with the base numeric types like `Double`, `Float`, and `Int`, because they also have an implicit `Ordering`.

### Other solutions

If the type an `Array` is holding doesn't have an implicit `Ordering`, you can either modify it to mix in the `Ordered` trait (which gives it an implicit `Ordering`), or sort it using the `sorted`, `sortWith`, or `sortBy` methods. These approaches are shown in Recipe 10.29.

Also, there are no unique sorting approaches for an `ArrayBuffer`, so see Recipe 10.29 for an example of how to sort it as well.

## See Also

The Scaladoc for the `Ordered` and `Ordering` traits is very good. The header information in both documents shows good examples of the approaches shown in this recipe and Recipe 10.29.

- The `Sorting` object (*http://bit.ly/13MzBeq*)
- The `Ordering` trait (*http://bit.ly/1bCFQSk*)
- The `Ordered` trait (*http://bit.ly/12ARfPx*)

# 11.11. Creating Multidimensional Arrays

## Problem

You need to create a multidimensional array, i.e., an array with two or more dimensions.

## Solution

There are two main solutions:

- Use `Array.ofDim` to create a multidimensional array. You can use this approach to create arrays of up to five dimensions. With this approach you need to know the number of rows and columns at creation time.

- Create arrays of arrays as needed.

Both approaches are shown in this solution.

### Using Array.ofDim

Use the `Array.ofDim` method to create the array you need:

```
scala> val rows = 2
rows: Int = 2

scala> val cols = 3
cols: Int = 3

scala> val a = Array.ofDim[String](rows, cols)
a: Array[Array[String]] = Array(Array(null, null, null), Array(null, null, null))
```

After declaring the array, add elements to it:

```
a(0)(0) = "a"
a(0)(1) = "b"
a(0)(2) = "c"
a(1)(0) = "d"
a(1)(1) = "e"
a(1)(2) = "f"
```

Access the elements using parentheses, similar to a one-dimensional array:

```
scala> val x = a(0)(0)
x: String = a
```

Iterate over the array with a `for` loop:

```
scala> for {
     |     i <- 0 until rows
     |     j <- 0 until cols
     | } println(s"($i)($j) = ${a(i)(j)}")
(0)(0) = a
(0)(1) = b
```

```
(0)(2) = c
(1)(0) = d
(1)(1) = e
(1)(2) = f
```

To create an array with more dimensions, just follow that same pattern. Here's the code for a three-dimensional array:

```
val x, y, z = 10
val a = Array.ofDim[Int](x,y,z)
for {
  i <- 0 until x
  j <- 0 until y
  k <- 0 until z
} println(s"($i)($j)($k) = ${a(i)(j)(k)}")
```

### Using an array of arrays

Another approach is to create an array whose elements are arrays:

```
scala> val a = Array( Array("a", "b", "c"), Array("d", "e", "f") )
a: Array[Array[String]] = Array(Array(a, b, c), Array(d, e, f))

scala> a(0)
res0: Array[String] = Array(a, b, c)

scala> a(0)(0)
res1: String = a
```

This gives you more control of the process, and lets you create "ragged" arrays (where each contained array may be a different size):

```
scala> val a = Array(Array("a", "b", "c"), Array("d", "e"))
a: Array[Array[String]] = Array(Array(a, b, c), Array(d, e))
```

You can declare your variable as a var and create the same array in multiple steps:

```
scala> var arr = Array(Array("a", "b", "c"))
arr: Array[Array[String]] = Array(Array(a, b, c))

scala> arr ++= Array(Array("d", "e"))

scala> arr
res0: Array[Array[String]] = Array(Array(a, b, c), Array(d, e))
```

Note in this example that the variable arr was created as a var, which lets you assign the output from the ++= operator back to it. This gives the illusion that you've modified the *contents* of arr, but in reality, you've modified arr's *reference* so it points at a new collection. (See Recipe 10.6, "Understanding Mutable Variables with Immutable Collections" for more information.)

## Discussion

Decompiling the `Array.ofDim` solution helps to understand how this works behind the scenes. Create the following Scala class in a file named *Test.scala*:

```
class Test {
  val arr = Array.ofDim[String](2, 3)
}
```

If you compile that class with `scalac`, and then decompile it with a tool like JAD, you can see the Java code that's created:

```
private final String arr[][];
```

Similarly, creating a Scala three-dimensional `Array` like this:

```
val arr = Array.ofDim[String](2, 2, 2)
```

results in a Java array like this:

```
private final String arr[][][];
```

As you might expect, the code generated by using the "array of arrays" approach is more complicated. This is a case where using a decompiler can help you understand how Scala works, i.e., what code it generates for you.

Finally, the `Array.ofDim` approach is unique to the `Array` class; there is no `ofDim` method on a `List`, `Vector`, `ArrayBuffer`, etc. But the "array of arrays" solution is not unique to the `Array` class. You can have a "list of lists," "vector of vectors," and so on.

# 11.12. Creating Maps

## Problem

You want to use a mutable or immutable `Map` in a Scala application.

## Solution

To use an immutable map, you don't need an import statement, just create a `Map`:

```
scala> val states = Map("AL" -> "Alabama", "AK" -> "Alaska")
states: scala.collection.immutable.Map[String,String] =
  Map(AL -> Alabama, AK -> Alaska)
```

This expression creates an immutable `Map` with type [`String`, `String`]. For the first element, the string `AL` is the key, and `Alabama` is the value.

As noted, you don't need an import statement to use a basic, immutable `Map`. The Scala `Predef` object brings the immutable `Map` trait into scope by defining a type alias:

```
type Map[A, +B] = immutable.Map[A, B]
val Map         = immutable.Map
```

To create a *mutable* map, either use an import statement to bring it into scope, or specify the full path to the `scala.collection.mutable.Map` class when you create an instance. You can define a mutable Map that has initial elements:

```
scala> var states = collection.mutable.Map("AL" -> "Alabama")
states: scala.collection.mutable.Map[String,String] = Map(AL -> Alabama)
```

You can also create an empty, mutable Map initially, and add elements to it later:

```
scala> var states = collection.mutable.Map[String, String]()
states: scala.collection.mutable.Map[String,String] = Map()

scala> states += ("AL" -> "Alabama")
res0: scala.collection.mutable.Map[String,String] = Map(AL -> Alabama)
```

## Discussion

Like maps in other programming languages, maps in Scala are a collection of key/value pairs. If you've used maps in Java, dictionaries in Python, or a hash in Ruby, Scala maps are straightforward. You only need to know a couple of new things, including the methods available on map classes, and the specialty maps that can be useful in certain situations, such as having a sorted map.

Note that the syntax that's used inside parentheses in a map creates a Tuple2:

```
"AL" -> "Alabama"
```

Because you can also declare a Tuple2 as ("AL", "Alabama"), you may also see maps created like this:

```
scala> val states = Map( ("AL", "Alabama"), ("AK", "Alaska") )
states: scala.collection.immutable.Map[String,String] =
  Map(AL -> Alabama, AK -> Alaska)
```

Use whichever style you prefer.

When I want to be clear that I'm using a mutable map, I normally specify the full path to the mutable Map class when I create the instance, as shown in the Solution. Another technique you can use it to give the mutable Map an alias when you import it, and then refer to it using that alias, as shown here:

```
import scala.collection.mutable.{Map => MMap}

object Test extends App {

  // MMap is really scala.collection.mutable.Map
  val m = MMap(1 -> 'a')
  for((k,v) <- m) println(s"$k, $v")

}
```

This technique is described more in Recipe 7.3, "Renaming Members on Import".

## See Also

- The `Map` trait (*http://bit.ly/18lkmuu*)
- The `Predef` object (*http://bit.ly/15C0L36*)

# 11.13. Choosing a Map Implementation

## Problem

You need to choose a map class for a particular problem.

## Solution

Scala has a wealth of map types to choose from, and you can even use Java map classes.

If you're looking for a basic map class, where sorting or insertion order doesn't matter, you can either choose the default, immutable `Map`, or import the mutable `Map`, as shown in the previous recipe.

If you want a map that returns its elements in sorted order by keys, use a `SortedMap`:

```
scala> import scala.collection.SortedMap
import scala.collection.SortedMap

scala> val grades = SortedMap("Kim" -> 90,
     | "Al" -> 85,
     | "Melissa" -> 95,
     | "Emily" -> 91,
     | "Hannah" -> 92
     | )
grades: scala.collection.SortedMap[String,Int] =
    Map(Al -> 85, Emily -> 91, Hannah -> 92, Kim -> 90, Melissa -> 95)
```

If you want a map that remembers the insertion order of its elements, use a `LinkedHashMap` or `ListMap`. Scala only has a *mutable* `LinkedHashMap`, and it returns its elements in the order you inserted them:

```
scala> import scala.collection.mutable.LinkedHashMap
import scala.collection.mutable.LinkedHashMap

scala> var states = LinkedHashMap("IL" -> "Illinois")
states: scala.collection.mutable.LinkedHashMap[String,String] =
  Map(IL -> Illinois)

scala> states += ("KY" -> "Kentucky")
res0: scala.collection.mutable.LinkedHashMap[String,String] =
  Map(IL -> Illinois, KY -> Kentucky)
```

```
scala> states += ("TX" -> "Texas")
res1: scala.collection.mutable.LinkedHashMap[String,String] =
  Map(IL -> Illinois, KY -> Kentucky, TX -> Texas)
```

Scala has both mutable and immutable ListMap classes. They return elements in the opposite order in which you inserted them, as though each insert was at the head of the map (like a List):

```
scala> import scala.collection.mutable.ListMap
import scala.collection.mutable.ListMap

scala> var states = ListMap("IL" -> "Illinois")
states: scala.collection.mutable.ListMap[String,String] =
  Map(IL -> Illinois)

scala> states += ("KY" -> "Kentucky")
res0: scala.collection.mutable.ListMap[String,String] =
  Map(KY -> Kentucky, IL -> Illinois)

scala> states += ("TX" -> "Texas")
res1: scala.collection.mutable.ListMap[String,String] =
  Map(TX -> Texas, KY -> Kentucky, IL -> Illinois)
```

The LinkedHashMap implements a mutable map using a hashtable, whereas a ListMap is backed by a list-based data structure. (Personally, I don't use the List class very often, so I prefer the LinkedHashMap.)

## Discussion

Table 11-1 shows a summary of the basic Scala map classes and traits, and provides a brief description of each.

*Table 11-1. Basic map classes and traits*

| Class or trait | Description |
| --- | --- |
| collection.immutable.Map | This is the default, general-purpose immutable map you get if you don't import anything. |
| collection.mutable.Map | A mutable version of the basic map. |
| collection.mutable.LinkedHashMap | All methods that traverse the elements will visit the elements in their insertion order. |
| collection.immutable.ListMap collection.mutable.ListMap | Per the Scaladoc (*http://bit.ly/15iqY79*), "implements immutable maps using a list-based data structure." As shown in the examples, elements that are added are prepended to the head of the list. |
| collection.SortedMap | Keys of the map are returned in sorted order. Therefore, all traversal methods (such as foreach) return keys in that order. |

Although those are the most commonly used maps, Scala offers even more map types. They are summarized in Table 11-2.

*Table 11-2. More map classes and traits*

| Class or trait | Description |
| --- | --- |
| collection.immutable.HashMap | From the Scaladoc (*http://bit.ly/15C0Uno*), "implements immutable maps using a hash trie." |
| collection.mutable.ObservableMap | From the Scaladoc (*http://bit.ly/18iQITo*): "This class is typically used as a mixin. It adds a subscription mechanism to the Map class into which this abstract class is mixed in." |
| collection.mutable.MultiMap | From the Scaladoc (*http://bit.ly/15C0Yn8*): "A trait for mutable maps with multiple values assigned to a key." |
| collection.mutable.SynchronizedMap | From the Scaladoc (*http://bit.ly/14Wammz*): This trait "should be used as a mixin. It synchronizes the map functions of the class into which it is mixed in." |
| collection.immutable.TreeMap | From the Scaladoc (*http://bit.ly/13MzFLg*): "implements immutable maps using a tree." |
| collection.mutable.WeakHashMap | A wrapper around java.util.WeakHashMap, "a map entry is removed if the key is no longer strongly referenced." |

But wait, there's still more. Beyond these types, Scala also offers several more map types that have parallel/concurrent implementations built into them:

- collection.parallel.immutable.ParHashMap
- collection.parallel.mutable.ParHashMap
- collection.concurrent.TrieMap

## See Also

- Map methods (*http://bit.ly/13lzu1T*)
- When map performance is important, see Recipe 10.4, "Understanding the Performance of Collections"
- Scala's parallel collections (*http://bit.ly/1dCbKfX*)

# 11.14. Adding, Updating, and Removing Elements with a Mutable Map

## Problem

You want to add, remove, or update elements in a *mutable* map.

## Solution

Add elements to a mutable map by simply assigning them, or with the += method. Remove elements with -= or --=. Update elements by reassigning them.

Given a new, mutable Map:

```
scala> var states = scala.collection.mutable.Map[String, String]()
states: scala.collection.mutable.Map[String,String] = Map()
```

You can add an element to a map by assigning a key to a value:

```
scala> states("AK") = "Alaska"
```

You can also add elements with the += method:

```
scala> states += ("AL" -> "Alabama")
res0: scala.collection.mutable.Map[String,String] =
  Map(AL -> Alabama, AK -> Alaska)
```

Add multiple elements at one time with +=:

```
scala> states += ("AR" -> "Arkansas", "AZ" -> "Arizona")
res1: scala.collection.mutable.Map[String,String] =
  Map(AL -> Alabama, AR -> Arkansas, AK -> Alaska, AZ -> Arizona)
```

Add multiple elements from another collection using ++=:

```
scala> states ++= List("CA" -> "California", "CO" -> "Colorado")
res2: scala.collection.mutable.Map[String,String] = Map(CO -> Colorado,
  AZ -> Arizona, AL -> Alabama, CA -> California, AR -> Arkansas,
  AK -> Alaska)
```

Remove a single element from a map by specifying its key with the -= method:

```
scala> states -= "AR"
res3: scala.collection.mutable.Map[String,String] =
  Map(AL -> Alabama, AK -> Alaska, AZ -> Arizona)
```

Remove multiple elements by key with the -= or --= methods:

```
scala> states -= ("AL", "AZ")
res4: scala.collection.mutable.Map[String,String] = Map(AK -> Alaska)

// remove multiple with a List of keys
scala> states --= List("AL", "AZ")
res5: scala.collection.mutable.Map[String,String] = Map(AK -> Alaska)
```

Update elements by reassigning their key to a new value:

```
scala> states("AK") = "Alaska, A Really Big State"

scala> states
res6: scala.collection.mutable.Map[String,String] =
  Map(AK -> Alaska, A Really Big State)
```

There are other ways to add elements to maps, but these examples show the most common uses.

## Discussion

The methods shown in the Solution demonstrate the most common approaches. You can also use put to add an element (or replace an existing element); retain to keep only the elements in the map that match the predicate you supply; remove to remove an element by its key value; and clear to delete all elements in the map. These methods are shown in the following examples:

```scala
scala> val states = collection.mutable.Map(
     |    "AK" -> "Alaska",
     |    "IL" -> "Illinois",
     |    "KY" -> "Kentucky"
     | )
states: collection.mutable.Map[String,String] =
  Map(KY -> Kentucky, IL -> Illinois, AK -> Alaska)

scala> states.put("CO", "Colorado")
res0: Option[String] = None

scala> states.retain((k,v) => k == "AK")
res1: states.type = Map(AK -> Alaska)

scala> states.remove("AK")
res2: Option[String] = Some(Alaska)

scala> states
res3: scala.collection.mutable.Map[String,String] = Map()

scala> states.clear

scala> states
res4: scala.collection.mutable.Map[String,String] = Map()
```

As shown, the remove method returns an Option that contains the value that was removed. It's not shown in the example, but if the element put into the collection by put replaced another element, that value would be returned. Because this example didn't replace anything, it returned None.

## See Also

The Scala mutable Map trait (*http://bit.ly/1dCbM7y*)

# 11.15. Adding, Updating, and Removing Elements with Immutable Maps

## Problem

You want to add, update, or delete elements when working with an *immutable* map.

## Solution

Use the correct operator for each purpose, remembering to assign the results to a new map.

To be clear about the approach, the following examples use an immutable map with a series of val variables. First, create an immutable map as a val:

```
scala> val a = Map("AL" -> "Alabama")
a: scala.collection.immutable.Map[String,String] =
    Map(AL -> Alabama)
```

Add one or more elements with the + method, assigning the result to a new Map variable during the process:

```
// add one element
scala> val b = a + ("AK" -> "Alaska")
b: scala.collection.immutable.Map[String,String] =
    Map(AL -> Alabama, AK -> Alaska)

// add multiple elements
scala> val c = b + ("AR" -> "Arkansas", "AZ" -> "Arizona")
c: scala.collection.immutable.Map[String,String] =
    Map(AL -> Alabama, AK -> Alaska, AR -> Arkansas, AZ -> Arizona)
```

To update a key/value pair with an immutable map, reassign the key and value while using the + method, and the new values replace the old:

```
scala> val d = c + ("AR" -> "banana")
d: scala.collection.immutable.Map[String,String] =
    Map(AL -> Alabama, AK -> Alaska, AR -> banana, AZ -> Arizona)
```

To remove one element, use the - method:

```
scala> val e = d - "AR"
e: scala.collection.immutable.Map[String,String] =
    Map(AL -> Alabama, AK -> Alaska, AZ -> Arizona)
```

To remove multiple elements, use the - or -- methods:

```
scala> val f = e - "AZ" - "AL"
f: scala.collection.immutable.Map[String,String] =
    Map(AK -> Alaska)
```

## Discussion

You can also declare an immutable map as a var. Doing so has a dramatic difference on how you can treat the map:

```
scala> var x = Map("AL" -> "Alabama")
x: scala.collection.mutable.Map[String,String] = Map(AL -> Alabama)

// add one element
scala> x += ("AK" -> "Alaska"); println(x)
Map(AL -> Alabama, AK -> Alaska)

// add multiple elements
scala> x += ("AR" -> "Arkansas", "AZ" -> "Arizona"); println(x)
Map(AZ -> Arizona, AL -> Alabama, AR -> Arkansas, AK -> Alaska)

// add a tuple to a map (replacing the previous "AR" key)
scala> x += ("AR" -> "banana"); println(x)
Map(AZ -> Arizona, AL -> Alabama, AR -> banana, AK -> Alaska)

// remove an element
scala> x -= "AR"; println(x)
Map(AZ -> Arizona, AL -> Alabama, AK -> Alaska)

// remove multiple elements (uses varargs method)
scala> x -= ("AL", "AZ"); println(x)
Map(AK -> Alaska)

// reassign the map that 'x' points to
scala> x = Map("CO" -> "Colorado")
x: scala.collection.mutable.Map[String,String] = Map(CO -> Colorado)
```

It's important to understand that when you create an immutable map as a var, you still have an immutable map. For instance, you can't reassign an element in the map:

```
scala> x("AL") = "foo"
<console>:9: error: value update is not a member of scala.collection.immutable.↵
Map[String,String]
              x("AL") = "foo"
              ^
```

What's really happening in the previous examples is that because x was defined as a var, it's being reassigned during each step in the process. This is a subtle but important distinction to understand. See Recipe 10.6, "Understanding Mutable Variables with Immutable Collections" for more information.

## See Also

The immutable Map class (*http://bit.ly/13MzP5e*)

# 11.16. Accessing Map Values

## Problem

You want to access individual values stored in a map. You may have tried this and run into an exception when a key didn't exist, and want to see how to avoid that exception.

## Solution

Given a sample map:

```
scala> val states = Map("AL" -> "Alabama", "AK" -> "Alaska", "AZ" -> "Arizona")
states: scala.collection.immutable.Map[String,String] =
  Map(AL -> Alabama, AK -> Alaska, AZ -> Arizona)
```

Access the value associated with a key in the same way you access an element in an array:

```
scala> val az = states("AZ")
az: String = Arizona
```

However, be careful, because if the map doesn't contain the requested key, a `java.util.NoSuchElementException` exception is thrown:

```
scala> val s = states("FOO")
java.util.NoSuchElementException: key not found: FOO
```

One way to avoid this problem is to create the map with the `withDefaultValue` method. As the name implies, this creates a default value that will be returned by the map whenever a key isn't found:

```
scala> val states = Map("AL" -> "Alabama").withDefaultValue("Not found")
states: scala.collection.immutable.Map[String,String] =
  Map(AL -> Alabama)

scala> states("foo")
res0: String = Not found
```

Another approach is to use the `getOrElse` method when attempting to find a value. It returns the default value you specify if the key isn't found:

```
scala> val s = states.getOrElse("FOO", "No such state")
s: String = No such state
```

You can also use the `get` method, which returns an `Option`:

```
scala> val az = states.get("AZ")
az: Option[String] = Some(Arizona)

scala> val az = states.get("FOO")
az: Option[String] = None
```

To loop over the values in a map, see the next recipe.

---

## See Also

- Recipe 11.20, "Testing for the Existence of a Key or Value in a Map".
- Recipe 20.6, "Using the Option/Some/None Pattern", shows how to work with Option, Some, and None values.

# 11.17. Traversing a Map

## Problem

You want to iterate over the elements in a map.

## Solution

There are several different ways to iterate over the elements in a map. Given a sample map:

```
val ratings = Map("Lady in the Water"-> 3.0,
                  "Snakes on a Plane"-> 4.0,
                  "You, Me and Dupree"-> 3.5)
```

my preferred way to loop over all of the map elements is with this for loop syntax:

```
for ((k,v) <- ratings) println(s"key: $k, value: $v")
```

Using a match expression with the foreach method is also very readable:

```
ratings.foreach {
  case(movie, rating) => println(s"key: $movie, value: $rating")
}
```

The following approach shows how to use the Tuple syntax to access the key and value fields:

```
ratings.foreach(x => println(s"key: ${x._1}, value: ${x._2}"))
```

If you just want to use the keys in the map, the keys method returns an Iterable you can use:

```
ratings.keys.foreach((movie) => println(movie))
```

For simple examples like this, that expression can be reduced as follows:

```
ratings.keys.foreach(println)
```

In the same way, use the values method to iterate over the values in the map:

```
ratings.values.foreach((rating) => println(rating))
```

Note: Those are not my movie ratings. They are taken from the book, *Programming Collective Intelligence* (O'Reilly), by Toby Segaran.

### Operating on map values

If you want to traverse the map to perform an operation on its values, the `mapValues` method may be a better solution. It lets you perform a function on each map value, and returns the modified map:

```
scala> var x = collection.mutable.Map(1 -> "a", 2 -> "b")
x: scala.collection.mutable.Map[Int,String] = Map(2 -> b, 1 -> a)

scala> val y = x.mapValues(_.toUpperCase)
y: scala.collection.Map[Int,String] = Map(2 -> B, 1 -> A)
```

The `transform` method gives you another way to create a new map from an existing map. Unlike `mapValues`, it lets you use both the key and value to write a transformation method:

```
scala> val map = Map(1 -> 10, 2 -> 20, 3 -> 30)
map: scala.collection.mutable.Map[Int,Int] = Map(2 -> 20, 1 -> 10, 3 -> 30)

scala> val newMap = map.transform((k,v) => k + v)
newMap: map.type = Map(2 -> 22, 1 -> 11, 3 -> 33)
```

# 11.18. Getting the Keys or Values from a Map

## Problem

You want to get all of the keys or values from a map.

## Solution

To get the keys, use `keySet` to get the keys as a `Set`, `keys` to get an `Iterable`, or `keysIterator` to get the keys as an iterator:

```
scala> val states = Map("AK" -> "Alaska", "AL" -> "Alabama", "AR" -> "Arkansas")
states: scala.collection.immutable.Map[String,String] =
  Map(AK -> Alaska, AL -> Alabama, AR -> Arkansas)

scala> states.keySet
res0: scala.collection.immutable.Set[String] = Set(AK, AL, AR)

scala> states.keys
res1: Iterable[String] = Set(AK, AL, AR)

scala> states.keysIterator
res2: Iterator[String] = non-empty iterator
```

To get the values from a map, use the `values` method to get the values as an `Iterable`, or `valuesIterator` to get them as an `Iterator`:

```
scala> states.values
res0: Iterable[String] = MapLike(Alaska, Alabama, Arkansas)
```

```
scala> states.valuesIterator
res1: Iterator[String] = non-empty iterator
```

As shown in these examples, keysIterator and valuesIterator return an iterator from the map data. I tend to prefer these methods because they don't create a new collection; they just provide an iterator to walk over the existing elements.

# 11.19. Reversing Keys and Values

## Problem

You want to reverse the contents of a map, so the values become the keys, and the keys become the values.

## Solution

You can reverse the keys and values of a map with a *for comprehension*, being sure to assign the result to a new variable:

```
val reverseMap = for ((k,v) <- map) yield (v, k)
```

But be aware that values don't have to be unique and keys must be, so you might lose some content. As an example of this, reversing the following map—where two values are $5—results in one of the items being dropped when the keys and values are reversed:

```
scala> val products = Map(
     |    "Breadsticks" -> "$5",
     |    "Pizza" -> "$10",
     |    "Wings" -> "$5"
     | )
products: scala.collection.mutable.Map[String,String] =
   Map(Wings -> $5, Pizza -> $10, Breadsticks -> $5)

scala> val reverseMap = for ((k,v) <- products) yield (v, k)
reverseMap: scala.collection.mutable.Map[String,String] =
   Map($5 -> Breadsticks, $10 -> Pizza)
```

As shown, the $5 wings were lost when the values became the keys, because both the breadsticks and the wings had the String value $5.

## See Also

- Recipe 3.4, "Creating a for Comprehension (for/yield Combination)"
- Recipe 10.13, "Transforming One Collection to Another with for/yield"

# 11.20. Testing for the Existence of a Key or Value in a Map

## Problem

You want to test whether a map contains a given key or value.

## Solution

To test for the existence of a key in a map, use the `contains` method:

```
scala> val states = Map(
     |   "AK" -> "Alaska",
     |   "IL" -> "Illinois",
     |   "KY" -> "Kentucky"
     | )
states: scala.collection.immutable.Map[String,String] =
  Map(AK -> Alaska, IL -> Illinois, KY -> Kentucky)

scala> if (states.contains("FOO")) println("Found foo") else println("No foo")
No foo
```

To test whether a value exists in a map, use the `valuesIterator` method to search for the value using `exists` and `contains`:

```
scala> states.valuesIterator.exists(_.contains("ucky"))
res0: Boolean = true

scala> states.valuesIterator.exists(_.contains("yucky"))
res1: Boolean = false
```

This works because the `valuesIterator` method returns an `Iterator`:

```
scala> states.valuesIterator
res2: Iterator[String] = MapLike(Alaska, Illinois, Kentucky)
```

and `exists` returns `true` if the function you define returns `true` for at least one element in the collection. In the first example, because at least one element in the collection contains the `String` literal ucky, the `exists` call returns true.

## Discussion

When chaining methods like this together, be careful about intermediate results. In this example, I originally used the `values` methods to get the values from the map, but this produces a new collection, whereas the `valuesIterator` method returns a lightweight iterator.

## See Also

- Recipe 11.16, "Accessing Map Values", shows how to avoid an exception while accessing a map key.
- Recipe 11.18, "Getting the Keys or Values from a Map", demonstrates the values and valuesIterator methods.

# 11.21. Filtering a Map

## Problem

You want to filter the elements contained in a map, either by directly modifying a mutable map, or by applying a filtering algorithm on an immutable map to create a new map.

## Solution

Use the retain method to define the elements to retain when using a mutable map, and use filterKeys or filter to filter the elements in a mutable or immutable map, remembering to assign the result to a new variable.

### Mutable maps

You can filter the elements in a *mutable* map using the retain method to specify which elements should be retained:

```scala
scala> var x = collection.mutable.Map(1 -> "a", 2 -> "b", 3 -> "c")
x: scala.collection.mutable.Map[Int,String] = Map(2 -> b, 1 -> a, 3 -> c)

scala> x.retain((k,v) => k > 1)
res0: scala.collection.mutable.Map[Int,String] = Map(2 -> b, 3 -> c)

scala> x
res1: scala.collection.mutable.Map[Int,String] = Map(2 -> b, 3 -> c)
```

As shown, retain modifies a mutable map in place. As implied by the anonymous function signature used in that example:

```scala
(k,v) => ...
```

your algorithm can test both the key and value of each element to decide which elements to retain in the map.

In a related note, the transform method doesn't filter a map, but it lets you transform the elements in a mutable map:

```scala
scala> x.transform((k,v) => v.toUpperCase)
res0: scala.collection.mutable.Map[Int,String] = Map(2 -> B, 3 -> C)
```

```
scala> x
res1: scala.collection.mutable.Map[Int,String] = Map(2 -> B, 3 -> C)
```

Depending on your definition of "filter," you can also remove elements from a map using methods like `remove` and `clear`, which are shown in Recipe 11.15.

## Mutable and immutable maps

When working with a mutable or immutable map, you can use a predicate with the `filterKeys` methods to define which map elements to retain. When using this method, remember to assign the filtered result to a new variable:

```
scala> val x = Map(1 -> "a", 2 -> "b", 3 -> "c")
x: scala.collection.mutable.Map[Int,String] = Map(2 -> b, 1 -> a, 3 -> c)

scala> val y = x.filterKeys(_ > 2)
y: scala.collection.Map[Int,String] = Map(3 -> c)
```

The predicate you supply should return `true` for the elements you want to keep in the new collection and `false` for the elements you don't want.

If your algorithm is longer, you can define a function (or method), and then use it in the `filterKeys` call, rather than using an anonymous function. First define your method, such as this method, which returns `true` when the value the method is given is 1:

```
scala> def only1(i: Int) = if (i == 1) true else false
only1: (i: Int)Boolean
```

Then pass the method to the `filterKeys` method:

```
scala> val x = Map(1 -> "a", 2 -> "b", 3 -> "c")
x: scala.collection.mutable.Map[Int,String] = Map(2 -> b, 1 -> a, 3 -> c)

scala> val y = x.filterKeys(only1)
y: scala.collection.Map[Int,String] = Map(1 -> a)
```

In an interesting use, you can also use a `Set` with `filterKeys` to define the elements to retain:

```
scala> var m = Map(1 -> "a", 2 -> "b", 3 -> "c")
m: scala.collection.immutable.Map[Int,String] = Map(1 -> a, 2 -> b, 3 -> c)

scala> val newMap = m.filterKeys(Set(2,3))
newMap: scala.collection.immutable.Map[Int,String] = Map(2 -> b, 3 -> c)
```

You can also use all of the filtering methods that are shown in Chapter 10. For instance, the map version of the `filter` method lets you filter the map elements by either key, value, or both. The `filter` method provides your predicate a `Tuple2`, so you can access the key and value as shown in these examples:

```
scala> var m = Map(1 -> "a", 2 -> "b", 3 -> "c")
m: scala.collection.immutable.Map[Int,String] = Map(1 -> a, 2 -> b, 3 -> c)
```

```
// access the key
scala> m.filter((t) => t._1 > 1)
res0: scala.collection.immutable.Map[Int,String] = Map(2 -> b, 3 -> c)

// access the value
scala> m.filter((t) => t._2 == "c")
res1: scala.collection.immutable.Map[Int,String] = Map(3 -> c)
```

The take method lets you "take" (keep) the first N elements from the map:

```
scala> m.take(2)
res2: scala.collection.immutable.Map[Int,String] = Map(1 -> a, 2 -> b)
```

See the filtering recipes in Chapter 10 for examples of other methods that you can use, including takeWhile, drop, slice, and more.

# 11.22. Sorting an Existing Map by Key or Value

## Problem

You have an unsorted map and want to sort the elements in the map by the key or value.

## Solution

Given a basic, immutable Map:

```
scala> val grades = Map("Kim" -> 90,
     |     "Al" -> 85,
     |     "Melissa" -> 95,
     |     "Emily" -> 91,
     |     "Hannah" -> 92
     | )
grades: scala.collection.immutable.Map[String,Int] =
  Map(Hannah -> 92, Melissa -> 95, Kim -> 90, Emily -> 91, Al -> 85)
```

You can sort the map by *key*, from low to high, using sortBy:

```
scala> import scala.collection.immutable.ListMap
import scala.collection.immutable.ListMap

scala> ListMap(grades.toSeq.sortBy(_._1):_*)
res0: scala.collection.immutable.ListMap[String,Int] =
  Map(Al -> 85, Emily -> 91, Hannah -> 92, Kim -> 90, Melissa -> 95)
```

You can also sort the keys in ascending or descending order using sortWith:

```
// low to high
scala> ListMap(grades.toSeq.sortWith(_._1 < _._1):_*)
res0: scala.collection.immutable.ListMap[String,Int] =
  Map(Al -> 85, Emily -> 91, Hannah -> 92, Kim -> 90, Melissa -> 95)

// high to low
```

```scala
scala> ListMap(grades.toSeq.sortWith(_._1 > _._1):_*)
res1: scala.collection.immutable.ListMap[String,Int] =
   Map(Melissa -> 95, Kim -> 90, Hannah -> 92, Emily -> 91, Al -> 85)
```

You can sort the map by *value* using sortBy:

```scala
scala> ListMap(grades.toSeq.sortBy(_._2):_*)
res0: scala.collection.immutable.ListMap[String,Int] =
   Map(Al -> 85, Kim -> 90, Emily -> 91, Hannah -> 92, Melissa -> 95)
```

You can also sort by value in ascending or descending order using sortWith:

```scala
// low to high
scala> ListMap(grades.toSeq.sortWith(_._2 < _._2):_*)
res0: scala.collection.immutable.ListMap[String,Int] =
   Map(Al -> 85, Kim -> 90, Emily -> 91, Hannah -> 92, Melissa -> 95)

// high to low
scala> ListMap(grades.toSeq.sortWith(_._2 > _._2):_*)
res1: scala.collection.immutable.ListMap[String,Int] =
   Map(Melissa -> 95, Hannah -> 92, Emily -> 91, Kim -> 90, Al -> 85)
```

In all of these examples, you're not sorting the existing map; the sort methods result in a new sorted map, so the output of the result needs to be assigned to a new variable. Also, you can use either a ListMap or a LinkedHashMap in these recipes. This example shows how to use a LinkedHashMap and assign the result to a new variable:

```scala
scala> val x = collection.mutable.LinkedHashMap(grades.toSeq.sortBy(_._1):_*)
x: scala.collection.mutable.LinkedHashMap[String,Int] =
   Map(Al -> 85, Emily -> 91, Hannah -> 92, Kim -> 90, Melissa -> 95)

scala> x.foreach(println)
(Al,85)
(Emily,91)
(Hannah,92)
(Kim,90)
(Melissa,95)
```

## Discussion

To understand these solutions, it's helpful to break them down into smaller pieces. First, start with the basic immutable Map:

```scala
scala> val grades = Map("Kim" -> 90,
     |    "Al" -> 85,
     |    "Melissa" -> 95,
     |    "Emily" -> 91,
     |    "Hannah" -> 92
     | )
grades: scala.collection.immutable.Map[String,Int] =
   Map(Hannah -> 92, Melissa -> 95, Kim -> 90, Emily -> 91, Al -> 85)
```

Next, this is what grades.toSeq looks like:

```
scala> grades.toSeq
res0: Seq[(String, Int)] =
   ArrayBuffer((Hannah,92), (Melissa,95), (Kim,90), (Emily,91), (Al,85))
```

You make the conversion to a Seq because it has sorting methods you can use:

```
scala> grades.toSeq.sortBy(_._1)
res0: Seq[(String, Int)] =
   ArrayBuffer((Al,85), (Emily,91), (Hannah,92), (Kim,90), (Melissa,95))

scala> grades.toSeq.sortWith(_._1 < _._1)
res1: Seq[(String, Int)] =
   ArrayBuffer((Al,85), (Emily,91), (Hannah,92), (Kim,90), (Melissa,95))
```

Once you have the map data sorted as desired, store it in a ListMap to retain the sort order:

```
scala> ListMap(grades.toSeq.sortBy(_._1):_*)
res0: scala.collection.immutable.ListMap[String,Int] =
   Map(Al -> 85, Emily -> 91, Hannah -> 92, Kim -> 90, Melissa -> 95)
```

The LinkedHashMap also retains the sort order of its elements, so it can be used in all of the examples as well:

```
scala> import scala.collection.mutable.LinkedHashMap
import scala.collection.mutable.LinkedHashMap

scala> LinkedHashMap(grades.toSeq.sortBy(_._1):_*)
res0: scala.collection.mutable.LinkedHashMap[String,Int] =
   Map(Al -> 85, Emily -> 91, Hannah -> 92, Kim -> 90, Melissa -> 95)
```

There are both mutable and immutable versions of a ListMap, but LinkedHashMap is only available as a mutable class. Use whichever is best for your situation.

## About that _*

The _* portion of the code takes a little getting used to. It's used to convert the data so it will be passed as multiple parameters to the ListMap or LinkedHashMap. You can see this a little more easily by again breaking down the code into separate lines. The sortBy method returns a Seq[(String, Int)], i.e., a sequence of tuples:

```
scala> val x = grades.toSeq.sortBy(_._1)
x: Seq[(String, Int)] =
   ArrayBuffer((Al,85), (Emily,91), (Hannah,92), (Kim,90), (Melissa,95))
```

You can't directly construct a ListMap with a sequence of tuples, but because the apply method in the ListMap companion object accepts a Tuple2 varargs parameter, you can adapt x to work with it, i.e., giving it what it wants:

```
scala> ListMap(x: _*)
res0: scala.collection.immutable.ListMap[String,Int] =
   Map(Al -> 85, Emily -> 91, Hannah -> 92, Kim -> 90, Melissa -> 95)
```

Attempting to create the ListMap without using this approach results in an error:

```
scala> ListMap(x)
<console>:16: error: type mismatch;
 found    : Seq[(String, Int)]
 required: (?, ?)
              ListMap(x)
                  ^
```

Another way to see how _* works is to define your own method that takes a varargs parameter. The following printAll method takes one parameter, a varargs field of type String:

```
def printAll(strings: String*) {
    strings.foreach(println)
}
```

If you then create a List like this:

```
// a sequence of strings
val fruits = List("apple", "banana", "cherry")
```

you won't be able to pass that List into printAll; it will fail like the previous example:

```
scala> printAll(fruits)
<console>:20: error: type mismatch;
 found    : List[String]
 required: String
              printAll(fruits)
                  ^
```

But you can use _* to adapt the List to work with printAll, like this:

```
// this works
printAll(fruits: _*)
```

If you come from a Unix background, it may be helpful to think of _* as a "splat" operator. This operator tells the compiler to pass each element of the sequence to printAll as a separate argument, instead of passing fruits as a single List argument.

## See Also

- The immutable ListMap class (*http://bit.ly/1bkkkDB*)
- The immutable ListMap companion object (*http://bit.ly/12tYmWw*)
- The mutable ListMap class (*http://bit.ly/149431d*)
- The mutable LinkedHashMap class (*http://bit.ly/190DOMw*)

# 11.23. Finding the Largest Key or Value in a Map

## Problem

You want to find the largest value of a key or value in a map.

## Solution

Use the `max` method on the map, or use the map's `keysIterator` or `valuesIterator` with other approaches, depending on your needs.

For example, given this map:

```
val grades = Map("Al" -> 80, "Kim" -> 95, "Teri" -> 85, "Julia" -> 90)
```

the key is type `String`, so which key is "largest" depends on your definition. You can find the "largest" key using the natural `String` sort order by calling the `max` method on the map:

```
scala> grades.max
res0: (String, Int) = (Teri,85)
```

Because the "T" in "Teri" is farthest down the alphabet in the names, it is returned.

You can also call `keysIterator` to get an iterator over the map keys, and call its `max` method:

```
scala> grades.keysIterator.max
res1: String = Teri
```

You can find the same maximum by getting the `keysIterator` and using `reduceLeft`:

```
scala> grades.keysIterator.reduceLeft((x,y) => if (x > y) x else y)
res2: String = Teri
```

This approach is flexible, because if your definition of "largest" is the longest string, you can compare string lengths instead:

```
scala> grades.keysIterator.reduceLeft((x,y) => if (x.length > y.length) x else y)
res3: String = Julia
```

Because the values in the map are of type `Int` in this example, you can use this simple approach to get the largest value:

```
scala> grades.valuesIterator.max
res4: Int = 95
```

You can also use the `reduceLeft` approach, if you prefer:

```
scala> grades.valuesIterator.reduceLeft(_ max _)
res5: Int = 95
```

You can also compare the numbers yourself, which is representative of what you may need to do with more complex types:

```
scala> grades.valuesIterator.reduceLeft((x,y) => if (x > y) x else y)
res6: Int = 95
```

To find minimum keys and values, just reverse the algorithms in these examples.

## See Also

Recipe 11.18, "Getting the Keys or Values from a Map"

# 11.24. Adding Elements to a Set

## Problem

You want to add elements to a mutable set, or create a new set by adding elements to an immutable set.

## Solution

Mutable and immutable sets are handled differently, as demonstrated in the following examples.

### Mutable set

Add elements to a *mutable* Set with the +=, ++=, and add methods:

```
// use var with mutable
scala> var set = scala.collection.mutable.Set[Int]()
set: scala.collection.mutable.Set[Int] = Set()

// add one element
scala> set += 1
res0: scala.collection.mutable.Set[Int] = Set(1)

// add multiple elements
scala> set += (2, 3)
res1: scala.collection.mutable.Set[Int] = Set(2, 1, 3)

// notice that there is no error when you add a duplicate element
scala> set += 2
res2: scala.collection.mutable.Set[Int] = Set(2, 6, 1, 4, 3, 5)

// add elements from any sequence (any TraversableOnce)
scala> set ++= Vector(4, 5)
res3: scala.collection.mutable.Set[Int] = Set(2, 1, 4, 3, 5)

scala> set.add(6)
res4: Boolean = true
```

```
scala> set.add(5)
res5: Boolean = false
```

The last two examples demonstrate a unique characteristic of the add method on a set:
It returns true or false depending on whether or not the element was added. The other
methods silently fail if you attempt to add an element that's already in the set.

You can test to see whether a set contains an element before adding it:

```
set.contains(5)
```

But as a practical matter, I use += and ++=, and ignore whether the element was already
in the set.

Whereas the first example demonstrated how to create an empty set, you can also add
elements to a mutable set when you declare it, just like other collections:

```
scala> var set = scala.collection.mutable.Set(1, 2, 3)
set: scala.collection.mutable.Set[Int] = Set(2, 1, 3)
```

### Immutable set

The following examples show how to create a new immutable set by adding elements
to an existing immutable set.

First, create an immutable set:

```
scala> val s1 = Set(1, 2)
s1: scala.collection.immutable.Set[Int] = Set(1, 2)
```

Create a new set by adding elements to a previous set with the + and ++ methods:

```
// add one element
scala> val s2 = s1 + 3
s2: scala.collection.immutable.Set[Int] = Set(1, 2, 3)

// add multiple elements (+ method has a varargs field)
scala> val s3 = s2 + (4, 5)
s3: scala.collection.immutable.Set[Int] = Set(5, 1, 2, 3, 4)

// add elements from another sequence
scala> val s4 = s3 ++ List(6, 7)
s4: scala.collection.immutable.Set[Int] = Set(5, 1, 6, 2, 7, 3, 4)
```

I showed these examples with immutable variables just to be clear about how the approach works. You can also declare your variable as a var, and reassign the resulting set
back to the same variable:

```
scala> var set = Set(1, 2, 3)
set: scala.collection.immutable.Set[Int] = Set(1, 2, 3)

scala> set += 4
```

```
scala> set
res0: scala.collection.immutable.Set[Int] = Set(1, 2, 3, 4)
```

See Recipe 10.6, "Understanding Mutable Variables with Immutable Collections" for more information on the difference between mutable/immutable *variables* and mutable/immutable *collections*.

# 11.25. Deleting Elements from Sets

## Problem

You want to remove elements from a mutable or immutable set.

## Solution

Mutable and immutable sets are handled differently, as demonstrated in the following examples.

### Mutable set

When working with a *mutable* Set, remove elements from the set using the -= and --= methods, as shown in the following examples:

```
scala> var set = scala.collection.mutable.Set(1, 2, 3, 4, 5)
set: scala.collection.mutable.Set[Int] = Set(2, 1, 4, 3, 5)

// one element
scala> set -= 1
res0: scala.collection.mutable.Set[Int] = Set(2, 4, 3, 5)

// two or more elements (-= has a varags field)
scala> set -= (2, 3)
res1: scala.collection.mutable.Set[Int] = Set(4, 5)

// multiple elements defined in another sequence
scala> set --= Array(4,5)
res2: scala.collection.mutable.Set[Int] = Set()
```

You can also use other methods like retain, clear, and remove, depending on your needs:

```
// retain
scala> var set = scala.collection.mutable.Set(1, 2, 3, 4, 5)
set: scala.collection.mutable.Set[Int] = Set(2, 1, 4, 3, 5)

scala> set.retain(_ > 2)

scala> set
res0: scala.collection.mutable.Set[Int] = Set(4, 3, 5)

// clear
```

```
scala> var set = scala.collection.mutable.Set(1, 2, 3, 4, 5)
set: scala.collection.mutable.Set[Int] = Set(2, 1, 4, 3, 5)

scala> set.clear

scala> set
res1: scala.collection.mutable.Set[Int] = Set()

// remove
scala> var set = scala.collection.mutable.Set(1, 2, 3, 4, 5)
set: scala.collection.mutable.Set[Int] = Set(2, 1, 4, 3, 5)

scala> set.remove(2)
res2: Boolean = true

scala> set
res3: scala.collection.mutable.Set[Int] = Set(1, 4, 3, 5)

scala> set.remove(40)
res4: Boolean = false
```

As shown, the remove method provides feedback as to whether or not any elements were removed.

### Immutable set

By definition, when using an *immutable* Set you can't remove elements from it, but you can use the - and - - operators to remove elements while assigning the result to a new variable:

```
scala> val s1 = Set(1, 2, 3, 4, 5, 6)
s1: scala.collection.immutable.Set[Int] = Set(5, 1, 6, 2, 3, 4)

// one element
scala> val s2 = s1 - 1
s2: scala.collection.immutable.Set[Int] = Set(5, 6, 2, 3, 4)

// multiple elements
scala> val s3 = s2 - (2, 3)
s3: scala.collection.immutable.Set[Int] = Set(5, 6, 4)

// multiple elements defined in another sequence
scala> val s4 = s3 -- Array(4, 5)
s4: scala.collection.immutable.Set[Int] = Set(6)
```

You can also use all of the filtering methods shown in Chapter 10. For instance, you can use the filter or take methods:

```
scala> val s1 = Set(1, 2, 3, 4, 5, 6)
s1: scala.collection.immutable.Set[Int] = Set(5, 1, 6, 2, 3, 4)

scala> val s2 = s1.filter(_ > 3)
s2: scala.collection.immutable.Set[Int] = Set(5, 6, 4)
```

```
scala> val firstTwo = s1.take(2)
firstTwo: scala.collection.immutable.Set[Int] = Set(5, 1)
```

# 11.26. Using Sortable Sets

## Problem

You want to be able to store and retrieve items from a set in a sorted order.

## Solution

To retrieve values from a set in sorted order, use a SortedSet. To retrieve elements from a set in the order in which elements were inserted, use a LinkedHashSet.

A SortedSet returns elements in a sorted order:

```
scala> val s = scala.collection.SortedSet(10, 4, 8, 2)
s: scala.collection.SortedSet[Int] = TreeSet(2, 4, 8, 10)

scala> val s = scala.collection.SortedSet("cherry", "kiwi", "apple")
s: scala.collection.SortedSet[String] = TreeSet(apple, cherry, kiwi)
```

A LinkedHashSet saves elements in the order in which they were inserted:

```
scala> var s = scala.collection.mutable.LinkedHashSet(10, 4, 8, 2)
s: scala.collection.mutable.LinkedHashSet[Int] = Set(10, 4, 8, 2)
```

## Discussion

The SortedSet is available only in an immutable version. If you need a mutable version, use the java.util.TreeSet. The LinkedHashSet is available only as a mutable collection.

The examples shown in the Solution work because the types used in the sets have an implicit Ordering. Custom types won't work unless you also provide an implicit Ordering. For example, the following code won't work because the Person class is just a basic class:

```
class Person (var name: String)

import scala.collection.SortedSet
val aleka = new Person("Aleka")
val christina = new Person("Christina")
val molly = new Person("Molly")
val tyler = new Person("Tyler")

// this won't work
val s = SortedSet(molly, tyler, christina, aleka)
```

In the REPL, the last line of code fails with this error:

```
scala> val s = SortedSet(molly, tyler, christina, aleka)
<console>:17: error: No implicit Ordering defined for Person.
       val s = SortedSet(molly, tyler, christina, aleka)
                ^
```

To solve this problem, modify the Person class to extend the Ordered trait, and implement a compare method:

```
class Person (var name: String) extends Ordered [Person]
{
  override def toString = name

  // return 0 if the same, negative if this < that, positive if this > that
  def compare (that: Person) = {
    if (this.name == that.name)
      0
    else if (this.name > that.name)
      1
    else
      -1
  }

}
```

With this new Person class definition, sorting works as desired:

```
scala> val s = SortedSet(molly, tyler, christina, aleka)
s: scala.collection.SortedSet[Person] = TreeSet(Aleka, Christina, Molly, Tyler)
```

For more information about the Ordered and Ordering traits, see Recipe 10.28, "Sorting a Collection" and the links in the See Also section.

## See Also

- The SortedSet trait (*http://bit.ly/12tYs0n*)
- The LinkedHashSet class (*http://bit.ly/11TyOXS*)
- The Ordering trait (*http://bit.ly/1bCFQSk*)
- The Ordered trait (*http://bit.ly/12ARfPx*)

# 11.27. Using a Queue

## Problem

You want to use a queue data structure in a Scala application.

## Solution

A queue is a first-in, first-out (FIFO) data structure. Scala offers both an immutable queue and mutable queue. This recipe demonstrates the *mutable* queue.

You can create an empty, mutable queue of any data type:

```
import scala.collection.mutable.Queue
var ints = Queue[Int]()
var fruits = Queue[String]()
var q = Queue[Person]()
```

You can also create a queue with initial elements:

```
scala> val q = Queue(1, 2, 3)
q: scala.collection.mutable.Queue[Int] = Queue(1, 2, 3)
```

Once you have a mutable queue, add elements to it using +=, ++=, and enqueue, as shown in the following examples:

```
scala> import scala.collection.mutable.Queue
import scala.collection.mutable.Queue

// create an empty queue
scala> var q = new Queue[String]
q: scala.collection.mutable.Queue[String] = Queue()

// add elements to the queue in the usual ways
scala> var q = new Queue[String]
q: scala.collection.mutable.Queue[String] = Queue()

scala> q += "apple"
res0: scala.collection.mutable.Queue[String] = Queue(apple)

scala> q += ("kiwi", "banana")
res1: scala.collection.mutable.Queue[String] = Queue(apple, kiwi, banana)

scala> q ++= List("cherry", "coconut")
res2: scala.collection.mutable.Queue[String] =
  Queue(apple, kiwi, banana, cherry, coconut)

// can also use enqueue
scala> q.enqueue("pineapple")

scala> q
res3: scala.collection.mutable.Queue[String] =
  Queue(apple, kiwi, banana, cherry, coconut, pineapple)
```

Because a queue is a FIFO, you typically remove elements from the head of the queue, one element at a time, using dequeue:

```
// take an element from the head of the queue
scala> val next = q.dequeue
next: String = apple
```

```
// 'apple' is removed from the queue
scala> q
res0: scala.collection.mutable.Queue[String] = Queue(kiwi, banana, cherry, ↵
coconut, pineapple)

// take the next element
scala> val next = q.dequeue
next: String = kiwi

// 'kiwi' is removed from the queue
scala> q
res1: scala.collection.mutable.Queue[String] = Queue(banana, cherry, coconut, ↵
pineapple)
```

You can also use the dequeueFirst and dequeueAll methods to remove elements from the queue by specifying a predicate:

```
scala> q.dequeueFirst(_.startsWith("b"))
res2: Option[String] = Some(banana)

scala> q
res3: scala.collection.mutable.Queue[String] = Queue(cherry, coconut, pineapple)

scala> q.dequeueAll(_.length > 6)
res4: scala.collection.mutable.Seq[String] = ArrayBuffer(coconut, pineapple)

scala> q
res5: scala.collection.mutable.Queue[String] = Queue(cherry)
```

A Queue is a collection class that extends from Iterable and Traversable, so it has all the usual collection methods, including foreach, map, etc. See the Queue Scaladoc for more information.

## See Also

- The mutable Queue class (*http://bit.ly/10YbKV5*)
- The immutable Queue class (*http://bit.ly/15lrxhh*)

# 11.28. Using a Stack

## Problem

You want to use a stack data structure in a Scala application.

# Solution

A stack is a last-in, first-out (LIFO) data structure. In most programming languages you add elements to a stack using a push method, and take elements off the stack with pop, and Scala is no different.

Scala has both immutable and mutable versions of a stack, as well as an `ArrayStack` (discussed shortly). The following examples demonstrate how to use the *mutable* `Stack` class.

Create an empty, mutable stack of any data type:

```
import scala.collection.mutable.Stack
var ints = Stack[Int]()
var fruits = Stack[String]()

case class Person(var name: String)
var people = Stack[Person]()
```

You can also populate a stack with initial elements when you create it:

```
val ints = Stack(1, 2, 3)
```

Once you have a mutable stack, push elements onto the stack with push:

```
// create a stack
scala> var fruits = Stack[String]()
fruits: scala.collection.mutable.Stack[String] = Stack()

// add one element at a time
scala> fruits.push("apple")
res0: scala.collection.mutable.Stack[String] = Stack(apple)

scala> fruits.push("banana")
res1: scala.collection.mutable.Stack[String] = Stack(banana, apple)

// add multiple elements
scala> fruits.push("coconut", "orange", "pineapple")
res2: scala.collection.mutable.Stack[String] =
  Stack(pineapple, orange, coconut, banana, apple)
```

To take elements off the stack, pop them off the top of the stack:

```
scala> val next = fruits.pop
next: String = pineapple

scala> fruits
res3: scala.collection.mutable.Stack[String] =
  Stack(orange, coconut, banana, apple)
```

You can peek at the next element on the stack without removing it, using top:

```
scala> fruits.top
res4: String = orange
```

```
// 'orange' is still on the top
scala> fruits
res5: scala.collection.mutable.Stack[String] =
  Stack(orange, coconut, banana, apple)
```

Stack extends from Seq, so you can inspect it with the usual methods:

```
scala> fruits.size
res6: Int = 4

scala> fruits.isEmpty
res7: Boolean = false
```

You can empty a mutable stack with clear:

```
scala> fruits.clear

scala> fruits
res8: scala.collection.mutable.Stack[String] = Stack()
```

## Discussion

There's also an ArrayStack class, and according to the Scala documentation, "It provides fast indexing and is generally slightly more efficient for most operations than a normal mutable stack."

Although I haven't used an immutable Stack, I've seen several people recommend using a List instead of an immutable Stack for this use case. A List has at least one less layer of code, and you can push elements onto the List with :: and access the first element with the head method.

## See Also

- The mutable Stack class (*http://bit.ly/13MA28x*)
- The immutable Stack class (*http://bit.ly/12SHete*)
- The ArrayStack class (*http://bit.ly/13q90MV*)

# 11.29. Using a Range

## Problem

You want to use a Range in a Scala application.

## Solution

Ranges are often used to populate data structures, and to iterate over for loops. Ranges provide a lot of power with just a few methods, as shown in these examples:

```
scala> 1 to 10
res0: scala.collection.immutable.Range.Inclusive =
  Range(1, 2, 3, 4, 5, 6, 7, 8, 9, 10)

scala> 1 until 10
res1: scala.collection.immutable.Range = Range(1, 2, 3, 4, 5, 6, 7, 8, 9)

scala> 1 to 10 by 2
res2: scala.collection.immutable.Range = Range(1, 3, 5, 7, 9)

scala> 'a' to 'c'
res3: collection.immutable.NumericRange.Inclusive[Char] = NumericRange(a, b, c)
```

You can use ranges to create and populate sequences:

```
scala> val x = (1 to 10).toList
x: List[Int] = List(1, 2, 3, 4, 5, 6, 7, 8, 9, 10)

scala> val x = (1 to 10).toArray
x: Array[Int] = Array(1, 2, 3, 4, 5, 6, 7, 8, 9, 10)

scala> val x = (1 to 10).toSet
x: scala.collection.immutable.Set[Int] = Set(5, 10, 1, 6, 9, 2, 7, 3, 8, 4)
```

Some sequences have a range method in their objects to perform the same function:

```
scala> val x = Array.range(1, 10)
x: Array[Int] = Array(1, 2, 3, 4, 5, 6, 7, 8, 9)

scala> val x = Vector.range(1, 10)
x: collection.immutable.Vector[Int] = Vector(1, 2, 3, 4, 5, 6, 7, 8, 9)

scala> val x = List.range(1, 10)
x: List[Int] = List(1, 2, 3, 4, 5, 6, 7, 8, 9)

scala> val x = List.range(0, 10, 2)
x: List[Int] = List(0, 2, 4, 6, 8)

scala> val x = collection.mutable.ArrayBuffer.range('a', 'd')
x: scala.collection.mutable.ArrayBuffer[Char] = ArrayBuffer(a, b, c)
```

Ranges are also commonly used in for loops:

```
scala> for (i <- 1 to 3) println(i)
1
2
3
```

## Discussion

In addition to the approaches shown, a Range can be combined with the map method to populate a collection:

```scala
scala> val x = (1 to 5).map { e => (e + 1.1) * 2 }
x: scala.collection.immutable.IndexedSeq[Double] =
    Vector(4.2, 6.2, 8.2, 10.2, 12.2)
```

While discussing ways to populate collections, the tabulate method is another nice approach:

```scala
scala> val x = List.tabulate(5)(_ + 1)
x: List[Int] = List(1, 2, 3, 4, 5)

scala> val x = List.tabulate(5)(_ + 2)
x: List[Int] = List(2, 3, 4, 5, 6)

scala> val x = Vector.tabulate(5)(_ * 2)
x: scala.collection.immutable.Vector[Int] = Vector(0, 2, 4, 6, 8)
```

## See Also

The immutable Range class (*http://bit.ly/18lkQAQ*)

# CHAPTER 12

# Files and Processes

## 12.0. Introduction

When it comes to working with files, the `scala.io.Source` class and its companion object offer some nice simplifications compared to Java. Not only does `Source` make it easy to open and read text files, but it also makes it easy to accomplish other tasks, such as downloading content from URLs, or substituting a `String` for a `File`, which is useful for testing. The Scala `Console` class also simplifies console interaction, letting you print to the console (command line) and read from it very easily. In other cases, such as when reading a YAML file or working with directories, you simply fall back to use existing Java libraries.

Scala also makes it *much* easier to execute system commands. When it comes to interacting with system processes, the Scala API designers created a clean and familiar API to let you run external commands. This is useful for applications, and it's terrific for scripts.

## 12.1. How to Open and Read a Text File

### Problem

You want to open a plain-text file in Scala and process the lines in that file.

### Solution

There are two primary ways to open and read a text file:

- Use a concise, one-line syntax. This has the side effect of leaving the file open, but can be useful in short-lived programs, like shell scripts.

- Use a slightly longer approach that properly closes the file.

This solution shows both approaches.

### Using the concise syntax

In Scala shell scripts, where the JVM is started and stopped in a relatively short period of time, it may not matter that the file is closed, so you can use the Scala `scala.io.Source.fromFile` method as shown in the following examples.

To handle each line in the file as it's read, use this approach:

```
import scala.io.Source

val filename = "fileopen.scala"
for (line <- Source.fromFile(filename).getLines) {
  println(line)
}
```

As a variation of this, use the following approach to get all of the lines from the file as a `List` or `Array`:

```
val lines = Source.fromFile("/Users/Al/.bash_profile").getLines.toList
val lines = Source.fromFile("/Users/Al/.bash_profile").getLines.toArray
```

The `fromFile` method returns a `BufferedSource`, and its `getLines` method treats "any of \r\n, \r, or \n as a line separator (longest match)," so each element in the sequence is a line from the file.

Use this approach to get all of the lines from the file as one `String`:

```
val fileContents = Source.fromFile(filename).getLines.mkString
```

This approach has the side effect of leaving the file open as long as the JVM is running, but for short-lived shell scripts, this shouldn't be an issue; the file is closed when the JVM shuts down.

### Properly closing the file

To properly close the file, get a reference to the `BufferedSource` when opening the file, and manually close it when you're finished with the file:

```
val bufferedSource = Source.fromFile("example.txt")
for (line <- bufferedSource.getLines) {
  println(line.toUpperCase)
}
bufferedSource.close
```

For automated methods of closing the file, see the "Loan Pattern" examples in the Discussion.

## Discussion

The getLines method of the Source class returns a scala.collection.Iterator. The iterator returns each line without any newline characters. An iterator has many methods for working with a collection, and for the purposes of working with a file, it works well with the for loop, as shown.

### Leaving files open

As mentioned, the first solution leaves the file open as long as the JVM is running:

```
// leaves the file open
for (line <- io.Source.fromFile("/etc/passwd").getLines) {
  println(line)
}

// also leaves the file open
val contents = io.Source.fromFile("/etc/passwd").mkString
```

On Unix systems, you can show whether a file is left open by executing one of these fromFile statements in the REPL with a real file (like */etc/passwd*), and then running an lsof ("list open files") command like this at the Unix command line:

```
$ sudo lsof -u Al | grep '/etc/passwd'
```

That command lists all the open files for the user named Al, and then searches the output for the */etc/passwd* file. If this filename is in the output, it means that it's open. On my Mac OS X system I see a line of output like this when the file is left open:

```
java  17148  Al  40r  REG  14,2  1475 174214161 /etc/passwd
```

When I shut down the REPL—thereby stopping the JVM process—the file no longer appears in the lsof output. So while this approach has this flaw, it can be used in short-lived JVM processes, such as a shell script. (You can demonstrate the same result using a Scala shell script. Just add a Thread.sleep call after the for loop so you can keep the script running long enough to check the lsof command.)

### Automatically closing the resource

When working with files and other resources that need to be properly closed, it's best to use the Loan Pattern (*http://bit.ly/169sJU8*). According to this website, the pattern "ensures that a resource is deterministically disposed of once it goes out of scope."

In Scala, this can be ensured with a try/finally clause, which the Loan Pattern website shows like this:

```
def using[A](r : Resource)(f : Resource => A) : A =
  try {
    f(r)
  } finally {
    r.dispose()
  }
```

One way to implement the Loan Pattern when working with files is to use Joshua Suereth's ARM library (*https://github.com/jsuereth/scala-arm*). To demonstrate this library, create an SBT project, and then add the following line to its *build.sbt* file to pull in the required dependencies:

```
libraryDependencies += "com.jsuereth" %% "scala-arm" % "1.3"
```

Next, create a file named *TestARM.scala* in the root directory of your SBT project with these contents:

```
import resource._

object TestARM extends App {

  for (source <- managed(scala.io.Source.fromFile("example.txt"))) {
    for (line <- source.getLines) {
      println(line)
    }
  }

}
```

This code prints all of the lines from the file named *example.txt*. The managed method from the ARM library makes sure that the resource is closed automatically when the resource goes out of scope. The ARM website shows several other ways the library can be used.

A second way to demonstrate the Loan Pattern is with the using method described on the Loan Pattern website. The best implementation I've seen of a using method is in the book *Beginning Scala* (Apress), by David Pollak. The following code is a slight modification of his code:

```
object Control {

  def using[A <: { def close(): Unit }, B](resource: A)(f: A => B): B =
    try {
      f(resource)
    } finally {
      resource.close()
    }

}
```

This using method takes two parameters:

- An object that has a close() method
- A block of code to be executed, which transforms the input type A to the output type B

The body of this using method does exactly what's shown on the Loan Pattern web page, wrapping the block of code it's given in a try/finally block.

The following code demonstrates how to use this method when reading from a file:

```
import Control._

object TestUsing extends App {

  using(io.Source.fromFile("example.txt")) { source => {
      for (line <- source.getLines) {
        println(line)
      }
    }
  }

}
```

Both the ARM library and the using method end up with the same result, implementing the Loan Pattern to make sure your resource is closed automatically.

## Handling exceptions

You can generate exceptions any time you try to open a file, and if you want to handle your exceptions, use Scala's try/catch syntax:

```
import scala.io.Source
import java.io.{FileNotFoundException, IOException}

val filename = "no-such-file.scala"
try {
  for (line <- Source.fromFile(filename).getLines) {
    println(line)
  }
} catch {
  case e: FileNotFoundException => println("Couldn't find that file.")
  case e: IOException => println("Got an IOException!")
}
```

The following code demonstrates how the fromFile method can be used with using to create a method that returns the entire contents of a file as a List[String], wrapped in an Option:

```
import Control._

def readTextFile(filename: String): Option[List[String]] = {
  try {
    val lines = using(io.Source.fromFile(filename)) { source =>
      (for (line <- source.getLines) yield line).toList
    }
    Some(lines)
  } catch {
    case e: Exception => None
```

```
    }
  }
```

This method returns a `Some(List[String])` on success, and `None` if something goes wrong, such as a `FileNotFoundException`. It can be used in the following ways:

```
val filename = "/etc/passwd"

println("--- FOREACH ---")
val result = readTextFile(filename)
result foreach { strings =>
  strings.foreach(println)
}

println("\n--- MATCH ---")
readTextFile(filename) match {
  case Some(lines) => lines.foreach(println)
  case None => println("couldn't read file")
}
```

If the process of opening and reading a file fails, you may prefer to return a `Try` or an empty `List[String]`. See Recipes 20.5 and 20.6 for examples of those approaches.

### Multiple fromFile methods

In Scala 2.10, there are eight variations of the `fromFile` method that let you specify a character encoding, buffer size, codec, and URI. For instance, you can specify an expected character encoding for a file like this:

```
// specify the encoding
Source.fromFile("example.txt", "UTF-8")
```

See the Scaladoc for the `scala.io.Source` object (not the `Source` class, which is an abstract class) for more information.

 Because Scala works so well with Java, you can use the Java `FileReader` and `BufferedReader` classes, as well as other Java libraries, like the Apache Commons FileUtils library.

## See Also

- The Source object (*http://bit.ly/1bkl0bX*).
- The Loan Pattern (*https://wiki.scala-lang.org/display/SYGN/Loan*).
- Joshua Suereth's ARM library (*https://github.com/jsuereth/scala-arm*).
- David Pollak's book, *Beginning Scala*.

- A detailed discussion of David Pollak's using method (*http://bit.ly/12JL0Fp*).
- The Apache Commons FileUtils project has many methods (*http://bit.ly/18iRijX*) for reading and writing files that can be used with Scala.

# 12.2. Writing Text Files

## Problem

You want to write plain text to a file, such as a simple configuration file, text data file, or other plain-text document.

## Solution

Scala doesn't offer any special file writing capability, so fall back and use the Java PrintWriter or FileWriter approaches:

```
// PrintWriter
import java.io._
val pw = new PrintWriter(new File("hello.txt" ))
pw.write("Hello, world")
pw.close

// FileWriter
val file = new File(canonicalFilename)
val bw = new BufferedWriter(new FileWriter(file))
bw.write(text)
bw.close()
```

## Discussion

Although I normally use a FileWriter to write plain text to a file, a good post at coderanch.com (*http://bit.ly/13gi8rN*) describes some of the differences between PrintWriter and FileWriter. For instance, while both classes extend from Writer (*http://bit.ly/1bFri4o*), and both can be used for writing plain text to files, FileWriter throws IOExceptions, whereas PrintWriter does not throw exceptions, and instead sets Boolean flags that can be checked. There are a few other differences between the classes; check their Javadoc for more information.

## See Also

- My Java file utilities (*http://bit.ly/11TzgoP*) and my Scala file utilities (*https://github.com/alvinj/FileUtils*)
- The Java FileWriter class (*http://bit.ly/18lkZnN*)

- The Java PrintWriter class (*http://bit.ly/1apShzo*)
- The coderanch.com PrintWriter versus FileWriter page (*http://bit.ly/13gi8rN*)

# 12.3. Reading and Writing Binary Files

## Problem

You want to read data from a binary file or write data to a binary file.

## Solution

Scala doesn't offer any special conveniences for reading or writing binary files, so use the Java FileInputStream and FileOutputStream classes.

To demonstrate this, the following code is a close Scala translation of the CopyBytes class on the Oracle Byte Streams tutorial (*http://bit.ly/1ahHPtP*):

```scala
import java.io._

object CopyBytes extends App {

  var in = None: Option[FileInputStream]
  var out = None: Option[FileOutputStream]

  try {
    in = Some(new FileInputStream("/tmp/Test.class"))
    out = Some(new FileOutputStream("/tmp/Test.class.copy"))
    var c = 0
    while ({c = in.get.read; c != -1}) {
      out.get.write(c)
    }
  } catch {
    case e: IOException => e.printStackTrace
  } finally {
    println("entered finally ...")
    if (in.isDefined) in.get.close
    if (out.isDefined) out.get.close
  }

}
```

In this code, in and out are populated in the try clause. It's safe to call in.get and out.get in the while loop, because if an exception had occurred, flow control would have switched to the catch clause, and then the finally clause before leaving the method.

Normally I tell people that I think the `get` and `isDefined` methods on `Option` would be deprecated, but this is one of the few times where I think their use is acceptable and they lead to more readable code.

Another difference between this code and Oracle's example is the `while` loop, which is slightly different in Scala. This change is required because a Java statement like `c = in.read` has a type of `Unit` in Scala, and will therefore never be equal to `-1` (or any other value). There are several other ways to work around this difference, but this example shows a fairly direct translation.

### See Also

- The Oracle Byte Streams tutorial (*http://bit.ly/1ahHPtP*)
- The Apache Commons FileUtils project (*http://bit.ly/18iRijX*) has many methods for reading and writing files that can be used with Scala

# 12.4. How to Process Every Character in a Text File

## Problem

You want to open a text file and process every character in the file.

## Solution

If performance isn't a concern, write your code in a straightforward, obvious way:

```
val source = io.Source.fromFile("/Users/Al/.bash_profile")
for (char <- source) {
  println(char.toUpper)
}
source.close
```

However, be aware that this code may be slow on large files. For instance, the following method that counts the number of lines in a file takes 100 seconds to run on an Apache access logfile that is ten million lines long:

```
// run time: took 100 secs
def countLines1(source: io.Source): Long = {
  val NEWLINE = 10
  var newlineCount = 0L
  for {
    char <- source
    if char.toByte == NEWLINE
  } newlineCount += 1
  newlineCount
}
```

The time can be significantly reduced by using the `getLines` method to retrieve one line at a time, and then working through the characters in each line. The following line-counting algorithm counts the same ten million lines in just 23 seconds:

```
// run time: 23 seconds
// use getLines, then count the newline characters
// (redundant for this purpose, i know)
def countLines2(source: io.Source): Long = {
  val NEWLINE = 10
  var newlineCount = 0L
  for {
    line <- source.getLines
    c <- line
    if c.toByte == NEWLINE
  } newlineCount += 1
  newlineCount
}
```

Both algorithms work through each byte in the file, but by using `getLines` in the second algorithm, the run time is reduced dramatically.

Notice that there's the equivalent of two for loops in the second example. If you haven't seen this approach before, here's what the code looks like with two explicit for loops:

```
for (line <- source.getLines) {
  for {
    c <- line
    if c.toByte == NEWLINE
  } newlineCount += 1
}
```

The two approaches are equivalent, but the first is more concise.

# 12.5. How to Process a CSV File

## Problem

You want to process the lines in a CSV file, either handling one line at a time or storing them in a two-dimensional array.

## Solution

Combine Recipe 12.1, "How to Open and Read a Text File" with Recipe 1.3, "Splitting Strings". Given a simple CSV file like this named *finance.csv*:

```
January, 10000.00, 9000.00, 1000.00
February, 11000.00, 9500.00, 1500.00
March, 12000.00, 10000.00, 2000.00
```

you can process the lines in the file with the following code:

```
object CSVDemo extends App {

  println("Month, Income, Expenses, Profit")
  val bufferedSource = io.Source.fromFile("/tmp/finance.csv")
  for (line <- bufferedSource.getLines) {
    val cols = line.split(",").map(_.trim)
    // do whatever you want with the columns here
    println(s"${cols(0)}|${cols(1)}|${cols(2)}|${cols(3)}")
  }
  bufferedSource.close

}
```

The magic in that code is this line:

```
val cols = line.split(",").map(_.trim)
```

It splits each line using the comma as a field separator character, and then uses the map method to trim each field to remove leading and trailing blank spaces. The resulting output looks like this:

```
January|10000.00|9000.00|1000.00
February|11000.00|9500.00|1500.00
March|12000.00|10000.00|2000.00
```

If you prefer named variables instead of accessing array elements, you can change the for loop to look like this:

```
for (line <- bufferedSource.getLines) {
  val Array(month, revenue, expenses, profit) = line.split(",").map(_.trim)
  println(s"$month $revenue $expenses $profit")
}
```

If the first line of the file is a header line and you want to skip it, just add drop(1) after getLines:

```
for (line <- bufferedSource.getLines.drop(1)) { // ...
```

If you prefer, you can also write the loop as a foreach loop:

```
bufferedSource.getLines.foreach { line =>
  rows(count) = line.split(",").map(_.trim)
  count += 1
}
```

If you'd like to assign the results to a two-dimensional array, there are a variety of ways to do this. One approach is to create a 2D array, and then use a counter while assigning each line to a row. To do this, you need to know the number of rows in the file before creating the array:

```
object CSVDemo2 extends App {
```

```
val nrows = 3
val ncols = 4
val rows = Array.ofDim[String](nrows, ncols)

val bufferedSource = io.Source.fromFile("/tmp/finance.csv")
var count = 0
for (line <- bufferedSource.getLines) {
  rows(count) = line.split(",").map(_.trim)
  count += 1
}
bufferedSource.close

// print the rows
for (i <- 0 until nrows) {
  println(s"${rows(i)(0)} ${rows(i)(1)} ${rows(i)(2)} ${rows(i)(3)}")
}

}
```

Rather than use a counter, you can do the same thing with the zipWithIndex method. This changes the loop to:

```
val bufferedSource = io.Source.fromFile("/tmp/finance.csv")
for ((line, count) <- bufferedSource.getLines.zipWithIndex) {
  rows(count) = line.split(",").map(_.trim)
}
bufferedSource.close
```

If you don't know the number of rows ahead of time, read each row as an Array[String], adding each row to an ArrayBuffer as the file is read. That approach is shown in this example, which uses the using method introduced in the Solution:

```
import scala.collection.mutable.ArrayBuffer

object CSVDemo3 extends App {

  // each row is an array of strings (the columns in the csv file)
  val rows = ArrayBuffer[Array[String]]()

  // (1) read the csv data
  using(io.Source.fromFile("/tmp/finance.csv")) { source =>
    for (line <- source.getLines) {
      rows += line.split(",").map(_.trim)
    }
  }

  // (2) print the results
  for (row <- rows) {
    println(s"${row(0)}|${row(1)}|${row(2)}|${row(3)}")
  }

  def using[A <: { def close(): Unit }, B](resource: A)(f: A => B): B =
    try {
```

```
        f(resource)
      } finally {
        resource.close()
      }
    }
```

An `Array[String]` is used for each row because that's what the `split` method returns. You can convert this to a different collection type, if desired.

## Discussion

As you can see, there are a number of ways to tackle this problem. Of all the examples shown, the `zipWithIndex` method probably requires some explanation. The `Iterator` Scaladoc denotes that it creates an iterator that pairs each element produced by this iterator with its index, counting from 0.

So the first time through the loop, `line` is assigned the first line from the file, and `count` is 0. The next time through the loop, the second line of the file is assigned to `line`, and `count` is 1, and so on. The `zipWithIndex` method offers a nice solution for when you need a line counter.

In addition to these approaches, a quick search for "scala csv parser" will turn up a number of competing open source projects that you can use.

## See Also

- Recipe 12.1, "How to Open and Read a Text File", shows both manual and automated ways of closing file resources.
- Recipe 10.11, "Using zipWithIndex or zip to Create Loop Counters", provides more examples of the `zipWithIndex` method.
- The `Iterator` trait (*http://bit.ly/1dzYcSo*).

# 12.6. Pretending that a String Is a File

## Problem

Typically for the purposes of testing, you want to pretend that a `String` is a file.

## Solution

Because `Scala.fromFile` and `Scala.fromString` both extend `scala.io.Source`, they are easily interchangeable. As long as your method takes a `Source` reference, you can pass it the `BufferedSource` you get from calling `Source.fromFile`, or the `Source` you get from calling `Source.fromString`.

For example, the following method takes a Source object and prints the lines it contains:

```
import io.Source

def printLines(source: Source) {
  for (line <- source.getLines) {
    println(line)
  }
}
```

It can be called when the source is constructed from a String:

```
val s = Source.fromString("foo\nbar\n")
printLines(s)
```

It can also be called when the source is a file:

```
val f = Source.fromFile("/Users/Al/.bash_profile")
printLines(f)
```

## Discussion

When writing unit tests, you might have a method like this that you'd like to test:

```
package foo

object FileUtils {

  def getLinesUppercased(source: io.Source): List[String] = {
    (for (line <- source.getLines) yield line.toUpperCase).toList
  }

}
```

As shown in the following ScalaTest tests, you can test the getLinesUppercased method by passing it either a Source from a file or a String:

```
package foo

import org.scalatest.{FunSuite, BeforeAndAfter}
import scala.io.Source

class FileUtilTests extends FunSuite with BeforeAndAfter {

  var source: Source = _
  after { source.close }

  // assumes the file has the string "foo" as its first line
  test("1 - foo file") {
    source = Source.fromFile("/Users/Al/tmp/foo")
    val lines = FileUtils.getLinesUppercased(source)
    assert(lines(0) == "FOO")
  }
```

```
    test("2 - foo string") {
      source = Source.fromString("foo\n")
      val lines = FileUtils.getLinesUppercased(source)
      assert(lines(0) == "FOO")
    }
  }
```

If you're interested in making your method easily testable with a String instead of a file, define your method to take a Source instance.

### See Also

- The Source class (*http://bit.ly/15is1E7*)
- The Source object (*http://bit.ly/1bkl0bX*)
- The BufferedSource class (*http://bit.ly/1aLATc1*)

# 12.7. Using Serialization

## Problem

You want to serialize a Scala class and save it as a file, or send it across a network.

## Solution

The general approach is the same as Java, but the syntax to make a class serializable is different.

To make a Scala class serializable, extend the Serializable trait and add the @SerialVersionUID annotation to the class:

```
@SerialVersionUID(100L)
class Stock(var symbol: String, var price: BigDecimal)
extends Serializable {
  // code here ...
}
```

Because Serializable is a trait, you can mix it into a class, even if your class already extends another class:

```
@SerialVersionUID(114L)
class Employee extends Person with Serializable ...
```

After marking the class serializable, use the same techniques to write and read the objects as you did in Java, including the Java "deep copy" technique that uses serialization (*http://bit.ly/12Dkd13*).

## Discussion

The following code demonstrates the proper approach. The comments in the code explain the process:

```
import java.io._

// create a serializable Stock class
@SerialVersionUID(123L)
class Stock(var symbol: String, var price: BigDecimal)
extends Serializable {
  override def toString = f"$symbol%s is ${price.toDouble}%.2f"
}

object SerializationDemo extends App {

  // (1) create a Stock instance
  val nflx = new Stock("NFLX", BigDecimal(85.00))

  // (2) write the instance out to a file
  val oos = new ObjectOutputStream(new FileOutputStream("/tmp/nflx"))
  oos.writeObject(nflx)
  oos.close

  // (3) read the object back in
  val ois = new ObjectInputStream(new FileInputStream("/tmp/nflx"))
  val stock = ois.readObject.asInstanceOf[Stock]
  ois.close

  // (4) print the object that was read back in
  println(stock)

}
```

This code prints the following output when run:

```
NFLX is 85.00
```

## See Also

- The Serializable trait (*http://bit.ly/1aLR3Cn*)
- Recipe 17.3, "Using @SerialVersionUID and Other Annotations"
- My Java "Deep Copy/Clone" example (*http://bit.ly/12SSwxR*)

# 12.8. Listing Files in a Directory

## Problem

You want to get a list of files that are in a directory, potentially limiting the list of files with a filtering algorithm.

## Solution

Scala doesn't offer any different methods for working with directories, so use the `listFiles` method of the Java `File` class. For instance, this method creates a list of all files in a directory:

```
def getListOfFiles(dir: String):List[File] = {
  val d = new File(dir)
  if (d.exists && d.isDirectory) {
    d.listFiles.filter(_.isFile).toList
  } else {
    List[File]()
  }
}
```

The REPL demonstrates how you can use this method:

```
scala> import java.io.File
import java.io.File

scala> val files = getListOfFiles("/tmp")
files: List[java.io.File] = List(/tmp/foo.log, /tmp/Files.scala.swp)
```

Note that if you're sure that the file you're given is a directory and it exists, you can shorten this method to just the following code:

```
def getListOfFiles(dir: File):List[File] =
  dir.listFiles.filter(_.isFile).toList
```

## Discussion

If you want to limit the list of files that are returned based on their filename extension, in Java, you'd implement a `FileFilter` with an `accept` method to filter the filenames that are returned. In Scala, you can write the equivalent code without requiring a `FileFilter`. Assuming that the `File` you're given represents a directory that is known to exist, the following method shows how to filter a set of files based on the filename extensions that should be returned:

```
import java.io.File

def getListOfFiles(dir: File, extensions: List[String]): List[File] =
{
  dir.listFiles.filter(_.isFile).toList.filter { file =>
```

```
        extensions.exists(file.getName.endsWith(_))
    }
}
```

You can call this method as follows to list all WAV and MP3 files in a given directory:

```
val okFileExtensions = List("wav", "mp3")
val files = getListOfFiles(new File("/tmp"), okFileExtensions)
```

As long as this method is given a directory that exists, this method will return an empty List if no matching files are found:

```
scala> val files = getListOfFiles(new File("/Users/Al"), okFileExtensions)
files: List[java.io.File] = List()
```

This is nice, because you can use the result normally, without having to worry about a null value:

```
scala> files.foreach(println)

(no output or errors, because an empty List was returned)
```

### See Also

The Java File class (*http://bit.ly/15KfbRd*)

# 12.9. Listing Subdirectories Beneath a Directory

## Problem

You want to generate a list of subdirectories in a given directory.

## Solution

Use a combination of the Java File class and Scala collection methods:

```
// assumes that dir is a directory known to exist
def getListOfSubDirectories(dir: File): List[String] =
    dir.listFiles
        .filter(_.isDirectory)
        .map(_.getName)
        .toList
```

This algorithm does the following:

- Uses the listFiles method of the File class to list all the files in the given directory as an Array[File].

- The filter method trims that list to contain only directories.

- map calls `getName` on each file to return an array of directory names (instead of `File` instances).
- `toList` converts that to a `List[String]`.

Calling `toList` isn't necessary, but if it isn't used, the method should be declared to return `Array[String]`.

This method can be used like this:

```
getListOfSubDirectories(new File("/Users/Al")).foreach(println)
```

As mentioned, this method returns a `List[String]`. If you'd rather return a `List[File]`, write the method as follows, dropping the `map` method call:

```
dir.listFiles.filter(_.isDirectory).toList
```

## Discussion

This problem provides a good way to demonstrate the differences between writing code in a functional style versus writing code in an imperative style.

When a developer first comes to Scala from Java, she might write a more Java-like (imperative) version of that method as follows:

```
def getListOfSubDirectories1(dir: File): List[String] = {
  val files = dir.listFiles
  val dirNames = collection.mutable.ArrayBuffer[String]()
  for (file <- files) {
    if (file.isDirectory) {
      dirNames += file.getName
    }
  }
  dirNames.toList
}
```

After getting more comfortable with Scala, she'd realize the code can be shortened. One simplification is that she can eliminate the need for the `ArrayBuffer` by using a `for` loop with a `yield` expression. Because the method should return a `List[String]`, the `for` loop is made to yield `file.getName`, and the `for` loop result is assigned to the variable `dirs`. Finally, `dirs` is converted to a `List` in the last line of the method, and it's returned from there:

```
def getListOfSubDirectories2(dir: File): List[String] = {
  val files = dir.listFiles
  val dirs = for {
    file <- files
    if file.isDirectory
  } yield file.getName
  dirs.toList
}
```

Although there's nothing wrong with this code—indeed, some programmers prefer writing for comprehensions to using map—at some point, as the developer gets more comfortable with the Scala collections and FP style, she'll realize the *intention* of the code is to create a filtered list of files, and using the filter method on the collection to return only directories will come to mind. Also, when she sees a for/yield combination, she should think, "map method," and in short order, she'll be at the original solution.

# 12.10. Executing External Commands

## Problem

You want to execute an external (system) command from within a Scala application. You're not concerned about the output from the command, but you are interested in its exit code.

## Solution

To execute external commands, use the methods of the scala.sys.process package. There are three primary ways to execute external commands:

- Use the ! method to execute the command and get its exit status.
- Use the !! method to execute the command and get its output.
- Use the lines method to execute the command in the background and get its result as a Stream.

This recipe demonstrates the ! method, and the next recipe demonstrates the !! method. The lines method is shown in the Discussion of this recipe.

To execute a command and get its exit status, import the necessary members and run the desired command with the ! method:

```
scala> import sys.process._
import sys.process._

scala> "ls -al".!
total 64
drwxr-xr-x  10 Al  staff   340 May 18 18:00 .
drwxr-xr-x   3 Al  staff   102 Apr  4 17:58 ..
-rw-r--r--   1 Al  staff   118 May 17 08:34 Foo.sh
-rw-r--r--   1 Al  staff  2727 May 17 08:34 Foo.sh.jar
res0: Int = 0
```

When using the ! method, you can get the exit code of the command that was run:

```
scala> val exitCode = "ls -al".!
total 64
drwxr-xr-x  10 Al  staff   340 May 18 18:00 .
```

```
drwxr-xr-x   3 Al   staff    102 Apr  4 17:58 ..
-rw-r--r--   1 Al   staff    118 May 17 08:34 Foo.sh
-rw-r--r--   1 Al   staff   2727 May 17 08:34 Foo.sh.jar
result: Int = 0

scala> println(exitCode)
0
```

Both of those examples work because of an implicit conversion that adds the ! method
to a String when you add the import statement shown.

## Discussion

I use this technique to execute the afplay system command on Mac OS X systems to
play sound files in one of my Scala applications, as shown in this method:

```
def playSoundFile(filename: String): Int = {
  val cmd = "afplay " + filename
  val exitCode = cmd.!
  exitCode
}
```

That method attempts to play the given filename as a sound file with the afplay command, and returns the exitCode from the command. This method can be shortened to
just one line, but I prefer the approach shown because it's easy to read, especially if you
don't execute system processes very often.

To execute system commands I generally just use ! after a String, but the Seq approach
is also useful. The first element in the Seq should be the name of the command you want
to run, and subsequent elements are considered to be arguments to it, as shown in these
examples:

```
val exitCode = Seq("ls", "-al").!
val exitCode = Seq("ls", "-a", "-l").!
val exitCode = Seq("ls", "-a", "-l", "/tmp").!
```

I've omitted the output from each of those examples, but each command provides the
same directory listing you'd get at the Unix command line.

You can also create a Process object to execute an external command, if you prefer:

```
val exitCode = Process("ls").!
```

When running these commands, be aware of whitespace around your command and
arguments. All of the following examples fail because of extra whitespace:

```
// beware leading whitespace
scala> " ls".!
java.io.IOException: Cannot run program "": error=2,
  No such file or directory
  at java.lang.ProcessBuilder.start(ProcessBuilder.java:460)
```

```
scala> val exitCode = Seq(" ls ", "-al").!
java.io.IOException: Cannot run program " ls ": error=2,
  No such file or directory

// beware trailing whitespace
scala> val exitCode = Seq("ls", " -al ").!
ls:  -al : No such file or directory
exitCode: Int = 1
```

If you enter the strings yourself, leave the whitespace out, and if you get the strings from user input, be sure to trim them.

### Using the lines method

The `lines` method is an interesting alternative to the `!` and `!!` commands. With `lines`, you can immediately execute a command in the background. For instance, the following command will run for a long time on a Unix system and result in a large amount of output:

```
val process = Process("find / -print").lines
```

The variable `process` in this example is a `Stream[String]`. With `lines` running the process in the background, you can either work with the result immediately or at some later point. For instance, you can read from the stream like this:

```
process.foreach(println)
```

The `lines` method throws an exception if the exit status of the command is nonzero. You can catch that with a `try`/`catch` expression, but if this is a problem, or if you also want to retrieve the standard error from the command, use the `lines_!` method instead of `lines`. The `lines_!` method is demonstrated in Recipe 12.11 and discussed in Table 12-1 in Recipe 12.19.

### External commands versus built-in commands

As a final note, you can run any external command from Scala that you can run from the Unix command line. However, there's a big difference between an *external* command and a shell *built-in* command. The `ls` command is an external command that's available on all Unix systems, and can be found as a file in the */bin* directory:

```
$ which ls
/bin/ls
```

Some other commands that can be used at a Unix command line, such as the `cd` or `for` commands in the Bash shell, are actually built into the shell; you won't find them as files on the filesystem. Therefore, these commands can't be executed unless they're executed from within a shell. See Recipe 12.13, "Building a Pipeline of Commands" for an example of how to execute a shell built-in command.

# 12.11. Executing External Commands and Using STDOUT

## Problem

You want to run an external command and then use the standard output (STDOUT) from that process in your Scala program.

## Solution

Use the !! method to execute the command and get the standard output from the resulting process as a String.

Just like the ! command in the previous recipe, you can use !! after a String to execute a command, but !! returns the STDOUT from the command rather than the exit code of the command. This returns a multiline string, which you can process in your application:

```
scala> import sys.process._
import sys.process._

scala> val result = "ls -al" !!
result: String =
"total 64
drwxr-xr-x  10 Al   staff    340 May 18 18:00 .
drwxr-xr-x   3 Al   staff    102 Apr  4 17:58 ..
-rw-r--r--   1 Al   staff    118 May 17 08:34 Foo.sh
-rw-r--r--   1 Al   staff   2727 May 17 08:34 Foo.sh.jar
"

scala> println(result)
total 64
drwxr-xr-x  10 Al   staff    340 May 18 18:00 .
drwxr-xr-x   3 Al   staff    102 Apr  4 17:58 ..
-rw-r--r--   1 Al   staff    118 May 17 08:34 Foo.sh
-rw-r--r--   1 Al   staff   2727 May 17 08:34 Foo.sh.jar
```

If you prefer, you can do the same thing with a Process or Seq instead of a String:

```
val result = Process("ls -al").!!
val result = Seq("ls -al").!!
```

As shown in the previous recipe, using a Seq is a good way to execute a system command that requires arguments:

```
val output = Seq("ls", "-al").!!
val output = Seq("ls", "-a", "-l").!!
val output = Seq("ls", "-a", "-l", "/tmp").!!
```

The first element in the Seq is the name of the command to be run, and subsequent elements are arguments to the command. The following code segment shows how to run a complex Unix find command:

```
val dir = "/Users/Al/tmp"
val searchTerm = "dawn"

val results = Seq("find", dir, "-type", "f", "-exec", "grep", "-il",
                  searchTerm, "{}", ";").!!
println(results)
```

This code is the equivalent of running the following find command at the Unix prompt:

```
find /Users/Al/tmp -type f -exec grep -il dawn {} \;
```

If you're not familiar with Unix commands, this command can be read as, "Search all files under the *Users/Al/tmp* directory for the string dawn, ignoring case, and print the names of all files where a match is found."

## Discussion

Use the ! method to get the exit code from a process, or !! to get the standard output from a process.

Be aware that attempting to get the standard output from a command exposes you to exceptions that can occur. As a simple example, if you write the following statement to get the exit code of a command using the ! operator, even though a little extra STDERR information is printed in the REPL, out is just assigned a nonzero exit code:

```
scala> val out = "ls -l fred" !
ls: fred: No such file or directory
out: Int = 1
```

But if you attempt to get the standard output from the same command using the !! method, an exception is thrown, and out is not assigned:

```
scala> val out = "ls -l fred" !!
ls: fred: No such file or directory
java.lang.RuntimeException: Nonzero exit value: 1
  many more lines of output ...
```

### Unexpected newline characters

When running an external command, you may expect a one-line string to be returned, but you can get a newline character as well:

```
scala> val dir = "pwd" !!
dir: String =
"/Users/Al/Temp
"
```

When this happens, just trim the result:

```
scala> val dir = "pwd".!!.trim
dir: java.lang.String = /Users/Al/Temp
```

### Using the lines_! method

You may want to check to see whether an executable program is available on your system. For instance, suppose you wanted to know whether the hadoop2 executable is available on a Unix-based system. A simple way to handle this situation is to use the Unix which command with the ! method, where a nonzero exit code indicates that the command isn't available:

```scala
scala> val executable = "which hadoop2".!
executable: Int = 1
```

If the value is nonzero, you know that the executable is not available on the current system. More accurately, it may be on the system, but it's not on the PATH (or much less likely, the which command is not available).

Another way to handle this situation is to use the lines_! method. This can be used to return a Some or None, depending on whether or not the hadoop command is found by which. The syntax for the lines_! method is shown in this example:

```scala
val executable = "which hadoop2".lines_!.headOption
```

In the Scala REPL, you can see that if the executable isn't available on the current system, this expression returns None:

```scala
scala> val executable = "which hadoop2".lines_!.headOption
executable: Option[String] = None
```

Conversely, if the command is found, the expression returns a Some:

```scala
scala> val executable = "which ls".lines_!.headOption
executable: Option[String] = Some(/bin/ls)
```

Note the call to the headOption method at the end of this pipeline. You call this method because the lines_! method returns a Stream, but you want the Option immediately.

See Recipe 12.19 for a description of the lines_! method.

# 12.12. Handling STDOUT and STDERR for External Commands

## Problem

You want to run an external command and get access to both its STDOUT and STDERR.

## Solution

The simplest way to do this is to run your commands as shown in previous recipes, and then capture the output with a ProcessLogger. This Scala shell script demonstrates the approach:

```
#!/bin/sh
exec scala "$0" "$@"
!#

import sys.process._

val stdout = new StringBuilder
val stderr = new StringBuilder

val status = "ls -al FRED" ! ProcessLogger(stdout append _, stderr append _)
println(status)
println("stdout: " + stdout)
println("stderr: " + stderr)
```

When this script is run, the status variable contains the exit status of the command. The stdout variable contains the STDOUT if the command is successful (such as with ls -al), and stderr contains the STDERR from the command if there are problems. If the command you're running writes to both STDOUT and STDERR, both stdout and stderr will contain data.

For instance, assuming you don't run the following command as root, changing the status expression in the script to the following code should generate output to both STDOUT and STDERR on a Unix system:

```
val status = Seq("find", "/usr", "-name", "make") ! ↵
ProcessLogger(stdout append _, stderr append _)
```

Running the script with this command on a Mac OS X (Unix) system, I correctly get the following exit status, STDOUT, and STDERR output:

```
scala> val status = Seq("find", "/usr", "-name", "make") ! ProcessLogger(stdout↵
append _, stderr append _)
status: Int = 1

scala> println(stdout)
/usr/bin/make

scala> println(stderr)
find: /usr/local/mysql-5.0.67-osx10.5-x86/data: Permission denied
```

Depending on your needs, this can get much more complicated very quickly. The Scaladoc states, "If one desires full control over input and output, then a ProcessIO can be used with run." See the scala.sys.process API documentation for the ProcessLogger and ProcessIO classes for more examples.

## See Also

The process package object documentation (*http://bit.ly/13MI5Cl*) includes many details and examples.

# 12.13. Building a Pipeline of Commands

## Problem

You want to execute a series of external commands, redirecting the output from one command to the input of another command, i.e., you want to pipe the commands together.

## Solution

Use the #| method to pipe the output from one command into the input stream of another command. When doing this, use ! at the end of the pipeline if you want the exit code of the pipeline, or !! if you want the output from the pipeline.

The !! approach is shown in the following example where the output from the ps command is piped as the input to the wc command:

```
import sys.process._
val numProcs = ("ps auxw" #| "wc -l").!!.trim
println(s"#procs = $numProcs")
```

Because the output from the ps command is piped into a line count command (wc -l), that code prints the number of processes running on a Unix system. The following command creates a list of all Java processes running on the current system:

```
val javaProcs = ("ps auxw" #| "grep java").!!.trim
```

There are other ways to write these commands, but because I usually end up trimming the result I get back from commands, I find this syntax to be the most readable approach.

## Discussion

If you come from a Unix background, the #| command is easy to remember because it's just like the Unix pipe symbol, but preceded by a # character (#|). In fact, with the exception of the ### operator (which is used instead of the Unix ; symbol), the entire library is consistent with the equivalent Unix commands.

Note that attempting to pipe commands together inside a String and then execute them with ! won't work:

```
// won't work
val result = ("ls -al | grep Foo").!!
```

This doesn't work because the piping capability comes from a shell (Bourne shell, Bash, etc.), and when you run a command like this, you don't have a shell.

To execute a series of commands in a shell, such as the Bourne shell, use a Seq with multiple parameters, like this:

```
val r = Seq("/bin/sh", "-c", "ls | grep .scala").!!
```

This approach runs the `ls | grep .scala` command inside a Bourne shell instance. A quick run in the REPL demonstrates this:

```
scala> val r = Seq("/bin/sh", "-c", "ls | grep .scala").!!
r: String =
"Bar.scala
Baz.scala
Foo.scala
"
```

However, note that when using `!!`, you'll get the following exception if there are no *.scala* files in the directory:

```
java.lang.RuntimeException: Nonzero exit value: 1
```

I've found it best to wrap commands executed with `!!` in a `try/catch` expression.

### See Also

My tutorial, "How to Execute a System Command Pipeline in Java," (*http://bit.ly/15KflrJ*) discusses the need for a shell when piping commands.

# 12.14. Redirecting the STDOUT and STDIN of External Commands

## Problem

You want to redirect the standard output (STDOUT) and standard input (STDIN) when running external commands. For instance, you may want to redirect STDOUT to log the output of an external command to a file.

## Solution

Use #> to redirect STDOUT, and #< to redirect STDIN.

When using #>, place it after your command and before the filename you want to write to, just like using > in Unix:

```
import sys.process._
import java.io.File

("ls -al" #> new File("files.txt")).!
("ps aux" #> new File("processes.txt")).!
```

You can also pipe commands together and then write the resulting output to a file:

```
("ps aux" #| "grep http" #> new File("http-processes.out")).!
```

Get the exit status from a command like this:

```
val status = ("cat /etc/passwd" #> new File("passwd.copy")).!
println(status)
```

You can also download a URL and write its contents to a file:

```
import sys.process._
import scala.language.postfixOps
import java.net.URL
import java.io.File

new URL("http://www.google.com") #> new File("Output.html") !
```

I don't redirect STDIN too often, but this example shows one possible way to read the contents of the */etc/passwd* file into a variable using #< and the Unix cat command:

```
import scala.sys.process._
import java.io.File

val contents = ("cat" #< new File("/etc/passwd")).!!
println(contents)
```

## Discussion

The #> and #< operators generally work like their equivalent > and < Unix commands, though you can also use them for other purposes, such as using #> to write from one ProcessBuilder to another, like a pipeline:

```
val numLines = ("cat /etc/passwd" #> "wc -l").!!.trim
println(numLines)
```

The ProcessBuilder Scaladoc states that #> and #< "may take as input either another ProcessBuilder, or something else such as a java.io.File or a java.lang.InputStream."

As mentioned, the Scala process commands are consistent with the standard Unix redirection symbols, so you can also append to a file with the #>> method:

```
// append to a file
("ps aux" #>> new File("ps.out")).!
```

Regarding the use of the URL and File classes, the Scaladoc states that instances of java.io.File and java.net.URL can be used as input to other processes, and a File instance can also be used as output. This was demonstrated in the Solution with the ability to download the contents from a URL and write it to a file with the #> operator.

## See Also

- The `process` package object (*http://bit.ly/13MI5Cl*)
- The Scala `ProcessBuilder` trait (*http://bit.ly/17iya4p*)
- The Scala `Process` trait (*http://bit.ly/10Yk0UY*)

# 12.15. Using AND (&&) and OR (||) with Processes

## Problem

You want to use the equivalent of the Unix && and || commands to perform an `if`/`then`/`else` operation when executing external commands.

## Solution

Use the Scala operators #&& and #||, which mirror the Unix && and || operators:

```
val result = ("ls temp" #&& "rm temp" #|| "echo 'temp' not found").!!.trim
```

This command can be read as, "Run the `ls` command on the file *temp*, and if it's found, remove it, otherwise, print the 'not found' message."

In practice, this can be a little more difficult than shown, because these commands usually involve the use of a wildcard operator. For instance, even if there are *.scala* files in the current directory, the following attempt to compile them using #&& and #|| will fail because of the lack of wildcard support:

```
scala> ("ls *.scala" #&& "scalac *.scala" #|| "echo no files to compile").!
ls: *.scala: No such file or directory
no files to compile
res0: Int = 0
```

To get around this problem, use the formula shared in Recipe 12.16, "Handling Wildcard Characters in External Commands" running each command in a shell (and also separating each command to make the #&& and #|| command readable):

```
#!/bin/sh
exec scala "$0" "$@"
!#

import scala.sys.process._

val filesExist = Seq("/bin/sh", "-c", "ls *.scala")
val compileFiles = Seq("/bin/sh", "-c", "scalac *.scala")
(filesExist #&& compileFiles #|| "echo no files to compile").!!
```

That script compiles all *.scala* files in the current directory.

# 12.16. Handling Wildcard Characters in External Commands

## Problem

You want to use a Unix shell wildcard character, such as *, in an external command.

## Solution

In general, the best thing you can do when using a wildcard character like * is to run your command while invoking a Unix shell. For instance, if you have *.scala* files in the current directory and try to list them with the following command, the command will fail:

```
scala> import scala.sys.process._
import scala.sys.process._

scala> "ls *.scala".!
ls: *.scala: No such file or directory
res0: Int = 1
```

But by running the same command inside a Bourne shell, the command now correctly shows the *.scala* files (and returns the exit status of the command):

```
scala> val status = Seq("/bin/sh", "-c", "ls *.scala").!
AndOrTest.scala
Console.scala
status: Int = 0
```

## Discussion

Putting a shell wildcard character like * into a command doesn't work because the * needs to be interpreted and expanded by a shell, like the Bourne or Bash shells. In this example, even though there are files in the current directory named *AndOrTest.scala* and *Console.scala*, the first attempt doesn't work. These other attempts will also fail as a result of the same problem:

```
scala> "echo *".!
*
res0: Int = 0

scala> Seq("grep", "-i", "foo", "*.scala").!
grep: *.scala: No such file or directory
res1: Int = 2

scala> Seq("ls", "*.scala").!
```

```
ls: *.scala: No such file or directory
res2: Int = 1
```

In each example, you can make these commands work by invoking a shell in the first two parameters to a Seq:

```
val status = Seq("/bin/sh", "-c", "echo *").!
val status = Seq("/bin/sh", "-c", "ls *.scala").!
val status = Seq("/bin/sh", "-c", "grep -i foo *.scala").!
```

An important part of this recipe is using the -c argument of the */bin/sh* command. The sh manpage describes this parameter as follows:

```
-c string

If the -c option is present, then commands are read from string.
If there are arguments after the string, they are assigned to the
positional parameters, starting with $0.
```

As an exception to this general rule, the -name option of the find command may work because it treats the * character as a wildcard character itself. As a result, the following find command finds the two files in the current directory without having to be run in a shell:

```
scala> val status = Seq("find", ".", "-name", "*.scala", "-type", "f").!
./AndOrTest.scala
./Console.scala
status: Int = 0
```

However, as shown, other commands generally require that the * wildcard character be interpreted and expanded by a shell.

## See Also

- "How to Execute a Command Pipeline in Java" (*http://bit.ly/15KflrJ*)
- "Execute System Processes with Java Process and ProcessBuilder" (*http://bit.ly/16GAKPp*)

# 12.17. How to Run a Process in a Different Directory

## Problem

You want to use another directory as the base directory when running an external command.

## Solution

Use one of the Process factory methods, setting your command and the desired directory, then running the process with the usual ! or !! commands. The following example runs the ls command with the -al arguments in the /var/tmp directory:

```
import sys.process._
import java.io.File

object Test extends App {

  val output = Process("ls -al", new File("/tmp")).!!
  println(output)

}
```

To run that same command in the current directory, just remove the second parameter when creating the Process:

```
val p = Process("ls -al")
```

You can use another Process factory method to set system environment variables, i.e., those that can be seen at the shell command line with set or env. See the next recipe for examples of that method.

# 12.18. Setting Environment Variables When Running Commands

## Problem

You need to set one or more environment variables when running an external command.

## Solution

Specify the environment variables when calling a Process factory method (an apply method in the Process object).

The following example shows how to run a shell script in a directory named /home/al/bin while also setting the PATH environment variable:

```
val p = Process("runFoo.sh",
        new File("/Users/Al/bin"),
        "PATH" -> ".:/usr/bin:/opt/scala/bin")

val output = p.!!
```

To set multiple environment variables at one time, keep adding them at the end of the Process constructor:

```
val output = Process("env",
                     None,
                     "VAR1" -> "foo",
                     "VAR2" -> "bar")
```

These examples work because of the overloaded `apply` methods in the `Process` object. For instance, one method takes a `File` for the directory parameter, and another method takes an `Option[File]` for that parameter. This second approach lets you use `None` to indicate the current directory.

The ability to specify multiple environment variables when calling a `Process` factory method works because the `apply` methods accept a varargs argument of the type `(String, String)*` for their last argument. This means "a variable number of tuple arguments."

## See Also

The `Process` object (*http://bit.ly/149qL9t*)

# 12.19. An Index of Methods to Execute External Commands

The following tables list the methods of the `scala.sys.process` package that you can use when running external (system) commands.

Table 12-1 lists the methods that you can use to execute system commands.

*Table 12-1. Methods to execute system commands*

| Method | Description |
|---|---|
| ! | Runs the command and returns its exit code. Blocks until all external commands exit. If used in a chain, returns the exit code of the last command in the chain. |
| !! | Runs the command (or command pipe/chain), and returns the output from the command as a `String`. Blocks until all external commands exit. Warning: throws exceptions when the command's exit status is nonzero. |
| run | Returns a `Process` object immediately while running the process in the background. The `Process` can't currently be polled to see if it has completed. |
| lines | Returns immediately, while running the process in the background. The output that's generated is provided through a `Stream[String]`. Getting the next element of the `Stream` may block until it becomes available. Throws an exception if the return code is not zero; if this isn't desired, use the `lines_!` method. Example:<br><br>`scala> `**`val x = Process("ls").lines`**<br>`x: Stream[String] = Stream(Bar.scala, ?)` |
| lines_! | Like the `lines` method, but `STDERR` output is sent to the `ProcessLogger` you provide. Per the Scaladoc, "If the process exits with a nonzero value, the `Stream` will provide all lines up to termination but will not throw an exception." Demonstrated in Recipe 12.11. |

Table 12-2 lists the methods that you can use to redirect STDIN and STDOUT when external commands are executed.

*Table 12-2. Methods to redirect STDIN and STDOUT*

| Methods | Description |
|---------|-------------|
| #< | Read from STDIN |
| #> | Write to STDOUT |
| #>> | Append to STDOUT |

Table 12-3 lists the methods that you can use to combine (pipe) external commands.

*Table 12-3. Methods to combine external commands*

| Methods | Description |
|---------|-------------|
| cmd1 #\| cmd2 | The output of the first command is used as input to the second command, like a Unix shell pipe. |
| cmd1 ### cmd2 | cmd1 and cmd2 will be executed in sequence, one after the other. This is like the Unix ; operator, but ; is a reserved keyword in Scala. |
| cmd1 #> cmd2 | Normally used to write to STDOUT but can be used like #\| to chain commands together. Example:<br><br>`scala> ("ps aux" #> "grep java" #> "wc -l").!!.trim`<br>`res0: String = 2` |
| cmd1 #&& cmd2 | Run cmd2 if cmd1 runs successfully (i.e., it has an exit status of 0). |
| cmd1 #\|\| cmd2 | Run cmd2 if cmd1 has an unsuccessful (nonzero) exit status. |
| cmd1 #&& cmd2 #\|\| cmd3 | Run cmd2 is cmd1 has a successful exit status, otherwise, run cmd3. |

The primary online documentation for the Scala process API is at these URLs:

- The scala.sys.process package object (*http://bit.ly/13MI5Cl*)
- The ProcessBuilder trait (*http://bit.ly/17iya4p*)

# CHAPTER 13
# Actors and Concurrency

## Introduction

In Scala you can still use Java threads, but the Actor model is the preferred approach for concurrency. The Actor model is at a much higher level of abstraction than threads, and once you understand the model, it lets you focus on solving the problem at hand, rather than worrying about the low-level problems of threads, locks, and shared data.

Although earlier versions of Scala included its original Actors library, Scala 2.10.0 began the official transition to the Akka actor library (*http://akka.io/*) from Typesafe, which is more robust than the original library. Scala 2.10.1 then deprecated the original *scala.actors* library.

In general, actors give you the benefit of offering a high level of abstraction for achieving concurrency and parallelism. Beyond that, the Akka actor library adds these additional benefits:

- Lightweight, event-driven processes. The documentation states that there can be approximately 2.7 million actors per gigabyte of RAM.
- Fault tolerance. Akka actors can be used to create "self-healing systems." (The Akka "team blog" is located at *http://letitcrash.com/*.)
- Location transparency. Akka actors can span multiple JVMs and servers; they're designed to work in a distributed environment using pure message passing.

A "high level of abstraction" can also be read as "ease of use." It doesn't take very long to understand the Actor model, and once you do, you'll be able to write complex, concurrent applications much more easily than you can with the basic Java libraries. I wrote a speech interaction application (speech recognition input, text-to-speech output) named SARAH (*http://alvinalexander.com/sarah*) that makes extensive use of Akka actors, with agents constantly working on tasks in the background. Writing this code with actors was *much* easier than the equivalent threading approach.

I like to think of an actor as being like a web service on someone else's servers that I can't control. I can send messages to that web service to ask it to do something, or I can query it for information, but I can't reach into the web service to directly modify its state or access its resources; I can only work through its API, which is just like sending immutable messages. In one way, this is a little limiting, but in terms of safely writing parallel algorithms, this is very beneficial.

## The Actor Model

Before digging into the recipes in this chapter, it can help to understand the Actor model.

The first thing to understand about the Actor model is the concept of an *actor*:

- An actor is the smallest unit when building an actor-based system, like an object in an OOP system.
- Like an object, an actor encapsulates state and behavior.
- You can't peek inside an actor to get its state. You can send an actor a message requesting state information (like asking a person how they're feeling), but you can't reach in and execute one of its methods, or access its fields.
- An actor has a mailbox (an inbox), and its purpose in life is to process the messages in its mailbox.
- You communicate with an actor by sending it an immutable message. These messages go into the actor's mailbox.
- When an actor receives a message, it's like taking a letter out of its mailbox. It opens the letter, processes the message using one of its algorithms, then moves on to the next letter in the mailbox. If there are no more messages, the actor waits until it receives one.

In an application, actors form hierarchies, like a family, or a business organization:

- The Typesafe team recommends thinking of an actor as being like a person, such as a person in a business organization.
- An actor has one parent (supervisor): the actor that created it.
- An actor may have children. Thinking of this as a business, a president may have a number of vice presidents. Those VPs will have many subordinates, and so on.
- An actor may have siblings. For instance, there may be 10 VPs in an organization.
- A best practice of developing actor systems is to "delegate, delegate, delegate," especially if behavior will block. In a business, the president may want something

done, so he delegates that work to a VP. That VP delegates work to a manager, and so on, until the work is eventually performed by one or more subordinates.

- Delegation is important. Imagine that the work takes several man-years. If the president had to handle that work himself, he couldn't respond to other needs (while the VPs and other employees would all be idle).

A final piece of the Actor model is handling failure. When performing work, something may go wrong, and an exception may be thrown. When this happens, an actor suspends itself and all of its children, and sends a message to its supervisor, signaling that a failure has occurred. (A bit like Scotty calling Captain Kirk with a problem.)

Depending on the nature of the work and the nature of the failure, the supervising actor has a choice of four options at this time:

- Resume the subordinate, keeping its internal state
- Restart the subordinate, giving it a clean state
- Terminate the subordinate
- Escalate the failure

In addition to those general statements about actors, there are a few important things to know about Akka's implementation of the Actor model:

- You can't reach into an actor to get information about its state. When you instantiate an `Actor` in your code, Akka gives you an `ActorRef`, which is essentially a façade between you and the actor.
- Behind the scenes, Akka runs actors on real threads; many actors may share one thread.
- There are different mailbox implementations to choose from, including variations of unbounded, bounded, and priority mailboxes. You can also create your own mailbox type.
- Akka does not let actors scan their mailbox for specific messages.
- When an actor terminates (intentionally or unintentionally), messages in its mailbox go into the system's "dead letter mailbox."

Hopefully these notes about the general Actor model, and the Akka implementation specifically, will be helpful in understanding the recipes in this chapter.

## Other Features

Scala offers other conveniences for writing code that performs operations in parallel. A *future* can be used for simple, "one off" tasks that require concurrency. The Scala collections library also includes special *parallel collections*, which can be used to improve the performance of large collections and certain algorithms.

 There are interesting debates about what the terms *concurrency* and *parallelism* mean. I tend to use them interchangeably, but for one interesting discussion of their differences—such as concurrency being one vending machine with two lines, and parallelism being two vending machines and two lines—see this blog post (*http://bit.ly/12u8azO*).

# 13.1. Getting Started with a Simple Actor

## Problem

You want to begin using actors to build concurrency into your applications.

## Solution

Create an actor by extending the `akka.actor.Actor` class and writing a `receive` method in your class. The `receive` method should be implemented with a `case` statement that allows the actor to respond to the different messages it receives.

To demonstrate this, create an SBT project directory named *HelloAkka*, move into that directory, and then add the necessary Akka resolver and dependency information to your *build.sbt* file:

```
name := "Hello Test #1"

version := "1.0"

scalaVersion := "2.10.0"

resolvers += "Typesafe Repository" at ↵
  "http://repo.typesafe.com/typesafe/releases/"

libraryDependencies += "com.typesafe.akka" %% "akka-actor" % "2.1.2"
```

 At the time of this writing, the Akka actor library is being migrated into the Scala distribution, but it's still necessary to include the library as a dependency in your SBT *build.sbt* file (or download the necessary JAR files manually). This may change in the future, in which case the dependencies shown in this chapter may not be necessary.

Next, define an actor that responds when it receives the String literal hello as a message. To do this, save the following source code to a file named *Hello.scala* in the root directory of your SBT project. Notice how the literal hello is used in the first case statement in the receive method of the HelloActor class:

```scala
import akka.actor.Actor
import akka.actor.ActorSystem
import akka.actor.Props

class HelloActor extends Actor {
  def receive = {
    case "hello" => println("hello back at you")
    case _       => println("huh?")
  }
}

object Main extends App {

  // an actor needs an ActorSystem
  val system = ActorSystem("HelloSystem")

  // create and start the actor
  val helloActor = system.actorOf(Props[HelloActor], name = "helloactor")

  // send the actor two messages
  helloActor ! "hello"
  helloActor ! "buenos dias"

  // shut down the system
  system.shutdown

}
```

Then run the application like this:

```
$ sbt run
```

After SBT downloads the Akka JAR files and their dependencies, you should see the following output from the println statements in the HelloActor class:

```
[info] Running Main
hello back at you
huh?
```

## Discussion

Here's a step-by-step description of the code:

- The import statements import the members that are needed.
- An Actor named HelloActor is defined.

- HelloActor's behavior is implemented by defining a `receive` method, which is implemented using a match expression.

- When `HelloActor` receives the `String` literal `hello` as a message, it prints the first reply, and when it receives any other type of message, it prints the second reply.

- The `Main` object is created to test the actor.

- In `Main`, an `ActorSystem` is needed to get things started, so one is created. The `ActorSystem` takes a `name` as an argument, so give the system a meaningful name. The name must consist of only the `[a-zA-Z0-9]` characters, and zero or more hyphens, and a hyphen can't be used in the leading space.

- Actors can be created at the `ActorSystem` level, or inside other actors. At the `ActorSystem` level, actor instances are created with the `system.actorOf` method. The `helloActor` line shows the syntax to create an `Actor` with a constructor that takes no arguments.

- Actors are automatically started (asynchronously) when they are created, so there's no need to call any sort of "start" or "run" method.

- Messages are sent to actors with the ! method, and `Main` sends two messages to the actor with the ! method: `hello` and `buenos dias`.

- `helloActor` responds to the messages by executing its `println` statements.

- The `ActorSystem` is shut down.

That's all you need to create and use your first Akka `Actor`.

### Details

When implementing the behavior of an Akka actor, you should define a `receive` method using a match expression, as shown in the example. Your method should handle all potential messages that can be sent to the actor; otherwise, an `UnhandledMessage` will be published to the `ActorSystem`'s `EventStream`. As a practical matter, this means having the catch-all `case _` line in your match expression.

In this example, messages were sent to the `HelloActor` class as `String` literals, but other recipes will show how to send messages to actors using other types. Messages should be immutable, so for simple examples, a `String` works well.

### ActorSystem

The API documentation describes an `ActorSystem` like this:

> "An actor system is a hierarchical group of actors which share common configuration, e.g. dispatchers, deployments, remote capabilities and addresses. It is also the entry point for creating or looking up actors."

An `ActorSystem` is the structure that allocates one or more threads for your application, so you typically create one `ActorSystem` per (logical) application.

As an example, I wrote a "speech interaction" application named SARAH that lets me interact with a Mac OS X computer using only voice commands. Besides allowing interactive commands, SARAH also runs background tasks to check my email, notify me of Facebook and Twitter events, stock prices, etc.

SARAH uses a plug-in architecture, so there are plug-ins for each major area of functionality (such as an email plug-in, Facebook plug-in, Twitter plug-in, etc.). A plug-in typically has one parent actor that delegates work to child actors as necessary. All of these plug-ins run under one ActorSystem. When SARAH starts, it starts the ActorSystem using the same method shown in the Solution. Once started, it creates three main actors named brain, ears, and mouth, and then starts its plug-ins.

As an interesting experiment with the ActorSystem, remove the system.shutdown line at the end of the Main object. You'll see that the application doesn't terminate, because the actors and system are still running. (Press Control-C to terminate the application.)

### ActorRef

When you call the actorOf method on an ActorSystem, it starts the actor asynchronously and returns an instance of an ActorRef. This reference is a "handle" to the actor, which you can think of as being a façade or broker between you and the actual actor. This façade keeps you from doing things that would break the Actor model, such as reaching into the Actor instance and attempting to directly mutate variables. Tasks like this should only be done by passing messages to the actor, and the hands-off approach of an ActorRef helps reinforce proper programming practices.

(Again, think of an actor as a person you can only communicate with by placing messages in his mailbox.)

The Akka documentation states that an ActorRef has these qualities:

- It is immutable.
- It has a one-to-one relationship with the Actor it represents.
- It is serializable and network-aware. This lets you pass the ActorRef around the network.

## See Also

- The introductory Akka actor documentation (*http://bit.ly/14Wm54w*)
- The ActorSystem class (*http://bit.ly/17iyzE7*)
- The ActorRef class (*http://bit.ly/1bFDp1q*)

# 13.2. Creating an Actor Whose Class Constructor Requires Arguments

## Problem

You want to create an Akka actor, and you want your actor's constructor to have one or more arguments.

## Solution

Create the actor using the syntax shown here, where `HelloActor` takes one constructor parameter:

```
val helloActor = system.actorOf(Props(new HelloActor("Fred")), ↵
name = "helloactor")
```

## Discussion

When creating an actor whose constructor takes one or more arguments, you still use the `Props` class to create the actor, but with a different syntax than when creating an actor whose constructor takes no arguments.

The following code demonstrates the difference between creating an actor with a no-args constructor and an actor that takes at least one constructor parameter:

```
// an actor with a no-args constructor
val helloActor = system.actorOf(Props[HelloActor], name = "helloactor")

// an actor whose constructor takes one argument
val helloActor = system.actorOf(Props(new HelloActor("Fred")), ↵
name = "helloactor")
```

To demonstrate these differences, the following source code is a modified version of the example in Recipe 13.1. Comments are included in the code to highlight the changes:

```
import akka.actor._

// (1) constructor changed to take a parameter
class HelloActor(myName: String) extends Actor {
  def receive = {
    // (2) println statements changed to show the name
    case "hello" => println(s"hello from $myName")
    case _       => println(s"'huh?', said $myName")
  }
}

object Main extends App {
  val system = ActorSystem("HelloSystem")
  // (3) use a different version of the Props constructor
```

```
    val helloActor = system.actorOf(
                    Props(new HelloActor("Fred")), name = "helloactor")
    helloActor ! "hello"
    helloActor ! "buenos dias"
    system.shutdown
}
```

As shown in this example, if your actor takes more than one argument, include those arguments in the constructor call. If the `HelloActor` constructor required both a first and last name, you'd specify them like this:

```
Props(new HelloActor("John", "Doe")), name = "helloactor")
```

Remember that an actor instance is instantiated and started when the `actorOf` method is called, so the only ways to set a property in an actor instance are:

- By sending the actor a message
- In the actor's constructor
- In its `preStart` method

You've already seen how to send a message to an actor and use its constructor. The `preStart` method is demonstrated in Recipe 13.4, "Understanding the Methods in the Akka Actor Lifecycle".

## See Also

The `Props` class (*http://bit.ly/1aq25JW*)

# 13.3. How to Communicate Between Actors

## Problem

You're building an actor-based application and want to send messages between actors.

## Solution

Actors should be sent immutable messages with the ! method.

When an actor receives a message from another actor, it also receives an implicit reference named `sender`, and it can use that reference to send a message back to the originating actor.

The general syntax to send a message to an actor is:

```
actorInstance ! message
```

For example, if you have an actor instance named `car`, you can send it a `start` message like this:

```
car ! "start"
```

In this case, the message is the `String` literal `start`. The `car` actor should receive this message in a match expression in its `receive` method, and from there it can send a message back to whoever sent the `start` message. A simplified version of a `receive` method for `car` might look like this:

```
def receive = {
  case "start" =>
      val result = tryToStart()
      sender ! result
  case _ => // do nothing

}
```

As mentioned, the `sender` instance is implicitly made available to your actor. If you just want to send a message back to the code that sent you a message, that's all you have to do.

## Discussion

To demonstrate a more complicated example of actors communicating, the following code shows how to send messages back and forth between Akka actors. It was inspired by the "Ping Pong" threading example in the book by James Gosling et al., *The Java Programming Language* (Addison-Wesley Professional):

```
import akka.actor._

case object PingMessage
case object PongMessage
case object StartMessage
case object StopMessage

class Ping(pong: ActorRef) extends Actor {
  var count = 0
  def incrementAndPrint { count += 1; println("ping") }
  def receive = {
    case StartMessage =>
        incrementAndPrint
        pong ! PingMessage
    case PongMessage =>
        incrementAndPrint
        if (count > 99) {
          sender ! StopMessage
          println("ping stopped")
          context.stop(self)
        } else {
          sender ! PingMessage
```

```
        }
      case _ => println("Ping got something unexpected.")
    }
  }

  class Pong extends Actor {
    def receive = {
      case PingMessage =>
          println("  pong")
          sender ! PongMessage
      case StopMessage =>
          println("pong stopped")
          context.stop(self)
      case _ => println("Pong got something unexpected.")
    }
  }

  object PingPongTest extends App {
    val system = ActorSystem("PingPongSystem")
    val pong = system.actorOf(Props[Pong], name = "pong")
    val ping = system.actorOf(Props(new Ping(pong)), name = "ping")
    // start the action
    ping ! StartMessage

    // commented-out so you can see all the output
    //system.shutdown
  }
```

Actors should communicate by sending immutable messages between each other. In this case there are four messages, and they're defined using case objects: PingMessage, PongMessage, StartMessage, and StopMessage.

The PingPongTest object performs the following work:

1. Creates an ActorSystem.

2. Creates pong, an instance of the Pong actor. (The pong object is actually an instance of ActorRef, though I loosely refer to it as an actor, or actor instance.) The Pong actor constructor does not require any arguments, so the noargs Props syntax is used.

3. Creates ping, an instance of the Ping actor. The Ping actor constructor takes one argument, an ActorRef, so a slightly different version of the Props syntax is used.

4. Starts the ping/pong action by sending a StartMessage to the ping actor.

Once ping receives the StartMessage, the actors send messages back and forth between each other as fast as they can until the counter limit in ping is reached. Messages are sent using the usual ! method.

To get things started, the `Ping` class needs an initial reference to the `Pong` actor, but once the action starts, the two actors just send a `PingMessage` and `PongMessage` to each other using the `sender` references they implicitly receive, until the `Ping` actor count limit is reached. At that time, it sends a `StopMessage` to the `Pong` actor, and then both actors call their `context.stop` methods. The `context` object is implicitly available to all actors, and can be used to stop actors, among other uses.

In addition to demonstrating how to communicate between actors using immutable messages, this example provides several examples of an `ActorRef`. The `ping` and `pong` instances are `ActorRef` instances, as is the `sender` variable.

A great thing about an `ActorRef` is that it hides the actor instance from you. For instance, the `Pong` actor can't directly execute `ping.incrementAndPrint`; the two actors can only send messages between each other. Although this seems limiting at first, once you understand the model, you'll see that it's a terrific way to *safely* implement concurrency in your applications.

 Messages can also be sent between actors using the ? or ask methods, but those should be used only rarely. See Recipe 13.10, "Sending a Message to an Actor and Waiting for a Reply" for examples of those methods.

# 13.4. Understanding the Methods in the Akka Actor Lifecycle

## Problem

You're creating more complicated actors, and need to understand when the methods on an `Actor` are called.

## Solution

In addition to its constructor, an `Actor` has the following lifecycle methods:

- `receive`
- `preStart`
- `postStop`
- `preRestart`
- `postRestart`

To demonstrate when these methods are called, basic implementations of these methods have been created in the Kenny actor of the following example:

```scala
import akka.actor._

class Kenny extends Actor {
  println("entered the Kenny constructor")
  override def preStart { println("kenny: preStart") }
  override def postStop { println("kenny: postStop") }
  override def preRestart(reason: Throwable, message: Option[Any]) {
    println("kenny: preRestart")
    println(s"  MESSAGE: ${message.getOrElse("")}")
    println(s"  REASON: ${reason.getMessage}")
    super.preRestart(reason, message)
  }
  override def postRestart(reason: Throwable) {
    println("kenny: postRestart")
    println(s"  REASON: ${reason.getMessage}")
    super.postRestart(reason)
  }
  def receive = {
    case ForceRestart => throw new Exception("Boom!")
    case _ => println("Kenny received a message")
  }
}

case object ForceRestart

object LifecycleDemo extends App {
  val system = ActorSystem("LifecycleDemo")
  val kenny = system.actorOf(Props[Kenny], name = "Kenny")

  println("sending kenny a simple String message")
  kenny ! "hello"
  Thread.sleep(1000)

  println("make kenny restart")
  kenny ! ForceRestart
  Thread.sleep(1000)

  println("stopping kenny")
  system.stop(kenny)

  println("shutting down system")
  system.shutdown
}
```

The output from this program shows when the lifecycle methods are invoked:

```
[info] Running LifecycleDemo
sending kenny a simple String message
entered the Kenny constructor
kenny: preStart
```

```
Kenny received a message
make kenny restart
[ERROR] [05/14/2013 10:21:54.953] [LifecycleDemo-akka.actor.default-dispatcher-4]
[akka://LifecycleDemo/user/Kenny] Boom!
java.lang.Exception: Boom!
  at Kenny$$anonfun$receive$1.applyOrElse(Test.scala:19)
  (many more lines of exception output ...)

kenny: preRestart
  MESSAGE: ForceRestart
  REASON: Boom!
kenny: postStop
entered the Kenny constructor
kenny: postRestart
  REASON: Boom!
kenny: preStart
stopping kenny
shutting down system
kenny: postStop
[success]
```

## Discussion

As shown in the `println` statement at the beginning of the Kenny actor, the body of an Akka `Actor` is a part of the constructor, just like any regular Scala class. Along with an actor's constructor, the `pre*` and `post*` methods can be used to initialize and close resources that your actor requires.

Notice that `preRestart` and `postRestart` call the super versions of their methods. This is because the default implementation of `postRestart` calls `preRestart`, and I want that default behavior in this application.

Table 13-1 provides a description of each lifecycle method, including an actor's constructor.

*Table 13-1. Akka actor lifecycle methods*

| Method | Description |
| --- | --- |
| The actor's constructor | An actor's constructor is called just like any other Scala class constructor, when an instance of the class is first created. |
| preStart | Called right after the actor is started. During restarts it's called by the default implementation of postRestart. |
| postStop | Called after an actor is stopped, it can be used to perform any needed cleanup work. According to the Akka documentation, this hook "is guaranteed to run after message queuing has been disabled for this actor." |
| preRestart | According to the Akka documentation, when an actor is restarted, the old actor is informed of the process when preRestart is called with the exception that caused the restart, and the message that triggered the exception. The message may be None if the restart was not caused by processing a message. |

| Method | Description |
| --- | --- |
| postRestart | The postRestart method of the new actor is invoked with the exception that caused the restart. In the default implementation, the preStart method is called. |

## See Also

The Akka actors documentation (*http://bit.ly/14Wm54w*)

# 13.5. Starting an Actor

## Problem

You want to start an Akka actor, or attempt to control the start of an actor.

## Solution

This is a bit of a tricky problem, because Akka actors are started asynchronously when they're passed into the actorOf method using a Props. At the ActorSystem level of your application, you create actors by calling the system.actorOf method. Within an actor, you create a child actor by calling the context.actorOf method.

As demonstrated in Recipe 13.1, you can create an actor at the ActorSystem level by passing your actor class name (such as HelloActor) to the system.actorOf method, using the Props case class:

```
val system = ActorSystem("HelloSystem")

// the actor is created and started here
val helloActor = system.actorOf(Props[HelloActor], name = "helloactor")

helloActor ! "hello"
```

The process of creating a child actor from within another actor is almost identical. The only difference is that you call the actorOf method on the context object instead of on an ActorSystem instance. The context object is implicitly available to your actor instance:

```
class Parent extends Actor {
  val child = context.actorOf(Props[Child], name = "Child")
  // more code here ...
}
```

## Discussion

The following complete example demonstrates how to create actors both at the system level and from within another actor:

```
package actortests.parentchild

import akka.actor._

case class CreateChild (name: String)
case class Name (name: String)

class Child extends Actor {
  var name = "No name"
  override def postStop {
    println(s"D'oh! They killed me ($name): ${self.path}")
  }
  def receive = {
    case Name(name) => this.name = name
    case _ => println(s"Child $name got message")
  }
}

class Parent extends Actor {
  def receive = {
    case CreateChild(name) =>
      // Parent creates a new Child here
      println(s"Parent about to create Child ($name) ...")
      val child = context.actorOf(Props[Child], name = s"$name")
      child ! Name(name)
    case _ => println(s"Parent got some other message.")
  }
}

object ParentChildDemo extends App {

  val actorSystem = ActorSystem("ParentChildTest")
  val parent = actorSystem.actorOf(Props[Parent], name = "Parent")

  // send messages to Parent to create to child actors
  parent ! CreateChild("Jonathan")
  parent ! CreateChild("Jordan")
  Thread.sleep(500)

  // lookup Jonathan, then kill it
  println("Sending Jonathan a PoisonPill ...")
  val jonathan = actorSystem.actorSelection("/user/Parent/Jonathan")
  jonathan ! PoisonPill
  println("jonathan was killed")

  Thread.sleep(5000)
  actorSystem.shutdown
}
```

Here's a brief description of that code:

- At the beginning of the code, the `CreateChild` and `Name` case classes are created. They'll be used to send messages to the actors.
- The `Child` actor has a `receive` method that can handle a `Name` message. It uses that message to set its `name` field.
- The `receive` method of the `Parent` actor can handle a `CreateChild` message. When it receives that message, it creates a new `Child` actor with the given name. Notice that it calls `context.actorOf` to do this.
- The `ParentChildDemo` object creates a new `ActorSystem`, and then creates the `Parent` actor using the `ActorSystem` reference. It then sends two `CreateChild` messages to the `parent` actor reference. After a brief pause, it looks up the `Child` actor named `Jonathan`, and then sends it a `PoisonPill` message. After another pause, it shuts down the system using the `ActorSystem` reference.

Although it isn't required, in this case, the child actor instance is created in the constructor of the `Parent` actor. The `Child` actor could have been created when the `Parent` actor received a message, so in a sense, that gives you a way to control when an actor instance is created.

# 13.6. Stopping Actors

## Problem

You want to stop one or more running Akka actors.

## Solution

There are several ways to stop Akka actors. The most common ways are to call `system.stop(actorRef)` at the `ActorSystem` level or `context.stop(actorRef)` from inside an actor.

There are other ways to stop an actor.

- Send the actor a `PoisonPill` message.
- Program a `gracefulStop`.

To demonstrate these alternatives, at the `ActorSystem` level you can stop an actor by using the `ActorSystem` instance:

```
actorSystem.stop(anActor)
```

Within an actor, you can stop a child actor by using the `context` reference:

```
context.stop(childActor)
```

An actor can also stop itself:

```
context.stop(self)
```

You can stop an actor by sending it a `PoisonPill` message:

```
actor ! PoisonPill
```

The `gracefulStop` is a little more complicated and involves the use of a future. See the Discussion for a complete example.

## Discussion

Table 13-2 provides a summary of the methods that you can use to stop an actor.

*Table 13-2. Ways to stop actors*

| Message | Description |
|---|---|
| `stop` method | The actor will continue to process its current message (if any), but no additional messages will be processed. See additional notes in the paragraphs that follow. |
| `PoisonPill` message | A `PoisonPill` message will stop an actor when the message is processed. A `PoisonPill` message is queued just like an ordinary message and will be handled after other messages queued ahead of it in its mailbox. |
| `gracefulStop` method | Lets you attempt to terminate actors gracefully, waiting for them to timeout. The documentation states that this is a good way to terminate actors in a specific order. |

As noted in Table 13-2, a major difference between calling the `stop` method on an actor and sending it a `PoisonPill` message is in how the actor is stopped. The `stop` method lets the actor finish processing *the current message* in its mailbox (if any), and then stops it. The `PoisonPill` message lets the actors process *all* messages that are in the mailbox ahead of it before stopping it.

Calling `actorSystem.stop(actor)` and `context.stop(actor)` are the most common ways to stop an actor. The following notes on this process are from the official Akka actor documentation (*http://bit.ly/15CoDUk*):

- Termination of an actor is performed asynchronously; the `stop` method may return before the actor is actually stopped.

- The actor will continue to process its current message, but no additional messages will be processed.

- An actor terminates in two steps. First, it suspends its mailbox and sends a `stop` message to all of its children. Then it processes termination messages from its children until they're all gone, at which point it terminates itself. If one of the actors doesn't respond (because it's blocking, for instance), the process has to wait for that actor and may get stuck.

- When additional messages aren't processed, they're sent to the deadLetters actor of the ActorSystem (though this can vary depending on the mailbox implementation). You can access these with the deadLetters method on an ActorSystem.

- As shown in the following examples, the postStop lifecycle method is invoked when an actor is fully stopped, which lets you clean up resources, as needed.

The following subsections demonstrate examples of each of these approaches.

### system.stop and context.stop

This is a complete example that shows how to stop an actor by using the stop method of an ActorSystem:

```
package actortests

import akka.actor._

class TestActor extends Actor {
  def receive = {
    case _ => println("a message was received")
  }
}

object SystemStopExample extends App {
  val actorSystem = ActorSystem("SystemStopExample")
  val actor = actorSystem.actorOf(Props[TestActor], name = "test")
  actor ! "hello"

  // stop our actor
  actorSystem.stop(actor)
  actorSystem.shutdown
}
```

As mentioned, using context.stop(actorRef) is similar to using actorSystem.stop(actorRef); just use context.stop(actorRef) from within an actor. The context variable is implicitly available inside an Actor. This is demonstrated in Recipe 13.5, "Starting an Actor".

### PoisonPill message

You can also stop an actor by sending it a PoisonPill message. This message will stop the actor when the message is processed. The message is queued in the mailbox like an ordinary message.

Here is a PoisonPill example:

```
package actortests

import akka.actor._

class TestActor extends Actor {
```

```
    def receive = {
      case s:String => println("Message Received: " + s)
      case _ => println("TestActor got an unknown message")
    }
    override def postStop { println("TestActor::postStop called") }
  }

  object PoisonPillTest extends App {
    val system = ActorSystem("PoisonPillTest")
    val actor = system.actorOf(Props[TestActor], name = "test")

    // a simple message
    actor ! "before PoisonPill"

    // the PoisonPill
    actor ! PoisonPill

    // these messages will not be processed
    actor ! "after PoisonPill"
    actor ! "hello?!"

    system.shutdown
  }
```

As shown in the comments, the second `String` message sent to the actor won't be received or processed by the actor because it will be in the mailbox after the `PoisonPill`. The only output from running this program will be:

```
Message Received: before PoisonPill
TestActor::postStop called
```

### gracefulStop

As its name implies, you can use the `gracefulStop` approach if you want to wait for a period of time for the termination process to complete gracefully. The following code shows a complete example of the `gracefulStop` approach:

```
package actortests.gracefulstop

import akka.actor._
import akka.pattern.gracefulStop
import scala.concurrent.{Await, ExecutionContext, Future}
import scala.concurrent.duration._
import scala.language.postfixOps


class TestActor extends Actor {
  def receive = {
    case _ => println("TestActor got message")
  }
  override def postStop { println("TestActor: postStop") }
}
```

```
object GracefulStopTest extends App {
  val system = ActorSystem("GracefulStopTest")
  val testActor = system.actorOf(Props[TestActor], name = "TestActor")

  // try to stop the actor gracefully
  try {
    val stopped: Future[Boolean] = gracefulStop(testActor, 2 seconds)(system)
    Await.result(stopped, 3 seconds)
    println("testActor was stopped")
  } catch {
    case e:Exception => e.printStackTrace
  } finally {
    system.shutdown
  }

}
```

Per the Scaladoc, gracefulStop(actorRef, timeout) "Returns a Future that will be completed with success when existing messages of the target actor has [sic] been processed and the actor has been terminated." If the actor isn't terminated within the timeout, the Future results in an ActorTimeoutException. To keep this example simple, I use Await.result, so the time period it waits for should be just slightly longer than the timeout value given to gracefulStop.

If the order in which actors are terminated is important, using gracefulStop can be a good way to attempt to terminate them in a desired order. The "Akka 2 Terminator" example (*http://bit.ly/10YksCP*) referenced in the See Also section demonstrates a nice technique for killing child actors in a specific order using gracefulStop and flatMap.

### "Killing" an actor

As you dig deeper into Akka actors, you'll get into a concept called "supervisor strategies." When you implement a supervisor strategy, you can send an actor a Kill message, which can actually be used to restart the actor. The Akka documentation states that sending a Kill message to an actor, "will restart the actor through regular supervisor semantics."

With the default supervisory strategy, the Kill message does what its name states, terminating the target actor. The following example shows the semantics for sending a Kill message to an actor:

```
package actortests

import akka.actor._

class Number5 extends Actor {
  def receive = {
    case _ => println("Number5 got a message")
  }
  override def preStart { println("Number5 is alive") }
```

```
  override def postStop { println("Number5::postStop called") }
  override def preRestart(reason: Throwable, message: Option[Any]) {
    println("Number5::preRestart called")
  }
  override def postRestart(reason: Throwable) {
    println("Number5::postRestart called")
  }
}

object KillTest extends App {
  val system = ActorSystem("KillTestSystem")
  val number5 = system.actorOf(Props[Number5], name = "Number5")
  number5 ! "hello"
  // send the Kill message
  number5 ! Kill
  system.shutdown
}
```

Running this code results in the following output:

```
Number5 is alive
Number5 got a message
[ERROR] [16:57:02.220] [KillTestSystem-akka.actor.default-dispatcher-2]
[akka://KillTestSystem/user/Number5] Kill (akka.actor.ActorKilledException)
Number5::postStop called
```

This code demonstrates the Kill message so you can see an example of it. In general, this approach is used to kill an actor to allow its supervisor to restart it. If you want to stop an actor, use one of the other approaches described in this recipe.

## See Also

- The "Akka 2 Terminator" example (*http://bit.ly/10YksCP*).

- This Google Groups thread (*http://goo.gl/F3mIP*) discusses how a Kill message is turned into an exception that is handled in the default supervision strategy so it doesn't restart the actor.

- The Akka actors documentation (*http://bit.ly/14Wm54w*) provides more examples of these approaches.

- The gracefulStop method is described on this Scaladoc page (*http://bit.ly/149s744*).

# 13.7. Shutting Down the Akka Actor System

## Problem

You want to shut down the Akka actor system, typically because your application is finished, and you want to shut it down gracefully.

## Solution

Call the `shutdown` method on your `ActorSystem` instance:

```
object Main extends App {
  // create the ActorSystem
  val system = ActorSystem("HelloSystem")

  // put your actors to work here ...

  // shut down the ActorSystem when the work is finished
  system.shutdown
}
```

## Discussion

When you're finished using actors in your application, you should call the `shutdown` method on your `ActorSystem` instance. As shown in the examples in this chapter, if you comment out the `system.shutdown` call, your application will continue to run indefinitely.

In my SARAH application (*http://alvinalexander.com/sarah*), which is a Swing application, I call `actorSystem.shutdown` when the user shuts down the GUI.

If you want to stop your actors before shutting down the actor system, such as to let them complete their current work, see the examples in Recipe 13.6, "Stopping Actors".

# 13.8. Monitoring the Death of an Actor with watch

## Problem

You want an actor to be notified when another actor dies.

## Solution

Use the `watch` method of an actor's `context` object to declare that the actor should be notified when an actor it's monitoring is stopped.

In the following code snippet, the `Parent` actor creates an actor instance named kenny, and then declares that it wants to "watch" kenny:

---

```
class Parent extends Actor {
  val kenny = context.actorOf(Props[Kenny], name = "Kenny")
  context.watch(kenny)
  // more code here ...
```

(Technically, kenny is an `ActorRef` instance, but it's simpler to say "actor.")

If kenny is killed or stopped, the `Parent` actor is sent a `Terminated(kenny)` message. This complete example demonstrates the approach:

```
package actortests.deathwatch

import akka.actor._

class Kenny extends Actor {
  def receive = {
    case _ => println("Kenny received a message")
  }
}

class Parent extends Actor {
  // start Kenny as a child, then keep an eye on it
  val kenny = context.actorOf(Props[Kenny], name = "Kenny")
  context.watch(kenny)

  def receive = {
    case Terminated(kenny) => println("OMG, they killed Kenny")
    case _ => println("Parent received a message")
  }
}

object DeathWatchTest extends App {

  // create the ActorSystem instance
  val system = ActorSystem("DeathWatchTest")

  // create the Parent that will create Kenny
  val parent = system.actorOf(Props[Parent], name = "Parent")

  // lookup kenny, then kill it
  val kenny = system.actorSelection("/user/Parent/Kenny")
  kenny ! PoisonPill

  Thread.sleep(5000)
  println("calling system.shutdown")
  system.shutdown
}
```

When this code is run, the following output is printed:

```
OMG, they killed Kenny
calling system.shutdown
```

## Discussion

Using the `watch` method lets an actor be notified when another actor is stopped (such as with the `PoisonPill` message), or if it's killed with a `Kill` message or `gracefulStop`. This can let the watching actor handle the situation, as desired.

An important thing to understand is that if the Kenny actor throws an exception, this doesn't kill it. Instead it will be restarted. You can confirm this by changing the Kenny actor code to this:

```
case object Explode

class Kenny extends Actor {
  def receive = {
    case Explode => throw new Exception("Boom!")
    case _ => println("Kenny received a message")
  }
  override def preStart { println("kenny: preStart") }
  override def postStop { println("kenny: postStop") }
  override def preRestart(reason: Throwable, message: Option[Any]) {
    println("kenny: preRestart")
    super.preRestart(reason, message)
  }
  override def postRestart(reason: Throwable) {
    println("kenny: postRestart")
    super.postRestart(reason)
  }
}
```

Also, change this line of code in the `DeathWatchTest` object:

```
kenny ! PoisonPill
```

to this:

```
kenny ! Explode
```

When you run this code, in addition to the error messages that are printed because of the exception, you'll also see this output:

```
kenny: preRestart
kenny: postStop
kenny: postRestart
kenny: preStart
calling system.shutdown
kenny: postStop
```

What you won't see is the "OMG, they killed Kenny" message from the `Parent` actor, because the exception didn't kill kenny, it just forced kenny to be automatically restarted. You can verify that kenny is restarted after it receives the explode message by sending it another message:

```
kenny ! "Hello?"
```

It will respond by printing the "Kenny received a message" string in the default _ case of its `receive` method.

### Looking up actors

This example also showed one way to look up an actor:

```
val kenny = system.actorSelection("/user/Parent/Kenny")
```

As shown, you look up actors with the `actorSelection` method, and can specify a full path to the actor in the manner shown. The `actorSelection` method is available on an `ActorSystem` instance and on the `context` object in an `Actor` instance.

You can also look up actors using a relative path. If `kenny` had a sibling actor, it could have looked up `kenny` using its own `context`, like this:

```
// in a sibling actor
val kenny = context.actorSelection("../Kenny")
```

You can also use various implementations of the `actorFor` method to look up actors. The `kenny` instance could be looked up from the `DeathWatchTest` object in these ways:

```
val kenny = system.actorFor("akka://DeathWatchTest/user/Parent/Kenny")
val kenny = system.actorFor(Seq("user", "Parent", "Kenny"))
```

It could also be looked up from a sibling like this:

```
val kenny = system.actorFor(Seq("..", "Kenny"))
```

# 13.9. Simple Concurrency with Futures

## Problem

You want a simple way to run one or more tasks concurrently, including a way to handle their results when the tasks finish. For instance, you may want to make several web service calls in parallel, and then work with their results after they all return.

## Solution

A *future* gives you a simple way to run an algorithm concurrently. A future starts running concurrently when you create it and returns a result at some point, well, in the future. In Scala, it's said that a future returns *eventually*.

The following examples show a variety of ways to create futures and work with their eventual results.

### Run one task, but block

This first example shows how to create a future and then block to wait for its result. Blocking is not a good thing—you should block only if you really have to—but this is useful as a first example, in part, because it's a little easier to reason about, and it also gets the bad stuff out of the way early.

The following code performs the calculation 1 + 1 at some time in the future. When it's finished with the calculation, it returns its result:

```
package actors

// 1 - the imports
import scala.concurrent.{Await, Future}
import scala.concurrent.duration._
import scala.concurrent.ExecutionContext.Implicits.global

object Futures1 extends App {

  // used by 'time' method
  implicit val baseTime = System.currentTimeMillis

  // 2 - create a Future
  val f = Future {
    sleep(500)
    1 + 1
  }

  // 3 - this is blocking (blocking is bad)
  val result = Await.result(f, 1 second)
  println(result)

  sleep(1000)
}
```

Here's how this code works:

- The import statements bring the code into scope that's needed.

- The ExecutionContext.Implicits.global import statement imports the "default global execution context." You can think of an *execution context* as being a thread pool, and this is a simple way to get access to a thread pool.

- A Future is created after the second comment. Creating a future is simple; you just pass it a block of code you want to run. This is the code that will be executed at some point in the future.

- The Await.result method call declares that it will wait for up to one second for the Future to return. If the Future doesn't return within that time, it throws a java.util.concurrent.TimeoutException.

- The sleep statement at the end of the code is used so the program will keep running while the Future is off being calculated. You won't need this in real-world programs, but in small example programs like this, you have to keep the JVM running.

I created the sleep method in my package object while creating my future and concurrency examples, and it just calls Thread.sleep, like this:

```
def sleep(time: Long) { Thread.sleep(time) }
```

As mentioned, blocking is bad; you shouldn't write code like this unless you have to. The following examples show better approaches.

The code also shows a time duration of 1 second. This is made available by the *scala.concurrent.duration._* import. With this library, you can state time durations in several convenient ways, such as 100 nanos, 500 millis, 5 seconds, 1 minute, 1 hour, and 3 days. You can also create a duration as Duration(100, MILLISECONDS), Duration(200, "millis").

### Run one thing, but don't block—use callback

A better approach to working with a future is to use its callback methods. There are three callback methods: onComplete, onSuccess, and onFailure. The following example demonstrates onComplete:

```
import scala.concurrent.{Future}
import scala.concurrent.ExecutionContext.Implicits.global
import scala.util.{Failure, Success}
import scala.util.Random

object Example1 extends App {

  println("starting calculation ...")
  val f = Future {
    sleep(Random.nextInt(500))
    42
  }

  println("before onComplete")
  f.onComplete {
    case Success(value) => println(s"Got the callback, meaning = $value")
    case Failure(e) => e.printStackTrace
  }

  // do the rest of your work
  println("A ..."); sleep(100)
  println("B ..."); sleep(100)
  println("C ..."); sleep(100)
  println("D ..."); sleep(100)
  println("E ..."); sleep(100)
  println("F ..."); sleep(100)

  sleep(2000)

}
```

This example is similar to the previous example, though it just returns the number 42 after a random delay. The important part of this example is the f.onComplete method call and the code that follows it. Here's how that code works:

- The f.onComplete method call sets up the callback. Whenever the Future completes, it makes a callback to onComplete, at which time that code will be executed.

- The Future will either return the desired result (42), or an exception.

- The println statements with the slight delays represent other work your code can do while the Future is off and running.

Because the Future is off running concurrently somewhere, and you don't know exactly when the result will be computed, the output from this code is nondeterministic, but it can look like this:

```
starting calculation ...
before onComplete
A ...
B ...
C ...
D ...
E ...
Got the callback, meaning = 42
F ...
```

Because the Future returns eventually, at some nondeterministic time, the "Got the callback" message may appear anywhere in that output.

### The onSuccess and onFailure callback methods

There may be times when you don't want to use onComplete, and in those situations, you can use the onSuccess and onFailure callback methods, as shown in this example:

```
import scala.concurrent.{Future}
import scala.concurrent.ExecutionContext.Implicits.global
import scala.util.{Failure, Success}
import scala.util.Random

object OnSuccessAndFailure extends App {

  val f = Future {
    sleep(Random.nextInt(500))
    if (Random.nextInt(500) > 250) throw new Exception("Yikes!") else 42
  }

  f onSuccess {
    case result => println(s"Success: $result")
  }

  f onFailure {
    case t => println(s"Exception: ${t.getMessage}")
```

```
  }

  // do the rest of your work
  println("A ..."); sleep(100)
  println("B ..."); sleep(100)
  println("C ..."); sleep(100)
  println("D ..."); sleep(100)
  println("E ..."); sleep(100)
  println("F ..."); sleep(100)

  sleep(2000)

}
```

This code is similar to the previous example, but this Future is wired to throw an exception about half the time, and the onSuccess and onFailure blocks are defined as partial functions; they only need to handle their expected conditions.

### Creating a method to return a Future[T]

In the real world, you may have methods that return futures. The following example defines a method named longRunningComputation that returns a Future[Int]. Declaring it is new, but the rest of this code is similar to the previous onComplete example:

```
import scala.concurrent.{Await, Future, future}
import scala.concurrent.ExecutionContext.Implicits.global
import scala.util.{Failure, Success}

object Futures2 extends App {

  implicit val baseTime = System.currentTimeMillis

  def longRunningComputation(i: Int): Future[Int] = future {
    sleep(100)
    i + 1
  }

  // this does not block
  longRunningComputation(11).onComplete {
    case Success(result) => println(s"result = $result")
    case Failure(e) => e.printStackTrace
  }

  // keep the jvm from shutting down
  sleep(1000)
}
```

The future method shown in this example is another way to create a future. It starts the computation asynchronously and returns a Future[T] that will hold the result of the computation. This is a common way to define methods that return a future.

## Run multiple things; something depends on them; join them together

The examples so far have shown how to run one computation in parallel, to keep things simple. You may occasionally do something like this, such as writing data to a database without blocking the web server, but many times you'll want to run several operations concurrently, wait for them all to complete, and then do something with their combined results.

For example, in a stock market application I wrote, I run all of my web service queries in parallel, wait for their results, and then display a web page. This is faster than running them sequentially.

The following example is a little simpler than that, but it shows how to call an algorithm that may be running in the cloud. It makes three calls to Cloud.runAlgorithm, which is defined elsewhere to return a Future[Int]. For the moment, this algorithm isn't important, other than to know that it prints its result right before returning it.

The code starts those three futures running, then joins them back together in the for comprehension:

```
import scala.concurrent.{Future, future}
import scala.concurrent.ExecutionContext.Implicits.global
import scala.util.{Failure, Success}
import scala.util.Random

object RunningMultipleCalcs extends App {

  println("starting futures")
  val result1 = Cloud.runAlgorithm(10)
  val result2 = Cloud.runAlgorithm(20)
  val result3 = Cloud.runAlgorithm(30)

  println("before for-comprehension")
  val result = for {
    r1 <- result1
    r2 <- result2
    r3 <- result3
  } yield (r1 + r2 + r3)

  println("before onSuccess")
  result onSuccess {
    case result => println(s"total = $result")
  }

  println("before sleep at the end")
  sleep(2000)  // keep the jvm alive

}
```

Here's a brief description of how this code works:

- The three calls to `Cloud.runAlgorithm` create the `result1`, `result2`, and `result3` variables, which are of type `Future[Int]`.

- When those lines are executed, those futures begin running, just like the web service calls in my stock market application.

- The for comprehension is used as a way to join the results back together. When all three futures return, their `Int` values are assigned to the variables `r1`, `r2`, and `r3`, and the sum of those three values is returned from the yield expression, and assigned to the result variable.

- Notice that `result` can't just be printed after the for comprehension. That's because the for comprehension returns a new future, so `result` has the type `Future[Int]`. (This makes sense in more complicated examples.) Therefore, the correct way to print the example is with the `onSuccess` method call, as shown.

When this code is run, the output is nondeterministic, but looks something like this:

```
starting futures
before for-comprehension
before onSuccess
before sleep at end
returning result from cloud: 30
returning result from cloud: 20
returning result from cloud: 40
total = 90
```

Notice how all of the `println` statements in the code print before the `total` is printed. That's because they're running in sequential fashion, while the future is off and running in parallel, and returns at some indeterminate time ("eventually").

I mentioned earlier that the `Cloud.runAlgorithm` code wasn't important—it was just something running "in the cloud,"—but for the sake of completeness, here's that code:

```
object Cloud {

  def runAlgorithm(i: Int): Future[Int] = future {
    sleep(Random.nextInt(500))
    val result = i + 10
    println(s"returning result from cloud: $result")
    result
  }

}
```

In my real-world code, I use a future in a similar way to get information from web services. For example, in a Twitter client, I make multiple calls to the Twitter web service API using futures:

```
// get the desired info from twitter
val dailyTrendsFuture = Future { getDailyTrends(twitter) }
```

```
val usFuture = Future { getLocationTrends(twitter, woeidUnitedStates) }
val worldFuture = Future { getLocationTrends(twitter, woeidWorld) }
```

I then join them in a for comprehension, as shown in this example. This is a nice, simple way to turn single-threaded web service calls into multiple threads.

# Discussion

Although using a future is straightforward, there are also many concepts behind it. The following sections summarize the most important concepts.

### A future and ExecutionContext

The following statements describe the basic concepts of a future, as well as the ExecutionContext that a future relies on.

- A Future[T] is a container that runs a computation concurrently, and at some future time may return either (a) a result of type T or (b) an exception.

- Computation of your algorithm starts at some nondeterministic time after the future is created, running on a thread assigned to it by the execution context.

- The result of the computation becomes available once the future completes.

- When it returns a result, a future is said to be *completed*. It may either be *successfully completed*, or *failed*.

- As shown in the examples, a future provides an interface for reading the value that has been computed. This includes callback methods and other approaches, such as a for comprehension, map, flatMap, etc.

- An ExecutionContext executes a task it's given. You can think of it as being like a thread pool.

- The ExecutionContext.Implicits.global import statement shown in the examples imports the default global execution context.

### Callback methods

The following statements describe the use of the callback methods that can be used with futures.

- Callback methods are called asynchronously when a future completes.

- The callback methods onComplete, onSuccess, onFailure, are demonstrated in the Solution.

- A callback method is executed by some thread, some time after the future is completed. From the Scala Futures documentation (*http://bit.ly/12STMkt*), "There is no guarantee that it will be called by the thread that completed the future or the thread that created the callback."

- The order in which callbacks are executed is not guaranteed.

- `onComplete` takes a callback function of type `Try[T] => U`.

- `onSuccess` and `onFailure` take partial functions. You only need to handle the desired case. (See Recipe 9.8, "Creating Partial Functions" for more information on partial functions.)

- `onComplete`, `onSuccess`, and `onFailure` have the result type `Unit`, so they can't be chained. This design was intentional, to avoid any suggestion that callbacks may be executed in a particular order.

### For comprehensions (combinators: map, flatMap, filter, foreach, recoverWith, fallbackTo, andThen)

As shown in the Solution, callback methods are good for some purposes. But when you need to run multiple computations in parallel, and join their results together when they're finished running, using *combinators* like `map`, `foreach`, and other approaches, like a for comprehension, provides more concise and readable code. The for comprehension was shown in the Solution.

The `recover`, `recoverWith`, and `fallbackTo` combinators provide ways of handling failure with futures. If the future they're applied to returns successfully, you get that (desired) result, but if it fails, these methods do what their names suggest, giving you a way to recover from the failure.

As a short example, you can use the `fallbackTo` method like this:

```
val meaning = calculateMeaningOfLife() fallbackTo 42
```

The `andThen` combinator gives you a nice syntax for running whatever code you want to run when a future returns, like this:

```
var meaning = 0
future {
  meaning = calculateMeaningOfLife()
} andThen {
  println(s"meaning of life is $meaning")
}
```

See the Scala Futures documentation (*http://bit.ly/12STMkt*) for more information on their use.

## See Also

- The Scala Futures documentation (*http://bit.ly/12STMkt*)

- These examples (and more) are available at my GitHub repository (*https://github.com/alvinj/ScalaFutureExamples*).

- As shown in these examples, you can read a result from a future, and a *promise* is a way for some part of your software to put that result in there. I've linked to the best article I can find (*http://bit.ly/18zUuI8*).

# 13.10. Sending a Message to an Actor and Waiting for a Reply

## Problem

You have one actor that needs to ask another actor for some information, and needs an immediate reply. (The first actor can't continue without the information from the second actor.)

## Solution

Use the ? or ask methods to send a message to an Akka actor and wait for a reply, as demonstrated in the following example:

```
import akka.actor._
import akka.pattern.ask
import akka.util.Timeout
import scala.concurrent.{Await, ExecutionContext, Future}
import scala.concurrent.duration._
import scala.language.postfixOps

case object AskNameMessage

class TestActor extends Actor {
  def receive = {
    case AskNameMessage => // respond to the 'ask' request
                           sender ! "Fred"
    case _ => println("that was unexpected")
  }
}

object AskTest extends App {

  // create the system and actor
  val system = ActorSystem("AskTestSystem")
  val myActor = system.actorOf(Props[TestActor], name = "myActor")

  // (1) this is one way to "ask" another actor for information
  implicit val timeout = Timeout(5 seconds)
  val future = myActor ? AskNameMessage
  val result = Await.result(future, timeout.duration).asInstanceOf[String]
  println(result)
```

```
// (2) a slightly different way to ask another actor for information
val future2: Future[String] = ask(myActor, AskNameMessage).mapTo[String]
val result2 = Await.result(future2, 1 second)
println(result2)

system.shutdown

}
```

## Discussion

Both the ? or ask methods use the Future and Await.result approach demonstrated
in Recipe 13.9, "Simple Concurrency with Futures". The recipe is:

1. Send a message to an actor using either ? or ask instead of the usual ! method.

2. The ? and ask methods create a Future, so you use Await.result to wait for the
   response from the other actor.

3. The actor that's called should send a reply back using the ! method, as shown in
   the example, where the TestActor receives the AskNameMessage and returns an
   answer using sender ! "Fred".

To keep the previous example simple, only one actor is shown, but the same approach
is used by two actors. Just use the ? or ask method in your actor, like this:

```
class FooActor extends Actor {
  def receive = {
    case GetName =>
        val future: Future[String] = ask(otherActor, AskNameMessage).mapTo↵
[String]
        val result = Await.result(future, 1 second)
    case _ => // handle other messages
  }
}
```

Be careful when writing code that waits for immediate responses like this. This causes
your actor to block, which means that it can't respond to anything else while it's in this
state. When you need to perform work like this, the mantra is, "Delegate, delegate,
delegate."

# 13.11. Switching Between Different States with become

## Problem

You want a simple mechanism to allow an actor to switch between the different states
it can be in at different times.

## Solution

Use the Akka "become" approach. To do this, first define the different possible states the actor can be in. Then, in the actor's `receive` method, switch between the different states based on the messages it receives.

The following example shows how the actor named `DavidBanner` might switch between its `normalState` and its `angryState` (when he becomes The Hulk):

```
package actortests.becometest

import akka.actor._

case object ActNormalMessage
case object TryToFindSolution
case object BadGuysMakeMeAngry

class DavidBanner extends Actor {
  import context._

  def angryState: Receive = {
    case ActNormalMessage =>
        println("Phew, I'm back to being David.")
        become(normalState)
  }

  def normalState: Receive = {
    case TryToFindSolution =>
        println("Looking for solution to my problem ...")
    case BadGuysMakeMeAngry =>
        println("I'm getting angry...")
        become(angryState)
  }

  def receive = {
    case BadGuysMakeMeAngry => become(angryState)
    case ActNormalMessage => become(normalState)
  }
}

object BecomeHulkExample extends App {
  val system = ActorSystem("BecomeHulkExample")
  val davidBanner = system.actorOf(Props[DavidBanner], name = "DavidBanner")
  davidBanner ! ActNormalMessage // init to normalState
  davidBanner ! TryToFindSolution
  davidBanner ! BadGuysMakeMeAngry
  Thread.sleep(1000)
  davidBanner ! ActNormalMessage
  system.shutdown
}
```

Here's a description of the code:

1. The davidBanner actor instance is created, as shown in previous recipes.

2. The davidBanner instance is sent the ActNormalMessage to set an initial state.

3. After sending davidBanner a TryToFindSolution message, it sends a BadGuysMakeMeAngry message.

4. When davidBanner receives the BadGuysMakeMeAngry message, it uses become to switch to the angryState.

5. In the angryState the only message davidBanner can process is the ActNormalMessage. (In the real world, er, entertainment world, it should be programmed to receive other messages, like SmashThings.)

6. When davidBanner receives the final ActNormalMessage, it switches back to the normalState, again using the become method.

## Discussion

As shown, the general recipe for using the become approach to switch between different possible states is:

- Define the different possible states, such as the normalState and angryState.
- Define the receive method in the actor to switch to the different states based on the messages it can receive. As shown in the example, this is handled with a match expression.

It's important to note that the different states can only receive the messages they're programmed for, and those messages can be different in the different states. For instance, the normalState responds to the messages TryToFindSolution and BadGuys-MakeMeAngry, but the angryState can only respond to the ActNormal-Message.

## See Also

The Akka actors documentation (*http://bit.ly/14Wm54w*) shows a become example.

# 13.12. Using Parallel Collections

## Problem

You want to improve the performance of algorithms by using parallel collections.

## Solution

When creating a collection, use one of the Scala's parallel collection classes, or convert an existing collection to a parallel collection. In either case, test your algorithm to make sure you see the benefit you're expecting.

You can convert an existing collection to a parallel collection. To demonstrate this, first create a sequential collection, such as a `Vector`:

```
scala> val v = Vector.range(0, 10)
v: scala.collection.immutable.Vector[Int] = Vector(0, 1, 2, 3, 4, 5, 6, 7, 8, 9)
```

Next, print the sequence, and you'll see that it prints as usual:

```
scala> v.foreach(print)
0123456789
```

As expected, that example prints the string `0123456789`. No matter how many times you print it, you'll always see that same result; that's the linear world you're used to.

Next, call the `par` method on your collection to turn it into a parallel collection, and repeat the experiment:

```
scala> v.par.foreach(print)
5678901234

scala> v.par.foreach(print)
0123456789

scala> v.par.foreach{ e => print(e); Thread.sleep(50) }
0516273894
```

Whoa. Sometimes the collection prints in order, other times it prints in a seemingly random order. That's because it's now using an algorithm that runs concurrently. Welcome to the brave, new, parallel world.

That example showed how to convert a "normal" collection to a parallel collection. You can also create a parallel collection directly:

```
scala> import scala.collection.parallel.immutable.ParVector
import scala.collection.parallel.immutable._

scala> val v = ParVector.range(0, 10)
v: scala.collection.parallel.immutable.ParVector[Int] =
    ParVector(0, 1, 2, 3, 4, 5, 6, 7, 8, 9)

scala> v.foreach{ e => Thread.sleep(100); print(e) }
0516273849
```

## Discussion

As shown, you can create parallel collections in two ways:

- Convert a "normal" collection to its parallel counterpart
- Instantiate them directly, just like their nonparallel counterparts

You can create a new instance of a parallel collection directly. As with the "normal" collection classes that are discussed in Chapter 10 and Chapter 11, there are both immutable and mutable parallel collections. Here's a list of some of the immutable parallel collection classes:

```
ParHashMap    ParHashSet    ParIterable    ParMap
ParRange      ParSeq        ParSet         ParVector
```

In addition to these, the mutable collection has other classes and traits, including `ParArray`.

 For a full list of Scala's parallel collections, see the Scala website (*http://bit.ly/1dCbKfX*).

### Where are parallel collections useful?

To understand where a parallel collection can be useful, it helps to think about how they work. Conceptually, you can imagine a collection being split into different chunks; your algorithm is then applied to the chunks, and at the end of the operation, the different chunks are recombined.

For instance, in the Solution, a `ParVector` was created like this:

```
scala> val v = ParVector.range(0, 10)
v: scala.collection.parallel.immutable.ParVector[Int] =
    ParVector(0, 1, 2, 3, 4, 5, 6, 7, 8, 9)
```

The elements in the `ParVector` were then printed like this:

```
scala> v.foreach{ e => Thread.sleep(100); print(e) }
0516273849
```

This makes sense if you imagine that the original `ParVector` is split into two sequences before the printing operation begins:

```
(0,1,2,3,4)
(5,6,7,8,9)
```

In this case you can imagine the `foreach` method taking (or receiving) the 0 from the first sequence, printing it; getting the 5 from the second sequence, printing it; then getting the 1 from the first sequence, etc.

To summarize the basic concept:

- Collection elements are split into different groups.
- The operation is performed.
- The elements are recombined.

The impact of this approach is that it must be okay that your algorithm receives elements in an arbitrary order. This means that algorithms like `sum`, `max`, `min`, `mean`, and `filter` will all work fine.

Conversely, any algorithm that depends on the collection elements being received in a predictable order should not be used with a parallel collection. A simple demonstration of this is the `foreach` examples that have been shown: if it's important that the collection elements are printed in a particular order, such as the order in which they were placed in the collection, using a parallel collection isn't appropriate.

The official Scala documentation refers to this as "side-effecting operations." The Parallel Collections Overview URL (*http://bit.ly/1dCbKfX*) in the See Also section discusses this in detail.

### Performance

Using parallel collections won't always make your code faster. It's important to test your algorithm with and without a parallel collection to make sure your algorithm is faster with a parallel collection. The "Measuring Performance" URL (*http://bit.ly/190QUtd*) in the See Also section has a terrific discussion about how to properly benchmark JVM performance.

For a parallel algorithm to provide a benefit, a collection usually needs to be fairly large. The documentation states:

> "As a general heuristic, speed-ups tend to be noticeable when the size of the collection is large, typically several thousand elements."

Finally, if using a parallel collection won't solve your problem, using Akka actors and futures can give you complete control over your algorithms.

## See Also

- Immutable parallel collections (*http://bit.ly/15iEXd9*)
- Mutable parallel collections (*http://bit.ly/12GQ10p*)
- Parallel collections overview (*http://bit.ly/1dCbKfX*)
- Measuring the performance of parallel collections (*http://bit.ly/190QUtd*)

CHAPTER 14

# Command-Line Tasks

## 14.0. Introduction

Scala offers a number of tools to let you work at the command line, including the Read-Eval-Print-Loop, or *REPL*. As shown in Figure 14-1, the REPL lets you execute Scala expressions in an interactive environment.

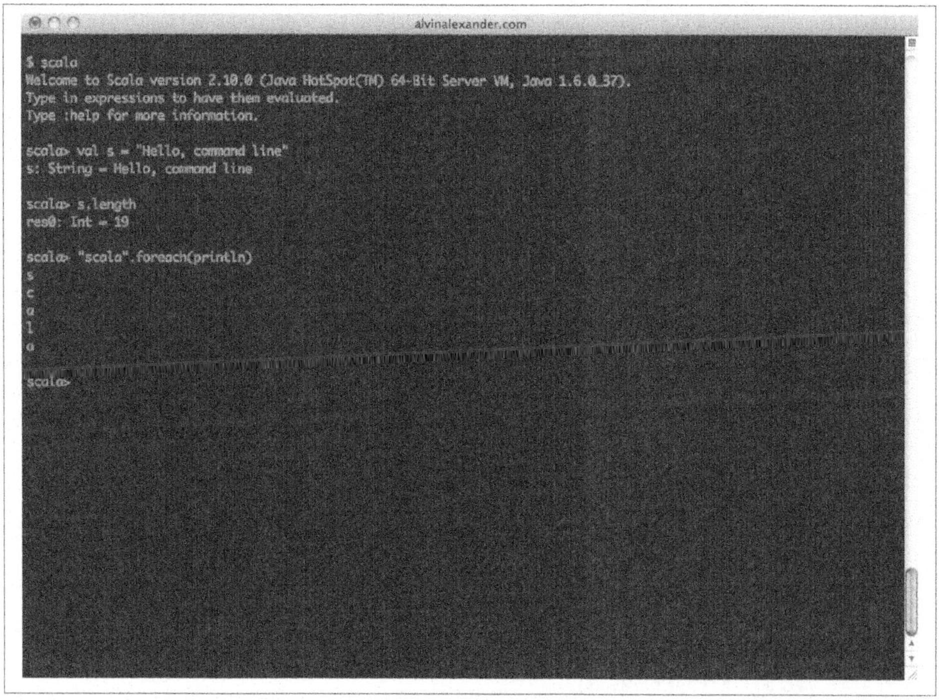


*Figure 14-1. The REPL lets you execute Scala expressions in an interactive environment*

If you've used an interactive interpreter before (such as Ruby's *irb* tool), the Scala REPL will seem very familiar.

When it comes to building your projects, you'll be well served to use the Simple Build Tool (SBT), so that's covered in Chapter 18. But there are still times when you'll want to use `scalac`, `fsc`, `scaladoc`, and other command-line tools, and this chapter demonstrates all of those tools.

The name "Scala" comes from the word "scalable," and Scala does indeed scale from small shell scripts to the largest, highest-performance applications in the world. On the low end of that scale, this chapter demonstrates how to create your own shell scripts, prompt for input from your scripts, and then make them run faster.

# 14.1. Getting Started with the Scala REPL

## Problem

You want to get started using the Scala REPL, including understanding some of its basic features, such as tab completion, starting the REPL with different options, and dealing with errors.

## Solution

To start the Scala REPL, type `scala` at your operating system command line:

```
$ scala
```

You'll see a welcome message and Scala prompt:

```
Welcome to Scala version 2.10.0
Type in expressions to have them evaluated.
Type :help for more information.

scala> _
```

Welcome, you're now using the Scala REPL.

Inside the REPL environment, you can try all sorts of different experiments and expressions:

```
scala> val x, y = 1
x: Int = 1
y: Int = 1

scala> x + y
res0: Int = 2

scala> val a = Array(1, 2, 3)
a: Array[Int] = Array(1, 2, 3)
```

```
scala> a.sum
res1: Int = 6
```

As shown in the second example, if you don't assign the result of an expression to a variable, the REPL creates its own variable, beginning with res0, then res1, etc. You can use these variable names just as though you had created them yourself:

```
scala> res1.getClass
res2: Class[Int] = int
```

Writing tests like this in the REPL is a great way to run experiments outside of your IDE or editor.

There are a few simple tricks that can make using the REPL more effective. One trick is to use *tab completion* to see the methods that are available on an object. To see how tab completion works, create a String object, type a decimal, and then press the Tab key. With Scala 2.10, the REPL shows that more than 30 methods are available on a String instance:

```
scala> "foo".[Tab]
+                 asInstanceOf      charAt       codePointAt
codePointBefore   codePointCount    compareTo

// a total of thirty methods listed here ...
```

If you press the Tab key again, the REPL expands the list to more than 50 methods:

```
scala> "foo".[Tab][Tab]
// 51 methods now listed ...
```

Similarly, the Int object expands from 25 to 34 methods when you press the Tab key twice.

When you press the Tab key the first time, the REPL filters out many common methods, but by pressing the Tab key the second time, it removes those filters and increases the verbosity of its output. You can find an explanation of how this works at the JLineCompletion class link in the See Also section of this recipe.

You can also limit the list of methods that are displayed by typing the first part of a method name and then pressing the Tab key. For instance, if you know that you're interested in the to* methods on a Scala List, type a decimal and the characters to after a List instance, and then press Tab:

```
scala> List(1,2,3).to[Tab]
toByte   toChar   toDouble   toFloat   toInt   toLong   toShort   toString
```

These are all the List methods that begin with the letters to.

Although the REPL tab-completion feature is good, it currently doesn't show methods that are available to an object that results from implicit conversions. For instance, when you invoke the tab-completion feature on a `String` instance, the REPL doesn't show the methods that are available to the `String` that come from the implicit conversions defined in the `StringOps` class.

To see methods available from the `StringOps` class, you currently have to do something like this:

```scala
scala> val s = new collection.immutable.StringOps("")
s: scala.collection.immutable.StringOps = s
```

```scala
scala> s.[Tab]
```

After pressing the Tab key, you'll see dozens of additional methods that are available to a `String` object, such as all the `to*` and collection methods.

The REPL also doesn't show method signatures. Hopefully features like this will be added to future versions of the REPL. In the meantime, these are most easily seen in an IDE.

## Discussion

I use the REPL to create many small experiments, and it also helps me understand some type conversions that Scala performs automatically. For instance, when I first started working with Scala and typed the following code into the REPL, I didn't know what type the variable x was:

```scala
scala> val x = (3, "Three", 3.0)
x: (Int, java.lang.String, Double) = (3,Three,3.0)
```

With the REPL, it's easy to run tests like this, and then call `getClass` on a variable to see its type:

```scala
scala> x.getClass
res0: java.lang.Class[_ <: (Int, java.lang.String, Double)] = class scala.Tuple3
```

Although some of that result line is hard to read when you first start working with Scala, the text on the right side of the = lets you know that the type is a `Tuple3`.

Though this is a simple example, when you're working with more complicated code or a new library, you'll find yourself running many small tests like this in the REPL.

A `Tuple3` is a specific instance of a *tuple*. A tuple is a container for heterogeneous objects. A `Tuple3` is simply a tuple that contains three elements. Here's a `Tuple2` that holds a `String` and a `Char`:

```
scala> val y = ("Foo", 'a')
y: (java.lang.String, Char) = (Foo,a)

scala> y.getClass
res1: java.lang.Class[_ <: (java.lang.String, Char)]
    = class scala.Tuple2
```

See Recipe 10.27, "Tuples, for When You Just Need a Bag of Things" for more information.

### REPL command-line options

If you need to set Java properties when starting the Scala interpreter, you can do so like this on Unix systems:

```
$ env JAVA_OPTS="-Xmx512M -Xms64M" scala
```

That command sets the maximum and initial size of the Java memory allocation pool. You can confirm this by looking at the maximum available memory in the REPL:

```
scala> Runtime.getRuntime.maxMemory / 1024
res0: Long = 520064
```

When starting the Scala 2.10 REPL without any options, the same command yields a different result:

```
scala> Runtime.getRuntime.maxMemory / 1024
res0: Long = 258880
```

You can also use the `-J` command-line argument to set parameters. I ran into a `java.lang.OutOfMemoryError` in the REPL while processing a large XML dataset, and fixed the problem by starting the REPL with this command:

```
$ scala -J-Xms256m -J-Xmx512m
```

The `scala` command you're running in these examples is actually a shell script, so if you need to modify these parameters permanently, just edit that script. (On Unix systems, you can also create a wrapper script or an alias.)

### Deprecation and feature warnings

From time to time, you may see a message that suggests starting the REPL with the `-deprecation` or `-feature` option enabled. For instance, attempting to create an octal value by entering an integer value with a leading zero generates a deprecation warning:

```
scala> 012
warning: there were 1 deprecation warnings; re-run with -deprecation for details
res0: Int = 10
```

To see the error, you *could* restart the REPL with the `-deprecation` option, like this:

```
$ scala -deprecation
```

Fortunately, restarting the REPL isn't usually necessary. Beginning with Scala 2.10, it's usually easier to ask the REPL to show the message with the `:warning` command:

```
scala> 012
warning: there were 1 deprecation warnings; re-run with -deprecation for details
res0: Int = 10

scala> :warning
<console>:8: warning: Treating numbers with a leading zero as octal is deprecated.
       012
       ^
```

The REPL documentation states that the `:warning` command shows "the suppressed warnings from the most recent line."

If you run into the similar `feature` warning message, you can also issue the `:warning` command to see the error. If necessary, you can also restart the REPL with the `-feature` option:

```
$ scala -feature
```

## The Scala Worksheet

If you're using Eclipse with the Scala IDE plug-in, you can also run a REPL session in a Scala Console panel. Another alternative is to use the Scala Worksheet (*http://bit.ly/1aq2RXe*). The Worksheet is a plug-in that's available for Eclipse and IntelliJ IDEA. It works like the REPL, but runs inside the IDE. Figure 14-2 shows what the Worksheet looks like in Eclipse.

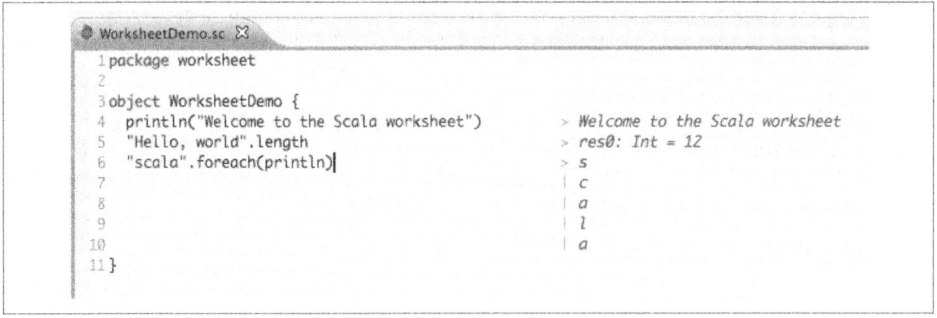

*Figure 14-2. The Scala Worksheet plug-in works like the REPL*

## See Also

- Source code for the `JLineCompletion` class (*http://bit.ly/12DmhpW*)
- The `Tuple3` class (*http://bit.ly/1aq2VWU*)

# 14.2. Pasting and Loading Blocks of Code into the REPL

## Problem

You want to experiment with some code in the Scala REPL, and typing it in or trying to paste it into the REPL won't work.

## Solution

The REPL is "greedy" and consumes the first full statement you type in, so attempting to paste blocks of code into it can fail. To solve the problem, either use the `:paste` command to paste blocks of code into the REPL, or use the `:load` command to load the code from a file into the REPL.

### The :paste command

Attempting to paste the following `if`/`else` block into the REPL will cause an error:

```
if (true)
    print("that was true")
else
    print("that was false")
```

But by issuing the `:paste` command before pasting in the code, the code will be interpreted properly:

```
scala> :paste
// Entering paste mode (ctrl-D to finish)

if (true)
    print("that was true")
else
    print("false")

[Ctrl-D]

// Exiting paste mode, now interpreting.
that was true
```

As shown, follow these steps to paste your code into the REPL:

1. Type the `:paste` command in the REPL.

2. Paste in your block of code (Command-V on a Mac, Ctrl-V on Windows).

3. Press Ctrl-D, and the REPL will evaluate what you pasted in.

### The :load command

Similarly, if you have source code in a file that you want to read into the REPL environment, you can use the `:load` command. For example, assume you have the following source code in a file named *Person.scala* in the same directory where you started the REPL:

```
case class Person(name: String)
```

You can load that source code into the REPL environment like this:

```
scala> :load Person.scala
Loading /Users/Al/ScalaTests/Person.scala...
defined class Person
```

Once the code is loaded into the REPL, you can create a new `Person` instance:

```
scala> val al = Person("Alvin Alexander")
al: Person = Person(Alvin Alexander)
```

Note, however, that if your source code has a package declaration:

```
// Person.scala source code
package com.alvinalexander.foo
case class Person(name: String)
```

the `:load` command will fail:

```
scala> :load /Users/Al/ProjectX/Person.scala
Loading /Users/Al/ProjectX/Person.scala...
<console>:1: error: illegal start of definition
       package com.alvinalexander.foo
       ^
defined class Person
```

You can't use packages in the REPL, so for situations like this, you'll need to compile your file(s) and then include them on the classpath, as shown in Recipe 14.3, "Adding JAR Files and Classes to the REPL Classpath".

## Discussion

Although the REPL is incredibly helpful, its greedy nature can cause multiline statements to fail. Imagine that you want to type the following block of code into the REPL:

```
if (true)
  't'
else
  'f'
```

If you try typing this code in one line at a time, the REPL will cut you off as soon as it sees a complete statement:

```
scala> if (true)
     |   't'
res0: AnyVal = t
```

In this simple example, you can get around the problem by adding curly braces to the expression, in which case the REPL recognizes that the expression isn't finished:

```
scala> if (true) {
     |     't'
     | } else {
     |     'f'
     | }
res0: Char = t
```

But you can't always do this. In the cases where this fails, use one of the approaches shown in the Solution.

### Scala's -i option

Another approach you can use is to load your source code with the -i argument when starting the Scala REPL. See Recipe 14.4, "Running a Shell Command from the REPL" for more information on that approach.

## See Also

Recipe 14.3, "Adding JAR Files and Classes to the REPL Classpath"

# 14.3. Adding JAR Files and Classes to the REPL Classpath

## Problem

You want to add individual classes or one or more JAR files to the REPL classpath so you can use them in a REPL session.

## Solution

If you know that you want to use code from a JAR file when you start the REPL session, add the -cp or -classpath argument to your scala command when you start the session. This example shows how to load and use my *DateUtils.jar* library:

```
$ scala -cp DateUtils.jar

scala> import com.alvinalexander.dateutils._
import com.alvinalexander.dateutils._
```

```
scala> DateUtils.getCurrentDate
res0: String = Saturday, March 16
```

If you realize you need a JAR file on your classpath *after* you've started a REPL session, you can add one dynamically with the :cp command:

```
scala> :cp DateUtils.jar
Added '/Users/Al/Projects/Scala/Tests/DateUtils.jar'.
Your new classpath is:
".:/Users/Al/Projects/Scala/Tests/DateUtils.jar"

scala> import com.alvinalexander.dateutils._
import com.alvinalexander.dateutils._

scala> DateUtils.getCurrentDate
res0: String = Saturday, March 16
```

Compiled class files in the current directory (*.class) are automatically loaded into the REPL environment, so if a simple Person.class file is in the current directory when you start the REPL, you can create a new Person instance without requiring a classpath command:

```
scala> val p = new Person("Bill")
p: Person = Person(Bill)
```

However, if your class files are in a subdirectory, you can add them to the environment when you start the session, just as with JAR files. If all the class files are located in a subdirectory named classes, you can include them by starting your REPL session like this:

```
$ scala -cp classes
```

If the class files you want to include are in several different directories, you can add them all to your classpath:

```
$ scala -cp "../Project1/bin:../Project2/classes"
```

(This command works on Unix systems, but it may be slightly different on Windows.)

These approaches let you add JAR files and other compiled classes to your REPL environment, either at startup or as the REPL is running.

# 14.4. Running a Shell Command from the REPL

## Problem

You want to be able to run a shell command from within the Scala REPL, such as listing the files in the current directory.

# Solution

Run the command using the `:sh` REPL command, then print the output. The following example shows how to run the Unix `ls -al` command from within the REPL, and then show the results of the command:

```
scala> :sh ls -al
res0: scala.tools.nsc.interpreter.ProcessResult = `ls -al` (6 lines, exit 0)

scala> res0.show
total 24
drwxr-xr-x    5 Al   staff   170 Jul 14 17:14 .
drwxr-xr-x   29 Al   staff   986 Jul 14 15:27 ..
-rw-r--r--    1 Al   staff   108 Jul 14 15:34 finance.csv
-rw-r--r--    1 Al   staff   469 Jul 14 15:38 process.scala
-rw-r--r--    1 Al   staff   412 Jul 14 16:24 process2.scala
```

Alternatively you can import the `scala.sys.process` package, and then use the normal `Process` and `ProcessBuilder` commands described in Recipe 12.10, "Executing External Commands":

```
scala> import sys.process._
import sys.process._

scala> "ls -al" !
total 24
drwxr-xr-x    5 Al   staff   170 Jul 14 17:14 .
drwxr-xr-x   29 Al   staff   986 Jul 14 15:27 ..
-rw-r--r--    1 Al   staff   108 Jul 14 15:34 finance.csv
-rw-r--r--    1 Al   staff   469 Jul 14 15:38 process.scala
-rw-r--r--    1 Al   staff   412 Jul 14 16:24 process2.scala
res0: Int = 0
```

## Scala's -i option

Although those examples show the correct approach, you can improve the situation by loading your own custom code when you start the Scala interpreter. For instance, I always start the REPL in my */Users/Al/tmp* directory, and I have a file in that directory named *repl-commands* with these contents:

```
import sys.process._

def clear = "clear".!
def cmd(cmd: String) = cmd.!!
def ls(dir: String) { println(cmd(s"ls -al $dir")) }
def help {
  println("\n=== MY CONFIG ===")
  "cat /Users/Al/tmp/repl-commands".!
}

case class Person(name: String)
val nums = List(1, 2, 3)
```

```
val strings = List("sundance", "rocky", "indigo")

// lets me easily see the methods from StringOps
// with tab completion
val so = new collection.immutable.StringOps("")
```

With this setup, I start the Scala interpreter with the -i argument, telling it to load this file when it starts:

```
$ scala -i repl-commands
```

This makes those pieces of code available to me inside the REPL. For instance, I can clear my terminal window by invoking the clear method:

```
scala> clear
```

My ls method provides a directory listing:

```
scala> ls("/tmp")
```

With my cmd method I can run other external commands:

```
scala> cmd("cat /etc/passwd")
```

The help method uses the system cat command to display this file, which is helpful if I haven't used it in a while. The nums and strings variables and Person class also make it easy to run quick experiments.

This approach is similar to using a startup file to initialize a Unix login session, like a *.bash_profile* file for Bash users, and I highly recommend it. As you use the REPL more and more, use this technique to customize its behavior.

To make this even easier, I created the following Unix alias and put it in my *.bash_profile* file:

```
alias repl="scala -i /Users/Al/tmp/repl-commands"
```

I now use this alias to start a REPL session, rather than starting it by typing scala:

```
$ repl
```

## See Also

The "Executing external commands" recipes in Chapter 12 for more examples of executing external commands from Scala code

## 14.5. Compiling with scalac and Running with scala

### Problem

Though you normally use the Simple Build Tool (SBT) to build Scala applications, you may want to use more basic tools to compile and run small test programs, in the same way you might use `javac` and `java` with small Java applications.

### Solution

Compile programs with `scalac`, and run them with `scala`. For example, given a Scala source code file named *Hello.scala*:

```
object Hello extends App {
  println("Hello, world")
}
```

Compile it from the command line with `scalac`:

```
$ scalac Hello.scala
```

Then run it with `scala`:

```
$ scala Hello
Hello, world
```

### Discussion

Compiling and executing classes is basically the same as Java, including concepts like the classpath. For instance, if you have a class named `Pizza` in a file named *Pizza.scala*, it may depend on a `Topping` class:

```
class Pizza (var toppings: Topping*) {
  override def toString = toppings.toString
}
```

Assuming that the `Topping` class is compiled to a file named *Topping.class* in a subdirectory named *classes*, compile *Pizza.scala* like this:

```
$ scalac -classpath classes Pizza.scala
```

In a more complicated example, you may have your source code in subdirectories under a *src* folder, one or more JAR files in a *lib* directory, and you want to compile your output class files to a *classes* folder. In this case, your files and directories will look like this:

```
./classes
./lib/DateUtils.jar
./src/com/alvinalexander/pizza/Main.scala
./src/com/alvinalexander/pizza/Pizza.scala
./src/com/alvinalexander/pizza/Topping.scala
```

The *Main.scala*, *Pizza.scala*, and *Topping.scala* files will also have package declarations corresponding to the directories they are located in, i.e.:

```
package com.alvinalexander.pizza
```

Given this configuration, to compile your source code files to the *classes* directory, use the following command:

```
$ scalac -classpath lib/DateUtils.jar -d classes ↵ src/com/alvinalexander/pizza/*
```

Assuming *Main.scala* is an object that extends App, *Pizza.scala* is a regular class file, and *Topping.scala* is a case class, your *classes* directory will contain these files after your `scalac` command:

```
./classes/com/alvinalexander/pizza/Main$.class
./classes/com/alvinalexander/pizza/Main$delayedInit$body.class
./classes/com/alvinalexander/pizza/Main.class
./classes/com/alvinalexander/pizza/Pizza.class
./classes/com/alvinalexander/pizza/Topping$.class
./classes/com/alvinalexander/pizza/Topping.class
```

Once the files have been compiled in this manner, you can run the application like this:

```
$ scala -classpath classes:lib/DateUtils.jar com.alvinalexander.pizza.Main
```

As you can imagine, this process gets more and more difficult as you add new classes and libraries, and it's strongly recommended that you use a tool like SBT, Maven, or Ant to manage your application's build process. The examples shown in this recipe are shown for the "one off" cases where you might want to compile and run a small application or test code.

For other useful command-line options, see the manpages for the `scalac` and `scala` commands.

# 14.6. Disassembling and Decompiling Scala Code

## Problem

In the process of learning Scala, or trying to understand a particular problem, you want to examine the bytecode the Scala compiler generates from your source code.

## Solution

You can use several different approaches to see how your Scala source code is translated:

- Use the `javap` command to disassemble a *.class* file to look at its signature.
- Use `scalac` options to see how the compiler converts your Scala source code to Java code.
- Use a decompiler to convert your class files back to Java source code.

All three solutions are shown here.

### Using javap

Because your Scala source code files are compiled into regular Java class files, you can use the `javap` command to disassemble them. For example, assume that you've created a file named *Person.scala* that contains the following source code:

```
class Person (var name: String, var age: Int)
```

If you compile that file with `scalac`, you can disassemble the resulting class file into its signature using `javap`, like this:

```
$ javap Person
Compiled from "Person.scala"
public class Person extends java.lang.Object implements scala.ScalaObject{
    public java.lang.String name();
    public void name_$eq(java.lang.String);
    public int age();
    public void age_$eq(int);
    public Person(java.lang.String, int);
}
```

This shows the signature of the `Person` class, which is basically its public API, or interface. Even in a simple example like this you can see the Scala compiler doing its work for you, creating methods like `name()`, `name_$eq`, `age()`, and `age_$eq`.

### Using scalac print options

Depending on your needs, another approach is to use the "print" options available with the `scalac` command. These are demonstrated in detail in Recipe 3.1, "Looping with for and foreach".

As that recipe shows, you begin with a file named *Main.scala* that has these contents:

```
class Main {
    for (i <- 1 to 10) println(i)
}
```

Next, compile this code with the `scalac -Xprint:parse` command:

```
$ scalac -Xprint:parse Main.scala

[[syntax trees at end of parser]] // Main.scala
package <empty> {
    class Main extends scala.AnyRef {
        def <init>() = {
```

```
      super.<init>();
      ()
    };
    1.to(10).foreach(((i) => println(i)))
  }
}
```

Recipe 3.1 demonstrates that the initial Scala for loop is translated into a foreach method call, as shown by this line in the compiler output:

```
1.to(10).foreach(((i) => println(i)))
```

If you want to see more details, use the -Xprint:all option instead of -Xprint:parse. For this simple class, this command yields more than 200 lines of output. A portion of the code at the end of the output looks like this:

```
class Main extends Object {
  def <init>(): Main = {
    Main.super.<init>();
    RichInt.this.to$extension0(scala.this.Predef.intWrapper(1),
    10).foreach$mVc$sp({
      (new anonymous class anonfun$1(Main.this): Function1)
    });
    ()
  }
};
```

As you can see, your beautiful Scala code gets translated into something quite different, and this is only part of the output.

Whereas scalac -Xprint:all prints a *lot* of output, the basic scalac -print command only prints the output shown at the very end of the -Xprint:all output. The scalac manpage states that this print option, "Prints program with all Scala-specific features removed." View the manpage for the scalac command to see other -Xprint options that are available.

### Use a decompiler

Depending on class versions and legal restrictions, you may be able to take this approach a step further and decompile a class file back to its Java source code representation using a Java decompiler tool, such as *JAD*. Continuing from the previous example, you can decompile the *Main.class* file like this:

```
$ jad Main

Parsing Main...Parsing inner class Main$$anonfun$1.class...
Generating Main.jad
```

The *Main.jad* file that results from this process contains the following Java source code:

```
import scala.*;
import scala.collection.immutable.Range;
import scala.runtime.*;
```

```
public class Main
{

  public Main()
  {
    RichInt$.MODULE$.to$extension0(Predef$.MODULE$.intWrapper(1),
      10).foreach$mVc$sp(new Serializable() {

      public final void apply(int i)
      {
        apply$mcVI$sp(i);
      }

      public void apply$mcVI$sp(int v1)
      {
        Predef$.MODULE$.println(BoxesRunTime.boxToInteger(v1));
      }

      public final volatile Object apply(Object v1)
      {
        apply(BoxesRunTime.unboxToInt(v1));
        return BoxedUnit.UNIT;
      }

      public static final long serialVersionUID = 0L;

    });
  }
}
```

Though you may have to be careful with legal issues when using a decompiler, when you're first learning Scala, a tool like JAD (*http://bit.ly/10Yl4IC*) or the Java Decompiler Project (*http://java.decompiler.free.fr/*) can really help to see how your Scala source code is converted into Java source code. Additionally, both Eclipse and IntelliJ offer decompiler plug-ins that are based on JAD or the Java Decompiler Project.

## Discussion

Disassembling class files with `javap` can be a helpful way to understand how Scala works. As you saw in the first example with the `Person` class, defining the constructor parameters `name` and `age` as `var` fields generates quite a few methods for you.

As a second example, take the `var` attribute off both of those fields, so you have this class definition:

```
class Person (name: String, age: Int)
```

Compile this class with `scalac`, and then run `javap` on the resulting class file. You'll see that this results in a much shorter class signature:

```
$ javap Person
Compiled from "Person.scala"public class Person extends java.lang.Object↵
implements scala.ScalaObject{
    public Person(java.lang.String, int);
}
```

Conversely, leaving var on both fields and turning the class into a case class significantly
expands the amount of code Scala generates on your behalf. To see this, change the code
in *Person.scala* so you have this case class:

```
case class Person (var name: String, var age: Int)
```

When you compile this code, it creates two output files, *Person.class* and *Person$.class*.
Disassemble these two files using javap:

```
$ javap Person
Compiled from "Person.scala"
public class Person extends java.lang.Object implements scala.ScalaObject,scala.↵
Product,scala.Serializable{
    public static final scala.Function1 tupled();
    public static final scala.Function1 curry();
    public static final scala.Function1 curried();
    public scala.collection.Iterator productIterator();
    public scala.collection.Iterator productElements();
    public java.lang.String name();
    public void name_$eq(java.lang.String);
    public int age();
    public void age_$eq(int);
    public Person copy(java.lang.String, int);
    public int copy$default$2();
    public java.lang.String copy$default$1();
    public int hashCode();
    public java.lang.String toString();
    public boolean equals(java.lang.Object);
    public java.lang.String productPrefix();
    public int productArity();
    public java.lang.Object productElement(int);
    public boolean canEqual(java.lang.Object);
    public Person(java.lang.String, int);
}

$ javap Person$
Compiled from "Person.scala"
public final class Person$ extends scala.runtime.AbstractFunction2 implements ↵
scala.ScalaObject,scala.Serializable{
    public static final Person$ MODULE$;
    public static {};
    public final java.lang.String toString();
    public scala.Option unapply(Person);
    public Person apply(java.lang.String, int);
    public java.lang.Object readResolve();
    public java.lang.Object apply(java.lang.Object, java.lang.Object);
}
```

As shown, when you define a class as a *case class*, Scala generates a *lot* of code for you. This output shows the signature for that code. See Recipe 4.14, "Generating Boilerplate Code with Case Classes" for a detailed discussion of this code.

## See Also

- Information on the JAD decompiler (*http://bit.ly/10Yl4IC*)
- The Java Decompiler project (*http://java.decompiler.free.fr/*)

# 14.7. Finding Scala Libraries

## Problem

Ruby has the RubyGems package manager, which lets developers easily distribute and manage the installation of Ruby libraries; does Scala have anything like this?

## Solution

Prior to Scala 2.9.2, a tool named `sbaz` shipped with Scala, but it wasn't very popular. Instead, most tools are "discovered" by paying attention to the mailing lists, using a search engine, and being aware of a few key websites.

As discussed in Chapter 18, once you've found a tool you want to use, you usually add it as a dependency to your project with SBT. For instance, to include libraries into your project, such as ScalaTest and Mockito, just add lines like this to your SBT *build.sbt* file:

```
resolvers += "Typesafe Repository" at↵
    "http://repo.typesafe.com/typesafe/releases/"

libraryDependencies ++= Seq(
  "org.scalatest" %% "scalatest" % "1.8" % "test",
  "org.mockito" % "mockito-core" % "1.9.0" % "test"
)
```

SBT has become the de facto tool for building Scala applications and managing dependencies. Possibly because of this success, a system like RubyGems hasn't evolved, or been necessary.

Some of the top ways of finding Scala libraries are:

- Searching for libraries using a search engine, or ls.implicit.ly (*http://ls.implicit.ly/*).
- Asking questions and searching the *scala-tools@googlegroups.com* and *scala-language@googlegroups.com* mailing lists.
- New software is also announced at the "scala-announce" mailing list; you can find a list of Scala mailing lists online (*http://www.scala-lang.org/node/199*).
- Viewing tools listed at the Scala wiki (*http://bit.ly/1aLUmJM*).
- Scala project updates are often noted at *http://notes.implicit.ly/*, the archive is at *http://notes.implicit.ly/archive*, and you can search for tools at *http://ls.implicit.ly/*.
- Asking questions on StackOverflow.com (*http://stackoverflow.com*).

The search engine at ls.implicit.ly (*http://ls.implicit.ly/*) is interesting. The owners advertise the site as "A card catalog for Scala libraries." As they state on their website, they make two assumptions regarding their search process:

- The library you're looking for is an open source library that's hosted at GitHub.
- You build your projects with SBT (*http://www.scala-sbt.org/*).

For instance, if you search for "logging," the website currently shows tools like the "Grizzled-SLF4J" library.

# 14.8. Generating Documentation with scaladoc

## Problem

You've annotated your Scala code with Scaladoc, and you want to generate developer documentation for your API.

## Solution

To generate Scaladoc API documentation, document your code using Scaladoc tags, and then create the documentation using an SBT task or the `scaladoc` command.

You can mark up your source code using Scaladoc tags (*http://bit.ly/13qCk5U*) as well as a wiki-like syntax (*http://bit.ly/18j2ugh*). The following code shows many of the Scaladoc tags and a few of the wiki-style markup tags:

```scala
package com.acme.foo

/**
 * A class to represent a ''human being''.
 *
 * Specify the `name`, `age`, and `weight` when creating a new `Person`,
 * then access the fields like this:
 * {{{
 * val p = Person("Al", 42, 200.0)
 * p.name
 * p.age
 * p.weight
 * }}}
 *
 * Did you know: The [[com.acme.foo.Employee]] extends this class.
 *
 * @constructor Create a new person with a `name`, `age`, and `weight`.
 * @param name The person's name.
 * @param age The person's age.
 * @param weight The person's weight.
 * @author Alvin Alexander
 * @version 1.0
 * @todo Add more functionality.
 * @see See [[http://alvinalexander.com alvinalexander.com]] for more
 * information.
 */
@deprecated("The `weight` field is going away", "1.0")
class Person (var name: String, var age: Int, var weight: Double) {

  /**
   * @constructor This is an auxiliary constructor. Just need a `name` here.
   */
  def this(name: String) {
    this(name, 0, 0.0)
  }

  /**
   * @return Returns a greeting based on the `name` field.
   */
  def greet = s"Hello, my name is $name"

}
```

```
/**
 * @constructor Create a new `Employee` by specifying their `name`, `age`,
 * and `role`.
 * @param name The employee's name.
 * @param age The employee's age.
 * @param role The employee's role in the organization.
 * @example val e = Employee("Al", 42, "Developer")
 */
class Employee(name: String, age: Int, role: String) extends Person(name, age, 0)
{

    /**
     * @throws boom Throws an Exception 100% of the time, be careful.
     */
    @throws(classOf[Exception])
    def boom { throw new Exception("boom") }

    /**
     * @return Returns a greeting based on the `other` and `name` fields.
     * @param other The name of the person we're greeting.
     */
    override def greet(other: String) = s"Hello $other, my name is $name"

}
```

With this code saved to a file named *Person.scala*, generate the Scaladoc documentation with the `scaladoc` command:

```
$ scaladoc Person.scala
```

This generates a root *index.html* file and other related files for your API documentation.

Similarly, if you're using SBT, generate Scaladoc API documentation by running the `sbt doc` command in the root directory of your project:

```
$ sbt doc
```

This generates the same API documentation, and places it under the *target* directory of your SBT project. With Scala 2.10 and SBT 0.12.3, the root file is located at *target/scala-2.10/api/index.html*.

Figure 14-3 shows the resulting Scaladoc for the Person class, and Figure 14-4 shows the Scaladoc for the Employee class. Notice how the Scaladoc and wiki tags affect the documentation.

**com.acme.foo**

# Person

class **Person** extends AnyRef

A class to represent a *human being*.

Specify the name, age, and weight when creating a new Person, then access the fields like this:

```
val p = Person("Al", 42, 200.0)
p.name
p.age
p.weight
```

Did you know: The com.acme.foo.Employee extends this class.

| | |
|---|---|
| Annotations | @deprecated |
| Deprecated | (Since version 1.0) The weight field is going away |
| Version | 1.0 |
| To do | Add more functionality. |
| See also | See alvinalexander.com for more information. |

▸ Linear Supertypes

▸ Known Subclasses

---

🔍 ❌

| | | | |
|---|---|---|---|
| **Ordering** | Alphabetic | By inheritance | |
| **Inherited** | Person | AnyRef | Any |
| | Hide All | Show all | Learn more about member selection |
| **Visibility** | Public | All | |

## Instance Constructors

new **Person**(name: String)

▾ new **Person**(name: String, age: Int, weight: Double)

Create a new person with a name, age, and weight.

| | |
|---|---|
| **name** | The person's name. |
| **age** | The person's age. |
| **weight** | The person's weight. |

## Value Members

var **age**: Int

The person's age.

▾ def **greet**: String

| | |
|---|---|
| **returns** | Returns a greeting based on the name field. |

var **name**: String

The person's name.

var **weight**: Double

The person's weight.

*Figure 14-3. The Scaladoc for the Person class*

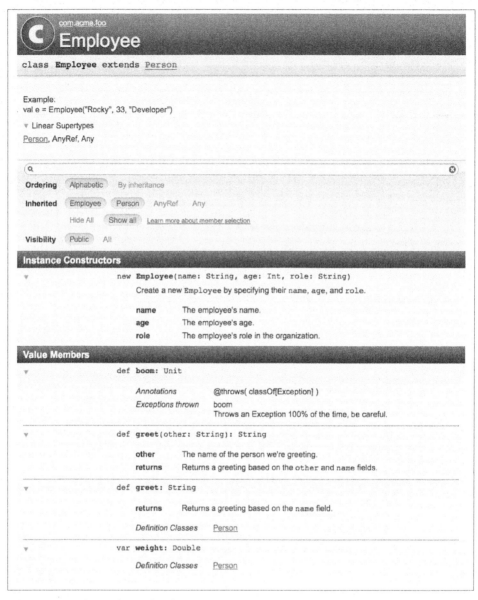

*Figure 14-4. The Scaladoc for the Employee class*

## Discussion

Most Scaladoc tags are similar to Javadoc tags. Common Scaladoc tags are shown in Table 14-1.

---

*Table 14-1. Common Scaladoc tags*

| Tag | Description | Number allowed |
|---|---|---|
| @author | The author of the class. | Multiple tags are allowed |
| @constructor | Documentation you want to provide for the constructor. | One (does not currently work on auxiliary constructors) |
| @example | Provide an example of how to use a method or constructor. | Multiple |
| @note | Document pre- and post-conditions, and other requirements. | Multiple |
| @param | Document a method or constructor parameter. | One per parameter |
| @return | Document the return value of a method. | One |
| @see | Describe other sources of related information. | Multiple |
| @since | Used to indicate that a member has been available since a certain version release. | One |
| @todo | Document "to do" items for a method or class. | Multiple |
| @throws | Document an exception type that can be thrown by a method or constructor. | Multiple |
| @version | The version of a class. | One |

These are just some of the common tags. Other tags include @define, @migration, @tparam, and @usecase. Other Scala annotation tags like @deprecated and @throws also result in output to your documentation.

As shown in the source code, you can format your documentation using wiki-like tags. Table 14-2 shows the most common wiki *character* formatting tags, and Table 14-3 shows the most common wiki *paragraph* formatting tags.

*Table 14-2. Scaladoc wiki character formatting tags*

| Format | Tag example |
|---|---|
| Bold | `'''foo'''` |
| Italic | `''foo''` |
| Monospace (fixed-width) | `` `foo` `` |
| Subscript | `,,foo,,` |
| Superscript | `^foo^` |
| Underline | `__foo__` |

*Table 14-3. Scaladoc wiki paragraph formatting tags*

| Format | Tag example |
|---|---|
| Headings | `=heading1=`<br>`==heading2==`<br>`===heading3===` |
| New paragraph | A blank line starts a new paragraph |

| Format | Tag example |
|---|---|
| Source code block | `// all on one line`<br>`{{{ if (foo) bar else    baz }}}`<br><br>`// multiple lines`<br>`{{{`<br>`val p =    Person("Al", 42)`<br>`p.name`<br>`p.age`<br>`}}}` |

Table 14-4 shows how to create hyperlinks in Scaladoc.

*Table 14-4. Scaladoc hyperlink tags*

| Link type | Tag example |
|---|---|
| Link to a Scala type | `[[scala.collection.immutable.List]]` |
| Link to an external web page | `[[http://alvinalexander.com My website]]` |

The Scaladoc tags and annotations are described in more detail in the Scala wiki (*http://bit.ly/13qCk5U*), as well as the Wiki markup tags (*http://bit.ly/18j2ugh*).

### Generating Scaladoc documentation with SBT

SBT has several commands that can be used to generate project documentation. See Recipe 18.8, "Generating Project API Documentation" for a tabular listing of those commands.

## See Also

- Recipe 5.8, "Declaring That a Method Can Throw an Exception" and Recipe 17.2, "Add Exception Annotations to Scala Methods to Work with Java" for demonstrations of the `@throws` annotation
- Scaladoc wiki-like syntax (*http://bit.ly/18j2ugh*)
- Scaladoc tags (*http://bit.ly/13qCk5U*)
- The Scaladoc page in the Scala Style Guide (*http://docs.scala-lang.org/style/scaladoc.html*)
- Recipe 18.8, "Generating Project API Documentation" for details on generating Scaladoc documentation with SBT

# 14.9. Faster Command-Line Compiling with fsc

## Problem

You're making changes to a project and recompiling it with `scalac`, and you'd like to reduce the compile time.

## Solution

Use the `fsc` command instead of `scalac` to compile your code:

```
$ fsc *.scala
```

The `fsc` command works by starting a compilation daemon and also maintains a cache, so compilation attempts after the first attempt run much faster than `scalac`.

## Discussion

Although the primary advantage is that compile times are significantly improved when recompiling the same code, it's important to be aware of a few caveats, per the `fsc` manpage:

- "The tool is especially effective when repeatedly compiling with the same class paths, because the compilation daemon can reuse a compiler instance."
- "The compilation daemon is smart enough to flush its cached compiler when the class path changes. However, if the contents of the class path change, for example due to upgrading a library, then the daemon should be explicitly shut down with `-shutdown`."

As an example of the second caveat, if the JAR files on the classpath have changed, you should shut down the daemon, and then reissue your `fsc` command:

```
$ fsc -shutdown
[Compile server exited]
```

```
$ fsc *.scala
```

On Unix systems, running `fsc` creates a background process with the name `CompileServer`. You can see information about this process with the following `ps` command:

```
$ ps auxw | grep CompileServer
```

See the `fsc` manpage for more information.

## See Also

- The `fsc` manpage (type `man fsc` at the command line).
- When using SBT, you can achieve similar performance improvements by working in the SBT shell instead of your operating system's command line. See Recipe 18.2, "Compiling, Running, and Packaging a Scala Project with SBT" for more information.

# 14.10. Using Scala as a Scripting Language

## Problem

You want to use Scala as a scripting language on Unix systems, replacing other scripts you've written in a Unix shell (Bourne Shell, Bash), Perl, PHP, Ruby, etc.

## Solution

Save your Scala code to a text file, making sure the first three lines of the script contain the lines shown, which will execute the script using the `scala` interpreter:

```
#!/bin/sh
exec scala "$0" "$@"
!#

println("Hello, world")
```

To test this, save the code to a file named *hello.sh*, make it executable, and then run it:

```
$ chmod +x hello.sh

$ ./hello.sh
Hello, world
```

As detailed in the next recipe, command-line parameters to the script can be accessed via an `args` array, which is implicitly made available to you:

```
#!/bin/sh
exec scala "$0" "$@"
!#

args.foreach(println)
```

## Discussion

Regarding the first three lines of a shell script:

---

- The #! in the first line is the usual way to start a Unix shell script. It invokes a Unix Bourne shell.

- The exec command is a shell built-in. $0 expands to the name of the shell script, and $@ expands to the positional parameters.

- The !# characters as the third line of the script is how the header section is closed.

A great thing about using Scala in your scripts is that you can use all of its advanced features, such as the ability to create and use classes in your scripts:

```
#!/bin/sh
exec scala "$0" "$@"
!#

class Person(var firstName: String, var lastName: String) {
  override def toString = firstName + " " + lastName
}

println(new Person("Nacho", "Libre"))
```

### Using the App trait or main method

To use an App trait in a Scala script, start the script with the usual first three header lines, and then create an object that extends the App trait:

```
#!/bin/sh
exec scala "$0" "$@"
!#

object Hello extends App {
  println("Hello, world")
  // if you want to access the command line args:
  //args.foreach(println)
}

Hello.main(args)
```

The last line in that example shows how to pass the script's command-line arguments to the implicit main method in the Hello object. As usual in an App trait object, the arguments are available via a variable named args.

You can also define an object with a main method to kick off your shell script action:

```
#!/bin/sh
exec scala "$0" "$@"
!#

object Hello {
  def main(args: Array[String]) {
    println("Hello, world")
    // if you want to access the command line args:
    //args.foreach(println)
```

```
    }
}

Hello.main(args)
```

## Building the classpath

If your shell script needs to rely on external dependencies (such as JAR files), add them to your script's classpath using this syntax:

```
#!/bin/sh
exec scala -classpath "lib/htmlcleaner-2.2.jar:lib/scalaemail_2.10.0-↵
1.0.jar:lib/stockutils_2.10.0-1.0.jar" "$0" "$@"
!#
```

You can then import these classes into your code as usual. The following code shows a complete script I wrote that retrieves stock quotes and mails them to me:

```
#!/bin/sh
exec scala -classpath "lib/htmlcleaner-2.2.jar:lib/scalaemail_2.10.0-↵
1.0.jar:lib/stockutils_2.10.0-1.0.jar" "$0" "$@"
!#

import java.io._
import scala.io.Source
import com.devdaily.stocks.StockUtils
import scala.collection.mutable.ArrayBuffer

object GetStocks {

  case class Stock(symbol: String, name: String, price: BigDecimal)

  val DIR = System.getProperty("user.dir")
  val SLASH = System.getProperty("file.separator")
  val CANON_STOCKS_FILE = DIR + SLASH + "stocks.dat"
  val CANON_OUTPUT_FILE = DIR + SLASH + "quotes.out"

  def main(args: Array[String]) {

    // read the stocks file into a list of strings ("AAPL|Apple")
    val lines = Source.fromFile(CANON_STOCKS_FILE).getLines.toList

    // create a list of Stock from the symbol, name, and by
    // retrieving the price
    var stocks = new ArrayBuffer[Stock]()
    lines.foreach{ line =>
      val fields = line.split("\\|")
      val symbol = fields(0)
      val html = StockUtils.getHtmlFromUrl(symbol)
      val price = StockUtils.extractPriceFromHtml(html, symbol)
      val stock = Stock(symbol, fields(1), BigDecimal(price))
      stocks += stock
    }
```

```
    // build a string to output
    var sb = new StringBuilder
    stocks.foreach { stock =>
      sb.append("%s is %s\n".format(stock.name, stock.price))
    }
    val output = sb.toString

    // write the string to the file
    val pw = new PrintWriter(new File(CANON_OUTPUT_FILE))
    pw.write(output)
    pw.close

  }
}

GetStocks.main(args)
```

I run this script twice a day through a crontab entry on a Linux server. The *stocks.dat* file it reads has entries like this:

```
AAPL|Apple
KKD|Krispy Kreme
NFLX|Netflix
```

## See Also

- More about the first three lines of these shell script examples at my site (*http://bit.ly/1bkJW2V*)

- Recipe 14.13, "Make Your Scala Scripts Run Faster" for a way to make your scripts run faster

# 14.11. Accessing Command-Line Arguments from a Script

## Problem

You want to access the command-line arguments from your Scala shell script.

## Solution

Use the same script syntax as shown in Recipe 14.8, "Generating Documentation with scaladoc", and then access the command-line arguments using args, which is a List[String] that is implicitly made available:

```
#!/bin/sh
exec scala "$0" "$@"
!#
```

```
args.foreach(println)
```

Save this code to a file named *args.sh*, make the file executable, and run it like this:

```
$ ./args.sh a b c
a
b
c
```

## Discussion

Because the implicit field `args` is a `List[String]`, you can perform all the usual operations on it, including getting its size, and accessing elements with the usual syntax.

In a more "real-world" example, you'll check for the number of command-line arguments, and then assign those arguments to values. This is demonstrated in the following script:

```
#!/bin/sh
exec scala "$0" "$@"
!#

if (args.length != 2) {
  Console.err.println("Usage: replacer <search> <replace>")
  System.exit(1)
}

val searchPattern = args(0)
val replacePattern = args(1)

println(s"Replacing $searchPattern with $replacePattern ...")

// more code here ...
```

When this script is run from the command line without arguments, the result looks like this:

```
$ ./args.sh
Usage: replacer <search> <replace>
```

When it's run with the correct number of arguments, the result looks like this:

```
$ ./args.sh foo bar
Replacing foo with bar ...
```

If you decide to use the `App` trait in your script, make sure you pass the command-line arguments to your `App` object, as shown in the `Hello.main(args)` line in this example:

```
#!/bin/sh
exec scala "$0" "$@"
!#
```

```
object Hello extends App {
  println("Hello, world")
  // if you want to access the command line args:
  //args.foreach(println)
}

Hello.main(args)
```

Use the same syntax if you use a main method instead of an App object.

# 14.12. Prompting for Input from a Scala Shell Script

## Problem

You want to prompt a user for input from a Scala shell script and read her responses.

## Solution

Use the readLine, print, printf, and Console.read* methods to read user input, as demonstrated in the following script. Comments in the script describe each method:

```
#!/bin/sh
exec scala "$0" "$@"
!#

// write some text out to the user with Console.println
Console.println("Hello")

// Console is imported by default, so it's not really needed, just use println
println("World")

// readLine lets you prompt the user and read their input as a String
val name = readLine("What's your name? ")

// readInt lets you read an Int, but you have to prompt the user manually
print("How old are you? ")
val age = readInt()

// you can also print output with printf
println(s"Your name is $name and you are $age years old.")
```

## Discussion

The readLine method lets you prompt a user for input, but the other read* methods don't, so you need to prompt the user manually with print, println, or printf.

You can list the Console.read* methods in the Scala REPL:

```
scala> Console.read
readBoolean   readByte   readChar   readDouble   readFloat
```

```
readInt          readLine    readLong    readShort    readf
readf1           readf2      readf3
```

Be careful with the methods that read numeric values; as you might expect, they can all throw a NumberFormatException.

Although these methods are thorough, if you prefer, you can also fall back and read input with the Java Scanner class:

```
// you can also use the Java Scanner class, if desired
val scanner = new java.util.Scanner(System.in)
print("Where do you live? ")
val input = scanner.nextLine()
print(s"I see that you live in $input")
```

### Reading multiple values from one line

If you want to read multiple values from one line of user input (such as a person's name, age, and weight), there are several approaches to the problem.

To my surprise, I prefer to use the Java Scanner class. The following code demonstrates the Scanner approach:

```
import java.util.Scanner

// simulated input
val input = "Joe 33 200.0"

val line = new Scanner(input)
val name = line.next
val age = line.nextInt
val weight = line.nextDouble
```

To use this approach in a shell script, replace the input line with a readLine() call, like this:

```
val input = readLine()
```

Of course if the input doesn't match what you expect, an error should be thrown. The Scanner next* methods throw a java.util.InputMismatchException when the data doesn't match what you expect, so you'll want to wrap this code in a try/catch block.

I initially assumed that one of the readf methods on the Console object would be the best solution to this problem, but unfortunately they return their types as Any, and then you have to cast them to the desired type. For instance, suppose you want to read the same name, age, and weight information as the previous example. After prompting the user, you read three values with the readf3 method like this:

```
val(a,b,c) = readf3("{0} {1,number} {2,number}")
```

If the user enters a string followed by two numbers, a result is returned, but if he enters an improperly formatted string, such as 1 a b, the expression fails with a ParseException:

```
java.text.ParseException: MessageFormat parse error!
  at java.text.MessageFormat.parse(MessageFormat.java:1010)
  at scala.Console$.readf(Console.scala:413)
  at scala.Console$.readf3(Console.scala:445)
```

Unfortunately, even if the user enters the text as desired, you still need to cast the values to the correct type, because the variables a, b, and c are of type Any. You can try to cast them with this approach:

```
val name = a
val age = b.asInstanceOf[Long]
val weight = c.asInstanceOf[Double]
```

Or convert them like this:

```
val name = a.toString
val age = b.toString.toInt
val weight = c.toString.toDouble
```

But for me, the Scanner is cleaner and easier.

A third approach is to read the values in as a String, and then split them into tokens. Here's what this looks like in the REPL:

```
scala> val input = "Michael 54 250.0"
input: String = Michael 54 250.0

scala> val tokens = input.split(" ")
tokens: Array[String] = Array(Michael, 54, 250.0)
```

The split method creates an Array[String], so access the array elements and cast them to the desired types to create your variables:

```
val name = tokens(0)
val age = tokens(1).toInt
val weight = tokens(2).toDouble
```

Note that the age and weight fields in this example can throw a NumberFormatException.

A fourth way to read the user's input is by specifying a regular expression to match the input you expect to receive. Using this technique, you again receive each variable as a String, and then cast it to the desired type. The process looks like this in the REPL:

```
scala> val ExpectedPattern = "(.*) (\\d+) (\\d*\\.?\\d*)".r
ExpectedPattern: scala.util.matching.Regex = (.*) (\d+) (\d*\.?\d*)

// you would use readLine() here
scala> val input = "Paul 36 180.0"
input: String = Paul 36 180.0

scala> val ExpectedPattern(a, b, c) = input
a: String = Paul
```

```
b: String = 36
c: String = 180.0
```

Now that you have the variables as strings, cast them to the desired types, as before:

```
val name = a
val age = b.toInt
val weight = c.toDouble
```

The ExpectedPattern line in this example will fail with a scala.MatchError if the input doesn't match what's expected.

Hopefully with all of these examples you'll find your own preferred way to read in multiple values at one time.

### Fun with output

Use print, printf, or println to write output. As shown in the Solution, the readLine method also lets you prompt a user for input.

The Console object contains a number of fields that you can use with the print methods to control the display. For instance, if you want your entire line of output to be underlined, change the last lines of the script to look like this:

```
val qty = 2
val pizzaType = "Cheese"
val total = 20.10

print(Console.UNDERLINED)
println(f"$qty%d $pizzaType pizzas coming up, $$$total%.2f.")
print(Console.RESET)
```

This prints the following string, underlined:

```
2 Cheese pizzas coming up, $20.10.
```

Other displayable attributes include colors and attributes such as BLINK, BOLD, INVISIBLE, RESET, REVERSED, and UNDERLINED. See the Console object Scaladoc page for more options.

## See Also

- Recipe 1.8, "Extracting Parts of a String That Match Patterns" for more examples of the pattern-matching technique shown in this recipe.
- The Java Scanner class (*http://bit.ly/14WoFaM*)
- The Java Pattern class (*http://bit.ly/17iBhJG*)
- The Scala Console object (*http://bit.ly/1aLWLEh*) provides the read* methods

# 14.13. Make Your Scala Scripts Run Faster

## Problem

You love using Scala as a scripting language, but you'd like to eliminate the lag time in starting up a script.

## Solution

Use the `-savecompiled` argument of the Scala interpreter to save a compiled version of your script.

A basic Scala script like this:

```
#!/bin/sh
exec scala "$0" "$@"
!#

println("Hello, world!")
args foreach println
```

consistently runs with times like this on one of my computers:

```
real    0m1.573s
user    0m0.574s
sys     0m0.089s
```

To improve this, add the `-savecompiled` argument to the Scala interpreter line:

```
#!/bin/sh
exec scala -savecompiled "$0" "$@"
!#

println("Hello, world!")
args foreach println
```

Then run the script once. This generates a compiled version of the script. After that, the script runs with a consistently lower real time (wall clock) on all subsequent runs:

```
real    0m0.458s
user    0m0.487s
sys     0m0.075s
```

Precompiling your script shaves a nice chunk of time off the runtime of your script, even for a simple example like this.

## Discussion

When you run your script the first time, Scala generates a JAR file that matches the name of your script. For instance, I named my script *test1.sh*, and then ran it like this:

```
$ ./test1.sh
```

After running the script, I looked at the directory contents and saw that Scala created a file named *test1.sh.jar*. Scala creates this new file and also leaves your original script in place.

On subsequent runs, Scala sees that there's a JAR file associated with the script, and if the script hasn't been modified since the JAR file was created, it runs the precompiled code from the JAR file instead of the source code in the script. This results in a faster runtime because the source code doesn't need to be compiled.

You can look at the contents of the JAR file using the `jar` command:

```
$ jar tvf test1.sh.jar
 43 Wed Jul 25 15:44:26 MDT 2012 META-INF/MANIFEST.MF
965 Wed Jul 25 15:44:26 MDT 2012 Main$$anon$1$$anonfun$1.class
725 Wed Jul 25 15:44:26 MDT 2012 Main$$anon$1.class
557 Wed Jul 25 15:44:26 MDT 2012 Main$.class
646 Wed Jul 25 15:44:26 MDT 2012 Main.class
```

In this example, I didn't include a `main` method in an object or use the `App` trait with an object, so Scala assumed the name `Main` for the main/primary object that it created to run my script.

# CHAPTER 15

# Web Services

## Introduction

Between the Java web services libraries and the newer Scala libraries and frameworks that are available, Scala easily handles web service tasks. You can rapidly create web service clients to send and receive data using these general libraries, or solve problems with more specific libraries, such as creating a Twitter client with the Twitter4J library. There are also several good JSON libraries available, so you can easily convert between data JSON strings and Scala objects.

When it comes to creating your own RESTful web services, you can use lightweight frameworks like Scalatra (*http://scalatra.org/*) or Unfiltered (*http://unfiltered.databind er.net/Unfiltered.html*) and have web services up and running in a matter of minutes. But you have many choices, so you can also use the Play Framework (Play) (*http://www.playframework.com/*), Lift Framework (*http://liftweb.net/*), or other Scala libraries to create web services, as well as all of the previously available Java web service libraries.

As demonstrated in Chapter 16, Scala has nice support for the MongoDB (*http://www.mongodb.org/*) database, and this chapter demonstrates how to provide a complete web services solution using Scalatra and MongoDB. This chapter shares a few recipes that are specific to using Play to create web services.

Finally, although the Scala libraries offer some nice convenience classes and methods for connecting to web services, the trusty old Java Apache HttpClient library (*http://hc.apache.org/httpclient-3.x/*) is still very useful, and it's also demonstrated in several recipes.

# 15.1. Creating a JSON String from a Scala Object

## Problem

You're working outside of a specific framework, and want to create a JSON string from a Scala object.

## Solution

If you're using the Play Framework, you can use its library to work with JSON, as shown in Recipes 15.13 and 15.14, but if you're using JSON outside of Play, you can use the best libraries that are available for Scala and Java:

- Lift-JSON (*https://github.com/lift/framework/tree/master/core/json*)
- The Google Gson library (*https://code.google.com/p/google-gson/*) (Java)
- Json4s (*https://github.com/json4s/json4s*)
- spray-json (*https://github.com/spray/spray-json*)

This recipe demonstrates the Lift-JSON and Gson libraries. (Json4s is a port of Lift-JSON, so it shares the same API.)

### Lift-JSON solution

To demonstrate the Lift-JSON library, create an empty SBT test project. With Scala 2.10 and SBT 0.12.x, configure your *build.sbt* file as follows:

```
name := "Basic Lift-JSON Demo"

version := "1.0"

scalaVersion := "2.10.0"

libraryDependencies += "net.liftweb" %% "lift-json" % "2.5+"
```

Next, in the root directory of your project, create a file named *LiftJsonTest.scala*:

```
import scala.collection.mutable._
import net.liftweb.json._
import net.liftweb.json.Serialization.write

case class Person(name: String, address: Address)
case class Address(city: String, state: String)

object LiftJsonTest extends App {

  val p = Person("Alvin Alexander", Address("Talkeetna", "AK"))

  // create a JSON string from the Person, then print it
  implicit val formats = DefaultFormats
```

```
val jsonString = write(p)
println(jsonString)

}
```

This code creates a JSON string from the Person instance, and prints it. When you run the project with the sbt run command, you'll see the following JSON output:

```
{"name":"Alvin Alexander","address":{"city":"Talkeetna","state":"AK"}}
```

### Gson solution

To demonstrate the Gson library, follow similar steps. Create an empty SBT test project, then download the Gson JAR file from the Gson website (*http://code.google.com/p/google-gson/*), and place it in your project's *lib* directory.

In the root directory of the project, create a file named *GsonTest.scala* with these contents:

```
import com.google.gson.Gson

case class Person(name: String, address: Address)
case class Address(city: String, state: String)

object GsonTest extends App {
  val p = Person("Alvin Alexander", Address("Talkeetna", "AK"))

  // create a JSON string from the Person, then print it
  val gson = new Gson
  val jsonString = gson.toJson(p)
  println(jsonString)
}
```

In a manner similar to the first example, this code converts a Person instance to a JSON string and prints the string. When you run the project with sbt run, you'll see the same output as before:

```
{"name":"Alvin Alexander","address":{"city":"Talkeetna","state":"AK"}}
```

## Discussion

The Lift-JSON project is a subproject of the Lift Framework (*http://liftweb.net/*), which is a complete Scala web framework. Fortunately the library has been created as a separate module you can download and use on its own.

In addition to working with simple classes, it works well with Scala collections. The following example shows how to generate JSON strings from a simple Scala Map:

```
import net.liftweb.json.JsonAST
import net.liftweb.json.JsonDSL._
import net.liftweb.json.Printer.{compact,pretty}
```

```
object LiftJsonWithCollections extends App {

  val json = List(1, 2, 3)
  println(compact(JsonAST.render(json)))

  val map = Map("fname" -> "Alvin", "lname" -> "Alexander")
  println(compact(JsonAST.render(map)))

}
```

That program prints the following output:

```
[1,2,3]
{"fname":"Alvin","lname":"Alexander"}
```

When communicating with other computer systems you'll want to use the `compact` method as shown, but when a human needs to look at your JSON strings, use the `pretty` method instead:

```
println(pretty(JsonAST.render(map)))
```

This changes the `map` output to look like this:

```
{
  "fname":"Alvin",
  "lname":"Alexander"
}
```

The Lift-JSON examples in this recipe work well for either objects or collections, but when you have an object that *contains* collections, such as a `Person` class that has a list of friends defined as `List[Person]`, it's best to use the Lift-JSON DSL. This is demonstrated in Recipe 15.2.

Gson (*http://code.google.com/p/google-gson/*) is a Java library that you can use to convert back and forth between Scala objects and their JSON representation. From the Gson documentation:

> There are a few open-source projects that can convert Java objects to JSON. However, most of them require that you place Java annotations in your classes; something that you can not do if you do not have access to the source-code. Most also do not fully support the use of Java Generics. Gson considers both of these as very important design goals.

I used Gson to generate JSON for a while, but because it's written in Java, it has a few issues when trying to work with Scala collections. One such problem is demonstrated in Recipe 15.2.

## See Also

- The Lift-JSON library (*https://github.com/lift/framework/tree/master/core/json*)
- The Gson library (*http://code.google.com/p/google-gson/*)

- A project named Json4s (*http://json4s.org/*) aims to provide a unified interface for all Scala JSON projects. The current package is a port of Lift-JSON, with support for using the Java Jackson library as a backend as well.

- spray-json (*https://github.com/spray/spray-json*) is another popular Scala JSON library.

# 15.2. Creating a JSON String from Classes That Have Collections

## Problem

You want to generate a JSON representation of a Scala object that contains one or more collections, such as a Person class that has a list of friends or addresses.

## Solution

Once classes start containing collections, converting them to JSON becomes more difficult. In this situation, I prefer to use the Lift-JSON domain-specific library (DSL) to generate the JSON.

### Lift-JSON version 1

The Lift-JSON library uses its own DSL for generating JSON output from Scala objects. As shown in the previous recipe, this isn't necessary for simple objects, but it is necessary once objects become more complex, specifically once they contain collections. The benefit of this approach is that you have complete control over the JSON that is generated.

The following example shows how to generate a JSON string for a Person class that has a friends field defined as List[Person]:

```
import net.liftweb.json._
import net.liftweb.json.JsonDSL._

case class Person(name: String, address: Address) {
  var friends = List[Person]()
}

case class Address(city: String, state: String)

object LiftJsonListsVersion1 extends App {

  //import net.liftweb.json.JsonParser._
  implicit val formats = DefaultFormats

  val merc = Person("Mercedes", Address("Somewhere", "KY"))
```

```
val mel = Person("Mel", Address("Lake Zurich", "IL"))
val friends = List(merc, mel)
val p = Person("Alvin Alexander", Address("Talkeetna", "AK"))
p.friends = friends

// define the json output
val json =
  ("person" ->
    ("name" -> p.name) ~
    ("address" ->
      ("city" -> p.address.city) ~
      ("state" -> p.address.state)) ~
    ("friends" ->
      friends.map { f =>
        ("name" -> f.name) ~
        ("address" ->
          ("city" -> f.address.city) ~
          ("state" -> f.address.state))
      })
  )

println(pretty(render(json)))

}
```

The JSON output from this code looks like this:

```
{
  "person":{
    "name":"Alvin Alexander",
    "address":{
      "city":"Talkeetna",
      "state":"AK"
    },
    "friends":[{
      "name":"Mercedes",
      "address":{
        "city":"Somewhere",
        "state":"KY"
      }
    },{
      "name":"Mel",
      "address":{
        "city":"Lake Zurich",
        "state":"IL"
      }
    }]
  }
}
```

The JSON-generating code is shown after the "define the json output" comment, and is repeated here:

```
val json =
  ("person" ->
    ("name" -> p.name) ~
    ("address" ->
      ("city" -> p.address.city) ~
      ("state" -> p.address.state)) ~
    ("friends" ->
      friends.map { f =>
        ("name" -> f.name) ~
        ("address" ->
          ("city" -> f.address.city) ~
          ("state" -> f.address.state))
      })
  )
```

As you can see, Lift uses a custom DSL to let you generate the JSON, and also have control over how the JSON is generated (as opposed to using reflection to generate the JSON). Although you'll want to read the details of the DSL to take on more difficult tasks, the basics are straightforward.

The first thing to know is that any `Tuple2` generates a JSON field, so a code snippet like (`"name" -> p.name`) produces this output:

```
"name":"Alvin Alexander"
```

The other important thing to know is that the `~` operator lets you join fields. You can see from the example code and output how it works.

You can also refer to objects and methods when generating the JSON. You can see this in sections of the code like `p.address.city` and `friends.map { f =>`. Writing JSON-generating code like this feels just like writing other Scala code.

### Lift-JSON Version 2

As your classes grow, creating a larger JSON generator in one variable becomes hard to read and maintain. Fortunately, with the Lift-JSON DSL you can break your JSON-generating code down into small chunks to keep the code maintainable. The following code achieves the same result as the previous example, but I've broken the JSON-generating code down into small methods that are easier to maintain and reuse:

```
import net.liftweb.json._
import net.liftweb.json.JsonDSL._

object LiftJsonListsVersion2 extends App {

    val merc = Person("Mercedes", Address("Somewhere", "KY"))
    val mel = Person("Mel", Address("Lake Zurich", "IL"))
    val friends = List(merc, mel)
    val p = Person("Alvin Alexander", Address("Talkeetna", "AK"))
    p.friends = friends

    val json =
```

```
      ("person" ->
        ("name" -> p.name) ~
        getAddress(p.address) ~
          getFriends(p)
      )

    println(pretty(render(json)))

    def getFriends(p: Person) = {
      ("friends" ->
        p.friends.map { f =>
          ("name" -> f.name) ~
          getAddress(f.address)
        })
    }

    def getAddress(a: Address) = {
      ("address" ->
        ("city" -> a.city) ~
        ("state" -> a.state))
    }

  }

case class Person(name: String, address: Address) {
  var friends = List[Person]()
}

case class Address(city: String, state: String)
```

As shown, this approach lets you create methods that can be reused. The `getAddress` method, for instance, is called several times in the code.

## Discussion

As shown in Recipe 15.1, Gson works via reflection, and it works well for simple classes. However, I've found it to be harder to use when your classes have certain collections. For instance, the following code works fine when the list of friends is defined as an `Array[Person]`:

```
import com.google.gson.Gson
import com.google.gson.GsonBuilder

case class Person(name: String, address: Address) {
  var friends: Array[Person] = _
}

case class Address(city: String, state: String)

/**
 * This approach works with Array.
```

```
  */
object GsonWithArray extends App {

  val merc = Person("Mercedes", Address("Somewhere", "KY"))
  val mel = Person("Mel", Address("Lake Zurich", "IL"))
  val friends = Array(merc, mel)
  val p = Person("Alvin Alexander", Address("Talkeetna", "AK"))
  p.friends = friends
  val gson = (new GsonBuilder()).setPrettyPrinting.create
  println(gson.toJson(p))

}
```

Because a Scala `Array` is backed by a Java array, that code works well, generating JSON output that is similar to Lift-JSON. However, if you change the `Array[Person]` to `List[Person]`, Gson removes the list of friends from the output:

```
{
  "name": "Alvin Alexander",
  "address": {
    "city": "Talkeetna",
    "state": "AK"
  },
  "friends": {}
}
```

Changing the `Array` to an `ArrayBuffer` also causes problems and exposes the internal implementation of an `ArrayBuffer`:

```
{
  "name": "Alvin Alexander",
  "address": {
    "city": "Talkeetna",
    "state": "AK"
  },
  "friends": {
    "initialSize": 16,
    "array": [
      {
        "name": "Mercedes",
        "address": {
          "city": "Somewhere",
          "state": "KY"
        }
      },
      {
        "name": "Mel",
        "address": {
          "city": "Lake Zurich",
          "state": "IL"
        }
      },
      null,  // this line is repeated 13 more times
```

```
      ...
      ...
      null
   ],
   "size0": 2
  }
}
```

An `ArrayBuffer` begins with 16 elements, and when Gson generates the JSON for the list of friends, it correctly includes the two friends, but then outputs the word `null` 14 times, along with including the other output shown.

If you like the idea of generating JSON from your code using reflection, see the Gson User Guide link in the See Also section for information on how to try to resolve these issues by writing custom serializers (creating a JSON string from an object) and deserializers (creating an object from a JSON string).

### See Also

- The Lift-JSON library (*https://github.com/lift/framework/tree/master/core/json*).
- The Gson User Guide (*https://sites.google.com/site/gson/gson-user-guide*) shows how to write serializers and deserializers.

# 15.3. Creating a Simple Scala Object from a JSON String

## Problem

You need to convert a JSON string into a simple Scala object, such as a Scala case class that has no collections.

## Solution

Use the Lift-JSON library to convert a JSON string to an instance of a case class. This is referred to as *deserializing* the string into an object.

The following code shows a complete example of how to use Lift-JSON to convert a JSON string into a case class named `MailServer`. As its name implies, `MailServer` represents the information an email client needs to connect to a server:

```
import net.liftweb.json._

// a case class to represent a mail server
case class MailServer(url: String, username: String, password: String)

object JsonParsingExample extends App {
```

```
implicit val formats = DefaultFormats

// simulate a json string
val jsonString = """
{
  "url": "imap.yahoo.com",
  "username": "myusername",
  "password": "mypassword"
}
"""

// convert a String to a JValue object
val jValue = parse(jsonString)

// create a MailServer object from the string
val mailServer = jValue.extract[MailServer]
println(mailServer.url)
println(mailServer.username)
println(mailServer.password)

}
```

In this example, the `jsonString` contains the text you'd expect to receive if you called a web service asking for a `MailServer` instance. That string is converted into a Lift-JSON `JValue` object with the `parse` function:

```
val jValue = parse(jsonString)
```

Once you have a `JValue` object, use its `extract` method to create a `MailServer` object:

```
val mailServer = jValue.extract[MailServer]
```

The `JValue` class is the root class in the Lift-JSON abstract syntax tree (AST), and its `extract` method builds a case class instance from a JSON string.

Working with objects that have collections is a little more difficult, and that process is covered in the next recipe.

## See Also

- The Lift-JSON library (*https://github.com/lift/framework/tree/master/core/json*)
- Lift-JSON documentation (*http://bit.ly/1aJ22ZN*)

# 15.4. Parsing JSON Data into an Array of Objects

## Problem

You have a JSON string that represents an array of objects, and you need to deserialize it into objects you can use in your Scala application.

## Solution

Use a combination of methods from the Lift-JSON library. The following example demonstrates how to deserialize the string `jsonString` into a series of `EmailAccount` objects, printing each object as it is deserialized:

```scala
import net.liftweb.json.DefaultFormats
import net.liftweb.json._

// a case class to match the JSON data
case class EmailAccount(
  accountName: String,
  url: String,
  username: String,
  password: String,
  minutesBetweenChecks: Int,
  usersOfInterest: List[String]
)

object ParseJsonArray extends App {

  implicit val formats = DefaultFormats

  // a JSON string that represents a list of EmailAccount instances
  val jsonString ="""
{
  "accounts": [
  { "emailAccount": {
    "accountName": "YMail",
    "username": "USERNAME",
    "password": "PASSWORD",
    "url": "imap.yahoo.com",
    "minutesBetweenChecks": 1,
    "usersOfInterest": ["barney", "betty", "wilma"]
  }},
  { "emailAccount": {
    "accountName": "Gmail",
    "username": "USER",
    "password": "PASS",
    "url": "imap.gmail.com",
    "minutesBetweenChecks": 1,
    "usersOfInterest": ["pebbles", "bam-bam"]
  }}
```

```
    ]
  }
  """

  // json is a JValue instance
  val json = parse(jsonString)

  val elements = (json \\ "emailAccount").children
  for (acct <- elements) {
    val m = acct.extract[EmailAccount]
    println(s"Account: ${m.url}, ${m.username}, ${m.password}")
    println("  Users: " + m.usersOfInterest.mkString(","))
  }

}
```

Running this program results in the following output:

```
Account: imap.yahoo.com, USERNAME, PASSWORD
  Users: barney,betty,wilma
Account: imap.gmail.com, USER, PASS
  Users: pebbles,bam-bam
```

## Discussion

I use code like this in my SARAH application (*http://alvinalexander.com/sarah*) to notify me when I receive an email message from people in the usersOfInterest list. SARAH scans my email inbox periodically, and when it sees an email message from people in this list, it speaks, "You have new email from Barney and Betty."

This example begins with some sample JSON stored in a string named jsonString. This string is turned into a JValue object named json with the parse function. The json object is then searched for all elements named emailAccount using the \\ method. This syntax is nice, because it's consistent with the XPath-like methods used in Scala's XML library.

The for loop iterates over the elements that are found, and each element is extracted as an EmailAccount object, and the data in that object is then printed.

Notice that the EmailAccount class has the usersOfInterest field, which is defined as List[String]. The Lift-JSON library converts this sequence easily, with no additional coding required.

## See Also

- The Lift-JSON library is well-documented on GitHub (*https://github.com/lift/framework/tree/master/core/json*) and Assembla (*http://www.assembla.com/spaces/liftweb/wiki/JSON_Support*).

- SARAH (*http://alvinalexander.com/sarah*) is a voice-interaction application written in Scala.

# 15.5. Creating Web Services with Scalatra

## Problem

You want to be able to build new web services with Scalatra (*http://www.scalatra.org/*), a lightweight Scala web framework similar to the Ruby Sinatra (*http://www.sina trarb.com/*) library.

## Solution

The recommended approach to create a new Scalatra project is to use Giter8 (*https://github.com/n8han/giter8*), a great tool for building SBT directories for new projects.

Assuming you have Giter8 installed, use the g8 command to create a new project with a Scalatra template:

```
$ g8 scalatra/scalatra-sbt
organization [com.example]: com.alvinalexander
package [com.example.app]: com.alvinalexander.app
name [My Scalatra Web App]:
scalatra_version [2.2.0]:
servlet_name [MyScalatraServlet]:
scala_version [2.10.0]:
version [0.1.0-SNAPSHOT]:

Template applied in ./my-scalatra-web-app
```

When Giter8 finishes, move into the new directory it created:

```
$ cd my-scalatra-web-app
```

Start SBT in that directory, and then issue the container:start command to start the Jetty server:

```
$ sbt

> container:start
// a lot of output here ...
[info] Started SelectChannelConnector@0.0.0.0:8080
[success] Total time: 11 s, completed May 13, 2013 4:32:08 PM
```

Then use the following command to enable continuous compilation:

```
> ~ ;copy-resources;aux-compile
1. Waiting for source changes... (press enter to interrupt)
```

That command is nice; it automatically recompiles your source code when it changes.

The Jetty server starts on port 8080 by default. If you switch to a browser and go to the URL *http://localhost:8080/*, you should see some default "Hello, world" output, indicating that Scalatra is running.

The content displayed at this URL comes from a class named `MyScalatraServlet`, located in the project's *src/main/scala/com/alvinalexander/app* directory:

```
package com.alvinalexander.app

import org.scalatra._
import scalate.ScalateSupport

class MyScalatraServlet extends MyScalatraWebAppStack {

  get("/") {
    <html>
      <body>
        <h1>Hello, world!</h1>
        Say <a href="hello-scalate">hello to Scalate</a>.
      </body>
    </html>
  }

}
```

That's the entire servlet. If you're used to building web services with "heavier" tools, this can be quite a shock.

The get method shown declares that it's listening to GET requests at the / URI. If you try accessing another URL like *http://localhost:8080/foo* in your browser, you'll see output like this in the browser:

```
Requesting "GET /foo" on servlet "" but only have:
GET /
```

This is because `MyScalatraServlet` only has one method, and it's programmed to listen for a GET request at the / URI.

### Add a new service

To demonstrate how the process of adding a new web service works, add a new method that listens to GET requests at the */hello* URI. To do this, just add the following method to the servlet:

```
get("/hello") {
  <p>Hello, world!</p>
}
```

A few moments after saving this change to `MyScalatraServlet`, you should see some output in your SBT console. An abridged version of the output looks like this:

```
[info] Compiling 1 Scala source to target/scala-2.10/classes...
[success] Total time: 8 s
```

```
[info] Generating target/scala-2.10/resource_managed/main/rebel.xml.
[info] Compiling Templates in Template Directory:
  src/main/webapp/WEB-INF/templates
[success] Total time: 1 s, completed May 28, 2013 1:56:36 PM
2. Waiting for source changes... (press enter to interrupt)
```

As a result of the ~ aux-compile command, SBT automatically recompiles your source code. Once the code is recompiled, you can go to the *http://localhost:8080/hello* URL in your browser, where you'll see the new output.

Congratulations. By following the steps in this recipe, you should have a web service up and running in a matter of minutes.

## Discussion

Giter8 is a tool for creating SBT project directory structures based on templates. The template used in this example is just one of many Giter8 templates (*https://github.com/ n8han/giter8/wiki/giter8-templates*). Giter8 requires SBT (*http://www.scala-sbt.org/*) and another tool named Conscript (*https://github.com/n8han/conscript*). Despite these requirements, the overall installation process is simple, and is described in Recipe 18.1.

In addition to the MyScalatraServlet class, this list shows some of the most important files in your project:

```
project/build.scala
project/plugins.sbt
src/main/resources/logback.xml
src/main/scala/com/alvinalexander/app/MyScalatraServlet.scala
src/main/scala/com/alvinalexander/app/MyScalatraWebAppStack.scala
src/main/scala/ScalatraBootstrap.scala
src/main/webapp/WEB-INF/web.xml
src/main/webapp/WEB-INF/templates/layouts/default.jade
src/main/webapp/WEB-INF/templates/views/hello-scalate.jade
src/test/scala/com/alvinalexander/app/MyScalatraServletSpec.scala
```

Notice that this includes a *WEB-INF/web.xml* file. If you're used to the Java web programming world, you'll find that this is a normal *web.xml* file, albeit a very small one. Excluding the boilerplate XML, it has only this entry:

```
<listener>
  <listener-class>org.scalatra.servlet.ScalatraListener</listener-class>
</listener>
```

You'll rarely need to edit this file. Recipe 15.6, "Replacing XML Servlet Mappings with Scalatra Mounts" shows one instance where you'll need to make a small change to it, but that's it.

As shown in the list of files, an interesting thing about the current Giter8 template for Scalatra is that it uses a *project/build.scala* file rather than a *build.sbt* file. You can find all of Scalatra's dependencies in that file, including the use of tools such as the Scalate template engine (*http://scalate.fusesource.org/*), specs2 (*http://etorreborre.github.io/specs2/*), Logback (*http://logback.qos.ch/*), and Jetty (*http://www.eclipse.org/jetty/*).

## See Also

- The Scalatra website (*http://www.scalatra.org/*)
- The Giter8 website (*https://github.com/n8han/giter8/*)
- Recipe 18.1, "Creating a Project Directory Structure for SBT" for how to install Giter8, and use it in other scenarios

# 15.6. Replacing XML Servlet Mappings with Scalatra Mounts

## Problem

You want to add new servlets to your Scalatra application, and need to know how to add them, including defining their URI namespace.

## Solution

Scalatra provides a nice way of getting you out of the business of declaring your servlets and servlet mappings in the *web.xml* file. Simply create a boilerplate *web.xml* file like this in the *src/main/webapp/WEB-INF* directory:

```
<?xml version="1.0" encoding="UTF-8"?>
<web-app xmlns="http://java.sun.com/xml/ns/javaee"
     xmlns:xsi="http://www.w3.org/2001/XMLSchema-instance"
     xsi:schemaLocation="http://java.sun.com/xml/ns/javaee ↵
http://java.sun.com/xml/ns/javaee/web-app_3_0.xsd"
     version="3.0">
  <listener>
    <listener-class>org.scalatra.servlet.ScalatraListener</listener-class>
  </listener>

  <servlet-mapping>
    <servlet-name>default</servlet-name>
    <url-pattern>/img/*</url-pattern>
    <url-pattern>/css/*</url-pattern>
    <url-pattern>/js/*</url-pattern>
    <url-pattern>/assets/*</url-pattern>
  </servlet-mapping>
</web-app>
```

Next, assuming that you're working with the application created in Recipe 15.5, edit the *src/main/scala/ScalatraBootstrap.scala* file so that it has these contents:

```
import org.scalatra._
import javax.servlet.ServletContext
import com.alvinalexander.app._

class ScalatraBootstrap extends LifeCycle {
  override def init(context: ServletContext) {

    // created by default
    context.mount(new MyScalatraServlet, "/*")

    // new
    context.mount(new StockServlet, "/stocks/*")
    context.mount(new BondServlet, "/bonds/*")
  }
}
```

The two new `context.mount` lines shown tell Scalatra that a class named `StockServlet` should handle all URI requests that begin with *stocks/*, and another class named `BondServlet` should handle all URI requests that begin with *bonds/*.

Next, create a file named *src/main/scala/com/alvinalexander/app/OtherServlets.scala* to define the `StockServlet` and `BondServlet` classes:

```
package com.alvinalexander.app

import org.scalatra._
import scalate.ScalateSupport

class StockServlet extends MyScalatraWebAppStack {
  get("/") {
    <p>Hello from StockServlet</p>
  }
}

class BondServlet extends MyScalatraWebAppStack {
  get("/") {
    <p>Hello from BondServlet</p>
  }
}
```

Assuming your project is still configured to recompile automatically, when you access the *http://localhost:8080/stocks/* and *http://localhost:8080/bonds/* URLs, you should see the content from your new servlets.

## Discussion

Scalatra refers to this configuration process as "mounting" the servlets, and if you've used a filesystem technology like NFS, it does indeed feel similar to the process of mounting a remote filesystem.

---

As a result of the configuration, new methods in the StockServlet and BondServlet will be available under the */stocks/* and */bonds/* URIs. For example, if you define a new method like this in the StockServlet:

```
get("/foo") {
  <p>Foo!</p>
}
```

you'll be able to access this method at the */stocks/foo* URI, e.g., the *http://localhost:8080/stocks/foo* URL, if you're running on port 8080 on your local computer.

In the end, this approach provides the same functionality as servlet mappings, but it's more concise, with the added benefit that you're working in Scala code instead of XML, and you can generally forget about the *web.xml* file after the initial configuration.

## See Also

Scalatra configuration and deployment guide (*http://www.scalatra.org/2.2/guides/deployment/configuration.html*)

# 15.7. Accessing Scalatra Web Service GET Parameters

## Problem

When creating a Scalatra web service, you want to be able to handle parameters that are passed into a method using a GET request.

## Solution

If you want to let parameters be passed into your Scalatra servlet with a URI that uses traditional ? and & characters to separate data elements, like this:

```
http://localhost:8080/saveName?fname=Alvin&lname=Alexander
```

you can access them through the implicit params variable in a get method:

```
/**
 * The URL
 * http://localhost:8080/saveName?fname=Alvin&lname=Alexander
 * prints: Some(Alvin), Some(Alexander)
 */
get("/saveName") {
  val firstName = params.get("fname")
  val lastName = params.get("lname")
  <p>{firstName}, {lastName}</p>
}
```

However, Scalatra also lets you use a "named parameters" approach, which can be more convenient, and also documents the parameters your method expects to receive. Using this approach, callers can access a URL like this:

```
http://localhost:8080/hello/Alvin/Alexander
```

You can handle these parameters in a get method like this:

```
get("/hello/:fname/:lname") {
  <p>Hello, {params("fname")}, {params("lname")}</p>
}
```

As mentioned, a benefit of this approach is that the method signature documents the expected parameters.

With this approach, you can use wildcard characters for other needs, such as when a client needs to pass in a filename path, where you won't know the depth of the path beforehand:

```
get("/getFilename/*.*") {
  val data = multiParams("splat")
  <p>{data.mkString("[", ", ", "]")}</p>
}
```

You can understand this method by looking at a specific example. Imagine a GET request to the *http://localhost:8080/getFilename/Users/Al/tmp/file.txt* URL. The comments in the following code show how this URL is handled:

```
/**
 * (1) GET http://localhost:8080/getFilename/Users/Al/tmp/file.txt
 */
get("/getFilename/*.*") {

  // (2) creates a Vector(Users/Al/tmp/file, txt)
  val data = multiParams("splat")

  // (3) prints: [Users/Al/tmp/file, txt]
  <pre>{data.mkString("[", ", ", "]")}</pre>

}
```

This code works because the multiParams method with the splat argument creates a Vector that contains two elements: the strings Users/Al/tmp/file and txt. Next, the information is printed back to the browser with the data.mkString line. In a real-world program, you can put the filename back together by merging data(0) and data(1), and then using the filename as needed.

There are more methods for parsing GET request parameters with Scalatra, including additional uses of wildcard characters, and Rails-like pattern matching. See the latest Scalatra documentation (*http://scalatra.org/guides/*) for more information.

# 15.8. Accessing POST Request Data with Scalatra

## Problem

You want to write a Scalatra web service method to handle POST data, such as handling JSON data sent as a POST request.

## Solution

To handle a POST request, write a post method in your Scalatra servlet, specifying the URI the method should listen at:

```
post("/saveJsonStock") {
  val jsonString = request.body
  // deserialize the JSON ...
}
```

As shown, access the data that's passed to the POST request by calling the request.body method.

The Discussion shows an example of how to process JSON data received in a post method, and two clients you can use to test a post method: a Scala client, and a command-line client that uses the Unix curl command.

## Discussion

Recipe 15.3 shows how to convert a JSON string into a Scala object using the Lift-JSON library, in a process known as deserialization. In a Scalatra post method, you access a JSON string that has been POSTed to your method by calling request.body. Once you have that string, deserialize it using the approach shown in Recipe 15.3.

For instance, the post method in the following StockServlet shows how to convert the JSON string it receives as a POST request and deserialize it into a Stock object. The comments in the code explain each step:

```
package com.alvinalexander.app

import org.scalatra._
import scalate.ScalateSupport
import net.liftweb.json._

class StockServlet extends MyScalatraWebAppStack {

  /**
   * Expects an incoming JSON string like this:
   * {"symbol":"GOOG","price":"600.00"}
   */
  post("/saveJsonStock") {
```

```
// get the POST request data
val jsonString = request.body

// needed for Lift-JSON
implicit val formats = DefaultFormats

// convert the JSON string to a JValue object
val jValue = parse(jsonString)

// deserialize the string into a Stock object
val stock = jValue.extract[Stock]

// for debugging
println(stock)

// you can send information back to the client
// in the response header
response.addHeader("ACK", "GOT IT")

  }

}

// a simple Stock class
class Stock (var symbol: String, var price: Double) {
  override def toString = symbol + ", " + price
}
```

The last step to get this working is to add the Lift-JSON dependency to your project. Assuming that you created your project as an SBT project as shown in Recipe 15.1, add this dependency to the libraryDependencies declared in the *project/build.scala* file in your project:

```
"net.liftweb" %% "lift-json" % "2.5+"
```

### Test the POST method with Scala code

As shown in the code comments, the post method expects a JSON string with this form:

```
{"symbol":"GOOG","price":600.00}
```

You can test your post method in a variety of ways, including (a) a Scala POST client or (b) a simple shell script. The following PostTester object shows how to test the post method with a Scala client:

```
import net.liftweb.json._
import net.liftweb.json.Serialization.write
import org.apache.http.client.methods.HttpPost
import org.apache.http.entity.StringEntity
import org.apache.http.impl.client.DefaultHttpClient

object PostTester extends App {
```

```
// create a Stock and convert it to a JSON string
val stock = new Stock("AAPL", 500.00)
implicit val formats = DefaultFormats
val stockAsJsonString = write(stock)

// add the JSON string as a StringEntity to a POST request
val post = new HttpPost("http://localhost:8080/stocks/saveJsonStock")
post.setHeader("Content-type", "application/json")
post.setEntity(new StringEntity(stockAsJsonString))

// send the POST request
val response = (new DefaultHttpClient).execute(post)

// print the response
println("--- HEADERS ---")
response.getAllHeaders.foreach(arg => println(arg))

}

class Stock (var symbol: String, var price: Double)
```

The code starts by creating a `Stock` object and converting the object to a JSON string using Lift-JSON. It then uses the methods of the Apache HttpClient library to send the JSON string as a POST request: it creates an `HttpPost` object, sets the header content type, then wraps the JSON string as a `StringEntity` object before sending the POST request and waiting for the response.

When this test object is run against the Scalatra `saveJsonStock` method, it results in the following output:

```
--- HEADERS ---
ACK: GOT IT
Content-Type: text/html;charset=UTF-8
Content-Length: 0
Server: Jetty(8.1.8.v20121106)
```

Note that it receives the ACK message that was returned by the Scalatra `post` method. This isn't required, but it gives the client a way to confirm that the data was properly received and processed by the server method (or that it failed).

### Test the POST method with a curl command

Another way to test the `post` method is with a Unix shell script. The following `curl` command sets the `Content-type` header, and sends a sample JSON string to the Scalatra `StockServlet` `post` method as a POST request:

```
curl \
  --header "Content-type: application/json" \
  --request POST \
  --data '{"symbol":"GOOG", "price":600.00}' \
  http://localhost:8080/stocks/saveJsonStock
```

On Unix systems, save this command to a file named *postJson.sh*, and then make it executable:

```
$ chmod +x postJson.sh
```

Then run it to test your Scalatra web service:

```
$ ./postJson.sh
```

You won't see any output from this command, but you should see the correct debugging output printed by the `StockServlet` in its output window. Assuming that you're running your Scalatra web service using SBT, the debug output will appear there.

### Notes

Recent versions of Scalatra use the Json4s library to deserialize JSON. This library is currently based on Lift-JSON, so the deserialization code will be similar, if not exactly the same. Either library will have to be added as a dependency.

The other important parts about this recipe are:

- Knowing to use the `post` method to handle a `POST` request
- Using `request.body` to get the `POST` data
- Using `response.addHeader("ACK", "GOT IT")` to return a success or failure message to the client (though this is optional)
- Having `POST` request client programs you can use

# 15.9. Creating a Simple GET Request Client

## Problem

You want an HTTP client you can use to make `GET` request calls.

## Solution

There are many potential solutions to this problem. This recipe demonstrates three approaches:

- A simple use of the `scala.io.Source.fromURL` method
- Adding a timeout wrapper around `scala.io.Source.fromURL` to make it more robust
- Using the Apache HttpClient library

These solutions are demonstrated in the following sections.

---

### A simple use of scala.io.Source.fromURL

If it doesn't matter that your web service client won't time out in a controlled manner, you can use this simple method to download the contents from a URL:

```
/**
 * Returns the text (content) from a URL as a String.
 * Warning: This method does not time out when the service is non-responsive.
 */
def get(url: String) = scala.io.Source.fromURL(url).mkString
```

This GET request method lets you call the given RESTful URL to retrieve its content. You can use it to download web pages, RSS feeds, or any other content using an HTTP GET request.

Under the covers, the `Source.fromURL` method uses classes like `java.net.URL` and `java.io.InputStream`, so this method can throw exceptions that extend from `java.io.IOException`. As a result, you may want to annotate your method to indicate that:

```
@throws(classOf[java.io.IOException])
def get(url: String) = io.Source.fromURL(url).mkString
```

### Setting the timeout while using scala.io.Source.fromURL

As mentioned, that simple solution suffers from a significant problem: it doesn't time out if the URL you're calling is unresponsive. If the web service you're calling isn't responding, your code will become unresponsive at this point as well.

Therefore, a better approach is to write a similar method that allows the setting of a timeout value. By using a combination of *java.net* classes and the method `io.Source.fromInputStream`, you can create a more robust method that lets you control both the *connection* and *read* timeout values:

```
/**
 * Returns the text (content) from a REST URL as a String.
 * Inspired by http://matthewkwong.blogspot.com/2009/09/↵
scala-scalaiosource-fromurl-blockshangs.html
 * and http://alvinalexander.com/blog/post/java/how-open-url-↵
read-contents-httpurl-connection-java
 *
 * The `connectTimeout` and `readTimeout` comes from the Java URLConnection
 * class Javadoc.
 * @param url The full URL to connect to.
 * @param connectTimeout Sets a specified timeout value, in milliseconds,
 * to be used when opening a communications link to the resource referenced
 * by this URLConnection. If the timeout expires before the connection can
 * be established, a java.net.SocketTimeoutException
 * is raised. A timeout of zero is interpreted as an infinite timeout.
 * Defaults to 5000 ms.
 * @param readTimeout If the timeout expires before there is data available
 * for read, a java.net.SocketTimeoutException is raised. A timeout of zero
```

```
 * is interpreted as an infinite timeout. Defaults to 5000 ms.
 * @param requestMethod Defaults to "GET". (Other methods have not been tested.)
 *
 * @example get("http://www.example.com/getInfo")
 * @example get("http://www.example.com/getInfo", 5000)
 * @example get("http://www.example.com/getInfo", 5000, 5000)
 */
@throws(classOf[java.io.IOException])
@throws(classOf[java.net.SocketTimeoutException])
def get(url: String,
        connectTimeout:Int =5000,
        readTimeout:Int =5000,
        requestMethod: String = "GET") = {
  import java.net.{URL, HttpURLConnection}
  val connection = (new URL(url)).openConnection.asInstanceOf[HttpURLConnection]
  connection.setConnectTimeout(connectTimeout)
  connection.setReadTimeout(readTimeout)
  connection.setRequestMethod(requestMethod)
  val inputStream = connection.getInputStream
  val content = io.Source.fromInputStream(inputStream).mkString
  if (inputStream != null) inputStream.close
  content
}
```

As the Scaladoc shows, this method can be called in a variety of ways, including this:

```
try {
  val content = get("http://localhost:8080/waitForever")
  println(content)
} catch {
  case ioe: java.io.IOException =>  // handle this
  case ste: java.net.SocketTimeoutException => // handle this
}
```

I haven't tested this method with other request types, such as PUT or DELETE, but I have allowed for this possibility by making the requestMethod an optional parameter.

### Using the Apache HttpClient

Another approach you can take is to use the Apache HttpClient library. Before I learned about the previous approaches, I wrote a getRestContent method using this library like this:

```
import java.io._
import org.apache.http.{HttpEntity, HttpResponse}
import org.apache.http.client._
import org.apache.http.client.methods.HttpGet
import org.apache.http.impl.client.DefaultHttpClient
import scala.collection.mutable.StringBuilder
import scala.xml.XML
import org.apache.http.params.HttpConnectionParams
import org.apache.http.params.HttpParams
```

```
/**
 * Returns the text (content) from a REST URL as a String.
 * Returns a blank String if there was a problem.
 * This function will also throw exceptions if there are problems trying
 * to connect to the url.
 *
 * @param url A complete URL, such as "http://foo.com/bar"
 * @param connectionTimeout The connection timeout, in ms.
 * @param socketTimeout The socket timeout, in ms.
 */
def getRestContent(url: String,
                   connectionTimeout: Int,
                   socketTimeout: Int): String = {
  val httpClient = buildHttpClient(connectionTimeout, socketTimeout)
  val httpResponse = httpClient.execute(new HttpGet(url))
  val entity = httpResponse.getEntity
  var content = ""
  if (entity != null) {
    val inputStream = entity.getContent
    content = io.Source.fromInputStream(inputStream).getLines.mkString
    inputStream.close
  }
  httpClient.getConnectionManager.shutdown
  content
}

private def buildHttpClient(connectionTimeout: Int, socketTimeout: Int):
DefaultHttpClient = {
  val httpClient = new DefaultHttpClient
  val httpParams = httpClient.getParams
  HttpConnectionParams.setConnectionTimeout(httpParams, connectionTimeout)
  HttpConnectionParams.setSoTimeout(httpParams, socketTimeout)
  httpClient.setParams(httpParams)
  httpClient
}
```

This requires significantly more code than the Source.fromURL approaches, as well as the HttpClient library. If you're already using the Apache HttpClient library for other purposes, this is a viable alternative. As shown in Recipes 15.11 and 15.12, the HttpClient library definitely has advantages in situations such as working with request headers.

## Discussion

There are several other approaches you can take to handle this timeout problem. One is to use the Akka Futures as a wrapper around the Source.fromURL method call. See Recipe 13.9, "Simple Concurrency with Futures" for an example of how to use that approach.

Also, new libraries are always being released. A library named Newman (*https://github.com/stackmob/newman*) was released by StackMob as this book was in the production process, and looks promising. The Newman DSL was inspired by the Dispatch library, but uses method names instead of symbols, and appears to be easier to use as a result. It also provides separate methods for the GET, POST, PUT, DELETE, and HEAD request methods.

### See Also

- Matthew Kwong's Source.fromURL timeout approach (*http://bit.ly/18lwkV3*).
- If you prefer asynchronous programming, you can mix this recipe with Scala Futures, which are demonstrated in Chapter 13. Another option is the Dispatch library. As its documentation (*http://dispatch.databinder.net/Dispatch.html*) states, "Dispatch is a library for asynchronous HTTP interaction. It provides a Scala vocabulary for Java's async-http-client."
- Newman, from StackMob (*https://github.com/stackmob/newman*).

# 15.10. Sending JSON Data to a POST URL

## Problem

You want to send JSON data (or other data) to a POST URL, either from a standalone client, or when using a framework that doesn't provide this type of service.

## Solution

Create a JSON string using your favorite JSON library, and then send the data to the POST URL using the Apache HttpClient library. In the following example, the Gson library is used to construct a JSON string, which is then sent to a server using the methods of the HttpClient library:

```
import java.io._
import org.apache.commons._
import org.apache.http._
import org.apache.http.client._
import org.apache.http.client.methods.HttpPost
import org.apache.http.impl.client.DefaultHttpClient
import java.util.ArrayList
import org.apache.http.message.BasicNameValuePair
import org.apache.http.client.entity.UrlEncodedFormEntity
import com.google.gson.Gson

case class Person(firstName: String, lastName: String, age: Int)
```

```
object HttpJsonPostTest extends App {

  // create our object as a json string
  val spock = new Person("Leonard", "Nimoy", 82)
  val spockAsJson = new Gson().toJson(spock)

  // add name value pairs to a post object
  val post = new HttpPost("http://localhost:8080/posttest")
  val nameValuePairs = new ArrayList[NameValuePair]()
  nameValuePairs.add(new BasicNameValuePair("JSON", spockAsJson))
  post.setEntity(new UrlEncodedFormEntity(nameValuePairs))

  // send the post request
  val client = new DefaultHttpClient
  val response = client.execute(post)
  println("--- HEADERS ---")
  response.getAllHeaders.foreach(arg => println(arg))

}
```

## Discussion

The Gson library is used to construct a JSON string in this code because this is a simple example. For more complex cases, you'll probably want to use the Lift-JSON library, as discussed in the first several recipes of this chapter.

In this example, once you've constructed a JSON string from a Scala object, the Apache HttpClient NameValuePair, BasicNameValuePair, and UrlEncodedFormEntity classes are used to set an Entity on an HttpPost object. In the last lines of the code, the POST request is sent using the client.execute call, the response is received, and the response headers are printed (though this isn't necessary).

## See Also

- Recipe 15.1, "Creating a JSON String from a Scala Object" and Recipe 15.2, "Creating a JSON String from Classes That Have Collections".
- The Lift-JSON library (*https://github.com/lift/framework/tree/master/core/json*).
- The Google Gson library (*http://code.google.com/p/google-gson/*).
- Dispatch (*http://dispatch.databinder.net/Dispatch.html*) is a "library for asynchronous HTTP interaction."

# 15.11. Getting URL Headers

## Problem

You need to access the HTTP response headers after making an HTTP request.

## Solution

Use the Apache HttpClient library, and get the headers from the `HttpResponse` object after making a request:

```
import org.apache.http.client.methods.HttpGet
import org.apache.http.impl.client.DefaultHttpClient

object FetchUrlHeaders extends App {

  val get = new HttpGet("http://alvinalexander.com/")
  val client = new DefaultHttpClient
  val response = client.execute(get)
  response.getAllHeaders.foreach(header => println(header))

}
```

Running that program prints the following header output:

```
Server: nginx/1.0.10
Date: Sun, 15 Jul 2012 19:10:19 GMT
Content-Type: text/html; charset=utf-8
Connection: keep-alive
Keep-Alive: timeout=20
Content-Length: 28862
Cache-Control: no-store, no-cache, must-revalidate, post-check=0, pre-check=0
Expires: Sun, 19 Nov 1978 05:00:00 GMT
Vary: Accept-Encoding
```

## Discussion

When I worked with a Single Sign-On (SSO) system named OpenSSO from Sun (now known as OpenAM (*http://www.forgerock.com/openam.html*)), much of the work in the sign-on process involved setting and reading header information. The HttpClient library greatly simplifies this process.

## See Also

- Apache HttpClient library (*http://hc.apache.org/httpclient-3.x/*).

- You may also be able to use the Dispatch library (*http://dispatch.databinder.net/ Dispatch.html*) for this purpose.

# 15.12. Setting URL Headers When Sending a Request

## Problem

You need to set URL headers when making an HTTP request.

## Solution

Use the Apache HttpClient library to set the headers before making the request, as shown in this example:

```
import org.apache.http.client.methods.HttpGet
import org.apache.http.impl.client.DefaultHttpClient

object SetUrlHeaders extends App {

  val url = "http://localhost:9001/baz"
  val httpGet = new HttpGet(url)

  // set the desired header values
  httpGet.setHeader("KEY1", "VALUE1")
  httpGet.setHeader("KEY2", "VALUE2")

  // execute the request
  val client = new DefaultHttpClient
  client.execute(httpGet)

  client.getConnectionManager.shutdown

}
```

## Discussion

If you don't have a web server to test against, you can use a tool like HttpTea (*http://httptea.sourceforge.net/*) to see the results of running this program. HttpTea helps to simulate a server in a test environment.

Start HttpTea at the command line to listen on port 9001 like this:

```
$ java -jar HttpTea.jar -l 9001
```

Now when you run your client program—such as the program shown in the Solution—you should see the following output from HttpTea, including the headers that were set:

```
Client>>>
GET /baz HTTP/1.1
KEY1: VALUE1
KEY2: VALUE2
Host: localhost:9001
Connection: Keep-Alive
User-Agent: Apache-HttpClient/4.1.3 (java 1.5)
```

### See Also

- HttpTea (*http://httptea.sourceforge.net/*).
- Apache HttpClient library (*http://hc.apache.org/httpclient-3.x/*).
- You may also be able to use the Dispatch library (*http://dispatch.databinder.net/Dispatch.html*) for this purpose.

# 15.13. Creating a GET Request Web Service with the Play Framework

## Problem

You want to create a GET request web service using the Play Framework, such as returning a JSON string when the web service URI is accessed.

## Solution

When working with RESTful web services, you'll typically be converting between one or more model objects and their JSON representation.

To demonstrate how a GET request might be used to return the JSON representation of an object, create a new Play project with the `play new` command:

```
$ play new WebServiceDemo
```

Respond to the prompts to create a new Scala application, and then move into the *WebServiceDemo* directory that's created.

Next, assume that you want to create a web service to return an instance of a Stock when a client makes a GET request at the */getStock* URI. To do this, first add this line to your *conf/routes* file:

```
GET    /getStock    controllers.Application.getStock
```

Next, create a method named `getStock` in the default `Application` controller (*apps/controllers/Application.scala*), and have it return a JSON representation of a Stock object:

```
package controllers

import play.api._
import play.api.mvc._
import play.api.libs.json._
import models.Stock

object Application extends Controller {
```

```
def index = Action {
  Ok(views.html.index("Your new application is ready."))
}

def getStock = Action {
  val stock = Stock("GOOG", 650.0)
  Ok(Json.toJson(stock))
}

}
```

That code uses the Play `Json.toJson` method. Although the code looks like you can create `Stock` as a simple case class, attempting to use only a case class will result in this error when you access the */getStock* URI:

No Json deserializer found for type `models.Stock`. Try to implement an implicit Writes or Format for this type.

To get this controller code to work, you need to create an instance of a `Format` object to convert between the `Stock` model object and its JSON representation. To do this, create a model file named *Stock.scala* in the *app/models* directory of your project. (Create the directory if it doesn't exist.)

In that file, define the `Stock` case class, and then implement a `play.api.libs.json.Format` object. In that object, define a `reads` method to convert from a JSON string to a `Stock` object and a `writes` method to convert from a `Stock` object to a JSON string:

```
package models

case class Stock(symbol: String, price: Double)

object Stock {

  import play.api.libs.json._

  implicit object StockFormat extends Format[Stock] {

    // convert from JSON string to a Stock object (de-serializing from JSON)
    def reads(json: JsValue): JsResult[Stock] = {
      val symbol = (json \ "symbol").as[String]
      val price = (json \ "price").as[Double]
      JsSuccess(Stock(symbol, price))
    }

    // convert from Stock object to JSON (serializing to JSON)
    def writes(s: Stock): JsValue = {
      // JsObject requires Seq[(String, play.api.libs.json.JsValue)]
      val stockAsList = Seq("symbol" -> JsString(s.symbol),
                            "price" -> JsNumber(s.price))
      JsObject(stockAsList)
```

```
        }

      }

    }
```

The comments in that code help to explain how the `reads` and `writes` methods work.

With this code in place, you can now access the `getStock` web service. If you haven't already done so, start the Play console from within the root directory of your project, then issue the `run` command:

```
$ play

[WebServiceDemo] $ run 8080
```

Play runs on port 9000 by default, but this collides with other services on my system, so I run it on port 8080, as shown. Assuming that you're running on port 8080, access the *http://localhost:8080/getStock* URL from a web browser. You should see this result in the browser:

```
{"symbol":"GOOG","price":650.0}
```

## Discussion

When converting from a `Stock` object to its JSON representation, the `writes` method of your `Format` object is implicitly used in this line of code:

```
Json.toJson(stock)
```

Although there are other approaches to converting between objects and their JSON representation, implementing the `reads` and `writes` methods of a `Format` object provides a straightforward means for this serialization and deserialization process.

## See Also

The Play `json` package object (*http://bit.ly/12ubzOT*)

# 15.14. POSTing JSON Data to a Play Framework Web Service

## Problem

You want to create a web service using the Play Framework that lets users send JSON data to the service using the `POST` request method.

## Solution

Follow the steps from the previous recipe to create a new Play project, controller, and model.

Whereas the previous recipe used the writes method of the Format object in the model, this recipe uses the reads method. When JSON data is received in a POST request, the reads method is used to convert from the JSON string that's received to a Stock object. Here's the code for the reads method:

```
def reads(json: JsValue): JsResult[Stock] = {
  val symbol = (json \ "symbol").as[String]
  val price = (json \ "price").as[Double]
  JsSuccess(Stock(symbol, price))
}
```

This method creates a Stock object from the JSON value it's given. (The complete code for the model object is shown in the previous recipe.)

With this method added to the model, create a saveStock method in the Application controller:

```
import play.api._
import play.api.mvc._

object Application extends Controller {

  import play.api.libs.json.Json

  def saveStock = Action { request =>
    val json = request.body.asJson.get
    val stock = json.as[Stock]
    println(stock)
    Ok
  }

}
```

The saveStock method gets the JSON data sent to it from the request object, and then converts it with the json.as method. The println statement in the method is used for debugging purposes, and prints to the Play command line (the Play console).

Finally, add a route that binds a POST request to the desired URI and the saveStock method in the Application controller by adding this line to the *conf/routes* file:

```
POST    /saveStock     controllers.Application.saveStock
```

If you haven't already done so, start the Play console from within the root directory of your project, and issue the run command:

```
$ play

[WebServicesDemo] $ run 8080
```

With the Play server running, use the following Unix `curl` command to POST a sample JSON string to your `saveStock` web service:

```
curl \
  --header "Content-type: application/json" \
  --request POST \
  --data '{"symbol":"GOOG", "price":900.00}' \
  http://localhost:8080/saveStock
```

If everything works properly, you should see this output in your Play console window:

```
STOCK: Stock(GOOG,900.0)
```

## Discussion

A few notes about the code:

- The `request` object is a `play.api.mvc.AnyContent` object.
- The `request.body` is also a `play.api.mvc.AnyContent` object.
- The `request.body.asJson` returns an instance of the following: `Option[play.api.libs.json.JsValue]`.
- `request.body.asJson.get` returns a `JsValue`.

In a real-world web service, once you've converted the JSON string to an object, you can do anything else you need to do with it, such as saving it to a database.

## See Also

- The Play `json` package object (*http://bit.ly/12ubzOT*)
- The Play `Request` trait (*http://bit.ly/16GF3uf*)

# CHAPTER 16

# Databases and Persistence

## Introduction

With Scala, you can interact with traditional relational databases using their JDBC drivers, just like you do in Java. As an example of this, the first recipe in this chapter demonstrates how to connect to a MySQL database using the "plain old JDBC" approach.

In the real world, once applications grow in size, few people use plain old JDBC to work with databases. Typically on those projects you use a library, such as the Spring Framework (*http://www.springsource.org/spring-framework*), to make development easier and handle issues like connection pooling. Therefore, this chapter also demonstrates the few changes you'll need to make to use the Spring JDBC library with Scala. As an added benefit, by showing the changes needed to instantiate a bean from a Spring application context file, this recipe will help you use other Spring libraries with Scala as well. You can use other technologies with Scala, such as the Java Persistence API (JPA) and Hibernate, with just a few changes.

The Scala community is also developing new approaches to database development. The Squeryl (*http://squeryl.org/*) and Slick (*http://slick.typesafe.com/*) libraries both take "type-safe" approaches to writing database code. The Squeryl documentation states that it's a "Scala ORM and DSL." In a manner similar to Hibernate, Squeryl lets you write database code like this:

```
// insert
val bill = people.insert(new Person("Bill"))
val candy = people.insert(new Person("Candy"))

// update
stock.price = 500.00
stocks.update(stock)
```

With Squeryl's DSL, you can also write statements like this:

---

```
update(stocks)(s =>
  where(s.symbol === "AAPL")
  set(s.price := 500.00)
)
```

Slick isn't an object-relational mapping (ORM) tool, but with its type-safe approach, it lets you write database access code almost like you're working with a collection. This approach is demonstrated in the last recipe in this chapter.

When you get to "big data" projects, it's nice to know that Scala works there as well. There are several Scala drivers available for the MongoDB (*http://www.mongodb.org/*) database, including Casbah (*https://github.com/mongodb/casbah*) and ReactiveMongo (*http://reactivemongo.org/*). The recipes in this chapter demonstrate how to use the Casbah driver to insert, update, read, and delete objects in a MongoDB collection with Scala.

If you want to use Scala to work with Hadoop, Twitter has created a project named Scalding (*https://github.com/twitter/scalding*) that "makes it easy to specify Hadoop MapReduce jobs." Scalding is analogous to the Apache Pig project (*http://pig.apache.org/*), but is tightly integrated with Scala. Scalding and Hadoop are not covered in this chapter, but the Scalding source code tutorials (*https://github.com/twitter/scalding/tree/master/tutorial*) can help you quickly get up and running with Scalding.

# 16.1. Connecting to MySQL with JDBC

## Problem

You want to connect to a MySQL database (or any other database with a JDBC driver) from a Scala application using "plain old JDBC."

## Solution

Use JDBC just like you would in a Java application. Download the MySQL JDBC driver, and then access your database with code like this:

```
package tests

import java.sql.{Connection,DriverManager}

object ScalaJdbcConnectSelect extends App {

  // connect to the database named "mysql" on port 8889 of localhost
  val url = "jdbc:mysql://localhost:8889/mysql"
  val driver = "com.mysql.jdbc.Driver"
  val username = "root"
  val password = "root"
  var connection:Connection = _
```

```
try {
  Class.forName(driver)
  connection = DriverManager.getConnection(url, username, password)
  val statement = connection.createStatement
  val rs = statement.executeQuery("SELECT host, user FROM user")
  while (rs.next) {
    val host = rs.getString("host")
    val user = rs.getString("user")
    println("host = %s, user = %s".format(host,user))
  }
} catch {
  case e: Exception => e.printStackTrace
}
connection.close

}
```

That code shows how to query a database table named user in a database named mysql. That database name and table name are standard in any MySQL installation.

As shown in the example, the format of the MySQL JDBC URL string is:

```
jdbc:mysql://HOST:PORT/DATABASE
```

In this code I have MySQL running on port 8889 on my computer because it's the default port when using MAMP (*http://www.mamp.info/en/index.html*), a tool that makes it easy to run MySQL, Apache, and PHP on Mac OS X systems. If you have MySQL running on its standard port (3306), just drop the port off the URL string.

## Discussion

The easiest way to run this example is to use the Simple Build Tool (*https://github.com/ harrah/xsbt/wiki*) (SBT). To do this, create an SBT directory structure as described in Recipe 18.1, "Creating a Project Directory Structure for SBT", then add the MySQL JDBC dependency to the *build.sbt* file:

```
libraryDependencies += "mysql" % "mysql-connector-java" % "5.1.24"
```

Copy and paste the code shown in this recipe into a file named *Test1.scala* in the root directory of your project, and then run the program:

```
$ sbt run
```

You should see some output like this:

```
host = localhost, user =
host = localhost, user = fred
```

That output will vary depending on the users actually defined in your MySQL database.

This recipe works well for small applications where you want one connection to a database, and you don't mind running simple JDBC SQL queries using the Statement,

`PreparedStatement`, and `ResultSet` classes. For larger applications, you'll want to use a tool that gives you connection pooling capabilities, and possibly DSL or ORM capabilities to simplify your SQL queries.

If you're using a different relational database, the approach is the same as long as the database provides a JDBC driver. For instance, to use PostgreSQL (*http://www.post gresql.org/*), just use the PostgreSQL JDBC driver (*http://jdbc.postgresql.org/*) and this information to create a connection:

```
Class.forName("org.postgresql.Driver")
val url = "jdbc:postgresql://HOST/DATABASE"
val conn = DriverManager.getConnection(url,"username", "password")
```

Of course your database tables will be different, but the process of connecting to the database is the same.

## See Also

- The MySQL JDBC driver (*http://dev.mysql.com/downloads/connector/j/*).
- MAMP (*http://www.mamp.info/*).
- The Simple Build Tool (SBT) (*http://www.scala-sbt.org/*).
- Recipe 18.1, "Creating a Project Directory Structure for SBT" shows how to create an SBT directory structure.
- If you're new to MySQL and JDBC, I wrote a series of MySQL JDBC tutorials (*http://alvinalexander.com/java/java-mysql-examples*) that can help you get started.

# 16.2. Connecting to a Database with the Spring Framework

## Problem

You want to connect to a database using the Spring Framework (*http://www.spring source.org/*). This gives you a nice way to add connection pooling and other capabilities to your SQL code.

## Solution

Use the same Spring Framework configuration you've used in Java applications, but convert your Java source code to Scala. The biggest changes involve the differences in class casting between Java and Scala, and conversions between Java and Scala collections.

## Discussion

To demonstrate this, create a basic Spring JDBC example. Start by creating a simple SBT project directory structure as demonstrated in Recipe 18.1, "Creating a Project Directory Structure for SBT".

Once the SBT directory structure is created, place this Spring *applicationContext.xml* file in the *src/main/resources* directory:

```
<?xml version="1.0" encoding="UTF-8"?>
<!DOCTYPE beans PUBLIC "-//SPRING//DTD BEAN//EN"
  "http://www.springframework.org/dtd/spring-beans.dtd">

<beans>

  <bean id="testDao" class="springtests.TestDao">
    <property name="dataSource" ref="basicDataSource"/>
  </bean>

  <bean id="basicDataSource" class="org.apache.commons.dbcp.BasicDataSource">
    <property name="driverClassName" value="com.mysql.jdbc.Driver" />
    <property name="url" value="jdbc:mysql://localhost/mysql" />
    <property name="username" value="root" />
    <property name="password" value="root" />
    <property name="initialSize" value="1" />
    <property name="maxActive" value="5" />
  </bean>

</beans>
```

This file declares that you'll have a class named `TestDao` in a package named *springtests*. This bean declaration will be used in the `Main` object, which you'll create shortly.

This file also lets you connect to a MySQL database named `mysql`, on the default port (3306) of the `localhost` server, with the username and password both set to `root`. The `initialSize` and `maxActive` settings let you control the database connection pool settings. Change those properties as needed for your system.

You'll need to add a number of dependencies to your *build.sbt* file to get Spring to work:

```
name := "MySQLTest1"

version := "1.0"

scalaVersion := "2.10.1"

libraryDependencies ++= Seq(
  "mysql" % "mysql-connector-java" % "5.1.+",
  "commons-dbcp" % "commons-dbcp" % "1.4",
  "org.springframework" % "spring-core" % "3.1+",
```

```
            "org.springframework" % "spring-beans" % "3.1+",
            "org.springframework" % "spring-jdbc" % "3.1+",
            "org.springframework" % "spring-tx" % "3.1+"
        )
```

Alternatively, you can manually download the JAR files that are needed and put them in your *lib* directory.

Next, create a file named *Main.scala* in your root SBT directory with the following contents:

```
package springtests

import org.springframework.context.support.ClassPathXmlApplicationContext

object Main extends App {

    // read the application context file
    val ctx = new ClassPathXmlApplicationContext("applicationContext.xml")

    // get a testDao instance
    val testDao = ctx.getBean("testDao").asInstanceOf[TestDao]
    val numUsers = testDao.getNumUsers
    println("You have this many users: " + numUsers)

}
```

Note how an instance of the `TestDao` is instantiated in this object. This code is similar to Java, except for the way class casting is handled. As shown, Scala uses the `asInstanceOf` method to declare that the `testDao` bean is of the type `TestDao`.

Next, create another file in the root directory of the project named *TestDao.scala* with these contents:

```
package springtests

import org.springframework.jdbc.core.simple._

class TestDao
extends SimpleJdbcDaoSupport {

    def getNumUsers: Int  = {
        val query = "select count(1) from user"
        return getJdbcTemplate.queryForInt(query)
    }

}
```

Now run the project with the `sbt run` command. You should see some simple output, including the number of records in your MySQL user database table.

Although this example was created to demonstrate how to use the Spring JDBC support with Scala, you can use the steps in this recipe to use other Spring libraries in your Scala applications.

## See Also

- The Spring Framework (*http://www.springsource.org/*).
- MAMP (*http://mamp.info/en/index.html*).
- Recipe 18.1, "Creating a Project Directory Structure for SBT".
- A project named "Spring Scala" is being created to make it easier to use Spring in Scala applications (*http://blog.springsource.org/2012/12/10/introducing-spring-scala/*).

# 16.3. Connecting to MongoDB and Inserting Data

## Problem

You want to use the MongoDB database with a Scala application, and want to learn how to connect to it, and insert and retrieve data.

## Solution

If you don't already have a MongoDB (*http://www.mongodb.org/*) installation, download and install the MongoDB software per the instructions on its website. (It's simple to install.) Once it's running, use the Casbah driver (*https://github.com/mongodb/casbah*) with your Scala application to interact with MongoDB.

In development, I start my test instance of MongoDB from its installation directory with this command:

```
$ bin/mongod -vvvv --dbpath /Users/Al/data/mongodatabases
```

This starts the MongoDB server in a verbose mode, using the directory shown for its databases. After a lot of output, the last few lines from the mongod command look like this:

```
Sun Sep 16 14:27:34 [websvr] admin web console waiting for connections
    on port 28017
Sun Sep 16 14:27:34 [initandlisten] waiting for connections on port 27017
```

To demonstrate Casbah, build a small application. First, create a simple SBT project directory structure, as demonstrated in Recipe 18.1, "Creating a Project Directory Structure for SBT"."

You can follow along by cloning my GitHub project (*https://github.com/alvinj/ScalaCasbahMongoDB*).

Second, create your *build.sbt* file, specifically including the Casbah driver dependency:

```
name := "MongoDBDemo1"

version := "1.0"

scalaVersion := "2.10.0"

libraryDependencies ++= Seq(
  "org.mongodb" %% "casbah" % "2.6.0",
  "org.slf4j" % "slf4j-simple" % "1.6.4"
)

scalacOptions += "-deprecation"
```

The SLF4J library shown isn't necessary for a simple example, but including it gets rid of a few warning messages.

Next, put the following code in a file named *MongoFactory.scala* in the root directory of your SBT project:

```
import com.mongodb.casbah.MongoCollection
import com.mongodb.casbah.MongoConnection

object MongoFactory {

  private val SERVER = "localhost"
  private val PORT   = 27017
  private val DATABASE = "portfolio"
  private val COLLECTION = "stocks"

  val connection = MongoConnection(SERVER)
  val collection = connection(DATABASE)(COLLECTION)

}
```

This object helps to simplify the interactions with a MongoDB database. You won't need all of its functionality for this recipe, but it will be used completely in other recipes. If your MongoDB instance is running on the default port on localhost, those settings will work fine. If you already have a database named portfolio, be sure to use a different name.

Next, put the following code in a file named *Common.scala*, also in the root directory of your SBT project:

```
import com.mongodb.casbah.Imports._

case class Stock (symbol: String, price: Double)

object Common {

  /**
   * Convert a Stock object into a BSON format that MongoDb can store.
   */
  def buildMongoDbObject(stock: Stock): MongoDBObject = {
    val builder = MongoDBObject.newBuilder
    builder += "symbol" -> stock.symbol
    builder += "price" -> stock.price
    builder.result
  }

}
```

That code includes a simple case class to represent a Stock, and the buildMongoDbObject method in the Common object does the work of converting a Stock into a MongoDBObject that can be stored in a MongoDB database. The method converts the fields in the Stock object into key/value pairs that correspond to the MongoDB "document" paradigm. The MongoDBObject from the Casbah driver simplifies the conversion process.

With this code in place, it's time to create a simple test program to insert several Stock instances into the database. Put the following code into a file named *Insert.scala* in the root directory of your SBT project:

```
import com.mongodb.casbah.Imports._
import Common._

object Insert extends App {

  // create some Stock instances
  val apple = Stock("AAPL", 600)
  val google = Stock("GOOG", 650)
  val netflix = Stock("NFLX", 60)

  // save them to the mongodb database
  saveStock(apple)
  saveStock(google)
  saveStock(netflix)

  // our 'save' method
  def saveStock(stock: Stock) {
    val mongoObj = buildMongoDbObject(stock)
    MongoFactory.collection.save(mongoObj)
  }

}
```

The interesting part of this code is the saveStock method. It does the following work:

- It takes a Stock object as an input parameter.
- It converts the Stock object to a MongoDBObject with the buildMongoDbObject method.
- It saves the mongoObj object to the database collection with the save method of the collection instance. The collection is an instance of MongoCollection, which is obtained from the MongoFactory.

With everything in place, run this object with sbt run, and it will quietly insert the data into the collection.

## Discussion

In Recipe 16.5, "Searching a MongoDB Collection", you'll see how to search a MongoDB collection using Scala and Casbah, but for the time being, if you open up the MongoDB command-line client and switch to the portfolio database, you can see the new documents in the stocks collection.

To do this, move to your MongoDB installation *bin* directory, start the mongo command-line client, move to the portfolio database, and list all the documents in the stocks collection, using these commands:

```
$ mongo

> use portfolio

> db.stocks.find()
{"_id" : ObjectId("5023fad43004f32afda0b550"), "symbol" : "AAPL", "price" : 600 }
{"_id" : ObjectId("5023fad43004f32afda0b551"), "symbol" : "GOOG", "price" : 650 }
{"_id" : ObjectId("5023fad43004f32afda0b552"), "symbol" : "NFLX", "price" : 60 }
```

This shows the three objects the Insert application inserted. You can remove those objects with the following command if you'd like to modify and run the program again:

```
> db.stocks.remove()
```

To help you work with MongoDB, I've created a Scala + MongoDB + Casbah example project on GitHub (*https://github.com/alvinj/ScalaCasbahMongoDB*) that includes the source code shown in this recipe, as well as additional code from the Find, Update, and Delete recipes in this chapter.

## See Also

- MongoDB (*http://www.mongodb.org/*)
- Casbah (*http://api.mongodb.org/scala/casbah/current/*)
- The `MongoCollection` API (*http://api.mongodb.org/scala/casbah/current/scala doc/#com.mongodb.casbah.MongoCollection*)

# 16.4. Inserting Documents into MongoDB with insert, save, or +=

## Problem

You want to save documents to a MongoDB collection from a Scala application.

## Solution

Use the `insert`, `save`, or `+=` methods of the Casbah `MongoCollection` class.

In order to save a document to your MongoDB collection, you can use the `MongoCollection` `insert` method:

```
collection.insert(buildMongoDbObject(apple))
collection.insert(buildMongoDbObject(google))
collection.insert(buildMongoDbObject(netflix))
```

You can also use the `save` method:

```
collection.save(buildMongoDbObject(apple))
collection.save(buildMongoDbObject(google))
collection.save(buildMongoDbObject(netflix))
```

And you can also use the `+=` method:

```
collection += buildMongoDbObject(apple)
collection += buildMongoDbObject(google)
collection += buildMongoDbObject(netflix)
collection += buildMongoDbObject(amazon)
```

The intention of the `insert` and `save` methods is obvious; you're inserting/saving data to your MongoDB collection. The third approach is a little different; it looks like what you're doing is adding an object to a collection. In fact, you're saving your object to the database collection with each `+=` call.

Here's what the `+=` approach looks like in a complete program:

```
import com.mongodb.casbah.Imports._
import Common._
```

```
object Insert2 extends App {

  val collection = MongoFactory.collection

  // create some Stock instances
  val apple = Stock("AAPL", 600)
  val google = Stock("GOOG", 650)
  val netflix = Stock("NFLX", 60)
  val amazon = Stock("AMZN", 220)

  // add them to the collection (+= does the save)
  collection += buildMongoDbObject(apple)
  collection += buildMongoDbObject(google)
  collection += buildMongoDbObject(netflix)
  collection += buildMongoDbObject(amazon)

}
```

To use the insert or save methods, simply replace the += lines with their equivalent lines.

## Discussion

If you'd like to experiment with this code, just add it to the SBT project that you started in Recipe 16.3. The buildMongoDbObject method in the Common class of that recipe converts a Scala object to a MongoDBObject that can be saved to the database using save, insert, or +=.

When choosing between save, insert, or +=, there's obviously a big difference in style between += and the other methods. The save and insert methods accept a variety of different parameters and both return a WriteResult, so you have a number of options to choose from.

You'll encounter the WriteResult and WriteConcern classes while working with the Casbah driver. These classes come from the MongoDB Java driver, which Casbah wraps. WriteResult lets you access the results of the previous write, and has methods like getField, getError, and getLastError.

WriteConcern provides options to let you control the write behavior, including behavior about network errors, slaves, timeouts, and forcing fsync to disk.

## See Also

- The WriteResult Javadoc (*http://bit.ly/18lGsNu*)
- The WriteConcern Javadoc (*http://bit.ly/13gNwpY*)

# 16.5. Searching a MongoDB Collection

## Problem

You want to find objects in your MongoDB collection using Scala and the Casbah driver.

## Solution

Use the `find*` methods of the `MongoCollection` class to get the elements you want, specifically the `find` and `findOne` methods.

Assuming that you have everything set up as shown in Recipe 16.3, the following code demonstrates these techniques:

- How to find all the documents in a collection
- How to find one document that matches your search criteria
- How to find all documents that match your search criteria
- How to limit the number of results returned by a `find` query

Here's the code:

```
import com.mongodb.casbah.Imports._

object Find extends App {

    val collection = MongoFactory.collection

    // (1) find all stocks with find()
    // -----------------------------
    println("\n___ all stocks ___")
    var stocks = collection.find
    stocks.foreach(println)

    // (2) search for an individual stock
    // ---------------------------------
    println("\n___ .findOne(query) ___")
    val query = MongoDBObject("symbol" -> "GOOG")
    val result = collection.findOne(query)          // Some
    val stock = convertDbObjectToStock(result.get)  // convert it to a Stock
    println(stock)

    // (3) find all stocks that meet a search criteria
    // ----------------------------------------------
    println("\n___ price $gt 500 ___")
    stocks = collection.find("price" $gt 500)
    stocks.foreach(println)

    // (4) find all stocks that match a search pattern
```

```
// ------------------------------------------------
println("\n___ stocks that begin with 'A' ___")
stocks = collection.find(MongoDBObject("symbol" -> "A.*".r))
stocks.foreach(println)

// (5) find.limit(2)
// ------------------------------
println("\n___ find.limit(2) ___")
stocks = collection.find.limit(2)
stocks.foreach(println)

// warning: don't use the 'get' method in real-world code
def convertDbObjectToStock(obj: MongoDBObject): Stock = {
  val symbol = obj.getAs[String]("symbol").get
  val price = obj.getAs[Double]("price").get
  Stock(symbol, price)
}

}
```

Save that code to a file named *Find.scala* in the root directory of your SBT project, and then run the object with SBT:

```
$ sbt run
```

If you've been working through the MongoDB recipes in this chapter, or you cloned my Scala + Casbah + MongoDB project from GitHub (*https://github.com/alvinj/Scala CasbahMongoDB*), you may have multiple main methods in your project. If so, SBT detects those main methods and asks which one you want to run. To run the Find object, select it from the list SBT displays:

```
Multiple main classes detected, select one to run:

[1] Find
[2] Insert
[3] Insert2

Enter number: 1
```

Running the Find object after populating the database in the earlier recipes results in the following output:

```
___ all stocks ___
{ "_id" : { "$oid" : "502683283004b3802ec47df2"} , "symbol" : "AAPL" ,
  "price" : 600.0}
{ "_id" : { "$oid" : "502683283004b3802ec47df3"} , "symbol" : "GOOG" ,
  "price" : 650.0}
{ "_id" : { "$oid" : "502683283004b3802ec47df4"} , "symbol" : "NFLX" ,
  "price" : 60.0}
{ "_id" : { "$oid" : "502683283004b3802ec47df5"} , "symbol" : "AMZN" ,
  "price" : 220.0}

___ .findOne(query) ___
```

```
Stock(GOOG,650.0)

___ price $gt 500 ___
{ "_id" : { "$oid" : "502683283004b3802ec47df2"} , "symbol" : "AAPL" ,
  "price" : 600.0}
{ "_id" : { "$oid" : "502683283004b3802ec47df3"} , "symbol" : "GOOG" ,
  "price" : 650.0}

___ stocks that begin with 'A' ___
{ "_id" : { "$oid" : "502683283004b3802ec47df2"} , "symbol" : "AAPL" ,
  "price" : 600.0}
{ "_id" : { "$oid" : "502683283004b3802ec47df5"} , "symbol" : "AMZN" ,
  "price" : 220.0}

___ find.limit(2) ___
{ "_id" : { "$oid" : "502683283004b3802ec47df2"} , "symbol" : "AAPL" ,
  "price" : 600.0}
{ "_id" : { "$oid" : "502683283004b3802ec47df3"} , "symbol" : "GOOG" ,
  "price" : 650.0}
```

## Discussion

In the first query, the find method returns all documents from the specified collection. This method returns a MongoCursor, and the code iterates over the results using that cursor.

In the second query, the findOne method is used to find one stock that matches the search query. The query is built by creating a MongoDBObject with the desired attributes. In this example, that's a stock whose symbol is GOOG. The findOne method is called to get the result, and it returns an instance of Some[MongoDBObject].

In this example, result.get is called on the next line, but in the real world, it's a better practice to use a for loop or a match expression:

```
collection.findOne(query) match {
  case Some(Stock) =>
      // convert it to a Stock
      println(convertDbObjectToStock(result.get))
  case None =>
      println("Got something else")
}
```

Of course, how you implement that will vary depending on your needs.

The convertDbObjectToStock method does the reverse of the buildMongoDbObject method shown in the earlier recipes, and converts a MongoDBObject to a Stock instance.

The third query shows how to search for all stocks whose price is greater than 500:

```
stocks = collection.find("price" $gt 500)
```

This again returns a MongoCursor, and all matches are printed.

Casbah includes other methods besides `$gt`, such as `$gte`, `$lt`, and `$lte`. You can use multiple operators against one field like this:

```
"price" $gt 50 $lte 100
```

You can also query against multiple fields by joining tuples:

```
val query: DBObject = ("price" $gt 50 $lte 100) ++ ("priceToBook" $gt 1)
```

See the Casbah documentation (*http://api.mongodb.org/scala/casbah/current/tutori al.html*) for more examples of creating Casbah-style queries.

In the fourth query, a simple regular expression pattern is used to search for all stocks whose symbol begins with the letter A:

```
stocks = collection.find(MongoDBObject("symbol" -> "A.*".r))
```

Notice that the `r` method is called on a `String` to create the query. This converts the `String` to a `Regex`, as demonstrated in the REPL:

```
scala> "A.*".r
res0: scala.util.matching.Regex = A.*
```

The fifth query demonstrates how to use the `limit` method to limit the number of results that are returned:

```
stocks = collection.find.limit(2)
```

Because MongoDB is typically used to store a *lot* of data, you'll want to use `limit` to control the amount of data you get back from a query.

The `MongoCollection` class also has a `findByID` method that you can use when you know the ID of your object. Additionally, there are `findAndModify` and `findAndRemove` methods, which are discussed in other recipes in this chapter.

## See Also

- Casbah documentation (*http://mongodb.github.io/casbah/*)
- The `MongoCollection` class (*http://bit.ly/1aMhTKC*)
- The MongoDB tutorial (*http://docs.mongodb.org/manual/tutorial/getting-started/*)

# 16.6. Updating Documents in a MongoDB Collection

## Problem

You want to update one or more documents in a MongoDB collection.

## Solution

Use either the `findAndModify` or `update` methods from the Casbah `MongoCollection` class, as shown in this example:

```
import com.mongodb.casbah.Imports._
import Common._

object Update extends App {

  val collection = MongoFactory.collection

  // findAndModify
  // ------------

  // create a new Stock object
  val google = Stock("GOOG", 500)
  // search for an existing document with this symbol
  var query = MongoDBObject("symbol" -> "GOOG")
  // replace the old document with one based on the 'google' object
  val res1 = collection.findAndModify(query, buildMongoDbObject(google))
  println("findAndModify: " + res1)

  // update
  // ------

  // create a new Stock
  var apple = Stock("AAPL", 1000)
  // search for a document with this symbol
  query = MongoDBObject("symbol" -> "AAPL")
  // replace the old document with the 'apple' instance
  val res2 = collection.update(query, buildMongoDbObject(apple))
  println("update: " + res2)

}
```

In both cases, you build a document object to replace the existing document in the database, and then create a query object, which lets you find what you want to replace. Then you call either `findAndModify` or `update` to perform the update.

For instance, in the `findAndModify` example, a new `Stock` instance named `google` is created, and it's used to replace the old document in the database whose symbol is GOOG. The `buildMongoDbObject` method is used to convert the `google` instance into a MongoDB document before the `update` method is called.

The difference between the two methods can be seen in the output:

```
findAndModify: Some({ "_id" : { "$oid" : "502683283004b3802ec47df3"} ,
   "symbol" : "GOOG" , "price" : 500.0})
update: N/A
```

Whereas the findAndModify method returns the old document (the document that was replaced), the update method returns a WriteResult instance.

If you've been following along with the MongoDB recipes in this chapter, save that file as *Update.scala* in the root directory of your project, and run it with sbt run.

# 16.7. Accessing the MongoDB Document ID Field

## Problem

You want to get the ID field for a document you've inserted into a MongoDB collection.

## Solution

Perform a query to get the document you want, and then call get("_ID") on the resulting MongoDBObject, like this:

```
basicDbObject.get("_id")
```

The following example shows how to get the ID field from a DBObject after inserting the object into the database. I first create a Stock as usual, convert the Stock to a MongoDBObject, perform the insert, and then get the ID value, which is added to the MongoDBObject after the insert operation is performed:

```
import com.mongodb.casbah.Imports._
import Common._

object InsertAndGetId extends App {

  val coll = MongoFactory.collection

  // get the _id field after an insert
  val amazon = Stock("AMZN", 220)
  val amazonMongoObject = buildMongoDbObject(amazon)
  coll.insert(amazonMongoObject)
  println("ID: " + amazonMongoObject.get("_id"))

}
```

If you just need to get the ID field from a MongoDBObject after performing a query, the following complete example shows how to do that with a match expression:

```
import com.mongodb.casbah.Imports._

object GetId extends App {

  val collection = MongoFactory.collection

  val query = MongoDBObject("symbol" -> "GOOG")
  collection.findOne(query) match {
```

```
    case Some(result) => println("ID: " + result.get("_id"))
    case None => println("Stock not found")
  }

}
```

A match expression is used in this example because the findOne(query) will return None if no matching documents are found in the collection. You can also use the usual getOrElse and foreach techniques to work with an Option.

If you've been following along with the MongoDB recipes in this chapter, save those files with the names *InsertAndGetId.scala* and *GetId.scala* in the root directory of your project, and run them with sbt run.

## See Also

Recipe 20.6, "Using the Option/Some/None Pattern" for many examples of working with methods that return an Option

# 16.8. Deleting Documents in a MongoDB Collection

## Problem

You want to delete one or more documents in a MongoDB collection.

## Solution

Use the findAndRemove method of the Casbah MongoCollection class to delete one document at a time, or use the remove method to delete one or more documents at a time.

The following code uses findAndRemove to delete the document whose symbol field is AAPL:

```
val query = MongoDBObject("symbol" -> "AAPL")
val result = collection.findAndRemove(query)
println("result: " + result)
```

When a document is deleted, the findAndRemove method returns the document that was deleted, wrapped in a Some:

```
result: Some({ "_id" : { "$oid" : "50255d1d03644925d83b3d07"} ,
  "symbol" : "AAPL" , "price" : 600.0})
```

If nothing is deleted, such as when you try to delete a document that doesn't exist, the result is None:

```
result: None
```

Therefore, you'll probably want to handle this using a match expression, as shown in the previous recipe.

To delete multiple documents from the collection, specify your search criteria when using the `remove` method, such as deleting all documents whose `price` field is greater than 500:

```
collection.remove("price" $gt 500)
```

The following method is dangerous: it shows how to delete all documents in the current collection:

```
// removes all documents
def deleteAllObjectsFromCollection(coll: MongoCollection) {
  coll.remove(MongoDBObject.newBuilder.result)
}
```

(Be careful with that one.)

## Discussion

If you've been following along with the MongoDB recipes in this chapter, you can experiment with these approaches by saving the following code to a file named *DeleteApple.scala* in the root directory of your SBT project:

```
import com.mongodb.casbah.Imports._

object DeleteApple extends App {

  var collection = MongoFactory.collection

  // delete AAPL
  val query = MongoDBObject("symbol" -> "AAPL")
  val result = collection.findAndRemove(query)
  println("result: " + result)

}
```

 You can also clone my complete Scala + Casbah + MongoDB project from GitHub (*https://github.com/alvinj/ScalaCasbahMongoDB*).

If your database has a document whose `symbol` field is AAPL, when you run this object with `sbt run`, the result will show the document that was deleted:

```
result: Some({ "_id" : { "$oid" : "5026b22c300478e85a145d43"} ,
  "symbol" : "AAPL" , "price" : 600.0})
```

The following complete code shows how to delete multiple documents:

```
import com.mongodb.casbah.Imports._

object DeleteMultiple extends App {

  var collection = MongoFactory.collection

  // delete all documents with price > 200
  collection.remove("price" $gt 200)

}
```

In this case, the remove method doesn't return anything interesting, so I don't assign it
to a result.

## See Also

My Scala + Casbah + MongoDB sample project (*https://github.com/alvinj/Scala CasbahMongoDB*)

# 16.9. A Quick Look at Slick

When it comes to working with relational databases, you can use the wealth of Java
solutions that are available, but other tools are emerging to provide a "Scala way" of
working with databases. One of these solutions is a library named Slick (*http://slick.type safe.com/*), from Typesafe (*http://typesafe.com/*), a company that was founded by the
creators of the Scala language. According to their documentation, Slick provides a
"modern database query and access library."

This recipe doesn't cover Slick in depth because it's well documented on the Typesafe
website, but instead offers a quick look at what Slick offers.

In short, Slick lets you define database table objects in your code like this:

```
object Authors extends Table[(Int, String, String)]("AUTHORS") {
  def id        = column[Int]("ID", O.PrimaryKey)
  def firstName = column[String]("FIRST_NAME")
  def lastName  = column[String]("LAST_NAME")
  def * = id ~ firstName ~ lastName
}

object Books extends Table[(Int, String)]("BOOKS") {
  def id    = column[Int]("ID", O.PrimaryKey)
  def title = column[String]("TITLE")
  def * = id ~ title
}

object BookAuthors extends Table[(Int, Int, Int)]("BOOK_AUTHORS") {
  def id        = column[Int]("ID", O.PrimaryKey)
  def bookId    = column[Int]("BOOK_ID")
```

```
    def authorId   = column[Int]("AUTHOR_ID")
    def bookFk      = foreignKey("BOOK_FK", bookId, Books)(_.id)
    def authorFk    = foreignKey("AUTHOR_FK", authorId, Authors)(_.id)
    def * = id ~ bookId ~ authorId
}
```

Having defined your tables in Scala code, you can refer to the fields in the tables in a type-safe manner. You can create your database tables using Scala code, like this:

```
(Books.ddl ++ Authors.ddl ++ BookAuthors.ddl).create
```

A simple query to retrieve all records from the resulting books database table looks like this:

```
val q = Query(Books)
q.list.foreach(println)
```

You can filter queries using a filter method:

```
val q = Query(Books).filter(_.title.startsWith("Zen"))
q.list.foreach(println)
```

You can write a join like this:

```
val q = for {
  b <- Books
  a <- Authors
  ba <- BookAuthors if b.id === ba.bookId && a.id === ba.authorId
} yield (b.title, a.lastName)
q.foreach(println)
```

Insert, update, and delete expressions follow the same pattern. Because you declared the database design in Scala code, Slick makes working with a database feel like working with collections.

Though I appreciate a good DSL, one thing I always look for in a database library is a way to break out of the library to let me write my own SQL queries, and Slick allows this as well.

As mentioned, the Slick documentation (*http://slick.typesafe.com/docs/*) is thorough, so it's not covered in this chapter. See the Slick website (*http://slick.typesafe.com/*) for more information.

# CHAPTER 17

# Interacting with Java

## Introduction

In general, the ability to easily mix Scala and Java code is pretty seamless and amazing. In most cases, you can create an SBT project, put your Scala code in *src/main/scala*, put your Java code in *src/main/java*, and it "just works." For instance, the recipes on web services in Chapter 15 provide many examples of calling existing Java libraries from Scala code.

In my Scala/Java interactions, the biggest issues I've run into deal with the differences between their collections libraries. However, I've always been able to work through those problems with Scala's `JavaConversions` object.

If you're going to be accessing Scala code from Java, the other problem you can run into is that there are things you can do in Scala that don't map well to Java. If you're going to use Scala features like implicit conversions and parameters, currying, traits that have implemented methods, and other advanced features, you'll want to keep that Scala code away from your public API.

Finally, for some cases such as serialization, methods with varargs parameters, and creating JavaBean-like classes in Scala, it's important to know the annotations that are available to you.

## 17.1. Going to and from Java Collections

### Problem

You're using Java classes in a Scala application, and those classes either return Java collections, or require Java collections in their method calls.

## Solution

Use the methods of Scala's `JavaConversions` object to make the conversions work.

For instance, the `java.util.ArrayList` class is commonly used in Java applications, and you can simulate receiving an `ArrayList` from a method in the REPL, like this:

```
scala> def nums = {
     |    var list = new java.util.ArrayList[Int]()
     |    list.add(1)
     |    list.add(2)
     |    list
     | }
nums: java.util.ArrayList[Int]
```

Even though this method is written in Scala, when it's called, it acts just as though it was returning an `ArrayList` from a Java method:

```
scala> val list = nums
list: java.util.ArrayList[Int] = [1, 2]
```

However, because it's a Java collection, I can't call the `foreach` method on it that I've come to know and love in Scala, because it isn't there:

```
scala> list.foreach(println)
<console>:10: error:
value foreach is not a member of java.util.ArrayList[Int]
              list.foreach(println)
                   ^
```

But by importing the methods from the `JavaConversions` object, the `ArrayList` magically acquires a `foreach` method:

```
scala> import scala.collection.JavaConversions._
import scala.collection.JavaConversions._

scala> list.foreach(println)
1
2
```

This "magic" comes from the power of Scala's implicit conversions, which are demonstrated in Recipe 1.10, "Add Your Own Methods to the String Class".

## Discussion

When you get a reference to a Java collections object, you can either use that object as a Java collection (such as using its `Iterator`), or you can convert that collection to a Scala collection. Once you become comfortable with Scala collection methods like `foreach`, `map`, etc., you'll definitely want to treat it as a Scala collection, and the way to do that is to use the methods of the `JavaConversions` object.

As a more thorough example of how the `JavaConversions` methods work, assume you have a Java class named `JavaExamples` with the following `getNumbers` method:

```java
// java
public static List<Integer> getNumbers() {
  List<Integer> numbers = new ArrayList<Integer>();
  numbers.add(1);
  numbers.add(2);
  numbers.add(3);
  return numbers;
}
```

You can attempt to call that method from Scala code, as shown in this example:

```
val numbers = JavaExamples.getNumbers()
numbers.foreach(println)  // this won't work
```

But this code will fail with the following compiler error:

```
value 'foreach' is not a member of java.util.List[Integer]
```

To solve this problem, you need to import the `JavaConversions.asScalaBuffer` method. When you do this, you can either explicitly call the `asScalaBuffer` method, or let it be used implicitly. The *explicit* call looks like this:

```
import scala.collection.JavaConversions.asScalaBuffer

val numbers = asScalaBuffer(JavaExamples.getNumbers)
numbers.foreach(println)

// prints 'scala.collection.convert.Wrappers$JListWrapper'
println(numbers.getClass)
```

The *implicit* use looks like this:

```
import scala.collection.JavaConversions.asScalaBuffer

val numbers = JavaExamples.getNumbers
numbers.foreach(println)

// prints 'java.util.ArrayList'
println(numbers.getClass)
```

The `println(numbers.getClass)` calls show that there's a slight difference in the result between the explicit and implicit uses. Using the explicit `asScalaBuffer` method call makes the `numbers` object an instance of `collection.convert.Wrappers$JListWrapper`, whereas the implicit use shows that `numbers` is an `ArrayList`. As a practical matter, you can use either approach, depending on your preferences about working with implicit conversions; they both let you call `foreach`, `map`, and other Scala sequence methods.

You can repeat the same example using a Java `Map` and `HashMap`. First, create this method in a `JavaExamples` class:

```
// java
public static Map<String, String> getPeeps() {
  Map<String, String> peeps = new HashMap<String, String>();
  peeps.put("captain", "Kirk");
  peeps.put("doctor", "McCoy");
  return peeps;
}
```

Then, before calling this method from your Scala code, import the appropriate JavaConversions method:

```
import scala.collection.JavaConversions.mapAsScalaMap
```

You can then call the mapAsScalaMap method explicitly, or allow it to be called implicitly:

```
// explicit call
val peeps1 = mapAsScalaMap(JavaExamples.getPeeps)

// implicit conversion
val peeps2 = JavaExamples.getPeeps
```

Again there is a difference between the types of the map objects. In this case, peeps1, which used the explicit method call, has a type of collection.convert.Wrappers$JMapWrapper, whereas peeps2 has a type of java.util.HashMap.

Note that the JavaConversions class has been through a number of changes, and although you'll see a large number of conversion methods in your IDE, many of them are deprecated. See the latest Scaladoc for the JavaConversions object (*http://bit.ly/ 13N4ZJO*) for up-to-date information.

### Conversion tables

One interesting thing that happens during the process of converting Java collections is that you learn more about the Scala collections. For instance, given their names, you might expect a Scala List and a Java List to convert back and forth between each other, but that isn't the case. A Java List is much more like a Scala Seq or a mutable Buffer.

This is shown in Table 17-1, which shows the two-way conversions that the JavaConversions object allows between Java and Scala collections. This table is adapted from the JavaConversions documentation (*http://bit.ly/13N4ZJO*).

*Table 17-1. The two-way conversions provided by the JavaConversions object*

| Scala collection | Java collection |
| --- | --- |
| collection.Iterable | java.lang.Iterable |
| collection.Iterable | java.util.Collection |
| collection.Iterator | java.util.{Iterator, Enumeration} |
| collection.mutable.Buffer | java.util.List |
| collection.mutable.Set | java.util.Set |
| collection.mutable.Map | java.util.{Map, Dictionary} |

| Scala collection | Java collection |
|---|---|
| `collection.mutable.ConcurrentMap` | `java.util.concurrent.ConcurrentMap` |

As an example of the two-way conversions shown in Table 17-1, the `JavaConversions` object provides methods that convert between a Java `List` and a Scala `Buffer`. The `asScalaBuffer` method converts a Java `List` to a Scala `Buffer`, and `bufferAsJavaList` converts in the opposite direction, from a `Buffer` to a `List`.

### Going from Scala collections to Java collections

So far you've looked primarily at converting Java collections to Scala collections. You may also need to go in the other direction, from a Scala collection to a Java collection.

If you're converting a Scala collection to a Java collection, in addition to the two-way conversions shown in Table 17-1, the one-way conversions shown in Table 17-2 are available. Again, these have been adapted from the `JavaConversions` Scaladoc.

*Table 17-2. The Scala to Java one-way conversions provided by the JavaConversions class*

| Scala collection | Java collection |
|---|---|
| `collection.Seq` | `java.util.List` |
| `collection.mutable.Seq` | `java.util.List` |
| `collection.Set` | `java.util.Set` |
| `collection.Map` | `java.util.Map` |
| `collection.mutable.Map[String,String]` | `java.util.Properties` |

For example, assume you want to call the following `sum` method declared in a Java class named `ConversionExamples`, which expects a `java.util.List<Integer>`:

```java
// java
public static int sum(List<Integer> list) {
    int sum = 0;
    for (int i: list) { sum = sum + i; }
    return sum;
}
```

Putting the conversion tables to work, the following examples show how to pass a `Seq`, `ArrayBuffer`, and `ListBuffer` to the `sum` method:

```
import scala.collection.JavaConversions._
import scala.collection.mutable._

val sum1 = ConversionExamples.sum(seqAsJavaList(Seq(1, 2, 3)))
val sum2 = ConversionExamples.sum(bufferAsJavaList(ArrayBuffer(1,2,3)))
val sum3 = ConversionExamples.sum(bufferAsJavaList(ListBuffer(1,2,3)))
```

There are many other collection conversion possibilities, and hopefully these examples will get you started on the right path.

### The JavaConverters object

The Scala `JavaConverters` object (*http://bit.ly/13rwXU4*) lets you perform conversions in a manner similar to the examples shown, though they don't offer implicit conversions. Instead they require you to explicitly call `asJava` or `asScala` methods to perform the conversions. Be careful, because the object also contains many deprecated methods.

## See Also

- The `JavaConversions` object (*http://bit.ly/190DRry*)
- The `JavaConverters` object (*http://bit.ly/18jroMN*)

# 17.2. Add Exception Annotations to Scala Methods to Work with Java

## Problem

You want to let Java users know that a method can throw one or more exceptions so they can handle those exceptions with `try/catch` blocks.

## Solution

Add the `@throws` annotation to your Scala methods so Java consumers will know which methods can throw exceptions and what exceptions they throw.

For example, the following Scala code shows how to add an `@throws` annotation to let callers know that the exceptionThrower method can throw an `Exception`:

```
// scala
class Thrower {

  @throws(classOf[Exception])
  def exceptionThrower {
    throw new Exception("Exception!")
  }

}
```

With your Scala method annotated like that, it will work just like a Java method that throws an exception. If you attempt to call exceptionThrower from a Java class without wrapping it in a `try/catch` block, or declaring that your Java method throws an exception, the compiler (or your IDE) will give you the following error:

```
unreported exception java.lang.Exception; must be caught or declared to be thrown
```

In your Java code, you'll write a `try/catch` block as usual to handle the exception:

---

```java
// java
Thrower t = new Thrower();
try {
  t.exceptionThrower();
} catch (Exception e) {
  System.err.println("Caught the exception.");
  e.printStackTrace();
}
```

If you want to declare that your Scala method throws multiple exceptions, add an annotation for each exception:

```scala
@throws(classOf[IOException])
@throws(classOf[LineUnavailableException])
@throws(classOf[UnsupportedAudioFileException])
def playSoundFileWithJavaAudio {
  // exception throwing code here ...
}
```

## Discussion

If you don't mark the Scala `exceptionThrower` method with the `@throws` annotation, a Java developer *can* call it without using a `try`/`catch` block in her method, or declaring that her method throws an exception. For example, you can define the Scala method as follows, without declaring that it throws an exception:

```scala
//scala
def exceptionThrower {
  throw new Exception("Exception!")
}
```

This method can then be called from Java:

```java
// java
public static void main(String[] args) {
  Thrower t = new Thrower();
  t.exceptionThrower();
}
```

However, when the Java developer calls `exceptionThrower`, the uncaught exception will cause the Java method to fail:

```
[error] (run-main) java.lang.Exception: Exception!
java.lang.Exception: Exception!
    at Thrower.exceptionThrower(Thrower.scala:6)
    at Main.main(Main.java:9)
```

As shown, if a Java consumer doesn't know an exception can be thrown, it can wreak havoc on her application.

# 17.3. Using @SerialVersionUID and Other Annotations

## Problem

You want to specify that a class is serializable, and set the serialVersionUID. More generally, you want to know the syntax for using annotations in your Scala code, and know which annotations are available.

## Solution

Use the Scala @SerialVersionUID annotation while also having your class extend the Serializable trait:

```
@SerialVersionUID(1000L)
class Foo extends Serializable {
  // class code here
}
```

Note that Scala has a serializable annotation, but it has been deprecated since version 2.9.0. The serializable annotation Scaladoc (*http://bit.ly/17j1zLG*) includes the following note:

```
instead of @serializable class C, use class C extends Serializable
```

## Discussion

In addition to the @SerialVersionUID annotation and the Serializable trait, Scala has other annotations that should be used for various purposes, including the cloneable, remote, transient, and volatile annotations. Based primarily on the "A Tour of Scala Annotations" web page (*http://bit.ly/12uB5nl*), Table 17-3 shows a mapping of Scala annotations to their Java equivalents.

*Table 17-3. Scala annotations and their Java equivalents*

| Scala | Java |
|---|---|
| scala.beans.BeanProperty | No equivalent. When added to a class field, it results in getter and setter methods being generated that match the JavaBean specification. |
| scala.cloneable | java.lang.Cloneable |
| scala.deprecated | java.lang.Deprecated |
| scala.inline | Per the Scaladoc, @inline "requests that the compiler should try especially hard to inline the annotated method." |
| scala.native | The Java native keyword. |
| scala.remote | java.rmi.Remote |
| scala.serializable | java.io.Serializable |
| scala.SerialVersionUID | serialVersionUID field. |

| Scala | Java |
|---|---|
| `scala.throws` | `throws` keyword. |
| `scala.transient` | `transient` keyword. |
| `scala.unchecked` | No equivalent. According to its Scaladoc, it designates that "the annotated entity should not be considered for additional compiler checks." |
| `scala.annotation.varargs` | Used on a field in a method, it instructs the compiler to generate a Java varargs-style parameter. |
| `scala.volatile` | `volatile` keyword. |

As one example of these annotations, the current nightly version of the Scala Remote Scaladoc (*http://bit.ly/15Dcq1z*) states that the following Scala code and Java code are equivalent:

```
// scala
@remote trait Hello {
  def sayHello(): String
}

// java
public interface Hello extends java.rmi.Remote {
  String sayHello() throws java.rmi.RemoteException;
}
```

Recipe 17.6, "When Java Code Requires JavaBeans" provides examples of the `BeanProperty` annotation.

## See Also

- The `Serializable` trait is deprecated (*http://bit.ly/15DctKQ*)
- "A Tour of Scala Annotations" (*http://www.scala-lang.org/node/106*)
- Recipe 17.5 discusses the `@varargs` annotation, and Recipe 17.6 discusses JavaBeans

# 17.4. Using the Spring Framework

## Problem

You want to use the Java Spring Framework library in your Scala application.

## Solution

In my experience, the only real changes in using the Spring Framework in Scala applications involve how you cast the objects you instantiate from your Spring application context file, and that's only because the casting processes in Scala and Java are different.

To demonstrate this, create an empty SBT project. (See Recipe 18.1, if necessary.) Within that project, create a Spring *applicationContext.xml* file in the *src/main/resources* directory with the following contents:

```
<?xml version="1.0" encoding="UTF-8"?>
<!DOCTYPE beans PUBLIC "-//SPRING//DTD BEAN//EN" ↵
   "http://www.springframework.org/dtd/spring-beans.dtd">

<beans>

  <bean id="dog" class="scalaspring.Dog">
    <constructor-arg value="Fido" />
  </bean>

  <bean id="cat" class="scalaspring.Cat">
    <constructor-arg value="Felix" />
  </bean>

</beans>
```

This file declares that there are two classes, one named `Dog` and the other named `Cat`, in a package named `scalaspring`. You can't tell it from looking at this file, but as you'll see shortly, both the `Dog` and `Cat` classes extend a base `Animal` class.

Next, create a simple Scala object in a file named *SpringExample.scala* in the root directory of your project with a `main` method to read the *applicationContext.xml* file and create instances of the `Dog` and `Cat` classes:

```
package scalaspring

import org.springframework.context.support.ClassPathXmlApplicationContext

object ScalaSpringExample extends App {

  // open & read the application context file
  val ctx = new ClassPathXmlApplicationContext("applicationContext.xml")

  // instantiate the dog and cat objects from the application context
  val dog = ctx.getBean("dog").asInstanceOf[Animal]
  val cat = ctx.getBean("cat").asInstanceOf[Animal]

  // let them speak
  dog.speak
  cat.speak

}
```

In this code, the *applicationContext.xml* file is loaded, the `dog` and `cat` instances are created from their bean definitions in the application context, and their speak methods are executed.

Next, define the `Dog` and `Cat` classes in a file named *Animals.scala*, along with their abstract parent class `Animal`. You can also save this file in the root directory of your SBT project:

```
package scalaspring

abstract class Animal(name: String) {
  def speak: Unit      // asbtract
}

class Dog(name: String) extends Animal(name) {
  override def speak {
    println(name + " says Woof")
  }
}

class Cat(name: String) extends Animal(name) {
  override def speak {
    println(name + " says Meow")
  }
}
```

The base `Animal` class requires that the concrete classes have a `speak` method, and the `Dog` and `Cat` classes define their `speak` methods in different ways. The `Dog` and `Cat` classes are defined using a one-argument constructor, and if you look back at the application context file, you'll see that the names `Fido` and `Felix` are used in their Spring bean definitions.

Next, add Spring as a dependency to your *build.sbt* file. A basic file looks like this:

```
name := "Scala Spring Example"

version := "1.0"

scalaVersion := "2.10.0"

libraryDependencies += "org.springframework" % "spring" % "2.5.6"
```

As mentioned, you should place the *applicationContext.xml* file in your project's *src/main/resources* folder. This listing shows all the files in my project:

```
./Animals.scala
./build.sbt
./SpringExample.scala
./src/main/resources/applicationContext.xml
```

With everything in place, run the project with the usual `sbt run` command. You'll see a lot of output, including these lines, showing that the program ran successfully:

```
$ sbt run
```

```
Fido says Woof
Felix says Meow
```

 You can put the two Scala source files under the *src/main/scala* directory if you prefer, but for simple examples like this, I put them in the
root directory of my SBT project.

## Discussion

Although there was a bit of boilerplate work in this example, the only major differences
between using Scala and Java are these two lines of code in the `ScalaSpringExample`
object:

```
val dog = ctx.getBean("dog").asInstanceOf[Animal]
val cat = ctx.getBean("cat").asInstanceOf[Animal]
```

That's because this is how you cast classes in Scala. In Java, these same lines of code
would look like this:

```
Animal dog = (Animal)ctx.getBean("dog");
Animal cat = (Animal)ctx.getBean("cat");
```

## See Also

- Recipe 6.1 provides other examples of casting in Scala
- Recipe 16.2, "Connecting to a Database with the Spring Framework" shows another
  Scala Spring example
- The "Spring Scala" project aims to make it easier to use the Spring Framework in
  Scala (*http://blog.springsource.org/2012/12/10/introducing-spring-scala/*)

# 17.5. Annotating varargs Methods

## Problem

You've created a Scala method with a varargs field, and would like to be able to call that
method from Java code.

## Solution

When a Scala method has a field that takes a variable number of arguments, mark it
with the `@varargs` annotation.

For example, the `printAll` method in the following Scala class is marked with `@varargs` so it can be called as desired from Java:

```
package varargs

import scala.annotation.varargs

class Printer {

  @varargs def printAll(args: String*) {
    args.foreach(print)
    println
  }

}
```

The `printAll` method can now be called from a Java program with a variable number of parameters, as shown in this example:

```
package varargs;

public class Main {

  public static void main(String[] args) {
    Printer p = new Printer();
    p.printAll("Hello");
    p.printAll("Hello, ", "world");
  }

}
```

When this code is run, it results in the following output:

```
Hello
Hello, world
```

## Discussion

If the `@varargs` annotation isn't used on the `printAll` method, the Java code shown won't even compile, failing with the following compiler errors:

```
Main.java:7: printAll(scala.collection.Seq<java.lang.String>) in
varargs.Printer cannot be applied to (java.lang.String)
[error]     p.printAll("Hello");
[error]      ^

Main.java:8: printAll(scala.collection.Seq<java.lang.String>) in
varargs.Printer cannot be applied to (java.lang.String,java.lang.String)
[error]     p.printAll("Hello, ", "world");
[error]      ^
```

Without the `@varargs` annotation, from a Java perspective, the `printAll` method appears to take a `scala.collection.Seq<java.lang.String>` as its argument.

# 17.6. When Java Code Requires JavaBeans

## Problem

You need to interact with a Java class or library that accepts only classes that conform to the JavaBean specification.

## Solution

Use the `@BeanProperty` annotation on your fields, also making sure you declare each field as a `var`.

The `@BeanProperty` annotation can be used on fields in a Scala class constructor:

```
import scala.reflect.BeanProperty

class Person(@BeanProperty var firstName: String,
             @BeanProperty var lastName: String) {
  override def toString = s"Person: $firstName $lastName"
}
```

It can also be used on the fields in a Scala class:

```
import scala.reflect.BeanProperty

class EmailAccount {
  @BeanProperty var username: String = ""
  @BeanProperty var password: String = ""
  override def toString = s"Email Account: ($username, $password)"
}
```

To demonstrate this, create an SBT project, then save the following code to a file named *Test.scala* in the root directory of the project:

```
package foo

import scala.reflect.BeanProperty

class Person(@BeanProperty var firstName: String,
             @BeanProperty var lastName: String) {
}

class EmailAccount {
  @BeanProperty var username: String = ""
  @BeanProperty var password: String = ""
}
```

This code shows how to use the `@BeanProperty` annotation on class constructor parameters, as well as the fields in a class.

Next, create a directory named *src/main/java/foo*, and save the following Java code in a file named *Main.java* in that directory:

```java
package foo;

public class Main {

    public static void main(String[] args) {

        // create instances
        Person p = new Person("Regina", "Goode");
        EmailAccount acct = new EmailAccount();

        // demonstrate 'setter' methods
        acct.setUsername("regina");
        acct.setPassword("secret");

        // demonstrate 'getter' methods
        System.out.println(p.getFirstName());
        System.out.println(p.getLastName());
        System.out.println(acct.getUsername());
        System.out.println(acct.getPassword());

    }

}
```

This Java code demonstrates how to create instances of the Scala `Person` and `EmailAccount` classes, and access the JavaBean methods of those classes. When the code is run with `sbt run`, you'll see the following output, showing that all the getter and setter methods work:

```
$ sbt run
[info] Running foo.Main
Regina
Goode
regina
secret
```

## Discussion

You can see how the `@BeanProperty` annotation works by compiling a simple class and then disassembling it. First, save these contents to a file named *Person.scala*:

```scala
import scala.reflect.BeanProperty

class Person(@BeanProperty var name: String,
             @BeanProperty var age: Int) {
}
```

Then compile the class:

```
$ scalac Person.scala
```

After it's compiled, disassemble it with the `javap` command:

```
$ javap Person

Compiled from "Person.scala"
public class Person extends java.lang.Object implements scala.ScalaObject{
  public java.lang.String name();
  public void name_$eq(java.lang.String);
  public void setName(java.lang.String);
  public int age();
  public void age_$eq(int);
  public void setAge(int);
  public int getAge();
  public java.lang.String getName();
  public Person(java.lang.String, int);
}
```

As you can see from the disassembled code, the methods `getName`, `setName`, `getAge`, and `setAge` have all been generated because of the `@BeanProperty` annotation.

Note that if you declare your fields as type `val`, the "setter" methods (`setName`, `setAge`) won't be generated:

```
Compiled from "Person.scala"
public class Person extends java.lang.Object implements scala.ScalaObject{
  public java.lang.String name();
  public int age();
  public int getAge();
  public java.lang.String getName();
  public Person(java.lang.String, int);
}
```

Without these methods, your class will not follow the JavaBean specification.

As a final example, if the `@BeanProperty` annotation is removed from all fields, you're left with this code:

```
class Person(var firstName: String, var lastName: String)
```

When you compile this code with `scalac` and then disassemble it with `javap`, you'll see that no getter or setter methods are generated (except for those that follow the Scala convention):

```
Compiled from "Person.scala"
public class Person extends java.lang.Object{
  public java.lang.String firstName();
  public void firstName_$eq(java.lang.String);
  public java.lang.String lastName();
  public void lastName_$eq(java.lang.String);
  public Person(java.lang.String, java.lang.String);
}
```

## See Also

My tutorial about using the Java SnakeYaml library in Scala (*http://bit.ly/13h3kcc*) shows more examples of the @BeanProperty annotation.

# 17.7. Wrapping Traits with Implementations

## Problem

You've written a Scala trait with implemented methods and need to be able to use those methods from a Java application.

## Solution

You can't use the implemented methods of a Scala trait from Java, so wrap the trait in a class.

Assuming you have a Scala trait named MathTrait with a method named sum that you want to access from Java code, create a Scala class named MathTraitWrapper that wraps MathTrait:

```scala
// scala
package foo

// the original trait
trait MathTrait {
  def sum(x: Int, y: Int) =  x + y
}

// the wrapper class
class MathTraitWrapper extends MathTrait
```

In your Java code, extend the MathTraitWrapper class, and access the sum method:

```java
// java
package foo;

public class JavaMath extends MathTraitWrapper {

  public static void main(String[] args) {
    new JavaMath();
  }

  public JavaMath() {
    System.out.println(sum(2,2));
  }

}
```

This code works as expected, printing the number 4 when it is run.

# Discussion

A Java class can't extend a Scala trait that has implemented methods. To demonstrate the problem, first create a trait with a simple implemented method named sum:

```
package foo

trait MathTrait {
  def sum(x: Int, y: Int) =  x + y
}
```

Next, to attempt to use this trait from Java, you have a choice of trying to extend it or implement it. Let's first try to *extend* it:

```
package foo;

public class JavaMath extends MathTrait {}
```

By the time you finish typing that code, you see the following compiler error message:

```
The type MathTrait cannot be the superclass of JavaMath;
a superclass must be a class
```

Next, you can attempt to *implement* the trait, but intuitively you know that won't work, because in Java you implement *interfaces*, and this trait has implemented behavior, so it's not a regular Java interface:

```
package foo;

public class JavaMath implements MathTrait {}
```

This code leads to the following compiler error:

```
The type JavaMath must implement the inherited abstract method
MathTrait.sum(int, int)
```

You *could* implement a sum method in your JavaMath class, but that defeats the purpose of trying to use the sum method that's already written in the Scala MathTrait.

## Other attempts

You can try other things, such as attempting to create an instance of the MathTrait and trying to use the sum method, but this won't work either:

```
// java
package foo;

public static void main(String[] args) {
  MathTrait trait = new MathTrait();   // error, won't compile
  int sum = trait.sum(1,2);
  System.out.println("SUM = " + sum);
}
```

Trying to instantiate a MathTrait instance results in this compiler error:

```
foo.MathTrait is abstract; cannot be instantiated
[error] MathTrait trait = new MathTrait();
[error]                        ^
```

You may already know what the problem is, but to be clear, let's see what class files are generated on the Scala side. In an SBT project, the class files are located in the following directory:

```
$PROJECT/target/scala-2.10.0/classes/foo
```

If you move into that directory and list the files, you'll see that two files related to the Scala MathTrait trait have been created:

```
MathTrait.class
MathTrait$class.class
```

You can see the problem by disassembling these files with javap. First, the *MathTrait.class* file:

```
$ javap MathTrait
Compiled from "MathTrait.scala"
public interface foo.MathTrait{
    public abstract int sum(int, int);
}
```

Next, the *MathTrait$class.class* file:

```
$ javap MathTrait\$class
Compiled from "MathTrait.scala"
public abstract class foo.MathTrait$class extends java.lang.Object{
    public static int sum(foo.MathTrait, int, int);
    public static void $init$(foo.MathTrait);
}
```

The problem with trying to work with the Scala MathTrait from a Java perspective is that MathTrait looks like an interface, and MathTrait$class looks like an abstract class. Neither one will let you use the logic in the sum method.

Because MathTrait looks like just an interface, you realize you might be able to create a Java class that implements that interface, and then override the sum method:

```
// java
package foo;

public class JavaMath implements MathTrait {

  public int sum(int x, int y) {
    return x + y;
  }
}
```

```
public static void main(String[] args) {
  JavaMath math = new JavaMath();
  System.out.println(math.sum(1,1));
}

}
```

This does indeed work, but for the purposes of this recipe, it doesn't really matter. The purpose of trying to use the trait was to use the behavior of the trait's sum method, and there's no way to do this from Java without creating a Scala wrapper class.

In a last desperate attempt, you might try to call super.sum(x,y) from your Java method, like this:

```
// java
public int sum(int x, int y) {
  return super.sum(x, y);
}
```

But that won't work either, failing with the following error message:

```
cannot find symbol
[error] symbol   : method sum(int,int)
[error] location: class java.lang.Object
[error]     return super.sum(x,y);
[error]                 ^
```

The only way to solve the problem is to wrap the trait with a class on the Scala side, which was demonstrated in the Solution.

To summarize: If you're writing a Scala API that will be used by Java clients, don't expose traits that have implemented behavior in your public API. If you have traits like that, wrap them in a class for your Java consumers.

# CHAPTER 18

# The Simple Build Tool (SBT)

## Introduction

Although you can use Ant and Maven to build your Scala projects, SBT, or the Simple Build Tool (*http://www.scala-sbt.org/*), is the de facto build tool for Scala applications. SBT makes the basic build and dependency management tasks simple, and lets you use the Scala language itself to conquer more difficult tasks.

SBT uses the same directory structure as Maven, and like Maven, it uses a "convention over configuration" approach that makes the build process incredibly easy for basic projects. Because it provides a well-known, standard build process, if you work on one Scala project that's built with SBT, it's easy to move to another project that also uses SBT. The project's directory structure will be the same, and you'll know that you should look at the *build.sbt* file and the optional *project/\*.scala* files to see how the build process is configured.

Like Maven, under the covers, SBT's dependency management system is handled by Apache Ivy (*http://ant.apache.org/ivy/*). This means that all those Java projects that have been created and packaged for use with Maven over the years can easily be used by SBT. Additionally, other JAR files not in an Ivy/Maven repository can simply be placed in your project's *lib* folder, and SBT will automatically find them.

As a result of all these features, with very little effort on your part, SBT lets you build projects that contain both Scala and Java code, unit tests, and both managed and unmanaged dependencies.

 All examples in this chapter were tested with SBT version 0.12.3.

# 18.1. Creating a Project Directory Structure for SBT

## Problem

SBT doesn't include a command to create a new project, and you'd like to quickly and easily create the directory structure for a new project.

## Solution

Use either a shell script or a tool like Giter8 (*https://github.com/n8han/giter8*) to create your project's directory structure. Both approaches are shown here.

### Use a shell script

SBT uses the same directory structure as Maven, and for simple needs, you can generate a compatible structure using a shell script. For example, the following Unix shell script creates the initial set of files and directories you'll want for most projects:

```
#!/bin/sh
mkdir -p src/{main,test}/{java,resources,scala}
mkdir lib project target

# create an initial build.sbt file
echo 'name := "MyProject"

version := "1.0"

scalaVersion := "2.10.0"' > build.sbt
```

Just save that code as a shell script on Unix systems (or Cygwin on Windows), make it executable, and run it inside a new project directory to create all the subdirectories SBT needs, as well as an initial *build.sbt* file.

Assuming this script is named `mkdirs4sbt`, and it's on your path, the process looks like this:

```
/Users/Al/Projects> mkdir MyNewProject

/Users/Al/Projects> cd MyNewProject

/Users/Al/Projects/MyNewProject> mkdirs4sbt
```

If you have the `tree` command on your system and run it from the current directory, you'll see that the basic directory structure looks like this:

```
.
|-- build.sbt
|-- lib
|-- project
|-- src
|   |-- main
|   |   |-- java
|   |   |-- resources
|   |   |-- scala
|   |-- test
|       |-- java
|       |-- resources
|       |-- scala
|-- target
```

This is just a simple starter script, but it helps to show how easy it is to create a basic SBT directory structure.

 The *build.sbt* file is SBT's basic configuration file. You define most settings that SBT needs in this file, including specifying library dependencies, repositories, and any other basic settings your project requires. I'll demonstrate many examples of it in the recipes in this chapter.

## Use Giter8

Although that script shows how simple building a basic directory structure is, Giter8 (*https://github.com/n8han/giter8*) is an excellent tool for creating SBT directory structures with specific project needs. It's based on a template system, and the templates usually contain everything you need to create a skeleton SBT project that's preconfigured to use one or more Scala tools, such as ScalaTest, Scalatra, and many others.

The Giter8 templates that you can use are listed on GitHub (*https://github.com/n8han/giter8/wiki/giter8-templates*). As a demonstration of how this works, the following example shows how to use the `scalatra/scalatra-sbt` template.

To create a project named "NewApp," Giter8 prompts you with a series of questions, and then creates a *newapp* folder for your project. To demonstrate this, move to a directory where you normally create your projects, then start Giter8 with the `g8` command, giving it the name of the template you want to use:

```
/Users/Al/Projects> g8 scalatra/scalatra-sbt

organization [com.example]: com.alvinalexander
package [com.example.app]: com.alvinalexander.newapp
name [My Scalatra Web App]: NewApp
scalatra_version [2.2.0]:
servlet_name [MyScalatraServlet]: NewAppServlet
```

```
scala_version [2.10.0]:
version [0.1.0-SNAPSHOT]:

Template applied in ./newapp
```

Because I answered the `name` prompt with `NewApp`, Giter8 creates a subdirectory under the current directory named *newapp*. It contains the following files and directories:

```
newapp/.gitignore
newapp/project/build.properties
newapp/project/build.scala
newapp/project/plugins.sbt
newapp/README.md
newapp/sbt
newapp/src/main/resources/logback.xml
newapp/src/main/scala/com/alvinalexander/newapp/NewAppServlet.scala
newapp/src/main/scala/com/alvinalexander/newapp/NewappStack.scala
newapp/src/main/scala/ScalatraBootstrap.scala
newapp/src/main/webapp/WEB-INF/templates/layouts/default.jade
newapp/src/main/webapp/WEB-INF/templates/views/hello-scalate.jade
newapp/src/main/webapp/WEB-INF/web.xml
newapp/src/test/scala/com/alvinalexander/newapp/NewAppServletSpec.scala
```

In this example, Giter8 creates all the configuration files and Scalatra stub files you need to have a skeleton Scalatra project up and running in just a minute or two.

### Giter8 notes

At the time of this writing, I had a problem with the current Scalatra template, and had to add this line to the *build.sbt* file in my root project directory to get the template to work:

```
scalaVersion := "2.10.0"
```

To run a Scalatra project, enter the SBT shell from your operating system command line, and then run the `container:start` command:

```
/Users/Al/Projects/newapp> sbt
```

```
> container:start
```

This command starts the Jetty server running on port 8080 on your computer, so you can easily test your installation by accessing the *http://localhost:8080/* URL from a browser.

In the case of using a new template like this, SBT may have a *lot* of files to download. Fear not—once they're downloaded, your new Scalatra project should be up and running, and all of these downloads are required only during the first sbt run.

# Discussion

As shown in the Solution, because the SBT directory structure is standard and based on the Maven directory structure, you can create your own tool, or use other tools that are built for this purpose.

For simple SBT projects, I've created an improved version of the shell script shown in the Solution. I named it *sbtmkdirs*, and you can download it from the URL shown in the See Also section. Like Giter8, this script prompts you with several questions, and optionally creates *.gitignore* and *README.md* files, along with a full *build.sbt* file. I use this script whenever I want to create a Scala project where I don't need a template.

As demonstrated, Giter8 works by downloading project templates from GitHub. Giter8 requires SBT and another tool named Conscript, so to install and use Giter8, you'll need to follow these steps:

1. Install SBT (*http://www.scala-sbt.org/*).
2. Install Conscript (*https://github.com/n8han/conscript/*).
3. Install Giter8 (*https://github.com/n8han/giter8*).

Fortunately those projects are well documented, and it takes just a few minutes to install all three tools.

There have been a couple of times when I've used Giter8 and it failed to download a project template. I don't remember the exact error messages, but this was the most recent one:

```
$ g8 scalatra/scalatra-sbt

Unable to find github repository: scalatra/scalatra-sbt.g8 (master)
```

Each time this has happened, I've upgraded Conscript and Giter8 to their latest versions, and the problem has gone away.

> Conscript is an interesting tool that works with GitHub projects for the purpose of "installing and updating Scala programs." Its purpose and installation process are well documented at its website.
>
> Giter8 currently uses a Java installer. Installing it on a Mac OS X system failed when I double-clicked the JAR file, but when I ran it from the command line (using the `java -jar` approach), it installed successfully.

## See Also

- The SBT website (*http://www.scala-sbt.org*)
- Information about installing SBT (*http://bit.ly/1bGe3Au*)
- My `sbtmkdirs` script (*http://alvinalexander.com/scala/sbtmkdirs-script*)
- The Giter8 website (*https://github.com/n8han/giter8*)
- There are currently over thirty Giter8 templates (*https://github.com/n8han/giter8/wiki/giter8-templates*)
- The Conscript website (*https://github.com/n8han/conscript/*)

# 18.2. Compiling, Running, and Packaging a Scala Project with SBT

## Problem

You want to use SBT to compile and run a Scala project, and package the project as a JAR file.

## Solution

Create a directory layout to match what SBT expects, then run `sbt compile` to compile your project, `sbt run` to run your project, and `sbt package` to package your project as a JAR file.

To demonstrate this, create a new SBT project directory structure as shown in Recipe 18.1, and then create a file named *Hello.scala* in the *src/main/scala* directory with these contents:

```
package foo.bar.baz

object Main extends App {
  println("Hello, world")
}
```

Unlike Java, in Scala, the file's package name doesn't have to match the directory name. In fact, for simple tests like this, you can place this file in the root directory of your SBT project, if you prefer.

From the root directory of the project, you can compile the project:

```
$ sbt compile
```

Run the project:

```
$ sbt run
```

Package the project:

```
$ sbt package
```

## Discussion

The first time you run SBT, it may take a while to download all the dependencies it needs, but after that first run, it will download new dependencies only as needed. The commands executed in the Solution, along with their output, are shown here:

```
$ sbt compile
```

```
[info] Loading global plugins from /Users/Al/.sbt/plugins
[info] Set current project to Basic (in build file:/Users/Al/SbtTests/)
[success] Total time: 0 s
```

```
$ sbt run
```

```
[info] Loading global plugins from /Users/Al/.sbt/plugins
[info] Set current project to Basic (in build file:/Users/Al/SbtTests/)
[info] Running foo.bar.baz.Main
Hello, world
[success] Total time: 1 s
```

```
$ sbt package
```

```
[info] Loading global plugins from /Users/Al/.sbt/plugins
[info] Set current project to Basic (in build file:/Users/Al/SbtTests/)
[info] Packaging /Users/Al/SbtTests/target/scala-2.10/basic_2.10-1.0.jar ...
[info] Done packaging.
[success] Total time: 0 s
```

Because compile is a dependency of run, you don't have to run compile before each run; just type sbt run.

The JAR file created with sbt package is a normal Java JAR file. You can list its contents with the usual jar tvf command:

```
$ jar tvf target/scala-2.10/basic_2.10-1.0.jar
   261 Sat Apr 13 13:58:44 MDT 2013 META-INF/MANIFEST.MF
     0 Sat Apr 13 13:58:44 MDT 2013 foo/
     0 Sat Apr 13 13:58:44 MDT 2013 foo/bar/
     0 Sat Apr 13 13:58:44 MDT 2013 foo/bar/baz/
  2146 Sat Apr 13 13:57:52 MDT 2013 foo/bar/baz/Main$.class
  1003 Sat Apr 13 13:57:52 MDT 2013 foo/bar/baz/Main.class
   759 Sat Apr 13 13:57:52 MDT 2013 foo/bar/baz/Main$delayedInit$body.class
```

You can also execute the main method in the JAR file with the Scala interpreter:

```
$ scala target/scala-2.10/basic_2.10-1.0.jar
Hello, world
```

## SBT commands

As with any Java-based command, there can be a little startup lag time involved with running SBT commands, so when you're using SBT quite a bit, it's common to run these commands in interactive mode from the SBT shell prompt to improve the speed of the process:

```
$ sbt

> compile
> run
> package
```

You can run multiple commands at one time, such as running clean before compile:

```
> clean compile
```

At the time of this writing, there are 247 SBT commands available (which I just found out by hitting the Tab key at the SBT shell prompt, which triggered SBT's tab completion). Table 18-1 shows a list of the most common commands.

*Table 18-1. Descriptions of the most common SBT commands*

| Command | Description |
| --- | --- |
| clean | Removes all generated files from the *target* directory. |
| compile | Compiles source code files that are in *src/main/scala*, *src/main/java*, and the root directory of the project. |
| ~ compile | Automatically recompiles source code files while you're running SBT in interactive mode (i.e., while you're at the SBT command prompt). |
| console | Compiles the source code files in the project, puts them on the classpath, and starts the Scala interpreter (REPL). |
| doc | Generates API documentation from your Scala source code using scaladoc. |
| help <command> | Issued by itself, the help command lists the common commands that are currently available. When given a command, help provides a description of that command. |
| inspect <setting> | Displays information about <setting>. For instance, inspect library-dependencies displays information about the libraryDependencies setting. (Variables in *build.sbt* are written in camelCase, but at the SBT prompt, you type them using this hyphen format instead of camelCase.) |
| package | Creates a JAR file (or WAR file for web projects) containing the files in *src/main/scala*, *src/main/java*, and resources in *src/main/resources*. |
| package-doc | Creates a JAR file containing API documentation generated from your Scala source code. |
| publish | Publishes your project to a remote repository. See Recipe 18.15, "Publishing Your Library". |
| publish-local | Publishes your project to a local Ivy repository. See Recipe 18.15, "Publishing Your Library". |

| Command | Description |
|---|---|
| reload | Reloads the build definition files (*build.sbt*, *project/\*.scala*, and *project/\*.sbt*), which is necessary if you change them while you're in an interactive SBT session. |
| run | Compiles your code, and runs the `main` class from your project, in the same JVM as SBT. If your project has multiple `main` methods (or objects that extend App), you'll be prompted to select one to run. |
| test | Compiles and runs all tests. |
| update | Updates external dependencies. |

There are many other SBT commands available, and when you use plug-ins, they can also make their own commands available. For instance, Recipe 18.7, "Using SBT with Eclipse" shows that the sbteclipse plug-in adds an `eclipse` command. See the SBT documentation (*https://github.com/harrah/xsbt/wiki/Command-Line-Reference*) for more information.

### Continuous compiling

As mentioned, you can eliminate the SBT startup lag time by starting the SBT interpreter in "interactive mode." To do this, type `sbt` at your operating system command line:

```
$ sbt

>
```

When you issue your commands from the SBT shell, they'll run noticeably faster.

As shown in the Solution, you can issue the `compile` command from within the SBT shell, but you can also take this a step further and continuously compile your source code by using the `~ compile` command instead. When you issue this command, SBT watches your source code files, and automatically recompiles them whenever it sees the code change.

To demonstrate this, start the SBT shell from the root directory of your project:

```
$ sbt
```

Then issue the `~ compile` command:

```
> ~ compile
[info] Compiling 1 Scala source to /Users/Al/SbtTests/target/scala-2.10/classes
[success] Total time: 4 s, completed Apr 13, 2013 2:34:23 PM
1. Waiting for source changes... (press enter to interrupt)
```

Now, any time you change and save a source code file, SBT automatically recompiles it. You'll see these new lines of output when SBT recompiles the code:

```
[info] Compiling 1 Scala source to /Users/Al/SbtTests/target/scala-2.10/classes
[success] Total time: 2 s, completed Apr 13, 2013 2:34:32 PM
2. Waiting for source changes... (press enter to interrupt)
```

### Use last to get more information on the last command

From time to time when working in the SBT shell you may have a problem, such as with incremental compiling. When issues like this come up, you may be able to use the shell's `last` command to see what happened.

For instance, you may issue a `compile` command, and then see something wrong in the output:

```
> compile
[info] Updating ...
[info] Resolving com.typesafe#config;1.0.0 ...
[info] Compiling 1 Scala source to
YIKES!
```

I made up the YIKES! part, but you get the idea; something goes wrong. To see what happened, issue the `last compile` command:

```
> last compile
[debug]
[debug] Initial source changes:
[debug]   removed:Set()
[debug]   added: Set(/Users/Al/Projects/Scala/Foo/Test.scala)
[debug]   modified: Set()
[debug] Removed products: Set()
[debug] Modified external sources: Set()

many more lines of debug output here ...
```

The `last` command prints logging information for the last command that was executed. This can help you understand what's happening, including understanding why something is being recompiled over and over when using incremental compilation.

Typing `help last` in the SBT interpreter shows a few additional details, including a note about the `last-grep` command, which can be useful when you need to filter a large amount of output.

## See Also

- The SBT command-line reference (*http://bit.ly/178Zztv*).
- Information on publishing an SBT project (*http://bit.ly/12DYQNk*).
- Incremental compiling can often be much (much!) faster than compiling an entire project. See the Scala website (*http://bit.ly/1blueEQ*) for more details on how it works in SBT.
- Typesafe has made SBT's incremental compiler available as a standalone tool named Zinc (*http://bit.ly/12HthNJ*), which can be used with other tools, like Maven.

# 18.3. Running Tests with SBT and ScalaTest

## Problem

You want to set up an SBT project with ScalaTest, and run the tests with SBT.

## Solution

Create a new SBT project directory structure as shown in Recipe 18.1, and then add the ScalaTest library dependency to your *build.sbt* file, as shown here:

```
name := "BasicProjectWithScalaTest"

version := "1.0"

scalaVersion := "2.10.0"

libraryDependencies += "org.scalatest" % "scalatest_2.10" % "1.9.1" % "test"
```

Add your Scala source code under the *src/main/scala* folder, add your tests under the *src/test/scala* folder, and then run the tests with the SBT `test` command:

```
$ sbt test
```

## Discussion

The `libraryDependencies` tag in the *build.sbt* file shows the standard way of adding new dependencies to an SBT project:

```
libraryDependencies += "org.scalatest" % "scalatest_2.10" % "1.9.1" % "test"
```

You can write that line as shown, or this way:

```
libraryDependencies += "org.scalatest" %% "scalatest" % "1.9.1" % "test"
```

In the second example, I used the `%%` method to automatically append the project's Scala version (2.10) to the end of the artifact name (`scalatest`). These two options are explained more in Recipe 18.4, "Managing Dependencies with SBT", but hopefully the way they work is clear from those examples.

To demonstrate how ScalaTest integrates seamlessly with SBT, create a source file named *Hello.scala* with the following contents in the *src/main/scala* directory of your project:

```
package com.alvinalexander.testproject

object Hello extends App {
  val p = Person("Alvin Alexander")
  println("Hello from " + p.name)
}

case class Person(var name: String)
```

Then create a test file named *HelloTests.scala* in the *src/test/scala* directory of your project with these contents:

```
package com.alvinalexander.testproject

import org.scalatest.FunSuite

class HelloTests extends FunSuite {

  test("the name is set correctly in constructor") {
    val p = Person("Barney Rubble")
    assert(p.name == "Barney Rubble")
  }

  test("a Person's name can be changed") {
    val p = Person("Chad Johnson")
    p.name = "Ochocinco"
    assert(p.name == "Ochocinco")
  }
}
```

Next, run your tests from your project's root directory with SBT:

```
$ sbt test

[info] Loading global plugins from /Users/Al/.sbt/plugins
[info] Set current project to BasicProjectWithScalaTest (in build
       file:/Users/Al/Projects/BasicProjectWithScalaTest/)
[info] HelloTests:
[info] - the name is set correctly in constructor
[info] - a Person's name can be changed
[info] Passed: : Total 2, Failed 0, Errors 0, Passed 2, Skipped 0
[success] Total time: 0 s
```

This output shows that the two tests in the HelloTests test class were run.

As shown in these examples, there's nothing special you have to do to make ScalaTest work with SBT, other than adding it as a dependency in the *build.sbt* file; it just works.

 If you reused an existing SBT project folder to test this recipe, you may need to issue the SBT reload command. As described in Table 18-1, this command tells SBT to reload the project definition files, including the *build.sbt* file.

## See Also

- The ScalaTest "quick start" page (*http://www.scalatest.org/quick_start*).
- If you'd like a simple way to test this, you can download the code for this recipe from GitHub (*https://github.com/alvinj/BasicScalaSbtProjectWithScalatest*).

- specs2 (*http://etorreborre.github.com/specs2/*) is another popular Scala testing framework that integrates easily with SBT. It compares well to ScalaTest, and is also the default testing library for the Play Framework.
- The SBT Quick Configuration documentation (*http://bit.ly/1aqsveB*) shows dozens of *build.sbt* examples.

# 18.4. Managing Dependencies with SBT

## Problem

You want to use one or more external libraries in your Scala/SBT projects.

## Solution

You can use both managed and unmanaged dependencies in your SBT projects.

If you have JAR files (*unmanaged* dependencies) that you want to use in your project, simply copy them to the *lib* folder in the root directory of your SBT project, and SBT will find them automatically. If those JARs depend on other JAR files, you'll have to download those other JAR files and copy them to the *lib* directory as well.

If you have a single *managed* dependency, such as wanting to use the Java HtmlCleaner library (*http://htmlcleaner.sourceforge.net/*) in your project, add a libraryDependencies line like this to your *build.sbt* file:

```
libraryDependencies += "net.sourceforge.htmlcleaner" % "htmlcleaner" % "2.4"
```

Because configuration lines in *build.sbt* must be separated by blank lines, a simple but complete file with one dependency looks like this:

```
name := "BasicProjectWithScalaTest"

version := "1.0"

scalaVersion := "2.10.0"

libraryDependencies += "org.scalatest" %% "scalatest" % "1.9.1" % "test"
```

To add multiple managed dependencies to your project, define them as a Seq in your *build.sbt* file:

```
libraryDependencies ++= Seq(
  "net.sourceforge.htmlcleaner" % "htmlcleaner" % "2.4",
  "org.scalatest" % "scalatest_2.10" % "1.9.1" % "test",
  "org.foobar" %% "foobar" % "1.8"
)
```

Or, if you prefer, you can add them one line at a time to the file, separating each line by a blank line:

```
libraryDependencies += "net.sourceforge.htmlcleaner" % "htmlcleaner" % "2.4"

libraryDependencies += "org.scalatest" % "scalatest_2.10" % "1.9.1" % "test"

libraryDependencies += "org.foobar" %% "foobar" % "1.6"
```

As you might infer from these examples, entries in *build.sbt* are simple key/value pairs. SBT works by creating a large map of key/value pairs that describe the build, and when it parses this file, it adds the pairs you define to its map. The fields in this file named `version`, `name`, `scalaVersion`, and `libraryDependencies` are all SBT keys (and in fact are probably the most common keys).

## Discussion

A *managed dependency* is a dependency that's managed by your build tool, in this case, SBT. In this situation, if library *a.jar* depends on *b.jar*, and that library depends on *c.jar*, and those JAR files are kept in an Ivy/Maven repository along with this relationship information, then all you have to do is add a line to your *build.sbt* file stating that you want to use *a.jar*. The other JAR files will be downloaded and included into your project automatically.

When using a library as an *unmanaged dependency*, you have to manage this situation yourself. Given the same situation as the previous paragraph, if you want to use the library *a.jar* in your project, you must manually download *a.jar*, and then know about the dependency on *b.jar*, and the transitive dependency on *c.jar*, then download all those files yourself, and place them in your project's *lib* directory.

I've found that manually managing JAR files in the *lib* directory works fine for small projects, but as shown in Recipe 16.2, "Connecting to a Database with the Spring Framework", a few lines of managed dependency declarations can quickly explode into a large number of JAR files you'll need to manually track down and add to your *lib* folder.

Under the covers, SBT uses Apache Ivy as its dependency manager. Ivy is also used by Ant and Maven, and as a result, you can easily use the wealth of Java libraries that have been created over the years in your Scala projects.

There are two general forms for adding a managed dependency to a *build.sbt* file. In the first form, you specify the `groupID`, `artifactID`, and `revision`:

```
libraryDependencies += groupID % artifactID % revision
```

In the second form, you add an optional configuration parameter:

```
libraryDependencies += groupID % artifactID % revision % configuration
```

The groupID, artifactID, revision, and configuration strings correspond to what Ivy requires to retrieve the module you want. Typically, the module developer will give you the information you need. For instance, the specs2 website provides this string:

```
libraryDependencies += "org.specs2" %% "specs2" % "1.14" % "test"
```

It also provides this information, which shows how to use the same library with Maven:

```
<dependency>
  <groupId>org.specs2</groupId>
  <artifactId>specs2_2.10</artifactId>
  <version>1.14</version>
  <scope>test</scope>
</dependency>
```

The symbols +=, %, and %% used in *build.sbt* are part of the DSL defined by SBT. They're described in Table 18-2.

*Table 18-2. Common methods used in a build.sbt file*

| Method | Description |
| --- | --- |
| += | Appends to the key's value. The *build.sbt* file works with settings defined as key/value pairs. In the examples shown, libraryDependencies is a key, and it's shown with several different values. |
| % | A method used to construct an Ivy Module ID from the strings you supply. |
| %% | When used after the groupID, it automatically adds your project's Scala version (such as _2.10) to the end of the artifact name. |

As shown in the examples, you can use % or %% after the groupID. This example shows the % method:

```
libraryDependencies += "org.scalatest" % "scalatest_2.10" % "1.9.1" % "test"
```

This example shows the %% method:

```
libraryDependencies += "org.scalatest" %% "scalatest" % "1.9.1" % "test"
```

When using Scala 2.10, these two lines are equivalent. The %% method adds your project's Scala version to the end of the artifact name. The practice of adding the Scala version (in the format _2.10.0) to the artifactID is used because modules may be compiled for different Scala versions.

Note that in some of the examples, the string test is added after the revision:

```
"org.scalatest" % "scalatest_2.10" % "1.9.1" % "test"
```

This demonstrates the use of the "configuration" form for adding a dependency that was shown earlier:

```
libraryDependencies += groupID % artifactID % revision % configuration
```

As the SBT documentation states, this means that the dependency you're defining "will be added to the classpath only for the Test configuration, and won't be added in the

Compile configuration." This is useful for adding dependencies like ScalaTest, specs2, Mockito, etc., that will be used when you want to test your application, but not when you want to compile and run the application.

If you're not familiar with Apache Ivy, it can be helpful to know that managed dependencies are downloaded beneath a *.ivy2* directory in your home directory (*~/.ivy2/*) on your filesystem. See the Ivy documentation (*http://ant.apache.org/ivy/*) for more information.

### Repositories

SBT uses the standard Maven2 repository by default, so it can locate most libraries when you add a `libraryDependencies` line to a *build.sbt* file. In these cases, there's no need for you to tell SBT where to look for the file. However, when a library is not in a standard repository, you can tell SBT where to look for it. This process is referred to as adding a resolver, and it's covered in Recipe 18.11, "Telling SBT How to Find a Repository (Working with Resolvers)".

## See Also

- Apache Ivy (*http://ant.apache.org/ivy/*).
- The SBT Quick Configuration documentation (*http://bit.ly/1aqsveB*) shows dozens of *build.sbt* examples.
- Recipe 18.11, "Telling SBT How to Find a Repository (Working with Resolvers)".

# 18.5. Controlling Which Version of a Managed Dependency Is Used

## Problem

You want to make sure you always have the desired version of a managed dependency, including the latest integration release, milestone release, or other versions.

## Solution

The `revision` field in the `libraryDependencies` setting isn't limited to specifying a single, fixed version. According to the Apache Ivy documentation, you can specify terms such as `latest.integration`, `latest.milestone`, and other terms.

As one example of this flexibility, rather than specifying version `1.8` of a `foobar` module, as shown here:

```
libraryDependencies += "org.foobar" %% "foobar" % "1.8"
```

you can request the `latest.integration` version like this:

```
libraryDependencies += "org.foobar" %% "foobar" % "latest.integration"
```

The module developer will often tell you what versions are available or should be used, and Ivy lets you specify tags to control which version of the module will be downloaded and used. The Ivy "dependency" documentation states that the following tags can be used:

- `latest.integration`
- `latest.[any status]`, such as `latest.milestone`
- You can end the revision with a + character. This selects the latest subrevision of the dependency module. For instance, if the dependency module exists in revisions `1.0.3`, `1.0.7`, and `1.1.2`, specifying `1.0.+` as your dependency will result in `1.0.7` being selected.
- You can use "version ranges," as shown in the following examples:

```
[1.0,2.0] matches all versions greater or equal to 1.0 and lower or equal to
          2.0
[1.0,2.0[ matches all versions greater or equal to 1.0 and lower than 2.0
]1.0,2.0] matches all versions greater than 1.0 and lower or equal to 2.0
]1.0,2.0[ matches all versions greater than 1.0 and lower than 2.0
[1.0,) matches all versions greater or equal to 1.0
]1.0,) matches all versions greater than 1.0
(,2.0] matches all versions lower or equal to 2.0
(,2.0[ matches all versions lower than 2.0
```

(These configuration examples are courtesy of the Apache Ivy documentation. See the link in the See Also section for more information.)

To demonstrate a few of these tags, this example shows the `latest.milestone` tag:

```
libraryDependencies += "org.scalatest" %% "scalatest" % "latest.milestone" % ↵
"test"
```

At the time of this writing, it retrieves this file:

```
scalatest_2.10-2.0.M6-SNAP13.jar
```

This specification demonstrates the + tag:

```
libraryDependencies += "org.scalatest" %% "scalatest" % "1.9.+" % "test"
```

It currently retrieves this file:

```
scalatest_2.10-1.9.2-SNAP1.jar
```

## See Also

Apache Ivy revision documentation (*http://bit.ly/18jswQI*)

# 18.6. Creating a Project with Subprojects

## Problem

You want to configure SBT to work with a main project that depends on other subprojects you're developing.

## Solution

Create your subproject as a regular SBT project, but without a *project* subdirectory. Then, in your main project, define a *project/Build.scala* file that defines the dependencies between the main project and subprojects.

This is demonstrated in the following example, which I created based on the SBT Multi-Project documentation (*https://github.com/harrah/xsbt/wiki/Getting-Started-Multi-Project*):

```
import sbt._
import Keys._

/**
 * based on http://www.scala-sbt.org/release/docs/Getting-Started/Multi-Project
 */
object HelloBuild extends Build {

  // aggregate: running a task on the aggregate project will also run it
  // on the aggregated projects.
  // dependsOn: a project depends on code in another project.
  // without dependsOn, you'll get a compiler error: "object bar is not a
  // member of package com.alvinalexander".
  lazy val root = Project(id = "hello",
                      base = file(".")) aggregate(foo, bar) dependsOn(foo, bar)

  // sub-project in the Foo subdirectory
  lazy val foo = Project(id = "hello-foo",
                      base = file("Foo"))

  // sub-project in the Bar subdirectory
  lazy val bar = Project(id = "hello-bar",
                      base = file("Bar"))
}
```

To create your own example, you can either follow the instructions in the SBT Multi-Project documentation (*https://github.com/harrah/xsbt/wiki/Getting-Started-Multi-Project*) to create a main project with subprojects, or clone my SBT Subproject Example (*https://github.com/alvinj/SbtSubProjectsExample*) on GitHub, which I created to help you get started quickly.

# Discussion

Creating a main project with subprojects is well documented on the SBT website, and the primary glue that defines the relationships between projects is the *project/Build.scala* file you create in your main project.

In the example shown, my main project depends on two subprojects, which are in directories named *Foo* and *Bar* beneath my project's main directory. I reference these projects in the following code in my main project, so it's necessary to tell SBT about the relationship between the projects:

```
package com.alvinalexander.subprojecttests

import com.alvinalexander.bar._
import com.alvinalexander.foo._

object Hello extends App {
  println(Bar("I'm a Bar"))
  println(Bar("I'm a Foo"))
}
```

The following output from the Unix `tree` command shows what the directory structure for my project looks like, including the files and directories for the main project, and the two subprojects:

```
|-- Bar
|   |-- build.sbt
|   +-- src
|       |-- main
|       |   |-- java
|       |   |-- resources
|       |   +-- scala
|       |       +-- Bar.scala
|       +-- test
|           |-- java
|           +-- resources
|-- Foo
|   |-- build.sbt
|   +-- src
|       |-- main
|       |   |-- java
|       |   |-- resources
|       |   +-- scala
|       |       +-- Foo.scala
|       +-- test
|           |-- java
|           +-- resources
|-- build.sbt
|-- project
|   |-- Build.scala
|
```

```
+-- src
    |-- main
    |   |-- java
    |   |-- resources
    |   +-- scala
    |       +-- Hello.scala
    +-- test
        |-- java
        |-- resources
        +-- scala
            +-- HelloTest.scala
```

To experiment with this yourself, I encourage you to clone my GitHub project (*http://bit.ly/13bjik7*).

## See Also

- SBT Multi-Project documentation (*http://bit.ly/15gi9Mi*)
- My example "SBT Subprojects" code at GitHub (*http://bit.ly/13bjik7*)

# 18.7. Using SBT with Eclipse

## Problem

You want to use Eclipse with a project you're managing with SBT.

## Solution

Use the Scala IDE for Eclipse project (*http://scala-ide.org/*) so you can work on Scala projects in Eclipse, and use the sbteclipse plug-in (*https://github.com/typesafehub/sbteclipse*) to enable SBT to generate files for Eclipse.

The Scala IDE for Eclipse project lets you edit Scala code in Eclipse. With syntax highlighting, code completion, debugging, and many other features, it makes Scala development in Eclipse a pleasure.

To use the sbteclipse plug-in, download it per the instructions on the website. Once installed, when you're in the root directory of an SBT project, type `sbt eclipse` to generate the files Eclipse needs. You may see a lot of output the first time you run the command as SBT checks everything it needs, but at the end of the output you should see a "success" message, like this:

```
$ sbt eclipse

[info] Successfully created Eclipse project files for project(s):
[info] YourProjectNameHere
```

The plug-in generates the two files Eclipse needs, the *.classpath* and *.project* files.

Once these files are generated, go to Eclipse and follow the usual steps to import a project into the Eclipse workspace: File → Import → Existing Projects into Workspace. Your project will then appear in the Eclipse Navigator, Project Explorer, Package Explorer, and other views.

## Discussion

The *.classpath* file is an XML file that contains a number of <classpathentry> tags, like this:

```
<classpath>
  <classpathentry output="target/scala-2.10/classes"
   path="src/main/scala" kind="src"></classpathentry>
  <classpathentry output="target/scala-2.10/classes"
   path="src/main/java" kind="src"></classpathentry>
  <classpathentry output="target/scala-2.10/test-classes"
   path="src/test/scala" kind="src"></classpathentry>
  <classpathentry output="target/scala-2.10/test-classes"
   path="src/test/java" kind="src"></classpathentry>
  <classpathentry kind="con"
   path="org.scala-ide.sdt.launching.SCALA_CONTAINER"></classpathentry>
  <classpathentry
   path="/Users/Al/.ivy2/cache/com.typesafe/config/bundles/config-1.0.0.jar"
   kind="lib"></classpathentry>
  <classpathentry path="org.eclipse.jdt.launching.JRE_CONTAINER"
   kind="con"></classpathentry>
  <classpathentry path="bin" kind="output"></classpathentry>
</classpath>
```

The *.project* file is an XML file that describes your project and looks like this:

```
<projectDescription>
  <name>YourProjectName</name>
  <buildSpec>
    <buildCommand>
      <name>org.scala-ide.sdt.core.scalabuilder</name>
    </buildCommand>
  </buildSpec>
  <natures>
    <nature>org.scala-ide.sdt.core.scalanature</nature>
    <nature>org.eclipse.jdt.core.javanature</nature>
  </natures>
</projectDescription>
```

Any time you update your SBT build definition files (*build.sbt*, *project/\*.scala*, *project/\*.sbt*) you should rerun the `sbt eclipse` command to update the *.classpath* and *.project* files. Eclipse will also need to know that these files were regenerated, so this is really a two-step process:

- Run `sbt eclipse` from the command line.
- In Eclipse, select your project and then refresh it (using the F5 function key, or refreshing it with the menu commands).

### See Also

- The Scala IDE for Eclipse (*http://scala-ide.org/*)
- The sbteclipse plug-in (*https://github.com/typesafehub/sbteclipse/*)
- JetBrains (*http://plugins.jetbrains.com/*) also has plug-ins for IntelliJ IDEA

# 18.8. Generating Project API Documentation

## Problem

You've marked up your source code with Scaladoc comments, and want to generate the API documentation for your project.

## Solution

Use any of the commands listed in Table 18-3, depending on your needs.

*Table 18-3. Descriptions of SBT commands that generate project documentation*

| SBT command | Description |
| --- | --- |
| doc | Creates Scaladoc API documentation from the Scala source code files located in *src/main/scala*. |
| test:doc | Creates Scaladoc API documentation from the Scala source code files located in *src/test/scala*. |
| package-doc | Creates a JAR file containing the API documentation created from the Scala source code in *src/main/scala*. |
| test:package-doc | Creates a JAR file containing the API documentation created from the Scala source code in *src/test/scala*. |
| publish | Publishes artifacts to the repository defined by the `publish-to` setting. See Recipe 18.15, "Publishing Your Library". |
| publish-local | Publishes artifacts to the local Ivy repository as described. See Recipe 18.15, "Publishing Your Library". |

For example, to generate API documentation, use the doc command:

```
$ sbt doc
```

At the time of this writing, SBT doesn't show where the output from this command is written to, but with Scala 2.10.0, SBT 0.12.3 places the root *index.html* Scaladoc file at *target/scala-2.10/api/index.html* under the root directory of your project. Other commands, including package-doc and publish, do indicate where their output is located.

The following example shows that publish-local generates its output for a project named "Hello" to the *.ivy2* directory under your *$HOME* directory:

```
> sbt publish-local
[info] Loading global plugins from /Users/Al/.sbt/plugins
$HOME/.ivy2/local/hello/hello_2.10/1.0/poms/hello_2.10.pom
$HOME/.ivy2/local/hello/hello_2.10/1.0/jars/hello_2.10.jar
$HOME/.ivy2/local/hello/hello_2.10/1.0/srcs/hello_2.10-sources.jar
$HOME/.ivy2/local/hello/hello_2.10/1.0/docs/hello_2.10-javadoc.jar
$HOME/.ivy2/local/hello/hello_2.10/1.0/ivys/ivy.xml
```

See Recipe 18.15, "Publishing Your Library" for examples of how to use publish and publish-local.

For a detailed example of how to use Scaladoc, see Recipe 14.8, "Generating Documentation with scaladoc".

## See Also

- The SBT command-line reference (*http://bit.ly/178Zztv*) has more information on these commands

- When writing Scaladoc, you can use a Wiki-like syntax (*https://wiki.scala-lang.org/display/SW/Syntax*)

- The Scaladoc tags (@see, @param, etc.) are listed in the Scala wiki (*https://wiki.scala-lang.org/display/SW/Tags+and+Annotations*)

- Recipe 14.8, "Generating Documentation with scaladoc" provides more examples of the documentation publishing commands

- See Recipe 18.15, "Publishing Your Library" for examples of using publish and publish-local

# 18.9. Specifying a Main Class to Run

## Problem

You have multiple main methods in objects in your project, and you want to specify which main method should be run when you type sbt run, or specify the main method that should be invoked when your project is packaged as a JAR file.

## Solution

If you have multiple `main` methods in your project and want to specify which `main` method to run when typing `sbt run`, add a line like this to your *build.sbt* file:

```
// set the main class for 'sbt run'
mainClass in (Compile, run) := Some("com.alvinalexander.Foo")
```

This class can either contain a `main` method, or extend the `App` trait.

To specify the class that will be added to the manifest when your application is packaged as a JAR file, add this line to your *build.sbt* file:

```
// set the main class for packaging the main jar
mainClass in (Compile, packageBin) := Some("com.alvinalexander.Foo")
```

That setting tells SBT to add the following line to the *META-INF/MANIFEST.MF* file in your JAR when you run `sbt package`:

```
Main-Class: com.alvinalexander.Foo
```

### Using run-main

When running your application with SBT, you can also use SBT's `run-main` command to specify the class to run. Invoke it like this from your operating system command line:

```
$ sbt "run-main com.alvinalexander.Foo"
[info] Loading global plugins from /Users/Al/.sbt/plugins
[info] Running com.alvinalexander.Foo
hello
[success] Total time: 1 s
```

Invoke it like this from inside the SBT shell:

```
$ sbt

> run-main com.alvinalexander.Foo
[info] Running com.alvinalexander.Foo
hello
[success] Total time: 1 s
```

## Discussion

If you have only one `main` method in an object in your project (or one object that extends the `App` trait), SBT can automatically determine the location of that `main` method. In that case, these configuration lines aren't necessary.

If you have multiple `main` methods in your project and don't use any of the approaches shown in the Solution, SBT will prompt you with a list of objects it finds that have a `main` method or extend the `App` trait when you execute `sbt run`:

```
Multiple main classes detected, select one to run:

[1] com.alvinalexander.testproject.Foo
[2] com.alvinalexander.testproject.Bar
```

The following code shows what a *build.sbt* file with both of the `mainClass` settings looks like:

```
name := "Simple Test Project"

version := "1.0"

scalaVersion := "2.10.0"

// set the main class for packaging the main jar
mainClass in (Compile, packageBin) := Some("com.alvinalexander.testproject.Foo")

// set the main class for the main 'sbt run' task
mainClass in (Compile, run) := Some("com.alvinalexander.testproject.Foo")
```

## See Also

The SBT Quick Configuration documentation (*http://bit.ly/1aqsveB*) shows dozens of *build.sbt* examples.

# 18.10. Using GitHub Projects as Project Dependencies

## Problem

You want to use a Scala library project on GitHub as an SBT project dependency.

## Solution

Reference the GitHub project you want to include in your *project/Build.scala* file as a `RootProject`.

For example, assuming you want to use the Scala project at *https://github.com/alvinj/SoundFilePlayer* as a dependency, put the following contents in a file named *project/Build.scala* in your SBT project:

```
import sbt._

object MyBuild extends Build {

  lazy val root = Project("root", file(".")) dependsOn(soundPlayerProject)
  lazy val soundPlayerProject =
      RootProject(uri("git://github.com/alvinj/SoundFilePlayer.git"))

}
```

You can now use that library in your code, as shown in this little test program:

```
package githubtest

import com.alvinalexander.sound._
import javazoom.jlgui.basicplayer._
import scala.collection.JavaConversions._
import java.util.Map

object TestJavaSound extends App {

  val testClip = "/Users/al/Sarah/Sounds/HAL-mission-too-important.wav"
  val player = SoundFilePlayer.getSoundFilePlayer(testClip)
  player.play

}
```

With this configuration and a basic *build.sbt* file, you can run this code as usual with the sbt run command.

Including this GitHub project is interesting, because it has a number of JAR files in its own *lib* folder, and compiling and running this example works fine.

Note that although this works well for compiling and running your project, you can't package all of this code into a JAR file by just using the sbt package command. Unfortunately, SBT doesn't include the code from the GitHub project for you. However, a plug-in named sbt-assembly (*https://github.com/sbt/sbt-assembly*) does let you package all of this code together as a single JAR file. See Recipe 18.14, "Deploying a Single, Executable JAR File" for information on how to configure and use sbt-assembly.

## Discussion

Whereas the *build.sbt* file is used to define simple settings for your SBT project, the *project/Build.scala* file is used for "everything else." In this file you write Scala code using the SBT API to accomplish any other task you want to achieve, such as including GitHub projects like this.

To use multiple GitHub projects as dependencies, add additional RootProject instances to your *project/Build.scala* file:

```
import sbt._

object MyBuild extends Build {

  lazy val root = Project("root", file("."))
                      .dependsOn(soundPlayerProject)
                      .dependsOn(appleScriptUtils)

  lazy val soundPlayerProject =
      RootProject(uri("git://github.com/alvinj/SoundFilePlayer.git"))
```

```
lazy val appleScriptUtils =
    RootProject(uri("git://github.com/alvinj/AppleScriptUtils.git"))

}
```

## See Also

Recipe 18.6, "Creating a Project with Subprojects", and Recipe 18.16, "Using Build.scala Instead of build.sbt", show other examples of the *project/Build.scala* file.

# 18.11. Telling SBT How to Find a Repository (Working with Resolvers)

## Problem

You want to add a managed dependency to your project from an Ivy repository that SBT doesn't know about by default.

## Solution

Use the `resolvers` key in the *build.sbt* file to add any unknown Ivy repositories. Use this syntax to add one resolver:

```
resolvers += "Java.net Maven2 Repository" at ↵
"http://download.java.net/maven/2/"
```

You can use a Seq to add multiple resolvers:

```
resolvers ++= Seq(
  "Typesafe" at "http://repo.typesafe.com/typesafe/releases/",
  "Java.net Maven2 Repository" at "http://download.java.net/maven/2/"
)
```

Or, if you prefer, you can also add them one line at a time, making sure to separate them by a blank line:

```
resolvers += "Typesafe" at "http://repo.typesafe.com/typesafe/releases/"

resolvers += "Java.net Maven2 Repository" at ↵
"http://download.java.net/maven/2/"
```

## Discussion

If the module you're requesting is in the default Maven2 repository SBT knows about (*http://search.maven.org/#browse*), adding a managed dependency "just works." But if the module isn't there, the library's author will need to provide you with the repository information.

You define a new repository in the *build.sbt* file with this general format:

```
resolvers += "repository name" at "location"
```

As shown in the Solution, you can enter one resolver at a time with the += method, and you can add multiple resolvers with ++= and a Seq.

In addition to the default Maven2 repository, SBT is configured to know about the JavaNet1Repository (*http://download.java.net/maven/1/*). To use this repository in your SBT project, add this line to your *build.sbt* file:

```
resolvers += JavaNet1Repository
```

# 18.12. Resolving Problems by Getting an SBT Stack Trace

## Problem

You're trying to use SBT to compile, run, or package a project, and it's failing, and you need to be able to see the stack trace to understand why it's failing.

## Solution

When an SBT command silently fails (typically with a "Nonzero exit code" message), but you can't tell why, run your command from within the SBT shell, then use the last run command after the command that failed.

This pattern typically looks like this:

```
$ sbt run      // something fails here, but you can't tell what

$ sbt
> run          // failure happens again
> last run     // this shows the full stack trace
```

I've run into this on several projects where I was using JAR files and managing their dependencies myself, and in one specific case, I didn't know I needed to include the Apache Commons Logging JAR file. This was causing the "Nonzero exit code" error message, but I couldn't tell that until I issued the last run command from within the SBT shell. Once I ran that command, the problem was obvious from the stack trace.

Depending on the problem, another approach that can be helpful is to set the SBT logging level. See Recipe 18.13, "Setting the SBT Log Level" for more information.

# 18.13. Setting the SBT Log Level

## Problem

You're having a problem compiling, running, or packaging your project with SBT and need to adjust the SBT logging level to debug the problem. (Or, you're interested in learning about how SBT works.)

## Solution

Set the SBT logging level in your *build.sbt* file with this setting:

```
logLevel := Level.Debug
```

Or, if you're working interactively from the SBT command line and don't want to add this to your *build.sbt* file, use this syntax:

```
> set logLevel := Level.Debug
```

Changing the logging levels significantly changes the output SBT produces, which can help you debug problems. If you're just starting out with SBT, the output can also help you learn how SBT works.

Other logging levels are:

- `Level.Info`
- `Level.Warning`
- `Level.Error`

## See Also

The SBT FAQ (*http://www.scala-sbt.org/release/docs/faq*) shows the logging levels.

# 18.14. Deploying a Single, Executable JAR File

## Problem

You're building a Scala application, such as a Swing application, and want to deploy a single, executable JAR file to your users.

## Solution

The `sbt package` command creates a JAR file that includes the class files it compiles from your source code, along with the resources in your project (from *src/main/resources*), but there are two things it doesn't include in the JAR file:

- Your project dependencies (JAR files in your project's *lib* folder, or managed dependencies declared in *build.sbt*).
- Libraries from the Scala distribution that are needed to execute the JAR file with the `java` command.

This makes it difficult to distribute a single, executable JAR file for your application. There are three things you can do to solve this problem:

- Distribute all the JAR files necessary with a script that builds the classpath and executes the JAR file with the `scala` command. This requires that Scala be installed on client systems.
- Distribute all the JAR files necessary (including Scala libraries) with a script that builds the classpath and executes the JAR file with the `java` command. This requires that Java is installed on client systems.
- Use an SBT plug-in such as sbt-assembly (*https://github.com/sbt/sbt-assembly/*) to build a single, complete JAR file that can be executed with a simple `java` command. This requires that Java is installed on client systems.

This solution focuses on the third approach. The first two approaches are examined in the Discussion.

### Using sbt-assembly

The installation instructions for sbt-assembly may change, but at the time of this writing, just add these two lines of code to a *plugins.sbt* file in the *project* directory of your SBT project:

```
resolvers += Resolver.url("artifactory",
url("http://scalasbt.artifactoryonline.com/scalasbt/sbt-plugin-releases"))↵
(Resolver.ivyStylePatterns)

addSbtPlugin("com.eed3si9n" % "sbt-assembly" % "0.8.4")
```

You'll need to create that file if it doesn't already exist.

Then add these two lines to the top of your *build.sbt* file:

```
import AssemblyKeys._

// sbt-assembly
assemblySettings
```

That's the only setup work that's required. Now run sbt assembly to create your single, executable JAR file:

```
$ sbt assembly
```

When the assembly task finishes running it will tell you where the executable JAR file is located. For instance, when packaging my Blue Parrot application (*http://alvina lexander.com/blueparrot*), SBT prints the following lines of output that show the dependencies sbt-assembly is including, and the location of the final JAR file:

```
[info] Including akka-actor-2.0.1.jar
[info] Including scala-library.jar
[info] Including applescriptutils_2.9.1-1.0.jar
[info] Including forms-1.0.7.jar
[info] Including sounds_2.9.1-1.0.jar
[info] Packaging target/BlueParrot-assembly-1.0.jar ...
[info] Done packaging.
```

The sbt-assembly plug-in works by copying the class files from your source code, the class files from your dependencies, and the class files from the Scala library into one single JAR file that can be executed with the java interpreter. This can be important if there are license restrictions on a JAR file, for instance.

As noted, there are other plug-ins to help solve this problem, including One-JAR, but sbt-assembly worked best with several applications I've deployed as single, executable JAR files.

## Discussion

A JAR file created by SBT can be run by the Scala interpreter, but not the Java interpreter. This is because class files in the JAR file created by sbt package have dependencies on Scala class files (Scala libraries), which aren't included in the JAR file SBT generates. This is easily demonstrated.

First, create an empty SBT project directory. (See Recipe 18.1 for easy ways to do this.)

Then place the following code in a file named *Main.scala* in the root directory of the project:

```
package foo.bar.baz

object Main extends App {
  println("Hello, world")
}
```

Next, run sbt package to create the JAR file:

```
$ sbt package
[info] Loading global plugins from /Users/Al/.sbt/plugins
[info] Done updating.
[info] Compiling 1 Scala source to target/scala-2.10/classes...
```

```
[info] Packaging target/scala-2.10/basic_2.10-1.0.jar ...
[info] Done packaging.
[success] Total time: 6 s
```

Now attempt to run the JAR file with the `java -jar` command. This will fail:

```
$ java -jar target/scala-2.10/basic_2.10-1.0.jar
Exception in thread "main" java.lang.NoClassDefFoundError: scala/App
    at java.lang.ClassLoader.defineClass1(Native Method)
    ... 32 more
```

This fails because the Java interpreter doesn't know where the `scala/App` trait is.

Next, demonstrate that you can run the same JAR file with the Scala interpreter:

```
$ scala target/scala-2.10/basic_2.10-1.0.jar
Hello, world
```

This works fine.

For the Java interpreter to run your JAR file, it needs the *scala-library.jar* file from your Scala installation to be on its classpath. You can get this example to work with Java by including that JAR file on its classpath with this command:

```
$ java -cp "${CLASSPATH}:${SCALA_HOME}/lib/scala-library.jar:target/scala-2.10↵
/basic_2.10-1.0.jar" foo.bar.baz.Main
Hello, world
```

As shown, adding the *scala-library.jar* file lets the Java interpreter find the `scala/App` trait (which is a normal *.class* file), which lets it run the application successfully for you.

This is part of the work that sbt-assembly performs for you. It repackages the class files from *${SCALA_HOME}/lib/scala-library.jar* into your single, executable JAR file, and does the same thing with your other project dependencies. Note that if your application is more complicated, it may need additional JAR files from the *${SCALA_HOME}/lib* directory.

## See Also

- The sbt-assembly project (*https://github.com/sbt/sbt-assembly/*).

- My Blue Parrot application (*http://alvinalexander.com/blueparrot*) is written in Scala, and packaged with SBT and sbt-assembly.

- The One-JAR project (*https://github.com/sbt/sbt-onejar*).

# 18.15. Publishing Your Library

## Problem

You've created a Scala project or library with SBT that you want to share with other users, creating all the files you need for an Ivy repository.

## Solution

Define your repository information, then publish your project with `sbt publish` or `sbt publish-local`.

For my SoundFilePlayer library, I added this setting to my *build.sbt* file to define the location of my local repository:

```
publishTo := Some(Resolver.file("file", new File("/Users/al/tmp")))
```

I then ran `sbt publish`, and SBT generated the following files:

**$ sbt publish**

```
[info] Wrote
/Users/al/SoundFilePlayer/target/scala-2.10.0/sounds_2.10.0-1.0.pom
[info] :: delivering :: default#sounds_2.10.0;1.0 :: 1.0 :: release ::
[info]    delivering ivy file to
/Users/al/SoundFilePlayer/target/scala-2.10.0/ivy-1.0.xml
[info]    published sounds_2.10.0 to
/Users/al/tmp/default/sounds_2.10.0/1.0/sounds_2.10.0-1.0.pom
[info]    published sounds_2.10.0 to
/Users/al/tmp/default/sounds_2.10.0/1.0/sounds_2.10.0-1.0.jar
[info]    published sounds_2.10.0 to
/Users/al/tmp/default/sounds_2.10.0/1.0/sounds_2.10.0-1.0-sources.jar
[info]    published sounds_2.10.0 to
/Users/al/tmp/default/sounds_2.10.0/1.0/sounds_2.10.0-1.0-javadoc.jar
[success] Total time: 1s
```

Without doing anything to define a "local Ivy repository," I get the following results when running the `publish-local` task:

**$ sbt publish-local**

```
[info] Wrote /Users/al/SoundFilePlayer/target/scala-2.10.0/sounds_2.10.0-1.0.pom
[info] :: delivering :: default#sounds_2.10.0;1.0 :: 1.0 :: release ::
[info]    delivering ivy file to
/Users/al/SoundFilePlayer/target/scala-2.10.0/ivy-1.0.xml
[info]    published sounds_2.10.0 to
/Users/al/.ivy2/local/default/sounds_2.10.0/1.0/poms/sounds_2.10.0.pom
[info]    published sounds_2.10.0 to
/Users/al/.ivy2/local/default/sounds_2.10.0/1.0/jars/sounds_2.10.0.jar
[info]    published sounds_2.10.0 to
/Users/al/.ivy2/local/default/sounds_2.10.0/1.0/srcs/sounds_2.10.0-sources.jar
```

```
[info]    published sounds_2.10.0 to
/Users/al/.ivy2/local/default/sounds_2.10.0/1.0/docs/sounds_2.10.0-javadoc.jar
[info]    published ivy to
/Users/al/.ivy2/local/default/sounds_2.10.0/1.0/ivys/ivy.xml
[success] Total time: 1 s,
```

The "SBT Publishing" documentation provides these descriptions of the `publish` and `publish-local` tasks:

- The `publish` action is used to publish your project to a remote repository. To use publishing, you need to specify the repository to publish to and the credentials to use. Once these are set up, you can run `publish`.

- The `publish-local` action is used to publish your project to a local Ivy repository. You can then use this project from other projects on the same machine.

For more information on publishing to remote servers, repositories, and artifacts, see the SBT Publishing documentation (*http://www.scala-sbt.org/release/docs/Detailed-Topics/Publishing*).

# 18.16. Using Build.scala Instead of build.sbt

## Problem

You want to use the *project/Build.scala* file instead of *build.sbt* to define your Scala project, or you need some examples of how to use *Build.scala* to solve build problems that can't be handled in *build.sbt*.

## Solution

The recommended approach when using SBT is to define all your simple settings (key/value pairs) in the *build.sbt* file, and handle all other work, such as build logic, in the *project/Build.scala* file. However, it can be useful to use only the *project/Build.scala* file to learn more about how it works.

To demonstrate this, don't create a *build.sbt* file in your project, and then do create a *Build.scala* file in the *project* subdirectory by extending the SBT `Build` object:

```
import sbt._
import Keys._

object ExampleBuild extends Build {

  val dependencies = Seq(
    "org.scalatest" %% "scalatest" % "1.9.1" % "test"
  )

  lazy val exampleProject = Project("SbtExample", file(".")) settings(
```

```
      version       := "0.2",
      scalaVersion  := "2.10.0",
      scalacOptions := Seq("-deprecation"),
      libraryDependencies ++= dependencies
    )

  }
```

With just this *Build.scala* file, you can now run all the usual SBT commands in your project, including `compile`, `run`, `package`, and so on.

## Discussion

The *Build.scala* file shown in the Solution is equivalent to the following *build.sbt* file:

```
name := "SbtExample"

version := "0.2"

scalaVersion := "2.10.0"

scalacOptions += "-deprecation"

libraryDependencies += "org.scalatest" %% "scalatest" % "1.9.1" % "test"
```

As mentioned, the recommended approach when working with SBT is to define your basic settings in the *build.sbt* file, and perform all other work in a *Build.scala* file, so creating a *Build.scala* file with only settings in it is not a best practice. However, when you first start working with a *Build.scala* file, it's helpful to see a "getting started" example like this.

Also, although the convention is to name this file *Build.scala*, this is only a convention, which I use here for simplicity. You can give your build file any legal Scala filename, as long as you place the file in the *project* directory with a *.scala* suffix. Another convention is to name this file after the name of your project, so the Scalaz project (*http://bit.ly/ 1aMJeML*) uses the name *ScalazBuild.scala*.

### The Full Configuration Example in the SBT documentation

The Full Configuration Example (*https://github.com/harrah/xsbt/wiki/Full-Configuration-Example*) in the SBT documentation and the *ScalazBuild.scala* build file both show *many* more examples of what can be put in a *Build.scala* file. For instance, the Full Configuration Example shows how to add a series of resolvers to a project:

```
// build 'oracleResolvers'
object Resolvers {
  val sunrepo    = "Sun Maven2 Repo" at "http://download.java.net/maven/2"
  val sunrepoGF  = "Sun GF Maven2 Repo" at
                   "http://download.java.net/maven/glassfish"
  val oraclerepo = "Oracle Maven2 Repo" at "http://download.oracle.com/maven"
```

```
    val oracleResolvers = Seq (sunrepo, sunrepoGF, oraclerepo)
}

object CDAP2Build extends Build {
  import Resolvers._
  // more code here ...

  // use 'oracleResolvers' here
  lazy val server = Project (
    "server",
    file ("cdap2-server"),
    settings = buildSettings ++ Seq (resolvers := oracleResolvers,
                                     libraryDependencies ++= serverDeps)
  ) dependsOn (common)
```

This code is similar to the example shown in Recipe 18.11, "Telling SBT How to Find a Repository (Working with Resolvers)", where the following configuration line is added to a *build.sbt* file:

```
    resolvers += "Java.net Maven2 Repository" at "http://download.java.net/maven/2/"
```

The *ScalazBuild.scala* file also shows many examples of using TaskKey and SettingKey, which are different types of keys that can be used in SBT project definition files.

## See Also

- The Full Configuration Example in the SBT documentation (*http://bit.ly/1blwxHZ*).

- The *ScalazBuild.scala* file (*http://bit.ly/1aMJeML*).

- For more examples of using *Build.scala* files, see Recipe 18.6, "Creating a Project with Subprojects"; Recipe 18.10, "Using GitHub Projects as Project Dependencies"; and Recipe 18.11, "Telling SBT How to Find a Repository (Working with Resolvers)".

# 18.17. Using a Maven Repository Library with SBT

## Problem

You want to use a Java library that's in a Maven repository, but the library doesn't include information about how to use it with Scala and SBT.

# Solution

Translate the Maven `groupId`, `artifactId`, and `version` fields into an SBT `libraryDependencies` string.

For example, I wanted to use the Java HTMLCleaner project in a Scala/SBT project. The HTMLCleaner website (*http://htmlcleaner.sourceforge.net/*) provided the following Maven information, but no SBT information:

```
<dependency>
  <groupId>net.sourceforge.htmlcleaner</groupId>
  <artifactId>htmlcleaner</artifactId>
  <version>2.2</version>
</dependency>
```

Fortunately this translates into the following SBT `libraryDependencies` string:

```
libraryDependencies += "net.sourceforge.htmlcleaner" % "htmlcleaner" % "2.2"
```

After adding this line to my *build.sbt* file, I ran `sbt compile`, and watched as it downloaded the HTMLCleaner JAR file and dependencies:

```
[info] downloading http://repo1.maven.org/maven2/net/sourceforge/htmlcleaner/
   htmlcleaner/2.2/htmlcleaner-2.2.jar ...
[info]   [SUCCESSFUL ] net.sourceforge.htmlcleaner#htmlcleaner;2.2!htmlcleaner.jar
   (864ms)
[info] downloading http://repo1.maven.org/maven2/org/jdom/jdom/1.1/jdom-1.1.jar ...
[info]   [SUCCESSFUL ] org.jdom#jdom;1.1!jdom.jar (514ms)
[info] downloading
   http://repo1.maven.org/maven2/org/apache/ant/ant/1.7.0/ant-1.7.0.jar ...
[info]   [SUCCESSFUL ] org.apache.ant#ant;1.7.0!ant.jar (1997ms)
[info] downloading http://repo1.maven.org/maven2/org/apache/ant/ant-launcher/
   1.7.0/ant-launcher-1.7.0.jar ...
[info]   [SUCCESSFUL ] org.apache.ant#ant-launcher;1.7.0!ant-launcher.jar (152ms)
[info] Done updating.
[info] Compiling 1 Scala source to target/scala-2.10.0/classes...
[success] Total time: 13 s, completed Aug 10, 2012 9:22:38 PM
```

As mentioned in other recipes, because SBT and Maven both use Apache Ivy under the covers, and SBT also uses the standard Maven2 repository as a default resolver, SBT users can easily use Java libraries that are packaged for Maven.

As shown inRecipe 18.4, "Managing Dependencies with SBT", there are two formats for adding a `libraryDependencies` line to a *build.sbt* file. The first form was used in the Solution, and its general format looks like this:

```
libraryDependencies += groupID % artifactID % revision
```

As shown with the HTMLCleaner example, the `groupID`, `artifactID`, and `revision` fields correspond directly to the information you'll find in the documentation for a Maven library.

---

The second `libraryDependencies` form lets you add an optional `configuration` parameter:

```
libraryDependencies += groupID % artifactID % revision % configuration
```

Maven doesn't use the term `configuration`, instead using a `<scope>` tag for the same information. This field is optional, and is typically used for testing libraries such as ScalaTest and specs2, so when it's needed, the value is usually just `test`.

### See Also

The Java HTMLCleaner website (*http://htmlcleaner.sourceforge.net/*)

# 18.18. Building a Scala Project with Ant

## Problem

You want to use Ant to build your Scala project.

## Solution

Assuming you have a Maven- and SBT-like project directory structure as described in Recipe 18.1, create the following Ant *build.xml* file in the root directory of your project:

```
<project name="AntCompileTest" default="compile" basedir=".">

  <!-- mostly from: http://www.scala-lang.org/node/98 -->

  <property name="sources.dir" value="src" />
  <property name="scala-source.dir" value="main/scala" />
  <property name="scala-test.dir" value="main/test" />
  <property name="build.dir" value="classes" />

  <!-- set scala.home -->
  <property environment="env" />
  <property name="scala.home" value="${env.SCALA_HOME}" />

  <target name="init">
    <property name="scala-library.jar"
              value="${scala.home}/lib/scala-library.jar" />
    <property name="scala-compiler.jar"
              value="${scala.home}/lib/scala-compiler.jar" />
    <property name="scala.reflect"
              value="${scala.home}/lib/scala-reflect.jar"/>
    <path id="build.classpath">
      <pathelement location="${scala-library.jar}" />
      <pathelement location="${build.dir}" />
    </path>
    <taskdef resource="scala/tools/ant/antlib.xml">
```

```
    <classpath>
      <pathelement location="${scala-compiler.jar}" />
      <pathelement location="${scala-library.jar}" />
      <pathelement location="${scala.reflect}"/>
    </classpath>
  </taskdef>
</target>

<target name="compile" depends="init">
  <mkdir dir="${build.dir}" />
  <scalac srcdir="${sources.dir}"
          destdir="${build.dir}"
          classpathref="build.classpath"
          deprecation="on">
    <include name="${scala-source.dir}/**/*.scala" />
    <exclude name="${scala-test.dir}/**/*.scala" />
  </scalac>
</target>

</project>
```

You can then run the usual `ant` command, which by default will compile your files to a new *classes* folder under the root directory of your project. Running `ant` on a small project produces output like this:

```
$ ant
Buildfile: /Users/Al/Projects/AntExample/build.xml

init:

compile:
 [scalac] Compiling 1 source file to /Users/Al/Projects/AntExample/classes

BUILD SUCCESSFUL
Total time: 5 seconds
```

## Discussion

In general, when learning a new technology, it's best to learn the tools of that technology, and in this case, the preferred build tool for Scala projects is SBT. (As a friend once said, when we went from C to Java, we didn't attempt to bring make along with us.) Once you grasp the SBT concepts, you'll find that it's both a simple and powerful tool, and you can find a lot of support in the Scala community.

That being said, you're also hit with a lot of changes when first learning a new technology, and at the beginning, it can be helpful to use the tools you're already comfortable with, so this recipe demonstrates how to use Ant to compile a Scala project to help you get into Scala in a comfortable way.

Recommendation: If someone brought me into their organization to help them adopt Scala, SBT is one of the first things I'd teach. In this case, I think you're better off just diving into the water, so to speak. It doesn't take that long to grasp the SBT basics.

### The build.xml code

The secret sauce to this recipe is the `init` target, whose source code can be found on the official Scala website (*http://www.scala-lang.org/node/98*). This target does the work necessary to make the `scalac` Ant task available to you.

As you can see from the code, the `build` target depends on the `init` target, and uses `scalac` to compile all the files in the source directory, while skipping the files in the test directory. Of course that approach is completely optional, and you can adjust it to meet your needs.

The *antlib.xml* file referred to in the `taskdef` tag is shipped with the Scala distribution. You can demonstrate this on a Unix system with the following command:

```
$ jar tvf ${SCALA_HOME}/lib/scala-compiler.jar | grep -i antlib
```

The *build.xml* file shown here is slightly different than the file shown on the Scala website. Specifically, I found that the `scala.home` property needed to be set manually, and with Scala 2.10, it's also necessary to add the `scala.reflect` lines to the build file. The compilation process worked fine with Ant 1.8.4 once I made those changes.

In addition to this `scalac` Ant task, there are `fsc` and `scaladoc` tasks. See the Scala Ant Tasks page (*http://www.scala-lang.org/node/98*) on the official Scala website for more information.

### Creating a JAR file with Ant

Once you've compiled your Scala classes, you can treat them as normal Java class files. For instance, you can create a JAR file from them using the following simplified Ant task. This task shows how to create a JAR file named *hello.jar* from the compiled classes in the *classes* directory, and a simple manifest in a *Manifest.txt* file. Here's the `create-jar` task, which you can add to the earlier *build.xml* file:

```
<target name="create-jar" depends="compile">
  <jar basedir="classes"
       jarfile="hello.jar"
       manifest="Manifest.txt"/>
</target>
```

Assuming the `Hello` class in the `hello` package has the `main` method for your application (or extends the `App` trait), place this line in the *Manifest.txt* file:

```
Main-Class: hello.Hello
```

After adding this task to your *build.xml* file, you can run it as follows from the root directory of your project:

```
$ ant create-jar
```

That command creates a JAR file named *hello.jar* in the root directory. You can then run the JAR file with this Scala command:

```
$ scala hello.jar
```

This is similar to running `java -jar` on a JAR file created by a Java application, but because a Scala application has dependencies on its own JAR files, such as *$SCALA_HOME/lib/scala-library.jar*, you need to run the JAR file with the `scala` interpreter, as shown. You can run the JAR file with the Java interpreter, but this takes a bit more work. See Recipe 18.14, "Deploying a Single, Executable JAR File" for details on that process.

## See Also

The Scala Ant Tasks documentation (*http://bit.ly/13fICX5*)

# CHAPTER 19

# Types

## Introduction

As you can tell from one look at the Scaladoc for the collections classes, Scala has a powerful type system. However, unless you're the creator of a library, you can go a long way in Scala without having to go too far down into the depths of Scala types. But once you start creating collections-style APIs for other users, you will need to learn them.

This chapter provides recipes for the most common problems you'll encounter, but when you need to go deeper, I highly recommend the book, *Programming in Scala*, by Odersky, Spoon, and Venners. (Martin Odersky is the creator of the Scala programming language, and I think of that book as "the reference" for Scala.)

Scala's type system uses a collection of symbols to express different generic type concepts, including variance, bounds, and constraints. The most common of these symbols are summarized in the next sections.

## Variance

*Type variance* is a generic type concept, and defines the rules by which parameterized types can be passed into methods. The type variance symbols are briefly summarized in Table 19-1.

*Table 19-1. Descriptions of type variance symbols*

| Symbols | Name | Description |
|---------|------|-------------|
| Array[T] | Invariant | Used when elements in the container are mutable.<br>Example: Can *only* pass Array[String] to a method expecting Array[String]. |
| Seq[+A] | Covariant | Used when elements in the container are immutable. This makes the container more flexible.<br>Example: Can pass a Seq[String] to a method expected Seq[Any]. |

| Symbols | Name | Description |
|---|---|---|
| `Foo[-A]`<br>`Function1[-A, +B]` | Contravariant | Contravariance is essentially the opposite of covariance, and is rarely used. See Scala's Function1 trait (*http://bit.ly/11Uopv5*) for an example of how it is used. |

The following examples, showing what code will and won't compile with the Grandparent, Parent, and Child classes, can also be a helpful reference to understanding variance:

```scala
class Grandparent
class Parent extends Grandparent
class Child extends Parent

class InvariantClass[A]
class CovariantClass[+A]
class ContravariantClass[-A]

class VarianceExamples {

    def invarMethod(x: InvariantClass[Parent]) {}
    def covarMethod(x: CovariantClass[Parent]) {}
    def contraMethod(x: ContravariantClass[Parent]) {}

    invarMethod(new InvariantClass[Child])          // ERROR - won't compile
    invarMethod(new InvariantClass[Parent])         // success
    invarMethod(new InvariantClass[Grandparent])    // ERROR - won't compile

    covarMethod(new CovariantClass[Child])          // success
    covarMethod(new CovariantClass[Parent])         // success
    covarMethod(new CovariantClass[Grandparent])    // ERROR - won't compile

    contraMethod(new ContravariantClass[Child])       // ERROR - won't compile
    contraMethod(new ContravariantClass[Parent])      // success
    contraMethod(new ContravariantClass[Grandparent]) // success

}
```

# Bounds

Bounds let you place restrictions on type parameters. Table 19-2 shows the common bounds symbols.

*Table 19-2. Descriptions of Scala's bounds symbols*

| | Name | Description |
|---|---|---|
| `A <: B` | Upper bound | A must be a subtype of B. See Recipe 19.6. |
| `A >: B` | Lower bound | A must be a supertype of B. Not commonly used. See Recipe 19.8. |
| `A <: Upper >: Lower` | Lower and upper bounds used together | The type A has both an upper and lower bound. |

*Programming Scala* (O'Reilly) had a nice tip that helps me remember these symbols. The authors state that in UML diagrams, subtypes are shown below supertypes, so when I see A <: B, I think, "A is less than B ... A is under B ... A is a subtype of B."

Lower bounds are demonstrated in several methods of the collections classes. To find some lower bound examples, search the Scaladoc of classes like List (*http://bit.ly/15iqGNE*) for the >: symbol.

There are several additional symbols for bounds. For instance, a *view bound* is written as A <% B, and a *context bound* is written as T : M. These symbols are not covered in this book; see *Programming in Scala* for details and examples of their use.

## Type Constraints

Scala lets you specify additional type constraints. These are written with these symbols:

```
A =:= B  // A must be equal to B
A <:< B  // A must be a subtype of B
A <%< B  // A must be viewable as B
```

These symbols are not covered in this book. See *Programming in Scala* for details and examples. Twitter's Scala School Advanced Types page (*http://bit.ly/18juAbp*) also shows brief examples of their use, where they are referred to as "type relation operators."

## Type Examples in Other Chapters

Because types are naturally used in many solutions, you can find some recipes related to types in other chapters:

- Recipe 2.2, "Converting Between Numeric Types (Casting)" and Recipe 2.3 demonstrate ways to convert between types.

- Recipe 5.9, "Supporting a Fluent Style of Programming" demonstrates how to return this.type from a method.

- Implicit conversions let you add new behavior to closed types like String, which is declared final in Java. They are demonstrated in Recipe 1.10, "Add Your Own Methods to the String Class" and Recipe 2.1, "Parsing a Number from a String".

- Recipe 6.1, "Object Casting" demonstrates how to cast objects from one type to another.

Finally, Recipe 19.8, "Building Functionality with Types" combines several of the concepts described in this chapter, and also helps to demonstrate Scala's *call-by-name* feature.

# 19.1. Creating Classes That Use Generic Types

## Problem

You want to create a class (and associated methods) that uses a generic type.

## Solution

As a library writer, creating a class (and methods) that takes a generic type is similar to Java. For instance, if Scala didn't have a linked list class and you wanted to write your own, you could write the basic functionality like this:

```scala
class LinkedList[A] {

  private class Node[A] (elem: A) {
    var next: Node[A] = _
    override def toString = elem.toString
  }

  private var head: Node[A] = _

  def add(elem: A) {
    val n = new Node(elem)
    n.next = head
    head = n
  }

  private def printNodes(n: Node[A]) {
    if (n != null) {
      println(n)
      printNodes(n.next)
    }
  }

  def printAll() { printNodes(head) }

}
```

Notice how the generic type A is sprinkled throughout the class definition. This is similar to Java, but Scala uses [A] everywhere, instead of <T> as Java does. (More on the characters A versus T shortly.)

To create a list of integers with this class, first create an instance of it, declaring its type as Int:

```scala
val ints = new LinkedList[Int]()
```

Then populate it with Int values:

```scala
ints.add(1)
ints.add(2)
```

Because the class uses a generic type, you can also create a `LinkedList` of `String`:

```
val strings = new LinkedList[String]()
strings.add("Nacho")
strings.add("Libre")
strings.printAll()
```

Or any other type you want to use:

```
val doubles = new LinkedList[Double]()
val frogs = new LinkedList[Frog]()
```

At this basic level, creating a generic class in Scala is just like creating a generic class in Java, with the exception of the brackets.

## Discussion

When using generics like this, the container can take subtypes of the base type you specify in your code. For instance, given this class hierarchy:

```
trait Animal
class Dog extends Animal { override def toString = "Dog" }
class SuperDog extends Dog { override def toString = "SuperDog" }
class FunnyDog extends Dog { override def toString = "FunnyDog" }
```

you can define a `LinkedList` that holds `Dog` instances:

```
val dogs = new LinkedList[Dog]
```

You can then add `Dog` subtypes to the list:

```
val fido = new Dog
val wonderDog = new SuperDog
val scooby = new FunnyDog

dogs.add(fido)
dogs.add(wonderDog)
dogs.add(scooby)
```

So far, so good: you can add `Dog` subtypes to a `LinkedList[Dog]`. Where you might run into a problem is when you define a method like this:

```
def printDogTypes(dogs: LinkedList[Dog]) {
  dogs.printAll()
}
```

You can pass your current `dogs` instance into this method, but you won't be able to pass the following `superDogs` collection into `makeDogsSpeak`:

```
val superDogs = new LinkedList[SuperDog]
superDogs.add(wonderDog)

// error: this line won't compile
printDogTypes(superDogs)
```

The last line won't compile because (a) makeDogsSpeak wants a LinkedList[Dog], (b) LinkedList elements are mutable, and (c) superDogs is a LinkedList[SuperDog]. This creates a conflict the compiler can't resolve. This situation is discussed in detail in Recipe 19.5, "Make Immutable Collections Covariant".

In Scala 2.10, the compiler is even nice enough to tell you what's wrong in this situation, and points you toward a solution:

```
[error] Note: SuperDog <: Dog, but class LinkedList is invariant in type A.
[error] You may wish to define A as +A instead. (SLS 4.5)
```

### Type parameter symbols

If a class requires more than one type parameter, use the symbols shown in Table 19-3. For instance, in the official Java Generics documentation (*http://bit.ly/13rHoad*), Oracle shows an interface named Pair, which takes two types:

```
// from http://docs.oracle.com/javase/tutorial/java/generics/types.html
public interface Pair<K, V> {
    public K getKey();
    public V getValue();
}
```

You can port that interface to a Scala trait, as follows:

```
trait Pair[A, B] {
    def getKey: A
    def getValue: B
}
```

If you were to take this further and implement the body of a Pair class (or trait), the type parameters A and B would be spread throughout your class, just as the symbol A was used in the LinkedList example.

The same Oracle document lists the Java type parameter naming conventions. These are mostly the same in Scala, except that Java starts naming simple type parameters with the letter T, and then uses the characters U and V for subsequent types. The Scala standard is that simple types should be declared as A, the next with B, and so on. This is shown in Table 19-3.

*Table 19-3. Standard symbols for generic type parameters*

| Symbol | Description |
|---|---|
| A | Refers to a simple type, such as List[A]. |
| B, C, D | Used for the 2nd, 3rd, 4th types, etc. |
| | `// from the Scala Styleguide`<br>`class List[A] {`<br>`    def map[B](f: A => B): List[B] = ...`<br>`}` |
| K | Typically refers to a key in a Java map. Scala collections use A in this situation. |

| Symbol | Description |
|--------|-------------|
| N | Refers to a numeric value. |
| V | Typically refers to a value in a Java map. Scala collections use B in this situation. |

## See Also

- Oracle's Java "Generic Types" documentation (*http://bit.ly/13rHoad*).
- Recipe 19.4, "Make Mutable Collections Invariant".
- Recipe 19.5, "Make Immutable Collections Covariant".
- You can find a little more information on Scala's generic type naming conventions at the Scala Style Guide's Naming Conventions page (*http://docs.scala-lang.org/ style/naming-conventions.html*).

# 19.2. Creating a Method That Takes a Simple Generic Type

## Problem

You're not concerned about type variance, and want to create a method (or function) that takes a generic type, such as a method that accepts a Seq[A] parameter.

## Solution

As with Scala classes, specify the generic type parameters in brackets, like [A].

For example, when creating a lottery-style application to draw a random name from a list of names, you might follow the "Do the simplest thing that could possibly work" credo, and initially create a method without using generics:

```
def randomName(names: Seq[String]): String = {
  val randomNum = util.Random.nextInt(names.length)
  names(randomNum)
}
```

As written, this works with a sequence of String values:

```
val names = Seq("Aleka", "Christina", "Tyler", "Molly")
val winner = randomName(names)
```

Then, at some point in the future you realize that you could really use a general-purpose method that returns a random element from a sequence of any type. So, you modify the method to use a generic type parameter, like this:

```
def randomElement[A](seq: Seq[A]): A = {
  val randomNum = util.Random.nextInt(seq.length)
```

```
    seq(randomNum)
  }
```

With this change, the method can now be called on a variety of types:

```
randomElement(Seq("Aleka", "Christina", "Tyler", "Molly"))
randomElement(List(1,2,3))
randomElement(List(1.0,2.0,3.0))
randomElement(Vector.range('a', 'z'))
```

Note that specifying the method's return type isn't necessary, so you can simplify the signature slightly, if desired:

```
// change the return type from ':A =' to just '='
def randomElement[A](seq: Seq[A]) = { ...
```

## Discussion

This is a simple example that shows how to pass a generic collection to a method that doesn't attempt to mutate the collection. See Recipes 19.4 and 19.5 for more complicated situations you can run into.

# 19.3. Using Duck Typing (Structural Types)

## Problem

You're used to "Duck Typing" (structural types) from another language like Python or Ruby, and want to use this feature in your Scala code.

## Solution

Scala's version of "Duck Typing" is known as using a *structural type*. As an example of this approach, the following code shows how a callSpeak method can require that its obj type parameter have a speak() method:

```
def callSpeak[A <: { def speak(): Unit }](obj: A) {
  // code here ...
  obj.speak()
}
```

Given that definition, an instance of any class that has a speak() method that takes no parameters and returns nothing can be passed as a parameter to callSpeak. For example, the following code demonstrates how to invoke callSpeak on both a Dog and a Klingon:

```
class Dog { def speak() { println("woof") } }
class Klingon { def speak() { println("Qapla!") } }

object DuckTyping extends App {
```

```
def callSpeak[A <: { def speak(): Unit }](obj: A) {
  obj.speak()
}

callSpeak(new Dog)
callSpeak(new Klingon)

}
```

Running this code prints the following output:

```
woof
Qapla!
```

The class of the instance that's passed in doesn't matter at all. The only requirement for the parameter `obj` is that it's an instance of a class that has a `speak()` method.

## Discussion

The structural type syntax is necessary in this example because the `callSpeak` method invokes a `speak` method on the object that's passed in. In a statically typed language, there must be some guarantee that the object that's passed in will have this method, and this recipe shows the syntax for that situation.

Had the method been written as follows, it wouldn't compile, because the compiler can't guarantee that the type A has a `speak` method:

```
// won't compile
def callSpeak[A](obj: A) {
  obj.speak()
}
```

This is one of the great benefits of type safety in Scala.

It may help to break down the structural type syntax. First, here's the entire method:

```
def callSpeak[A <: { def speak(): Unit }](obj: A) {
  obj.speak()
}
```

The type parameter A is defined as a structural type like this:

```
[A <: { def speak(): Unit }]
```

The `<:` symbol in the code is used to define something called an *upper bound*. This is described in detail in Recipe 19.5, "Make Immutable Collections Covariant". As shown in that recipe, an upper bound is usually defined like this:

```
class Stack[A <: Animal] (val elem: A)
```

This states that the type parameter A must be a subtype of `Animal`.

However, in this recipe, a variation of that syntax is used to state that A must be a subtype of a type that has a `speak` method. Specifically, this code can be read as, "A must be a subtype of a type that has a `speak` method. The `speak` method (or function) can't take any parameters and must not return anything."

To demonstrate another example of the structural type signature, if you wanted to state that the `speak` method must take a `String` parameter and return a `Boolean`, the structural type signature would look like this:

```
[A <: { def speak(s: String): Boolean }]
```

As a word of warning, this technique uses reflection, so you may not want to use it when performance is a concern.

# 19.4. Make Mutable Collections Invariant

## Problem

You want to create a collection whose elements can be mutated, and want to know how to specify the generic type parameter for its elements.

## Solution

When creating a collection of elements that can be changed (mutated), its generic type parameter should be declared as `[A]`, making it *invariant*.

For instance, elements in a Scala `Array` or `ArrayBuffer` can be mutated, and their signatures are declared like this:

```
class Array[A] ...
class ArrayBuffer[A] ...
```

Declaring a type as invariant has several effects. First, the container can hold both the specified types as well as its subtypes. For example, the following class hierarchy states that the `Dog` and `SuperDog` classes both extend the `Animal` trait:

```
trait Animal {
  def speak
}

class Dog(var name: String) extends Animal {
  def speak { println("woof") }
  override def toString = name
}

class SuperDog(name: String) extends Dog(name) {
  def useSuperPower { println("Using my superpower!") }
}
```

With these classes, you can create a `Dog` and a `SuperDog`:

```
val fido = new Dog("Fido")
val wonderDog = new SuperDog("Wonder Dog")
val shaggy = new SuperDog("Shaggy")
```

When you later declare an ArrayBuffer[Dog], you can add both Dog *and* SuperDog instances to it:

```
val dogs = ArrayBuffer[Dog]()
dogs += fido
dogs += wonderDog
```

So a collection with an invariant type parameter can contain elements of the base type, and subtypes of the base type.

The second effect of declaring an invariant type is the primary purpose of this recipe. Given the same code, you can define a method as follows to accept an ArrayBuffer[Dog], and then have each Dog speak:

```
import collection.mutable.ArrayBuffer
def makeDogsSpeak(dogs: ArrayBuffer[Dog]) {
  dogs.foreach(_.speak)
}
```

Because of its definition, this works fine when you pass it an ArrayBuffer[Dog]:

```
val dogs = ArrayBuffer[Dog]()
dogs += fido
makeDogsSpeak(dogs)
```

However, the makeDogsSpeak call won't compile if you attempt to pass it an ArrayBuffer[SuperDog]:

```
val superDogs = ArrayBuffer[SuperDog]()
superDogs += shaggy
superDogs += wonderDog
makeDogsSpeak(superDogs)   // ERROR: won't compile
```

This code won't compile because of the conflict built up in this situation:

- Elements in an ArrayBuffer can be mutated.
- makeDogsSpeak is defined to accept a parameter of type ArrayBuffer[Dog].
- You're attempting to pass in superDogs, whose type is ArrayBuffer[SuperDog].
- If the compiler allowed this, makeDogsSpeak could replace SuperDog elements in superDogs with plain old Dog elements. This can't be allowed.

One of the reasons this problem occurs is that ArrayBuffer elements can be mutated. If you want to write a method to make all Dog types *and* subtypes speak, define it to accept a collection of immutable elements, such as a List, Seq, or Vector.

## Discussion

The elements of the `Array`, `ArrayBuffer`, and `ListBuffer` classes can be mutated, and they're all defined with invariant type parameters:

```
class Array[T]
class ArrayBuffer[A]
class ListBuffer[A]
```

Conversely, collections classes that are immutable identify their generic type parameters differently, with the + symbol, as shown here:

```
class List[+T]
class Vector[+A]
trait Seq[+A]
```

The + symbol used on the type parameters of the immutable collections defines their parameters to be *covariant*. Because their elements can't be mutated, adding this symbol makes them more flexible, as discussed in the next recipe.

## See Also

You can find the source code for Scala classes by following the "Source code" links in their Scaladoc. The source code for the `ArrayBuffer` class isn't too long, and it shows how the type parameter A ends up sprinkled throughout the class:

```
ArrayBuffer class Scaladoc (http://bit.ly/18YoNuP)
```

# 19.5. Make Immutable Collections Covariant

## Problem

You want to create a collection whose elements can't be changed (they're immutable), and want to understand how to specify it.

## Solution

You *can* define a collection of immutable elements as invariant, but your collection will be much more flexible if you declare that your type parameter is *covariant*. To make a type parameter covariant, declare it with the + symbol, like [+A].

Covariant type parameters are shown in the Scaladoc for immutable collection classes like `List`, `Vector`, and `Seq`:

```
class List[+T]
class Vector[+A]
trait Seq[+A]
```

By defining the type parameter to be covariant, you create a situation where the collection can be used in a more flexible manner.

To demonstrate this, modify the example from the previous recipe slightly. First, define the class hierarchy:

```
trait Animal {
  def speak
}

class Dog(var name: String) extends Animal {
  def speak { println("Dog says woof") }
}

class SuperDog(name: String) extends Dog(name) {
  override def speak { println("I'm a SuperDog") }
}
```

Next, define a `makeDogsSpeak` method, but instead of accepting a mutable `ArrayBuffer[Dog]` as in the previous recipe, accept an immutable `Seq[Dog]`:

```
def makeDogsSpeak(dogs: Seq[Dog]) {
  dogs.foreach(_.speak)
}
```

As with the `ArrayBuffer` in the previous recipe, you can pass a sequence of type `[Dog]` into `makeDogsSpeak` without a problem:

```
// this works
val dogs = Seq(new Dog("Fido"), new Dog("Tanner"))
makeDogsSpeak(dogs)
```

However, in this case, you can also pass a `Seq[SuperDog]` into the `makeDogsSpeak` method successfully:

```
// this works too
val superDogs = Seq(new SuperDog("Wonder Dog"), new SuperDog("Scooby"))
makeDogsSpeak(superDogs)
```

Because `Seq` is immutable and defined with a covariant parameter type, `makeDogsSpeak` can now accept collections of both `Dog` and `SuperDog`.

## Discussion

You can demonstrate this by creating a collection class with a covariant type parameter. To do this, create a collection class that can hold one element. Because you don't want the collection element to be mutated, define the element as a `val`, and make the type parameter covariant with +A:

```
class Container[+A] (val elem: A)
```

Using the same type hierarchy as shown in the Solution, modify the makeDogsSpeak method to accept a Container[Dog]:

```
def makeDogsSpeak(dogHouse: Container[Dog]) {
  dogHouse.elem.speak()
}
```

With this setup, you can pass a Container[Dog] into makeDogsSpeak:

```
val dogHouse = new Container(new Dog("Tanner"))
makeDogsSpeak(dogHouse)
```

Finally, to demonstrate the point of adding the + symbol to the parameter, you can also pass a Container[SuperDog] into makeDogsSpeak:

```
val superDogHouse = new Container(new SuperDog("Wonder Dog"))
makeDogsSpeak(superDogHouse)
```

Because the Container element is immutable and its mutable type parameter is marked as covariant, all of this code works successfully. Note that if you change the Container's type parameter from +A to A, the last line of code won't compile.

As demonstrated in these examples, defining an immutable collection to take a covariant generic type parameter makes the collection more flexible and useful throughout your code.

# 19.6. Create a Collection Whose Elements Are All of Some Base Type

## Problem

You want to specify that a class or method takes a type parameter, and that parameter is limited so it can only be a base type, or a subtype of that base type.

## Solution

Define the class or method by specifying the type parameter with an *upper bound*.

To demonstrate this, create a simple type hierarchy:

```
trait CrewMember
class Officer extends CrewMember
class RedShirt extends CrewMember
trait Captain
trait FirstOfficer
trait ShipsDoctor
trait StarfleetTrained
```

Then create a few instances:

```
val kirk = new Officer with Captain
val spock = new Officer with FirstOfficer
val bones = new Officer with ShipsDoctor
```

Given this setup, imagine that you want to create a collection of officers on a ship, like this:

```
val officers = new Crew[Officer]()
officers += kirk
officers += spock
officers += bones
```

The first line lets you create officers as a collection that can only contain types that are an Officer, or subtype of an Officer.

In this example, those who are of type RedShirt won't be allowed in the collection, because they don't extend Officer:

```
val redShirt = new RedShirt
officers += redShirt  // ERROR: this won't compile
```

To enable this functionality and let Crew control which types are added to it, define it with an *upper bound* while extending ArrayBuffer:

```
class Crew[A <: CrewMember] extends ArrayBuffer[A]
```

This states that any instance of Crew can only ever have elements that are of type CrewMember. In this example, this lets you define officers as a collection of Officer, like this:

```
val officers = new Crew[Officer]()
```

It also prevents you from writing code like this, because String does not extend CrewMember:

```
// error: won't compile
val officers = new Crew[String]()
```

In addition to creating a collection of officers, you can create a collection of RedShirts, if desired:

```
val redshirts = new Crew[RedShirt]()
```

(I don't know the names of any redshirts, otherwise I'd add a few to this collection.)

Typically you'll define a class like Crew so you can create specific instances as shown. You'll also typically add methods to a class like Crew that are specific to the type (CrewMember, in this case). By controlling what types are added to Crew, you can be assured that your methods will work as desired. For instance, Crew could have methods like beamUp, beamDown, goWhereNoOneElseHasGone, etc.—any method that makes sense for a CrewMember.

## Discussion

This type is referred to as a bound, specifically an *upper bound*.

(If you're working with an implicit conversion, you'll want to use a *view bound* instead of an upper bound. To do this, use the <% symbol instead of the <: symbol.)

You can use the same technique when you need to limit your class to take a type that extends multiple traits. For example, to create a Crew that only allows types that extend CrewMember and StarfleetTrained, declare the Crew like this:

```
class Crew[A <: CrewMember with StarfleetTrained] extends ArrayBuffer[A]
```

If you adapt the officers to work with this new trait:

```
val kirk = new Officer with Captain with StarfleetTrained
val spock = new Officer with FirstOfficer with StarfleetTrained
val bones = new Officer with ShipsDoctor with StarfleetTrained
```

you can still construct a list of officers, with a slight change to the Crew definition:

```
val officers = new Crew[Officer with StarfleetTrained]()
officers += kirk
officers += spock
officers += bones
```

This approach works as long as the instances have those types somewhere in their lineage (class hierarchy). For instance, you can define a new StarfleetOfficer like this:

```
class StarfleetOfficer extends Officer with StarfleetTrained
```

You could then define the kirk instance like this:

```
val kirk = new StarfleetOfficer with Captain
```

With this definition, kirk can still be added to the officers collection; the instance still extends Officer and StarfleetTrained.

### Methods

Methods can also take advantage of this syntax. For instance, you can add a little behavior to CrewMember and RedShirt:

```
trait CrewMember {
  def beamDown { println("beaming down") }
}
class RedShirt extends CrewMember {
  def putOnRedShirt { println("putting on my red shirt") }
}
```

With this behavior, you can write methods to work specifically on their types. This method works for any CrewMember:

```
def beamDown[A <: CrewMember](crewMember: Crew[A]) {
  crewMember.foreach(_.beamDown)
}
```

But this method will only work for RedShirt types:

```
def getReadyForDay[A <: RedShirt](redShirt: Crew[A]) {
  redShirt.foreach(_.putOnRedShirt)
}
```

In both cases, you control which type can be passed into the method using an appropriate upper bound definition on the method's type parameter.

## See Also

- Recipe 19.3, "Using Duck Typing (Structural Types)".

- Scala also includes a *lower type bound*, though it is used less frequently. A lower bound is briefly demonstrated in Recipe 19.8, "Building Functionality with Types". The page titled "A Tour of Scala: Lower Type Bounds" (*http://www.scala-lang.org/node/137*) also describes a situation where a lower type bound might be used.

# 19.7. Selectively Adding New Behavior to a Closed Model

## Problem

You have a closed model, and want to add new behavior to certain types within that model, while potentially excluding that behavior from being added to other types.

## Solution

Implement your solution as a *type class*.

To demonstrate the problem and solution, when I first came to Scala, I thought it would be easy to write a single add method that would add any two numeric parameters, regardless of whether they were an Int, Double, Float, or other numeric value. Unfortunately I couldn't get this to work—until I learned about type classes.

Because a Numeric type class already exists in the Scala library, it turns out that you can create an add method that accepts different numeric types like this:

```
def add[A](x: A, y: A)(implicit numeric: Numeric[A]): A = numeric.plus(x, y)
```

Once defined, this method can be used with different numeric types like this:

```
println(add(1, 1))
println(add(1.0, 1.5))
println(add(1, 1.5F))
```

The add method works because of some magic in the scala.math.Numeric trait. To see how this magic works, create your own type class.

## Creating a type class

The process of creating a type class is a little complicated, but there is a formula:

- Usually you start with a need, such as having a closed model to which you want to add new behavior.

- To add the new behavior, you define a type class. The typical approach is to create a base trait, and then write specific implementations of that trait using implicit objects.

- Back in your main application, create a method that uses the type class to apply the behavior to the closed model, such as writing the add method in the previous example.

To demonstrate this, assume that you have a closed model that contains Dog and Cat types, and you want to make a Dog more human-like by giving it the capability to speak. However, while doing this, you don't want to make a Cat more human-like. (Everyone knows that dogs are human-like and can speak; see YouTube for examples.)

The closed model is defined in a class named *Animals.scala*, and looks like this:

```
package typeclassdemo

// an existing, closed model
trait Animal
final case class Dog(name: String) extends Animal
final case class Cat(name: String) extends Animal
```

To begin making a new speak behavior available to a Dog, create a type class that implements the speak behavior for a Dog, but not a Cat:

```
package typeclassdemo

object Humanish {

  // the type class.
  // defines an abstract method named 'speak'.
  trait HumanLike[A] {
    def speak(speaker: A): Unit
  }

  // companion object
  object HumanLike {
    // implement the behavior for each desired type. in this case,
```

```
      // only for a Dog.
      implicit object DogIsHumanLike extends HumanLike[Dog] {
        def speak(dog: Dog) { println(s"I'm a Dog, my name is ${dog.name}") }
      }
    }

  }
```

With this behavior defined, use the new functionality back in your main application:

```
package typeclassdemo

object TypeClassDemo extends App {

  import Humanish.HumanLike

  // create a method to make an animal speak
  def makeHumanLikeThingSpeak[A](animal: A)(implicit humanLike: HumanLike[A]) {
    humanLike.speak(animal)
  }

  // because HumanLike implemented this for a Dog, it will work
  makeHumanLikeThingSpeak(Dog("Rover"))

  // however, the method won't compile for a Cat (as desired)
  //makeHumanLikeThingSpeak(Cat("Morris"))

}
```

The comments in the code explain why this approach works for a Dog, but not a Cat.

There are a few other things to notice from this code:

- The makeHumanLikeThingSpeak is similar to the add method in the first example.

- In the first example, the Numeric type class already existed, so you could just use it to create the add method. But when you're starting from scratch, you need to create your own type class (the code in the HumanLike trait).

- Because a speak method is defined in the DogIsHumanLike implicit object, which extends HumanLike[Dog], a Dog can be passed into the makeHumanLikeThingSpeak method. But because a similar implicit object has not been written for the Cat class, it can't be used.

# Discussion

Despite the name "class," a type class doesn't come from the OOP world; it comes from the FP world, specifically Haskell. As shown in the examples, one benefit of a type class is that you can add behavior to a closed model.

Another benefit is that it lets you define methods that take generic types, and provide control over what those types are. For instance, in the first example, the add method takes Numeric types:

```
def add[A](x: A, y: A)(implicit numeric: Numeric[A]): A = numeric.plus(x, y)
```

Because the numeric.plus method is implemented for all the different numeric types, you can create an add method that works for Int, Double, Float, and other types:

```
println(add(1, 1))
println(add(1.0, 1.5))
println(add(1, 1.5F))
```

This is great; it works for all numeric types, as desired. As an additional benefit, the add method is type safe. If you attempted to pass a String into it, it won't compile:

```
// won't compile
add("1", 2.0)
```

In the second example, the makeHumanLikeThingSpeak method is similar to the add method. However, in this case, it lets a Dog type speak, but because the HumanLike trait didn't define a similar behavior for a Cat, a Cat instance can't currently be used by the method. You can resolve this by adding a speak method for a Cat type as another implicit object, or keep the code as it's currently written to prevent a Cat from speaking.

## See Also

- If you dig into the source code for Scala's Numeric trait, you'll find that it's implemented in a manner similar to what's shown here. You can find the source code for Scala's Numeric trait by following the "Source code" link on its Scaladoc page (*http://bit.ly/16HeYLy*).

- Recipe 1.10, "Add Your Own Methods to the String Class" demonstrates how to add new functionality to closed classes using implicit conversions.

# 19.8. Building Functionality with Types

To put what you've learned in this chapter to use, let's create two examples. First, you'll create a "timer" that looks like a control structure and works like the Unix time command. Second, you'll create another control structure that works like the Scala 2.10 Try/Success/Failure classes.

## Example 1: Creating a Timer

On Unix systems you can run a time command (timex on some systems) to see how long commands take to execute:

```
$ time find . -name "*.scala"
```

That command returns the results of the find command it was given, along with the time it took to run. This can be a helpful way to troubleshoot performance problems.

You can create a similar timer method in Scala to let you run code like this:

```
val (result, time) = timer(someLongRunningAlgorithm)
println(s"result: $result, time: $time")
```

In this example, the timer runs a method named longRunningAlgorithm, and then returns the result from the algorithm, along with the algorithm's execution time. You can see how this works by running a simple example in the REPL:

```
scala> val (result, time) = timer{ Thread.sleep(500); 1 }
result: Int = 1
time: Double = 500.32
```

As expected, the code block returns the value 1, with an execution time of about 500 ms.

The timer code is surprisingly simple, and involves the use of a generic type parameter:

```
def timer[A](blockOfCode: => A) = {
  val startTime = System.nanoTime
  val result = blockOfCode
  val stopTime = System.nanoTime
  val delta = stopTime - startTime
  (result, delta/1000000d)
}
```

The timer method uses Scala's *call-by-name* syntax to accept a block of code as a parameter. Rather than declare a specific return type from the method (such as Int), you declare the return type to be a generic type parameter. This lets you pass all sorts of algorithms into timer, including those that return nothing:

```
scala> val (result, time) = timer{ println("Hello") }
Hello
result: Unit = ()
time: Double = 0.544
```

Or an algorithm that reads a file and returns an iterator:

```
scala> def readFile(filename: String) = io.Source.fromFile(filename).getLines
readFile: (filename: String)Iterator[String]

scala> val (result, time) = timer{ readFile("/etc/passwd") }
result: Iterator[String] = non-empty iterator
time: Double = 32.119
```

This is a simple use of specifying a generic type in a noncollection class, and helps you get ready for the next example.

# Example 2: Writing Your Own "Try" Classes

Imagine the days back before Scala 2.10 when there was no such thing as the Try, Success, and Failure classes in *scala.util*. (They were available from Twitter, but just ignore that for now.) In those days, you might have come up with your own solution that you called Attempt, Succeeded, and Failed that would let you write code like this:

```
val x = Attempt("10".toInt)    // Succeeded(10)
val y = Attempt("10A".toInt)   // Failed(Exception)
```

To enable this basic API, you realize you'll need a class named Attempt, and because you know you don't want to use the new keyword to create a new instance, you know that you need a companion object with an apply method. You further realize that you need to define Succeeded and Failed, and they should extend Attempt. Therefore, you begin with this code, placed in a file named *Attempt.scala*:

```
// version 1
sealed class Attempt[A]

object Attempt {

  def apply[A](f: => A): Attempt[A] =
    try {
      val result = f
      return Succeeded(result)
    } catch {
      case e: Exception => Failed(e)
    }

}

final case class Failed[A](val exception: Throwable) extends Attempt[A]
final case class Succeeded[A](value: A) extends Attempt[A]
```

In a manner similar to the previous timer code, the apply method takes a call-by-name parameter, and the return type is specified as a generic type parameter. In this case, the type parameter ends up sprinkled around in other areas. Because apply returns a type of Attempt, it's necessary there; because Failed and Succeeded extend Attempt, it's propagated there as well.

This first version of the code lets you write the basic x and y examples. However, to be really useful, your API needs a new method named getOrElse that lets you get the information from the result, whether that result happens to be a type of Succeeded or Failed.

The getOrElse method will be called like this:

```
val x = Attempt(1/0)
val result = x.getOrElse(0)
```

Or this:

```
val y = Attempt("foo".toInt).getOrElse(0)
```

To enable a `getOrElse` method, make the following changes to the code:

```
// version 2
sealed abstract class Attempt[A] {
  def getOrElse[B >: A](default: => B): B = if (isSuccess) get else default
  var isSuccess = false
  def get: A
}

object Attempt {
  def apply[A](f: => A): Attempt[A] =
    try {
      val result = f
      Succeeded(result)
    } catch {
      case e: Exception => Failed(e)
    }
}

final case class Failed[A](val exception: Throwable) extends Attempt[A] {
  isSuccess = false
  def get: A = throw exception
}

final case class Succeeded[A](result: A) extends Attempt[A] {
  isSuccess = true
  def get = result
}
```

The variable `isSuccess` is added to `Attempt` so it can be set in `Succeeded` or `Failed`. An abstract method named `get` is also declared in `Attempt` so it can be implemented in the two subclasses. These changes let the `getOrElse` method in `Attempt` work.

The `getOrElse` method signature is the most interesting thing about this new code:

```
def getOrElse[B >: A](default: => B): B = if (isSuccess) get else default
```

Because of the way `getOrElse` works, it can either return the type A, which is the result of the expression, or type B, which the user supplies, and is presumably a substitute for A. The expression B >: A is a *lower bound*. Though it isn't commonly used, a lower bound declares that a type is a supertype of another type. In this code, the term B >: A expresses that the type parameter B is a supertype of A.

### The Scala 2.10 Try classes

You could keep developing your own classes, but the `Try`, `Success`, and `Failure` classes in the `scala.util` package were introduced in Scala 2.10, so this is a good place to stop.

However, it's worth noting that these classes can be a great way to learn about Scala types. For instance, the getOrElse method in the Attempt code is the same as the getOrElse method declared in Try:

```
def getOrElse[U >: T](default: => U): U = if (isSuccess) get else default
```

The map method declared in Success shows how to define a call-by-name parameter that transforms a type T to a type U:

```
def map[U](f: T => U): Try[U] = Try[U](f(value))
```

Its flatten method uses the <:< symbol that wasn't covered in this chapter. When used as A <:< B, it declares that "A must be a subtype of B." Here's how it's used in the Success class:

```
def flatten[U](implicit ev: T <:< Try[U]): Try[U] = value
```

When it comes to learning about generic parameter types, these classes are very interesting to study. They're self-contained and surprisingly short. The Scala collections classes also demonstrate many more uses of generics.

# CHAPTER 20

# Idioms

## Introduction

When I first came to Scala from Java, I was happy with the small things, including eliminating a lot of ;, ( ), and { } characters, and writing more concise, Ruby-like code. These were nice little wins that made for "a better Java."

Over time, I wanted to add more to my repertoire and use Scala the way it's intended to be used. As Ward Cunningham said in the book, *Clean Code* (Prentice Hall), I wanted to write code that "makes it look like the language was made for the problem."

That's what this chapter is about—trying to share some of the best practices of Scala programming so you can write code in "the Scala way."

Before digging into the recipes in this chapter, here's a short summary of Scala's best practices.

At the application level:

- At the big-picture, application-design level, follow the 80/20 rule, and try to write 80% of your application as pure functions, with a thin layer of other code on top of those functions for things like I/O.
- Learn "Expression-Oriented Programming" (Recipe 20.3).
- Use the Actor classes to implement concurrency (Chapter 13).
- Move behavior from classes into more granular traits. This is best described in the Scala Stackable Trait pattern (*http://bit.ly/17fZTma*).

At the coding level:

- Learn how to write pure functions. At the very least, they simplify testing.
- Learn how to pass functions around as variables (Recipes 9.2 to 9.4).

- Learn how to use the Scala collections API. Know the most common classes and methods (10 and 11).
- Prefer immutable code. Use `vals` and immutable collections first (Recipe 20.2).
- Drop the `null` keyword from your vocabulary. Use the `Option/Some/None` and `Try/Success/Failure` classes instead (Recipe 20.6).
- Use TDD and/or BDD testing tools like ScalaTest and specs2.

Outside the code:

- Learn how to use SBT. It's the de-facto Scala build tool (Chapter 18).
- Keep a REPL session open while you're coding (or use the Scala Worksheet (*http://bit.ly/1aq2RXe*)), and constantly try small experiments (Recipes 14.1 to 14.4, and many examples throughout the book).

## Other Resources

In addition to the practices shared in this chapter, I highly recommend reading Twitter's *Effective Scala* document (*http://bit.ly/1c3BpjS*). The Twitter team has been a big user and proponent of Scala, and this document summarizes their experiences.

The Scala Style Guide (*http://docs.scala-lang.org/style/*) is a good resource that shares examples of how to write code in the Scala "style."

# 20.1. Create Methods with No Side Effects (Pure Functions)

## Problem

In keeping with the best practices of Functional Programming (FP), you want to write "pure functions."

## Solution

In general, when writing a function (or method), your goal should be to write it as a pure function. This raises the question, "What is a pure function?" Before we tackle that question we need to look at another term, *referential transparency*, because it's part of the description of a pure function.

## Referential transparency

If you like algebra, you'll like referential transparency. An expression is referentially transparent (RT) if it can be replaced by its resulting value without changing the behavior of the program. This must be true regardless of where the expression is used in the program.

For instance, assume that x and y are immutable variables within some scope of an application, and within that scope they're used to form this expression:

```
x + y
```

You can assign this expression to a third variable, like this:

```
val z = x + y
```

Now, throughout the given scope of your program, anywhere the expression x + y is used, it can be replaced by z without affecting the result of the program.

Note that although I stated that x and y are immutable variables, they can also be the result of RT functions. For instance, "hello".length + "world".length will always be 10. This result could be assigned to z, and then z could be used everywhere instead of this expression.

Although this is a simple example, this is referential transparency in a nutshell.

## Pure functions

Wikipedia defines a pure function as follows:

1. The function always evaluates to the same result value given the same argument value(s). It cannot depend on any hidden state or value, and it cannot depend on any I/O.

2. Evaluation of the result does not cause any semantically observable side effect or output, such as mutation of mutable objects or output to I/O devices.

The book *Functional Programming in Scala* by Chiusano and Bjarnason (Manning Publications), states this a little more precisely:

> "A function f is *pure* if the expression f(x) is referentially transparent for all referentially transparent values x."

To summarize, a pure function is referentially transparent and has no side effects.

Regarding side effects, the authors of the book, *Programming in Scala*, make a great observation:

> "A telltale sign of a function with side effects is that its result type is Unit."

From these definitions, we can make these statements about pure functions:

- A pure function is given one or more input parameters.
- Its result is based solely off of those parameters and its algorithm. The algorithm will not be based on any hidden state in the class or object it's contained in.
- It won't mutate the parameters it's given.
- It won't mutate the state of its class or object.
- It doesn't perform any I/O operations, such as reading from disk, writing to disk, prompting for input, or reading input.

These are some examples of pure functions:

- Mathematical functions, such as addition, subtraction, multiplication.
- Methods like `split` and `length` on the `String` class.
- The `to*` methods on the `String` class (`toInt`, `toDouble`, etc.)
- Methods on immutable collections, including `map`, `drop`, `take`, `filter`, etc.
- The functions that extract values from an HTML string in Recipe 20.3.

The following functions are not pure functions:

- Methods like `getDayOfWeek`, `getHour`, or `getMinute`. They return a different value depending on when they are called.
- A `getRandomNumber` function.
- A function that reads user input or prints output.
- A function that writes to an external data store, or reads from a data store.

If you're coming to Scala from a pure OOP background, it can be difficult to write pure functions. Speaking for myself, historically my code has followed the OOP paradigm of encapsulating data and behavior in classes, and as a result, my methods often mutated the internal state of objects.

At this point you may be wondering how you can get anything done in a program consisting only of pure functions. If you can't read input from a user or database, and can't write output, how will your application ever work?

The best advice I can share about FP is to follow the 80/20 rule: write 80% of your program using pure functions (the "cake"), then create a 20% layer of other code on top of the functional base (the "icing") to handle the user interface, printing, database interactions, and other methods that have "side effects".

Obviously any interesting application will have I/O, and this balanced approach lets you have the best of both worlds.

## The Java approach

To look at how to write pure functions, you'll convert the methods in an OOP class into pure functions. The following code shows how you might create a `Stock` class that follows the Java/OOP paradigm. The following class intentionally has a few flaws. It not only has the ability to store information about a `Stock`, but it can also access the Internet to get the current stock price, and further maintains a list of historical prices for the stock:

```scala
// a poorly written class

class Stock (var symbol: String, var company: String,
             var price: BigDecimal, var volume: Long) {

  var html: String = _
  def buildUrl(stockSymbol: String): String = { ... }
  def getUrlContent(url: String):String = { ... }

  def setPriceFromHtml(html: String) { this.price = ... }
  def setVolumeFromHtml(html: String) { this.volume = ... }
  def setHighFromHtml(html: String) { this.high = ... }
  def setLowFromHtml(html: String) { this.low = ... }

  // some dao-like functionality
  private val _history: ArrayBuffer[Stock] = { ... }
  val getHistory = _history

}
```

Beyond attempting to do too many things, from an FP perspective, it has these other problems:

- All of its fields are mutable.
- All of the set methods mutate the class fields.
- The getHistory method returns a mutable data structure.

The getHistory method is easily fixed by only sharing an immutable data structure, but this class has deeper problems. Let's fix them.

### Fixing the problems

The first fix is to separate two concepts that are buried in the class. First, there should be a concept of a Stock, where a Stock consists only of a symbol and company name. You can make this a case class:

```
case class Stock(symbol: String, company: String)
```

Examples of this are Stock("AAPL", "Apple") and Stock("GOOG", "Google").

Second, at any moment in time there is information related to a stock's performance on the stock market. You can call this data structure a StockInstance, and also define it as a case class:

```
case class StockInstance(symbol: String,
                         datetime: String,
                         price: BigDecimal,
                         volume: Long)
```

A StockInstance example looks like this:

```
StockInstance("AAPL", "Nov. 2, 2012 5:00pm", 576.80, 20431707)
```

Going back to the original class, the getUrlContent method isn't specific to a stock, and should be moved to a different object, such as a general-purpose NetworkUtils object:

```
object NetworkUtils {
  def getUrlContent(url: String): String = { ... }
}
```

This method takes a URL as a parameter and returns the HTML content from that URL.

Similarly, the ability to build a URL from a stock symbol should be moved to an object. Because this behavior is specific to a stock, you'll put it in an object named StockUtils:

```
object StockUtils {
  def buildUrl(stockSymbol: String): String = { ... }
}
```

The ability to extract the stock price from the HTML can also be written as a pure function and should be moved into the same object:

```
object StockUtils {
  def buildUrl(stockSymbol: String): String = { ... }
```

```scala
    def getPrice(html: String): String = { ... }
}
```

In fact, all of the methods named set* in the previous class should be get* methods in StockUtils:

```scala
object StockUtils {
    def buildUrl(stockSymbol: String): String = { ... }
    def getPrice(symbol: String, html: String): String = { ... }
    def getVolume(symbol: String, html: String): String = { ... }
    def getHigh(symbol: String, html: String): String = { ... }
    def getLow(symbol: String, html: String): String = { ... }
}
```

The methods getPrice, getVolume, getHigh, and getLow are all pure functions: given the same HTML string and stock symbol, they will always return the same values, and they don't have side effects.

Following this thought process, the date and time are moved to a DateUtils object:

```scala
object DateUtils {
    def currentDate: String = { ... }
    def currentTime: String = { ... }
}
```

With this new design, you create an instance of a Stock for the current date and time as a simple series of expressions. First, retrieve the HTML that describes the stock from a web page:

```scala
val stock = new Stock("AAPL", "Apple")
val url = StockUtils.buildUrl(stock.symbol)
val html = NetUtils.getUrlContent(url)
```

Once you have the HTML, extract the desired stock information, get the date, and create the Stock instance:

```scala
val price = StockUtils.getPrice(html)
val volume = StockUtils.getVolume(html)
val high = StockUtils.getHigh(html)
val low = StockUtils.getLow(html)
val date = DateUtils.currentDate
val stockInstance = StockInstance(symbol, date, price, volume, high, low)
```

Notice that all of the variables are immutable, and each line is an expression.

The code is simple, so you can eliminate all the intermediate variables, if desired:

```scala
val html = NetUtils.getUrlContent(url)
val stockInstance = StockInstance(
    symbol,
    DateUtils.currentDate,
    StockUtils.getPrice(html),
    StockUtils.getVolume(html),
```

```
        StockUtils.getHigh(html),
        StockUtils.getLow(html))
```

As mentioned earlier, the methods `getPrice`, `getVolume`, `getHigh`, and `getLow` are all pure functions. But what about methods like `getDate`? It's not a pure function, but the fact is, you need the date and time to solve the problem. This is part of what's meant by having a healthy, balanced attitude about pure functions.

As a final note about this example, there's no need for the `Stock` class to maintain a mutable list of stock instances. Assuming that the stock information is stored in a database, you can create a `StockDao` to retrieve the data:

```
object StockDao {
  def getStockInstances(symbol: String): Vector[StockInstance] = { ... }
  // other code ...
}
```

Though `getStockInstances` isn't a pure function, the `Vector` class is immutable, so you can feel free to share it without worrying that it might be modified somewhere else in your application.

Although I use the prefix `get` in many of those method names, it's not at all necessary to follow a JavaBeans-like naming convention. In fact, in part because you write "setter" methods in Scala without beginning their names with `set`, and also to follow the Uniform Access Principle (*http://en.wikipedia.org/wiki/Uniform_access_principle*), many Scala APIs don't use `get` or `set` at all.

For example, think of case classes. The accessors and mutators they generate don't use `get` or `set`:

```
case class Person(name: String)
val p = Person("Mark")
p.name              // accessor
p.name = "Bubba"    // mutator
```

That being said, although it's best to follow the Scala standards, use whatever method names best fit your API.

## Discussion

A benefit of this coding style is that pure functions are easier to test. For instance, attempting to test the `set*` methods in the original code is harder than it needs to be. For each field (`price`, `volume`, `high`, and `low`), you have to follow these steps:

1. Set the `html` field in the object.

2. Call the current `set` method, such as `setPriceFromHtml`.

3. Internally, this method reads the private `html` class field.

---

4. When the method runs, it mutates a field in the class (`price`).

5. You have to "get" that field to verify that it was changed.

6. In more complicated classes, it's possible that the `html` and `price` fields may be mutated by other methods in the class.

The test code for the original class looks like this:

```
val stock = new Stock("AAPL", "Apple", 0, 0)
stock.buildUrl
val html = stock.getUrlContent
stock.getPriceFromHtml(html)
assert(stock.getPrice == 500.0)
```

This is a simple example of testing one method that has side effects, but of course this can get much more complicated in a large application.

By contrast, testing a pure function is easier:

1. Call the function, passing in a known value.

2. Get a result back from the function.

3. Verify that the result is what you expected.

The functional approach results in test code like this:

```
val url = NetUtils.buildUrl("AAPL")
val html = NetUtils.getUrlContent(url)
val price = StockUtils.getPrice(html)
assert(price == 500.0)
```

Although the code shown isn't much shorter, it is much simpler.

### StockUtils or Stock object?

The methods that were moved to the `StockUtils` class in the previous examples could be placed in the companion object of the `Stock` class. That is, you could have placed the `Stock` class and object in a file named *Stock.scala*:

```
case class Stock(symbol: String, company: String)

object Stock {
  def buildUrl(stockSymbol: String): String = { ... }
  def getPrice(symbol: String, html: String): String = { ... }
  def getVolume(symbol: String, html: String): String = { ... }
  def getHigh(symbol: String, html: String): String = { ... }
  def getLow(symbol: String, html: String): String = { ... }
}
```

For the purposes of this example, I put these methods in a `StockUtils` class to be clear about separating the concerns of the `Stock` *class* and *object*. In your own practice, use whichever approach you prefer.

## See Also

- Pure Functions (*http://en.wikipedia.org/wiki/Pure_function*)
- Referential Transparency (*http://bit.ly/12E47nU*)
- The Uniform Access Principle (*http://en.wikipedia.org/wiki/Uniform_access_prin ciple*)

# 20.2. Prefer Immutable Objects

## Problem

You want to reduce the use of mutable objects and data structures in your code.

## Solution

Begin with this simple philosophy, stated in the book, *Programming in Scala*:

> "Prefer `val`s, immutable objects, and methods without side effects. Reach for them first."

Then use other approaches with justification.

There are two components to "prefer immutability":

- Prefer immutable collections. For instance, use immutable sequences like `List` and `Vector` before reaching for the mutable `ArrayBuffer`.
- Prefer immutable variables. That is, prefer `val` to `var`.

In Java, mutability is the default, and it can lead to unnecessarily dangerous code and hidden bugs. In the following example, even though the `List` parameter taken by the `trustMeMuHaHa` method is marked as `final`, the method can still mutate the collection:

```java
// java

class EvilMutator {

  // trust me ... mu ha ha (evil laughter)
  public static void trustMeMuHaHa(final List<Person> people) {
    people.clear();
  }

}
```

Although Scala treats method arguments as `val`s, you leave yourself open to the exact same problem by passing around a mutable collection, like an `ArrayBuffer`:

```
def evilMutator(people: ArrayBuffer[Person]) {
  people.clear()
}
```

Just as with the Java code, the evilMutator method can call clear because the contents of an ArrayBuffer are mutable.

Though nobody would write malicious code like this intentionally, accidents do happen. To make your code safe from this problem, if there's no reason for a collection to be changed, don't use a mutable collection class. By changing the collection to a Vector, you eliminate the possibility of this problem, and the following code won't even compile:

```
def evilMutator(people: Vector[Person]) {
  // ERROR - won't compile
  people.clear()
}
```

Because Vector is immutable, any attempt to add or remove elements will fail.

## Discussion

There are at least two major benefits to using immutable variables (val) and immutable collections:

- They represent a form of defensive coding, keeping your data from being changed accidentally.
- They're easier to reason about.

The examples shown in the Solution demonstrate the first benefit: if there's no need for other code to mutate your reference or collection, don't let them do it. Scala makes this easy.

The second benefit can be thought of in many ways, but I like to think about it when using actors and concurrency. If I'm using immutable collections, I can pass them around freely. There's no concern that another thread will modify the collection.

### Using val + mutable, and var + immutable

As mentioned several times in this chapter, it's important to have a balanced attitude. I generally use that expression in regards to pure functions, but it also has meaning when discussing "prefer immutability."

For instance, some developers like to use these combinations:

- A mutable collection field declared as a val.
- An immutable collection field declared as a var.

These approaches generally seem to be used as follows:

- A mutable collection field declared as a `val` is typically made private to its class (or method).
- An immutable collection field declared as a `var` in a class is more often made publicly visible, that is, it's made available to other classes.

As an example of the first approach, the current Akka FSM class (*scala.akka.actor.FSM*) defines several mutable collection fields as private `vals`, like this:

```
private val timers = mutable.Map[String, Timer]()

// some time later ...
timers -= name
timers.clear()
```

This is safe to do, because the `timers` field is private to the class, so its mutable collection isn't shared with others.

An approach I used on a recent project is a variation of this theme:

```
class Pizza {

  private val _toppings = new collection.mutable.ArrayBuffer[Topping]()

  def toppings = _toppings.toList
  def addTopping(t: Topping) { _toppings += t }
  def removeTopping(t: Topping) { _toppings -= t }

}
```

This code defines `_toppings` as a mutable `ArrayBuffer`, but makes it a `val` that's private to the `Pizza` class. Here's my rationale for this approach:

- I made `_toppings` an `ArrayBuffer` because I knew that elements (toppings) would often be added and removed.
- I made `_toppings` a `val` because there was no need for it to ever be reassigned.
- I made it `private` so its accessor wouldn't be visible outside of my class.
- I created the methods `toppings`, `addTopping`, and `removeTopping` to let other code manipulate the collection.
- When other code calls the `toppings` method, I can give them an immutable copy of the toppings.

I intentionally didn't use the "val + mutable collection" approach, which would have looked like this:

```
// did not do this
val toppings = new collection.mutable.ArrayBuffer[Topping]()
```

I didn't use this approach because I didn't want to expose `toppings` as an immutable collection outside of my `Pizza` class, which would have happened here, because the `val` would have generated an accessor method. In using an OOP design, you think, "Who should be responsible for managing the toppings on the pizza?" and `Pizza` clearly has the responsibility of maintaining its toppings.

I also didn't choose this "var + immutable collection" design:

```
var toppings = Vector[Topping]()
```

The benefits of this approach are (a) it automatically shares `toppings` as an immutable collection, and (b) it lets me add toppings like this:

```
def addTopping(t: Topping) = toppings :+ t
```

But the approach suffers, because it's a little cumbersome to remove an element from a `Vector` (you have to filter the undesired toppings out of the originating `Vector` while assigning the result to a new `Vector`), and it lets `toppings` be reassigned outside of the `Pizza` class, which I don't want:

```
// bad: other code can mutate 'toppings'
pizza.toppings = Vector(Cheese)
```

You *can* remove elements with this approach by using the `filter` method and then reassigning the result back to `toppings`, like this:

```
toppings = toppings.filter(_ != Pepperoni)
```

But if you create a "double pepperoni" pizza by having two instances of `Pepperoni` in `toppings`, and then want to change it to a regular pepperoni pizza, the earlier `ArrayBuffer` approach is simpler.

### Summary

In summary, always begin with the "prefer immutability" approach, and relax that philosophy when it makes sense for the current situation, that is, when you can properly rationalize your decision.

## See Also

Recipe 10.6, "Understanding Mutable Variables with Immutable Collections"

# 20.3. Think "Expression-Oriented Programming"

## Problem

You're used to writing *statements* in another programming language, and want to learn how to write *expressions* in Scala, and the benefits of the expression-oriented programming (EOP) philosophy.

## Solution

To understand EOP, you have to understand the difference between a *statement* and an *expression*. Wikipedia provides a concise distinction between the two:

> "Statements do not return results and are executed solely for their side effects, while expressions always return a result and often do not have side effects at all."

So statements are like this:

```
order.calculateTaxes()
order.updatePrices()
```

Expressions are like this:

```
val tax = calculateTax(order)
val price = calculatePrice(order)
```

On Wikipedia's EOP page, it also states:

> "An expression-oriented programming language is a programming language where every (or nearly every) construction is an expression, and thus yields a value."

As you might expect, it further states that all pure FP languages are expression-oriented.

The following example helps to demonstrate EOP. This recipe is similar to Recipe 20.1, so it reuses the class from that recipe to show a poor initial design:

```
// an intentionally bad example

class Stock (var symbol: String,
             var company: String,
             var price: String,
             var volume: String,
             var high: String,
             var low: String) {

    var html: String = _
    def buildUrl(stockSymbol: String): String = { ... }
    def getUrlContent(url: String):String = { ... }
    def setPriceUsingHtml() { this.price = ... }
    def setVolumeUsingHtml() { this.volume = ... }
    def setHighUsingHtml() { this.high = ... }
    def setLowUsingHtml() { this.low = ... }

}
```

Although I didn't show it in that recipe, using this class would result in code like this:

```
val stock = new Stock("GOOG", "Google", "", "", "", "")
val url = buildUrl(stock.symbol)
stock.html = stock.getUrlContent(url)

// a series of calls on an object ('statements')
stock.setPriceUsingHtml
```

```
stock.setVolumeUsingHtml
stock.setHighUsingHtml
stock.setLowUsingHtml
```

Although the implementation code isn't shown, all of these "set" methods extract data from the HTML that was downloaded from a Yahoo Finance (*http://finance.yahoo.com/*) page for a given stock, and then update the fields in the current object.

After the first two lines, this code is not expression-oriented at all; it's a series of calls on an object to populate (mutate) the class fields, based on other internal data. These are statements, not expressions; they don't yield values.

Recipe 20.1 showed that by refactoring this class into several different components, you would end up with the following code:

```
// a series of expressions
val url = StockUtils.buildUrl(symbol)
val html = NetUtils.getUrlContent(url)
val price = StockUtils.getPrice(html)
val volume = StockUtils.getVolume(html)
val high = StockUtils.getHigh(html)
val low = StockUtils.getLow(html)
val date = DateUtils.getDate
val stockInstance = StockInstance(symbol, date, price, volume, high, low)
```

This code is expression-oriented. It consists of a series of simple expressions that pass values into pure functions (except for getDate), and each function returns a value that's assigned to a variable. The functions don't mutate the data they're given, and they don't have side effects, so they're easy to read, easy to reason about, and easy to test.

## Discussion

In Scala, most expressions are obvious. For instance, the following two expressions both return results, which you expect:

```
scala> 2 + 2
res0: Int = 4

scala> List(1,2,3,4,5).filter(_ > 2)
res1: List[Int] = List(3, 4, 5)
```

However, it can be more of a surprise that an if/else expression returns a value:

```
val greater = if (a > b) a else b
```

Match expressions also return a result:

```
val evenOrOdd = i match {
  case 1 | 3 | 5 | 7 | 9 => println("odd")
  case 2 | 4 | 6 | 8 | 10 => println("even")
}
```

Even a try/catch block returns a value:

```
val result = try {
  "1".toInt
} catch {
  case _ => 0
}
```

Writing expressions like this is a feature of functional programming languages, and Scala makes using them feel natural and intuitive, and also results in concise, expressive code.

### Benefits

Because expressions always return a result, and generally don't have side effects, there are several benefits to EOP:

- The code is easier to reason about. Inputs go in, a result is returned, and there are no side effects.

- The code is easier to test.

- Combined with Scala's syntax, EOP also results in concise, expressive code.

- Although it has only been hinted at in these examples, expressions can often be executed in any order. This subtle feature lets you execute expressions in parallel, which can be a big help when you're trying to take advantage of modern multicore CPUs.

### See Also

- The Wikipedia definition of a statement, and the difference between a statement and an expression (*http://bit.ly/10YJKAM*)

- Expression-Oriented Programming (EOP) (*http://bit.ly/1b7B6FE*)

# 20.4. Use Match Expressions and Pattern Matching

## Problem

Match expressions (and pattern matching) are a major feature of the Scala programming language, and you want to see examples of the many ways to use them.

# Solution

Match expressions (match/case statements) and pattern matching are a major feature of the Scala language. If you're coming to Scala from Java, the most obvious uses are:

- As a replacement for the Java `switch` statement
- To replace unwieldy `if/then` statements

However, pattern matching is so common, you'll find that match expressions are used in many more situations:

- In `try/catch` expressions
- As the body of a function or method
- With the `Option/Some/None` coding pattern
- In the `receive` method of actors

The following examples demonstrate these techniques.

### Replacement for the Java switch statement and unwieldy if/then statements

Recipe 3.8 showed that a match expression can be used like a Java `switch` statement:

```
val month = i match {
  case 1  => "January"
  case 2  => "February"

  // more months here ...

  case 11 => "November"
  case 12 => "December"
  case _  => "Invalid month"  // the default, catch-all
}
```

It can be used in the same way to replace unwieldy `if/then/else` statements:

```
i match {
  case 1 | 3 | 5 | 7 | 9 => println("odd")
  case 2 | 4 | 6 | 8 | 10 => println("even")
}
```

These are simple uses of match expressions, but they're a good start.

### In try/catch expressions

It helps to become comfortable with match expressions, because you'll use them with Scala's `try/catch` syntax. The following example shows how to write a `try/catch` expression that returns an `Option` when lines are successfully read from a file, and `None` if an exception is thrown during the file-reading process:

```
def readTextFile(filename: String): Option[List[String]] = {
  try {
    Some(Source.fromFile(filename).getLines.toList)
  } catch {
    case e: Exception => None
  }
}
```

To catch multiple exceptions in a try/catch expression, list the exception types in the catch clause, just like a match expression:

```
def readTextFile(filename: String): Option[List[String]] = {
  try {
    Some(Source.fromFile(filename).getLines.toList)
  } catch {
    case ioe: IOException =>
        logger.error(ioe)
        None
    case fnf: FileNotFoundException =>
        logger.error(fnf)
        None
  }
}
```

Note that if the specific error is important in a situation like this, use the Try/Success/Failure approach to return the error information to the caller, instead of Option/Some/None. See Recipe 20.6 for both Option and Try examples.

### As the body of a function or method

As you get comfortable with match expressions, you'll use them as the body of your methods, such as this method that determines whether the value it's given is true, using the Perl definition of "true":

```
def isTrue(a: Any) = a match {
  case 0 | "" => false
  case _ => true
}
```

In general, a match expression used as the body of a function will accept a parameter as input, match against that parameter, and then return a value:

```
def getClassAsString(x: Any):String = x match {
  case s: String => "String"
  case i: Int => "Int"
  case l: List[_] => "List"
  case p: Person => "Person"
  case Dog() => "That was a Dog"
  case Parrot(name) => s"That was a Parrot, name = $name"
  case _ => "Unknown"
}
```

As shown in Recipe 9.8, a match expression can also be used to create a partial function (i.e., working only for a subset of possible inputs):

```
val divide: PartialFunction[Int, Int] = {
  case d: Int if d != 0 => 42 / d
}
```

See that recipe for more details on this approach.

### Use with Option/Some/None

Match expressions work well with the Scala Option/Some/None types. For instance, given a method that returns an Option:

```
def toInt(s: String): Option[Int] = {
  try {
    Some(s.toInt)
  } catch {
    case e: Exception => None
  }
}
```

You can handle the result from toInt with a match expression:

```
toInt(aString) match {
  case Some(i) => println(i)
  case None => println("Error: Could not convert String to Int.")
}
```

In a similar way, match expressions are a popular way of handling form verifications with the Play Framework:

```
verifying("If age is given, it must be greater than zero",
  model =>
    model.age match {
      case Some(age) => age < 0
      case None => true
    }
)
```

### In actors

Match expressions are baked into actors as *the way* to handle incoming messages:

```
class SarahsBrain extends Actor {
  def receive = {
    case StartMessage => handleStartMessage
    case StopMessage => handleStopMessage
    case SetMaxWaitTime(time) => helper ! SetMaxWaitTime(time)
    case SetPhrasesToSpeak(phrases) => helper ! SetPhrasesToSpeak(phrases)
    case _ => log.info("Got something unexpected.")
  }

  // other code here ...
}
```

### Summary

Match expressions are an integral part of the Scala language, and as shown, they can be used in many ways. The more you use them, the more uses you'll find for them.

## See Also

- Match expressions are demonstrated in many examples in Chapter 3.
- Chapter 13 demonstrates the use of match expressions when writing actors.

# 20.5. Eliminate null Values from Your Code

## Problem

Tony Hoare, inventor of the null reference way back in 1965, refers to the creation of the null value as his "billion dollar mistake." (*http://en.wikipedia.org/wiki/Tony_Hoare*) In keeping with modern best practices, you want to eliminate null values from your code.

## Solution

David Pollak, author of the book *Beginning Scala*, offers a wonderfully simple rule about null values:

> "Ban null from any of your code. Period."

Although I've used null values in this book to make some examples easier, in my own practice, I no longer use them. I just imagine that there is no such thing as a null, and write my code in other ways.

There are several common situations where you may be tempted to use null values, so this recipe demonstrates how *not* to use null values in those situations:

- When a var field in a class or method doesn't have an initial default value, initialize it with Option instead of null.
- When a method doesn't produce the intended result, you may be tempted to return null. Use an Option or Try instead.
- If you're working with a Java library that returns null, convert it to an Option, or something else.

Let's look at each of these techniques.

## Initialize var fields with Option, not null

Possibly the most tempting time to use a null value is when a field in a class or method won't be initialized immediately. For instance, imagine that you're writing code for the next great social network app. To encourage people to sign up, during the registration process, the only information you ask for is an email address and a password. Because everything else is initially optional, you might write some code like this:

```
case class Address (city: String, state: String, zip: String)

class User(email: String, password: String) {
  var firstName: String = _
  var lastName: String = _
  var address: Address = _
}
```

This is bad news, because firstName, lastName, and address are all declared to be null, and can cause problems in your application if they're not assigned before they're accessed.

A better approach is to define each field as an Option:

```
case class Address (city: String, state: String, zip: String)

class User(email: String, password: String) {
  var firstName = None: Option[String]
  var lastName = None: Option[String]
  var address = None: Option[Address]
}
```

Now you can create a User like this:

```
val u = new User("al@example.com", "secret")
```

At some point later you can assign the other values like this:

```
u.firstName = Some("Al")
u.lastName = Some("Alexander")
u.address = Some(Address("Talkeetna", "AK", "99676"))
```

Later in your code, you can access the fields like this:

```
println(firstName.getOrElse("<not assigned>"))
```

Or this:

```
u.address.foreach { a =>
  println(a.city)
  println(a.state)
  println(a.zip)
}
```

In both cases, if the values are assigned, they'll be printed. With the example of printing the firstName field, if the value isn't assigned, the string <not assigned> is printed.

In the case of the `address`, if it's not assigned, the `foreach` loop won't be executed, so the print statements are never reached. This is because an `Option` can be thought of as a collection with zero or one elements. If the value is `None`, it has zero elements, and if it is a `Some`, it has one element—the value it contains.

On a related note, you should also use an `Option` in a constructor when a field is optional:

```
case class Stock (id: Long,
                  var symbol: String,
                  var company: Option[String])
```

### Don't return null from methods

Because you should never use `null` in your code, the rule for returning `null` values from methods is easy: don't do it.

If you can't return `null`, what can you do? Return an `Option`. Or, if you need to know about an error that may have occurred in the method, use `Try` instead of `Option`.

With an `Option`, your method signatures should look like this:

```
def doSomething: Option[String] = { ... }
def toInt(s: String): Option[Int] = { ... }
def lookupPerson(name: String): Option[Person] = { ... }
```

For instance, when reading a file, a method could return `null` if the process fails, but this code shows how to read a file and return an `Option` instead:

```
def readTextFile(filename: String): Option[List[String]] = {
  try {
    Some(io.Source.fromFile(filename).getLines.toList)
  } catch {
    case e: Exception => None
  }
}
```

This method returns a `List[String]` wrapped in a `Some` if the file can be found and read, or `None` if an exception occurs.

As mentioned, if you want the error information instead of a `Some` or `None`, use the `Try/Success/Failure` approach instead:

```
import scala.util.{Try, Success, Failure}

object Test extends App {

  def readTextFile(filename: String): Try[List[String]] = {
    Try(io.Source.fromFile(filename).getLines.toList)
  }

  val filename = "/etc/passwd"
  readTextFile(filename) match {
    case Success(lines) => lines.foreach(println)
```

```
      case Failure(f) => println(f)
  }

}
```

This code prints the lines from the */etc/passwd* file if the code succeeds, or prints an error message like this if the code fails:

```
java.io.FileNotFoundException: Foo.bar (No such file or directory)
```

As a word of caution (and balance), the Twitter *Effective Scala* page recommends not overusing Option, and using the Null Object Pattern (*http://en.wikipedia.org/wiki/ Null_Object_pattern*) where it makes sense. As usual, use your own judgment, but try to eliminate all null values using one of these approaches.

 A *Null Object* is an object that extends a base type with a "null" or neutral behavior. Here's a Scala implementation of Wikipedia's Java example of a Null Object:

```
trait Animal {
  def makeSound()
}

class Dog extends Animal {
  def makeSound() { println("woof") }
}

class NullAnimal extends Animal {
  def makeSound() {}
}
```

The makeSound method in the NullAnimal class has a neutral, "do nothing" behavior. Using this approach, a method defined to return an Animal can return NullAnimal rather than null.

This is arguably similar to returning None from a method declared to return an Option, especially when the result is used in a foreach loop.

### Converting a null into an Option, or something else

The third major place you'll run into null values is in working with legacy Java code. There is no magic formula here, other than to capture the null value and return something else from your code. That may be an Option, a Null Object, an empty list, or whatever else is appropriate for the problem at hand.

For instance, the following getName method converts a result from a Java method that may be null and returns an Option[String] instead:

```
def getName: Option[String] = {
  var name = javaPerson.getName
  if (name == null) None else Some(name)
}
```

### Benefits

Following these guidelines leads to these benefits:

- You'll eliminate `NullPointerExceptions`.
- Your code will be safer.
- You won't have to write `if` statements to check for `null` values.
- Adding an `Option[T]` return type declaration to a method is a terrific way to indicate that something is happening in the method such that the caller may receive a `None` instead of a `Some[T]`. This is a much better approach than returning `null` from a method that is expected to return an object.
- You'll become more comfortable using `Option`, and as a result, you'll be able to take advantage of how it's used in the collection libraries and other frameworks.

## See Also

- Tony Hoare's Billion Dollar Mistake (*http://en.wikipedia.org/wiki/Tony_Hoare#Quotations*)
- The "Null Object Pattern" (*http://en.wikipedia.org/wiki/Null_Object_pattern*)

# 20.6. Using the Option/Some/None Pattern

## Problem

For a variety of reasons, including removing `null` values from your code, you want to use what I call the `Option/Some/None` pattern. Or, if you're interested in a problem (exception) that occurred while processing code, you may want to return `Try/Success/Failure` from a method instead of `Option/Some/None`.

## Solution

There is some overlap between this recipe and the previous recipe, "Eliminate null Values from Your Code". That recipe shows how to use `Option` instead of `null` in the following situations:

- Using `Option` in method and constructor parameters
- Using `Option` to initialize class fields (instead of using `null`)
- Converting `null` results from other code (such as Java code) into an `Option`

See that recipe for examples of how to use an `Option` in those situations.

This recipe adds these additional solutions:

- Returning an Option from a method
- Getting the value from an Option
- Using Option with collections
- Using Option with frameworks
- Using Try/Success/Failure when you need the error message (Scala 2.10 and newer)
- Using Either/Left/Right when you need the error message (pre-Scala 2.10)

### Returning an Option from a method

The toInt method used in this book shows how to return an Option from a method. It takes a String as input and returns a Some[Int] if the String is successfully converted to an Int, otherwise it returns a None:

```
def toInt(s: String): Option[Int] = {
  try {
    Some(Integer.parseInt(s.trim))
  } catch {
    case e: Exception => None
  }
}
```

Although this is a simple method, it shows the common pattern, as well as the syntax. For a more complicated example, see the readTextFile example in Recipe 20.5.

This is what toInt looks like in the REPL when it succeeds and returns a Some:

```
scala> val x = toInt("1")
x: Option[Int] = Some(1)
```

This is what it looks like when it fails and returns a None:

```
scala> val x = toInt("foo")
x: Option[Int] = None
```

### Getting the value from an Option

The toInt example shows how to declare a method that returns an Option. As a consumer of a method that returns an Option, there are several good ways to call it and access its result:

- Use getOrElse
- Use foreach
- Use a match expression

To get the actual value if the method succeeds, or use a default value if the method fails, use getOrElse:

```scala
scala> val x = toInt("1").getOrElse(0)
x: Int = 1
```

Because an Option is a collection with zero or one elements, the foreach method can be used in many situations:

```scala
toInt("1").foreach{ i =>
  println(s"Got an int: $i")
}
```

That example prints the value if toInt returns a Some, but bypasses the println statement if toInt returns a None.

Another good way to access the toInt result is with a match expression:

```scala
toInt("1") match {
  case Some(i) => println(i)
  case None => println("That didn't work.")
}
```

### Using Option with Scala collections

Another great feature of Option is that it plays well with Scala collections. For instance, starting with a list of strings like this:

```scala
val bag = List("1", "2", "foo", "3", "bar")
```

imagine you want a list of all the integers that can be converted from that list of strings. By passing the toInt method into the map method, you can convert every element in the collection into a Some or None value:

```scala
scala> bag.map(toInt)
res0: List[Option[Int]] = List(Some(1), Some(2), None, Some(3), None)
```

This is a good start. Because an Option is a collection of zero or one elements, you can convert this list of Int values by adding flatten to map:

```scala
scala> bag.map(toInt).flatten
res1: List[Int] = List(1, 2, 3)
```

As shown in Recipe 10.16, "Combining map and flatten with flatMap", this is the same as calling flatMap:

```scala
scala> bag.flatMap(toInt)
res2: List[Int] = List(1, 2, 3)
```

The collect method provides another way to achieve the same result:

```scala
scala> bag.map(toInt).collect{case Some(i) => i}
res3: List[Int] = List(1, 2, 3)
```

That example works because the collect method takes a partial function, and the anonymous function that's passed in is only defined for Some values; it ignores the None values.

These examples work for several reasons:

- toInt is defined to return Option[Int].
- Methods like flatten, flatMap, and others are built to work well with Option values.
- You can pass anonymous functions into the collection methods.

## Using Option with other frameworks

Once you begin working with third-party Scala libraries, you'll see that Option is used to handle situations where a variable may not have a value. For instance, they're baked into the Play Framework's Anorm database library, where you use Option/Some/None for database table fields that can be null. In the following example, the third field may be null in the database, so it's handled using Some and None, as shown:

```scala
def getAll() : List[Stock] = {
  DB.withConnection { implicit connection =>
      sqlQuery().collect {
          // the 'company' field has a value
          case Row(id: Int, symbol: String, Some(company: String)) =>
                  Stock(id, symbol, Some(company))
          // the 'company' field does not have a value
          case Row(id: Int, symbol: String, None) =>
                  Stock(id, symbol, None)
      }.toList
  }
}
```

The Option approach is also used extensively in Play validation methods:

```scala
verifying("If age is given, it must be greater than zero",
  model =>
    model.age match {
      case Some(age) => age < 0
      case None => true
    }
)
```

The scala.util.control.Exception object gives you another way to use an Option, depending on your preferences and needs. For instance, the try/catch block was removed from the following method and replaced with an allCatch method:

```
import scala.util.control.Exception._

def readTextFile(f: String): Option[List[String]] =
    allCatch.opt(Source.fromFile(f).getLines.toList)
```

allCatch is described as a Catch object "that catches everything." The opt method returns None if an exception is caught (such as a FileNotFoundException), and a Some if the block of code succeeds.

Other allCatch methods support the Try and Either approaches. See the Exception object Scaladoc (*http://bit.ly/10YJQIt*) for more information.

If you like the Option/Some/None approach, but want to write a method that returns error information in the failure case (instead of None, which doesn't return any error information), there are two similar approaches:

- Try, Success, and Failure (introduced in Scala 2.10)
- Either, Left, and Right

I prefer the new Try/Success/Failure approach, so let's look at it next.

### Using Try, Success, and Failure

Scala 2.10 introduced scala.util.Try as an approach that's similar to Option, but returns failure information rather than a None.

The result of a computation wrapped in a Try will be one of its subclasses: Success or Failure. If the computation succeeds, a Success instance is returned; if an exception was thrown, a Failure will be returned, and the Failure will hold information about what failed.

To demonstrate this, first import the new classes:

```
import scala.util.{Try,Success,Failure}
```

Then create a simple method:

```
def divideXByY(x: Int, y: Int): Try[Int] = {
  Try(x / y)
}
```

This method returns a successful result as long as y is not zero. When y is zero, an ArithmeticException happens. However, the exception isn't thrown out of the method; it's caught by the Try, and a Failure object is returned from the method.

---

The method looks like this in the REPL:

```
scala> divideXByY(1,1)
res0: scala.util.Try[Int] = Success(1)

scala> divideXByY(1,0)
res1: scala.util.Try[Int] = Failure(java.lang.ArithmeticException: / by zero)
```

As with an Option, you can access the Try result using getOrElse, a foreach method, or a match expression. If you don't care about the error message and just want a result, use getOrElse:

```
// Success
scala> val x = divideXByY(1, 1).getOrElse(0)
x: Int = 1

// Failure
scala> val y = divideXByY(1, 0).getOrElse(0)
y: Int = 0
```

Using a foreach method also works well in many situations:

```
scala> divideXByY(1, 1).foreach(println)
1

scala> divideXByY(1, 0).foreach(println)
(no output printed)
```

If you're interested in the Failure message, one way to get it is with a match expression:

```
divideXByY(1, 1) match {
  case Success(i) => println(s"Success, value is: $i")
  case Failure(s) => println(s"Failed, message is: $s")
}
```

Another approach is to see if a Failure was returned, and then call its toString method (although this doesn't really follow the "Scala way"):

```
scala> if (x.isFailure) x.toString
res0: Any = Failure(java.lang.ArithmeticException: / by zero)
```

The Try class has the added benefit that you can chain operations together, catching exceptions as you go. For example, the following code won't throw an exception, regardless of what the values of x and y are:

```
val z = for {
  a <- Try(x.toInt)
  b <- Try(y.toInt)
} yield a * b

val answer = z.getOrElse(0) * 2
```

If x and y are `String` values like "1" and "2", this code works as expected, with answer resulting in an `Int` value. If x or y is a `String` that can't be converted to an `Int`, z will have this value:

```
z: scala.util.Try[Int] =
    Failure(java.lang.NumberFormatException: For input string: "one")
```

If x or y is `null`, z will have this value:

```
z: scala.util.Try[Int] = Failure(java.lang.NumberFormatException: null)
```

In either `Failure` case, the `getOrElse` method protects us, returning the default value of 0.

The `readTextFile` method in Recipe 20.5 shows another `Try` example. The method from that example is repeated here:

```
def readTextFile(filename: String): Try[List[String]] = {
  Try(Source.fromFile(filename).getLines.toList)
}
```

If the `readTextFile` method runs successfully, the lines from the */etc/passwd* file are printed, but if an exception happens while trying to open and read the file, the `Failure` line in the match expression prints the error, like this:

```
java.io.FileNotFoundException: Foo.bar (No such file or directory)
```

The `Try` class includes a nice collection of methods that let you handle situations in many ways, including:

- Collection-like implementations of `filter`, `flatMap`, `flatten`, `foreach`, and `map`
- `get`, `getOrElse`, and `orElse`
- `toOption`, which lets you treat the result as an `Option`
- `recover`, `recoverWith`, and `transform`, which let you gracefully handle `Success` and `Failure` results

As you can see, `Try` is a powerful alternative to using `Option`/`Some`/`None`.

### Using Either, Left, and Right

Prior to Scala 2.10, an approach similar to `Try` was available with the `Either`, `Left`, and `Right` classes. With these classes, `Either` is analogous to `Try`, `Right` is similar to `Success`, and `Left` is similar to `Failure`.

The following method demonstrates how to implement the `Either` approach:

```
def divideXByY(x: Int, y: Int): Either[String, Int] = {
  if (y == 0) Left("Dude, can't divide by 0")
  else Right(x / y)
}
```

As shown, your method should be declared to return an `Either`, and the method body should return a `Right` on success and a `Left` on failure. The `Right` type is the type your method returns when it runs successfully (an `Int` in this case), and the `Left` type is typically a `String`, because that's how the error message is returned.

As with `Option` and `Try`, a method returning an `Either` can be called in a variety of ways, including `getOrElse` or a match expression:

```
val x = divideXByY(1, 1).right.getOrElse(0)   // returns 1
val x = divideXByY(1, 0).right.getOrElse(0)   // returns 0

// prints "Answer: Dude, can't divide by 0"
divideXByY(1, 0) match {
  case Left(s) => println("Answer: " + s)
  case Right(i) => println("Answer: " + i)
}
```

You can also access the error message by testing the result with `isLeft`, and then accessing the `left` value, but this isn't really the Scala way:

```
scala> val x = divideXByY(1, 0)
x: Either[String,Int] = Left(Dude, can't divide by 0)

scala> x.isLeft
res0: Boolean = true

scala> x.left
res1: scala.util.Either.LeftProjection[String,Int] =
    LeftProjection(Left(Dude, can't divide by 0))
```

Although the `Either` classes offered a potential solution prior to Scala 2.10, I now use the `Try` classes in all of my code instead of `Either`.

## Discussion

As shown in the Solution, if there's a weakness of using `Option`, it's that it doesn't tell you *why* something failed; you just get a `None` instead of a `Some`. If you need to know why something failed, use `Try` instead of `Option`.

### Don't use the get method with Option

When you first come to Scala from Java, you may be tempted to use the `get` method to access the result:

```
scala> val x = toInt("5").get
x: Int = 5
```

However, this isn't any better than a `NullPointerException`:

```
scala> val x = toInt("foo").get
java.util.NoSuchElementException: None.get
// long stack trace omitted ...
```

Your next thought might be to test the value before trying to access it:

```
// don't do this
scala> val x = if (toInt("foo").isDefined) toInt("foo") else 0
x: Any = 0
```

As the comment says, don't do this. In short, it's a best practice to never call `get` on an `Option`. The preferred approaches are to use `getOrElse`, a match expression, or `foreach`. (As with `null` values, I just imagine that `get` doesn't exist.)

## See Also

- The `Option` class (*http://bit.ly/12uGdb2*)
- The `Try` class (*http://bit.ly/12TttL0*)
- The `Either` class (*http://bit.ly/12E4y1t*)

# Index

## Symbols

! method
    executing command and getting exit code, 394, 398
    sending messages to actors, 416
!! method, executing command and getting output, 394, 397, 398, 401
" (quotation marks, double), """" surrounding multiline strings, 6
#&& (AND) operator, 404
#:: method, constructing a Stream, 331
#< operator, redirecting STDIN, 402
#> operator, redirecting STDOUT, 402
#>> method, appending to a file, 403
#| method, pipelining commands, 401
#|| (OR) operator, 404
$ (dollar sign)
    preceding variable names, 9
$ { }, including expressions inside a string, 10
% method, in build.sbt file, 583
%% method, in build.sbt file, 583
( ) (parentheses), forcing callers to leave off accessor methods, 161
*= method, 40
+ method
    adding elements to immutable Map, 348
    adding elements to immutable Set, 363
++ method, 302, 304
    adding elements to immutable Set, 363

merging two lists, 330
++= method, 302
    adding elements to ArrayBuffer, 335
    adding elements to mutable Queue, 368
    adding elements to mutable Set, 362
    adding multiple elements to mutable maps, 346
+= method
    adding elements to ArrayBuffer, 335
    adding elements to mutable maps, 346
    adding elements to mutable Queue, 368
    adding elements to mutable Set, 362
    inserting documents into MongoDB, 537
    on Int and other numeric types, 40
    use in build.sbt file, 583
, (comma), adding to numbers, 50
- method
    removing elements from immutable Map, 348
    removing elements from immutable Set, 365
-- method, 304
    removing elements from immutable Map, 348
    removing elements from immutable Set, 365
--= method
    deleting elements from mutable Set, 364
    deleting multiple elements from a ListBuffer, 329

*We'd like to hear your suggestions for improving our indexes. Send email to index@oreilly.com.*

# A

using to create array whose size can change, 335

ArrayList class (Java), 550

arrays
  accessing and changing values by index position, 334
  Array and ArrayBuffer classes, 321
  assigning CSV file processing results to 2D array, 385
  converting findAllIn method results to Array, 18
  converting Range object to Array, 48
  creating array whose size can change (ArrayBuffer), 335
  creating multidimensional arrays, 339
    using array of arrays, 340
  deleting elements from an Array, 337
  different ways to define and populate an Array, 333
  extracting sequence of elements from, 291
  iterating over, using for loop, 54
  looping over elements, xiv
  manually specifying the type, 264
  of objects, parsing JSON data into, 502
  performance of an Array, 261
  sorting, 338

ArrayStack class, 371

asInstanceOf method
  casting numeric types, 173
  object casting with, 172

ask method (of Akka actors), 445

assignment, adding elements to mutable maps, 346

auxiliary constructors
  defining, 108–111
  eliminating need for, 114
  subclass, inability to call superclass constructor, 128

Await.result method, 431, 437, 446

# B

base and radix, handling in conversions of strings to integers, 33

@BeanProperty annotation, 117, 562–565

"become" approach for actors to switch states, 446

best practices in Scala, 635–666
  creating methods with no side effects (pure functions), 636–644

eliminating null values from code, 654–658
  expression-oriented programming (EOP), 647–650
  prefer immutable objects, 644–647
  using match expressions (and pattern matching), 650–654
  using Option/Some/None pattern, 658–666

BigDecimal, 43
  conversions to other numeric types, 44
  creating directly from strings, 33

BigDecimal class (Java), 44
  currency formatting with, 51

BigInt, 43
  conversions to other numeric types, 44
  creating directly from strings, 33

BigInteger class (Java), 44

binary files, reading and writing, 382

Boolean test to break out of loops, 69

bounds, 612
  upper bound, 624, 626
  view bound, 626

Bourne shell, 481

break and continue, implementing in Scala, 65–71
  break example, 66
  continue example, 67
    better way to solve problem, 68
  general syntax, 67
  nested loops and labeled breaks, 68
  ways to avoid using break and continue, 69

break method, 66

breakable method, 66

BreakControl exception, 66

BufferedSource class, 376
  close method, 376

build tools, 466

build.sbt file, 579
  adding multiple dependencies, 581
  common methods used in, 583
  entries as key/value pairs, 582
  entry for sbt-assembly plug-in, 598
  example file with one dependency, 581
  logLevel setting, 597
  mainClass settings, 593
  resolvers key, 595
  specifying man method to run, 592
  using Build.scala file instead of, 602–604

Build.scala file (see project/Build.scala file)

build.xml file (Ant), 606
    init target, 608
by method, setting step in ranges, 47
Byte type, 31

## C

callback methods, futures, 443
    onSuccess and onFailure, 439
canEqual method, 142
Casbah driver, 533
    creating Casbah-style queries, 542
case classes, 99, 640
    adding uninitialized var field to, 122
    as inner class, 143
    constructor parameters, val by default, 107
    creating new class instances without new
        keyword, 186
    extracting case class fields in match expres-
        sions, 88
    final, 644
    generating auxiliary constructors for, 110
    generating boilerplate code with, 136–140
    in match expressions, 86–87
        with variable-binding pattern, 84
    MailServer, generating from JSON string,
        500
    methods generated by, 140–143
    providing multiple constructors for, 187–189
    toString implementation, 137
    used to match JSON data with Lift-JSON,
        492
case statements
    adding if expressions (guards) to, 87
    matching multiple conditions with single
        statement, 76
    pattern matching examples, 79
case-insensitive string comparisons, 5
casting
    from one numeric type to another, 36
    object, 172
catch clause, 92
    (see also try/catch/finally)
    throwing exception from, 92
chaining methods, 4
Char type, 31
charAt method, 24
checked exceptions, 165
    in Java, 166
Child actor, 427

class members
    renaming on import, 196
    static imports of, 197
ClassCastException, 173
classes, 99
    adding to REPL classpath, 462
    assigning field to a block or function, 121
    calling superclass constructor, 127
    controlling visibility of constructor fields,
        104–108
    creating inner classes, 143
    creating primary constructor for, 100–104
    default values for constructor parameters,
        114
    defining auxiliary constructors, 108–111
    defining equals method to compare object
        instances, 140–143
    defining properties in abstract base class,
        131
    determining class of an object, 174
    extending traits, 203
    generating boilerplate code with case classes,
        136–140
    handling constructor parameters when ex-
        tending, 124–127
    hiding during import process, 196
    importing into current program scope, 193
    making serializable, 389
    mixing traits in, 208
    multiple, in a single file, 201
    overriding default accessors and mutators,
        116–119
    preventing accessor and mutator methods
        from being generated, 119
    providing private primary constructor, 112
    renaming on import, 195
    setting uninitialized var field types, 122
    traits can be mixed into, limiting, 209
    traits inheriting from, 210
    use of @BeanProperty annotation on fields,
        562
    using a trait by inheritance, limiting, 209
    using generic types, 614–617
    when to use abstract class, 129
classOf function, 174
classpath
    building for Scala shell script, 482
    REPL, adding JAR files and classes to, 461

clear method
 deleting all elements in a map, 347
 emptying mutable Stack with, 371
 removing all elements from ArrayBuffer, 337
 using with mutable Set, 364
closing files
 automatically, 377
 manually closing BufferedSource, 376
closures, 229–234
 comparison to techniques in Java, 233
 defined, 230
 using with other data types, 232
code blocks
 assigning class field to, 121
 for/yield processing after yield keyword, 274
 import statements in, 199
 pasting and loading into REPL, 459–461
code examples, using, xxii
code listings in this book, xxi
collect method, taking partial function as input, 241
collections, xv, 245–319
 building new collection from input collection, using for/yield, 55
 choosing a collection class, 250
  main categories of classes, 250
  maps, 253
  sequences, 250
  sets, 253
  strict and lazy collections, 254
  types acting like collections, 254
 choosing a collection method to solve a problem, 255
  common collection methods, 256
  common methods for maps, 259
  immutable collection operators, 259
  methods organized by category, 255
  mutable collection methods, 258
 classes containing, generating JSON string from, 495–500
 collection features in String, 3
 combining map and flatten with flatMap method, 286–289
 converting iterators to, 279
 converting to string with mkString, 318
 creating and using enumerations, 311
 creating lazy view on, 306–309
 creating whose elements are all of some base type, 624–627

declaring type when creating, 264
deleting documents from MongoDB collection, 545
extracting sequence of elements from, 291–293
extracting unique elements from a sequence, 300
filtering with filter method, 289
flattening list of lists with flatten, 285
important concepts when working with methods of classes, 245
iterating over, using collection methods, 57
iterating over, using for and for/yield loops, 56
Java, going to and from, 549–554
 conversion tables, 552
 going from Scala collections to Java collections, 553
looping over, 54
looping over with for loop, 272–276
looping over with foreach, 270
making ArrayBuffer your go to mutable sequence, 268
making immutable collections covariant, 622
making mutable collections invariant, 620
making Vector your go to immutable sequence, 266
merging sequential collections, 302
merging two sequential collections into pairs with zip, 304
mutable and immutable, 266
mutable variables with immutable collections, 265
performance of, 261–264
 maps and sets, 263
 performance characteristic keys, 261
 sequential collections, 262
populating
 using Range with map method, 373
 using tabulate method, 373
 with a Range, 309
random-length collection of printable characters, 47
Scala collections hierarchy, 246
 high-level view of collections, 247
 maps, 249
 more collection classes, 250
 sequences, 248
 sets, 249

if/then/else statements, match expressions as replacement for, 651
immutable collections
    common operators (methods) on, 259
    maps
        common methods for, 259
    mutable variables with, 265
    Vector class, go to immutable sequence, 266
immutable objects
    case classes as immutable records, 138
    preferring, 644–647
        using val + mutable and var + immutable, 645
imperative programming, 15, 393
implicit classes
    defining, 25
    defining methods on, 27
        annotating method return type, 28
        returning other types, 29
    putting in package objects, 26
    putting into objects, 25
implicit conversions, 2
    using to add methods to closed String class, 3
    using to add methods to String class, 25–29
implied loops, 246
import statements, using anywhere in Scala, 194, 199
imports
    hiding a class during import process, 196
    one or more members into current program scope, 193
    renaming members on import, 195
    static, 197
incrementing and decrementing numbers replacements for ++ and --, 39–41
indexed sequences, 327
    ArrayBuffer class, 268
IndexedSeq, 248, 252
    creating instance of, returning a Vector, 268
infix notation, 48
informational methods (collections), 256
inheritance
    classes using a trait by inheritance, limiting, 209
init method, 293
inner classes, creating, 143
Inner.breakable, 69

input, prompting users for, from Scala shell script, 485–489
InputStream class (Java), 515
insert method, Casbah MongoCollection class, 537
Insert object, 535
Int type, 31
Integer class (Java), parseInt method, 33
interfaces
    extending Java interface like a trait, 216
    traits versus, 203
    using traits as, 203
interpreter
    -savecompiled argument for Scala interpreter, 489
    starting Scala interpreter in REPL, 463
intersect method, 302
intersection of two sets, subtracting, 304
invariant, declaring a type as, 620
IOException (Java), 515
isDefinedAt method, 241
isInstanceOf method, using match expression instead of, 88
isValid methods, 37
Iterable trait, 247
iterators
    converting to collections, 279
    creating for tuples, 314
    keysIterator and valuesIterator methods on maps, 353
    using in Scala application, 278
    working with text files, 377

## J

JAD (decompiler), 468
JAR files
    adding to REPL classpath, 461
    creating with Ant, 608
    deploying single, executable file from SBT, 597–601
    generated for Scala scripts, 490
    SBT projects packaged as, specifying main method to run, 591
Java
    arrays, 334
    BigInteger and BigDecimal classes, 44
    checked exceptions, 166
    .class, 174
    class declaration, comparison with Scala, 102

adding exception annotations to work with Java, 554

assigning class field to results of, 121

assigning existing method to a function variable, 222

avoiding returning nulll from, 656

calling on a superclass or trait, 152–154
    selecting the trait, 153

chaining, 4

collection (see collections)

controlling scope, 148–152
    object-private scope, 148
    package scope, 150
    package-level control, additional, 150
    private scope, 149
    protected scope, 149
    public scope, 151

declaring can throw exceptions, 165

declaring in traits, 203

defined in object, not a class, 179

defining method that takes function as parameter, 223–225
    more complex functions, 226–229

differences between Java and Scala, 147

forcing callers to leave parentheses off accessor methods, 161

functions versus, 16

implemented methods of Scala traits, Java and, 565

match expressions as body of, 652

passing a class to, 174

requiring implementation by class attempting to mix in a trait, 213

returning multiple items (tuples), 159–161

returning Option from, 659

setting default values for parameters, 154–157

static, creating on a class, 180

symbols implemented as, in Scala, 41

taking simple generic type, 617

taking variable-argument fields, 163–165

throwing exceptions in Scala, 34

traits providing method implementations, 205

upper bound definition on type parameter, 626

using like anonymous functions, 221

using parameter names when calling, 157

vararg, annotating, 560

without side effects (see pure functions)

mixins, using traits as, 208

mkString method, 256
    converting collection to a String, 318

mongo command-line client, 536

MongoCollection class, 536, 537
    find and findOne methods, 539
    find* methods, 542
    findAndModify or update methods, 543
    findAndRemove method, 545

MongoCursor, 541

MongoDB, 491
    accessing document ID field, 544
    connecting to and inserting data, 533–537
    deleting documents from collection, 545
    inserting documents with insert, save, or +=, 537
    searching a collection, 539–542
    updating documents in a collection, 542

MongoDBObject, 535
    getting document ID from, 544

mounting servlets, 508

multidimensional arrays, creating, 339

multiline strings, creating, 6

mutable collections
    common methods on, 258
    maps, common methods for, 259
    sequences, making ArrayBuffer go to sequence, 268

MySQL, connecting to, using JDBC, 528

# N

named parameters, 114
    using for constructors, 115
    using when calling methods, 156, 157

namespace collisions or confusion, avoiding, 195

NegativeInfinity, 45

nested break statements, 68

new keyword
    creating object instances without using, 110, 185–189

newline characters, 376
    replacing with blank spaces in multiline string creation, 7
    unexpected, in external command output, 398

Newman DSL, 518

Newton's Method, implementation of, 243–244

toString method
    case class implementation of, 137
    using on a collection, 319
traits, 203–216
    abstract classes versus, 129
    adding to object instance, 215
    calling a method on, 152–154
        selecting the trait, 153
    defining properties in, 131
    ensuring trait can only be added to type with
        method of given signature, 213
    extending another trait, 204
    FunctionN, 222
    inherited by Vector class, 247
    limiting classes using a trait by inheritance,
        209
    marking for use only by subclasses of certain
        type, 211
    sequence, commonly used in library APIs,
        252
    using abstract and concrete fields in, 206
    using as interface, 203
    using as simple mixins, 208
    using like abstract class, 207
    wrapping with implementations to use from
        Java, 565–568
transform method, Map
    creating new map from existing map, 352
    using with mutable map, 355
transformer methods, 254, 255
    calling on Stream, 331
    used with lazy collections, 306
    views on collections and, 308
transformer, => symbol, 218, 220
Traversable trait, 247
    looping over Traversable types with for loop,
        272
    methods common to all collections via, 256
TraversableOnce trait, 336
tree command, 570, 587
TreeSet class (Java), 366
trimming strings, 8
Try, Success, and Failure classes, 662
    Scala 2.10 Try classes, 633
    writing your own, 632
try/catch/finally
    closing files and resources with try/finally,
        377
    declaring a variable before using in, 92–95

handling exceptions when opening files, 379
    matching one or more exceptions with try/
        catch, 91
    reading and writing binary files, 382
    using match expressions in try/catch, 651
tuple patterns, in match expressions, 80, 83
Tuple2 class, 313
Tuple3 class, 456
tuples, 254, 312–315, 457
    converting to collections, 314
    returned by zipWithIndex and zip when
        used on sequences, 277
    returning multiple objects from a method,
        159
    returning sequence of Tuple2 elements using
        map method with a Range, 311
    treating as collection by creating iterator, 314
    using Tuple syntax to access key and values
        fields in maps, 351
    working with, 160
Twitter, Effective Scala document, 636
type ascription, 38
type class, 627–630
type erasure, 81
type patterns, 83
types, 611–634
    assigning manually to an Array, 333
    bounds, 612
    building functionality with, 630–634
        creating a timer, 630
        writing your own Try classes, 632–634
    creating a collection whose elements are all
        of some base type, 624–627
    creating a method that takes generic type,
        617
    creating classes that use generic types, 614–
        617
        type parameter symbols, 616
    declaring a type when creating collections,
        264
    inferred by Scala for most expressions, 271
    making immutable collections covariant, 622
    selectively adding new behavior to closed
        model, 627–630
    type constraints, 613
    type examples in other chapters, 613
    type variance, 611
Typesafe
    Akka actor library, 411

# W

# X

# Y

# Z

## About the Author

**Alvin** took the circuitous route to software development. He managed to get a degree in Aerospace Engineering from Texas A&M University, while all he was really trying to do was play baseball. Once he became a practicing engineer, he realized he liked software and programming more than engineering. So, in approximate order, he taught himself Fortran, C, Unix and network administration, sed, awk, Perl, Java, Python, Ruby, JRuby, Groovy, PHP, and Scala. During this process, he started a software consulting firm, grew it to 15 people, sold it, and moved to Alaska for a few years. After returning to the "Lower 48," he self-published two books (*How I Sold My Business: A Personal Diary* and *Zen and the Art of Consulting*). He also created DevDaily.com, which receives millions of page views every year, started a new software consulting business, Valley Programming (*http://valleyprogramming.com*), and started a nonprofit organization named Zen Foundation (*http://zenfoundation.org*).

## Colophon

The animal on the cover of *Scala Cookbook* is a long-beaked echidna (*Zaglossus bruijnii, Z. bartoni,* and *Z. attenboroughi*), a genus of three mammal species found only on the island of New Guinea. Weighing up to 35 pounds, long-beaked echidnas are nocturnal insectivores that prefer to live in forests at higher altitudes.

The first specimen was found in 1961 on New Guinea's Cyclops Mountains, and the entire species was thought to be extinct in that area until evidence of their activity was found in 2007. According to data collected in 1982, only 1.6 echidnas existed per square kilometer of suitable habitat across New Guinea, adding up to a total of 300,000 individuals. Since then, that number has dropped significantly due to habitat loss as large areas are exploited for farming, logging, and mining. Hunting also remains a large problem since the long-beaked echidna is considered a delicacy to locals in Papua New Guinea. The low population numbers and rapid destruction of habitat make the long-beaked echidna an endangered species, while the short-beaked variety fares slightly better in both New Guinea and Australia.

The echidna is classified as a "monotreme," or a mammal that lays eggs. The mother holds one egg at a time in her body, providing it with nutrients and a place to live after it hatches. The only surviving monotremes are the four species of echidna and the platypus. All of these mammals are native to Australia and New Guinea, although there is evidence that they were once more widespread. With origins in the Jurassic era some 60 million years ago, monotremes offer evidence of mammal evolution away from reptilian forms of reproduction.

Instead of having teeth, echidnas' tongues are covered in spikes that help draw earthworms and ants into the mouth. The entire body is also covered in fur and spikes that are used for protection; much like a hedgehog, echidnas can curl up into a spiny ball when threatened. Although very little echidna behavior has been observed in the wild, they are believed to be solitary creatures; the short-beaked echidna displays little evidence of grooming, aggression, courting, or maternal behavior. In captivity, these creatures can live up to 30 years.

The cover image is from *Cassell's Natural History*. The cover font is Adobe ITC Garamond. The text font is Adobe Minion Pro; the heading font is Adobe Myriad Condensed; and the code font is Dalton Maag's Ubuntu Mono.

# Get even more for your money.

**Join the O'Reilly Community, and register the O'Reilly books you own. It's free, and you'll get:**

- $4.99 ebook upgrade offer
- 40% upgrade offer on O'Reilly print books
- Membership discounts on books and events
- Free lifetime updates to ebooks and videos
- Multiple ebook formats, DRM FREE
- Participation in the O'Reilly community
- Newsletters
- Account management
- 100% Satisfaction Guarantee

**Signing up is easy:**

1. **Go to: oreilly.com/go/register**
2. **Create an O'Reilly login.**
3. **Provide your address.**
4. **Register your books.**

Note: English-language books only

**To order books online:**

oreilly.com/store

**For questions about products or an order:**

orders@oreilly.com

**To sign up to get topic-specific email announcements and/or news about upcoming books, conferences, special offers, and new technologies:**

elists@oreilly.com

**For technical questions about book content:**

booktech@oreilly.com

**To submit new book proposals to our editors:**

proposals@oreilly.com

**O'Reilly books are available in multiple DRM-free ebook formats. For more information:**

oreilly.com/ebooks

Spreading the knowledge of innovators                    oreilly.com

CPSIA information can be obtained at www.ICGtesting.com
Printed in the USA
BVOW09s1058231015

423870BV00014B/276/P